World
Development
Report

Knowledge for
Development

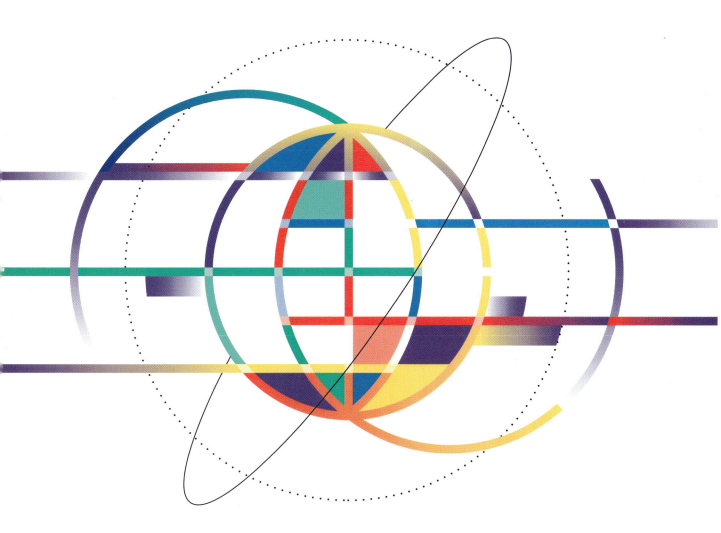

PUBLISHED FOR THE WORLD BANK

OXFORD UNIVERSITY PRESS

1998/99

Oxford University Press

OXFORD NEW YORK ATHENS AUCKLAND BANGKOK BOGOTA
BUENOS AIRES CALCUTTA CAPE TOWN CHENNAI DAR ES SALAAM
DELHI FLORENCE HONG KONG ISTANBUL KARACHI
KUALA LUMPUR MADRID MELBOURNE MEXICO CITY MUMBAI
NAIROBI PARIS SÃO PAULO SINGAPORE TAIPEI TOKYO
TORONTO WARSAW

and associated companies in

BERLIN IBADAN

© 1999 The International Bank for Reconstruction and
Development / The World Bank
1818 H Street, N.W., Washington, D.C. 20433, U.S.A.

Published by Oxford University Press, Inc.
200 Madison Avenue, New York, N.Y. 10016

Oxford is a registered trademark of Oxford University Press.

Cover and part opener design by
Communications Development Incorporated, Washington, D.C.,
with Grundy & Northedge of London.
Inside design and typesetting by
Barton Matheson Willse & Worthington, Baltimore.

Manufactured in the United States of America
First printing September 1998

ISBN 0-19-521119-7 clothbound
ISBN 0-19-521118-9 paperback
ISSN 0163-5085

Text printed on recycled paper that conforms to the American Standard
for Permanence of Paper for Printed Library Material Z39.48-1984.

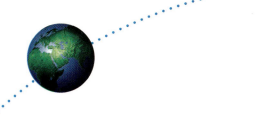

Foreword

THIS YEAR'S *World Development Report*, the twenty-first in this annual series, examines the role of knowledge in advancing economic and social well-being. It begins with the realization that economies are built not merely through the accumulation of physical capital and human skill, but on a foundation of information, learning, and adaptation. Because knowledge matters, understanding how people and societies acquire and use knowledge—and why they sometimes fail to do so—is essential to improving people's lives, especially the lives of the poorest.

The information revolution makes understanding knowledge and development more urgent than ever before. New communications technologies and plummeting computing costs are shrinking distance and eroding borders and time. The remotest village has the possibility of tapping a global store of knowledge beyond the dreams of anyone living a century ago, and more quickly and cheaply than anyone imagined possible only a few decades ago. And distance education offers the potential to extend learning opportunities to millions who would otherwise be denied a good education.

But with these opportunities come tremendous risks. The globalization of trade, finance, and information flows is intensifying competition, raising the danger that the poorest countries and communities will fall behind more rapidly than ever before. In our enthusiasm for the information superhighway, we must not forget the villages and slums without telephones, electricity, or safe water, or the primary schools without pencils, paper, or books. For the poor, the promise of the new information age—knowl-

edge for all—can seem as remote as a distant star. To bring that promise closer to reality, the implications of the information revolution must be thought through with care and made part of the development agenda.

As part of its contribution to such a daunting task, this *World Development Report* considers two sorts of knowledge: technical knowledge (for example, about farming, health, or accounting) and knowledge about attributes (the quality of a product, the credibility of a borrower, or the diligence of a worker). The Report calls the unequal distribution of technical know-how *knowledge gaps* and the uneven knowledge about attributes *information problems.* It argues that both types of problems are worse in developing than in more technologically advanced countries, and that they especially hurt the poor. This analysis suggests three lessons of particular importance to the welfare of the more than 4 billion people in developing countries:

First, developing countries must institute policies that will enable them to narrow the knowledge gaps that separate them from rich countries. Examples of such policies include making efficient public investments in lifelong education opportunities, maintaining openness to the world, and dismantling barriers to competition in the telecommunications sector.

Second, developing-country governments, bilateral donors, multilateral institutions, nongovernmental organizations, and the private sector must work together to strengthen the institutions needed to address information problems. As societies become more complex, mechanisms for reducing information problems, such as accounting standards, disclosure requirements, and credit rating agencies, and for enforcing contract performance, through effective laws and courts, become increasingly important.

Third, no matter how effective we are in these endeavors, problems with knowledge will persist. We cannot eliminate knowledge gaps and information failures, but by recognizing that knowledge is at the core of all our development efforts, we will sometimes discover unexpected solutions to seemingly intractable problems.

Putting knowledge at the center of our development efforts will bear fruit in two areas. The first is in increased social benefits—the more effective provision of public goods, including better air and water quality, greater educational attainment and higher enrollments, improved health and nutrition, and expanded access to essential infrastructure. These benefits will accrue to the poor as well as to others in society. The second is in better-functioning markets—for credit, education, housing, and land—that more efficiently coordinate resources and allocate opportunities across society. These improvements will benefit the poor the most, because they bear more than their share of the burden of information failures.

The widening access to knowledge brought about by the knowledge and information revolution is transforming relationships between expert and amateur, government and citizen, aid donor and recipient. Knowledge cannot be static, nor can it move in one direction only. Instead, it must flow constantly back and forth across an ever-changing web, involving all who create and use it. This is no less true of knowledge at the World Bank, and of this Report. Even as we attempt to share what we have learned, we know that there is much we do not know. Nonetheless, we hope that this Report will help to increase understanding of the complex relationship between knowledge and development. And that this understanding in turn will help us better apply the power of knowledge to the great challenge of eradicating poverty and improving people's lives.

James D. Wolfensohn
President
The World Bank

July 27, 1998

This Report has been prepared by a team led by Carl Dahlman with the support of Tara Vishwanath, who, along with Auguste Tano Kouame, served as a full-time team member. Other team members included Irfan Aleem, Francisco Ferreira, Yevgeny Kuznetsov, and Govindan Nair. Major contributions to chapters were made by Abhijit Banerjee, Jere Behrman, Gerard Caprio, Raffaello Cervigni, Stephen Denning, Samuel Fankhauser, Karla Hoff, Patrick Honohan, Emmanuel Jimenez, Lant Pritchett, Debraj Ray, Halsey Rogers, and David Wheeler. Valuable contributions were made by Harold Alderman, Carlos Braga, William Easterly, David Ellerman, Deon Filmer, Charles Kenny, Elizabeth King, Sanjaya Lall, Lawrence MacDonald, Saha Meyanathan, Sonia Plaza, Martin Ravallion, Francisco Sagasti, Claudia Paz Sepulveda, and Michael Walton. The team was assisted by Jesse Bump, Vajeera Dorabawila, Iyabode Fahm, Peter Lagerquist, Rohit Malhotra, Ambar Narayan, and Stratos Safioleas. Bruce Ross-Larson was the principal editor. The work was carried out under the general direction of Joseph Stiglitz and Lyn Squire.

Many others inside and outside the World Bank provided useful comments, wrote background papers and other contributions, and participated in consultation meetings. The Development Data Group contributed to the Appendix and was responsible for the Selected World Development Indicators.

The production staff of the Report included Jamila Abdelghani, Anne Hinterlong Dow, Joyce Gates, Stephanie Gerard, Jeffrey Lecksell, Brenda Mejia, Jenepher Moseley, Margaret Segears, Alison Smith, Michael Treadway, and Michael Zolandz. Rebecca Sugui served as executive assistant to the team, and Pansy Chintha, Paulina Flewitt, and Thomas Zorab as staff assistants. Maria Dolores Ameal served as administrative officer.

Contents

FIGURES

TABLES

APPENDIX TABLES

Definitions and data notes

The countries included in regional and income groupings used in this Report are listed in the Classification of economies table at the end of the Selected World Development Indicators. Income classifications are based on GNP per capita; thresholds for income classifications in this edition may be found in the Introduction to Selected World Development Indicators. Group averages reported in the figures and tables are unweighted averages of the countries in the group unless noted to the contrary. While this Report was in preparation, the income classifications of some economies changed, most notably that of China. Statistics reported for low-income economies may therefore include, and those for middle-income economies may exclude, data for China.

The use of the word "countries" to refer to economies implies no judgment by the World Bank about the legal or other status of a territory. The term "developing countries" includes low- and middle-income economies and thus may include economies in transition from central planning, as a matter of convenience. The term "advanced countries" may be used as a matter of convenience to denote the high-income economies.

Dollar figures are current U.S. dollars unless otherwise specified. "Billion" means 1,000 million; "trillion" means 1,000 billion.

The following abbreviations are used:

AIDS	Acquired immune deficiency syndrome
FDI	Foreign direct investment
GDP	Gross domestic product
GNP	Gross national product
IPRs	Intellectual property rights
NIE	Newly industrializing economy
NGO	Nongovernmental organization
OECD	Organisation for Economic Co-operation and Development
PPP	Purchasing power parity
R&D	Research and development

Overview

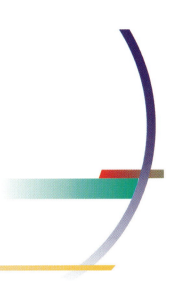

KNOWLEDGE IS LIKE LIGHT. Weightless and intangible, it can easily travel the world, enlightening the lives of people everywhere. Yet billions of people still live in the darkness of poverty—unnecessarily. Knowledge about how to treat such a simple ailment as diarrhea has existed for centuries—but millions of children continue to die from it because their parents do not know how to save them.

Poor countries—and poor people—differ from rich ones not only because they have less capital but because they have less knowledge. Knowledge is often costly to create, and that is why much of it is created in industrial countries. But developing countries can acquire knowledge overseas as well as create their own at home. Forty years ago, Ghana and the Republic of Korea had virtually the same income per capita. By the early 1990s Korea's income per capita was six times higher than Ghana's. Some reckon that half of the difference is due to Korea's greater success in acquiring and using knowledge.

Knowledge also illuminates every economic transaction, revealing preferences, giving clarity to exchanges, informing markets. And it is lack of knowledge that causes markets to collapse, or never to come into being. When some producers began diluting milk in India, consumers could not determine its quality before buying it. Without that knowledge, the overall quality of milk fell. Producers who did not dilute their milk were put at a disadvantage, and consumers suffered.

Poor countries differ from rich in having fewer institutions to certify quality, enforce standards and performance, and gather and disseminate information needed for business transactions. Often this hurts the poor. For example, village moneylenders often charge interest rates as high as 80 percent, because of the difficulty in assessing the creditworthiness of poor borrowers.

This *World Development Report* proposes that we look at the problems of development in a new way—from the perspective of knowledge. There are many types of knowledge. In this Report we focus on two sorts of knowledge and two types of problems that are critical for developing countries:

- *Knowledge about technology,* which we also call technical knowledge or simply know-how. Examples are nutrition, birth control, software engineering, and accountancy. Typically, developing countries have less of this know-how than industrial countries, and the poor have less than the nonpoor. We call these unequal distributions across and within countries *knowledge gaps.*
- *Knowledge about attributes,* such as the quality of a product, the diligence of a worker, or the creditworthiness of a firm—all crucial to effective markets. We call the difficulties posed by incomplete knowledge of attributes *information problems.* Mechanisms to alleviate information problems, such as product standards, training certificates, and credit reports, are fewer and weaker in developing countries. Information problems and the resulting market failures especially hurt the poor.

The relationship between knowledge gaps and information problems, their impact on development, and the ways that international institutions and developing-country governments can better address them are the central themes of this Report.

As we shall see, considering development from a knowledge perspective reinforces some well-known lessons, such as the value of an open trade regime and of universal basic education. It also focuses our attention on needs that have sometimes been overlooked: scientific and technical training, local research and development, and the critical importance of institutions to facilitate the flow of information essential for effective markets.

Approaching development from a knowledge perspective—that is, adopting policies to increase both types of knowledge, know-how and knowledge about attributes—can improve people's lives in myriad ways besides higher incomes. Better knowledge about nutrition can mean better health, even for those with little to spend on food. Knowledge about how to prevent the transmission of AIDS can save millions from debilitating illness and premature death. Public disclosure of information about industrial pollution can lead to a cleaner and more healthful environment. And microcredit programs can make it possible for poor people to invest in a better future for themselves and their children. In short, knowledge gives people greater control over their destinies.

The twin issues of knowledge gaps and information problems cannot be untangled in real life: to unleash the power of knowledge, governments must recognize and respond to both types of problems, often simultaneously. For the sake of clarity, however, we analyze these issues separately, beginning with knowledge gaps.

Narrowing knowledge gaps

Closing knowledge gaps will not be easy. Developing countries are pursuing a moving target, as the high-income industrial countries constantly push the knowledge frontier outward. Indeed, even greater than the knowledge gap is the gap in the capacity to create knowledge. Differences in some important measures of knowledge creation are far greater between rich and poor countries than the difference in income (Figure 1).

But developing countries need not reinvent the wheel—or the computer, or the treatment for malaria. Rather than re-create existing knowledge, poorer countries have the option of acquiring and adapting much knowledge already available in the richer countries. With communications costs plummeting, transferring knowledge is cheaper than ever (Figure 2). Given these advances, the stage appears to be set for a rapid narrowing of knowledge gaps and a surge in economic growth and human well-being. Why, then, isn't this transfer occurring as fast as we might expect? What conditions are necessary for developing countries to make fuller use of the global stock of knowledge?

Part One of the Report starts with a discussion of the importance of knowledge for development and of the

Figure 1

R&D spending and GDP per capita

Inequalities in the capacity to create knowledge exceed even those in income.

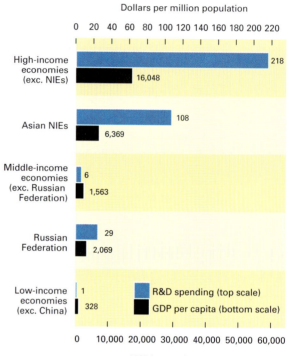

Note: Data are for 1991. Source: European Commission 1994.

risks and opportunities that the information revolution poses for developing countries (Chapter 1). It then examines three critical steps that developing countries must take to narrow knowledge gaps:

- *Acquiring knowledge* involves tapping and adapting knowledge available elsewhere in the world—for example, through an open trading regime, foreign investment, and licensing agreements—as well as creating knowledge locally through research and development, and building on indigenous knowledge (Chapter 2).
- *Absorbing knowledge* involves, for example, ensuring universal basic education, with special emphasis on extending education to girls and other traditionally disadvantaged groups; creating opportunities for lifelong learning; and supporting tertiary education, especially in science and engineering (Chapter 3).
- *Communicating knowledge* involves taking advantage of new information and communications technology—

through increased competition, private sector provision, and appropriate regulation—and ensuring that the poor have access (Chapter 4).

Just as knowledge gaps exist between developing and industrial countries, so too are there large gaps within countries. Strategies for closing these gaps often include the same elements, and applying them effectively will go a long way toward reducing inequality and eliminating poverty.

But even if knowledge gaps could be closed entirely, with everyone in developing countries enjoying access to the same know-how as well-educated people in the industrial countries, developing countries would still be at a disadvantage in another respect: knowledge about attributes. Because knowledge about attributes is required for every transaction, it must be generated on the spot and constantly refreshed. This requires a variety of market and nonmarket mechanisms to collect and disseminate information, many of which are weak or lacking in developing countries.

Addressing information problems

Without knowledge about attributes, markets cannot function properly. When the government steps in and addresses the problem, for example by establishing standards and certification (as it did for milk quality in India), the market functions better and everybody benefits.

Institutions, broadly defined to include governments, private organizations, laws, and social norms, contribute to establishing recognized standards and enforcing contracts, thus making possible transactions that would otherwise not occur. Rich countries have more-diverse and more-effective institutions to address information problems than do poor countries. These institutions make it possible for people to engage in economic transactions that improve their lives—from buying milk, to finding a job, to getting an education, to obtaining a loan. Information problems are often at the core of the difficulties that poor people in developing countries encounter in their daily struggle to survive and to improve their lives.

Part Two of the Report begins by discussing the nature and extent of these problems, noting that they are a major impediment to development—and especially severe for the poor (Chapter 5). The unequal distribution of information can never be entirely eliminated, but it can be ameliorated, in part through institutional innovations designed specifically for developing-country settings and the special problems confronting poor people. The rest of Part Two considers some specific problems involving information. It also describes some promising solutions in three areas where these problems are most severe, and where addressing them can make a major contribution to achieving sustainable growth that benefits the poor:

- *Processing the economy's financial information,* particularly by ensuring transparency through effective accounting and disclosure, and by designing regulatory approaches that work in information-scarce settings (Chapter 6)
- *Increasing our knowledge of the environment,* by conducting research to provide the underpinnings for effective environmental policies, and by disseminating information to create incentives for pollution reduction and responsible stewardship (Chapter 7)
- *Addressing information problems that hurt the poor,* and taking the time to learn about their needs and concerns, so that society can then offer them useful information and assist them in devising ways to reduce their isolation from markets and to improve their access to formal institutions (Chapter 8).

Most of the difficulties that developing countries face involve both knowledge gaps and information problems. To be effective, the solutions must address both issues—sometimes sequentially, often simultaneously. Because the

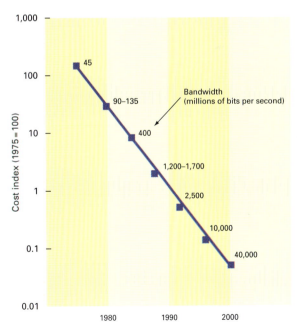

Figure 2

Cost trends in optical fiber transmission

The cost of sending information continues to plummet.

Note: The data underlying the index are in dollars per million bits transmitted 1 kilometer. The trendline is calculated logarithmically.
Source: Bond 1997a.

possibilities for improving human well-being are so immense, we return to these twin themes throughout the Report, beginning with the story of the green revolution, which shows dramatically how knowledge gaps and information problems—and their solutions—play out in the real world.

The green revolution: A paradigm of knowledge for development

Few stories better illustrate the potential of knowledge for development—or the obstacles to diffusing that knowledge—than that of the green revolution, the decades-long, worldwide movement dedicated to the creation and dissemination of new agricultural knowledge. This quest, breeding new seeds for enhanced agricultural productivity, was undertaken in the early postwar years by a vast array of agents—nonprofit organizations, governments, multilateral institutions, private firms, banks, village moneylenders, land-rich farmers, and landless laborers—all working, deliberately or not, to improve the daily bread (or rice, or maize) of people everywhere. The English economist Thomas Malthus had predicted in the 18th century that the population of any country would eventually outstrip its food supply. What the green revolution showed

instead was that Malthus had underestimated how quickly knowledge—in agriculture, in transportation, in mechanization—would transform food production. By the second half of the 20th century, world food supply was more than keeping up with population growth.

Since the early 1950s, Asia and South America have more than doubled yields of staple crops (Figure 3; Africa, which also lags in other measures of development and knowledge, has seen only modest yield increases). Global gains in output per hectare have been dramatic, particularly for wheat, maize, and rice (Figure 4). And although the impact of the green revolution on the poor was initially a matter of controversy, time has made it clear that poor people have benefited significantly, through higher incomes, cheaper food, and increased demand for their labor.

The early steps in the green revolution mostly involved narrowing knowledge gaps. The first step was to narrow the gap between what scientists already knew about plant genetics and the widespread ignorance on this score in developing countries, reflected in the unavailability there of new crop strains based on this knowledge. This gap was narrowed largely through the research and development efforts of governments and nonprofit organizations. But why was their action necessary? Why didn't private, for-profit firms make a greater effort to address food security? Why didn't they, for example, try to commercialize existing scientific knowledge about genetics by developing more productive plant varieties themselves?

The answer is that the knowledge embodied in the seed of a new plant variety is not easily appropriated by any breeder, seed company, farmer, or even country. The varieties most suitable for transfer to developing countries, once transferred, could be easily reproduced. Farmers had only to collect the seeds from the plants grown from the original seeds and replant them. That meant no repeat business for seed developers, and not enough profit to make their effort worthwhile.

Put another way, improved seeds, like many other research outputs, have many of the characteristics of a public good. A public good is one whose full benefits in the form of profits cannot be captured by its creator but instead leak out to society at large, without the creator receiving compensation. Because private entrepreneurs have diminished incentives to provide such goods, the tradition of entrusting public entities with providing them is long. (A good example is the agricultural research the U.S. government funded in the 19th century.) Indeed, it is widely recognized in many fields that, without some collective action, there will be far too little research into developing new knowledge.

After the first modern seed varieties proved successful in the early 1960s, many developing countries established national agriculture research organizations, as some had already done, mainly with public funding, to develop

Figure 3

Cereal yields by developing region

Yields have more than doubled in much of the developing world.

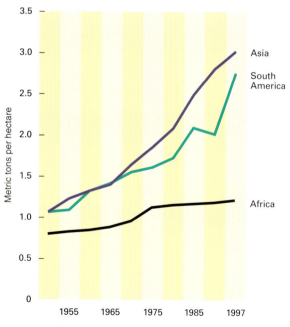

Source: FAO, various years.

second-generation varieties better suited to local conditions. As a result, the number of new varieties of rice and maize released by national research organizations doubled between 1966 and 1985.

To disseminate this knowledge, developing-country governments established agricultural extension services. At first the main job of the extension agents was to inform farmers about the new seeds and techniques. But the best extension agents—and the most effective extension services—quickly learned that listening was also an important part of the job. By listening to farmers and learning from them, extension agents not only gained a better understanding of the farmers' needs and concerns. They also sometimes stumbled upon seed varieties and cultivation techniques that the researchers had missed. This two-way flow of information furthered the local adoption and adaptation of green revolution technology.

At this point in the story, the focus shifts to information problems. The driving force in the early stages of the green revolution had been the creation, dissemination, and adaptation of agricultural know-how. But the potential of these innovations could not be unleashed until millions of small farmers planted the new seeds. For this to happen, a variety of information problems had to be addressed. In particular, what assurance did farmers have that the seeds would work? Why should a farmer risk his livelihood on the say-so of an extension agent? This uncertainty, coupled with the inability of the poor to obtain credit—another classic market failure closely related to information problems—had significant implications for the rate of adoption of the new seeds.

Large landholders and farmers with more education were among the first to try the new seeds, for a variety of reasons. Farmers with extensive landholdings could limit their risk by trying new seeds in test sowings on only a part of their land. They could also more quickly recover the fixed cost of their early adoption by applying what they learned across their larger farms. Educated farmers were better equipped to find out about the new varieties in the first place, and to learn the changes in cultivation practices needed to make the most of them. Perhaps most important, however, more-prosperous farmers had ready access to credit and the ability to absorb risk. Poor farmers, unable to borrow and lacking insurance or the savings to fall back on in the event of failure, could only watch and wait until their wealthier neighbors proved the value of the new seeds.

Why didn't banks or village moneylenders lend small farmers the money to buy the new seeds and fertilizer? Many poor people would repay small loans at reasonable interest, if such loans were available. But the costs of identifying the good credit risks among the poor are high relative to the size of the loans they would take out. Unsure which prospective borrowers will repay, lenders charge high interest and require collateral, which the poor often

Figure 4

Growth in yields for principal cereals

Productivity gains in some staple crops have been dramatic.

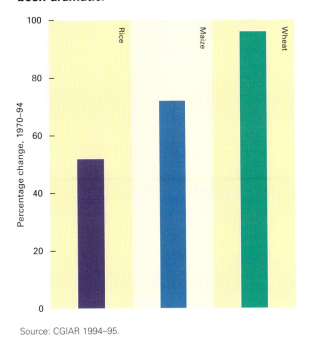

Source: CGIAR 1994–95.

lack. Even when the poor have assets (small landholdings) that could be pledged as collateral, weak legal infrastructure, including lack of land title and ineffective courts, means that enforcement of collateral pledges may be weak. Without enforcement, incentives to repay are limited, and this weakens incentives to lend. The result is that the poor often cannot borrow.

In recent years microcredit schemes have arisen to address these problems. But at the time of the green revolution, poor farmers' lack of credit, combined with their scant education (also partly attributable to lack of credit) and other factors, meant that they were often the last to adopt the new crop strains. The resulting lag between the introduction of new seeds and their widespread use can be seen in the slow expansion of areas sown with new varieties (Figure 5).

The costs of these delays were significant. If all the information problems could have been addressed—that is, if farmers could have been immediately persuaded of the potential of the new seeds, and if mechanisms had existed to provide credit to poor farmers—the productivity gains from the green revolution would have been even greater. One study found that, for a farm family with 3.7 hectares, the average loss of potential income over five years from

Figure 5

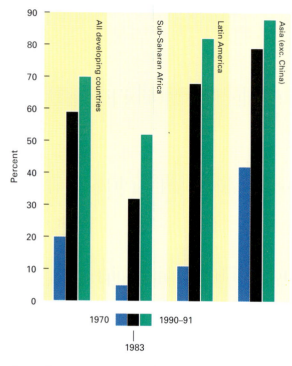

Cropland planted with new wheat varieties

New plant varieties took time to be adopted.

1970 ■ 1990–91

1983

Source: Byerlee and Moya 1993.

slow adoption and inefficient use of high-yielding varieties was nearly *four times* its annual farm income before the introduction of the new seeds.

Eventually the green revolution did boost the incomes of poor farmers and the landless. A survey in southern India concluded that, between 1973 and 1994, the average real income of small farmers increased by 90 percent, and that of the landless—among the poorest in the farm community—by 125 percent. The poor benefited greatly from increased demand for their labor, because the high-yielding varieties demanded labor-intensive cultivating techniques. Calorie intakes for small farmers and the landless rose 58 to 81 percent, and protein intakes rose 103 to 115 percent.

What knowledge gaps and information problems mean for development

The story of the green revolution shows how creating, disseminating, and using knowledge can narrow knowledge gaps. It also shows that know-how is only one part of what determines society's well-being. Information problems lead to market failures and impede efficiency and growth.

Development thus entails the need for an institutional transformation that improves information and creates incentives for effort, innovation, saving, and investment and enables progressively complex exchanges that span increased distances and time.

The relationship between knowledge gaps and information problems is clear from the history of the green revolution, because with time it became obvious that improved varieties of plants were necessary but not sufficient to improve the lives of the rural poor. The twin challenges of knowledge for development—knowledge gaps and information problems—are also illustrated in many other examples in this Report. How they will be manifested in the next green revolution, perhaps involving gene splicing and cloning, we can only guess. We can be sure, however, that whether or not new technologies are used in ways that help the poor will depend on how well society addresses knowledge gaps and information problems.

Part Three of the Report considers the policy options for responding to these challenges from two perspectives:

- *What can international institutions do?* Chapter 9 discusses how—by creating new knowledge, transferring and adapting knowledge to the needs of developing countries, and managing knowledge so that it is kept accessible and constantly refreshed—international institutions can help developing countries bridge knowledge gaps and resolve information problems.
- *What should governments do?* Drawing on the first two parts of the Report, Chapter 10 describes how the governments of developing countries can narrow knowledge gaps, address information problems, and design policies that take into account the reality that information and markets are always imperfect.

The rest of this Overview sketches the main conclusions from these two chapters.

What can international institutions do?

Development institutions have three roles in reducing knowledge gaps: to provide international public goods, to act as intermediaries in the transfer of knowledge, and to manage the rapidly growing body of knowledge about development.

Just as there are national public goods, so there are international ones, and many types of knowledge fall into this category. No single country will invest enough in the creation of such goods, because the benefits would accrue to all countries without the creating country receiving full compensation. But international institutions, acting on behalf of everyone, can fill this gap.

One of the best-known examples, the Consultative Group for International Agricultural Research, funded the green revolution through its worldwide sponsorship of agricultural research. It illustrates the standard response of public funding for research when there are large social returns (which exceed the private returns). Another response is to provide financial incentives for private researchers to focus on the needs of developing countries, such as the need for an affordable vaccine for AIDS.

Perhaps even more important is the role of development institutions as intermediaries. International research may produce knowledge useful for development, but the most important knowledge for development comes from developing countries themselves. Each change in policy in one country produces knowledge that may help another. Every project, successful or not, yields information about what works and what does not. Amassing this knowledge, assessing it, and making it available to others is a task beyond the capacity (and self-interest) of any single country. So the task falls to international institutions.

How well these institutions perform depends on their ability to manage vast amounts of information. For example, every World Bank staffer who works in a developing country accumulates knowledge about a particular sector or region or activity. Often this knowledge is used for the specific task requiring it, then shelved. Think how much more valuable it would be if that knowledge were made available to every other staff member working on similar issues and projects. Then add the much greater benefit to be had from sharing that knowledge with the rest of the world.

The information revolution is making it easier to manage this wealth of knowledge. By 2000, the World Bank intends that relevant parts of its knowledge base will be made available to clients, partners, and stakeholders around the world. The objective is to develop a dynamic knowledge management system capable of distilling knowledge and making it available for further adaptation and use in new settings. To do that effectively, however, also requires building the capability in developing countries to assess and adapt relevant policy and technical knowledge to local situations, and when necessary to create new knowledge, which in turn may be relevant for other countries.

International institutions can thus make important contributions. But it is what developing countries do themselves that will determine how effectively they make use of knowledge and deal with information failures. Different countries start from different positions and face different problems. But some generalizations can be made, and some are offered in the following sections.

What should governments do?

When development is considered from the perspective of knowledge, three key insights emerge:

- Because the market for knowledge often fails, there is a strong rationale for public action. The state is in a unique position to narrow knowledge gaps—for example, by adopting an open trade regime, supporting lifelong learning, or establishing a sound regulatory environment for a competitive telecommunications industry.
- Information is the lifeblood of markets, yet markets on their own do not always provide enough of it, because those who generate information cannot always appropriate the returns. Public action is thus required to provide information to verify quality, monitor performance, and regulate transactions to provide the foundation for successful market-based development.
- No matter how successful a government may be in this endeavor, knowledge gaps and information failures will remain. Every policy reform and every development program or project will be implemented in an environment that suffers from these problems to varying degrees. Even actions that on the surface have little to do with knowledge gaps or information failures are almost certain to be affected by them.

How should developing-country governments proceed, given the magnitude of knowledge gaps and the universality of information failures? Chapter 10 draws some policy conclusions from the discussions in the rest of the Report.

National strategies to narrow knowledge gaps

The Report considers a number of steps that governments can take to facilitate the acquisition, absorption, and communication of knowledge. Although it is useful for expository purposes to discuss each of them separately, in the real world they are intertwined. Policies adopted in one area have important repercussions on—and possible synergies with—each of the others. The acquisition of knowledge, whether imported from abroad or created at home, requires the absorption of knowledge, abetted by universal basic education and opportunities for lifelong learning. The exploding capacity and plummeting costs of communications technology greatly expand the potential for both the acquisition and the absorption of knowledge, creating new opportunities for two-way information flows. Government strategies to narrow knowledge gaps are most effective when they make the most of these synergies. But they also need to address information failures in their design and implementation.

Policies for acquiring knowledge

For developing countries, acquiring knowledge involves two complementary steps: obtaining knowledge by opening up to knowledge from abroad, and creating knowledge not readily available elsewhere. Three key means of facilitating the acquisition of knowledge from abroad are an open trading regime, foreign investment, and technology licensing.

Improving the policy and business environments to create conditions favorable to trade, especially exports, is one of the most important ways for countries to obtain knowledge from abroad. To compete in the global marketplace, exporting firms must meet international benchmarks for efficiency and design. As a result, exporters tend to invest more in knowledge than firms that do not export.

Openness to foreign direct investment goes hand in hand with an open trading regime, and it provides benefits for the acquisition of knowledge in its own right. Because multinational investors are global leaders in innovation, their activities in developing countries can be important in transmitting knowledge. Valuable knowledge spillovers can occur through their training of local staff and through contacts with domestic suppliers and subcontractors. Both are evident in Malaysia, where the local plant of the U.S. firm Intel Corporation now subcontracts a growing part of its production to new firms set up by former Intel engineers. Such spillovers are not limited to manufacturing; they also occur in relatively low-technology service industries, such as food services and hotels.

Technology licensing plays a growing role in developing countries' efforts to acquire knowledge. International licensing and royalties payments worldwide increased from $7 billion in 1976 to more than $60 billion in 1995. Technology licensing is an effective way to get access to some of the new proprietary technologies. Domestic firms can also use licensing to leverage technological development by negotiating access to the underlying design principles of the licensed technologies, as many Korean firms have done.

As the world moves toward a knowledge-based economy, there has been a trend toward stronger protection of intellectual property rights. This trend is reflected in the recently completed agreements in the World Trade Organization on the trade-related aspects of intellectual property rights. Intellectual property rights try to balance the incentives for the generation of new knowledge with those for its dissemination. That balance is difficult to achieve. The balance is also evolving, as new technologies bring new issues for negotiation, such as the protection of biotechnology, biodiversity, and computer and information technologies.

Developing countries should participate actively in continuing international negotiations on these issues, to express their concerns that tighter intellectual property rights shift bargaining power toward the producers of knowledge and increase the knowledge gap by slowing the rate of adaptation. These concerns about intellectual property rights have to be balanced against their advantages: they stimulate the creation of new knowledge in the world, including in developing countries. Many developing countries have found that by establishing and enforcing intellectual property rights standards that comply with international practice, they gain access to foreign markets and to foreign technology through direct investment and technology transfer.

Developing countries can take advantage of the large global stock of knowledge only if they develop the technological competence to search for appropriate technologies and to select, absorb, and adapt imported technology. The green revolution showed how new seed strains had to be further developed to suit local conditions. Even in manufacturing, knowledge produced in other countries often has to be adapted to local conditions, such as weather, consumer tastes, and the availability of complementary inputs. Similarly, progress in education, health care, and agricultural extension all require local knowledge that cannot be obtained from abroad.

In fostering the domestic creation of knowledge, governments have a special role in supporting potentially productive research, while establishing the necessary conditions for the private sector, in response to market forces, to apply the new knowledge created. Many developing countries are reforming their public research and development to make it more responsive to the market. Brazil, China, India, Korea, and Mexico have launched vast programs to help focus public laboratories on the needs of the productive sector. Their measures include corporatizing research institutes, improving the pay and recognition of researchers, and offering firms incentives to contract directly with the public labs.

Policies for absorbing knowledge

The explosion of new knowledge, accelerating technological progress, and ever-increasing competition make lifelong learning more important than ever. To narrow knowledge gaps, societies must ensure basic education for all and provide opportunities for people to continue to learn throughout their lives. Basic education is the foundation of a healthy, skilled, and agile labor force. Lifelong education beyond the basics enables countries to continually assess, adapt, and apply new knowledge.

In the past 30 years, developing countries have made enormous strides in expanding enrollments at all levels, particularly in primary school. These achievements have been invaluable and should be maintained and expanded. We have seen, for example, the importance of basic education in furthering the adoption of improved agricultural techniques. A growing economy, even a low-income one, needs people with up-to-date technical skills to participate in the global economy. Countries should consider supporting expanded adult education and training. In many cases the most cost-effective way of doing so is to support the private sector's activities in this area, for instance by establishing standards and accreditation procedures, and in some cases by providing subsidies, especially for the poor.

Improving the education of girls is particularly important in countries with large knowledge gaps. The benefits of female education, today widely recognized, include better child nutrition and health and reduced fertility. The recent success of a program in Bangladesh demonstrates that well-planned government actions can have far-reaching impacts, even in societies where girls' education has long been neglected. Nationwide, only about 20 percent of Bangladeshi women were literate in 1990, and only a third of students in secondary schools were girls. Since then a program to provide stipends and tuition grants to girls enrolled in secondary school has rapidly increased female enrollments. By 1996, half a million girls were receiving stipends, and as many girls as boys were enrolled in participating schools.

But to sustain economic growth and to compete in the global economy, countries must go beyond basic education, as Korea has done. By 1960 Korea had achieved universal primary education—the basis for a well-educated labor force—which fueled the economy's needs as it industrialized. Incentives were also put in place for extensive private investment in tertiary education, so that by 1995 more than half of college-age adults were enrolled in a college or university. Of these, more than 80 percent were enrolled in private institutions, and private spending on tertiary education exceeded public spending.

Tapping the private sector is one way to stretch limited government resources; a complementary measure is to improve the quality of public education. To do this, and to address some of the information failures afflicting education, many countries are experimenting with new approaches to providing it. These changes take several forms: decentralizing administration, increasing school autonomy, switching to demand-side financing, increasing information about individual educational institutions, and fostering competition among private, nongovernmental, and public providers. In El Salvador, after its civil war, the government improved and expanded the community-managed schools that had sprung up when the public system broke down. Even the poorest communities set up and managed such schools, actually improving quality. One reason is that parents monitor the teachers vigorously. As a result, students lose only about half as many days to teacher absenteeism as in conventional schools.

Policies for communicating knowledge in the information age

Advances in communications have transformed society before: movable type, photography and telegraphy, the telephone, television, and the fax machine all pushed out-ward the limits of our ability to store and transmit knowledge. Now the convergence of computing and telecommunications appears ready to shatter those limits, making it possible to send vast amounts of information anywhere in the world in seconds—at an ever-decreasing cost. This new technology greatly facilitates the acquisition and absorption of knowledge, offering developing countries unprecedented opportunities to enhance educational systems, improve policy formation and execution, and widen the range of opportunities for business and the poor. One of the great hardships endured by the poor, and by many others who live in the poorest countries, is their sense of isolation. The new communications technologies promise to reduce that sense of isolation, and to open access to knowledge in ways unimaginable not long ago.

A growing number of developing countries are taking advantage of these opportunities to leapfrog to the new technologies, largely skipping such intermediate stages as copper wires and analog telephones. Already Djibouti, Maldives, Mauritius, and Qatar all have fully digitized telephone networks. In this they have stolen a march on some industrial countries where half or more of the telephone network continues to rely on older technology, more expensive and lower in quality.

Throughout much of the developing world, however, access to even basic communications technology is available only to the fortunate few. South Asia and Sub-Saharan Africa have only about 1.5 telephone lines for every 100 people, compared with 64 lines per 100 in the United States. Lower incomes account for part of the difference, but many people in developing countries who are ready and willing to pay for a telephone are unable to obtain one. Standing in their way are inefficient state monopolies and regulatory regimes that unintentionally restrict supply. Worldwide, an estimated 28 million people, nearly all of them in developing countries, are on waiting lists for telephone installation. Given the long and uncertain delay, many others who want a telephone and could afford one simply have not bothered to apply.

Fortunately, countries can eliminate these bottlenecks—and lower the costs of telecommunications so that many more people benefit. This can be done by adopting a regulatory system that promotes and ensures competition, to prevent firms with monopoly power in some areas of service provision from using it to gain a stranglehold over others. In most cases, expanded competition should come before privatization, to avoid turning a state monopoly into a private one.

Developing countries are discovering that private involvement can rapidly extend telecommunications services, even when incomes are low. Before its reform, Ghana's telecommunications system was dominated by a money-losing state monopoly, only one in 400 people had a telephone, and there was a 10-year wait. The government sold 30 percent of the state firm to a consortium of domestic and Malaysian investors, approved a competing national franchise that also included foreign investors, licensed five new cellular providers, and approved several Internet service providers, one of which now has an aggressive program to provide rural access through collaboration with the post office. In 1997, the first year after the reforms, the number of fixed lines increased by 30 percent, to 120,000, and the pace of installation is expected to accelerate.

One problem that often remains with privatization is that some isolated rural communities are not served, because they have too few people stretched out across too much territory to attract private service providers. The problem for government is knowing how much subsidy is needed to encourage private service to these communities. Chile has had encouraging success with subsidy auctions, a market-like innovation that induces firms to reveal information about their costs, to the benefit of the poor. The government awarded subsidies on a competitive basis to firms providing telephone service to small and remote locales: firms bid against each other for the right to service these areas. Unexpectedly, for half the locales and nearly 60 percent of the target population, firms proved willing to provide pay phones at no subsidy at all. With additional rounds of bidding going forward, it is expected that 98 percent of Chileans will have access to pay phones by 2000.

Expanding telecommunications holds the promise to improve every developing country's capacity to absorb knowledge, for example by providing opportunities for high-quality, low-cost adult learning. The Virtual University of the Monterrey Institute of Technology in Mexico is a consortium of collaborating universities, including 13 outside the country. It enrolls 9,000 degree and 35,000 nondegree students each year in Mexico and other Latin American countries. It delivers courses through printed texts and live and prerecorded television broadcasts, with communication between students and faculty aided by computers and the Internet.

The African Virtual University, headquartered in Nairobi, seeks to increase university enrollments and improve the quality and relevance of instruction in business, science, and engineering throughout Africa. In each participating country, a local institution is competitively selected to oversee operations. This institution provides hardware and software for interactive courses, registers students, supervises study programs, offers a structured study environment, and awards local course credit. The university has installed 27 satellite receiver terminals throughout Africa and developed a digital library, to compensate for the dearth of scientific journals in African universities. Although it is too early to assess results, such initiatives are

reason to hope that new technology can make a big contribution to narrowing knowledge gaps.

Policies for addressing information failures

Part Two of the Report describes how markets thrive—or wither—depending on the flow of information, and how information failures are especially pervasive in developing countries. Although information failures can never be eliminated, recognizing and addressing them are crucial to effective markets and therefore fundamental to rapid, equitable, and sustainable growth. As the green revolution showed, information failures in the market for knowledge itself or in related markets (such as for credit) can limit the returns to acquiring knowledge. Put another way, countries can increase the return to acquiring and using knowledge by ensuring that markets function as well as possible.

Whatever actions governments undertake, significant information imperfections and the corresponding market failures will remain, and this fact has important implications for policy design. Because these imperfections are greater in developing countries, and the institutions for addressing them often more limited, market failure will also be more prevalent. Policies need to account for this. For instance, rural extension schemes should recognize that farmers may face credit rationing, may be able to borrow only at extremely high interest rates, and may have only limited ability to absorb risk. This will limit their ability to take advantage of new assistance, for example in the form of improved seeds.

A comprehensive strategy for the effective use of knowledge requires that governments seek ways to improve information flows. But governments suffer from information limits of their own, and an appreciation of these limits should inform decisions about the scope and nature of public action. It is not just the size of the market failure that matters—it is also the government's capacity to deal with it. But as the discussion below makes clear, developing-country governments have helped to improve markets in many ways by addressing information failures.

Part Two develops in detail the types of information problems that plague developing economies. It then explores the steps that governments can take to deal with those problems in three areas where information failures are especially severe: financial markets, the environment, and measures for the poor. Here we look at three approaches to information problems that cut across all these areas: providing information to help verify quality, monitoring and enforcing performance, and ensuring two-way information flows. We highlight throughout how governments are experimenting with innovative mechanisms to reduce the costs of collecting, analyzing, and applying information. By addressing information failures up front, governments are discovering new solutions to seemingly intractable problems, especially those that afflict the poor.

Providing information to help verify quality

Governments can smooth the workings of markets by requiring the disclosure of information that reduces the costs of market transactions, especially information about the quality of the good, service, or institution involved. In India in the 1950s, when rising production costs led producers to dilute milk, buyers were unable to determine the quality of milk sold in the market. Dairy producers who did not dilute their milk could no longer compete, leaving the market to low-quality producers. Milk quality was restored when the government took steps to ensure quality by establishing reputable brand names and distributing an inexpensive, handheld device for measuring butterfat. The results were not only more and better milk but also healthier children and higher incomes for dairy farmers.

In education and labor markets, accreditation and skills certification inform employers about the education and skills of prospective workers. Given the increased importance of lifelong learning and the increasing variety of settings in which education is provided, certification will become increasingly important, and governments should help set and validate the standards used.

In the financial sector, which is particularly prone to information problems, accounting and auditing standards make it possible for investors to compare information across firms. Standardization of balance sheets, income statements, cash flow statements, and the notes to these statements allows companies to report on their situation and activities in a consistent way, so that investors can make better-informed judgments about where to put their money. Developing-country governments can hasten the spread of good accounting standards by imposing accounting and disclosure requirements on publicly traded firms.

Similarly, common and rigorous standards make it possible to assess the health of banks, by enabling outsiders to assess the adequacy of loan-loss provisions, for example, and by ensuring that collateral is valued realistically. Improving such standards is important for an efficient financial system and for economic growth. Confidence in financial institutions enables them to attract more capital and avoid the dangers that arise from undercapitalized banks.

Improvements in accounting standards are important for the efficiency of the financial system—and for growth. Studies show that countries with sound accounting systems have more-developed financial intermediaries and faster growth. One study estimated that if Argentina had raised its accounting standards in the early 1990s to

the average then prevailing in a group of high-income economies, its annual GDP growth would have increased by 0.6 percentage point.

Governments can also promote specialized private institutions to verify the quality of goods and services. For example, the ISO 9000 quality certification procedures are private standards to which firms voluntarily adhere as a means of guaranteeing the quality of their processes and products. Such certification is especially valuable to developing-country exporters eager to establish a reputation for quality among skeptical buyers. In this case, governments need do little more than publicize the availability of the certification process.

This example shows that direct public action to set standards is not always necessary. Instead, governments can establish an institutional and legal environment, including trademark protection for brand names, that fosters private standards setting. Producers of goods whose quality is not fully apparent at the time of purchase—whether cola drinks, cars, or computer games—can use brand names to establish a reputation for quality. This enables producers to charge a premium for quality, which makes it worthwhile to market high-quality goods, which in turn benefits consumers. Of course, brand names can address information problems only if the government establishes and enforces legal standards to prevent brand piracy.

Generation of information by agents other than the government also shows promise in addressing complex environmental issues. The International Forestry Resources and Institutions Research Program in the United States brings together a network of collaborating research centers throughout the world. The centers agree on a common research method. They support the collection of primary data on forest conditions, management, and uses. And they interpret and analyze information gathered in the field. In this bottom-up approach, a university-based project serves as a clearinghouse for locally provided information with global implications.

Governments are also experimenting with self-revelation mechanisms to achieve disclosure of information at lower cost. The Chilean auction scheme already mentioned elicited information about the level of subsidy required without the government having to investigate the cost structure of each firm. A similar approach has been applied to social safety nets, ensuring that the benefits accrue to the poor while minimizing leakage to the nonpoor. Means-testing, the approach commonly used in industrial countries, is expensive and often unworkable in developing countries, because the household incomes of poor people cannot be reliably determined. An alternative that reveals the needed information at close to zero cost is self-targeting, whereby benefits—be they wages or food for work—are designed so that they are attractive only to the truly needy.

Monitoring and enforcing performance

Besides the means to verify the quality of the goods or services they buy or sell, participants in markets need a legal system to enforce contracts. Typically the problem in developing countries is not the absence of laws. Instead, it is the lack of credible enforcement: courts may be slow, and they are often corrupt, making judicial reform a necessary part of economic reform. Many countries would benefit from special courts to deal with various specialized legal issues, such as the enforcement of commercial contracts and the treatment of bankruptcy. In these countries, enforcement and, more broadly, laws that require disclosure are meaningful only if there are penalties against dishonesty and fraud.

But even when the legal system works, it is costly to use. So, in both industrial and developing countries, economic arrangements seek to be self-enforcing, to provide the right incentives on their own, with the legal system as the backdrop. Thus, credit markets are enhanced by a legal system that allows individuals to post collateral and other security for loans and allows creditors a reliable means of collecting debts when debtors fail to repay. Bankruptcy laws are therefore another essential part of a well-functioning legal system for modern private sector activity. Other government functions, such as land titling, also enhance the use of collateral. Similarly, land reform can ensure that more poor farmers have collateral, enhancing their access to credit.

The provisions of commercial law that determine the damages that may be collected if a party breaches a contract can provide important incentives to fulfill commitments. Again, achieving the right balance is crucial. If damages are too difficult to collect, there will be too few incentives to fulfill contracts; if too easy, and injured parties are overcompensated, parties may claim breach of contract under false pretenses. Criminal prosecution of fraud, undertaken when a party deliberately or repeatedly engages in promises that it does not intend to fulfill, can be an important supplement to civil action.

The government must also monitor and enforce performance, especially in finance and banking, where failure to comply with standards may not be readily apparent. Good accounting procedures are of little use if firms traded on the stock exchange are permitted to hide bad news or conceal profits. Monitoring and enforcement are also crucial in banking, given the risks of contagion (systemic risks from which the whole economy suffers) and the cost to taxpayers of banking failures. Government action in these areas can have repercussions for the entire economy. After suffering a costly banking crisis in the 1980s, Argentina adopted strict liquidity and capital requirements, which

have since helped maintain banking stability. In Thailand, relaxed limits on real estate lending led to a boom—and then a bust, which contributed to the Asian financial crisis of the late 1990s. Retaining ceilings on real estate lending might have helped avoid the problem.

In banking and finance, as in other areas, the appropriate approach to monitoring and enforcement depends both on the circumstances of the country, such as banks' capacities for risk management and the nature of the risks facing the country, and on the capabilities of the regulatory authorities. Simple rules such as ceilings on real estate lending, restrictions on the rate at which that lending may increase (speed limits), and limits on exposure to foreign exchange risk are often appropriate responses in countries that have limited regulatory capacity and face a volatile external environment. These countries may also favor stricter capital reserve requirements to provide incentives for prudent lending. Incentives for good behavior are important, because even the most effective monitoring and enforcement remain imperfect.

Countries with more sophisticated financial markets may find that the scope for evading certain regulations has increased with the arrival of new financial instruments, such as derivatives. They will have to adjust their regulations accordingly. In some cases they will have to abandon certain outmoded regulations, and in others increase disclosure requirements. Many industrial countries are shifting to regulation based on oversight of financial institutions' risk management systems. Although this can be an important complement to transaction-based regulation, they are not likely to be a perfect substitute, especially in developing countries. The dramatic failures of some financial institutions in the industrial world, large losses in others, and the questionable lending patterns of some banks—including their lending to risky countries around the world—cast doubt on the adequacy of these systems. The International Monetary Fund and the Bank for International Settlements are looking into new ways of ensuring the stability of these systems.

Just as government need not set standards directly, so it need not undertake all necessary monitoring and enforcement. Part of the success of Argentina's reforms comes from having "multiple eyes." By increasing the number of market players—such as subordinated debt holders, who have their own incentives to keep an eye on the banks—regulators have increased the chance that any failure to comply with the new standards will be detected and exposed.

One of the most promising innovations in third-party enforcement is the group lending exemplified by Bangladesh's Grameen Bank and Bolivia's Banco Solidario. In Grameen Bank's model, would-be borrowers first form small groups. Although the loans go to individuals, all members of a group understand that if any member defaults, none will receive subsequent loans. This gives them an incentive to monitor each other's performance, increasing the probability of repayment. Since the groups form voluntarily, borrowers can use their knowledge of their neighbors to exclude the riskiest, thus mitigating another common problem for lenders. Group lending also gives borrowers, many of whom have limited exposure to formal institutions of any type, an opportunity to learn in the company of neighbors about how credit works, and to keep abreast of each other's ideas and progress. Governments can promote group lending by incorporating the idea in public credit programs, by subsidizing the startup costs of nongovernment programs, and by providing general information about the approach.

Another innovative example of third-party monitoring is community enforcement of environmental standards. Environmental officials in Indonesia, frustrated with weak legal enforcement of water pollution standards, hit upon the idea of collecting information on compliance and disclosing it to the public. The resulting program, called PROPER, collected firm-level data on pollutants and compiled those data into a single index. A color-coding system assigned black to the worst establishments and green to the best (none of the firms earned gold, reserved for exemplary performance). Even before the information was made public, firms hurried to improve their ratings. After publication, citizens' groups used the ratings to pressure underperforming factories to clean up. Regulators, meanwhile, could focus their limited enforcement resources on the worst offenders. In the first 15 months of the program, roughly a third of the unsatisfactory performers came into compliance with the regulations.

Ensuring two-way information flows
Much of the discussion so far has focused on ways to facilitate the flow of knowledge from those who have much of it to those who have less: from industrial countries to developing, from governments to citizens, from teachers to students. But effective communication must be a two-way street. Sharing knowledge with the poor requires an understanding of their needs and concerns—and earning their trust. Only then can they be offered knowledge in a form that they can use and will accept. Almost always, listening to the poor is the first step in doing this well. And through listening, public action can benefit from knowledge that the poor themselves have to offer.

Building trust should be a priority for any program seeking to provide knowledge to the poor. Access to knowledge is of little benefit if people do not trust the source. Health workers can suggest good contraception techniques, but poor women might not use them because they suspect that the workers do not understand their life circumstances. Similar concerns lead many poor people to avoid schools and unfamiliar jobs.

Trust was essential in a health program in the state of Ceará, Brazil, where a third of the people live in extreme poverty. Starting in the 1980s, the government hired 7,300 workers (mostly women) as community health agents at minimum wage, with 235 nurses to supervise them. Recruiting people who already cared about health, the program gave them varied tasks and responsibility for results. It also launched a media campaign to raise awareness of the agents' efforts and the new health services. Mothers who previously had hidden their children from government health workers gradually began to see the agents as friends. As a result, vaccination rates for measles and polio rose from 25 percent to 90 percent, and infant mortality dropped from 102 per 1,000 live births to 65 per 1,000.

Because poor people know their own needs and circumstances, taking time to listen to them can greatly improve outcomes. In Rwanda in 1987, high charcoal prices created demand for more fuel-efficient stoves. A stove patterned on a Kenyan model proved unpopular in early trials; tests in 500 households led to changes in size, color, door design, and portability. Government assistance, managed by a team of women, involved publicity campaigns, market surveys, training programs for stovemakers, and limited initial assistance for modernizing stovemaking equipment. Private entrepreneurs then took over production and sales, without subsidies. Three years later, one in four urban households was using the redesigned stove, achieving fuel savings of 35 percent.

Scientists at the Institut des Sciences Agronomiques in Rwanda and at the Centro Internacional de Agricultura Tropical in Colombia collaborated with local women farmers to breed improved bean varieties, after they realized that listening to the women farmers in selecting crop varieties could greatly improve outcomes. The two or three varieties that the scientists first selected led to only modest increases in yields. The women were then invited to examine more than 20 bean varieties at the research stations and to take home and grow the two or three they thought most promising. They planted the selected varieties using their own methods for experimenting. Thanks largely to their better knowledge of the terrain and their personal interest in achieving higher yields with the breeds they had selected, their selections outperformed those of the scientists by 60 to 90 percent.

Beneficiary participation in the design and implementation of projects is another way of learning from the poor. The World Bank uses beneficiary assessments in its social fund projects, in which communities receive funding for projects they themselves have selected. In Zambia, for example, the views of the poor were incorporated through open consultations in public village meetings. Beneficiary participation has been shown to have a powerful impact on project outcomes. A study of 121 rural water supply projects in 49 countries found that 7 out of every 10 projects succeeded when the intended beneficiaries participated in project design, but only 1 in 10 succeeded when they did not.

Some jurisdictions have gone further in harnessing opportunities for participation. The city of Porto Alegre, Brazil, has pioneered a system of participatory budgeting that gives citizens a direct say in expenditure evaluation and allocation. Assemblies across the city account for and evaluate performance from past years; set priorities in education, health, transport, taxation, city planning, and urban development; and then elect representatives to a citywide participatory budget council. Through systematic evaluation of the relative needs of various regions and discussion of allocation criteria, the budgeting council establishes the city's investment plan. It is estimated that, in 1996, nearly 100,000 people, or about 8 percent of city residents, were involved in some stage of the budget deliberations. The changes have increased the resources available for investment; early reforms improved the efficiency of tax collection and were attended by the introduction of additional local taxes. By better identifying priorities and more effective means of investment, the participatory process put these resources to better use. The results have been striking. By 1996, sewerage services had been extended to 98 percent of households (up from half in 1989). Half the city's unpaved roads were paved. And the number of students enrolled in primary and secondary school doubled.

Threats and opportunities

Narrowing knowledge gaps and addressing information problems are clearly important, but neither is easy. Indeed, we know that these gaps and problems will persist, even in the industrial countries. For example, governments can never be sure of the long-run environmental impact of actions taken today. Nor will governments know fully how information failures will influence policy outcomes, even for policies that on the surface have little to do with information.

One challenge for governments everywhere, therefore, is to recognize the persistence and universality of knowledge gaps and information problems. The resulting uncertainty calls for caution and experimentation whenever possible. It should also induce a modicum of humility among those who offer policy advice—and a modicum of caution in those who receive it. Both should recognize that local conditions matter for the success of programs, that people on the ground have the most knowledge of local conditions, and that the challenge of knowledge for development is to combine local knowledge with the wealth of experience from around the world.

The challenge of recognizing the limits of what we know applies to our understanding of knowledge itself—and to this Report. The study of knowledge for development is a new field where much remains to be done. There is ongoing controversy, for example, about how to measure knowledge. Without a standard measure, we cannot determine whether knowledge gaps are growing or shrinking. Similarly, we lack a measure of a society's ability to address information problems and the resulting market failures. Finally, although the Report identifies many policies to improve the application of knowledge for development, additional work is needed. We hope that this Report will provide a starting point for future research on these and other unanswered questions about knowledge for development.

Yet governments and citizens in developing countries cannot wait for this analysis to be completed. The global explosion of knowledge presents urgent threats and opportunities. The globalization of trade, finance, and information flows may be making it easier in principle to narrow knowledge gaps between countries, but the accelerating pace of change in the industrial countries means in many cases a widening gap in practice. Modern life's disruption of traditional communities is dissipating informal channels of information exchange and only slowly supplying new institutions in their place. And some information problems, such as those associated with global financial flows, have been worsened by recent trends.

For developing countries, then, the global explosion of knowledge contains both threats and opportunities. If knowledge gaps widen, the world will be split further, not just by disparities in capital and other resources, but by the disparity in knowledge. Increasingly, capital and other resources will flow to those countries with the stronger knowledge bases, reinforcing inequality. There is also the danger of widening knowledge gaps within countries, especially developing ones, where a fortunate few surf the World Wide Web while others remain illiterate. But threat and opportunity are opposite sides of the same coin. If we can narrow knowledge gaps and address information problems, perhaps in ways suggested by this Report, it may be possible to improve incomes and living standards at a much faster pace than previously imagined.

Each country and community must address these challenges in its own way, taking into account the many ways in which knowledge is acquired, and the variety of institutions that can help to mitigate information failures. Poor people, who are hurt most by knowledge gaps and information problems, stand to gain the most from development strategies that take these problems into account. Knowledge of how to treat common illnesses and improve crop yields is critical, but the power of knowledge goes beyond the impact of specific techniques. As people grasp the ways in which knowledge can improve their lives, they are encouraged to seek out new knowledge and become agents of change themselves.

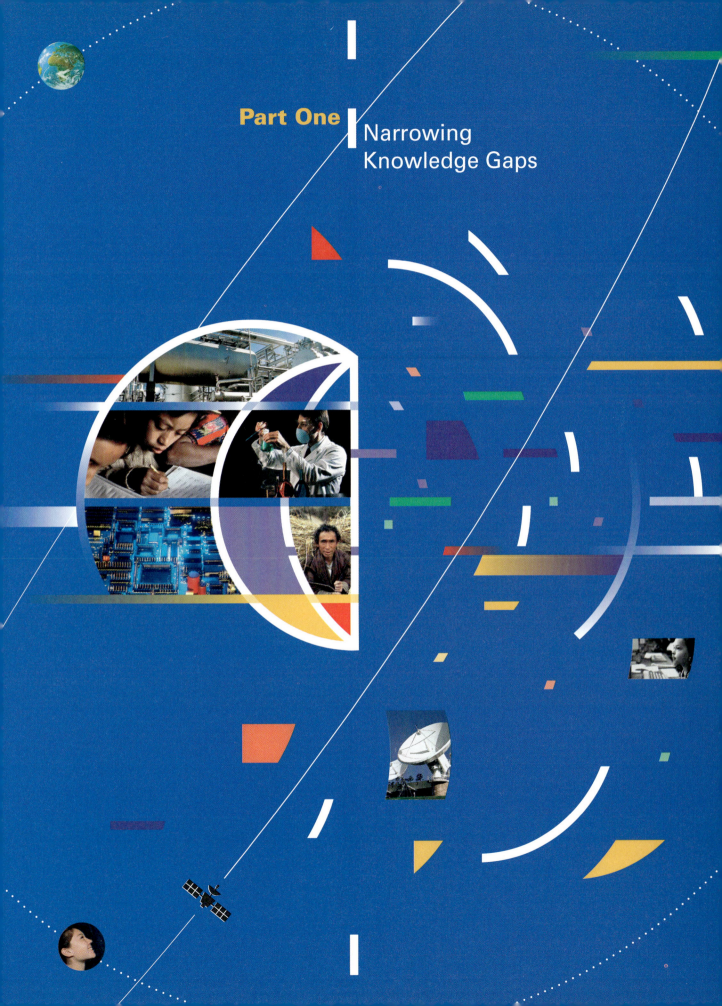

Part One | Narrowing
Knowledge Gaps

Chapter 1

The Power and Reach of Knowledge

KNOWLEDGE IS CRITICAL FOR DEVELOPMENT, because everything we do depends on knowledge. Simply to live, we must transform the resources we have into the things we need, and that takes knowledge. And if we want to live better tomorrow than today, if we want to raise our living standards as a household or as a country—and improve our health, better educate our children, and preserve our common environment—we must do more than simply transform *more* resources, for resources are scarce. We must use those resources in ways that generate ever-higher returns to our efforts and investments. That, too, takes knowledge, and in ever-greater proportion to our resources.

For countries in the vanguard of the world economy, the balance between knowledge and resources has shifted so far toward the former that knowledge has become perhaps the most important factor determining the standard of living—more than land, than tools, than labor. Today's most technologically advanced economies are truly knowledge-based. And as they generate new wealth from their innovations, they are creating millions of knowledge-related jobs in an array of disciplines that have emerged overnight: knowledge engineers, knowledge managers, knowledge coordinators.

The need for developing countries to increase their capacity to use knowledge cannot be overstated. Some are catching on, developing national knowledge strategies, and catching up. But most need to do much more, much faster, to increase their knowledge base, to invest in educating their people, and to take advantage of the new technologies for acquiring and disseminating knowledge. Countries that postpone these tasks will fall behind those

that move faster, and the unhappy consequences for their development prospects will be hard to remedy.

The quest for knowledge begins with the recognition that knowledge cannot easily be bought off the shelf, like cabbages or computers. The marketability of knowledge is limited by two features that distinguish it from more traditional commodities. The first is that one person's use of this or that bit of knowledge does not preclude the use of that same bit by others—it is, as economists say, *nonrivalrous*. This morning's weather forecast is as useful to me if I pass it on as if I keep it to myself. Not so this morning's cup of coffee. Thomas Jefferson understood this well. As he put it, "He who receives an idea from me, receives instruction himself without lessening mine; as he who lights his taper at mine, receives light without darkening me."

Second, when a piece of knowledge is already in the public domain, it is difficult for the creator of that knowledge to prevent others from using it—knowledge is *nonexcludable*. A new mathematical theorem or a new understanding of surface physics, once published, is at large, out there to be used by anyone, to improve a piece of software, for example, or to launch a new line of detergent. Ideas that resonate in the marketplace, from Venetian woolens and glassware in the 17th century to fast food and telemarketing today, can be quickly imitated.

These two properties of knowledge, the main characteristics of public goods, often make it possible for people to use knowledge without paying for it. This reduces the gains to innovators from creating knowledge—and in no small measure. The inability to appropriate all the returns to knowledge is the disincentive to its private supply. If anyone can use an innovation, the returns are diluted, and innovators have no incentive to invest in the costly research and development (R&D) to generate it in the first place. There will thus be too little investment in the creation of knowledge.

Precisely because knowledge is underprovided, governments often set up institutions to restore the incentives to create it. These take the form of patents, copyright, and other forms of intellectual property rights (IPRs), all of which are designed to provide innovators an opportunity to recoup the costs of creating knowledge and to earn a fair return. As knowledge becomes a critical asset for firms and individuals in the new, knowledge-based economy, the need to protect their rights with respect to those assets increases. At the same time, efforts to encourage the creation of knowledge must be balanced against the need to disseminate knowledge, especially to developing countries, and especially where the social returns exceed private returns.

There are many examples in health and environmental matters, to mention just two areas, where patents are not a solution because the social returns to an innovation (to all those benefiting from it) far exceed the private returns (to just those investing in it). Think of an innovation that might lead to a cure for such life-threatening diseases as AIDS and malaria, or reduce the threat of global warming. When the social returns exceed the private, investors, driven by the latter, invest too little from a social perspective in knowledge creation. And because of the large gaps between private returns and social returns, many governments have assumed responsibility—or provided financial incentives to the private sector—for creating some types of knowledge.

Given the special characteristics of knowledge, public action is sometimes required to provide the right incentives for its creation and dissemination by the private sector, as well as to directly create and disseminate knowledge when the market fails to provide enough. The payoffs to such public action have often been huge, as the following section will show for public health.

Knowledge and well-being

Over the past few decades, infant mortality has fallen dramatically worldwide. Higher incomes are a major factor behind the drop but do not account for all of it. Even parents earning the same real income as their parents or grandparents a few decades ago have better reason to expect that their children will live to see their first birthday. A country with an income per capita of $8,000 (adjusted for international purchasing power parity) in 1950 would have had, on average, an infant mortality rate of 45 per 1,000 live births. A country at that same real income in 1970 would have had an infant mortality rate of only 30 per 1,000, and in 1995 only 15 per 1,000 (Figure 1.1).

What explains this shifting relationship between infant mortality and real income? The growing power and reach of practical know-how goes a long way:

- The *invention* of antibacterial drugs and vaccines in the 1930s—and continuing progress in drugs, vaccines, and epidemiological knowledge—have helped tame most communicable diseases.
- *Education,* vital to the adoption and effective use of health knowledge, has expanded in almost every country. Many studies reveal that the amount of education attained by girls and women is an important determinant of children's health. A study of 45 developing countries found that the average mortality rate for children under 5 was 144 per 1,000 live births when their mothers had no education, 106 per 1,000 when they had primary education only, and 68 per 1,000 when they had some secondary education.

Figure 1.1

Infant mortality and real income per capita

As knowledge spreads, infant mortality falls—for rich and poor countries alike.

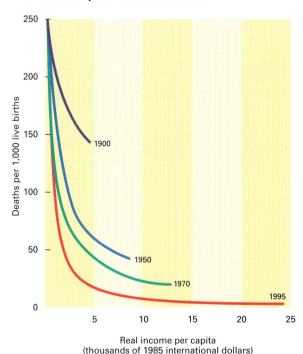

Note: Data are for 10 countries (1900), 59 countries (1950), 125 countries (1970), and 144 countries (1995) worldwide. Trendlines are calculated logarithmically. Source: Maddison 1995, Mitchell 1992, Summers and Heston 1994, World Bank 1997g.

■ Progress in information technologies has accelerated the *dissemination* of medical knowledge and sanitary information, spreading medical advice faster. The information revolution has expanded—and in some cases reinforced—traditional ways of disseminating health knowledge. More people can now reach a doctor or other medical practitioner by telephone. And telemedicine, which allows some surgical procedures to be performed electronically, at a distance, is reaching more and more countries.

Traditions and other social factors influence a community's absorption of medical knowledge. People will not accept modern medical knowledge unless those offering it show an understanding of local knowledge and a sensitivity to cultural norms. Thus efforts to integrate modern and traditional practices may help improve public health by increasing the social acceptability of modern knowledge and harnessing the curative power of traditional knowledge. Moreover, knowledge does not automatically find its way to all people and places that need it. Appropriate institutions, whether public or private, are often required to facilitate its acquisition and adoption, as in Costa Rica (Box 1.1).

Box 1.1

Institutional innovations to diffuse health knowledge in Costa Rica

With less than one-tenth the income per capita of the United States, Costa Rica boasts health indicators that compare favorably with those of many industrial countries. Costa Ricans live nine years longer than their income per capita would predict, and infant mortality rates have fallen to industrial-country levels.

These impressive results are no accident. Since the 1960s, Costa Rican governments have given high priority to the general dissemination of health and sanitation information. They have decentralized institutions to promote information about health and dispatched community health teams to disseminate preventive information. When cholera broke out in South and Central America in 1991, Costa Rica rapidly deployed education, sanitation, and information programs that kept the disease at bay.

Today, more than 400 integrated care teams are reinforcing the government's messages of prevention and health promotion. Schools are also helping get these messages to the public—an easier task than in other countries, because 93 percent of the country's school-age children attend elementary school, 54 percent of adolescents attend high school, and 60 percent of all Costa Ricans are registered in at least one educational program.

Table 1.1

Household spending per capita by level of education in Peru

(1991 new soles per year)

Highest level attained by head of household	Average expenditure per capita
None/initial	430
Completed primary	543
Some secondary	633
Completed secondary	808
Nonuniversity tertiary	969
Some university	1,160
Completed university	1,429
Average for all households	874

Note: Data are from a survey of 2,200 households. "Initial" means some preprimary or primary education.
Source: World Bank 1991.

Knowledge is important for individuals and households to raise children and to allocate time between home production and outside jobs. Knowledge of oral rehydration therapy reduces infant mortality. Knowledge of energy-efficient, less hazardous stoves reduces environmental degradation and improves safety. Household smoke contributes to acute respiratory infections, which, according to estimates, kill more than 4 million infants and children a year. Recurrent episodes of such infections show up in adults (mainly women) as chronic bronchitis and emphysema, often leading to heart failure. Better stoves with better exhaust systems can thus lead to significant health benefits for millions of women and children.

The knowledge of a parent can also raise the living standard of all family members. In Peru the education of the head of the household is strongly associated with household spending, which reflects household earning (Table 1.1). In Vietnam, people living in households headed by someone with no education have a poverty rate of 68 percent. Primary education for the household head brings the rate down to 54 percent, secondary education to 41 percent, and university education to 12 percent.

Knowledge and economic growth

Starting as low-income economies in the 1960s, a few economies in East Asia managed, in a few decades, to bridge all or nearly all of the income gap that separated them from the high-income economies of the Organisation for Economic Co-operation and Development (OECD). Meanwhile many other developing economies stagnated.

What made the difference? One way to grow is by developing hitherto unexploited land. Another is to accumulate physical capital: roads, factories, telephone networks. A third is to expand the labor force and increase its education and training. But Hong Kong (China) and Singapore had almost no land. They did invest heavily in physical capital and in educating their populations, but so did many other economies. During the 1960s through the 1980s the Soviet Union accumulated more capital as a share of its gross domestic product (GDP) than did Hong Kong (China), the Republic of Korea, Singapore, or Taiwan (China). And it increased the education of its population in no trivial measure. Yet the Soviets generated far smaller increases in living standards during that period than did these four East Asian economies.

Perhaps the difference was that the East Asian economies did not build, work, and grow harder so much as they built, worked, and grew smarter. Could knowledge, then, have been behind East Asia's surge? If so, the implications are enormous, for that would mean that knowledge is the key to development—that knowledge *is* development.

How important was knowledge for East Asia's growth spurt? This turned out not to be an easy question to answer. The many varieties of knowledge combine with its limited marketability to present a formidable challenge to anyone seeking to evaluate the effect of knowledge on economic growth.

How, after all, does one put a price tag on and add up the various types of knowledge? What common denominator lets us sum the knowledge that firms use in their production processes; the knowledge that policymaking institutions use to formulate, monitor, and evaluate policies; the knowledge that people use in their economic transactions and social interactions? What is the contribution of books and journals, of R&D spending, of the stock of information and communications equipment, of the learning and know-how of scientists, engineers, and students? Compounding the difficulty is the fact that many types of knowledge are accumulated and exchanged almost exclusively within networks, traditional groups, and professional associations. That makes it virtually impossible to put a value on such knowledge.

Reflecting these difficulties in quantifying knowledge, efforts to evaluate the aggregate impact of knowledge on growth have often proceeded indirectly, by postulating that knowledge explains the part of growth that cannot be explained by the accumulation of tangible and identifiable factors, such as labor or capital. The growth not accounted for by these factors of production—the residual in the calculation—is attributed to *growth in their productivity*, that is, using the other factors smarter, through knowledge. This residual is sometimes called the Solow residual, after the economist Robert M. Solow, who spearheaded the approach in the 1950s, and what it purports to measure is conventionally called total factor productivity (TFP) growth. Some also call the Solow residual a measure of our ignorance, because it represents what we cannot account for. Indeed, we must be careful not to attribute all of TFP growth to knowledge, for there may be other factors lurking in the Solow residual. Many other things do contribute to growth—institutions are an example—but are not reflected in the contributions of the more measurable factors. Their effect is (so far) inextricably woven into TFP growth.

In early TFP analyses, *physical capital* was modeled as the only country-specific factor that could be accumulated to better people's lives. Technical progress and other intangible factors were said to be universal, equally available to all people in all countries, and thus could not explain growth differences between countries. Their contributions to growth were lumped with the TFP growth numbers. Although this assumption was convenient, it quickly became obvious that physical capital was not the only factor whose accumulation drove economic growth. A study that analyzed variations in growth rates across a large number of countries showed that the accumulation of physical capital explained less than 30 percent of those variations. The rest—70 percent or more—was attributed directly or indirectly to the intangible factors that make up TFP growth (Table 1.2).

Table 1.2

Decomposition of cross-country variance in growth rates			
(percent)			
Source of variance	Nehru and Dhareshwar, 1960–88	King and Levine, 1960–85	King and Levine, 1980s
Growth in capital per capita	24	25	29
Unexplained by factor accumulation	76	75	71
Of which:			
TFP growth	60	57	79
Covariance of TFP growth and capital accumulation	16	18	−8

Source: Easterly, Levine, and Pritchett forthcoming. See the Technical Note.

Later attempts introduced *human capital* to better explain the causes of economic growth. A higher level of education in the population means that more people can learn to use better technology. Education was surely a key ingredient in the success of four of the fastest-growing East Asian economies: Hong Kong (China), the Republic of Korea, Singapore, and Taiwan (China). Before their transformation from developing into industrializing economies, their school enrollment rates had been much higher than those of other developing countries (Table 1.3). They had also emphasized advanced scientific and technical studies—as measured by their higher ratios of students in technical fields than in even some industrial countries—thus enhancing their capacity to import sophisticated technologies. Moreover, the importance of education for economic growth had long been recognized and established empirically. One study had found that growth in years of schooling explained about 25 percent of the increase in GDP per capita in the United States between 1929 and 1982.

Adding education reduced the part of growth that could not be explained, thus shrinking the haystack in which TFP growth (and knowledge) remained hidden. Some analysts even concluded, perhaps too quickly, that physical and human capital, properly accounted for, explained all or virtually all of the East Asian economies' rapid growth, leaving knowledge as a separate factor out of the picture (Box 1.2). One reason these analysts came up with low values for TFP growth is that they incorporated improvements in labor and equipment into their measurement of factor accumulation. So even their evidence of low TFP growth in East Asia does not refute the importance of closing knowledge gaps. Indeed, it shows that the fast-growing East Asian economies had a successful strategy to close knowledge gaps: by investing in the knowledge embodied in physical capital, and by investing in people and institutions to enhance the capability to absorb and use knowledge.

Looking beyond East Asia, other growth accounting studies have examined larger samples of countries. Even when human capital is accounted for, the unexplained part of growth remains high. One such study, of 98 countries with an unweighted average growth rate of output per worker of 2.24 percent, found that 34 percent (0.76 percentage point) of that growth came from physical capital accumulation, 20 percent (0.45 percentage point) from human capital accumulation, and as much as 46 percent (just over 1 percentage point) from TFP growth. Even more remains to be explained in *variations* in growth rates across countries. The same study found the combined role of human and physical capital to be as low as 9 percent, leaving the TFP residual at a staggering 91 percent. To take another example: Korea and Ghana had similarly low incomes per capita in the 1950s, but by 1991 Korea's income per capita was more than seven times Ghana's. Much of that gap remains unexplained even when human capital is taken into account (Figure 1.2).

All these results are subject to measurement problems. For example, the measured stock of human capital may overstate the actual quantity used in producing goods and services. High rates of school enrollment or attainment (years completed) may not translate into higher rates of economic growth if the quality of education is poor, or if educated people are not employed at their potential because of distortions in the labor market.

Moreover, it is now evident that education without openness to innovation and knowledge will not lead to economic development. The people of the former Soviet Union, like the people of the OECD countries and East Asia, were highly educated, with nearly 100 percent literacy. And for an educated population it is possible, through foreign direct investment and other means, to acquire and use information about the latest production and management innovations in other countries. But the Soviet Union placed severe restrictions on foreign investment, foreign collaboration, and innovation. Its work force did not adapt and change as new information became available elsewhere in the world, and consequently its economy suffered a decline.

Beyond growth accounting

Does our limited ability to fully account for knowledge in growth diminish its importance for development? Certainly not. Many would agree with the British economist Alfred Marshall that "While nature . . . shows a tendency to diminishing return, man . . . shows a tendency to increasing return. . . . Knowledge is our most powerful engine of production; it enables us to subdue nature and . . .

Table 1.3

Gross enrollment rates in primary school in selected economies			

(percent)

Economy	1970	1980	1990
Hong Kong, China	117	107	102
Korea, Rep. of	103	110	105
Singapore	105	108	104
Ghana	64	79	77
India	73	83	97

Note: Data are total primary enrollments divided by the number of children of official primary school age in the population. Rates can exceed 100 percent when persons younger or older than the official age are enrolled.

Source: World Bank 1998d.

Box 1.2

Knowledge in the East Asian miracle—an ongoing debate

Despite the financial crisis that continues to wreak havoc in much of Asia, the four original miracle economies—Hong Kong (China), Korea, Singapore, and Taiwan (China)—illustrate the possibilities for rapid growth. A key question is whether they achieved their high growth rates by intensively using large quantities of productive factors—physical capital and labor—or by using knowledge.

Several economists have suggested that the growth of most of the East Asian countries can be "fully accounted" for by the increases in their inputs. A high rate of saving in these economies led to high rates of capital accumulation. And their high levels of investment in education led to high rates of increase in human capital. In this view, there is no miracle.

This perspective is open to several criticisms, however:

- True, these economies did maintain high saving rates, but they also invested those savings efficiently. Some other countries—the centrally planned economies, for example—saved aggressively yet did not grow at East Asian rates, because they invested that saving inefficiently.
- The approach incorporates the improvements in knowledge embodied in human and physical capital in its measures of these factors. In other words, if firms invested in closing the knowledge gap by investing in worker training and new equipment, or by purchasing technology licenses, this would not show up, at least in the short run, as an increase in TFP growth (see figure).
- Improvements in knowledge may have sustained the high levels of investment. Without a shift in knowledge, diminishing returns would have set in, and the high rates of investment and saving would have flagged. Indeed, other researchers have found that when the effect of TFP growth on capital accumulation is taken into account, the contribution of TFP growth is significantly greater.
- Equally important, the TFP calculations are highly sensitive to how one measures increases in physical and human

Alternative calculations of TFP growth in four East Asian economies

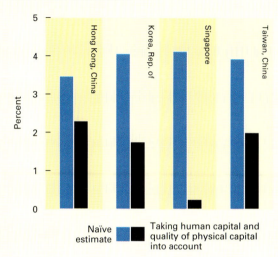

Note: Data are for 1966–90. Source: Young 1995.

capital and to the weights assigned to increases in those factors. Under certain idealized conditions (such as perfect competition), the observed shares of factors in GDP are the correct weights. But under imperfect competition the observed shares of capital and labor in GDP may not reflect the appropriate weights. For example, if wages were suppressed by direct government intervention in the labor market (as may have happened in Singapore), the observed share of labor in GDP may be too small and that of capital much too large. This, combined with faster accumulation of capital than of labor (as observed in East Asia), would understate the role of TFP growth.

satisfy our wants." If anything, recognition of the importance of knowledge has gained momentum, and there is a renewed impetus to integrate knowledge into countries' development strategies.

A key feature of growth in the 20th century has been the role of innovation and invention, as represented by the development of industrial research laboratories to promote innovation, and research universities to advance basic and applied science. Firms, and societies generally, have deliberately decided to allocate resources to improve productivity. Those decisions are much like those for other forms of investment: they are adversely affected by increases in the cost of capital. But because investments in R&D are typically not collateralized, and because they often require a

large upfront outlay, they may depend more on the investing firm's cash flow than, say, investment in real estate. That is why small firms, and firms in developing countries in particular, tend to invest less in R&D.

Firms have also become more sophisticated in their thinking about the adoption and adaptation of new technologies. Many know, for instance, that costs associated with new technologies follow a learning curve, decreasing with experience. This may make them willing to enter new areas of business, even when current costs might make it unprofitable, because they recognize the value of learning. The same considerations affect investment in the transfer of technology by developing countries, both at the firm level and economy-wide. The East Asian econ-

Figure 1.2

Trends in real GDP per capita in Ghana and the Republic of Korea

Differences in capital accumulation alone do not explain the wide divergence in growth.

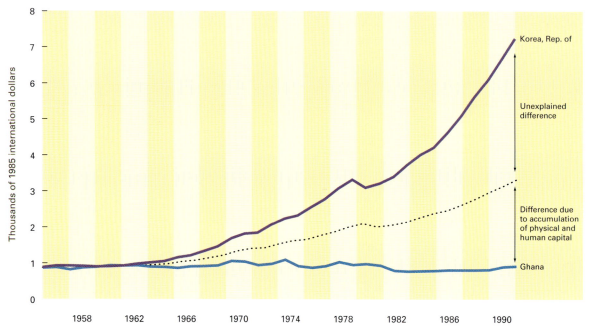

Source: Summers and Heston 1994 and World Bank staff calculations.

omies consciously made decisions to invest to close their knowledge gaps.

Some economists have incorporated in their growth models this purposeful investment in education, innovation, and adaptation of knowledge by people and firms as the main source of productivity growth, and thus as a key factor in economic growth. They see the world as a fertile field of nearly unbounded opportunity, where new ideas beget new products, new markets, and new possibilities for creating wealth. Although conceptually appealing, the approach stops short of providing a deeper empirical insight into explaining cross-country differences in economic growth. It, too, faces the challenge of usefully quantifying knowledge. But some studies have found that some knowledge-related factors affect countries' growth rates. In addition to human capital, they include investment in R&D, openness to trade, and the presence of infrastructure to disseminate information (Box 1.3).

Still other factors, not immediately associated with knowledge, probably add to growth as well. For instance, recent studies conclude that the quality of institutions and economic policies explains a significant part of economic growth. These institutions and policies foster the creation

of knowledge. Without protection of the ownership of physical capital and knowledge capital, little investment or research would take place, because investors would not expect to earn appropriate returns from their efforts. And good institutions and policies facilitate the transfer of knowledge and enhance the likelihood that it will be used effectively. Moreover, the relationship between knowledge and institutions goes two ways: supportive institutions facilitate the production and dissemination of knowledge, and knowledge, especially about the consequences of alternative institutional arrangements, can lead to more supportive institutions. These interactions make it all the more important for countries to develop institutions that complement markets in creating a climate for producing and supporting the free flow of knowledge and information.

Threats and opportunities in a fast-moving global economy

Three considerations argue for a deeper understanding of the interaction between knowledge and development. First, the world economy is becoming ever more integrated—more global—and countries have little leverage on global trends, nor can they isolate themselves from them for long. Between 1960 and 1995, international trade (exports plus imports) grew steadily from 24 percent of world GDP to 42 percent. Multinational corporations today dominate the global economic landscape: a third of world trade is now between multinationals and their affiliates. Improvements in international communications have made distance largely irrelevant.

Second, the share of high-technology industries in total manufacturing value added and exports has grown in almost all the OECD countries (Table 1.4). And it is estimated that more than half of GDP in the major OECD countries is based on the production and distribution of knowledge. This has obvious implications for the composition of the work force: in the United States, more workers are engaged in producing and distributing knowledge than in making physical goods. These indicators are available mainly for the OECD countries and may not apply to developing countries. But they provide useful insights about the importance of knowledge for firms and countries competing in the global economy.

The creation of technical knowledge—as measured by patents issued, although not all technical knowledge is patented—is expanding rapidly. The number of patent applications worldwide increased from 1.4 million in 1989 to 2 million in 1993. Continuous innovation, automation, and competition in the creation and use of knowledge have shortened product cycles in many industries. One study predicted that, between 1993 and 2000, the average product cycle in the automobile industry would drop from eight years to four in the United States, and from six years to four in Japan.

Third, information technologies are advancing at a tremendous rate. It has been said that if the aircraft industry had evolved as spectacularly as the computer industry since the mid-1960s, by the mid-1980s a Boeing 767 would have cost $500 and could have circled the globe in 20 minutes on 20 liters of fuel. Such technical advances reflect progress in technical knowledge. The information revolution spurs the creation of new knowledge by giving inventors and innovators quick access to knowledge, for them a critical input. It also facilitates the production of an increasing number of other goods and services. For example, the microchip content of GDP in the United States has skyrocketed (Figure 1.3). But more important,

Box 1.3

Growing faster with knowledge

Three indicators related to knowledge correlate significantly with growth rates: education, openness to trade, and the availability of communications infrastructure (as measured by telephone density, the ratio of telephone main lines to population). These three partial proxies for knowledge are by no means all there is to gauging access to knowledge or the ability to use it, but they do provide a rough approximation. They show that a country can add substantially to its growth rate by increasing the education of its people, its openness to international trade, and its supply of telecommunications infrastructure. The impact on growth can perhaps be as much as 4 percentage points for a country that moves from significantly below the average to significantly above the average on all these indicators (see figure).

These findings can be plausibly explained for each of the three factors:

■ Openness to trade relates to the opportunity to tap foreign knowledge embodied in traded goods and services. Trade also allows people to learn about business practices in other societies. These knowledge-related benefits of trade come in addition to the traditional, well-established gains from international trade.

■ The educational attainment of a population relates to people's capacity to use knowledge.

■ Telephone density relates to people's ability to access useful information when needed.

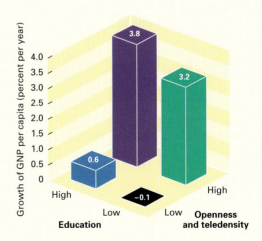

Impact of education, openness to trade, and telephone density on economic growth

Note: Each bar represents the average growth rate for a group of countries over the period 1965–95. Education is average years of education in the population. Openness is the sum of exports and imports divided by GDP. Teledensity is the number of main lines per 100 people. Countries with "high" or "low" values on these variables are those with values at least one standard deviation above or below the sample average, respectively. See the Technical Note for details of the calculation. Source: World Bank staff calculations.

Table 1.4

Share of high-technology goods in manufacturing value added and exports in high-income economies

(percent)

Economy	Value added		Exports	
	1970	1994	1970	1993
Australia	8.9	12.2	2.8	10.3
Austria	—	—	11.4	18.4
Belgium	—	—	7.2	10.9
Canada	10.2	12.6	9.0	13.4
Denmark	9.3	13.4	11.9	18.1
Finland	5.9	14.3	3.2	16.4
France	12.8	18.7	14.0	24.2
Germany	15.3	20.1	15.8	21.4
Greece	—	—	2.4	5.6
Ireland	—	—	11.7	43.6
Italy	13.3	12.9	12.7	15.3
Japan	16.4	22.2	20.2	36.7
Netherlands	15.1	16.8	16.0	22.9
New Zealand	—	5.4	0.7	4.6
Norway	6.6	9.4	4.7	10.7
Spain	—	13.7	6.1	14.3
Sweden	12.8	17.7	12.0	21.9
United Kingdom	16.6	22.2	17.1	32.6
United States	18.2	24.2	25.9	37.3

— Not available.
Source: OECD 1996b.

the information revolution provides untold opportunities for knowledge to be broadly disseminated. The volume of international telephone traffic rose on average by 15 percent a year between 1975 and 1995, thanks to higher-quality, more affordable telecommunications.

Even if more developing countries commit to boosting their investment in knowledge, they may have to run fast to stay in place. As more industrial countries develop artificial (and cheaper) substitutes for many of their traditional exports, the prices of these goods is likely to fall. Just as El Salvador suffered when the invention of chemical dyes made indigo, its principal export crop, obsolete, so many countries today face similar challenges. Copper cables are being replaced by fiber optics, cocoa by artificial cocoa flavorings, and so on. Unless developing countries improve their productivity and shift into the production of new goods—both of which involve acquiring new knowledge—they will face declining standards of living relative to the rest of the world.

Developing countries striving not just to stand pat but to improve their standards of living must do even more. They must move up the value-added chain to produce goods that typically require and embody higher levels of

technology, and to do that they must close the knowledge gap.

Today one country's advantage over others in certain lines of production and trade can no longer be viewed statically, in terms of such relatively unchanging tangible factors as relative supplies of labor, land, and natural resources. Once knowledge, and the potential to improve one's knowledge, are taken into account, *dynamic comparative advantage*—the relative advantage that countries can create for themselves—is what matters. Even dynamic comparative advantage suggests that developing countries will remain importers rather than principal producers of technical knowledge for some time. But the speed with which they do this—based on capacities and incentives—will have a major effect on living standards. Technological change has reduced the relative returns to unskilled labor, and countries that rely on unskilled labor and natural resource–based goods may thus face declining living standards. Countries that succeed in closing the knowl-

Figure 1.3

Real semiconductor content of the U.S. economy

The microchip's economic contribution is growing exponentially.

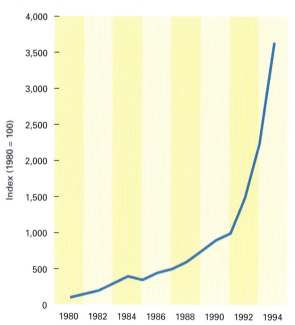

Note: This index is calculated by dividing real semiconductor output, as deflated by a semiconductor price index, by real GDP, and setting that value for 1980 equal to 100. It thus indicates real semiconductor content at 1980 prices per unit of real GDP. Source: Adapted from Flamm, background paper (b).

edge gap may, by contrast, seize a larger part of the returns to knowledge that account for much of the well-being of industrial countries.

Developing countries have tremendous opportunities to grow faster and possibly to catch up with the industrial countries. To take advantage of these opportunities in a fast-moving global economy, developing countries cannot afford to limit themselves to accumulating physical capital and educating their people. They must also be open to new ideas and capture the benefits of technological progress. They must therefore extend the power and reach of knowledge to close the gap in living standards. Some of the East Asian economies showed that the knowledge gap *can* be closed in a relatively short time, perhaps far less time than it takes to close the gap in physical capital. But there are strong complementarities between capital gaps and knowledge gaps, and the East Asian countries typically worked to close both gaps simultaneously.

Countries that fail to encourage investment in the effective use of global and local knowledge are likely to fall behind those that succeed in encouraging it. Some countries have recognized the potential of the global economy and have defined clear strategies to take advantage of it. Others will have to accept the reality of globalization more quickly than they might wish.

What it takes to close knowledge gaps

Successful development thus entails more than investing in physical capital, or closing the gap in capital. It also entails acquiring and using knowledge—closing the gaps in knowledge. The next three chapters address ways to close these gaps, arguing that developing countries have to position themselves to take advantage of the opportunities and to minimize the risks through effective strategies for acquiring and using knowledge. The main tasks are the following:

■ Acquiring and adapting global knowledge—and creating knowledge locally (the topic of Chapter 2)
■ Investing in human capital to increase the ability to absorb and use knowledge (Chapter 3), and
■ Investing in technologies to facilitate both the acquisition and the absorption of knowledge (Chapter 4).

Strategies for addressing these three tasks are complementary. Countries cannot access new technology unless they also invest in education. New technology spurs demand for education and makes it easier to obtain knowledge. Thus, effective policies for acquiring, absorbing, and communicating knowledge are mutually reinforcing components of an overall strategy for narrowing knowledge gaps.

Chapter 2

Acquiring Knowledge

PEOPLE, FIRMS, AND COUNTRIES use technical knowledge to improve their efficiency in the production of goods and services. Sometimes they create that knowledge themselves; at other times they adopt knowledge created by others. Their decision to create or adopt takes into account the constraints they face. Industrial countries, to expand their knowledge base, invest much time and money in research and development. Developing countries, with fewer resources at their disposal, invest less in R&D; instead, they typically expand their knowledge base by acquiring knowledge created elsewhere and adapting it to their needs.

Despite vast and growing opportunities for tapping knowledge created elsewhere, the income gap between rich and poor countries continues to grow. The challenge for developing countries is to reinforce their capabilities—both human and institutional—so that all sectors, firms, and individuals can acquire, adapt, and use knowledge effectively. The payoffs to doing this well should be enormous. But if it is done poorly or neglected, the knowledge gap between the industrial countries, with their huge capacity to create knowledge, and the developing countries will increase, and the income gap will continue to widen. Indeed, one reason the income gap has not been shrinking is that, in many developing countries, not enough has been done to close the knowledge gap. By contrast, those developing countries that have grown rapidly saw closing that gap as an essential part of their development strategy.

Narrowing knowledge gaps within countries is as important as narrowing those between them. Among 200 firms studied in Kenya, the most productive were found to be 40 times as efficient as the least productive—and the average firm did half as well as the best. If all the firms in the sample were as productive as the firm with the best practice, their total output would have been twice what it was. And if the sample is representative of Kenyan manufacturing generally, bringing all firms to local best practice would yield a 10 percent increase in GDP. Surveys in Ghana and Zimbabwe suggest similar potential gains (Figure 2.1).

The gains would be even greater if these developing countries could be pushed to international best practice. Average productivity in spinning in Kenya was found to be 66 percent that in England. Assuming a similar gap between best practice in Kenya and that in England (and using England as the reference for international best practice), Kenyan firms could enjoy a 50 percent jump in manufacturing output—and an additional 5 percent increase in GDP—if they were to produce at international best practice. This back-of-the-envelope calculation shows the large dividends available from closing knowledge gaps within and between countries.

Similarly large gains from making more effective use of existing knowledge can be achieved in such areas as health and agriculture. The technology already exists to deal with many of the infectious diseases that afflict developing countries. The challenge is to disseminate this knowledge effectively, especially to the poor.

This chapter has two main themes:

■ *Acquiring technical knowledge from the world.* For most developing countries, tapping into the global stock of knowledge is critical. And in their strategies for acquiring knowledge, they have to take intellectual property rights into account. For their part, national and international policymakers must strike the right balance between preserving incentives to create knowledge and discouraging efforts to disseminate it.

- *Creating technical knowledge at home.* If it is to be used productively, imported knowledge must be adapted to local circumstances. Moreover, developing countries must not only do better at adopting imported knowledge, but also create new knowledge and exploit the knowledge they have, to meet local needs. They also need to make better use of their own R&D.

Acquiring global technical knowledge

Industrial countries lead the way in the development of new products and processes. Eighty percent of the world's R&D and a similar share of its scientific publications come from the more industrialized nations. For developing countries, acquiring knowledge from abroad is the best way to enlarge the knowledge base. Indeed, one of the clearest lessons from Japan and the newly industrializing economies in East Asia is the value of importing—and building on—established technology from abroad. Developing countries, whatever their institutional disadvantages, have access to one great asset: the technological knowledge accumulated in industrial countries. They should tap this global stock of knowledge, and government should support the private sector in that endeavor.

Tapping global knowledge

The liberalization of trade and regulatory regimes in many countries and the falling costs of transportation and communications are making the world economy more interconnected—more global. Both trade in goods and services and foreign direct investment (FDI) have increased, as have international travel and migration. Here we briefly review the roles of trade, FDI, technology licensing, and the international movement of people as the principal channels for acquiring imported knowledge. (Others not discussed here include strategic alliances, technical assistance, and electronic interchange.)

International trade. Trade can bring greater awareness of new and better ways of producing goods and services: exports contribute to this awareness through the information obtained from buyers and suppliers, imports through access to the knowledge embodied in goods and services produced elsewhere. And as trade becomes ever more driven by knowledge, the opportunities for acquiring technical knowledge will expand. Since the 1970s the structure of international trade has changed significantly: formerly dominated by primary products (such as iron ore, coffee, and unprocessed cotton), it is now concentrated in technology-intensive goods (Figure 2.2). High-technology goods alone doubled their share of world merchandise exports from 11 percent in 1976 to 22 percent in 1996. Meanwhile the share of primary products dropped to less than 25 percent, from about 45 percent initially.

Exports expose firms to global benchmarks of quality and design. They allow firms to realize economies of scale, by expanding production beyond what is possible in the domestic market. An export orientation also induces efficiency, through pressures to compete in the global marketplace. And to compete with best-practice firms in other countries, exporters tend to invest more in knowledge than do firms that serve only the home market.

To expand their trade, countries also need good standards, measurement, testing, and quality control systems. These constitute the infrastructure for technical activity, and their significance grows as traded products and services increasingly have to conform to world standards and regu-

Figure 2.1

Productive efficiency in firms in three African countries

Productivity varies widely even within developing countries.

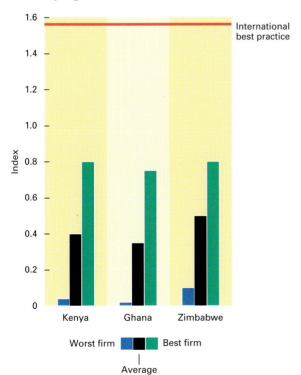

Worst firm ▮ Best firm
Average

Note: Data are from a survey of manufacturing firms in the three countries in 1992–93. The index is calculated such that 1 equals the maximum efficiency achievable, given the quality of available inputs and the policy environment, among all firms in the sample. Source: Biggs, Shah, and Srivastava 1995.

Figure 2.2

Goods in international trade by level of technological intensity

Technology goods have greatly expanded their share of global trade.

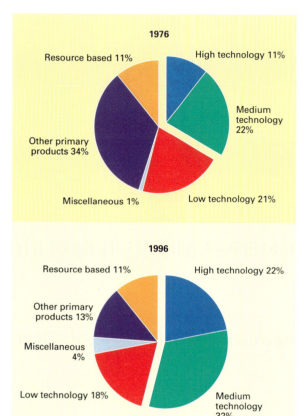

Note: Medium- and high-technology goods are those requiring intensive R&D as measured by R&D expenditure. Source: World Bank COMTRADE database.

size of their knowledge base is reflected in the fact that the 50 largest industrial-country multinationals accounted for 26 percent of all corporate patents granted in the United States from 1990 to 1996. The knowledge in multinationals spills over through learning by their workers and domestic suppliers and through technology sales (royalties, licenses, patent rights). In Malaysia the local affiliate of the U.S. firm Intel Corporation now subcontracts a range of its activities to firms set up by some of its former engineers.

The benefits to a developing country from FDI depend largely on its trade and investment policies. Countries with protected local markets are likely to attract such investment, but only for the purpose of jumping the tariff walls. The technology that enters is then likely to be the older and more inefficient kind, since it need compete only with similarly protected domestic firms. Countries with more-open trade regimes are more likely to attract competitive, outward-oriented foreign investment, which

Box 2.1

ISO 9000: Signaling quality and improving productivity

The ISO 9000 series of international quality management standards lays down detailed procedures for ensuring quality at all stages of production and requires strict documentation of adherence for firms seeking certification. In 1988 existing national standards of quality for manufacturing and services were adopted by the International Standards Organization (ISO) and published under the ISO 9000 name. ISO 9000 certification (which applies to the whole production process, not specific products) signals quality in markets, and international buyers often insist that their regular suppliers obtain this seal of approval.

A 1995 survey by the United Nations Industrial Development Organisation cited demand from overseas customers as the main impetus for ISO 9000 certification by Asian and Latin American exporters. Among 93 major Brazilian enterprises surveyed in 1994, 55 percent increased productivity as a result of ISO 9000, 35 percent improved the standardization of processes, 31 percent increased employee participation in quality control, and more than 20 percent reported an increase in client satisfaction.

Indian chemical companies have also worked to obtain ISO 9000 certification to reassure their Western buyers about the quality of their products. In 1993 Sudarshan Chemical Industries became the first Indian chemical company to receive certification. The process took 15 months, and before applying the company had been working on total quality management for about five years. More than 95 percent of its deliveries are now on time (up from 70 percent). And the margin of error in its product quality has been reduced from 6 percent to 1 percent, and that in new material quality from 4 percent to 1 percent.

lations. If consumers cannot readily distinguish between products or services of differing quality produced by different firms, poor quality by one producer in a market can damage all others, in extreme cases closing entire markets. In Latin America in recent years, substandard quality in a few export shipments—contaminated fruit, shrunken textiles—led North American retailers to shun all such exports from the originating country for months. Obtaining certification for meeting quality standards is especially important for countries with a reputation for poor products (Box 2.1).

Foreign direct investment. Large multinational firms are global leaders in innovation, and the worldwide spread of their productive activities is an important means of disseminating their knowledge to developing countries. The brings more efficient technology and management. Whether that investment also generates spillovers for the host country depends in part on the competitiveness of local suppliers, which in turn depends on their capabilities and access to inputs at world prices, and on the supporting domestic infrastructure (Box 2.2).

Spillovers also depend on linkages between the foreign-owned establishments and the rest of the economy. Yet often foreign companies operate in enclaves, with few local ties—and thus few opportunities to transfer knowledge. A prominent example is the *maquiladoras,* the assembly plants on the Mexican border with the United States. Maquiladoras operate in a wide variety of industries and range in size and sophistication from small plants stitching garments to sprawling electronics assembly plants with hundreds of employees. From their origins in 1965 employment in maquiladoras has grown to more than 800,000 workers at nearly 3,000 locations. Aside from this employment (mostly of low-skilled workers), the plants have few links with the Mexican economy, based as they are on processing imported U.S. inputs brought in under special tariff exemptions.

A major attraction to FDI in today's global economy is a sophisticated communications and transport infrastructure, and here developing countries are at a disadvantage. Many also suffer from an unstable economic, political, or social environment. As a consequence, despite the sizable increase in FDI to developing countries in the past decade, most of that investment goes to only a few countries. The majority of countries benefit only marginally, and Sub-Saharan Africa receives only around 1 percent of the total (Figure 2.3).

If developing countries are to get more global knowledge, they need to attract more FDI. Governments in countries where the investment climate is perceived to be risky can, in the short run, facilitate FDI by working with such international agencies as the Multilateral Investment Guarantee Agency (an affiliate of the World Bank), or with other insurance programs, public or private. But attracting FDI is more a matter of the long than the short run. Many countries, including some in Africa, have instituted policy reforms and maintained them over an extended period (five years or more), have achieved high levels of economic performance, and have worked hard to create an environment friendly to foreign investment. Yet that investment has been slow in coming. Investors also seem to be slow in distinguishing countries with good prospects from those with poor. Over time, however, investors should become better informed, and investment flows should increase to those countries that distinguish themselves by their sound policies.

Technology licensing. Licensing of foreign technology has become an important mechanism for developing countries

Box 2.2

How to attract technical knowledge through trade and foreign investment—and how not to

Openness to world markets makes it easier to acquire international technology, capital goods, and ideas—and to grow faster. A study of the factors driving economic growth in 130 countries found a statistically significant, positive relationship between growth in GDP per capita and the ratio of exports plus imports to GDP. In another study, exports of fast-growing economies averaged 32 percent of GDP; in the slower-growing economies that figure was only 20 percent. One of the prime reasons for the growth spurt of the East Asian economies was their ability to build strong links with world markets and acquire the technology flowing through them. They accomplished this with policies ranging from complete liberalization (in Singapore, for example) to aggressive export promotion (in Korea).

Countries in the Middle East and Africa have recently offered institutional incentives to exporters through free trade zones. However, these for the most part have been poorly managed, and tariffs on imports have remained relatively high. Exporters have faced prohibitive tariffs on the import of inputs (35 to 50 percent), and import licenses, where available, have been difficult to obtain.

Productivity growth and economic growth also come from openness to the foreign ideas and technology associated with FDI. This process typically begins with the local buying offices of international purchasers, which are an important source of production and marketing knowledge. Hong Kong (China), Indonesia, Malaysia, Singapore, Taiwan (China), and Thailand have been particularly welcoming to FDI, and their growth spurts have been closely associated with surges in foreign investment. These inflows can be attributed to a hospitable environment for foreign investment, along with favorable external conditions.

The opposite has been true in the Middle East and Africa. Countries there have received very little foreign investment, as a result of several impediments:

- Insecure property rights, a critical element of a market-friendly institutional environment
- Severe restrictions on the ownership of businesses by foreigners (and excessive regulation generally)
- Weak infrastructure, and
- An unhealthy macroeconomy, with chronically high fiscal deficits, high and unstable inflation, and fluctuating growth rates.

to acquire knowledge. Licensing and royalty payments increased from $6.8 billion in 1976 to more than $60 billion in 1995. Technology licensing is an effective way to get access to some of the new proprietary technologies and can be much more cost-effective than trying to develop an alternative technology. The learning that accrues from using more advanced technology can play an important role in closing the knowledge gap and thereby promote long-term

Figure 2.3

Trends in FDI flows in developing countries

FDI in developing countries has risen severalfold in this decade—but remains concentrated in a few markets.

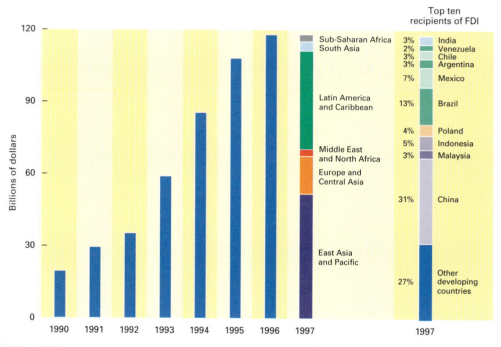

Source: World Bank 1998d.

development. Domestic firms can also use licensing explicitly to leverage their technological development by negotiating access to the underlying design principles of the licensed technologies in areas they are interested in developing further, as many Korean firms have done.

The information differences between the parties to a technology licensing agreement may, however, limit the agreement's potential scope. Not knowing the true cost and quality of the technology on offer, licensees risk choosing outdated or poor-quality technology. Licensers, for their part, may fear that licensees may try to renege on the contract after mastering the knowledge, and this, too, may block some transactions. Some countries have addressed this problem by creating information centers for domestic firms, where they can learn the ins and outs of foreign technology markets, and thus reduce their disadvantage in licensing negotiations. Another option is reputation building through the prospect of repeat contracts and linking royalties to the output of the licensee.

During the 1950s and 1960s, in an effort to weaken the bargaining power of foreign licensers, Japan's Ministry

of International Trade and Industry managed the source and type of technology licensing by Japanese firms. This reduced the cost of acquiring knowledge from abroad. Some developing countries have likewise tried to boost their bargaining power by restricting technology import contracts or capping royalty rates. But if countries lack market power, these restrictions can backfire: free to take their business elsewhere, licensers may not find it worthwhile to transfer technology under the restrictive terms.

Travel and migration. Some developing countries have experienced large inflows of skilled immigrants, who have brought with them specialized knowledge and in some cases have maintained knowledge links to their home countries. Other countries have imported technical knowledge embodied in the human capital of hired foreign experts. International technical assistance and international consulting also involve the movement across borders of people with specialized technical knowledge.

Developing countries can also benefit from (temporary) outflows of human capital: travel to the world's technological centers can be a very effective means of acquiring foreign knowledge. After World War II, under the Marshall Plan almost 20,000 Europeans traveled to U.S. plants to observe advanced manufacturing and management technologies firsthand. The trips proved very useful for setting up and improving the productivity of similar plants in Europe.

On a smaller scale, many businesses, universities, and research centers organize formal exchanges and study tours to share knowledge. These trips include visits to trade fairs, meetings of professional societies, and conventions. Governments, the World Bank, and other international development institutions also organize such visits, so that technicians and policymakers can learn about best practices from industrial countries or from other developing countries.

The opposite side of this coin is the still-ongoing brain drain from the developing to the industrial world. More than 1 million students from developing countries are getting their tertiary education abroad; many of them, especially those earning doctorates, never return home, finding the opportunities there few and the pay low. Some of the best students trained in the developing countries themselves also emigrate, for the same reasons. Both types of emigrants represent a serious loss, all the greater because their education is often fully or partly subsidized by their governments.

Some developing economies have launched programs to recoup these investments, with Korea and Taiwan, China, the most successful. Both have tried to repatriate brains by offering good job opportunities and strong financial and tax incentives to those who return home to teach or work. And some—such as China, India, and again Taiwan, China—have successfully tapped the expertise of their overseas nationals, even without bringing them back. Emigrés often work in high-technology firms and are well aware of market trends and niches. They are thus well placed to give useful technical and market information to producers back home. And they can serve as brokers in trade and other deals between home-country nationals and foreigners.

Another important source of knowledge is other developing countries. For knowledge flows do not just run in a single, one-way current from industrial to developing countries. A growing volume of knowledge is shared among developing countries. This includes technology that has been adapted for specific developing-country conditions as well as local knowledge. Countries now in the earlier stages of development have much to learn from the successes and failures of today's industrializers, for they, too, were on the lower rungs of the development ladder not so very long ago. Knowledge also flows from developing to industrial countries. These include not only indigenous knowledge—for example, about the curative properties of certain indigenous plants, the fruit of some developing countries' biodiversity—but also some modern technological innovations. All these flows—among developing countries and between developing and industrial countries—can be expected to increase.

Public support for technology transfer

Using and misusing incentives. To acquire knowledge through trade, FDI, or licensing, firms must often be encouraged to engage in a conscious and ongoing effort to learn and adapt technology. But the efforts of firms are difficult for government to monitor. Firms protected from price competition may fail to adapt rapidly and efficiently to new technologies or to lower long-run costs. By creating economic rents for incumbents in the protected industry, governments can induce wasteful lobbying as firms devote their efforts to seeking government favors rather than becoming competitive. Protection may dilute firms' incentive to search for the best technology, to invest in training, and to adapt and upgrade their designs.

For example, there is evidence of nonlearning due to misguided protection in the transfer of textile technology to certain African countries. Few resources were committed to searching for superior technological alternatives, and operating efficiency did not increase over a long period of high subsidies. By guaranteeing the profitability of the textile industry through tariffs, price harmonization, and import licensing, Côte d'Ivoire actually diminished the incentive to move toward more efficient production. Evidence from the early 1960s through the late 1970s shows that, despite extensive government intervention, Côte d'Ivoire's textile industry did not develop local technological capability, nor did it graduate from reliance on expensive expatriate staff or produce spillovers in the economy. The outcome was that improvements in labor productivity and capacity utilization rates, where data are available, were mostly slow.

Brazil's attempt to develop a national computer industry illustrates the difficulty of building an industry under a strong protectionist regime. In the mid-1970s the government reserved to national producers that segment of the computer market ranging from submicrocomputers to home computers, peripherals, and subassemblies. To do so it banned not only imports but also FDI. A government agency identified areas for national production, solicited bids from Brazilian firms, and awarded production licenses. It also set up a public research center for informatics and established special fiscal incentives for informatics R&D. By the mid-1980s this policy had succeeded in developing a large national industry. But protection left the industry too fragmented, with many manufacturers producing at less than efficient scale. The domestic component industry was also weak and inefficient, and exports

Box 2.3

Korea: The success of a strong interventionist state

A widespread view holds that Korea's growth was market-led, a result of opening to international markets. But some researchers argue that what is behind the emergence of this Asian "tiger" is a strong, interventionist state—a state that deliberately and abundantly granted tariff protection and subsidies, manipulated interest and exchange rates, managed investment, and controlled industry using both carrots and sticks. Relative prices were deliberately set "wrong," to generate and reap the benefits of evolving comparative advantage, instead of letting them adjust to the "right" levels by the free play of market forces. Korea's leaders judged that getting prices right would lead to short-run efficiency but long-run economic anemia.

Korea's development strategy has been mainly one of pragmatic trial and error, based on a twofold commitment: to the growth of exports and to the nurturing of selected infant industries through protection. The encouragement of exports, particularly manufactured exports, became an active policy in the early 1960s, following unsuccessful attempts at import substitution in the 1950s. It involved the establishment of virtual free trade regimes for exporters through detailed systems of duty drawbacks for direct and indirect exporters. The incentives available to exporters included direct tax reductions, privileged access to import licenses, and preferential interest rates. Thus export promotion entailed substantial government involvement.

Korea chose to focus first on low-technology products, in which the gap between the skills required and those available locally was not large. This had two effects: it encouraged learning-by-doing, and it made Korean firms less dependent on foreign expertise. In the early 1960s, targeted industries included cement, fertilizers, and petroleum refining. In the late 1960s and early 1970s the focus shifted to steel and petrochemicals, and in the late 1970s shipbuilding, capital goods, durable consumer goods, and chemicals were targeted. More recently, electronic and other component industries have been given preference.

At each stage, these industrial policies have engendered controversy. Advocates point to the bottom line: between 1955 and 1991, Korea's GDP per capita increased sixfold. Critics suggest that Korea's growth would have been more rapid still without these policies. To be sure, not every decision seems in retrospect to have been a good one; but the same can be said about any complex private enterprise, without government involvement. The investments in petrochemicals may have looked like a mistake after the huge increases in oil prices in 1973, but no one could have anticipated those price changes. Moreover, with oil prices lower today in real terms, Korea's petrochemical investments look much smarter—perhaps one has to take a longer perspective. In any case, these and other technology investments in the 1970s enabled Korea's petrochemical firms to move up the technology chain, closing the knowledge gap.

were low, consisting mostly of printers. Prices for Brazilian computers were significantly higher than international prices, and the computers were usually a generation behind the latest models abroad. This policy was finally reversed in 1992 with the liberalization of the informatics market.

A key role of a competitive price system is to reveal minimum costs of production. Markets with free entry are like contests: profits depend on performance. Governments that create protective walls around an industry remove this discipline and shut off the information flow that markets sustain. Policies that promote new industries must, to the extent that they replace the market contest system, find an alternative that ensures continuing efficiency if they are to succeed.

Many East Asian economies did this partly by granting subsidies largely on the basis of rules and performance, allowing little bureaucratic discretion. Firms that successfully entered export markets got preferential access to credit. There is some evidence that making subsidies contingent on export performance promoted the use of technology sophisticated enough to compete in world markets and ensure that learning kept pace with the technological frontier. East Asian governments also devised ways of better controlling the bureaucracy (for example, through job rotations), which limited the opportunities for corruption. Although export subsidies are not now permitted under World Trade Organization (WTO) rules, there is still much to learn from the strategies followed by the East Asian economies.

National strategies. Governments in many countries have played a large role in the development and application of technology. The U.S. government built the world's first telegraph line between Baltimore and Washington in 1842. Government-provided agricultural research and extension services are generally credited with much of the enormous increase in agricultural productivity in the 135 years since they were initiated. The Internet, which is changing the way information is exchanged throughout the world, was developed in the United States through public grants.

In the past 50 years, among the handful of economies that have come a long way toward closing the knowledge gap with the global technological leaders, government was active in several, including Japan, Korea, and Taiwan, China. Korea followed a strongly interventionist and nationalist route, keeping FDI to a minimum and relying instead on other modes of technology transfer and a concerted domestic technological effort (Box 2.3).

Although the government of Taiwan, China, was also actively involved in promoting industry, its policies differed in many ways from those of Korea. Rather than supporting a few large enterprises that were particularly successful in developing exports, the Taiwanese based their growth strategy on small and medium-size enterprises. Like Korea's giant *chaebol,* however, the small Taiwanese firms also sought to import high levels of technology. And although the Taiwanese did not erect the barriers to FDI that Korea did, neither did they base their development on the wholesale recruitment of FDI as some other economies have done.

Two other East Asian tigers followed more conventional outward policies and assigned a different role to government. Hong Kong, China, consistently a free trade economy, adopted a liberal stance toward technology acquisition, leaving private firms to choose whatever means they preferred. The city-state provided a free trade, low-tax, stable environment for all investors, regardless of origin. Coupled with a strong base of Chinese entrepreneurs and well-developed trade and financial sectors, this led to the growth of a vibrant, export-oriented industrial sector specializing in relatively low technology activities based largely on domestic enterprise. But the real success of Hong Kong, China, is as an entrepôt, a commercial trading post between China and the rest of the world.

Singapore, which also has a largely free trade regime, chose to rely on foreign investment, which it actively encouraged, and to move that investment into increasingly complex and scale-intensive technologies. Among develop-

ing countries, Singapore has relied the most on FDI, which it attracted initially with disciplined, low-cost labor. With this success in luring investment, wages rose. To continue to make Singapore an attractive location, the government has had to build physical infrastructure. Its seaport, airport, and telecommunications infrastructure are now among the most modern and efficient in the world. And having invested heavily in technical education and training, Singapore now boasts one of the world's most highly skilled labor forces.

The evolution of intellectual property rights
Many of the newly industrializing economies in East Asia imported much of their technical knowledge at a time when enforcement of IPRs was not as strong as it is today. Of late there has been a determined move, coming mainly from industrial countries, to strengthen IPRs. In 1994, at the conclusion of the Uruguay Round of multilateral trade negotiations that led to the creation of the WTO, a new agreement on trade-related aspects of intellectual property rights (TRIPs) strengthened IPRs in WTO member countries while allowing developing countries a transition period (Box 2.4).

IPRs are a compromise between preserving the incentive to create knowledge and the desirability of disseminating knowledge at little or no cost. Without a system

Box 2.4

TRIPs in a nutshell

Intellectual property rights are created by national law and thus apply only in a single national jurisdiction, independent of such rights granted elsewhere. Establishing a global IPR regime thus requires cooperation among national governments to harmonize their separate laws. Numerous international treaties to promote such cooperation have been negotiated over the past 100 years. Most are administered by the World Intellectual Property Organization (WIPO), a specialized agency of the United Nations. WIPO conventions—for example, the Paris Convention for industrial inventions and the Berne Convention for copyright of literature, art, and music—require their signatories to grant national treatment (foreign firms are treated the same as domestic ones) in the protection of IPRs, but typically do not impose common standards of protection. New global rules on IPRs are forcing a reassessment of past strategies for acquiring, disseminating, and using knowledge.

The 1994 TRIPs agreement builds on existing WIPO conventions and lays the foundation for global convergence toward higher standards of protection for IPRs. It requires signatories to apply the principles of national treatment and most-favored-nation (MFN) status to intellectual property protection. Unlike most other international agreements on IPRs, the TRIPs agreement sets minimum standards of protection for all forms of

intellectual property: copyright, trademarks, service marks, geographical indications, industrial designs, patents, layout designs for integrated circuits, and trade secrets.

In each area the agreement defines the main elements of protection: the subject matter to be protected, the rights to be conferred, and the permissible exceptions to those rights. For the first time ever in an international agreement on intellectual property, the TRIPs agreement addresses the enforcement of IPRs by establishing basic measures to ensure that legal remedies are available when infringement occurs. Disputes between WTO members over TRIPs obligations are subject to the same dispute settlement procedures that apply to other WTO agreements.

The provisions of the TRIPs agreement became applicable to all signatories at the beginning of 1996, although developing countries are entitled to a four-year transition period, except for obligations pertaining to national and MFN treatment. Developing countries are entitled to an additional five-year transition for product patents in fields of technology not protected before 1996 (this applies to pharmaceutical products). The least-developed countries are granted a transition period extending until 2006, again excepting for national and MFN treatment.

that protects the rights of those who create knowledge, it is unlikely that individuals and firms would spend much to do so, or at least as much as others do. Patents, for example, provide to knowledge creators the legally enforceable power to exclude others from using their knowledge for a specified period (17 years in the United States). However, the importance of patent protection differs across industries. It is more important in industries such as pharmaceuticals and specialty chemicals, where products tend to be long-lived and it is relatively easy to copy a formula, than in industries such as electronic products, where product cycles are very short and secrecy may be a more effective exclusion strategy. IPRs are important because the cost of developing new products can be quite high. In the pharmaceutical industry the investment necessary to develop, test, and market a new drug is estimated to average $200 million in the United States.

It is expected that stronger IPRs would lead to greater R&D effort in countries that offer such protection. There is limited empirical evidence, however, of the impact of IPR protection on increased investments in R&D, even in industrial countries. In part this reflects difficulties in establishing causality, for not only may IPRs stimulate more research, but also the demand for protection may be higher in countries that invest more in R&D. The benefits of patents, however, go beyond stimulating investment in R&D. Patents provide published information to other researchers, who can then develop innovations in similar directions to meet new needs.

It is also sometimes argued that stronger patent protection in developing countries could stimulate research in industrial countries on issues of concern to developing countries (such as tropical diseases). Once again, the empirical evidence is limited, although it is reasonable to expect that IPR protection may be a necessary, but not a sufficient condition for private companies to engage in such investment.

Because developing countries often use knowledge produced in industrial countries, they have a particular interest in its dissemination. But without some protection of intellectual property, firms in industrial countries will have no incentive to transfer knowledge, or even to make investments that might lead to such transfer. The level and quality of patent protection in developing countries therefore influence both FDI and direct technology transfers through licensing agreements and the vertical integration of multinational firms—both important for the diffusion of knowledge (Box 2.5). IPRs also help create a market for knowledge by providing a legal basis for technology sales and licensing. They signal to prospective investors that a country respects their intellectual property and is "open for business" according to accepted international norms. And IPRs can encourage multinational

Box 2.5

IPRs, investment, and technology transfer

A World Bank study found that the strength or weakness of a country's system of intellectual property protection has a substantial effect, particularly in high-technology industries, on the kinds of technology that many U.S., German, and Japanese firms transfer to that country. This strength or weakness also seems to influence the composition and extent of FDI in the country, although effects seem to differ from industry to industry.

In chemicals and pharmaceuticals, at least 25 percent of firms surveyed in all three countries felt that protection in Argentina, Brazil, Chile, India, Nigeria, and Thailand was too weak to allow them to invest in joint ventures where they contributed advanced technology. In machinery and electrical equipment, the same was true of Brazil, India, Nigeria, Taiwan (China), and Thailand.

More than a quarter of chemical and pharmaceutical firms in the three source countries felt that IPR protection in Argentina, Chile, and India was too weak to permit them to transfer their newest or most effective technology to a wholly owned subsidiary there. And more than 20 percent of machinery and electrical equipment firms in the source countries felt that this was the case in Brazil, Nigeria, and the Philippines. Hong Kong (China) and Singapore were felt to have the strongest protection among the major economies considered.

companies already established in a developing country to transfer more technology-intensive functions, including R&D, to their affiliates, as well as the knowledge embodied in products that are fairly easy to replicate.

Many developing countries have begun to reform their IPR regimes. The number of developing countries that have signed the Paris or the Berne Convention increased from almost 50 in the 1960s to more than 100 by the mid-1990s. As a result of the more stringent demands of the TRIPs agreement that went into effect in 1996, and of the increasing realization of the importance of knowledge in their own economic activity, one may expect that more developing countries will strengthen their IPR protection.

Despite the pluses, the effects of IPRs on developing countries raise several concerns. Tighter IPRs may lead to a higher cost of acquiring knowledge. They shift bargaining power toward producers of knowledge, and away from its users. Since knowledge is a key input in the production of more knowledge, stronger IPRs may adversely affect follow-on innovations, in developing as well as industrial countries, that draw on inventions whose patents have not yet expired. There is thus a concern that tighter IPRs may actually slow the overall pace of innovation. However, there is no systematic empirical evidence confirming this, just as there is none on the positive impact of IPRs on increased R&D. A related concern is that, with patented knowledge, the pace of imitation may be slowed, and the knowledge gap between industrial and developing countries may increase.

Tighter IPRs can thus disadvantage developing countries in two ways: by increasing the knowledge gap and by shifting bargaining power toward the producers of knowledge, most of whom reside in industrial countries. This raises a concern about the distributional effects. These may be particularly strong with respect to the effects of patents on the price of medicines, because of the relatively weak bargaining power of developing countries in negotiating prices with monopoly suppliers. Fears about this may be exaggerated, however. Some argue that the knowledge most needed by the poorest—for example, to produce most of the drugs they might use—is already in the public domain, mostly because the patents have expired. Moreover, these dangers have to be set against the advantages of tighter IPRs already described. A desirable IPR regime is one that balances the concerns of all parties affected by strengthened IPRs.

There are many dimensions to IPRs, and adjustments strengthening or weakening protection may affect developing countries in different ways. These should be taken into account as the IPR agreements evolve. The easiest to explain is the life of a patent: longer patent lives give the inventor more protection. Although patent lives have been standardized to a considerable degree, a variety of other issues remain. For instance, given the long delays in government approval, should the life of a drug patent begin only after the drug has received approval? or from the time the inventor applies for the patent? Standards for determining whether a product is novel enough to claim patent protection, and for determining how broadly such protection should apply to related products and processes, are complex issues, and changes can have enormous effects. Broad patents may, for instance, jeopardize the prospects of anyone attempting to adapt the technology in question to different circumstances.

Developing countries face new IPR challenges in biotechnology. Industrial-country breeders are relying on the regular patent systems for protection of agricultural biotechnology products and processes. Breeders enjoying such protection can prevent their competitors from using their protected material for breeding purposes—they can even prevent farmers from reusing harvested seed. In pharmaceuticals and biotechnology, shortly after the new research tools of molecular genetics were developed, patent systems in industrial countries began to provide protection for a variety of these innovations, such as the fundamental mechanism of gene splicing. These protections affect the processes for producing a variety of products and therefore go far beyond the protection of a specific pharmaceutical or other product.

Strong IPRs can also affect traditional knowledge. One issue is how to compensate local communities when industrial-country firms obtain patents on their indigenous knowledge (Box 2.6).

The rapid development of both science and intellectual property law presents the developing world with both opportunity and challenge. The opportunity is that the new technologies can be useful in developing products for tropical as well as for temperate zone diseases, and the expansion of the intellectual property system to developing countries will give the private sector greater incentive to develop these products. The challenge is that so many industrial-country firms are acquiring strong intellectual property positions, often covering fundamental research tools as well as marketable products, that it may prove hard for new firms and researchers to elbow into this new global industry. Developing-country firms and public research groups need to enter into agreements with industrial-country firms to obtain privately held technologies. And they need to understand how to negotiate these agreements and to participate in the continuing debate

Box 2.6

Providing local compensation when bioprospecting strikes gold

Madagascar's unique rose periwinkle plant was used to develop two anticancer drugs, vincristine and vinblastine, which together have generated more than $100 million in sales for a global pharmaceuticals company. Madagascar, however, got no financial return from these discoveries.

The example illustrates a growing concern, namely, that the strengthening of IPRs and their extension to biological materials will enable large multinationals engaged in bioprospecting to, in effect, appropriate valuable biomedical knowledge from indigenous peoples. Now, however, under pressure from nongovernmental organizations and environmental groups, large corporations are beginning to enter into contracts with local communities to provide compensation when the firm's innovations make use of the community's knowledge.

One of the best-known contracts is that negotiated between Merck & Company and INBio (Instituto Nacional de Biodiversidad), Costa Rica's nonprofit national biodiversity institute. Merck provided $1.1 million initially, plus a commitment to share royalties on any commercial products developed, in exchange for 2,000 to 10,000 extracts from plants, insects, and microorganisms in Costa Rica. INBio has now entered into nine research agreements giving companies limited access to biological resources in return for financial compensation and technology transfer.

about particular forms of intellectual property, to ensure that their interests and those of their country are taken into account.

The dawning of the digital era poses another set of problems. The merger of computer and telecommunications technologies has allowed the explosive growth of computer-mediated networks and the emergence of a global information infrastructure. In this new environment the frontiers between carriers and content providers become fuzzy. With a few keystrokes anyone can anonymously download copyrighted material from websites around the world. Prosecution of carriers who infringe on copyrights on digital information can discourage such infringement. But it may also inhibit the expansion of the value-added services that make the global information infrastructure so valuable.

In December 1996 WIPO convened a diplomatic conference to update the Berne Convention. The resulting WIPO Copyright Treaty and the WIPO Performance and Phonograms Treaty should facilitate the use of cyberspace for commercial applications by clarifying the rights of authors. For developing countries, joining these multilateral agreements can help advance the debate about reform in IPR laws to cope with the challenges of the digital age.

Stronger IPRs are a permanent feature of the new global economy, so it is important to find innovative ways of maintaining incentives to create knowledge while ensuring its broader diffusion. As Chapter 9 details, the initiatives in this direction range widely: from international public subsidies for research on technical knowledge of relevance for developing countries but not undertaken by the private sector, to partnerships between international organizations that want to see these technologies produced and the large private companies with the technical expertise to produce them.

Creating local knowledge

Developing countries cannot take advantage of the vast stock of global knowledge unless they develop the competence to search for appropriate technologies—and to select, absorb, and adapt what they find. The Overview showed that agricultural knowledge had to be adapted to local conditions for the green revolution to take hold. Even in manufacturing, knowledge produced in other countries often has to be adapted to differing conditions such as weather, consumer tastes, and the availability of complementary inputs. Making these adaptations often requires local research, which is also essential for following current developments in global knowledge and for selecting the most appropriate technology.

There is a strong complementarity between local technological efforts and technology imports. One recent study of technology institutions and policies gathered evidence from more than 2,750 firms in China, India, Japan, Korea, Mexico, and Taiwan, China. This study found, as did less extensive studies of Canada and Hungary, that firms with more in-house technical resources used more outside technological resources (such as those of technology institutions). It also found that the most important outside source of technology was long-term customers, followed by suppliers. Most of these customers and suppliers were foreign, confirming the importance of interaction through trade.

Similarly, firms with in-house R&D facilities were the most likely to receive technical assistance from customers in product and process innovations. This link seemed more valuable for firms catching up with international standards than for those already there. Foreign licensers were also very important sources for firms that had taken licenses, but licenses were considered costly both because of the high fees charged and the higher transactions costs. Consultants were also useful for firms that could afford the fees and transactions costs. Public technology institutes were very widely used, more by large companies than by small ones, because large companies could articulate their problems better.

Government-funded R&D

Since the private sector typically underinvests in R&D, governments have tried to encourage it either directly through public R&D or indirectly through incentives for private R&D. Direct government R&D includes that financed at universities, government research institutes, science parks, and research-oriented graduate schools. Indirect R&D interventions include preferential finance, tax concessions, matching grants, commercialization, and the promotion of national R&D projects. Developing countries spend a much smaller share of their GDP on R&D (an average of about 0.5 percent) than do the industrial countries (about 2.5 percent). And in the large majority of developing countries this R&D is funded by the government.

In most developing countries the allocation of public research funds to projects is haphazard, and fluctuations in research budgets undermine the continuity of projects, creating more inefficiency. But a few countries are strengthening research capacity, setting clearer research priorities, and establishing better systems for allocating public research funding on the basis of peer review. Some of the problems and reforms are well exemplified by Brazil, where the World Bank has been involved in a series of projects to strengthen capacity to produce, select, and adapt scientific and technological knowledge (Box 2.7).

Because adapting agricultural technology to local conditions is so important, and because the poorest developing economies are agriculturally based, most of their R&D is in agriculture, almost all of it publicly funded. As

Box 2.7

Changing the way Brazil does research

Brazil's scientific community is by far the largest in Latin America, yet the social and economic contribution from its research has been modest. The aims of a recent reform are to raise the standard of scientific and technological research to international levels, to improve the system for training high-level human resources, and to increase the relevance of the country's R&D for productive activity.

The Brazilian system exhibited all the flaws typical of developing-country research. Resources fluctuated dramatically with changing macroeconomic conditions, increasing the vulnerability of the system. Small grants of short duration, whose bureaucratic requirements lowered the productivity of researchers, were often awarded by administrators who lacked relevant expertise, not by scientific peers. Funds for equipment maintenance were scarce, import restrictions limited equipment availability, and inflation quickly eroded the value of grants. In addition, the system was strongly biased toward basic research, at the expense of applied work. Very little collaboration went on between researchers and firms. The system also lacked regional balance, with virtually all the world-class research being done in just a few of Brazil's southeastern states.

The Action Program for Science and Technology (known by its abbreviation in Portuguese, PADCT) grew out of the government's desire to equalize funding among disciplines in a system with a few dominant areas—notably physics—and many lagging ones. The World Bank helped develop two loans focusing broadly on reform of public funding for research, rather than on primarily rehabilitating select disciplines. The emphasis has been on appropriate "rules of the game" and on the long-term adoption of a transparent, merit-based system for allocating research resources.

Under the two loans, which totaled $479 million, 3,200 peer-reviewed research projects were awarded. A third loan, which was approved in 1997, will support a $360 million program to finance more than 1,000 projects in scientific research and technology development, with the emphasis on the latter.

Perhaps more important than the "how much," the PADCT has helped change "how" science is funded in Brazil. The peer review system of resource allocation has firmly established transparent, merit-based awarding of resources. And its rules have set a standard that other federal and state programs have adopted. The scientific community now does more in the way of planning and administration. Larger and longer-term grants are bringing Brazilian scientists closer to par with their colleagues in the industrial countries.

---

economies develop they increase their spending on R&D, but almost all of it continues to be publicly funded agricultural research. The average return to agricultural research has been around 60 percent, but the dispersion is high, reflecting the risks.

Unlike in much of industry, critical agricultural technologies (principally new seed varieties) are not well protected by IPRs, either globally or nationally. Therefore private investors do not provide enough R&D, especially for technologies applicable in the poorest countries, where information and market problems add to those of weak IPRs. The potential international spillovers that discourage private investors also enhance the economic effectiveness of international collective efforts in agricultural R&D, such as those undertaken through the system of international centers known as the Consultative Group for International Agricultural Research (see Chapter 9).

Only when developing countries come to have significant industrial sectors do they start to invest in industrial R&D, but for the most part even this continues to be publicly funded. Only as countries discover the need to upgrade their technology to compete in world markets does the private sector begin to invest in R&D.

Governments often lack information on the needs of the productive sector, and thus allocate funds for research inefficiently. As a result, many developing economies are reforming their public R&D institutes and making them more responsive to the market. Brazil, China, India, Korea, and Mexico have launched vast programs to reform public R&D laboratories and focus them on the needs of the productive sector. Reform measures include corporatizing these institutes, capping the government contribution to their budgets, improving researchers' pay and recognition, and giving firms direct incentives to place research contracts with the institutes.

China's reform program is a good example. With more than 1 million scientists and engineers and more than 5,000 research institutes, China has tremendous scientific and technological potential. With help from the World Bank the government is redirecting key assets of the country's large R&D infrastructure toward a results-oriented, market-based mode of operation that will increase productivity. Research laboratories and design institutions are being restructured and retooled to become true technology companies, some with the assistance of foreign investors or strategic partners. So far the government has invested in 47 engineering research centers, with 11 already operating as corporations. The balance sheet of each center has been sorted out, and each has a clear mandate from shareholders to innovate in the marketplace.

Private R&D

Private firms have taken a larger share of R&D in developing countries in the past 15 years. Basic scientific research is still done by highly qualified, specialized personnel—generally in academic institutions and public research laboratories, and mostly financed by government—while private research labs focus on applied R&D. The reason is simple: applied R&D, including engineering and product development efforts, leads to more directly appropriable results, whereas basic research, although it advances knowledge, usually does not. The public good features of basic research mean that usually only the government will provide it. In some cases, however, the cost of public R&D can be shared by private consortiums that benefit from commercialization. The private sector is also funding basic research in activities with potential for commercial applications, such as biotechnology.

Only a few developing economies—including Korea, Singapore, and Taiwan, China—have provided the right incentives for significant private R&D. Korea tops this list, with private R&D accounting for 2.3 percent of GDP (and 80 percent of the country's total R&D), one of the highest rates in the world. In 1975, when R&D spending was about 0.5 percent of GNP, and 80 percent of it public, the government launched a variety of incentives to promote private R&D. But what really spurred the increase was the need for more-advanced technology as the industrial sector matured in the 1980s. Acquiring this technology from abroad was becoming more difficult, so the private sector began to invest heavily in its own R&D to understand and acquire relevant technologies. As a result, Korea's publicly funded R&D institutes are redefining themselves, moving into more basic, precommercial research.

Building on local knowledge and local demand

For most developing countries, local research has to focus on more essential needs. And for local R&D to be relevant, particularly in agriculture and medicine, it should build on local knowledge, which can have tremendous value. In 1990 estimated world sales of medicines derived from plants discovered by indigenous peoples amounted to $43 billion. At least 25 percent of drugs prescribed in the United States use natural compounds derived from plants. For two-thirds of these the modern uses directly reflect the traditional applications.

In promoting local or adaptive research or in encouraging the adoption of modern technologies, care must be taken not to undermine useful traditional knowledge. Local technologies often require fewer material resources than imported technologies, allowing them to weather the vicissitudes of local shortages and material constraints. The oral rehydration solutions used to combat diarrhea provide an example. In some countries, aggressive promo-

tions of subsidized, ready-made industrial packets undercut the use of long-known home remedies. When the subsidies ended and health education efforts stopped, the rate of use fell. But households that might have then reverted to traditional home remedies did not, because confidence in them had been undermined by the promotion of the commercial remedy. To avoid such an outcome in Nepal, oral rehydration programs preserved local knowledge by encouraging the use of homemade simple solutions alongside the modern packet solution (see Chapter 8).

Just as developing countries profit from knowledge from the industrial world, so do they benefit from preserving and deploying the knowledge developed in the course of their own history. But efforts to harness that knowledge, or to reconcile it with new technologies, require the involvement of those who possess it. And for the knowledge generated by local adaptive research to be relevant and broadly adopted requires full participation of end users and local communities in design and implementation. Local women in Colombia and Rwanda proved to know more about how to breed improved bean varieties locally than did scientists from the countries' research institutes (Box 2.8).

It is also important to take into account local constraints and the availability of complementary inputs. The promise of simple, improved biomass stoves has sparked a spate of stove programs in more than 41 countries, including China, Ethiopia, India, Kenya, and Rwanda, since the early 1980s. Domestic stoves that burn biomass fuels more efficiently offer large benefits to developing countries, where overuse of these fuels is depleting resources, degrading local

Box 2.8

Building a better bean: How women farmers in Colombia and Rwanda outdid the researchers

Scientists at the Institut des Sciences Agronomiques in Rwanda and at the Centro Internacional de Agricultura Tropical in Colombia collaborated with local women farmers to breed improved bean varieties. The two or three varieties considered by the breeders to have the most potential had achieved only modest increases in yields. The women farmers were invited to examine more than 20 bean varieties at the research stations and to take home and grow the two or three they thought most promising. They planted the new varieties using their own methods of experimentation.

Although the women's criteria were not confined to yield, the breeders' primary measure for ranking, their selections outperformed those of the bean breeders by 60 to 90 percent. The farmers were still cultivating their choices six months later.

environments, exacting time to collect fuel, and creating indoor pollution that harms the most vulnerable in the household: women and children. But only a few programs have prompted widespread adoption and use. At the heart of this shortcoming lies the early failure of program sponsors to focus design and marketing efforts on the demands and constraints of local consumers and manufacturers. Fortunately, that has changed (Box 2.9).

• • •

To build their knowledge base, developing countries should explore all means of tapping the global stock of knowledge. Through their trade with the rest of the world, they can find new and better ways of producing goods and services. This is important as the structure of their trade shifts from primary to knowledge-intensive products. By attracting FDI, they can work with the global leaders in innovation, spurring all domestic producers to try to match their practice. But this will happen only with the right policies and appropriate infrastructure—for transport, for communications, for standards, indeed for doing business. Through licensing they can get access to new technology and can jump-start the accumulation of technological capital—if they negotiate to learn the underlying principles so that they can improve on what they are buying. And through the flow of people across borders, they can stay on top of the latest developments, often establishing lifelong relationships for the steady flow of know-how.

In all this, firms have to be encouraged to continue their search for the best techniques, to invest in training, and to upgrade their designs. Few things do more to encourage this than open, competitive markets—and few more to smother it than continuing subsidies. Also important is a balanced treatment of intellectual property that finds the right mix between providing incentives to create and acquire knowledge, and disseminating that knowledge at the lowest possible cost.

To take best advantage of the technology that comes in, and to spread successful practices throughout the economy, developing countries have to adapt that technology to local conditions. This should be the focus of government-funded R&D, initially in agriculture but increasingly in industry, as manufacturing develops. And in-

Box 2.9

Why better biomass stoves sold in Rwanda

The "Rondereza" charcoal stove was introduced in urban Rwanda in 1987, where high charcoal prices had created demand for more fuel-efficient stoves. Patterned on a popular Kenyan model, the Rondereza proved unpopular in early trials. What had worked in Kenya obviously did not work in Rwanda. The stove was then tested more extensively in 500 households and subsequently modified in terms of its size, valuation, quality, color, door design, and portability, in line with suggestions from householders and stovemakers.

Private entrepreneurs undertook (without subsidies) the production, distribution, and retailing of the stoves. This made the stove program oriented to consumers from the start. Government assistance, managed by a team of mostly Rwandan women, took the form of publicity campaigns, market surveys, training programs for stovemakers, and limited initial assistance for modernizing stove-making equipment.

The program's participatory, market-driven approach was quickly validated. Three years after its inception, 25 percent of urban households had the stove, which by then was widely available in market outlets and department stores. More than 90 percent of users surveyed indicated they would buy the stove again, citing not just its fuel economy but its cleanliness, long life, and ease of use. And the fuel savings achieved were on the order of 35 percent.

creasingly the incentives should be put in place for private firms to take on their own R&D, initially in adapting, understanding, and refining the technologies they are already using, but eventually moving into research in those areas where they are close to international best practice.

The opportunities to be had from moving to better practices—from narrowing the knowledge gaps within and between countries—are nothing short of stupendous, and they apply not only to industry but across all sectors. Seizing those opportunities requires openness to outside ideas, the right incentives and institutions, and local effort dedicated to acquiring, adopting, and using knowledge effectively.

Chapter 3

Absorbing Knowledge

FOR INDIVIDUALS AND FOR COUNTRIES, education is the key to creating, adapting, and spreading knowledge. Basic education increases people's capacity to learn and to interpret information. But that is just the start. Higher education and technical training are also needed, to build a labor force that can keep up with a constant stream of technological advances, which compress product cycles and speed the depreciation of human capital. And outside the classroom, people's working and living environments are the setting for still more learning, well beyond the ages associated with formal education. Moreover, the benefits of education can spread well beyond the educated. The education of a mother pays off in better health care and better nutrition for her children. Educated farmers tend to adopt new technologies first, and in so doing provide those who follow with valuable, free information about how best to use the new methods.

Recognizing these benefits, many countries have made great strides in expanding enrollment at all levels, and a good number have made primary and even secondary education universal. But the gains in access to education have been unevenly distributed, with the poor seldom getting their fair share. Quality is too often deficient in some countries, to the point that they fail to endow their people with the basic skills—literacy, numeracy, and the capacity for analytical reasoning—required to compete in future labor markets. And delivery is still too inefficient, with too little tangible return for what is spent.

Public action can address these challenges. Government, already a pervasive presence as a provider and funder of education, exerts a powerful influence on students, parents, teachers, employers—in short, on all who contri-

bute to educational outcomes. And only public action can ensure equitable access, take spillover effects into account, and overcome market failures in the provision of education. One of the gravest of these failures is in the market for information *about* education. Too often, decisions about investments in education are made by persons such as illiterate parents or ill-informed bureaucrats far from rural schools, who have insufficient information either about what is needed or about what is available. Reforms that confront these problems in education can go some way toward increasing its equity and efficiency.

Education as a lifelong process

Because each level and type of education—basic, tertiary, practical—plays an important role in the absorption of knowledge, the process affects all ages.

Basic education—the scaffolding for lifelong learning
Basic education (which in most countries means primary and secondary education) develops a person's capability for learning, for interpreting information, and for adapting knowledge to local conditions. And through its effects on economic productivity and on other aspects of life such as health, it helps determine a person's well-being.

One of education's most powerful effects is on wages. Studies of labor markets in Ghana, Kenya, Pakistan, South Africa, and Tanzania show that part of the association between higher wages and basic schooling can be directly attributed to the knowledge learned in school. But part is also due to the fact that acquiring education signals a worker's capacity and motivation for learning. Studies from Côte d'Ivoire, urban Pakistan, and Peru report significant "sheepskin" or credentialing effects: labor markets reward those who possess college degrees and other tangible signals of ability.

In performing this signaling role, the education system works to mitigate an important market imperfection. The information that schools provide about their alumni is valuable to employers, not only in selecting whom to hire but in matching workers with jobs that fit them best. And that is only the beginning:

- Schooling fosters agricultural innovation. Farmers with more basic education are more productive and more likely to profit from new technology. The benefit is therefore greatest in areas of faster innovation, because schooling provides the fundamental cognitive skills that farmers need to respond to changing circumstances and learn from new experience. Farmers who adopted the new plant varieties developed in the green revolution realized lower profits at first, compared with other farmers planting traditional varieties. But as experience with the new seeds increased, profits rose for all farmers using them—and they rose more for the more educated.
- Schooling enhances one's ability to reallocate resources in response to economic change—to weather price fluctuations or the peaks and troughs of business cycles. People with more schooling tend to be more venturesome and more willing to take the risks necessary to adapt quickly to a changing economic environment. In Slovenia, when employment and real wages fell in 1987–91, workers (especially women) with more education suffered a much smaller decline than those with less. Similar results hold in the wealthier industrial countries, such as the United States.
- Schooling promotes the use of new technologies in the home, for health, nutrition, learning, and contraception. In this the parents' schooling, especially the mother's, is critical. Child mortality declines and nutritional status rises with increased parental education, contributing greatly to children's welfare and development (Figure 3.1). Part of the reason is education's impact on earnings, but its effects go beyond that, since children in families with better-educated parents enjoy better health and nutrition at any given family income.

The influence of the mother's education begins in the womb and continues through the preschool period and beyond. Over the past 30 years, measured IQs have risen globally by about 20 points. This rise, too rapid to have been genetic, suggests that new child-rearing practices have affected children's innate ability and cognitive development, and thus improved educational outcomes (Box 3.1). This observation provides a compelling argument for governments to support early childhood programs that

Figure 3.1

Child mortality by educational attainment of the mother

Child mortality falls as mothers learn.

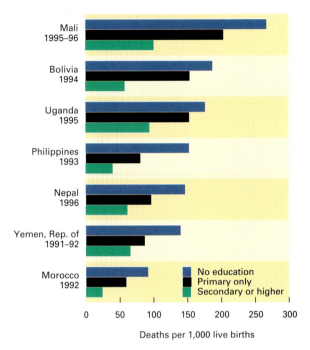

Note: Mortality data are for children under 5. Source: Macro International, various years.

raise lifelong learning potential, for example by ensuring that young children have access to adequate nutrition and health care, and by providing support and education to caregivers.

Schooling enables mothers to raise healthier children in four main ways:

- It imparts basic information about health and nutrition when such information is made part of the curriculum.
- It enables mothers to monitor their children's health more accurately and to read written instructions, from pamphlets distributed by health workers to the labels on bottles of medicine. Mothers who are literate and numerate can also acquire and process basic health information from newspapers, magazines, and other media.
- It helps to overcome some inhibiting traditional practices: women who have attended school tend to be less attached to traditional remedies for children's illnesses and thus more open to modern methods.
- It may also give mothers the self-confidence to use public health services when appropriate.

Box 3.1

Raising the potential for children to learn

Cognitive development starts well before a child enters school. It is influenced by the mother's health and nutrition during pregnancy and lactation, and by the early intellectual stimulation and the health care and nutrition the child receives. Much is now known about these effects. For example, maternal iodine deficiency has been shown to lead to irreversible mental impairment in children.

In Guatemala, a long-term study showed that protein deficiency works its effects both through the pregnant mother and directly on the child. High-protein or high-energy supplements were given to a random sample of pregnant women and of children under 7. By adolescence, those children who had received the protein supplement performed better on tests of general knowledge, numeracy, reading, and vocabulary than those who had received the energy supplement. And the earlier and longer the supplement was administered, the greater the effect. In other studies in Ghana, Pakistan, and the Philippines, malnutrition was shown to delay the entry of children into school.

Studies of families participating in programs of enhanced cognitive stimulation showed that children from such families completed more schooling, or received higher earnings as adults, or both. In Turkey, high school students whose parents were provided special training in child development performed better academically. In the United States, children who participated in the High/Scope center-based preschool program reap the benefits into their adult years.

Schooling thus complements health services, particularly when more-educated individuals are better able to use the services properly or more likely to know that they are available. In some cases, improved education may reduce the need for health services, for example when schooling teaches better sanitation or makes families more receptive to healthier diets. Educated mothers may be better able to shield their children from diarrhea and infectious disease. Such an effect has been observed in the Philippines, where the provision of maternity clinics and increased numbers of doctors was found to reduce child mortality mainly for children of educated mothers. Schooling also contributes to health by helping parents cope with economic shocks, such as a sudden job loss or the death of a spouse, that adversely affect the health of children.

The spread of the AIDS epidemic provides another dramatic illustration of the value of education. Surveys show that more-educated men and women are more likely to be aware of the protective effects of condoms. Moreover, among those with casual partners, the probability of condom use increases with years of schooling. In a Tanzanian survey, 20 percent of women with four to seven years of schooling, but only 6 percent of uneducated women, said they used a condom during sex with a casual partner.

These findings mean that the basic skills learned in primary school go a long way toward improving the lives of poor children and adults. These skills equip parents with the ability to take advantage of public health services when they are available. And they allow parents to cope better in the absence of these services: educated parents know what needs to be done and will improvise as best they can.

These findings also imply that basic health knowledge should be taught in primary school, because thereafter the rate at which girls begin to drop out accelerates sharply. Unfortunately, significant numbers of girls in poor countries never attend school and will someday join the ranks of illiterate mothers. So beyond the gains to public health from expanding enrollment, it is also worth reaching out, through adult education or mass media campaigns, to women who have never attended school. Even basic education can be a lifelong process.

Tertiary education—building knowledge for an information-based society

Basic education is thus critical for enhancing people's capabilities to harness knowledge, particularly in the poorest countries. But it should not monopolize a nation's attention as it becomes a player in global markets. For one thing, the tremendous enrollment gains in basic education in the past decade suggest that, in many countries, improvements in areas beyond basic education offer higher marginal returns. For another, new, information-based technologies are more demanding in skills for diffusing, interpreting, and applying knowledge. Besides teaching new and better skills, tertiary education and technical training produce people who can monitor technological trends, assess their relevance to the country's prospects, and help develop an appropriate national technological strategy. And countries at or near the technological frontier need strong tertiary education and research institutions to compete in the creation of new knowledge.

The appropriate strategy for most developing countries, as Chapter 2 argued, is to acquire foreign technology as cheaply and use it as effectively as they can, adapting it to local conditions. New knowledge in the form of scientific discoveries and inventions requires abundant financial resources, sophisticated human capabilities, and the business acumen to stay ahead of competitors—factors generally beyond the reach of developing countries. Being a technological "follower" did not hurt the East Asian economies, which began their spectacular rise by being very good at adapting foreign technology. But even a follower country needs a labor force with a relatively high level of technical education, especially when technologies are changing rapidly. A study of about a thousand inventors in India illustrates this point: almost 90 percent had a university degree, more than half had some graduate training, and nearly 30 percent had earned their doctorates.

There is also some evidence that the type of tertiary education provided matters for economic growth. The proportion of students majoring in mathematics, science, and engineering (but not the proportion majoring in prelaw) has been found to be positively associated with subsequent growth rates, suggesting higher returns to education investments in these fields than in others (Box 3.2). The content of education thus appears important for countries seeking to develop new technologies suitable for local conditions.

The production of new knowledge, as well as its adaptation to the setting of a particular country, is generally associated with higher-level teaching and research. In industrial countries university research accounts for a large share of domestic R&D. The same is true in most developing countries, but on a smaller scale. The best-known example is that of agricultural colleges and universities, where the bulk of scientists are engaged in agricultural R&D work. They have made important contributions in such countries as India, Malaysia, and the Philippines.

Of course, high and fast-growing university enrollments do not guarantee rapid growth. As Box 3.2 suggests, *what* students are taught may be at least as important as the number of years they spend in school. And without certain essential complementary inputs, even the best education system cannot lead to growth: some countries have found themselves with unemployed engineers because they failed to provide the other necessary ingredients to encourage private sector development to make use of these valuable skills. These ingredients include a healthy investment climate, a stable macroeconomy, and fewer state monopolies. What is clear, however, is that the aggressive investment in tertiary education that many of the East Asian economies made enabled them to sustain the new industries that provided the basis of their later growth. Those industries generated strong demand for engineers and other highly skilled workers. Thanks to these education investments, these economies were able to sustain their strategy of technology adoption in a world of constantly shifting knowledge (Box 3.3).

Universities thus serve a multiplicity of roles—not only enhancing the skills of future workers but also producing new knowledge and adapting knowledge produced elsewhere. The fact that universities throughout the world package these activities—teaching and research—suggests that there are strong complementarities between them. But this very multiplicity of activities can also give rise to conflicts of interest between those who supply and those who demand universities' output. Competition among

Box 3.2

Mathematics, science, and engineering studies may spur growth

A recent study investigated the relationship between the proportions of college students majoring in various disciplines in 1970 and subsequent real growth in GDP per capita. The study found a significant positive association between the proportion of engineering majors and later growth—but none between the proportion of prelaw students and growth. And for the 55 countries with college enrollments of at least 10,000 in 1970, the proportion of college students in engineering was significantly and positively associated with subsequent levels of physical capital investment and with primary schooling. Although these studies fall short of establishing a causal effect of science and engineering education on growth, they confirm that countries with a more technically skilled labor force do have faster growth.

This emphasis by some countries on higher scientific and technical studies has enhanced their capacity to import sophisticated technologies from the richer industrial countries—and helped maintain high rates of economic growth over a long period. When current tertiary enrollment is broken down by field, the East Asian economies show higher ratios in technical fields than the major industrial countries (see figure).

Tertiary enrollment in technical fields in selected economies

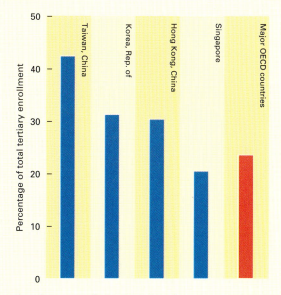

Note: Data are enrollments in mathematics, computer science, and engineering for various years from 1990 to 1994. Source: Lall, background paper (b).

Box 3.3

Korea's heavy investment in human capital

Most analysts agree that education and training were critical in sustaining Korea's economic growth over a remarkably long period. By 1960 Korea had achieved universal primary education, which provided the basis for a well-educated labor force that fueled the economy's growth as it industrialized.

Korea also invested heavily beyond the primary grades. By 1995 the gross enrollment rate for secondary education was 90 percent, and that for tertiary education was almost 55 percent, which compares favorably with most OECD countries. The dramatic rise in tertiary enrollment took place immediately after the economy took off in the 1970s (see figure). Many observers have concluded that the rapid growth in tertiary enrollment, rather than being the impetus to economic growth, was financed by the initial growth spurt, and thereafter played an important role in sustaining it. Also interesting is the fact that Korea's private sector has been responsible for much of the rapid increase in higher education. Enrollment at private colleges and universities reached 82 percent of total tertiary enrollment in 1995. In that year private spending on tertiary education, at 6 percent of GDP, outstripped the government's 5 percent share.

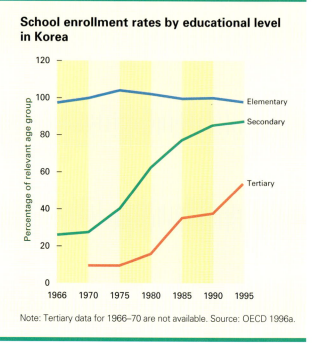

School enrollment rates by educational level in Korea

Note: Tertiary data for 1966–70 are not available. Source: OECD 1996a.

---

universities should ensure that curricula will be more attuned to the perceived demand of students and adapt faster to changing technologies. For instance, having long ago added computer science as a field of study, universities in the industrial countries have now integrated the use of computers throughout the curriculum. Students from developing countries who seek further training overseas will be at a severe disadvantage if the quality of education they receive at home falls far short of what they later encounter abroad.

To enhance the likelihood that their curricula and their research will remain relevant, many schools and universities are forging closer partnerships with industry. For example, universities in the United Kingdom have been building bridges to industry through curricula that include work-based learning components. Most Canadian universities now have an industrial liaison or technology transfer office. In fact, such partnerships enjoy widespread support within academia. In the United States, the OECD country with the largest share of university R&D spending in total R&D, a recent study shows that academics support research that directly leads to technological innovation, and that they are favorably disposed to consulting for private industry.

Because the returns to creating and adapting new knowledge are difficult for any individual (or any school, firm, or research institute) to appropriate, a spillover effect—an ex-

ternality—intrudes: there will be underinvestment not only in research itself (even research aimed at adaptation rather than creation) but in the key factor in the production of research, namely, researchers. That is one reason why universities and governments generally subsidize graduate students acquiring research degrees rather than those earning professional degrees—the latter already pay off handsomely to the degreeholder. A further reason for public support of advanced training, especially in research fields, is its high cost: with imperfect capital markets, prospective students may not be able to finance their education, even where they are able to appropriate the full returns (see "Helping poor people pay for education" below). The funding constraint is especially binding for children from poor families. Providing subsidies in these cases may increase not only economic efficiency and growth, by ensuring that talented students are better able to realize their potential, but equity as well. Of course, resource limitations imply that any such expenditures or subsidies should be carefully targeted to those areas where the externalities are greatest, or where capital market imperfections are most confining.

Vocational training and learning-by-doing
Productive learning does not just occur in the classroom—nor does it end with formal schooling. People continue to learn at work and through formal and informal job training. Learning-by-doing improves workers' performance.

And because experience provides opportunities for discovery, it increases the general stock of knowledge. Similarly, learning can lower the unit costs of production as workers discover better ways to use new technology, to organize production, or to monitor product quality. The observation that wages and productivity rise with experience in the initial stages of many jobs is consistent with such on-the-job learning. Again the green revolution provides telling evidence: farmers with basic schooling had little initial advantage in using the new seeds over farmers with none, but the more-educated farmers came to enjoy a substantial advantage as they gained more experience. This again points to the importance of learning-by-doing—and of basic schooling as its foundation.

Korea's path to technological mastery shows how the application of new knowledge can actually add to that knowledge. It has been argued that Korea's rapid industrial growth in the past two decades, by compressing the intervals between the construction of successive plants, permitted rapid technological learning in many industries. The first plants—which were often small relative to the market or to the size that would exhaust scale economies—were frequently built on a turnkey basis. Thus learning first came about through Korean workers operating plants built by others. But in the building of subsequent plants, local engineers and technicians assumed larger roles in design and implementation, and the newer plants were built to scales of production much closer to those achieved by the global market leaders. This developed Korean workers' capability to innovate. And it suggests that when technology is changing rapidly, the shop floor may be the best place to learn.

But learning-by-doing is not always enough. In some cases, formal training, whether undertaken inside or outside the firm, is far more important than work experience for acquiring technical knowledge and skills. The two may be complementary, of course: learning-by-doing may be more effective when preceded by appropriate preemployment training. Whatever the reason, larger firms around the world have found it useful (smaller firms less so) to provide workers with some formal training, perhaps because they have lower labor turnover rates and can thus realize more of the returns to training.

Why should countries—and especially governments—worry about education?

In the past three decades, many countries have made enormous strides in expanding enrollment at all levels. Yet despite these gains, new challenges have emerged as countries have had to absorb ever-expanding amounts of knowledge and information. Meanwhile other, older challenges persist, and indeed must often be given priority because they are so fundamental.

First, the gains in access to education have been unevenly distributed. Many countries still lag far behind in the pursuit of universal literacy, especially for girls and women (Figure 3.2).

Second, in many countries the poor get much less than their fair share of government spending on education. In Ghana the richest 20 percent of households appropriate 45 percent of subsidies to tertiary education, while the poorest fifth get only 6 percent. The distribution in Malawi is even more skewed: there the corresponding figures are 59 percent and 1 percent (Figure 3.3).

Third, education in many countries remains of poor or mediocre quality, particularly when it comes to the basic skills on which countries will depend to meet the needs of tomorrow's labor markets. One can infer this from well-known deficiencies in inputs—absentee teachers, an emphasis on rote learning, outdated curricula, and shortages of textbooks and other materials. But quality shortfalls are also showing up in output indicators such as the results of internationally comparable tests: in the Third International Mathematics and Science Study, for example, students in some developing countries did poorly (Figure 3.4). These results also show that resources alone do not determine performance: even some rich countries (notably the United States) did not fare as well as some East Asian high achievers (such as Singapore and Korea). One must be careful not to read too much into these results, since they fail to account for differences within countries (inner-city schools versus well-endowed suburban schools, for example) and test only a narrow set of skills, but they have been influential in drawing attention to real problems.

Fourth, schools at all levels still provide their services too inefficiently, especially when compared with institutions that must compete to survive. Studies show that not only are unit costs in public secondary schools higher than in their private counterparts, but the private school students score higher on standardized tests (Figure 3.5). Here, too, however, meaningful comparisons are often difficult, because the effects are confounded by background variables, some of which may be unobserved. Although the studies in question attempted to control for these variables statistically, some ambiguity remains about the magnitude of the difference in efficiency.

Reforming public policy is key to addressing these challenges. In the majority of countries more than 90 percent of primary and secondary students attend public rather than private school (although the variance is much higher at the secondary level; Figure 3.6). The government's extensive involvement in education is no accident. We have already explored two reasons for government action at the tertiary level: the presence of externalities and capital market imperfections (and their distributional

Figure 3.2

Illiteracy by gender and level of income

Large gaps in literacy persist both within and across countries.

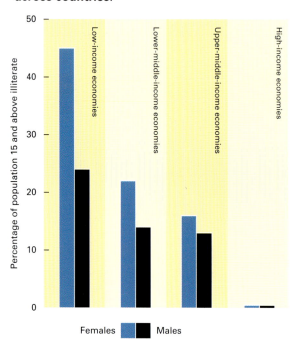

Note: Data are for 1995. Source: World Bank 1998d.

Figure 3.3

Shares of public educational subsidies received by rich and poor households in two African countries

The benefits of public education spending are often skewed toward the rich.

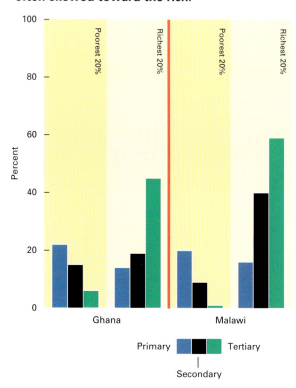

Note: Data are for 1992 for Ghana and 1994 for Malawi. Source: Castro-Leal and others 1997.

consequences). Yet these market failures arise not only there but throughout the educational process.

Passing knowledge on—the spillover benefits of education
The education of one individual often increases the learning of others in the family and the community. Best known is the intergenerational impact: the most reliable predictor of children's educational attainment is the level of education of their parents. Children of more-educated parents get more education than do children from households with similar incomes but less education, and they generally do better on tests. In some circumstances, as with primary schooling in Lahore, Pakistan, the education of the mother has a larger influence than that of the father, perhaps because of the mother's greater role in the home.

Even the education of other community members may affect how and what a person learns. Peer effects in a classroom can benefit all the children present by setting positive feedback cycles in motion, which enhance learning in the long run. But it is in the interest of those generating the positive feedbacks to set themselves apart, to try to internalize these externalities. The result can be socioeconomic stratification, which indeed has become a prime concern in many private elementary and secondary education systems (although some parochial schools have been quite effective in promoting both racial and socioeconomic integration).

Education also exhibits externalities in production. Recall from the discussion of the green revolution that farmers with more schooling were the first adopters of high-yielding varieties—and that their neighbors, learning from them, adopted new seeds more quickly than they would have otherwise. Such spillovers could lead to underinvestment both in schooling and in experimentation on the farm. In a study of villages in India, the proportion of educated households was significantly less than that which would best promote the adoption of new technology. The reason is straightforward: households do not base their educational choices on the uncompensated gains they provide to others when they explore new technologies.

Ultimately this underinvestment may lead to social and economic problems, the costs of which are likely to be borne at least in part by the government. For instance, one study in the United States showed that, on any given day in 1992, almost one-quarter of male dropouts between 18 and 34—but only 4 percent of high school graduates in that age group—were either in prison, on probation, or on parole. Here as always, interpreting causality is risky, but their lack of education surely limited the opportunities for these dropouts within the legal job market and encouraged them to turn to other ways of making a living. Conversely, higher levels of education have been found to lead to higher incomes, with government reaping part of the benefits in the form of higher tax payments.

These spillovers are an important reason for government to encourage education, because individuals may not take them into account in deciding whether to invest in education for themselves or for their children. In some cases they simply may not know about these external ef-

fects. In others, they know but lack the incentive to consider them.

Information issues within education

In all markets for knowledge-based services, consumers have a difficult time judging quality—not just before receiving the service, but even after. For their part, the providers of services may be tempted to exploit consumers' ignorance. Doctors can order excessive but (to them) remunerative tests. Mechanics can recommend unnecessary but (to them) remunerative repairs. Brokers can tout unprofitable but (to them) remunerative trades. Mechanisms arise to temper these perverse tendencies: competition among providers, government regulation of standards, professional self-policing, legal recourse against malprac-

Figure 3.5

Ratios of private to public education costs and test score achievement in four countries

Even for students of similar background, private schools often deliver better education at lower cost.

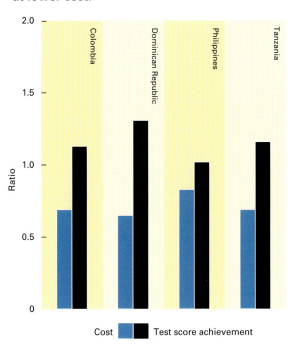

Note: Data are for 1981 (Colombia), 1982–83 (Dominican Republic), 1983 (the Philippines), and 1981 (Tanzania). Scores are from tests of mathematics and language skills, except in the Philippines (language skills only). Achievement is adjusted for differences in the background characteristics (such as urban or rural residence, gender, number of siblings, and parents' education, income, and occupation) of children from public and private schools. Source: Jimenez, Lockheed, and Paqueo 1991.

Figure 3.4

GNP per capita and mathematics test scores

Educational quality bears no obvious relationship to income.

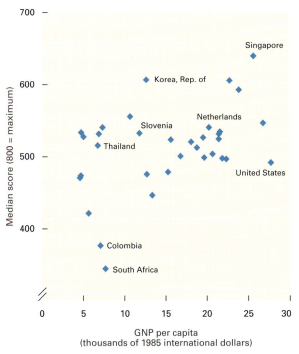

Note: Data are for 32 countries worldwide for 1994–95. Test scores are from the Third International Mathematics and Science Study. Source: Beanton and others 1996, World Bank 1998d.

Figure 3.6

Public sector shares of primary and secondary enrollments

Public education dominates the field in most countries.

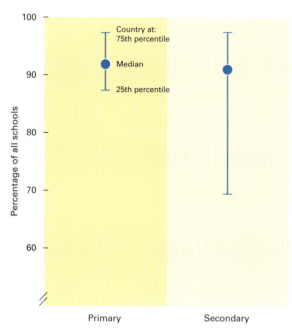

Note: Data are for 1995 and cover 113 countries (primary) and 100 countries (secondary) worldwide. Secondary enrollment is that in general secondary schools only. Source: UNESCO 1998.

the decisions about education (especially primary and secondary education) for their children—not the children themselves. But parents, however well intentioned, may be uninformed, or insufficiently informed, about the relative benefits of competing educational offerings—or about the value of education altogether. Conflicts of interest can also arise: parents may be eager to use their children's labor and may not fully appreciate the effects that forgoing education will have on their children's future. Government's role is to make up for these limits in the private market for education, and in the process to level the playing field for information.

Policy and information

Governments are, and should be, involved in education. But experience shows that designing the right policies, and then implementing them, is far from easy. Cross-country studies have found public spending on education to be unrelated to growth—worse yet, it is unrelated to educational outcomes, or at least such immediately measurable ones as scores on standardized mathematics and science tests (Figure 3.7). Care must be taken in interpreting these results, since higher test scores are not the ultimate purpose of education spending. But they are one of many indicators that show that it is the quality of spending, not the amount, that matters. Indeed, when funds are spent on inputs or programs that work, they can significantly improve outcomes. In Ghana, for example, spending for blackboards and classroom repairs has been shown to increase test scores—and raise wages by 20 percent.

Over the past decade, several editions of *World Development Report* have discussed the efficiency and equity issues bedeviling education. Too often, governments have invested in poor quality, done so at high cost, and failed to serve the needs of the poor or of other groups, such as girls, whose returns to education are potentially high. So there is much more to policy reform than simply spending more from the public purse. Governments have to make tradeoffs as they distribute limited resources across the array of educational vehicles associated with lifetime learning: preschool programs, formal schooling (basic and higher), formal training programs, on-the-job training, information dissemination programs, and informal education. The most effective public actions are those that focus directly on the source of the market failure or the distributional concern. For example, subsidies are warranted if individuals do not consider the positive effects their basic schooling may have on others. University research needs to be subsidized as well, since those undertaking it can seldom appropriate the gains.

The links between such market failures and policy reforms raise some general issues that lie beyond the scope of this Report—but are treated more comprehensively in such

tice. All share the same objective: to make providers accountable for outcomes and costs while preserving professional autonomy.

Markets for education and training face the same information problems on at least three levels: factual content (are teachers teaching the Pythagorean theorem correctly?), the appropriateness of that content (do students need to know the Pythagorean theorem?), and the pedagogical approach (are teachers teaching the Pythagorean theorem so that students can understand and apply it?). But markets for education are even more complex than those for medical services or car repairs, because so many actors jointly determine the outcome. Providers include not only teachers but also policymakers, central administrators and inspectors, their provincial or municipal counterparts, school administrators, and nonteaching staff. Just as important is the influence of parents and the local environment on the student, not to mention the student's own aptitude.

These decisionmakers possess widely varying amounts of information about the educational process—and about each other. For example, it is typically parents who make documents as the World Bank's recent strategy papers on education. Here the focus is on showing how addressing the market failures associated with information problems in education can go some way toward resolving the issues discussed above. Policy can address these market failures by:

- Empowering those with the most information—users and local providers—by decentralizing
- Making information about educational options more accessible, so that users and providers can make informed choices
- Helping poor people pay for their education—particularly tertiary education—so as to offset information failures in capital markets, and
- Using new knowledge to update curricula and new technologies, to improve the quality of education and broaden access.

Figure 3.7

Public education spending and mathematics test scores

Generous state spending does not guarantee quality education.

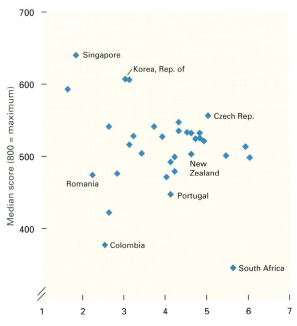

Note: Data are for 34 countries worldwide for 1994–95. Expenditure is that for preschool, primary, and secondary education. Since the share of education spending in GNP does not usually change quickly, these data are representative of spending over a longer period. Test scores are from the Third International Mathematics and Science Study. Source: Beanton and others 1996, UNESCO 1998.

Empowering informed stakeholders

Government provision of education creates three sets of stakeholders: citizens, educators, and governments themselves. Together these stakeholders must create a system that ensures that private and public money for education is well spent, while maintaining for educators the professional autonomy necessary for excellence. But to ensure accountability and efficiency, citizens—both as taxpayers and as consumers of education—must have adequate information to judge whether particular institutions are providing formal education efficiently.

Centralized education systems, despite their many remarkable successes, are beset by some basic information and accountability problems, leading to inefficiency and high costs. Quality is a continuing source of concern. It is difficult to discern the quality of education, because adequate assessments are generally lacking. But some assessments have been made, and many of them find that students have not mastered the skills the curriculum meant to impart. In some school systems—primary schools in Ghana and Kenya, for example—testing after several years of instruction reveals a significant percentage of children with scores no better than random guessing.

Perceptions of educational quality differ among the various stakeholders. A recent survey in Vietnam asked parents, teachers, and local commune leaders about school quality. Their assessments were correlated, but still quite different one from the other (Box 3.4).

To address the problems of information imbalance and limited accountability due to overcentralization, many systems are moving from a "top-down" to a "client-driven" model. These changes take several forms: decentralizing administration, increasing school autonomy, moving to demand-side financing (where the family rather than the government pays), increasing the information available about specific educational institutions, and relying on a mix of private, nongovernmental, and public providers. Although each of these reforms has its pluses and minuses, all seek to address perceived weaknesses in traditional systems.

Administrative decentralization means moving responsibilities to smaller jurisdictional units: from the nation to the province, from province to municipality, from municipality to the schools themselves and their clients. Decentralization can help countries and communities deal with information problems relating to differences in local preferences and conditions. It can also help improve the coordination and enforcement of education standards, because local jurisdictions are assumed to have the informational advantage in identifying cheaper, more appropriate ways of providing services to fit local preferences. They can also better monitor the performance of providers. Above all, decentralization can strengthen the account-

Box 3.4

Grading the teachers: Varying perceptions of school quality in Vietnam

A stratified random survey of 1,890 Vietnamese house-holds, when evaluated alongside the results of linked school and community surveys (which interviewed school headmasters and commune leaders), indicates how sharply perceptions can differ about school quality and what would most improve it. Among the findings:

■ At the primary and lower secondary levels, household-ers' evaluations tended to be lower than those of the headmasters. A systematic tendency was observed among those on the supply side to give more positive judgments than those on the demand side.

■ The headmasters' evaluations were much more in line with independently observed school characteristics than were the householders'. It may be that school heads are better informed than households about school inputs, or rather that households are concerned more with out-comes than with inputs.

In the judgment of the commune leaders, the two changes that would most improve the schools are better physical facilities (mentioned by 38 percent) and improved teacher training (34 percent), with more teachers (12 per-cent) and higher pay for teachers (10 percent) far behind. This differed from the perspective of the headmasters, who mentioned better teacher pay more than twice as often (20 to 23 percent).

These patterns are consistent with the possibility that headmasters face a conflict of interest between improving school quality and increasing staff compensation. This may lead them, but not other stakeholders, to give greater weight to increasing staff pay.

---

ability of local institutions, thus improving quality and cost-effectiveness.

But decentralization alone cannot solve all problems. Local governments and communities may lack the capac-ity to produce and manage high-quality education ser-vices. The information imbalance can work both ways: the central government may not know what to do; the local government may not know how to do it. That is why assessing local capacity is so important. The allocation of responsibilities between central and local government must be guided not just by the latter's informational ad-vantage, but also by local capacity to enhance the quality and efficient delivery of services.

Sometimes, however, the rhetoric of decentralization is used as a pretext to shift responsibility to lower levels of government without also transferring the necessary re-sources or revenue bases. This only widens regional in-

equality. But in other cases decentralization is genuinely viewed as an investment in the nation's future, which is worth enduring some short-run inefficiencies and in-equalities provided that, in the long run, a culture of par-ticipation and vigilance emerges at the community level, and quality improves.

Indeed, one of the lessons of past decentralizations is that going partway—from the central to the provincial or even the municipal level, for example—may not lead to as many gains as expected. The biggest potential gains come from promoting greater control of decisionmaking at the school level, typically through greater involvement of par-ents and the broader community in school management. In Nicaragua, an ambitious reform of public schools gives principals, teachers, and parents greater autonomy in managing their schools—the new regime places many de-cisions about staffing, supervision, administration, and pedagogy in the hands of a school council composed of local stakeholders. Not all schools have been transformed by this reform. But evaluations indicate that when local stakeholders rather than the central government do make more decisions affecting the school, and teachers feel they are better able to influence school operations, students perform better.

In El Salvador, the government that came to power in the wake of that country's devastating civil war formalized, improved, and expanded the community-managed schools that had arisen after the public system broke down. Initial evaluations show that even the poorest communities can set up and manage such schools—and improve quality in the process. One reason is that parents monitor teachers vigorously: students lose only about half as many days to teacher absenteeism as in conventional schools.

Subsidizing students or their families, rather than pro-viders, can also improve the availability of information and increase accountability by bolstering the voice of consumers. Subsidies can be routed either to providers through per-student grants in systems where students choose which schools to attend, or to consumers directly through schol-arships or vouchers. The results of voucher schemes remain controversial, however.

Providing information for better choice

For programs to be effective and suppliers to be held ac-countable, clients must have good information on which to base decisions. In addition to efficiency gains, there are likely to be distributional gains, because poorer families are likely to be the least informed under the status quo. Unsubsidized private providers are not likely to make suf-ficient information available about the effectiveness of ed-ucational alternatives.

Consider the provision of adequate health informa-tion. One form of government action, known as information, education, and communication (IEC), encompasses such activities as billboard advertising, pamphleting, and public service messages on radio and television. Nowhere is the role of IEC more critical than in the case of a fatal disease like AIDS, for which there is no cure but which can be prevented. Before the AIDS epidemic in Thailand, sex in brothels was popular recreation for local men and tourists, but condom use was low: only about 15 percent of commercial sex acts were protected in 1988. That figure rose to more than 50 percent in 1989–90, even before the launch of wide-ranging condom promotion campaigns, when the government informed the public that 44 percent of sex workers in the city of Chiang Mai were infected with the human immunodeficiency virus.

There may be high social payoffs from policies that improve the collection and dissemination of information about education and the opportunities open to more-educated people. Many countries are reforming their national training systems to include employers and private providers in planning and in coordinating provision. Such policies must be accompanied by efforts to put the information to good use (Box 3.5).

Governments have recently been doing more to provide information about, for example, test score improvements and placement records for students in particular schools and training programs. The reporting of nationally recognized test scores often impels parents and communities to action. The publication of national rankings based on the Third International Mathematics and Science Study has drawn the attention of many policymakers. Such comparisons, when done for schools within a country or district, might also better inform parents. These efforts would also, one hopes, stimulate debate about the overall objectives of the education system and the extent to which testing can capture them.

Another way that governments dispense information is through accreditation. Many industrial and some developing countries now have well-designed school inspection schemes in place, to provide a "stamp of approval" for schools that meet quality standards. Where the public sector does not, or cannot directly, accredit institutions, private voluntary accreditation agencies can be encouraged to take on this function. This has been done in the Philippines, and Brazil, Chile, Colombia, Mexico, South Africa, and Tanzania are following suit.

Helping poor people pay for education

Estimated private rates of return to education in developing countries—more than 30 percent a year for primary and about 20 percent a year for secondary and tertiary schooling—are enough to gladden the heart of any investment banker. Yet many would-be students in these countries cannot invest in their own education because

Box 3.5

From providing training to providing information

Retraining is vital for a country's economic restructuring. But mismatches between formal training programs and the evolving skill needs of employers have been a persistent problem, often resulting in very low rates of return to resources, public and private, devoted to such training. One way to improve performance is to move from direct provision to government intermediation between provider and trainee. This can reduce the information costs that can lead to such mismatching.

A program proposed in Madagascar will serve workers in 45 state enterprises facing restructuring, in preparation for their privatization or liquidation. A previous, failed attempt to facilitate these workers' redeployment was heavily centralized and information-intensive. The agency in charge had to identify the sectors and activities in which the soon-to-be-separated workers could work and then provide them with appropriate training. And it had to help those planning to launch their own microenterprises to design a business plan and buy the appropriate equipment. Many separated workers received their equipment years after losing their jobs. By that time they had moved on to other activities, so most of them simply sold the equipment. Despite costs of roughly $900 per worker, dissatisfaction with the program was widespread.

In the new redeployment program, the agency in charge provides a menu of training and redeployment services, but separated workers choose whether to "buy" those services. First, from a study of the labor market, the agency calculates the present value of the earnings loss each separated worker will experience. Simultaneously, the agency launches a tender for redeployment services, which is open to other government bodies, private providers, and nongovernmental organizations. Next, the agency runs a workshop at the plant, where all the retained bidders describe to the workers to be separated the redeployment service they propose. Finally, each separated worker decides which services to buy.

The government agency discounts the cost of these services from the amount of assistance allocated to each worker, pays the rest in cash, and pays the retained bidders upon delivery of their services. Workers have the right to get all their compensation in cash if they do not consider the services worth their cost. This minimizes the risk that large sums will be wasted in useless training and redeployment efforts.

they cannot pay for it. Education requires considerable private resources, even when it is "free" in the sense that no fees are charged. Perhaps most important are the opportunity costs: the time that a student spends in school, or a trainee in a training program, is time not spent working in the labor market, in the family enterprise, or in household activities such as care for younger siblings (a task that, because it often falls to girls, may contribute to their lower enrollment rates).

If credit markets for human resource investments are imperfect—as indeed they seem to be almost everywhere—households, particularly poor households, may not be able to finance investments in education, despite high expected rates of return. Their lack of access to credit reflects information problems. Would-be lenders cannot properly assess the returns to investing in human capital, nor can such capital be collateralized.

In such circumstances a poor student or trainee, even one with the brightest prospects, finds it difficult to mobilize the requisite funds. A recent survey of 42 studies from 21 mostly developing countries reports that income is a significant constraint in at least three-fifths of the studies. In Peru, children from lower-income households whose siblings are more closely spaced in age begin withdrawing from school at a younger age. In Vietnam a 10 percent increase in longer-run household income is associated with a 7 percent increase in educational attainment (grades attended) and an 8 percent increase in cognitive achievement.

This state of affairs is not only inequitable but inefficient as well. It deprives society of a larger pool of able people who have benefited from learning. Simulation analysis of data from Colombia in the 1980s concludes that, if the selection of students from secondary to tertiary education had been based on innate ability alone, the share of tertiary enrollment from the poorest 40 percent of the population would have increased significantly, and average verbal and mathematics test scores would have increased by 14 percent.

Credit constraints might also adversely affect the composition of educational offerings. In the Philippines—whose university system boasts one of the highest enrollment rates in the developing world, rivaling those of many industrial countries—the private sector provides 80 percent of tertiary education. But private schools must compete by offering only those courses that cover their costs. This works to the detriment of course offerings with high fixed costs for laboratory equipment and the like. Over 90 percent of enrollments in the Philippines are in vocational programs with a specific occupational goal. The most popular is business, which accounts for 40 percent of private sector tertiary enrollment (but only 21 percent of public sector enrollment). And mathematics and natural sciences are underemphasized: the enrollment rate in for-profit private schools is a minuscule 1 percent, compared with 4 percent in public schools. This is not necessarily a bad outcome: if private sector schools specialize in areas where demand is strong, that frees up scarce public resources for other areas where the externalities are greater.

The best solution to credit market failures is to relieve the credit constraint. Many countries have government-run (or government-backed) student loan programs covering tuition, living expenses, or both. These loans are supposed to be repaid from the borrower's earnings after graduation. But a review of 50 such schemes indicated that many were insolvent. The main problems were heavily subsidized interest rates, high default rates, and high administrative costs. In the first Brazilian student loan scheme in 1983, default rates were high despite generous real interest rates of –35 percent.

The few success stories of student loan schemes yield some important lessons:

- Subsidies should not be hidden in highly subsidized interest rates, but instead made transparent in the form of scholarships.
- Programs need to be well targeted to those in need.
- Combining loans with work-study programs helps lower-income students.
- Making repayment contingent on income after graduation does more to balance the imperative of cost recovery against the risk to the borrower (Box 3.6).
- Program solvency also requires fostering a "credit culture" that encourages borrowers to be conscientious about repaying their loans.

Should education be subsidized? And if so, how? Even when the credit constraint is removed, if credit markets redistribute risk imperfectly there may still be underinvestment in education, and thus subsidies may be warranted. The question is even more pressing in countries—and there are many—that lack effective student loan programs. Many developing countries subsidize both schooling and formal training programs too heavily and indiscriminately. In francophone Africa, allowances for noneducational expenses constitute, on average, 55 percent of the tertiary education budget. These subsidies contribute to even graver problems due to fiscal restraints. Some countries, unwilling or unable to provide subsidies to all, simply limit access to higher education. The result is that subsidies that are high on a per-student basis go to a few individuals, who are almost certainly not poor. Other countries offer broader access to education but dilute its quality.

A basic problem is that subsidies are seldom targeted to those who deserve them or to the fields of study that warrant subsidization for efficiency and distributional reasons. Such subsidies must be redirected. Scholarships should go to the credit-constrained and to those who, because of their talent or their choice of discipline, are likely to generate positive externalities. Means-tested targeting may itself be encumbered by information problems, but it

Box 3.6

Income-contingent loans for tertiary education in Australia and New Zealand

In 1989, in response to public demand to make tertiary education more effective and increase access for under-represented groups, Australia introduced its Higher Education Contribution Scheme. The scheme imposes a tuition fee at public universities but provides subsidized, income-contingent loans to help students defray the cost. Participating students defer repayment until their earnings after graduation reach a threshold, after which their payments are calculated as a percentage of their taxable income. The principal is indexed to the consumer price index, but the real interest rate is zero.

With repayment thus tied to income, default risk is reduced, and repayment can be stretched out over many years. And since the real interest rate is zero, those taking longer to repay the full amount (those less active in the labor force or who realize low returns to their schooling) receive more of a subsidy than those required to pay off the loan more quickly.

In 1992, New Zealand instituted an income-contingent loan program that does not completely subsidize the interest on the loan. As in Australia, only students with earnings above a given threshold are required to make repayments, but repayments are the same percentage of income (above the threshold) for all borrowers. Repayments are also adjusted for inflation. For those borrowers deemed able to afford it, the real interest rate is set equivalent to the government's cost of borrowing, thereby reducing the subsidy that a zero real interest rate represents.

may be less onerous for tertiary education than for lower levels, because the students are fewer.

Upgrading education systems through new content and new media

New curricula for a new world. Governments play an important role in adapting school curricula to foster national, regional, and global integration and to transmit new information to schools and educators. New perspectives on how students learn are regularly explored and the findings disseminated to teachers. And teachers are exposed to new technologies that may help them in the classroom—or beyond the classroom—through a variety of government-supported in-service training opportunities.

Beyond this, governments can serve as a conduit for new knowledge in rapidly evolving fields of science and technology, to ensure that curricula stay up to date. In Vietnam the draft primary curriculum includes information about computers (including the Internet), to prepare students to enter modern society. Governments may also promote the inclusion of fields of study already familiar

elsewhere but new to the country in question. In the transition economies of Europe and Central Asia such "new" fields may include economics, accounting, civil rights law, and business administration, as well as topics in history and geography previously proscribed. In these and other countries, curriculum expansion may also entail including material that has increased relevance in modern economies, such as environmental studies or the mathematical logic underlying the use of computers. A textbook recently approved by the Russian Federation's Ministry of Education for use in public schools, titled *The Adventures of a Little Man,* features a little green man who uses the court system to defend the environment against polluters and their powerful cronies.

Using new technology in the classroom. Today's technologies, as Chapter 4 will show, have enormous potential to increase access to education and reduce its unit costs. Radio distance education has already shown this for basic education.

Some education systems, especially in Latin America, have a long and well-documented history of using distance education. One approach, interactive radio instruction, delivers lessons by radio or audiocassette, accompanied by carefully integrated classroom activities facilitated by a teacher. Students respond to questions and do exercises while the program is on the air. The goal is mainly to improve educational quality, but the program also aims to increase access.

Interactive radio instruction was originally developed to teach primary school mathematics in Nicaragua in the mid-1970s. Analysts concluded from two controlled studies that these programs were more effective in increasing learning ability than an alternative program that simply provided additional textbooks. Following Nicaragua's lead, 18 other countries have since developed interactive radio programs for a range of subjects and learning environments. Test scores for students in these programs indicate gains of 10 to 40 percent over control groups. For some programs, the marginal resources employed are about two-thirds more effective in raising test scores than equivalent resources used for textbooks—and more than 10 times more effective than resources used for teacher education.

Computer-aided instruction has expanded substantially with the rapid decline in the costs of hardware and software. The most prominent use of computers in schools has been as a practice tool for basic skills. Many studies suggest that students show learning gains equivalent to one to eight months' worth of a year of traditional schooling when computer drills supplement traditional instruction. But the gains are much smaller when the computer replaces rather than deepens traditional instruction. Most studies also report increases in attendance, motivation, and attentiveness. More systematic studies analyzing the returns to such innovations, especially in controlled experiments, would be useful to determine the desirable levels of investment in these areas.

New technology for training teachers. Distance education has been advocated as a cost-effective means of increasing the number of qualified teachers—a major bottleneck limiting the expansion of formal schooling, particularly in South Asia and Sub-Saharan Africa. Several of these programs point to possible advantages over conventional teacher training, others to limits.

Distance education has been found to reach more teachers than conventional methods using the same amount of resources. Pass rates are in some cases similar, and in others notably higher or lower, than in conventional courses. In Indonesia, Sri Lanka, and Tanzania, teachers trained at a distance performed less well in science and mathematics than did those with conventional training.

These comparisons do not lead to definitive conclusions, because the underlying studies do not control well for other differences between teachers in the two groups. Given the limited success and much higher cost of conventional programs, however, the comparisons suggest that distance teacher training should be considered as a supplement, if not an alternative, to conventional programs.

Open universities. The most promising gains to new technology may come from its use in tertiary education. Pressure is mounting to increase access to tertiary education without diluting quality, especially in middle-income economies that have raised their secondary school graduation rates. These same countries confront the need to upgrade their labor force skills in the face of global competitive pressures. How can they provide relevant and good-quality higher education at an affordable cost? Here again, distance learning may be a viable alternative.

Distance education at the tertiary level has a long tradition in most industrial countries and in many developing countries, including China, Costa Rica, India, the Islamic Republic of Iran, Kenya, Pakistan, Tanzania, Thailand, and Venezuela. It can help developing countries with too few classrooms and teachers get around these resource constraints. Videoconferencing, for example, lets students from all parts of a country speak directly with the best teachers. Examinations can be administered on-line, and course materials and homework can be exchanged by e-mail. The virtual classroom is more effective, however, when complemented by face-to-face interaction between teacher and student. At a minimum, there is an ongoing need for teachers capable of customizing content to local needs and requirements.

Traditional universities are turning to distance learning to supplement their on-campus activities. In China, half of the 92,000 engineering and technology students who graduate each year do so through distance education from such traditional universities. Meanwhile a logical extension of the distance learning concept, the "open university," caters exclusively to distance learners. Open universities are growing in size and number. Today there are 11 so-called mega-universities—open universities enrolling more than 100,000 students per year—operating worldwide. Most have been established in the last quarter century, many of them patterned after the United Kingdom's Open University.

A variant of the open university, the virtual university, uses satellites and the Internet to deliver courses, allowing people in scattered locations to share resources. The Virtual University of the Monterrey Institute of Technology, in Mexico, is a consortium of collaborating universities, including 13 outside the country. Founded in 1989, the Virtual University enrolls 9,000 degree and 35,000 non-degree students each year throughout Mexico and several other Latin American countries. It delivers its courses through printed texts and live and prerecorded television broadcasts. Communication between students and faculty is facilitated by Internet connections.

Another virtual university is being established for Africa, with support from the World Bank (Box 3.7). As these experiments go forward, it will be important to assess the returns more precisely.

Lifelong learning. As the store of human knowledge continues to grow in size and complexity, and to be updated at an ever-faster pace, people the world over need to engage in structured and systematic learning throughout their lives. Lifelong learning is especially important in developing countries, where most adults never received basic education during their youth. For many of them, lifelong learning starts with basic literacy and numeracy. Modern communications technologies allow them to learn at their own pace outside school or the workplace. For example, women in a community group in South Africa, with the help of one of their peers who has the equivalent of two years of high school education, download information about adult education programs that they would otherwise not be able to afford. Thanks to advice they found on-line about vegetable farming, they recently harvested their first crop.

The picture of a society committed to lifelong learning, then, presents more than the familiar scene of 8-year-olds engaged full-time in learning the basics of reading, writing, and math. It also includes grandparents passing on their language and value systems to their grandchildren, while they in turn introduce their elders to the intricacies of the Internet, helping them gain access to information that will enlighten and give sustenance to their later years.

• • •

Basic education is the foundation for building a healthy, skilled, and agile labor force and for competing

Box 3.7

The African Virtual University

Many African universities lack top-quality professors, up-to-date materials, adequate facilities for teaching and research, and modern curricula, particularly in science and technology. And even these meager resources are accessible to only a privileged few—despite keen demand throughout Africa for qualified scientists, engineers, and business leaders.

The African Virtual University was launched in 1995 to remedy this shortfall by offering high-quality university education at a distance. Its mandate is to increase university enrollments and improve the quality and relevance of instruction in science, engineering, and business throughout the continent. In each participating country a local institution is competitively selected to oversee operations. It registers students, supervises study programs, and offers a structured study environment. It also helps with technology problems, provides hardware and software for interactive courses, and awards local credit for courses taken.

The African Virtual University's headquarters in Nairobi provides tutoring for students and training for professors and teaching assistants in the use of electronic teaching media. It installs and services all the required software and hardware, standardizes teaching practices and monitors quality control, sets price structures, and conducts marketing campaigns. And it purchases the best available distance education curricula and instructional materials from around the world and adapts them to local needs.

The university hopes to offer relevant short courses in high-demand subject areas at affordable prices. So far it has installed 27 satellite receiver terminals, with 12 each in English-speaking and French-speaking countries and three in Portuguese-speaking countries. And to compensate for the dearth of scientific journals in African universities, it has developed a digital library.

successfully in world markets. Education beyond the basics—both through teaching and through research—also has a role in securing the ability of countries to assess, adapt, and apply new, information-based technologies.

Despite the expansion of enrollments in recent decades, success in extending quality education to all has been limited, and new challenges have emerged. In still too many settings, some groups—the poor, girls, adults who have long since left school without learning basic skills—have not shared in the gains. Many school systems in developing countries fail to meet even basic academic standards. Meanwhile, demand for secondary and tertiary education is rising faster than the public sector can provide it.

Solving information problems in education systems is the key to addressing these challenges. Ignorance about the full benefits of education prevents individuals and their families from making optimal schooling decisions. Capital market imperfections that are rooted in lack of information about student borrowers stand in the way of appropriate private investments, especially in tertiary education. More public spending, if uninformed, is not likely to solve the quality problem. Given the limitations on resources and capacity in education systems, notable improvements in the quality of education may come only by involving consumers (parents and local communities) directly in school decisionmaking. Reforms that have embarked in this direction appear to have hit the mark. And finally, just as new technologies have broken age-old barriers in the production of goods and services, increasing yields or reducing costs, so too innovative methods of imparting skills and knowledge hold promise for breaking existing barriers to greater access and improved quality in education.

Chapter 4

Communicating Knowledge

REVOLUTIONS IN COMMUNICATION have often been at the center of changes in society. Movable type—the Gutenberg Bible—is widely considered to have ushered in the Renaissance, as it freed the sharing of written knowledge from the slow and laborious process of manual copying, which had for centuries sharply circumscribed access to books. Since Gutenberg, printed text has become the principal medium for sharing some types of knowledge. More recent breakthroughs in communications—the telegraph, the telephone, radio, television, the fax machine—have also wrought profound social and economic change. Today a new revolution is in full career, made possible by new technologies that can shuttle vast amounts of information almost anywhere in the world in mere seconds.

These advances in communication will enable the construction of whole new societies in cyberspace, linking individuals with common interests to share views and information. Already these technologies are enabling a new electronic commerce, which is rife with possibilities but also holds challenges. Transactions such as electronic settlement of accounts can now occur over distances previously unimaginable. The new technologies are creating a new global marketplace, where competition may be fiercer and winnow out weak firms quicker than ever before. This global marketplace opens up new opportunities for efficiency gains, as firms reap the advantages that come from a vastly expanded potential clientele.

The new information and communications technologies, from e-mail to cellular telephony to teleconferencing, let more and more people share knowledge without having to be in the same place. Sharing information through computers interlinked by telephone lines is quickly becoming commonplace in industrial countries, and increasingly so in developing countries as well.

In most developing countries, however, the use of the new technologies, although growing rapidly, is still limited. Low income, inadequate human capital, and weak competitive and regulatory environments slow their adoption. Sociocultural differences also pose a barrier, for people the world over tend to trust only what they know and feel at home with. That often means that modern knowledge must enter a traditional society through traditional channels. For example, community street theaters have proved more effective in several developing countries, such as Ethiopia and Namibia, for communicating information on AIDS prevention than have information brochures, television, or radio.

This chapter conveys two main messages:

- Although traditional channels of communication will remain important, the new information and communications technologies hold great potential for broadly disseminating knowledge at low cost, and for reducing knowledge gaps both within countries and between industrial and developing countries.
- Market competition can unleash the private sector to provide the communications infrastructure and services and expand the use of new communications technologies in developing countries. But governments have to ensure appropriate regulation to guard against private monopoly power, and supplement the market to ensure access for the poor.

Harnessing the potential of new technology

Demand for communication today is heavily driven by business relations, alliances, and exchanges that span countries. But it is also driven by personal relations—among friends and family members living in different cities, towns, or villages or traveling the globe. This heightened demand is paralleled—and perhaps boosted—by dramatic changes in information and communications technologies, which together constitute the information revolution.

Three main forces underlie this revolution: the expansion of computing power, the falling cost of transmitting information, and the convergence of computing and telecommunications:

■ Computing power per dollar invested has risen by a factor of 10,000 over the past 20 years. Even as the processing speed and transistor density of microchips are increasing, production costs are being pushed down by relentless technical innovation and by economies of scale in producing microchips.

■ The cost of voice transmission circuits has fallen by a factor of 10,000 over those same 20 years, mainly because of fiber optics, low-cost electronics, and wireless technology. A single optical fiber much thinner than a copper wire can carry thousands of telephone conversations, making the cost per voice circuit infinitesimal. The falling price of electronics has allowed for cheaper, more reliable telephone network exchanges. And wireless technology is offering the possibility of providing services without incurring the high fixed cost of installing lines. Together these technologies are shrinking the cost of reaching individual users.

■ Digital technologies have joined together the telecommunications and computing industries and merged segments of the information industry into services that manipulate voice, text, image, video, and data. This convergence opens huge opportunities for developing countries to connect their people quickly, using innovative technologies and private sector–led investment (Box 4.1). But it also poses huge challenges for regulation.

The world information technology market—whose products include personal computers and workstations, multiuser computer systems, data communications equipment, and packaged software—grew by about 12.2 percent a year in real terms between 1985 and 1995, almost five times faster than world GDP (Table 4.1). Although the production of information technology remains highly concentrated—with more than 90 percent in OECD countries—the use of modern communications media is expanding rapidly in other countries.

However, in many countries prices have not fallen nearly as fast as costs, partly because of incumbent national monopolies, and partly because prices for international connections are still set by a cartel-like system of international agreements between these national monopolies. Still, technical change is bringing in competition, which will eventually translate into affordable access for more people in more countries. Furthermore, as outmoded monopolies lose their hold on prices, consumers will enjoy a wider choice—between fixed lines and wireless or cellular, between fax and e-mail. Moreover, the larger a given network, the greater the opportunity for users to acquire and exchange information, and therefore the greater the appeal for even more to join.

Opportunities for leapfrogging

The opportunities are great for developing countries to take advantage of the new information and communications technologies in disseminating knowledge. New wireless technologies that require less fixed investment than traditional wire-based ones can be more cost-effective in countries with sparse populations, difficult terrain, and harsh climatic conditions, because they require less maintenance. Furthermore, some developing countries perceive—indeed, a few have already seized—an opportunity to leapfrog the industrial countries by going straight from underdeveloped networks to fully digitized networks, bypassing the traditional analog technology that still forms the backbone of the system in most industrial countries. In 1993 some two dozen or more developing economies already had fully digitized networks, while the level of digitization in the OECD countries averaged just 65 percent (37 percent in Germany, for example, and 72 percent in Japan; Figure 4.1).

Consumers in developing countries can indeed benefit from the new wireless technologies. Some who find it difficult to get a fixed telephone line can get a cellular phone instead. The number of cellular phones per fixed line is already as high in some low- and middle-income economies as in some industrial countries; some developing countries with low density in both traditional telephone service and cellular phones have recently invested in cellular technology at a very fast rate (Figure 4.2). The Philippines, a country with low telephone density (only 2.5 main lines per 100 people), has a higher ratio of mobile phone subscribers to main lines than Japan, the United Kingdom, the United States, or several other industrial countries with densities of more than 50 main lines per 100 people.

Opportunities for doing new things—and doing old things differently

People in developing countries can apply the new technologies to a vast range of activities, including education

Box 4.1

From the transistor to the integrated digital network

The invention of the transistor in 1947 and the complementary invention of the computer set in motion dramatic changes in the way people communicate. In 1959 came another major breakthrough: the first integrated circuits, multiple transistors connected on a single sliver of semiconductor material. In the years that followed, the cost of building and connecting these electronic components fell sharply as the number that could be squeezed on a chip rose. Successive manufacturing improvements allowed for ever smaller and cheaper yet also more powerful components to be stacked together. In 1972 the first microprocessor, the essentials of a simple computer packed onto a single chip, was introduced.

The revolution in information and communications technology then gained momentum, propelled by the ever-increasing ratio of computing power to computing cost, by the growth of digital communications, and by the rapidly declining costs of transmission over diverse media.

These trends made possible the convergence of computing and telephony. At first the various technologies evolved as separate networks: conventional analog telephone services used dedicated wireline networks, cable television providers strung their own coaxial cables, and data transmission systems built their own set of cables and satellites. Today, however, the world is heading toward a system where the telephone, the Internet, television, and data share a generalized digital information infrastructure consisting of interconnected systems: wireline, wireless, packet-switched, coaxial, and satellite (see figure).

This convergence demolishes the traditional view of telecommunications as a natural monopoly: competition is now

Convergence in the telecommunications industry

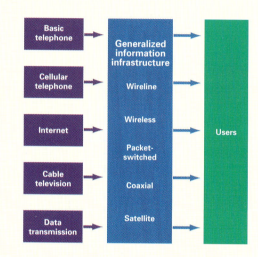

Source: Bond 1997a.

possible both between and within its different segments. Although this reduces governments' role in infrastructure provision, it also generates new challenges in designing market regulation. For example, by breaking down the division between broadcasting and telecommunications, convergence raises regulatory issues of privacy, decency, and intellectual property protection.

Table 4.1

Product and geographical composition of the world information technology market

(percent)

Product type or region	1985	1995	Average annual growth rate, 1985–95
By main product type			
Personal computers and workstations	20.9	30.5	17.2
Multiuser systems	29.5	13.0	4.0
Data communications equipment	3.0	4.3	17.0
Packaged software	13.5	18.4	16.3
Services	33.1	33.7	13.0
By region			
North America	59.2	43.5	9.4
Latin America	1.5	2.0	15.6
Western Europe	22.1	28.3	15.6
Eastern Europe, Middle East, and Africa	3.1	2.6	10.6
Other Asia and Pacific	14.0	23.7	18.9
World			12.2

Source: Mansell and Wehn 1998.

Figure 4.1

Economies ranked by share of the telephone network digitized

Some developing economies have leapfrogged over the richer industrial ones and installed fully digital networks.

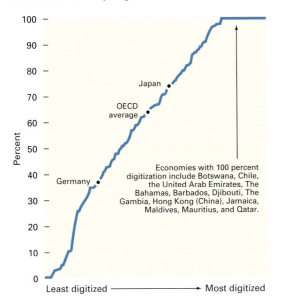

Note: Data are for 1993 for 164 economies worldwide. Source: International Telecommunication Union data.

Figure 4.2

Telephone density and mobile phone penetration

Mobile phones can complement a well-developed wire-based network—or substitute for an underdeveloped one.

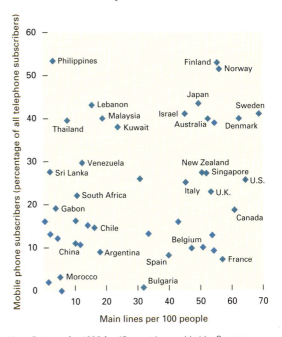

Note: Data are for 1996 for 45 countries worldwide. Source: International Telecommunication Union data.

(Chapter 3), finance (Chapter 6), the environment (Chapter 7), income generation by the poor (Chapter 8), and policymaking (Chapters 9 and 10).

Supporting lifelong learning. With the growing complexity of knowledge, the speed with which it is being updated, and the sheer quantity of information to be interpreted, people today need to engage in structured and systematic learning throughout their lives. As Chapter 3 argues, lifelong learning is especially important in developing countries, where many adults did not receive basic education during their youth. With modern communications technologies they can do so at their own pace, outside of school or the workplace. Also, schools and universities can share teaching materials and resources by e-mail and over the Internet, thus relaxing some of their resource constraints.

Taking advantage of investment opportunities. Many potential investors in developing countries remain excluded from formal financial transactions for lack of information about the instruments available. In China, however, more than 100 million people—farmers and housewives, bar-

maids and bureaucrats—now invest in stocks traded on the country's two exchanges in Shanghai and Shenzhen. Many are active investors, frequently seeking information about companies, markets, and opportunities. The traditional newspapers that provide stock market tips are no longer enough for these information-hungry investors, so the telephone company offers more than 100 pay-per-call hotlines analyzing the market's daily performance. There is also a separate hotline for each of the nearly 800 listed stocks. Investors can use bank debit cards to place trades at storefront brokerage offices, or trade using the keypads on their mobile telephones. More than 30 Chinese cities have electronic trading terminals that link them instantly to either exchange.

Helping the poor earn more income. The new technologies can help remove constraints that keep the poor living at subsistence levels. In a small business loan program in Vietnam, e-mail keeps the lender (a relief agency) in touch with borrowers (women in a small community) and helps coordinate loan payments, encouraging the lender to extend more loans. With the help of a nongovernmental organization (NGO) called Peoplink, women in Panama post pictures of their handicrafts on the Internet's World Wide Web, and thus gain access to a world market. And in West Africa, information technology helped eradicate river blindness, allowing millions to return to farming (Box 4.2).

Governments often lack the knowledge they need about the poor, their activities, and their needs. So, unfortunately, do those institutions whose mandate is to reduce poverty. The new technologies hold potential for teaching governments and institutions about the poor, for designing programs that benefit them, and for enhancing their participation and empowerment. Satellite technology, for example, can be used for computer mapping programs, to contribute to the clear titling to land that is crucial for small farmers and entrepreneurs seeking collateralized credit (Chapter 8). Care should be taken, however, to ensure that such programs are consistent with customary allocations of land rights, so that the titling is universally accepted.

Getting useful information to the poor. The information revolution offers great opportunities for informing the poor and empowering them to make decisions that affect their lives—provided political and legal impediments do not block the flow of information to the poor or weaken their ability to make their voices heard. The literate poor have greater and cheaper access to printed material and libraries than did their counterparts in today's industrial countries when they were at the same stage of development. In the Philippines, for example, a group of subsistence farmers have become pineapple specialists, using telex and fax machines to communicate directly with researchers and market representatives.

Providing information on markets and for small businesses. Small entrepreneurs and inhabitants of remote areas typically lack information about prices and market opportunities, about the successful replicable experiences of peers, or about financial systems. Information and communications technologies are a powerful instrument for remedying such information deficiencies:

Box 4.2

How information technology helped control river blindness

One of the most successful applications of information technology in developing countries has been in the Onchocerciasis Control Program (OCP), the international program to eradicate river blindness. River blindness is caused by a parasite, *Onchocerca volvulus,* that is carried from person to person by the blackfly. Because the parasite is concentrated along river beds, it had led over the years to the abandonment of large tracts of fertile land in West Africa.

The OCP was initiated in 1974 by seven West African countries: Benin, Burkina Faso, Côte d'Ivoire, Ghana, Mali, Niger, and Togo. Today 11 countries are partners in the program, which is executed by the World Health Organization. Twenty-one donor organizations (up from six originally) also participate, as well as several NGOs, community organizations, and a pharmaceutical company. The primary objectives of the program are twofold:

- To eliminate river blindness as a threat to public health and as an obstacle to socioeconomic development throughout the program area, and
- To assist in ensuring that the beneficiary countries are in a position to safeguard this achievement.

Over the past 20 years the OCP has eliminated the disease in the original seven member countries. In the 1980s the blackfly evolved resistance to the commonly used insecticide, but this was overcome by applying several insecticides in rotation. Over 30 million people are now protected from infection, and 185,000 who were already infected have been spared blindness. Fertile lands that were formerly vacant have now been resettled, and the inhabitants are thriving. A total of 25 million hectares (about 100,000 square miles) of riverine land is now available for settlement and cultivation. Under traditional technologies and agricultural practices, the reclaimed land is capable of feeding 17 million people.

The program was so successful because it pinpointed the peak times to spray, allowing systematic control of the blackfly population. Information was collected along 50,000 river kilometers, using sensors on the river bottom. Local inhabitants entered the data into computers, and the information was beamed to satellite radio transmitters and from there to a network of entomologists and laboratories, which in turn transmitted schedules to the airplane pilots responsible for spraying. Another element in the program's success was its use of epidemiological and environmental surveillance to ensure that the insecticides caused no damage to fish and invertebrate populations in the fast-flowing rivers.

Although the OCP was initially built around control of the parasite, in the last few years the discovery of the drug ivermectin has introduced a community-based dimension to the disease's control. The drug proved a real breakthrough: a single dose provides protection against the disease for a whole year. Ivermectin is provided free of cost by Merck & Company and distributed by national teams, with technical and logistical support from a committee comprising donor countries and NGOs. This combination of information technology, medical knowledge, community participation, and international support has greatly contributed to interrupting the transmission of river blindness and offers hope of eventually eliminating the disease.

- In rural Costa Rica small coffee growers use telecommunications to get marketing information from central cooperatives in the capital, which have computers linked to sources of information on national and international coffee prices.
- Farmers in Côte d'Ivoire use cellular phones to get international cocoa price quotations directly from Abidjan.
- Farmer associations in Mexico use computers to monitor the government's rural credit program; armed with that information, they can negotiate to make the program fairer and more effective.
- The introduction of telephone service to several rural towns and villages in Sri Lanka allowed small farmers to obtain current, firsthand information on wholesale and retail prices of fruits and other produce in Colombo, the capital. Before they obtained telephone service, they used to sell their crops at prices averaging 50 to 60 percent of the Colombo price. Now they regularly get 80 to 90 percent of that price.
- A small grocer in Rosario, Uruguay, who sold and delivered groceries to homes was able to expand his clientele beyond his immediate neighborhood when residential telephones became available locally and customers could order goods by telephone.
- A distributor of industrial spare parts and machinery in Nairobi saw his business expand 35 percent after additional lines were installed to his office from the local exchange. This permitted him to hire six new employees and add three light trucks to his company's fleet.

Improving governance. The new technologies can also improve governance by allowing policymaking institutions and think tanks to share knowledge. Officials of Kenya's Ministry of Agriculture brought a computer to budget meetings to show decisionmakers on the spot the consequences of adding or cutting projects as they were discussed. The result was a far better allocation of resources. In Morocco the government is using information and communications technology to enhance interministry coordination, tax administration, auditing, public investment planning and monitoring, and expenditure management. These tools have cut in half the time required to prepare the budget.

In most economies, industrial and developing, information and communications technologies are assuming a central role. In banking and international finance, tourism and travel, commodity trading, and export-oriented manufacturing, success depends on global information and efficient electronic exchange. The new technologies are also becoming a vital part of countries' economic infrastructure. At the port of Singapore, efforts to computerize port activities and customs clearance have dramatically boosted efficiency (Box 4.3).

To compete in the new global economy, developing countries must see the development and effective use of their information infrastructure as a key national objective. Indeed, a number of them have made effective use of information technologies a key thrust of their national development strategies. Malaysia, for example, has defined its information technology objectives and included them in its development strategy. The objectives include enhancing awareness of the new technologies among the population, ensuring widespread diffusion and application of information technology, expanding information technology training, and revising laws and regulations to facilitate and protect transactions that use electronic rather than paper-based modes of exchanging information. The ultimate goal is to make Malaysia into a global information hub.

Addressing the year 2000 problem. The information revolution and the technological progress that has accompanied it are bringing immense benefits to the world. But that same technology has generated one problem of its own that might affect today's technology-driven world quite dramatically. The year 2000 (Y2K) problem arises from the common practice in older computer programs of designating years by the last two digits only. This was done to economize on computer memory, which was then quite expensive. Computers so programmed will register the year 2000 as "00," which they then may interpret as "1900." A related problem is that computer programs with incorrect leap-year calculations will assume that the year 2000 has only 365 days instead of 366. Unless corrected, these programming flaws will cause devices containing embedded computer chips and related systems worldwide to fail or to behave in unpredictable ways.

The "millennium bug," as it is also called, is expected to affect systems in many different sectors, including communications, banking, public utilities, health care, and defense. It has the potential to seriously disrupt public and private sector operations at all levels. The precise dimensions of the Y2K problem are not known, but the global cost of fixing it is often estimated in the hundreds of billions of dollars.

Apart from the technological challenges, in many developing countries the problem is compounded by a lack of awareness. Whereas some countries have launched national programs to deal with the issue, others have yet to begin to address the problem. World Bank surveys as of August 1, 1998, indicated that only 29 out of 137 developing countries had put in place a national Y2K program. The lack of awareness and understanding means that solutions may not be implented in time, and failures may occur, causing serious disruptions.

Although Y2K is fundamentally a technical problem, choosing how to solve it is a business and regulatory issue. Accordingly, a special initiative has been launched by the

Box 4.3

How Singapore became the world's most efficient port

Singapore Network Services (SNS) manages and operates Tradenet, a networked information system that allows traders to declare imports and exports for customs directly from their office computers. Tradenet evolved from a five-person National Computer Board research project, begun in December 1986 with the aim of boosting Singapore's competitiveness in world markets. Fifty companies participated in a pilot launched in January 1988. The participants included traders, customs agents, and the Trade Development Board, which handles much of the documentation and licensing done in other countries by customs agencies.

With Tradenet, a trader's declaration is transmitted electronically to the Trade Development Board, which issues the necessary approvals within 15 minutes, after routing details to various government departments. Depending on the type of goods, as many as 20 agencies may be involved. On receiving approval, the trader prints and signs the document to obtain release of the cargo. Tradenet user software developed by SNS is offered through several approved Singaporean software houses. Software developed by others may be used instead but requires certification to ensure quality and compatibility.

Thanks to Tradenet, traders no longer have to leave their offices to obtain customs approvals. And because special trips to rectify errors or resolve disputes now hardly ever occur, traders have been able to trim their labor costs. With storage for goods awaiting clearance no longer necessary, goods can now go straight from the ship to the consignee—a particularly important consideration in Singapore, where space is at a premium.

Meanwhile a new port, container, and real-time vessel management system operated by the Port of Singapore Authority has further expedited the flow of goods. The result has been ship turnarounds of less than 10 hours, leading to huge improvements in the use of port and harbor facilities. This electronic preclearance has helped make Singapore's port the most efficient in the world. The Singapore government has valued these efficiencies at more than 1 percent of GDP.

Software from SNS is now also used for e-mail, information services, and bulletin boards, as well as a range of new services for health, legal systems, electronics, manufacturing, retail, and distribution. And the group is installing versions of its service in Canada, China, India, Malaysia, Mauritius, the Philippines, and Vietnam. Many of these installations are joint ventures with government departments (as in the case of Mauritius Network Services) or local commercial enterprises (as with Ayala in the Philippines). But how replicable the SNS experience is for countries with less human capital remains unclear.

World Bank's Information for Development program, in partnership with other multilateral development banks, some bilateral development agencies, and some private corporations. The program disseminates information to key stakeholders in developing countries on how to deal with the Y2K problem. It also provides limited financial support (in the form of grants) and technical assistance for remediation and for drawing up national Y2K plans, which will identify those aspects of the problem that merit the highest priority from an economic and a social perspective, and for providing targeted solutions. World Bank loans and credits are also available to address this problem. The use of new information technologies such as teleconferencing may also be effective in spreading awareness by promoting a broader dialogue on the issue (Box 4.4).

Although the first and necessary step in addressing the Y2K problem is to be aware of it, its solution will require resources, financial as well as human and technical. Many developing countries that have managed to develop awareness still face difficulties in mobilizing the resources necessary to begin modifying and converting their information systems.

Some caveats

Despite the great promise of the information revolution, some caveats are in order. As with the industrial revolu-

tion, gains will be fully realized only when ways of doing business have adapted more fully to the changed technology. For instance, videoconferencing may increasingly replace travel, saving large amounts of money and time. But even in industrial countries where individuals, firms, and other organizations have made large investments in new information and communications technologies, skeptics remain unconvinced about their eventual impact on economic growth. Skepticism is even more widespread in developing countries, where use of the new technologies is still sparse. The skeptics point out the dangers, and the costs, of information overload, including the huge costs involved in absorbing and sorting through vastly increased flows of information.

Another concern is that those who have access to the new technology may forge ahead, leaving those without access behind and widening gaps in well-being both between and within countries. Some worry that the wider marketplace of the global economy opens up opportunities for increased concentration of market power, and that the industrial, not the developing countries, will reap a disproportionate share of the profits.

In some countries and communities, language differences may inhibit the use of new information and communications technologies. For example, although the Internet is increasingly offering original material and on-line

Box 4.4

Teleconferencing to raise awareness of the year 2000 problem

To help raise developing countries' awareness about the Y2K problem, the World Bank is holding a series of interactive videoconferences on the topic. The first of these were produced for some countries in Africa. Originating from Bank headquarters in Washington, the conference consisted of briefings from a panel of experts from the Bank's Y2K group as well as from outside organizations. Policymakers and other decisionmakers, as well as representatives from ministries and the public and the private sector, took part. By June 1998 nine African countries—including both English- and French-speaking ones—had taken part.

These videoconferences have increased the level of awareness of the Y2K problem considerably. They have helped trigger action plans that could save these countries millions of dollars. Cameroon, Côte d'Ivoire, and Senegal have now set up national committees to examine the issue and define action plans. An ongoing dialogue is under way among organizations at the national level, as well as between the countries and the Bank. Through this dialogue, the Bank's Information for Development Program and its Information Solutions Group provide advice on how and where to find relevant information.

translations in a range of languages, English remains the dominant language on the World Wide Web. People who cannot read English therefore face much greater obstacles than others in accessing this growing store of knowledge.

Even if the ultimate impact of the information revolution turns out to be something less than the current excitement suggests, it is likely to have profound positive effects on the economy and on society. Developing countries are already reaping huge benefits in areas where lack of modern communications represented a real impediment. But reaping the full benefits of these new technolo-

gies will take longer, because they will take time to fully penetrate these economies.

Because of this, older means of communication are likely to remain important for the foreseeable future:

- Radio can reach large numbers of poor people because it is affordable and uses little electricity, which is in low supply in many countries and barely affordable for many of the poor.
- Television remains a powerful and influential medium, because it presents words and images together, reaching people regardless of their literacy.
- Newspapers cannot directly inform illiterate people, but they are one of the cheapest ways to communicate knowledge and are especially effective in reaching opinionmakers.

It may be some time, if ever, before the Internet displaces radio, television, and the print media as the dominant channel for reaching low-income households in developing countries. Policymakers thus need to pay due attention to these other media, provide the right competitive environment, encourage their free development and use, and facilitate the local provision of content.

Delays in adoption

The means for using information to be more productive in the new global economy are very unequally distributed. The average high-income economy has over 100 times more computers per capita than the average low-income economy. Similar gaps exist for telephones (Table 4.2). Hampering the potential of the new information and communications technologies in developing countries are inadequate human capital, low purchasing power, and poor competition and regulation. A lack of training in the new technologies, especially in their maintenance and repair, is a major bottleneck. A recent survey of Internet users in Africa found that low computer literacy and low

Table 4.2

Selected indicators of information and telecommunications penetration by country income level

Group	Telephone main lines per 1,000 people, 1995	Personal computers per 1,000 people, 1995	Internet users per 1,000 people, 1996
Low-income economies	25.7	1.6	0.01
Lower-middle-income economies	94.5	10.0	0.7
Upper-middle-income economies	130.1	24.2	3.5
Newly industrializing economies (NIEs)	448.4	114.8	12.9
High-income economies[a]	546.1	199.3	111.0

a. Excluding NIEs.
Source: World Bank 1998d.

skill with Internet programs correlated significantly with low use. Perpetuating this skills gap is a lack of educators knowledgeable in the new technology.

Income levels, which are often related to education, appear to influence the adoption of telecommunications. Eighty percent of cross-country differences in telephone density can be attributed to differences in income per capita (Figure 4.3). South Asia and Sub-Saharan Africa have roughly 1.5 telephone lines for every 100 people, compared with 64 per 100 in the United States. Although total annual investment in telecommunications in developing countries has doubled to $60 billion a year since the early 1990s, much remains to be done to meet growing demand.

Indeed, in most low-income economies the problem is not lack of demand but inadequate supply. Although many in developing countries cannot afford a telephone, many can. Yet too often a request for a telephone line can go unmet for months or even years. The ratio of telephones on order to telephones in service is much higher in countries with low telephone density (Figure 4.3). Almost all the 28 million people on waiting lists worldwide are in

developing countries, and their average wait is roughly one year. Moreover, some people do not bother to order a telephone line because they are sure they will not get it. In developing countries more than in industrial countries, the supply of telephones and of modern information technologies appears to be restrained by poor competition and regulation policies.

Competition and public policy

Telecommunications was long viewed as a natural monopoly. It was seen as most efficient to have one and only one producer. Because costs in this industry fall as the scale of production increases, the largest firm in the industry achieved the lowest costs and could underprice its rivals. As it did so, it would come eventually to dominate the industry. Most countries took the position that the only or at least the best way to prevent abuse of this monopoly power was for government to operate the telephone system.

Governments accordingly entered the arena. They then prevented the entry of competitors, arguing that they would wastefully duplicate existing facilities or provide

Figure 4.3

Telephone density, queuing for telephone service, and income per capita

The scarcity of telephones in developing countries reflects low income, but also unmet demand.

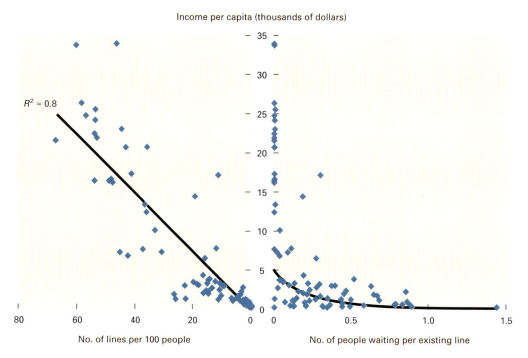

Note: Data are for 1993. Source: World Bank 1997g.

services only to low-cost users (typically those in urban areas, where the density of customers was high), thus inhibiting the government's ability to provide broad service at reasonable prices. Undercutting this argument, however, is the fact that capital costs of state telephone monopolies in developing countries often reach $4,000 per telephone line—three to four times the achievable cost.

Inefficiency and underinvestment by state telephone monopolies led to bad service, and little or none to the poor or to rural areas—an irony given that one of the justifications of government monopoly was that only government ownership could ensure universal service. Highly subsidized domestic calls meant low revenues and limited expansion. Low prices generated profits for businesses with access, which was unfair to those (usually small) businesses that had none. The authority to allocate scarce lines bred corruption. Thus a system designed to help the poor and to protect consumers did neither, and inefficient service inhibited economic growth.

The changing competitive environment in telecommunications

An equally important cause of the poor performance of many telecommunications providers has been a lack of competition combined with ineffective government regulation. Confronted with the failure of their public telecommunications monopolies, more than 70 developing countries are now shifting to private, competitive markets. Even when government retains control of the core of the telephone system, there is still enormous scope for private participation in cellular and value-added services. All too often, however, government policies restrict this participation. Partly because of these restrictions, in Sub-Saharan Africa, for instance, only 25 percent of telephone lines (outside South Africa) are privately provided. However, the World Trade Organization's recent agreements on telecommunications services offer the possibility for ever-larger gains from competition as telecommunications liberalization goes global (Box 4.5).

Since the 1980s, countries the world over have witnessed a sea change in the way information infrastructure is supplied, priced, financed, used, and regulated. The old telecommunications paradigm is crumbling fast. Recent technical advances allow for low-cost public access to a range of communications media. Although information infrastructure markets remain far from fully competitive, technology and increased demand have signed the national monopolies' death warrant. As already noted, natural monopolies occur when firms that produce more output have lower costs—they are said to achieve economies of scale. But when firms using the new technologies can have low costs even at a small scale of operation, there may be many effective competitors. Even a market as small as

---

Box 4.5

Telecommunications liberalization receives a global push

The World Trade Organization's General Agreement on Trade and Services, part of the 1994 Uruguay Round set of agreements, brought the services sector, including telecommunications, into multilateral trade negotiations for the first time. After the Uruguay Round, the Negotiating Group on Basic Telecommunications was created to continue the progress that the round had started. By February 1997, 69 WTO members, representing more than 90 percent of the world telecommunications market, had tabled internationally binding commitments to liberalize basic telephone services.

In these talks, 31 industrial and 24 developing countries made commitments to liberalize their voice telephone services. Other services to be liberalized included long-distance international and resale voice telephony, data transmission, private leased circuits, mobile and satellite services, and trunk services. Most participants made commitments to all or part of a set of procompetitive regulatory principles. The likely benefits for signatories include greater competitiveness, increased FDI, and a better price-quality mix of consumer services.

Sri Lanka's has shown that it can support four cellular operating companies offering globally competitive prices. That country now has some of the lowest cellular telephone tariffs in the world—and added 56,000 cellular lines between 1993 and 1996.

In many industrial countries and a handful of middle-income economies, this new trend is helping create a dynamic marketplace for new kinds of services, in which knowledge and information are rapidly tapped and disseminated over dense national and global networks. Many developing countries, too, are seizing opportunities to provide ever wider and broader access, to reduce gaps in the availability and affordability of information, and to connect their people to each other and the world through innovative technologies and private sector–led investment. But to keep from being passed by, countries have to introduce competition in their telecommunications sector. Indeed, in many segments of the telecommunications market, competition is not only feasible—it is inexorable. And governments will be able to maintain monopolies only with repressive measures.

Ongoing changes in technology, the competitive environment, and pricing are leading to a rebalancing of prices across different services: prices are falling for international calls and rising (as subsidies are removed) for domestic calls in many developing countries. Traditional pricing patterns have often given the wrong incentives to both

Box 4.6

Pressure to reform accounting rates for international calls

An international call used to be a service jointly provided by a telephone company in the country originating the call and its counterpart in the country receiving the call. Under traditional "accounting rates" established bilaterally between telephone companies in different countries, the originating company compensates the company at the receiving end for each call. The settlement payment is normally half the wholesale price for international calls. This price is usually higher than the actual cost of the call.

Developing countries typically receive more international telephone traffic than they originate. The reasons for this include differences in incomes, sizes of emigrant communities, and prices for international calls. As a result, telephone operating companies in, for example, China, India, Mexico, and the Philippines routinely receive substantial settlement payments from the United States, a net originator of international traffic.

Today, telephone companies in the United States and other countries that have introduced competition in international telephone services are under pressure to lower charges to customers. This pressure, combined with increased opportunities for arbitrage in international calling, through callback and calling card services, has produced substantial revenues for operating companies in many developing countries, which they are using to finance the development of information infrastructure. But this is hardly the ideal way to finance such investments, for the following reasons:

- Accounting rate payments benefit countries unequally. Mexico received more than 17 percent of U.S. settlement payments in 1995, Sub-Saharan Africa less than 2 percent. Canada, Germany, and Japan have also received net settlement payments from the United States, whereas Albania, Afghanistan, and Somalia have been net payers.
- Settlement payments have not always financed telecommunications development, but have gone instead to general government revenues.

Finally, by keeping the floor price of international calling charges artificially high, the settlements system hampers the development of new, information-intensive exports (such as in data entry services) and of other services such as tourism.

equipment is used for both), allocating to each the costs of the facilities they share is tricky. By most reckonings, international callers have traditionally paid more than their share, and domestic callers less. Experience has shown that high international charges usually translate into low monthly rentals for telephones and low charges or none for local calls. This discourages telephone companies from extending the network. And overpriced long-distance and international telephone services penalize subscribers with clients, friends, and families in distant cities or abroad. Now, however, competitive service provision is putting the old pricing systems under threat—and the international tariff structure under serious challenge (Box 4.6).

Access to telecommunications is widening, but still limited in many countries. Sub-Saharan Africa has just one pay phone for every 5,300 people, compared with one for every 100 in Singapore. Many people in poor countries often travel several miles to get to the nearest pay phone—if there is one available. For example:

- A couple in rural Jamaica lives 156 kilometers from their daughter, who has to call her parents' neighbors half a mile away to reach them. Their messages are relayed up and down the hill by younger members of the community.
- A Johannesburg resident reports that his parents in the Northern province, one of the poorest parts of South Africa, have to travel 5 kilometers to the nearest shopping center to make a telephone call. His parents do not even dream of getting a telephone in their own home, he says.
- Residents of a medium-size town in Albania wait along a concrete wall for the chance to make a long-distance call. They scribble on scraps of paper the telephone numbers of friends, businesses, or government agencies they wish to reach and pass them through a small opening in the wall. Behind the wall the operators of old-fashioned manual switchboards then wait to connect to one of the only two long-distance lines in town. Long delays and failed connections are frequent before a call is completed.

Traditional cross-subsidies from international to local calling have generally failed to provide universal access, because they have been neither transparent nor well targeted. Competition is likely to increase access. Widespread evidence suggests that, once privatization and competition are introduced, service provision expands (Figure 4.4). Chile allowed competition in all market segments in the 1980s, and in less than a decade its telephone density more than tripled, to over 15 lines per 100 inhabitants. The Philippines opened its private monopoly to competition in 1993, and by the end of 1996 the number of telephone main lines had risen from 785,000 to 3.4 million. Other countries are following their lead. Uganda has li-

users and suppliers. High charges for international calls have traditionally been justified on grounds that they subsidized local calls, ensuring access for all. But sometimes controversy arises over the extent of the subsidy, or even whether there is one: since domestic and international calls are, to some extent, produced jointly (much of the same censed a second national telecommunications operator, and its privatization agency will soon sell the original one.

Competition has also reduced costs to subscribers. In Ghana a second cellular operator brought 30 to 50 percent reductions in both connection charges and tariffs, besides inspiring a rapid expansion in the first operator's service provision plans. Soon thereafter, entry of a third operator induced the first two to improve service.

Ensuring competition in liberalized markets

In telecommunications, as in all industries, private ownership and competition are the two essentials, but neither is easy to achieve. The sequence in which privatization, competition, and regulation are introduced can affect the outcome. When a state monopoly is privatized without appropriate regulation, a private monopoly can emerge. And private monopolies, more often than not, seek to stifle further attempts to introduce competition. Economic rents may then be transferred from the public sector to the private, with no gain in efficiency, no lower prices, and no broader service. Experience also shows that allowing private companies to compete can put pressure on a state monopoly to become more efficient, and this may eventually facilitate its privatization (Box 4.7).

This suggests three principles. First, privatization should follow the establishment of a regulatory structure, to ensure that competition is maintained and that the terms of licenses are respected. Regulations need to ensure that any monopoly power after privatization does not restrict entry, and to guarantee that new service providers have access to the incumbent's infrastructure. But the need for regulatory reform should not be an excuse for undue delay in opening the telecommunications sector to private participation—privatization should not await the ideal regulatory system. Chile, Ghana, and New Zealand privatized before fine tuning their regulatory systems.

Second, wherever possible, privatization should follow the introduction of greater competition. This might be achieved by extending licenses to new private companies or by breaking up the telecommunications monopoly.

Third, it may be easier to introduce competition by privatizing only part of the system. Especially promising are moves in some Sub-Saharan African countries to lower costs by exploiting competition among international telephone providers. This they have accomplished through soliciting competitive bids for purchase of their systems' more commodity-like aspects, such as local lines.

Telecommunications companies in the industrial countries, often prime candidates to purchase publicly owned services in developing countries, are continually innovating and offering new services. And increasing competition in these companies' home markets makes it all the more likely that developing countries will enjoy more of the fruits of these innovations. But to realize these benefits, developing countries must ensure effective competition among international companies in their domestic markets as well. Each company has an incentive to persuade countries to give them the inside track, and some companies have tried, in a variety of ways.

In Poland the benefits of liberalization have been thwarted by poor regulation. About 200 new telecommunications licenses have been awarded since 1990, but only 12 were in use in 1996. Among the main impediments cited by licensees are unfavorable terms for revenue sharing with the dominant state operator, limited access to its network, and prohibitions against setting up their own transmission facilities. This suggests that an important new role for regulation is to ensure that the dominant operator does not engage in anticompetitive practices—for example, by withholding essential technical and commercial information needed to price interconnections. And even when

Figure 4.4

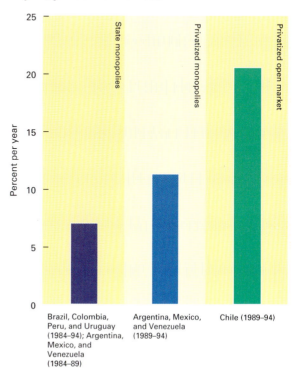

Growth in telephone main lines under differing market conditions in Latin America

Telephone networks have expanded faster in open, privatized markets.

Note: Data for monopolies are averages for the countries included.
Source: Wellenius 1997b.

Box 4.7

Competition before privatization in Ghana's telecommunications services

In less than four years Ghana has implemented one of the world's most ambitious telecommunications reform programs. In 1993 the industry was the exclusive domain of Ghana Posts and Telecommunications Corporation, then entirely state owned and losing money. Telephone density was extremely low, with only one main line for every 400 people. The average wait for a telephone line exceeded 10 years. Service was limited in range and poor in quality.

In 1997 Ghana became the first developing country to introduce privatization and competition in all areas of service, in all parts of the country. To raise financing, the government tapped international investors. It sold a 30 percent stake in Ghana Telecom Ltd., the company formed in 1995 by splitting telecommunications from the postal service, to a consortium of Telekom Malaysia and local investors. It granted a second national license to a consortium of two U.S. firms and the Ghana National Petroleum Corporation.

Ghana also issued national licenses to five cellular operating companies, to contain any monopoly power the consortia might attempt to wield. Three were operating at the end of 1997, providing 30 percent of the country's telephone lines. Ghana now has several privately owned Internet service providers, one with an aggressive program to provide access in rural areas through collaboration with the post office.

In 1997 alone the number of connected fixed lines increased from 90,000 to 120,000, while Ghana Telecom's revenue increased from around $55 million to $75 million. The company is now earning substantial profits for the first time in its history, and the government's remaining 70 percent holding is worth several times the value of the entire company before privatization. The company plans to meet its rollout obligation of 225,000 lines in three years, rather than the five allowed in the license.

Regulatory capacity was not strengthened before introducing competition, however, and there are worrying indications of poor performance by the regulator. Developing regulatory capacity is now Ghana's priority. Despite these problems, however, Ghana's model of competition with or before privatization is now being adopted by Madagascar, Nigeria, and Uganda.

these barriers are swept away, regulation is still necessary to ensure competition. For example, the United States, despite having one of the most competitive telecommunications industries in the world, does not yet have sufficient competition so that regulation can be put aside.

Although competition is increasing in telecommunications, it is still far from perfect. Of particular concern is that, typically, in certain vital parts of the industry there is still virtually no competition. This is especially true of the final wired connection to the local user (what is often called "the last mile"). Although cellular connections provide a partial substitute for these hard-wired connections, they remain an imperfect one. Regulators need to be concerned that the firm that controls the last mile does not abuse its market power by raising prices too high, or by restricting access. Access to existing networks is vital for any newcomer into the industry. A cellular phone company that could only connect its customers with each other would have a hard time garnering market share. Regulators have to ensure that the charges imposed for such interconnections are fair and that the quality of connection offered is good.

There is some controversy about what constitute "fair" access prices. In industrial countries with pro-competitive policies in information infrastructure—such as Australia, the United Kingdom, and the United States—regulators have used various approaches to estimate a "reasonable" price of access to the facilities of the dominant operator, to help prevent abuse of its market power.

Regulation will take different forms in countries at different stages of development and with different needs, but there is much to learn from the successes and failures in Chile, Ghana, Poland, New Zealand, and the United States. The task of the regulatory authority—independent of operators—is mainly to help competing operators reach a reasonable agreement when they cannot do so themselves. For instance, Guatemala requires the regulator to choose among the parties' final offers for connectivity charges. If one of the parties refuses to relinquish an unreasonable position, the regulator is likely to choose the other's price. (If regulatory skills are scarce, this task can be outsourced.) State-owned operators must also be deprived of the sovereign immunity that protects them from legal action, and new entrants should have recourse to the courts or to approved professional arbitrators to settle disputes.

Bringing access to the poor

The towns, small cities, and rural areas of many developing countries are underserved by telecommunications: in parts of Asia and Africa rural telephone density is a fifth that in the largest cities (Figure 4.5). But in some developing countries entrepreneurs have proved themselves capable of bringing telephones even to the poorest. Senegal in 1995 had more than 2,000 privately owned "telecenters," each with a pay phone and a fax machine; this was four times the number just two years before. But providing access to the rural poor often requires government support.

Governments can support such community facilities directly, thus leveraging poor people's willingness to pay,

Figure 4.5

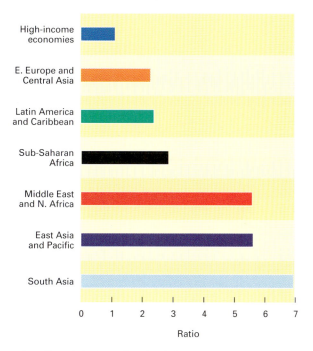

Ratios of urban to rural telephone density, by region

Telephones in the developing world are concentrated in the largest cities.

Note: The ratio is the number of main lines per 100 people in the largest cities divided by the number per 100 people outside the largest cities. Source: International Telecommunication Union data.

as in South Africa's multipurpose community information centers. The country's Universal Service Agency, established in 1996, provides each center two years' worth of startup costs, plus field workers to offer technical support. A 1997 survey of these centers found that 67 percent had a telephone, 31 percent a computer, and 8 percent Internet access.

Government can also work with the private sector to support services to low-income areas—markets, after all, have proved far more successful than traditional state monopolies in rolling out service. Even those who cannot afford the full cost are often willing to pay something to obtain access.

The proposition that market-supporting initiatives are likely to be more successful than direct subsidies is supported by Chile's competitive bidding for rural pay telephone subsidies. In 1994 a special fund, set to expire in 1998, began awarding subsidies competitively to projects providing telephone service to small and remote locales. By 1996 the fund had achieved 90 percent of its objectives while using only about half of its $4.3 million budget, largely because it received bids to provide service with no subsidy at all for projects accounting for half the locales and 59 percent of the targeted population. With successful completion of the bids, more than 97 percent of Chileans will likely have access to basic telecommunications by the end of 1998.

Chile's experiment suggests that private competition can greatly accelerate rural telecommunications development. By using market mechanisms, the government learned at low cost which projects required subsidies and how much. The experiment also shows that market mechanisms can give small subsidies tremendous leverage: with only half the designated budget, or roughly $2 million in public funds, the government triggered private investment equal to about $40 million. The average cost of installing a rural pay telephone dropped by 90 percent of the cost of direct public provision.

Monopoly power is a concern not only in telephone service but in the mass media as well. Again, different media are typically imperfect substitutes; each reaches a different audience. Some countries are increasingly concerned about concentration of ownership of television stations, or of print and broadcast media more broadly. Where there is such concentration, citizens may not get the diversity of viewpoints that is essential for a vibrant society. Media concentrated in the hands of a few may also fail to serve as an effective check on corruption, particularly if the owners are closely connected with the government. Worse still, such media may try to steer elections by distorting the positions of one or the other candidate. Monopoly power thus has more than strictly economic effects: it can thwart the flow of accurate information, or of at least the airing of competing views. The same concerns also arise when the media are state controlled, for there the government may use its control of information to maintain itself in power. Several countries are placing tighter restrictions on concentration in the media than in other industries, because the concern goes beyond just prices to the very functioning of an open society.

Another worry is that privatizing state-controlled media may curtail diversity. Providers who compete for a mass market tend to provide similar products, leaving those with more specialized interests without adequate service. This is one of the rationales for public radio and television. Fortunately the new information and communications technologies have the potential to enhance diversity: cable and satellite television can deliver far more stations at low cost than conventional broadcasting ever could. One private company, for example, is about to launch three satellites, one each to cover Africa, Latin America, and Asia, to beam a variety of world-class programs to low-income consumers.

• • •

For developing countries, the new information and communications technologies hold enormous potential. The new wireless technologies will extend modern communications into areas that conventional copper wires would have taken decades to reach—if they ever did. People in remote communities the world over can have access to knowledge beyond the dreams of anyone in the industrial countries even a quarter century ago.

Using privatization, competition, regulation, and selective public action, developing countries can supplement traditional media with these new tools for communicating knowledge. Indeed, to compete in the new global economy, developing countries must make the development and effective use of information infrastructure a top national objective. They have to seize the opportunities offered by the new technologies to enhance private provision of telecommunications services and extend the reach of the new technologies throughout society. If done well, these strategies promise to enhance educational systems, improve policy formation and execution, and widen the range of new opportunities for business.

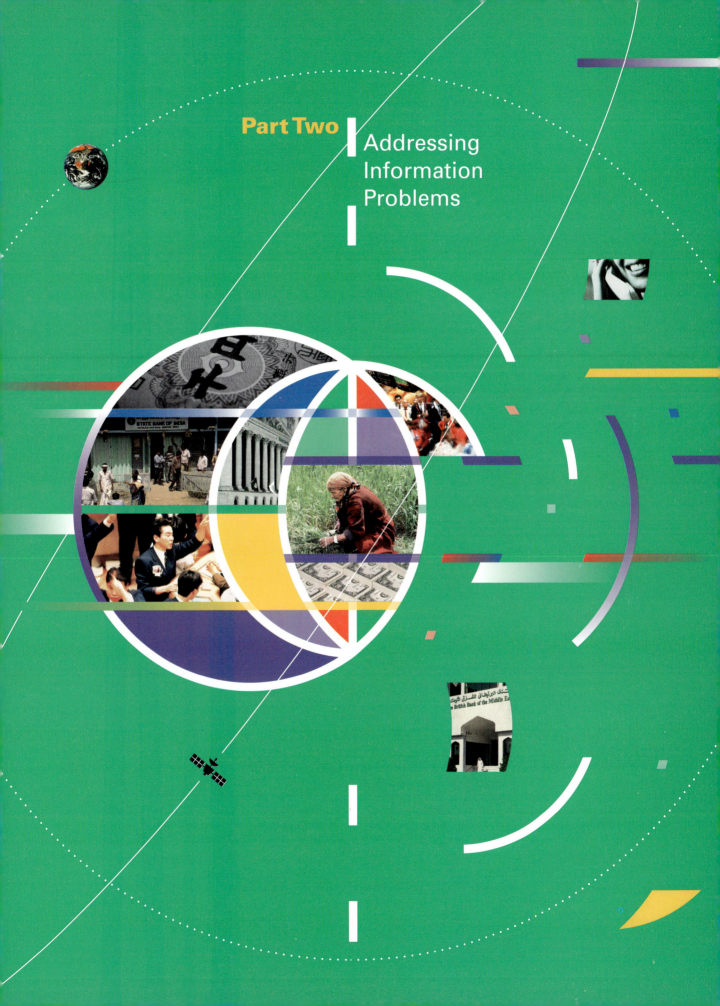

Part Two

Addressing
Information
Problems

Chapter 5

Information, Institutions, and Incentives

PART ONE OF THIS REPORT showed that narrowing knowledge gaps—by acquiring, absorbing, and communicating knowledge—can go a long way toward spurring economic growth and improving well-being in developing countries. Part Two argues that even if they could completely close the gaps in technical knowledge, developing countries would still be at a disadvantage with respect to the second type of knowledge, knowledge about attributes: about the quality of products, the diligence of workers, the creditworthiness of firms. This stems from the fact that developing countries have fewer institutions to ameliorate information problems, and the institutions they do have are weaker than the counterpart institutions in industrial countries. These institutional deficiencies mean that markets often wither rather than thrive, because people lack the incentive to enter into the transactions fundamental to rapid, equitable, and sustainable growth. And as we shall see, that institutional weakness often hurts the poor most.

Information is the lifeblood of every economy. In more traditional economies, information may be less codified, more often conveyed in personal interaction, but it is vital nonetheless. A farmer has to know the propitious time to plant. A moneylender has to know whether someone seeking a loan is likely to repay it. A landlord hiring a worker has to know whether the worker is skillful and diligent. And as countries develop, the requirements for information increase. A new seed is being offered by a government extension agent. Will it work? A farmer hears that some crop other than the traditional one can be sold in the market. Will it pay to switch?

The ways people get information, and the incentives they have to gather and provide it, are affected by the way society is organized: legal rules and social conventions, institutions and governments, all determine how much information people have and the quality (that is, the accuracy and completeness) of that information. Without reliable information, markets do not work well. If someone buying rice in a nearby market cannot tell whether stones have been added to increase the weight, sellers may be tempted to increase their profits by putting stones in. But then the buyer may decide to purchase rice only from a trusted seller, probably someone from the same village. That splinters markets, leaving them thin and less competitive. It can even make the market collapse, and otherwise profitable transactions will be forgone.

Traditional societies with little personal mobility often exhibit extraordinary information flows and an extraordinary ability to uphold social arrangements through various sanctions. But as countries develop, this traditional structure begins to disintegrate. People move from village to village, from village to town, from town to city in response to commerce and trade. Increasingly, they engage in transactions with strangers rather than neighbors. In this growing anonymity, traditional avenues of information sharing based on personal acquaintance must be replaced. But the new avenues—the sophisticated computer networks that track credit histories, or the efficient legal enforcement that makes contracts possible—may be a long time coming. So, in the course of development, information flows may deteriorate before they improve. Both traditional and modern societies may have a lot of good information, but societies in between may not.

This chapter sets out a simple, two-part taxonomy of information failure on which the rest of Part Two will draw. The first type of failure arises from the difficulty of *verifying quality* and the need to gather as much information about quality as is feasible or to find ways of reducing the need for it. The second type arises from the difficulty of *enforcing performance* and the need to find mechanisms to monitor transactions. These problems are universal, but they are far worse in developing countries than in industrial countries—and they are worst for the poor.

Verifying quality

Verifying quality means obtaining knowledge about the attributes of a good or service—the durability of a product, the productivity of a worker. In many transactions, such as those for durable goods, the problems associated with verifying quality—and the importance of doing so—are obvious. But goods, at least, can be inspected before purchase. Verifying the quality of services is harder, because a service comes into being only after it is purchased. An employer who is unsure of the skills of a prospective employee faces a difficult quality verification problem. So does the lender who is uncertain about the trustworthiness of a potential borrower.

Information about quality, like other forms of information examined throughout this Report, is costly to create but cheap to share. That is why societies typically exert considerable effort to make information about quality acquired by one person available to others. In small, closed communities, information about quality is spread by word of mouth. Buyers can identify and remember the supplier of a poor-quality good and warn their neighbors about that supplier. Employers can identify an inept worker and refuse to recommend that worker to other employers.

As communities grow and establish links with other communities, institutions of various kinds come into existence to share information about quality. In medieval Europe and in the Arab world until the late 19th century, guilds provided quality control, inspecting inputs and production processes and punishing dishonesty. *Amins,* the heads of local craft guilds in major cities throughout the Middle East and North Africa, were knowledgeable, respected individuals to whom consumers could turn to test sellers' claims about the authenticity and quality of their goods.

The uncertainty that consumers face in determining quality can create severe inefficiencies or even destroy a market. Government action to reduce such uncertainty, for example by establishing and enforcing standards, can improve the functioning of markets, to the benefit of all. Such was the case when India's National Dairy Development Board acted to ensure the quality of milk. Its program doubled the incomes of a million milk producers (Box 5.1).

The national and international expansion of markets in perishable fruits and vegetables also required the develop-

---

Box 5.1

Addressing information failures in India's milk market

In India in the 1950s, milk production could not keep pace with growing demand. Some milk vendors responded by watering down the milk. They could do this with relative impunity because consumers could not determine which milk was diluted before buying it. And because there were many vendors, and brand names were not clearly established, vendors who did not dilute their milk could not command a premium and were squeezed out of the market. The result was an overall drop in milk quality. Enter the National Dairy Development Board, which in the early 1970s launched Operation Flood, a multifaceted program to improve the functioning of the milk market by ensuring quality.

The board began by encouraging the creation of dairy cooperatives and helping them establish quality standards. The board distributed a simple, hand-operated device for testing butterfat content to each village cooperative that collected milk from farmers and to distributors and marketing agents. This strengthened the incentives for producing and marketing quality milk. Next the board took steps to improve and standardize milk quality by providing cooperatives with technical assistance, such as improved feed, veterinary services, and artificial insemination. The board also subsidized construction of modern processing plants and the provision of refrigerated transport. Finally, it encouraged the cooperatives to establish brand names. Taken together, these measures improved the quality of milk and by 1979 had doubled the incomes of a million milk producers in the target areas.

Who, in retrospect, was to blame for the widespread practice of watering down milk? Since any vendor in the unregulated market who did not dilute the milk would be at a competitive disadvantage, it is hard to blame the vendors, individually or collectively. The problem lay with the absence of institutions to verify quality. The National Dairy Development Board helped make the quality of milk verifiable and paid prices that reflected and rewarded quality. By defining standards, providing the means to meet and monitor them, and applying them honestly, the board helped India become the world's third-largest producer of milk. From 1970 to 1991, the number of milk producers participating in Operation Flood grew from 280,000 to 8 million.

---

ment of ways to monitor and assess quality. In the United States this process took several decades to complete. The innovation of refrigerated rail transport in the late 1800s transformed the American fresh fruit trade from a patchwork of small, isolated markets into a national market with fruit grown in regions far from major consumption centers. But shipping over long distances meant inserting middlemen between the farmers and the consumer, and this created opportunities for fraud. The farmer could deliver low-quality fruit and escape blame by claiming that the fruit was damaged during shipping. If the railroad allowed the fruit to rot, it could plausibly blame the farmer. And the distributor in the receiving market could claim that the quality of the goods received was lower than it actually was.

Without a means to verify quality at both the shipping point and the receiving point, written contracts based on delivered quality could not solve the information problem. Growers therefore asked the U.S. government for assistance, and it responded by establishing a shipping point inspection service. Today, the U.S. Agricultural Marketing Service provides inspections at the shipping point and the destination point on a voluntary, fee-for-service basis.

For many consumer goods in a modern economy, a respected brand name often replaces third-party institutions as a guarantor of quality. The institutional responsibilities for quality control shift from externally imposed standards to individual producers with an incentive to maintain their reputations, as embodied in their brand names. But institutional burdens do not disappear entirely: properly functioning courts must ensure that fraudulent imitation is deterred by the threat of swift legal retribution.

These problems of verifying quality go beyond the market for commodities. Labor markets raise many of the same issues and some new ones as well. In tasks involving sophisticated skills usually acquired through education, the conferral of a degree can signal quality. But even in markets for manual labor, employers care about quality: they want to know how hard the worker will work. They can learn this from experience, but this learning, if not shared with others, informs the employer about only a relatively few workers. Since employers would often rather draw on workers they know than gamble on those they do not, labor markets can become highly segmented.

A 1986 study of 80 villages in the state of West Bengal, India, found evidence of territorial segmentation of the market for casual agricultural labor: landlords typically hired workers in their own or immediately adjacent villages. This suggests that personal connections and trust may be stronger than wage differences in influencing the movement of labor. The West Bengal study reported that:

> . . . there are sometimes considerable wage differences on similar work across even neighbouring villages; and yet labourers often do not walk across to the next village to take advantage of higher wages. On the other hand, labourers occasionally go out to work in villages where the wage rate is not significantly higher. The boundaries of labour mobility across neighboring villages are sometimes significantly defined by territorial affinities and the relationships of trust and credit between labourers and their employers.

More generally, the problem of verifying quality may be resolved over time in communities with little personal mobility, through informal information-sharing and enforcement mechanisms based on personal exchange. The compactness of a small community also facilitates verification. With close and repeated contacts, people come to know the qualities of those they deal with. This extends not only to hiring workers but to other transactions as well: How much trouble will it be to get a loan repaid? How fertile is the land being put up for rent? But such a system is closed to outsiders, segmenting the market.

The problem of verifying quality is not restricted to goods or labor markets. It is especially acute in financial markets. The informational problem in a credit market may be reduced to a single question: how much, if any, of the loan will be repaid? The prudence of the borrower, whether he or she will repay, and the riskiness of the investment are the issues with which quality verification is concerned. The problem is compounded in poor communities where, whatever promises are made, liability is effectively limited: if the project fails, the loan taken out to finance it will not be repaid, because the borrower has few or no other resources. This limited liability is an important cause of high interest rates in informal credit markets, as it forces lenders to spend more time and effort to assess the creditworthiness of potential borrowers (Box 5.2). The high costs of verification in the case of the poor result in high interest rates, which in the end may be too high for the poor to pay.

The resulting segmentation in credit markets shows up in wide variations in interest rates and other terms of lending in the same geographical area. If information were perfect, a borrower being charged a high interest rate by one local lender might seek out another charging less. Arranging a new loan would make both of them better off. But the new lender will worry: is the current lender charging such a high interest rate because the borrower is unlikely to repay the loan? Thus the quality verification problem can keep capital markets highly segmented, with different borrowers paying markedly different interest rates, and with competitive forces remaining very weak.

As economies develop, they find various ways of reducing these problems of verifying quality. In many markets a variety of forms of certification evolve, from guild membership to membership in stock exchanges. A stock exchange, for example, certifies that firms raising funds on the exchange or whose shares trade there meet certain accounting requirements. By listing a firm, however, the exchange does not certify that the firm will not go bankrupt—indeed, many listed firms have gone bankrupt.

As a complement to these private efforts, to make them more effective, government action is often required. For example, brand names may be an important way of pro-

Box 5.2

The credit market in Chambar, Pakistan

Chambar is a flourishing commercial region in Pakistan served by roughly 60 moneylenders. Even though borrowers there seem to have access to many different lenders, each moneylender has built up a tight circle of trusted clients, outside of which the lender is rarely willing to lend because of the high cost of screening new clients.

Before accepting a new client, a moneylender usually takes certain precautions. Before advancing a loan, the lender often arranges to deal with the applicant in other transactions—for labor or for goods—for at least two seasons. Such dealings tell the moneylender much about the applicant's alertness, honesty, and ability to repay. New clients are also scrutinized extensively through visits to the client's village and through interviews with neighbors and previous business partners, to assess reliability and character.

If, after this intense screening and long wait, the lender decides to lend to the applicant (the rejection rate is around 50 percent), he usually begins with a small test loan. After all, no amount of inquiry can reveal what will happen in practice. Only when the test loan is repaid does the lender increase his trust and match the loan amount to the borrower's needs.

A study of moneylending activity in Chambar in the early 1980s found that the average interest rate charged was 79 percent a year. But this high average conceals considerable variation: from 18 percent (still higher than the 12 percent charged by banks) to 200 percent. Much of the interest covers the high costs of information and administration in the informal market. The researchers concluded that the rate of interest was roughly the same as the moneylenders' average cost of funds, implying that lenders made close to zero profit. The ease of entry into the lending business kept profits low, yet moneylenders enjoy some monopoly power over their established clientele, because their superior information about the characteristics of their longstanding clients gave them an edge over competing lenders.

viding quality assurance. But they also provide an incentive for the production of shoddy counterfeits. Governments can do much to protect firms against this theft of their reputation. Indeed, brand-name and trademark protection is an important aspect of intellectual property rights protection, as discussed in Chapter 2.

Moreover, whereas good firms have an incentive to disclose the attributes of their products, and even offer a guarantee of quality, less reputable firms may make false claims or fail to live up to their guarantees. How is a buyer to know whether the disclosures are truthful or the guarantees meaningful? Again, governments pass laws against fraud and to ensure truth in advertising, to provide customers some assurance, but these laws have to be enforced.

Governments sometimes act more directly to mitigate the quality verification problem. They may do so through disclosure requirements—for example, requiring manufacturers of food products to disclose their ingredients (again, laws need to ensure that the disclosures are honest). Or governments themselves may provide the certification. Government meat inspection arose at the demand of meat producers, who worried that concerns about food safety would deter consumers from buying meat. Government building inspectors verify that the builder has followed established building codes. Through all these actions, governments help make markets work.

Enforcing performance

Many transactions involve promises: a borrower promises to repay a loan, an employee to work hard. If such transactions are to occur and recur—as they must for an economy to function—these promises must be kept. If good information is not available on whether each party to the transaction has kept his or her side of the bargain, either the transaction will not occur, or an alternative mechanism must be found that demands less information. And even if perfect information were available, an enforcement mechanism is needed to ensure that promises are kept. Imperfect monitoring and difficulties with ensuring compliance together comprise the "enforcement problem." The ways of dealing with them are similar. For example, reputation, so important for quality assurance, can also enforce performance. A worker who risks losing his reputation (and hence the chances of finding another job) if he fails to work hard has an incentive to keep his promise to be diligent.

How do societies ensure the enforcement of performance in such transactions? And how do they cope with the fact that some enforcement will be imperfect at best? Incentives are at the core: rewards for fulfilling the promise, punishments for failing. Often the government plays an important role in enforcement: those who break a contract—a formal promise—can be taken to court. If there is enough information to prove this breach of promise legally, the contract breaker will be punished. The nature of the punishments that may be imposed is a key public policy issue, and the legal system has provided a variety of remedies, all of which depend on judgments about the cause and consequences of failure to live up to one's promises.

But resorting to legal remedies is costly, and in the normal course of affairs there is a clear preference to encourage compliance by other means. Firms, for instance, provide incentives to encourage workers to work hard and threaten to fire workers who shirk. Here we look at how developing economies address the problems of information and enforcement, and explore what their responses imply for economic performance and policy.

Sharecropping

Sharecropping provides a classic example of the information problems in a developing country, the way people cope with them, and the new problems to which the solution gives rise. Land ownership is often highly unequal in developing countries, with many poor farmers holding little or no land, and a few rich landowners holding more land than they can farm. To make full use of both the land and the labor available, either landlords have to hire workers, or workers have to rent land, or some other arrangement for matching land and workers has to be found. The arrangement that has evolved over much of the world is sharecropping, where land-poor farmers cultivate land belonging to a landlord, to whom they turn over a share of the harvest, keeping the rest for themselves. Typically the landlord's share is large, between one-third and two-thirds. The proportion of land under share tenancy is 30 percent in Thailand, 50 percent in India, and 60 percent in Indonesia. It is generally much lower in Latin America, except in Colombia (50 percent).

Why has this arrangement come to predominate in so much of the world? The answer has to do with information, risk, and, most important, contract enforcement. Consider the landowner who hires workers and pays them a fixed wage. This arrangement minimizes risk for the workers but maximizes it for the landlord. How can the landowner ensure that the workers will work hard? The landlord cannot spend all his time in the field supervising each worker. Nor can the landowner tell whether the workers have done a good job of weeding or whether seedlings have been planted with sufficient care. Even the size of the harvest does not tell whether the workers have done their job—a low yield could reflect poor weather, insect damage, or other factors. The landowner could hire many supervisors, but that would be costly, and in any case the same problem arises—how to supervise the supervisors?

The alternative possibility—the workers pay the landlord a fixed rent to use the land—simply shifts risk to the workers. In principle, the landlord gets the same share, regardless of the weather or the workers' effort. If the weather is bad and the harvest fails, the workers may starve or be forced to borrow. But credit markets in developing countries are typically highly imperfect—again for information reasons—and interest rates very high (as Box 5.2 showed). Without land of their own to offer as collateral, tenants may simply be unable to obtain credit. The alternative, practiced in some poor countries, is for tenants to sell themselves or their families into bonded labor. For the poor, in short, the risks of a rental contract may simply be intolerable.

In practice, however, the landlord may find the rental contract scarcely more attractive than the workers do. The landlord knows that if the crop is very bad, he will not receive the rent he is owed. Although unlike the workers he can bear the risk, the rent the landlord has to charge to compensate for this risk may be quite high. This may encourage the tenant to engage in risky methods of production, because if production fails, the rent is not paid, whereas if it succeeds, the tenant retains all the surplus.

One way to counter these problems is for the landlord to lower the rent when the crop fails and raise it when the harvest is good. This gives the tenant a stake when outcomes are bad, thereby curtailing the tendency to engage in high-risk production. And it provides incentives for effort, and so does not require the kind of close supervision that the wage contract does. Sharecropping is precisely such an arrangement. It is a compromise that works.

But sharecropping has a cost. If the sharecroppers' share of the harvest is 50 percent, they receive only 50 percent of the extra return from exerting greater effort. In some cases the sharecropping contract does not require that the landlord provide other inputs such as fertilizer. Then the sharecroppers will not have enough incentive to provide fertilizer, or higher-quality seed, or other inputs—again because they must pay the entire cost but will reap only 50 percent of the gain. It is not surprising, then, that sharecropped land is less productive than other land (Box 5.3).

This difference in productivity explains why, when tenants are wealthy enough to absorb the risk of renting land, they usually choose to do so. A study of farm tenancy in Tunisia found that richer tenants, with more working capital, tend to enter into fixed-rent tenancy arrangements, where they finance in advance both the land rental and the costs of other inputs, and they bear all the risk. The probability that tenants with twice the sample-average working capital will have a rental contract is two-thirds; that for households with no working capital is less than half. Thus the poor are more often obliged to accept share contracts, and the lower output that goes with that form of contract.

Problems with enforcement also help explain other aspects of the rural economy. In many cases the landlord provides credit as well as land. Landlords are in a better position to collect on loans to their sharecroppers than are outsiders: they are already engaged in enforcing sharecropping contracts, which requires being able to monitor output. The Tunisia study showed that poorer tenants were more likely not only to be sharecroppers, but also to obtain credit from the landlord and to repay in the form of a larger share of the crop (a kind of "equity" loan).

Where the landlord does not provide credit, the miller often does, again because of the ability to enforce performance. Because of high transport costs, a farmer typically

Box 5.3

Is sharecropping associated with lower yields?

A 1987 study in India tested the efficiency of sharecropping in inducing effort by carefully controlling for several other factors, such as irrigation and soil quality. The data, provided by the International Crops Research Institute for the Semi-Arid Tropics, permitted the study of households that own some land of their own and lease other plots under sharecropping. Because in such cases the sharecropper and the farmer who farms his or her own land are the same person, this experimental design automatically controls for systematic differences between households that own and those that sharecrop, such as ability to buy inputs up front.

The only remaining differences stem from the form of the tenancy contract—and they are striking: output per acre is 16 percent higher on owned than on sharecropped plots. Use of family male labor is 21 percent higher, that of family female labor 47 percent higher, and that of bullock labor 17 percent higher. The differences persist even when attention is restricted to sharecropper-owners who grow a single crop on the two types of plots. The study also found no systematic differences between plots under fixed rent and plots under owner cultivation.

has access to no more than a few millers, and farmers often develop an established relationship with a single miller. Millers are often willing to provide seeds and often other credit, because they are in a good position to ensure repayment at the time of milling.

One consequence of such interlinked transactions—between land rental and credit provision, or between milling and credit provision—is reduced competition. New moneylenders cannot easily enter the market, because they will find enforcement far more difficult and costly than do the already-established creditors. And tenants are reluctant to leave their landlord in search of better terms. The contractual arrangements may be highly stable, but they are also highly rigid.

Sharecropping has been a durable institution in low-income developing countries. Is there not some way to avoid the inefficiencies associated with it? If owner-cultivated farms are more productive than sharecropped farms, why don't landlords sell their land to the tenants? The reason is that the poor tenant would have to borrow the funds to buy the land, and this simply shifts the burden of enforcement from the landlord to the creditor. If the crop fails, the creditor will not be repaid. All the problems that applied to rental contracts for the land apply to the rental contract for money (the loan). As before, the poor tenant does not want to bear all the risk. Of course, the tenant might try to persuade the creditor to enter into a risk-

sharing contract, in which the creditor gets, say, a fixed share of the output (as in an equity contract). But then the contract becomes just like a sharecropping contract, and all the efficiency advantages of ownership disappear.

Can government do anything to increase the efficiency of sharecropping? Land reform might seem the obvious solution, but experience with land reform has often not been successful. Productivity actually seems to fall, and in many cases land ownership again becomes concentrated after a while.

One reason why land reforms have foundered is that they failed to take into account the nature of rural institutions and the information-related market imperfections. Productivity depends not just on land but on such other inputs as fertilizer and seeds. Obtaining these other inputs requires funds that poor tenants simply do not have. Nor can they obtain funds on credit markets, at least not at reasonable cost. So productivity falls. Today's land reforms in Brazil recognize these problems and, with World Bank assistance, are directly addressing them. The Land Reform and Poverty Alleviation Pilot Project, now being implemented in five northeastern Brazilian states, is designed to make loans available to groups to purchase land and inputs for production. Some 5,000 families are already taking part in the pilot, which will eventually involve some 15,000 families.

Labor contracts

The enforcement problem in the land market carries over, practically unchanged, to labor markets. Even in agriculture, where it might appear that harvesting and weeding are easy to monitor, several activities do not lend themselves to easy observation and monitoring. Plowing, regulating the flow of irrigation water, driving and looking after tractors, supervising and recruiting casual labor, operating threshers, tending livestock— all these tasks are difficult to monitor.

The problem is even more serious in industry and services, and sometimes sharecropping-style contracts are the response. Top-level managers who receive equity in the firm as part of their compensation package may be viewed as participating directly in the fortunes of the firm, and this increases their incentive to work hard. A variety of more or less easily monitorable services may be rewarded on a commission basis, an arrangement akin to sharecropping.

But in many situations it is not feasible to offer incentive contracts. There is then no substitute for direct monitoring of the worker's actions. But this monitoring is costly in two senses. First is the direct cost: someone's time must be devoted to observing the worker. Second is the question of what to do with a worker who has been caught shirking. The typical penalty for shirking is not to renew the worker's contract. But nonrenewal is costly to the worker only if his or her current contract offers more than the next-best alternative: for the stick of nonrenewal to be effective, the contract must have already offered a carrot.

In farming, an employer can carry out production tasks in any of several ways. First, the employer might entrust these tasks to family members, who have an interest in the farm's welfare. This is a good idea for small farms, but if the scale of operations is large, outsiders have to be hired. Second, the employer might hire casual labor to carry out these tasks. But then direct supervision becomes necessary, and even then it is not possible to keep track of the laborer's activities during every passing moment. So, to judge success or failure, one must rely on the final output, which is often an imprecise indicator of the worker's diligence. Third, the employer can hire workers on a permanent or "attached" basis, under the implicit or explicit understanding that this long-term relationship will be terminated if performance is consistently low. From this point of view, permanent labor may be seen as a response to the enforcement problem. And indeed, studies of permanent labor provide evidence that such contracts pay better than casual labor contracts.

How might one expect the prevalence of permanent labor arrangements to evolve with countries' development? Several factors are at work here, some running in opposite directions. The opening of markets for a product may increase the value of a stable labor force, leading to a rise in permanent labor. Similarly, certain types of technological change may increase the number of activities that go into the production process, causing monitoring difficulties. The mechanization of agriculture is one such shift. The use of large-scale, mechanized farming methods clearly brings more complexity into production. It may be more difficult to figure out who is to blame—person or machine—if something goes wrong (or, if more tasks are carried out jointly and with coordination, *which* person or machine). And if a mistake is made, the costs can be far higher; the need to ensure the development of reliable, job-specific knowledge then makes the need for long-term contracts all the greater.

The experience of some developing countries is consistent with these observations. The opening of markets for Chilean agricultural products in the late 19th century led to an increase in the proportion of permanent labor contracts there. It also appears that, in some regions of northern India where new technology was more widely diffused, permanent contracts constituted a larger share of the total than elsewhere.

But the increased mobility that comes with economic development may make it more difficult to shore up permanent contracts through the threat of firing or eviction. In closed societies with low mobility, a laborer's misdeeds

are recognized. The stigma of evicting a tenant worker who has failed to perform adequately is thus stronger, making it easier to support permanent contracts. Where mobility is on the increase, the stigma is likely to fade. This may help explain the long downward trend in the prevalence of permanent labor relationships in some places: the share of workers with permanent contracts fell from 52 percent to 21 percent between 1952 and 1976 in the Indian village of Kumbapettai, and from 74 percent to 20 percent in nearby Kirripur.

Collateral

Collateral is a widespread and straightforward means of ensuring the repayment of loans (thereby mitigating the problem of enforcement) and reducing the lender's need for information about the borrower (thereby mitigating the problem of quality verification). It may take many forms. Certain property rights may be transferred: land may be mortgaged to the lender, or use rights to the output of that land may be put in the lender's hands while the loan is outstanding. Labor may be mortgaged as well and used to pay off the loan. Useful though collateral is, it has its drawbacks. A lack of land registries may make it difficult to offer land as collateral. The slowness of courts to enforce the transfer of land after a default may also impede the collateralization of land.

More important, the use of collateral once again illustrates the tendency for information failures—and for attempts to overcome them—to work to the disadvantage of the poor. Poorer borrowers have less wealth to use as collateral and therefore less access to credit. Evidence from Thailand supports the contention that borrowers do not have equal access to all credit sources, particularly those in the formal sector, and that borrowers appear to be sorted by wealth and income (Table 5.1). In one survey 42 percent of households reported no credit transactions in the survey period, and these households included the poorest. Among people who did not borrow at all, only a small minority reported that they would like to borrow but were unable to, and their mean income was lower than that of those who were able to borrow. Well-to-do farmers were found more apt to obtain credit from formal sources, and households that borrowed from commercial banks clearly belonged to the richest strata. That different strata sort themselves in this way is not a choice of the borrowers but the result of sorting by lenders according to the availability of collateral. Poorer borrowers will have limited access to credit markets than wealthier borrowers with equally promising projects.

In some credit markets excessive reliance on collateral brings another set of problems. As Chapter 6 shows, many financial crises have their origins in real estate bubbles.

Table 5.1

Borrowing behavior	Number of households	Average assets or income (baht)		
		Assets per household	Gross income per household	Net income per capita
Borrowers				
From both sectors	26,671	204,702	47,673	4,413
From formal sector only	43,743	188,697	45,558	4,141
From informal sector only	88,145	126,754	30,626	3,171
Nonborrowers				
Unable to borrow	4,670	116,927	25,016	2,583
Unwilling to borrow	111,976	145,022	32,400	4,094

Assets and income of borrowers and nonborrowers in Nakhon Ratchasima Province, Thailand

Note: Extrapolated on the basis of data from a 1984–85 survey of households in 52 villages. Gross income is income before deducting farm production costs.
Source: Hoff and Stiglitz 1990.

High real estate prices are sustained by, and help sustain, high levels of borrowing. Lenders get a false sense of security from the collateral they receive. This leads them to fail to verify the ability of the borrower to repay—whether the investment will yield a stream of returns. And they fail to recognize that if the real estate bubble crashes, the collateral may be worth only a fraction of the value of the loan, and that this decline will happen just when the borrower is unable to repay, and just when the lender would like to draw on the collateral. The reliance on collateral feeds the excessive volatility of these markets: once the market starts to crash, borrowers are forced to sell their assets, and as these assets get dumped on the market, their prices plummet further.

Policy support for institutional development

Thus a variety of institutional arrangements emerges over time in response to verification and enforcement problems. These include, as we have seen, the guilds of medieval Europe and the premodern Arab world, long-term trading relationships, sharecropping, the interlinking of contracts across markets, permanent labor contracts, and collateral. Institutions that suffice at one time to support market exchange may not be adequate at another time. Modern economies face the same problems but have developed other solutions—such as sophisticated credit checks, brand names, stock exchanges, and accreditation of educational standards—while retaining some traditional solutions such as collateral. Thus, in order to grow, a country needs to have not only a good set of institutions but the capacity to change those institutions over time. In this sense, all countries are still developing.

Government can play an important role in developing institutions to address quality verification and enforcement problems. It can establish and enforce standards such as uniform weights and measures, disclosure rules, and credentialing systems. It can use law to facilitate credible commitments, for example by creating penalties for fraud. It can reform slow and corrupt courts. It can regulate banks to ensure their soundness. It can support land titling and registration programs. All these actions strengthen markets. And they provide the foundation for private efforts to flourish and contribute in their own right to resolving information problems.

This chapter has provided several examples of both verifying quality and enforcing performance. The next three chapters provide many more, covering three areas where information problems are especially severe: in financial markets, in environmental protection, and among the poor.

The informal financial sector has figured prominently throughout this chapter because finance is usually acknowledged to be the most information-intensive sector in the economy. Chapter 6 looks in more detail at how formal financial markets deal with information failures. It also examines how government can contribute to the smoother functioning of financial markets by insisting on good accounting practices and other forms of information disclosure (verifying quality) and by building a credible legal system (enforcing performance).

Providing information, setting standards, and enforcing performance are at the core of any sound environmental strategy. And nowhere are knowledge gaps likely to be larger—people often do not know about the pollution caused by a nearby factory; the world does not yet know the true impact of global warming. Chapter 7 shows how better knowledge is improving our ability to manage the environment, and how we are learning more about informationally efficient measures for environmental protection.

Whether in the labor market, the credit market, the land market, or commodity markets, the poor often suffer most from the consequences of information failure, and especially from the resulting market failure. It is the poor who are most likely to have difficulty gaining access to credit because they lack collateral, or who have to pay what seem like usurious interest rates when they do get loans. It is the poor who must resort to sharecropping contracts, which lower their productivity. It is the poor who are often limited to job opportunities in their immediate vicinity, where market segmentation holds their wages down. And it is the poor who are impoverished in many other ways, not least in their lack of access to information, which contributes to their sense of isolation. Chapter 8 shows how information failures and knowledge gaps hurt the poor, and what government can do to help.

Chapter 6

Processing the Economy's Financial Information

ALL FINANCE INVOLVES PARTING with money now in return for a promise of reward in the future, whether it is the West African marketwoman entrusting her morning's takings to a collector for safe-keeping, or an investor supplying funds to an Asian manufacturer seeking to expand exports. The promise may not be fulfilled, and when it is not, the consequences often extend well beyond the parties to the transaction. Any supplier of funds to the financial marketplace needs to assess the prospects of getting those funds back, along with a high enough return to compensate for the risk of loss.

It is because these exchanges of money now for money later are concluded only in the future that information about those prospects is always imperfect. Indeed, the rewards to gathering and processing information about risk and insulating against uncertainty have been the main force behind the development of financial markets and institutions. In this sense the financial system is central to how an economy copes with uncertainty, but it does so imperfectly. There is no guarantee that the outcome will be efficient, socially optimal, or even stable, for finance itself contributes to information-related economic problems.

Finance is important to every individual and firm, but good financial institutions are also vital for the functioning of the entire economy. If finance is an economy's nervous system, financial institutions are its brain. They make the decisions that tell scarce capital where to go, and they ensure that, once there, it is used in the most effective way. Research confirms that countries with more-developed financial institutions grow faster, and that countries with weak ones are more likely to have financial crises, with adverse effects on growth sometimes lasting years after.

The fixed costs of acquiring information about would-be borrowers and the difficulty of appropriating all the benefits of such information mean that lenders tend to have market power over borrowers and that less information is supplied than is socially optimal. The market for credit may not clear, because willingness to pay is a poor indicator of creditworthiness. And an economy can become highly vulnerable to small shifts in opinion or information, which can lead to large swings in asset prices.

A maxim among bank presidents is that a loan officer making good money for the bank needs to be watched closely; one making fantastic money should be fired, for the risks must be too great. If, as this maxim suggests, information failures are a familiar problem for financial intermediaries, they are even more of a problem for those outside: small shareholders, creditors of various types—and official regulators and supervisors.

For financial systems to cope with such information problems effectively requires supportive policies from government, especially in developing economies, where these problems are more severe. At the same time, the complexity of the incentive structures associated with handling financial information means that government needs to exert a restraining influence. Both these policy thrusts—the one supportive, the other restrictive—are crucial to good policy.

Chapter 5 has already discussed the high cost of accumulating information in informal finance. Certain informationally simple means of ensuring repayment—such as collateral, peer monitoring, and group lending—can help lower these costs and are covered in Chapter 8. Here we look at the many ways in which information supports the formal financial system and the economy—and how there can be perverse outcomes, starting with an example from East Asia.

Information and the East Asian financial crash

The financial crash that swept many East Asian economies in 1997 shows how information deficiencies can contribute to and amplify crises in asset markets. Company accounts in many of these economies were not transparent. Official supervisors lacked sufficient information on the condition of banks' balance sheets. Even the true size of an economy's foreign exchange reserves was not always known to market participants. A common factor affecting all these economies was their exposure to short-term foreign borrowing—more by banks and firms than by government. Most of this debt was denominated in foreign currency, making the borrowers doubly vulnerable: sudden and widespread capital outflows could present them both with refinancing difficulties and with a capital loss if the domestic currency collapsed.

Widespread capital outflows and currency collapse are precisely what occurred, and their scale and breadth reflected the pervasive lack of information throughout the world about finance in the region. The belated realization that many financial institutions had lent too much to firms investing in real estate was, by common consensus, a reason for the heightened anxiety of foreign and domestic lenders to lend to financial and nonfinancial firms alike. Indeed, the collapse in early 1997 of Finance One, a major Thai finance company that had invested heavily in real estate, can be seen as the trigger.

Yet the crisis cannot be attributed entirely to lack of available information; also to blame was the market's failure to process well and fully the information it had. Information about the high levels of investment in speculative real estate, the large current account deficits, and the weakness in financial intermediaries—all factors often now cited as central to the crisis—had long been in the public domain. Similarly, observers had commented for years about the riskiness of the high debt-equity ratios of Korean firms.

Unsound lending had been common throughout the region, and the financial sector had become fragile. But how fragile? And who was really uncreditworthy? Because of the lack of transparency and the general paucity of information, investors could not tell which firms, which banks, which economies could survive the crisis. So they abandoned them all. A bandwagon effect caused funds to be withdrawn and asset prices to be marked down across a wide front. The turnaround in capital flows amounted to more than $100 billion, or 10 percent of GDP in the economies most affected. Declining asset prices made the

panic self-fulfilling. Borrowers whose collateral value and earning power fell because of the general drop in asset prices became uncreditworthy. As some were forced to sell their assets, prices plummeted even more—a familiar pattern in financial crises.

One thing that might have helped avert the panic is greater accounting transparency, for greater confidence in the underlying information flows could have allowed a more discriminating response by investors. It could also have prompted much earlier corrective action, making the crisis less severe. Of course, transparency is not a foolproof protection against banking crises: the financial systems of the United States and Sweden were thought to be among the world's most transparent, yet both countries were hit with crises in recent years.

Even with the sophistication of modern information gathering and processing, then, information gaps and processing errors remain huge. The contagion that swept through industrial-country investors' holdings of emerging-market securities in the Asian crisis reflects a classic information failure and typifies the race for the exit when sentiment changes. Despite the public availability of much relevant information, the risk premium on Thai bonds before the crisis did not reflect that information, and the leading bond-rating agencies did not lower the rating of those bonds significantly until October 1997, three months after the Thai currency collapsed. Although some new information became available later—Thai reserves, it proved, were less than had been realized—the revision in risk premia seems larger than can be accounted for by this fact alone. Recalling Keynes' description of asset markets as beauty contests, it seems that market participants' concern was not with fundamental values but with what others thought.

How financial systems cope with information gaps

In financial markets the promised reward to a supplier of funds can take a variety of forms. Debt contracts promise to pay back a fixed amount, regardless of the circumstances. Equity contracts promise to pay a given fraction of the firm's profits. A wide variety of other promises are offered, many of which combine the features of debt and equity.

An essential problem facing the lender is assessing the value of the promise. For debt the question is, What is the probability of default, and if default occurs, how much will the lender be able to recover? For equity, the task is to estimate the future profits of the enterprise and their timing. These assessments are information problems, and institutions arise to address them. But they do so imperfectly, and the imperfections have important consequences.

Financial markets confront the usual information problems (raised in Chapter 5) of verifying quality and enforcing performance, and they deal with them in three related steps. Quality verification comes at the stages of *selecting* projects (who gets the funds?) and *monitoring* them (how are the funds being used?). Information about which projects will pay off and how funds are being used is not freely available, so good selection and monitoring improve both the quality of the portfolio of projects financed and that of the intermediary. Market participants are also concerned about *enforcing* the contract. Even if they know that the debtor can repay the debt, and even if they know the true value of the equity issuer's profits, can they be sure that they will receive what has been promised? Rigorous monitoring is linked inextricably with enforcement. Indeed, without good monitoring, enforcement is not credible, and it may come too late—the assets may be gone.

Almost all financial intermediation in low-income economies is accomplished through the banking system. As income and financial development increase, nonbank intermediaries—insurance companies, pension funds, finance companies, mutual funds—develop progressively (Figure 6.1). It is largely because of the ability of banks to cope with information and contracting problems that they dominate finance at low levels of country income, where these problems loom larger. That was the pattern in Europe, where the banking business of the Lombard merchants and London goldsmiths relied heavily on their accumulated knowledge of their customers' business.

Gathering and processing information

Even outside of formal financial markets, information is important in guiding decisions about whom to trust with funds. Tight-knit communities and families possess a wealth of information about the activities and the physical, intellectual, and moral attributes of their members. Accordingly, until formal institutions develop, the most common source of working capital for trading companies, or of venture capital for new enterprises, is funding from family members and friends. But if funds are to be advanced further afield or in large amounts, one must look to the formal financial sector, and it is there that acquiring and processing information become more important.

Lending markets are fundamentally different from other markets in that they are not run as simple auction markets, with the market interest rate determined at the intersection of the demand and supply curves. Nor can they be. The first rule of finance is that willingness to pay is no indicator of creditworthiness. On the contrary, those claiming to be willing to pay very high interest rates may be the least likely to repay the loan—if one expects to default anyway, what difference does a high interest rate make? Because charging a higher interest rate can lead to a worse mix of loan applicants, even after considerable screening, lenders may choose to charge a lower interest rate than

Figure 6.1

Financial structure of economies by income level

An economy's financial system tends to match its level of development.

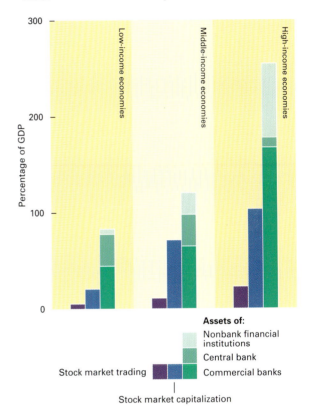

Note: Data are for 1990 for 12 low-income, 22 middle-income, and 14 high-income economies. Source: Levine 1997.

would clear the market. Lenders also know that borrowers may behave in a riskier fashion once funds are disbursed—as happens in insurance markets. So they may ration credit.

Similar issues arise in equity markets. Those most willing to sell their shares at the market price may be those who believe that the market has overvalued those shares. The consequences are similar to credit rationing: since investors know that owners are most willing to sell shares when they are overpriced, the announcement of a sale of new shares typically leads to a fall in the share price. Concern about the adverse signal makes firms reluctant to issue shares. That partly explains why, despite the principle that equity should provide better risk sharing than debt, new equity issues remain a relatively small source of new finance, even in the industrial countries.

Suppliers of credit sometimes seem to ignore the principle that willingness to pay high interest rates is a bad signal. For instance, Banco Latino in Venezuela was able to attract deposits by paying interest rates 5 percentage points above the rest of the market. Its collapse triggered one of the costlier episodes of bank failure. In this case depositors, counting on a government bailout, must have reasoned that there was little downside risk.

Assessing prospects. Unless convinced that the risks of their lending will be borne by others, bank loan officers—like investment fund managers, insurance underwriters, and venture capitalists—generally devote considerable resources to researching the prospects of would-be borrowers, policyholders, and startup companies. Although the growth in securitization and other means of reselling loans in the most advanced financial systems might suggest that this function is declining, closer examination reveals that much of the credit risk remains with the intermediary selling the loan. In the often riskier environment for entrepreneurs and their financiers in developing economies, risk assessment can be even more important.

In scrutinizing individual borrowers, a small set of objective indicators can go a long way toward predicting future capacity to repay. Proprietary software packages, used increasingly throughout the world, can automate much of the selection process (Box 6.1). For small corporate borrowers, however, such a mechanical approach is less reliable, implying the need for a heavy commitment of resources in preparing background, product, marketing, and macroeconomic appraisals.

Monitoring performance. Banks are particularly well placed to acquire ongoing information about the condition and performance of their borrowing clients. And they often prefer to lend short-term, so that, with good monitoring, they can intervene early if necessary to forestall a deteriorating situation. But what is good for the monitor is not always good for society. Evidence from countries as far apart as Ecuador and India suggests that borrowers with access to long-term credit (especially unsubsidized credit) achieve higher productivity. Furthermore, short-term credit, although it puts management on a short leash and thus prevents some kinds of abuses, also makes firms (and countries) highly vulnerable. A quick change in investor sentiment—which may have nothing to do with the firm's behavior or the release of new information about it—can lead to a withdrawal of credit and even bankruptcy. When sentiment changes in this way for many firms, the result can be a full-scale financial crisis. Once again, the financial system's solution to an information problem is—from the social point of view—at best partial.

Banks are not the only effective monitors. As financial markets deepen, they give rise to a coterie of specialized analysts who scrutinize various firms and securities. It is their close monitoring that opens the possibility for securities markets.

More generally, monitoring is multilayered, with many "watchful eyes." Managers monitor workers. Boards of directors and banks monitor management. Shareholders monitor the directors. Sometimes there is yet another level of monitoring: many corporate shares are owned by mutual funds, whose owners (the fund's shareholders) monitor the managers of the fund, who in turn monitor the directors and managers of the corporations they have invested in. Yet all this monitoring is imperfect, partly because of the public good problems discussed in earlier chapters, and partly because of inadequate legal protection.

Clearly, assessing borrowers' prospects and then monitoring them is not just a question of gathering and transmitting raw information. What is involved in all of this is *information processing,* or analyzing the implications of available information. Mathematical models of risk assessment are now being used quite widely, especially for marketed securities in at least the higher-income developing countries. Such models put risk assessment on a firmer basis, inasmuch as the available historical information is taken into account explicitly (Box 6.2).

Box 6.1

Technology eases credit decisions

Credit-scoring software packages try to approximate the information processing of seasoned credit professionals. Where there are enough data on borrowers' credit repayment history and other characteristics, they allow a high degree of automation in credit approvals, reducing processing costs and improving on conventional systems to screen credit risks. In place for consumer lending all over the world, and used by developing-country banks in all regions, these packages are also being used—although less extensively—for business loans and for pricing corporate bonds.

Automated credit scoring requires, as a first step, statistical analysis of the determinants of the probability of default. Attributes widely used for mortgage lending include the borrower's occupation, number of dependents, and income as a multiple of projected mortgage payments. Other factors typically entered include the terms of the loan (such as the loan-to-value ratio for a mortgage), the presence or absence of legal constraints on the bank's ability to foreclose, and prevailing economic conditions.

The next step is to use historical data to estimate the contribution of each factor to the probability of default. The bank uses the resulting equation to estimate the probability that each new applicant will prove slow-paying or delinquent, or will default. The prediction is sufficiently good on average (as good as the subjective judgments of trained loan officers) to lead to reliable decision rules for whether to lend and what default risk premium to apply to the interest rate.

Box 6.2

Value-at-risk: An approach to risk assessment

Until fairly recently most participants in financial markets controlled risk by procedural rules of thumb and qualitative assessments. The new complexity of financial instruments makes this approach inadequate. Fortunately, the cheaper computing power that contributed to this complexity has also made quantitative risk assessments more accessible, as Argentina, Canada, Chile, and other countries are finding.

One simple and attractive approach is to compute a portfolio's value-at-risk. Using historical asset price data, this approach projects the future variability of these asset prices and the degree to which they tend to move together. This is especially useful for derivative products, such as options and futures contracts, each of which represents a speculation on the future price of some underlying asset, whether equities, bonds, or foreign exchange. The method allows account to be taken of the correlation of a derivative with the price of its underlying security. Using calculations based on such projections, portfolio risk managers can arrive at statements such as "There is only a 1 percent chance that the portfolio will decline by more than $100 million over the next three months." This figure of $100 million would then be the value-at-risk, as estimated for the 1 percent level.

Attempts have also been made to determine the credit risk on nontraded bank loans. The attempt is complicated, however, by the fact that bank-customer relations are rarely long enough, or stable enough, to extract the necessary variability and correlation information reliably.

True, future variability cannot reliably be predicted on the basis of the past, and this method downplays the large occasional outliers that are really the source of serious problems to well-managed portfolios. Still, the method has value. Take Barings Bank, which lost $1.3 billion in unwise speculation by its Singapore subsidiary in 1995, wiping out its entire capital. The speculation had been that Japanese stock prices would rise, and that bond prices would fall. Official reports to Barings' senior management indicated no overall risk in the instruments being used to exploit this expectation (stock index futures leveraged by a short position in bond futures), suggesting instead that the leverage hedged the risk. But the correlation between these two asset prices was in fact negative, implying that the leveraged position was quite risky. A simple value-at-risk calculation would have shown a 5 percent probability of losing $800 million from the leveraged portfolio, not zero. That might have led management to take a different course.

Contracts and institutions to insulate against information gaps

Financial systems have developed a variety of means of dealing with information gaps, including contracts and institutions ranging from the simple to the elaborate.

Simple contracts: Collateral and debt. Simple rules or constraints on behavior are widely used to reduce the cost of information deficiencies and, more generally, to protect financial market participants from unfavorable outcomes. The standard debt contract calls for a fixed payment regardless of circumstances and gives the creditor the right to seize collateral in the event of default. The unconditional promise and the use of collateral reduce the creditor's need to verify the debtor's claims about its financial condition. Assuming adequate contract enforcement, then, debtors normally have no incentive to conceal their true financial condition, because if they are truly in a position to repay, it is in their interest to do so. But as noted earlier, the debt contract does not deal with other information problems.

If collateral is correctly priced from the outset, if it retains its value, and if it can be seized, it can insulate banks from errors in assessing the creditworthiness of the borrower. As mentioned in Chapter 5, collateral simplifies but does not eliminate the information problem, for the value and recoverability of the collateral still need to be assessed. The key issue is not the value of the collateral at the time the loan is made, but its likely value under the various circumstances that could lead to a default.

Some kinds of collateral are subject to severe problems. Property may unlock credit, but heavy reliance on real estate as collateral can increase an economy's fragility and its vulnerability to an economic downturn or an interest rate hike. Banks may believe that, because they have enough collateral to cover the loan, they do not have to inquire further into the nature of the asset. But market values for real estate are highly volatile and can collapse rapidly. Collateral-based lending sets up a dynamic that amplifies these fluctuations in values: as values fall, loans get called, forcing more real estate onto the market, which further depresses prices. A large fraction of the financial crises around the world in the last two decades have followed the collapse of a real estate boom.

Collateral provides no comfort either to the borrower unable to furnish it or to the lender unable to take possession after a default. Both sets of circumstances are especially prevalent in developing countries. This is a serious structural problem where land registration is deficient, where individual ownership of land is not widespread, or where property rights are fuzzy. In Botswana the collective ownership of tribal lands inhibited their use as collateral until recent legislation gave lenders the chance to foreclose, subject to the approval of local land boards. In transition economies, too, the uncertainty of land ownership and the lack of a comprehensive land registry present a barrier to private mortgage lending. And in countries where men hold most property, women have almost no access to collateral-based credit.

Collateral poses yet another problem: when banks rely on collateral, they may limit credit to other activities that yield high social returns but for which collateral is not available. Chapter 2 has already discussed the problems with financing R&D, and Chapter 3 the scarcity of credit (without government guarantees) to finance education.

Peer monitoring in informal markets. The screening processes of formal institutions do not seem to work well in many developing countries. Informal credit markets, however, have found some innovative and effective ways of solving the quality verification problem. One such solution is to recognize that relevant information may be available to third parties—say, to a borrower's neighbors who may themselves be interested in obtaining credit—and to give them a stake in the financial transaction. (Chapter 8 reviews the Grameen Bank and other group lending schemes.) The information available to these people helps lenders monitor and enforce lending contracts, even though they themselves have no direct access to it. Borrowers themselves have the incentive to use the information they have about each other to form groups for lending purposes. Knowing that they will be well monitored may actually make the monitoring easier. In a process known as self-selection, only those who believe they can repay and are planning to do so will choose to borrow.

Hedging, diversifying, and pooling risks. By facilitating the trading, hedging, diversifying, and pooling of risk, the financial system can reduce the cost of closing information gaps without actually gathering information. The simplest form is the insurance contract, where identifiable costly contingencies, such as the earlier-than-average death of a person, can be hedged explicitly. The insurance provider can offer such contracts by pooling diverse risks rather than by trying to fill the information gap about one policyholder.

Insurance intermediaries face other information problems, some of which they solve with simple contract rules. Policies often include covenants voiding the insurance if the insured party engages in risky behavior (such as driving a car off the road). This crude protection against cheating may have the additional advantage of greatly reducing monitoring requirements if violation can easily be detected in the case of a claim. Insurance contracts also routinely provide for voiding a contract if the insured's initial declarations prove to have been false. That reduces appraisal costs by removing the need to verify declarations unless and until a claim is made. (Lenders do not have this luxury, because it is too late to verify a borrower's condition when the loan has become unrecoverable.) Still, insurance lags behind banking in developing countries, not least where aggressive use of the "fine print" has meant that insurers are not trusted.

Organized markets and exchanges. Certain financial assets, such as commodity or currency futures, allow one to reduce or eliminate the risk of unknown future price movements in the underlying good. Or rather, they allow that risk to be transferred to others who can bear it better. This is useful, for example, for farmers waiting for their crop to ripen or for government debt managers trying to minimize the cost of exchange rate fluctuations. These instruments can also be used to speculate rather than to hedge, when investors feel they know which way prices are headed and want to bet on their beliefs or their superior information.

The market prices of financial assets can embody and communicate the information that first becomes available only to deep-pocketed, well-informed market participants. When news indicating an increase in the value of an asset becomes known to some, they find it advantageous to acquire that asset while it is still underpriced, bidding up its market price. But prices might not fully reveal such information. And to the extent they do, that reduces the incentive for market participants to expend resources in acquiring information about asset values. So capital markets are never perfectly efficient, in the sense that prices never perfectly aggregate or transfer the relevant information of participants.

The availability of liquid assets—whether in organized markets or from such intermediaries as banks—reduces the cost to savers of unforeseen needs for cash. In organized markets the main task is to pool the risk of unforeseen cash shortages. The bank in similar fashion pools the returns on many small loans extended to it (deposits) and acts as a monitor on behalf of the depositors, exploiting economies of scale in information processing.

Well-functioning payments systems dramatically reduce information costs, but they require confidence in the financial strength of the parties to the payments mechanism. Trade among the former Soviet republics suddenly collapsed by as much as 80 percent when the interrepublic payments system collapsed. Soon barter intermediaries emerged for both international and domestic trade to create and sustain elaborate multifirm chains of goods trading when money could not fully perform its normal function. Barter has also surfaced within the Russian Federation, especially outside the major cities, greatly increasing the costs of information processing (Box 6.3).

Why public action is required

The function of financial markets is to address information problems: to allocate scarce capital by selecting good projects and then monitoring them to ensure that the funds are used appropriately. But information is always imperfect. And no matter how good the contracting arrangements, information gaps will remain, and their consequences will be felt. Indeed, financial markets are rife with externalities, instances where the benefits and costs of transactions extend beyond the parties to the transaction, and these provide part of the reason for government action.

Box 6.3

Trading without banks: Money surrogates in the Russian Federation

Tax debtors in the Russian Federation are legally required to close all but one of their bank accounts, and that one must be registered with the tax authorities. So, once a firm becomes a tax debtor, the marginal tax rate on all of its revenues flowing through the banking system is 100 percent. Failure to make this transfer subjects the bank to criminal liability.

The stranglehold of these restrictions on the use of bank money is more serious than it would be in industrial market economies. Numerous taxes, onerous tax rates, excessive (until recently) penalty rates, and politically motivated exemptions encourage enterprises to evade taxes. Moreover, the State Tax Service estimates that 80 percent of firms are in arrears on their taxes. This estimate is probably high, but it shows that nearly all firms routinely confront blocked accounts, either their own or those of key trading partners. In response, many transactions are taking place outside the banking system, and barter has become common, having risen from 11 percent of sales in 1992 to 43 percent in 1997, according to a recent World Bank survey.

Barter, however, is very costly, particularly for firms that do not typically engage in repeated transactions and thus do not have good information about their trading partners. The cost of arranging most barter transactions is roughly 20 to 25 percent of the value of the transaction. To reduce this cost, private and public institutions use bills of exchange, or *veksels*, which after barter are the most common money surrogate. Banks, enterprises, and federal, provincial, and municipal authorities can issue these debt certificates, which in the spring of 1997 were estimated to amount to roughly two-thirds the stock of ruble-denominated money (as measured by the M2 monetary aggregate). They can perform the functions of a broad variety of debt instruments, including certificates of deposit, promissory notes, corporate bonds, and government bonds.

The value of a veksel depends on the reputation of the issuer and the ease with which it can be converted into a useful commodity. Enterprises typically view the veksels of well-regarded banks and firms with widely used products (such as natural monopolies) as close substitutes for money. Other veksels are subject to large discounts.

This widespread use of veksels complicates the conduct of monetary policy by weakening the central bank's direct control over liquidity in the economy. The move from money into barter and veksels reduces tax collections and dampens economic growth by increasing the cost of transactions. Just as damaging, their use clouds the financial position of enterprises, allowing managers to steal their income and assets. Property rights cannot be protected, and fraud is rampant.

Externalities and public goods in financial markets

Information externalities in finance take a variety of forms. When a bank grants a loan to a firm, and that information becomes public, others may presume that the bank has engaged in a screening process and that the firm has passed the test. Moreover, they know that, if the bank is solid, it is likely to monitor the firm while the loan is outstanding, preventing some of the worst abuses. Research shows that firms that establish good banking relationships do well. They pay less for their credit, pledge less collateral, and respond better to investment opportunities. The value of this accumulation of information also shows up in evidence that announcing a bank loan agreement tends to boost the stock market price of the borrowing firm.

If a large depositor closely monitors the managers of a bank and ensures that they neither engage in excessively risky behavior nor loot the bank's assets, all depositors benefit. Monitoring of banks is thus a public good, and one of the reasons why government should take primary responsibility for this function. But if the depositor discovers that there has been looting and withdraws funds before others do, this reduces what other stakeholders can recover—the positive externality becomes a negative one. And whether the depositor's judgment is correct or not, the withdrawal can set off a run on the bank, with adverse effects on other stakeholders.

Perhaps of greatest concern are the systemic risks of bank failures. The failure of one large or several medium-size banks can result in a financial crisis, precipitating a sharp and profound economic downturn. Although the effects can be mitigated through macroeconomic management, they are never eliminated, because policies take time to work their effect. Meanwhile innocent bystanders, such as bank employees and borrowers not engaged in activities that contributed to the crisis, may face heavy costs.

These systemic risks are important enough that governments typically act to contain bank crises, and those actions are typically costly. The costs, however, are borne only in part by those who caused the crisis. This large externality warrants government action to reduce the likelihood of such a crisis and its magnitude.

Contagion

One externality that has drawn broad attention in recent years is the so-called contagion effect: disturbances in one country's financial market can have consequences in others. Contagion can spread through trade: disturbances in the economy in financial crisis can affect its trading partners. It can also pass through the terms of trade: a financial crisis can affect the prices of commodities produced or purchased by the country or countries affected. But the most virulent contagion occurs through financial flows. Why a financial crisis in Mexico should affect Argentina, or why a crisis in Thailand should affect Russia, has often seemed a mystery. The direct contagion effects, through trade flows or terms-of-trade changes, are likely to be small. Contagion through the behavior of assetholders, hard though it is to observe or forecast, surely is part of the answer.

A well-known example of contagion is the bank panic. To see how a panic can occur, suppose that depositors cannot observe whether individual banks are solvent, but they can observe a shock that affects banks' portfolios and that causes at least one bank to close. They may then start runs on all banks, solvent and insolvent, causing even solvent banks to fail.

The idea that the price mechanism cannot cope easily with this kind of shock was put forward more than 100 years ago by Walter Bagehot, who emphasized the difficulty that a bank faces in transmitting credible information to the market during a crisis: "Every banker knows that if he has to prove that he is worthy of credit, however good may be his argument, in fact his credit is gone." If the price mechanism worked as it should in such cases, an increase in interest rates would compensate depositors for the increased risk of lending to a bank facing a crisis. But the same rise in interest rates may also signal an unsound position and therefore discourage potential depositors—as already noted, willingness to pay high interest is no indication of credit-worthiness. The market fails because of limited information on the bank's solvency.

Monopoly power

In loan markets borrowers typically face a very limited number of suppliers of funds, and they may not be able to switch easily from one to another. The reason is that information about whether a potential borrower is a good risk is costly to obtain, and easy for a bank to keep to itself once obtained. Thus different lenders are likely to face different costs for a new loan to any given borrower, and the borrower's current lender will be at an advantage. Each bank thus has specialized information about its customer base. A customer that has a long track record with one bank—and whom that bank therefore views as a good loan prospect—may be viewed as an unknown by another bank, and therefore a riskier prospect. To compensate for that risk, the second bank has to charge a higher interest rate, or it may simply refuse to lend.

Other considerations may deter a borrower from switching lenders. For example, the new bank may wonder why the customer wishes to switch banks. Is the old bank, with its superior knowledge, restricting credit to this customer? And does that mean it no longer regards the customer as creditworthy? Although customers can often persuade the new bank that there are good reasons for the switch, sometimes they cannot. Moreover, as Chapter 5 noted, many of the costs of information are sunk costs, which cannot be recovered if the loan is not made. This leads to a "local monopoly" relationship between a lender and a borrower.

The effect of screening, administrative, and enforcement costs on interest rates—and the imperfect competition that results—are also evident in recent studies of rural credit markets (see Box 5.2). As usual in monopolistic competition, each lender is operating at too small a scale of operation, spreading fixed costs over too small a clientele, and pushing interest rates up.

Undersupply of information

Markets by themselves are unlikely to supply enough of many types of information (although as we will see, they occasionally supply too much). This undersupply results from the public good nature of information already mentioned: the person or firm gathering it cannot capture all the returns. Even when the returns to information can be captured, the externalities can be large.

Those who have invested in acquiring information face two types of problems in trying to benefit from it. First, if they try to sell the information directly, they face a classic credibility problem: the potential buyer may not believe that the information is true. Second, the profits they might obtain from trading on their information might be too small relative to the cost of obtaining it. The profits might even be zero if prices in securities markets fully reveal an individual trader's private information.

Banks are generally better equipped than other financial intermediaries to address selection and monitoring problems for the projects they finance. They can profit from the information they produce by making private loans that are not traded. Other investors then have difficulty free-riding off their actions. Also, the costs to banks of collecting information are reduced by their ability to enter into long-term relationships with customers. And monitoring is easier because they can scrutinize the transactions of their borrowers who are also depositors. To discourage opportunism by borrowers during the life of the loan, banks can threaten to cut off future lending. The absence of a large supply of alternative lenders makes such threats effective. In developing countries, the greater difficulty of acquiring information on private firms makes banks an even more important part of the financial system than in industrial countries.

Some types of information, however, can be oversupplied. Examples are those that largely result in private returns for some and private losses for others, in redistributions that are neither wealth-creating nor productivity-enhancing. A trader who finds out a minute before everyone else that the government will soon issue a regulation affecting the value of XYZ stock may be able to buy or sell that stock at a profit, but these gains come at the expense of others. Much information gathering in secondary markets is directed at obtaining such information slightly before other market participants. Still, secondary markets provide liquidity, which is linked to financial and economic development. Shallow markets deter investors—the less the liquidity, the more difficult to get out of the market on short notice—encouraging them to hold wealth in safer forms.

Calls for greater transparency in financial markets—far greater disclosure of undersupplied information—reflect the belief that firms generally will not voluntarily disclose all the information that the market would like. Ironically, greater transparency can sometimes lead to greater volatility, as changing conditions or judgments quickly show up in market prices. Just as crying fire in a crowded theater can create a panic, whether or not the "fundamentals" are amiss, so too calling attention to certain financial variables may create a self-fulfilling crisis anytime those variables enter a "danger zone."

One of the most important pieces of information in chronic short supply is the total return to a project. Lenders focus not on the total return, but only on the return they expect to receive. That return is simply the principal plus the interest rate received, multiplied by the probability that it will be received, less the opportunity cost of funds. The total return to the project includes the (incremental) surplus accruing to the entrepreneur. The project with the highest expected return to the lender may not be the project with the highest total expected return. But it is the project with the highest expected return to the lender that gets funded. Thus, good projects may be rationed out of the market.

Supporting the financial system

The institutional and legal systems designed to address information issues in finance vary widely from country to country. In some countries, for example, the scope of activities permitted to banks is sharply circumscribed. Other countries (and not only developing ones) rely more heavily on banks, permitting them to carry out a broad range of commercial and investment activities, including owning and trading in stocks and placing directors on the boards of companies to which they have provided funds. Countries also differ in their approaches to achieving fair competition in securities markets and protecting the rights of shareholders. Some countries use government agencies for this, whereas others rely on self-regulation by the market.

Economies in transition face a particular challenge. Under central planning, banks did not perform the key functions associated with banking in market economies. They did not choose projects, nor did they make decisions about which firms should expand. They were not responsible for monitoring. Little more than bookkeepers, they provided finance at the direction of the planners. In moving to a market economy, these banks have had to transform themselves totally, and this has proved difficult.

Creating the preconditions for an effective equities market in these countries may be even more difficult. The early history of equity markets in today's industrial economies— before the establishment of strong government oversight—is replete with scandals that undermined confidence in these markets. Typically these debacles led to long periods in which equity markets almost ceased to be a source of new funds for corporations. Unfortunately, some of the economies in transition seem to be encountering the same problems (see Box 6.4 below).

For financial market participants to process information and design contracts that insulate the remaining information gaps, they need the support of public policies to develop accounting and disclosure systems and fraud (to help in information gathering) and to improve legal infrastructure (if contracts are to have any bite). Without these building blocks, the development of the formal financial system will be stymied. If instead countries provide reliable and comprehensive information about firms, and if their legal systems enforce contracts rapidly, effectively, and transparently, imposing penalties for fraud and breach of contract, they will enjoy greater financial development and faster economic growth.

Empirical evidence now shows (see next section) that, after taking account of all the usual factors that influence growth, the development of legal and accounting systems significantly explains the development of financial intermediaries. Countries with legal systems that give a high priority to secured creditors, rigorously enforce contracts, protect minority shareholders, and set accounting standards that produce comprehensive and comparable corporate financial statements have better-developed financial intermediaries and enjoy faster growth (Figure 6.2).

Accounting and auditing to ensure the flow of information
Accounting standards make it easier to interpret information about firms and compare it against information from other firms. They thus make it easier for investors to identify worthy firms and evaluate their managers. Many types of contracts also rely on accounting measures to trigger certain actions. For example, loan and bond covenants commonly include the option of immediate repayment if income or cash flow falls below a specified level. Such contracts can be enforced and will be written only if

Figure 6.2

Factors leading to financial development and growth

The pathway to financial development starts with the legal foundations.

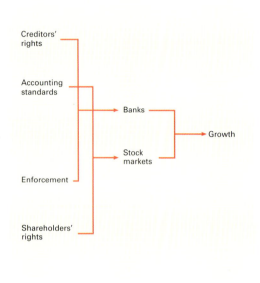

Source: Based on Levine, Loayza, and Beck 1998.

Figure 6.3

Accounting standards and GNP per capita

Poor countries tend to have weak legal and accounting systems.

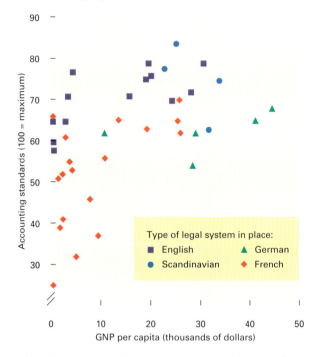

Note: Data are for 1996 for 39 countries worldwide. Source: La Porta and others 1998; Levine, Loayza, and Beck 1998; World Bank 1998d.

accounting measures are reasonably unambiguous and if auditors can verify them. Assessing the health of banks requires reliable information on loan classification and concentration, on the realistic valuation of collateral, on loan-loss provisioning, and on the rules for accruing interest in the bank's accounts when borrowers are in arrears. Accounting standards help in this regard as well.

Financial statements provide a wealth of information about a firm's past and present operations. Without them it is virtually impossible to assess the condition and credit-worthiness of an enterprise:

- Balance sheets show the breakdown of physical and financial assets and liabilities, including short- and long-term debt.
- Income statements portray revenues and expenses, including various costs and taxes.
- Cash flow statements, by showing the amount of cash flowing into and out of firms, can highlight when even solvent firms are experiencing liquidity difficulties.
- Notes to these statements can include additional information, for example about the off-balance-sheet activities of firms.

There are, of course, limits to the information revealed by financial statements. New financial instruments such as derivatives, other contingent liabilities, and stock options make it more difficult to provide accurate and timely assessments of the net worth of firms and financial institutions. Many types of derivatives are not regularly reported on the balance sheet, and their market value can change markedly in response to small changes in circumstances.

Accounting standards in the early 1990s differed significantly across countries, even countries with comparable incomes per capita (Figure 6.3). They also vary strongly with the type of legal system in effect (see below). Many of the lowest-income economies (not shown in the figure for lack of data) have the weakest accounting systems, often with few trained accountants and in some cases no uniform system of accounts. In these settings, formal markets are dominated by interchanges between foreign entities that have good sources of information (and recourse to offshore enforcement).

Despite recent gains by equities, financial markets in developing countries are still bank-dominated, partly because reliable information on company performance is lacking. In industrial countries, too, banks are the main source for net new finance. Governments around the world—especially after the recent rash of financial crises—are beginning to recognize the importance of the information they gather. Mexico embarked in 1997 on a major reform of its accounting disclosure standards aimed at convergence toward U.S. Generally Accepted Accounting Principles (GAAP). Authorities in some East Asian economies, having seen the damage done by high debt-equity ratios and too little arm's-length finance, are moving to improve their information environment as well. Better information alone will not prevent financial crises, however—the GAAP did not save Texas from a crisis in its banks and savings and loans in the 1980s—and as mentioned above, at times an abundance of information can itself trigger a crisis. But a better information environment can mitigate these costs, and this explains in part why crises generally have been less expensive in OECD countries than in other parts of the world.

One study suggests that had Argentina raised its accounting standards from levels prevailing in the early 1990s to the OECD average, it would have boosted the country's projected annual GDP growth rate by 0.6 percentage point. If the Arab Republic of Egypt could improve its enforcement to the level of that in Greece, its growth rate would be expected to rise by 0.9 percentage point a year. Overwhelmingly, growth is strongly influenced by infrastructure to support information gathering and by enforcing contracts based on such information.

Growth leads to financial market development. On this there is no doubt. But financial development also leads to growth. That is the conclusion of sophisticated economic studies at the industry and at the firm level. That conclusion is supported by historical case studies, as well as by the fact that countries with better-developed bank and equity markets at the start of a long period saw significantly faster development over that period, other factors held constant. It turns out that banking and equity markets are comple-

ments, most likely because both demand better-quality information and both supply it: banks through their decisions to make new loans or reschedule old ones, equity markets by revealing the worth of companies.

Balancing the interests of creditors, shareholders, and managers

The ability to write and enforce contracts confidently and inexpensively is fundamental to a well-functioning financial system. To the extent that the legal system makes it difficult to design mutually beneficial financial contracts and to settle claims quickly, surely, and fairly, financial services will be the poorer. The degree to which the interests of shareholders are protected also influences the degree to which equity funds are forthcoming.

Different legal systems protect creditors, shareholders, and managers in different ways—through their essential features and through the vigor of their enforcement (Table 6.1). Countries that use the British system of common law, whether adopted under colonial rule or by emulation, afford the best protection to creditors and shareholders. In contrast, the French code, used not just in its former colonies but also in those of Spain and Portugal (an enduring Napoleonic legacy), provides greater protection for managers and debtors. The Scandinavian and German systems afford the strongest enforcement.

Secured credit forms the bulk of intermediated finance, and the legal system can help by giving secured creditors a higher priority in claims against corporations going through a bankruptcy or reorganization. In Mexico, workers and government are first in line for repayment, ahead of secured creditors. Mexican law also imposes an automatic stay on the assets of firms filing for reorganization, so that lenders cannot easily take possession of collateral or liquidate a firm. Major banks in Mexico have tens of thousands of legal suits outstanding to collect past-due loans, many of which have been in the courts for years. Little surprise, then, that debt finance is not well developed.

Table 6.1

Ranking of legal systems on strength of protections and enforcement

Origin	Protection of creditors' rights	Protection of shareholders' rights	Enforcement
British	1	1	3
French	4	4	4
German	2	3	2
Scandinavian	3	2	1

Note: A ranking of 1 indicates best, and 4 worst, as calculated from average scores for countries with the indicated system in an assessment of 49 industrial and developing countries. For scores by country see Table A.2 in the Appendix.
Source: World Bank staff calculations based on La Porta and others 1998; Levine, Loayza, and Beck 1998.

In Malaysia, by contrast, secured creditors come first, and automatic stays on assets are not imposed. For a failing company pending reorganization, a party appointed by the court or the creditors replaces management. In some other countries existing management remains in charge pending the outcome of reorganization or bankruptcy proceedings. That reduces the likelihood that bank loans will be repaid and provides opportunities for managerial looting of the firm.

Shareholders also demand information from managers. A growing literature suggests that access to liquid stock exchanges—those where securities can be traded cheaply and confidently at posted prices—spurs economic development. And where shareholders are not well protected, equity markets tend to be underdeveloped and poorly functioning. Recent research also shows the concentration of ownership to be greater where minority shareholders are poorly protected.

Legal checks and transparency

The legal system can provide some check against gross abuse. If minority shareholders believe that the majority shareholders have deprived them of their fair share, they may be able to sue. And shareholders may be able to sue management for a violation of its fiduciary responsibilities. But strong protection of shareholders is far from universal.

In Venezuela a minority shareholder cannot vote by mail, is not protected from expropriation by the directors, and needs to amass 20 percent of the share capital to call an extraordinary shareholders' meeting. Shareholders in Colombia, Ecuador, Jordan, and Mexico need 25 percent of shares to call such a meeting, compared with 10 percent or less in countries with laws favoring minority shareholders.

Even where legal protections are in place, abuse of shareholder rights can remain a concern. The Czech Republic shows that these abuses can be greater in the absence of shareholder protections (Box 6.4). In the Russian Federation a widespread perception that minority shareholders have been poorly protected is thought to have contributed, along with poor transparency, to low stock market valuations of many Russian firms.

Laws are important, but so is their enforcement, and laws governing secured creditors and shareholders matter only if courts enforce them. Deficiencies in enforcement can manifest themselves as corruption, as uncertainty, and most commonly (as already noted in Mexico's case) as delay. Some legal districts in Mexico, however, have recently been enforcing contracts more effectively than others. Not surprisingly, banks are more active in those districts.

Recognizing the potential gains, a number of developing countries have been undertaking significant legal reforms. Argentina recently changed its bankruptcy law to

---

Box 6.4

Shareholders' rights and enterprise efficiency in the Czech privatization

In the hope of developing a robust equities market based on "people's capitalism," in the early 1990s the Czech Republic undertook voucher privatization, in which citizens were given vouchers to acquire shares in various firms. A concern, however, was that with share ownership thus dispersed, there would be too little oversight of managers. Since, as this chapter has shown, monitoring corporate managers is a kind of public good, there is a strong presumption that the Czech approach would lead to too little oversight. Having a single majority shareholder could go some way to rectifying this problem but would create another, for such a shareholder might advance his or her interests at the expense of the minority.

To head off this oversight problem, large holding companies (mutual funds) were formed, which would have an incentive to monitor the firms whose shares they held. Those that did a better job would have higher returns and would attract more investors. Market competition would thus ensure the efficiency of the capital market, and that of firms.

That was the theory; the experience turned out differently. Con artists promised far-fetched returns to those who turned over their vouchers to them. In a typical pyramid scheme, they then used funds from new investors to provide those returns to old investors—for a while. In the absence of effective fraud

and security laws, the more honest funds had to compete against the scurrilous ones. Some fund managers also diverted resources to themselves in a process called tunneling, whereby the underlying assets are removed, leaving nothing but a shell behind.

The holding companies were structured as closed-end mutual funds: shareholders could not redeem their shares at the net asset value but could only sell them in the secondary market, possibly at a discount. In fact, by 1997 shares in these companies were selling at discounts of 40 to 80 percent, no doubt reflecting the market's estimate of tunneling. Not surprisingly, confidence in the securities market declined, and it failed to perform its key function, that of raising capital for the creation of new enterprises and the expansion of existing ones.

Of equal importance, the funds failed to induce needed restructuring in the enterprises whose shares they held. Although the closed-end funds succeeded in buying firms with higher profit rates (they may have been effective in screening), they did not improve those profit rates. Firms with a strategic (large majority) owner often did improve their performance, but firms owned by the closed-end funds tended to let their performance slide. Opening the funds would make it easier for shareholders to exit and for corporate governance to improve.

give priority to secured creditors rather than workers. Many transition economies have had to establish bankruptcy and corporate laws to support a modern capitalist system, all in the context of far-ranging legal changes.

Even without far-reaching reforms in their legal codes, countries can take steps that improve the confidence of creditors and shareholders. Creditors can be protected in reorganization and bankruptcy courts that operate efficiently, quickly, and fairly. Even without strong legal codes, better reorganization and bankruptcy procedures would strengthen the position of secured lenders and bolster the development of financial intermediaries. Argentina materially improved its procedures in the 1990s, so that claims on troubled firms could be settled much more quickly and equitably than before.

Many countries have implemented reforms to improve the transparency and efficiency of their equity markets. Argentina, Brazil, and Chile have clarified the rules of conduct of participants in financial markets generally—and improved the functioning of their stock markets.

Many transition economies and others where the rule of corporate law is weak are finding it necessary to move beyond industrial-country models to devise a legal framework suitable for their situation. There is much to be said in such contexts for combining easily understood rules with strong sanctions for noncompliance. That kind of structure can be self-enforcing, because the higher penalties increase compliance, and behavior is more easily monitored. To the extent possible, the law should rely on action by direct participants in the corporate enterprise (shareholders, directors, managers) rather than by indirect participants (judges, regulators, legal and accounting professionals). For example, a better balance between shareholder protection and the need for business flexibility can be attained through procedural protections. Requiring that actions be approved by, say, independent directors could achieve a better balance than would flat prohibitions on entire categories of transactions.

The importance of ensuring transparency and consistency in the disclosure of information—and of improving creditors' and shareholders' confidence in exercising their rights—is clear. The supportive role of government in sustaining this informational infrastructure as a public good can hardly be questioned, even by proponents of laissez-faire. But more than support is needed.

Restraining the financial system

The failures and vulnerabilities of the financial system point clearly to the need for government to restrain its activities in certain specific ways. Financial markets are subject to major systemic risks, for example where failure in one bank can spill over to others—either directly through balance sheet linkages or through psychological conta-

gion—to the detriment of the economy. There are also the direct losses to depositors, most of which are often covered by public finances, whether through an explicit deposit protection scheme or through ad hoc compensation. The borrowers from failed banks suffer, too, as the informational capital they have built up through sustained dealings with the bank suddenly loses its value.

In the 1980s and early 1990s, priority went to reducing intrusive policy intervention that had distorted financial intermediation and had become counterproductive, especially in the face of technological developments that had outflanked the old regulatory regime. But such financial liberalization can increase enormously the informational requirements for financial stability and make it more difficult to collect information. These are two of the reasons behind the successive waves of banking crises in recent years, which have led to a reexamination of policies to restrain individual financial intermediaries.

Today, the issue is not deregulation but finding the *appropriate* regulatory structure. That structure should reflect the circumstances of the country, including the strengths and weaknesses of its financial system and the capacities of its regulators. Here the focus is on prudential regulation, to ensure a safe and sound banking system. But other important regulatory functions include promoting competition, protecting investors and depositors, and encouraging the provision of credit to underserved groups. Many of these functions are interlinked. If investors feel that they are fairly treated, that there is a level playing field, financial markets are likely to be deeper and more effective, and thus sounder.

Financial intermediaries help address information problems (such as determining which firms are good ones in which to invest), but they also give rise to a new set of information problems. Central among them is the difficulty that depositors and the authorities face in predicting bank failures.

The authorities can serve depositors by monitoring banks on their behalf, much as the well-managed bank monitors its borrowers. But government regulation goes beyond processing information and publishing the results. The regulator must not allow a bank to continue functioning when it is insolvent. One reason to step in is to avoid the fiscal costs when depositors are covered explicitly or implicitly by deposit insurance. Another is to avoid the wider systemic risks already discussed (Box 6.5). And in responding to banking failures, regulators need to ensure that the flow of credit is maintained and that the informational capital residing in banks—their knowledge of who is a good credit risk and of how to supervise borrowers—is preserved. Indeed, the inability of even the surviving banks in Indonesia to raise anything like enough capital to maintain the dollar value of their outstanding foreign currency lending led to a sharp credit squeeze there in the first half of 1998.

Box 6.5

Deposit insurance and risk taking

Depositors need to be reasonably confident about the safety of their deposits. Even having a central bank to act as lender of last resort did not provide enough assurance to U.S. depositors in the Great Depression. It is only since deposit insurance was instituted in the 1930s that bank runs have become a rarity in the United States.

Deposit insurance has its drawbacks, however. If governments do not provide adequate supervision, banks with deposit insurance have an incentive to engage in excessively risky activities. Their depositors have nothing to lose if the risks do not pan out, whereas the bank has everything to gain if they do. So depositors follow high interest rates, paying little or no attention to the riskiness of the bank's assets. Indeed, banks engaging in risky activities may be able, by offering higher interest rates, to drive rivals following a more conservative strategy out of business.

Three lines of defense can mitigate these risks:

- One is close supervision, to ensure that banks are not engaging in excessively risky behavior.
- Another is incentives to ensure that banks have enough of their own capital at risk so that they, too, have much to lose from a bankruptcy. Charging insurance premiums or imposing minimum capital requirements that vary with the riski-

ness of a bank's assets can help induce banks reduce their risks. Similarly, requiring a tier of externally held, uninsured debt brings in investors with an incentive to monitor the bank. The information so revealed can be of use to regulators and can itself put pressure on the bank.
- A third is to limit the bank's opportunities to invest in excessively risky assets (such as speculative real estate) or to offer high interest rates that can be justified only by high risk taking.

The notion that simply eliminating deposit insurance would restore discipline to the market and eliminate problems in the financial sector by reducing risk taking is misguided. Crises have hit numerous countries without explicit deposit insurance in recent times. Besides, most governments find it difficult in practice to avoid rescuing a major financial institution in crisis. As one commentator put it, there are two kinds of countries: those that have deposit insurance and know it, and those that have it but don't yet know it.

The fact that small depositors are not in a position to regularly inspect their bank's books makes monitoring a public good calling for collective action. Even without deposit insurance, banks with limited liability have to be adequately supervised to prevent excessive risk taking.

In addressing the information problems presented by the risk of financial institution failure, the authorities can draw on the same types of tools that the private financial system does. For this they need to work both directly to acquire and process information and indirectly to set policy rules and incentive structures that help align the banks' incentives with the social good. Informal finance, as Chapter 8 notes, solves the information problems by peer monitoring—the "watchful eyes" of many village members who stand to lose access to credit if any one of them defaults. In such settings enforcement is less problematic and more direct—although potentially more brutal.

Verifying and controlling transactions
Both direct and indirect tools have been used in supervising and regulating financial intermediaries. In many developing countries the banking authority was long concerned mainly with verifying mechanical compliance with simple constraints: to control inflation, for example, or to achieve sectoral policy goals. Many countries deployed a huge staff of bank regulators almost entirely devoted to such tasks. The regulator was not primarily concerned with ensuring sound banking.

Some simple constraints can reduce the risk of bank failure while requiring fairly little in the way of information acquisition or processing. For instance, rapid credit expansion is a definite warning signal of bank solvency problems, whether in one bank or the whole system. Nowadays, attempts to manage the rate of credit expansion of individual banks on a continuous basis will often be evaded or bypassed, at least in the more open and sophisticated financial systems. But it may be possible to make the financial system more robust by setting fairly high limits on credit growth. Countries might set those limits at a level that would not normally be reached but that could restrain occasional bursts of overexuberant and risky expansion, such as the unwise burst of credit to the property sector that led to solvency problems in Thailand and other East Asian economies.

Moving highly risky activities outside the banking system altogether could be desirable, even if it reduces the size of the banking sector. Crises in banks, which serve as the economy's payments mechanism and are thus central to its functioning, have larger systemic effects than losses in nonbank intermediaries. In practice, however, the less-regulated nonbank intermediaries are often owned by banks, which end up bearing the losses. Such financial connections can exist even if the subsidiaries move offshore. The issue, however, is not the location but the lack of regulation and the interdependence of balance sheets. Bank regulators need to monitor banks' consolidated balance sheets. They also need adequate information about the condition of large borrowers, notably about their foreign exchange exposure, which needs to be consolidated with that of the bank for an adequate overall picture.

With financial contracts becoming more complex, the traditional, transactions-based approach to assessing bank soundness becomes less effective. For example, countries commonly have simple rules limiting the exposure of banks to foreign exchange risk. The cost of such exposure shows up in crisis after crisis. The exposure also puts severe constraints on the scope of macroeconomic policy. Countries may face (or believe they face) the dilemma of either raising interest rates, inducing a recession, or allowing the exchange rate to fall, inducing a financial crisis and thereby also risking an economic downturn.

This provides a compelling reason for putting limits on the foreign exchange exposure of banks. But can such limits work? Consider the financial derivatives acquired by some Mexican banks shortly before that country's exchange rate crisis of late 1994. Although these derivatives were recorded as U.S. dollar claims, and as such did not appear to violate rules limiting each bank's net foreign exchange exposure, the complex contract terms defining the maturity value of these derivatives made them more like U.S. dollar liabilities. As long as the exchange rate remained stable, these instruments yielded a good return to Mexican banks. But when the peso fell, the contracts imposed severe losses. Only fantastically detailed and frequent on-site scrutiny of the files for these assets could have revealed their true riskiness, and then only to highly skilled supervisors, let alone the market.

Limiting such evasion of simple rules obviously requires more complex prohibitions. For example, such contracts could be made legally unenforceable against the banks unless fully disclosed on their balance sheets. Or such contracts could be assigned junior status in the event of a bank's liquidation. But some other, still simple rules, such as "speed bumps" restricting the rate of growth of lending to real estate, can do much in developing countries.

Assessing risk

The focus of regulation and supervisory practice is shifting toward risk assessment—and toward setting policy rules that better align the incentives of the supervised banks with the social good. This involves quite different types of information acquisition. Risk assessment for bank supervision uses a more forward-looking approach to solvency. It is designed to verify not just that the current financial situation of the bank is sound, but that the bank will continue to be sound and solvent. Statistical risk assessment techniques weigh the relative riskiness of different types of activity and different balance sheet components. But complementing these techniques is a greater emphasis on management and systems, including a qualitative assessment of the character and ability of the bank's directors and managers.

Supervisors have begun to prefer assessing the adequacy of a bank's internal risk control procedures over directly assessing its financial condition. The risk control department of a well-run bank should be the first to identify emerging problems and take corrective action. It is also best placed to establish operational rules and procedures that limit risk in the particular environment facing the bank. In this approach, then, much of the key information gathered and processed by the supervisor is about the bank's information-processing capacity and incentive structure.

Developing countries need to incorporate these risk assessment procedures into their operating procedures. Training bank personnel in the use of risk assessment techniques should be high on the agenda. But going down this road may require tougher penalties for infractions. Furthermore, the fact that many financial institutions in the industrial countries have failed dramatically in their risk management should serve as a caution against dismantling more direct supervision altogether.

Other arrangements

More subtle regulatory and institutional arrangements (that is, subtler than simple credit ceilings and other ratio controls) are also part of the toolbox of the prudential authorities. Risk-based capital adequacy requirements encourage banks to favor less risky forms of activity. There have also been some new experiments with rules to promote a parallel assessment of bank soundness by other market participants. Like the contractual arrangements devised by the private financial system, these rules help minimize the cost of the remaining information gaps facing the authorities. They work by aligning the incentives of market participants more closely with those of the authorities.

But in practice the ways in which capital adequacy standards are adjusted for risk have been very limited. Until recently, for example, international standards focused on credit risks to the exclusion of risks associated with capital asset values. For example, long-term U.S. Treasury bonds were treated as safe even though they carry significant interest rate risk. Furthermore, in arriving at rules for a bank's capital requirements, insufficient attention has gone to the correlation of returns on its various assets.

Banking crises in Chile and Mexico revealed, for newly privatized banks, that formal compliance with capital requirements is possible without the owners truly having as much at stake as it appears. For example, if owners finance their capital investment with a loan from the bank they are acquiring, they then have no real capital at stake. That the quality of capital was inadequate could not be verified until it was too late.

In some instances, increases in capital requirements could even lead banks to take *more* risks, because what is of concern to them is their total capital, which includes their franchise value, the present discounted value of future profits. Since the cost of the capital required to meet the capital adequacy standards may be high, increasing the capital adequacy requirements lowers the franchise value. In some cases the loss in franchise value may more than offset the increased capital, so that the bank actually assumes more risk. Normally, however, the net effect of increased capital requirements is to reduce the risk of failure without imposing excessive information costs on supervisors. This effect is strengthened when accompanied by graduated early intervention rules mandating the authorities to take corrective action when risk-weighted capital falls below the established threshold, even if capital is comfortably positive.

Capital requirements do not eliminate the need for supervisors to evaluate banks' assets, including the loan portfolio, and so do not eliminate the need for the regulator's information gathering. But by introducing a margin for error, they enhance the incentive for sound management of the bank—and help limit excessive risk taking (Box 6.6).

Enforcing more public disclosure of banks' accounts and requiring a tier of uninsured subordinated debt in each bank's portfolio are two ways of increasing the scope and incentive for complementary monitoring of bank soundness by the private sector. The holders of subordinated debt, first to lose in an insolvency, have a particularly strong incentive to watch for problems, especially if they have an arm's-length relationship with the bank owners. Although they may have little direct influence over management policy, a fall in the market price of this debt will indirectly communicate their concern to the regulator and to the market. The information burden is thus shared between the public regulator and other market participants. But the burden does not disappear, for regulators still have to ensure that the holders of subordinated debt are truly independent of the bank's insiders.

Multiplying the number of watchful eyes greatly reduces the risk that a bank will slip into insolvency without the problem becoming apparent in time to take corrective action. The same considerations apply to entire banking systems. More watchful eyes, including enhanced global

---

Box 6.6

Better bank regulation in Argentina

Reforms advanced significantly in Argentina after financial crises there in the 1980s resulted in losses estimated at 20 to 55 percent of GDP. As a result of additional measures in recent years, some as part of the fallout from the 1994–95 tequila crisis, Argentine banks are now characterized by:

- A minimum capital adequacy ratio of 11.5 percent, among the highest in the world
- A dramatic increase in the importance of foreign banks (about 45 percent of banking assets)
- Enhanced disclosure, including on-line information from the central bank on firms' balance sheets and income statements
- A requirement that banks issue uninsured subordinated debt
- High liquidity requirements (20 percent for most liabilities), and
- A much-strengthened supervisory function, with weaker banks closed or merged in the past three years.

Part of this drive to improve the safety and soundness of the banking system comes from the Argentine authorities' commitment to a fixed exchange rate with the U.S. dollar (evidenced by their adoption of a currency board). But it also reflects the shift to a "multiple eyes" approach. Higher capital requirements put owners' funds at risk. Reliance on reputable foreign banks gives the authorities some comfort that the quality of capital is high. Holders of subordinated debt provide market oversight and, with better information disclosure, a firmer basis for assessing creditworthiness. Supervision is now serious, and the liquidity cushion contributes to banking stability. Although it is too early to tell how successful this system will be, it has sailed on smoothly thus far despite the Asian storm, and in marked contrast to the shock Argentina experienced from the Mexican crisis.

---

surveillance by the International Monetary Fund and the initiatives of the Bank for International Settlements, combined with greater information in the hands of market participants, should help reduce the frequency and magnitude of crises. But if history is any guide, these measures almost surely will not eliminate them.

These elements do not exhaust the regulator's toolbox, nor can they. Financial technology keeps moving in response to regulatory change. The strategic game between regulator and regulated is ongoing. Market participants are always seeking ways to reduce the cost that regulation imposes, and the regulator must respond in turn.

Supervisors and regulators are unlikely to gather the necessary early-warning information needed to prevent bank failure if the incentive structure discourages early intervention—as it does when imprudent bankers have too much political influence. It may not be possible to turn the clock back to the early 19th century, when private bank supervisors in the highly successful Suffolk Bank system in New England had a strong incentive to avoid losses. Any such losses were paid out of the supervisors' deferred bonuses, which were thus similar to the bonds that senior bank officers used to post. But it is clear that the circle can be closed only where governments also have the incentive to act early on information that a bank is being run unsoundly.

Is the period immediately after financial liberalization associated with a significantly higher probability of financial crisis? The answer is yes, at least for countries with weak legal and regulatory institutions. One of the reasons is that such liberalizations erode franchise value and have not been accompanied by appropriate tightening of supervision. And one of the important lessons is that the pacing and sequencing of reforms—introducing better supervision before other restrictions are reduced—need more attention.

Imposing some constraints that increase franchise value could lead to safer and sounder banks. There is some evidence that mild restraints on deposit interest rates in some East Asian economies in earlier periods contributed to their growth. Although financial restrictions that lead to negative real interest rates hurt growth, and significant departures from market interest rates lead to actions to evade the constraints, mild financial constraints might be effective.

The East Asian crisis reopens the question of whether prudential regulation of banks is enough to insulate economies from the vulnerability that comes with high foreign currency indebtedness, especially short-term indebtedness, of banks and corporations. Beyond what is needed to finance trade, short-term capital flows may contribute little to economic growth while adding considerably to economic instability. Recent empirical studies find that capital account liberalization is associated with financial market vulnerability, but not with growth, and that international investors chase trends. And clearly there is a reluctance to undertake high-productivity, long-term investments with volatile short-term capital.

Outflows of short-term funds have imposed huge systemic risks on economies. Some have therefore recommended that the monetary authorities maintain enough foreign exchange reserves to cover the country's short-term foreign exchange liabilities in full. But if that were done, the country as a whole would be borrowing from the industrial world at high interest rates and redepositing the proceeds at the lower rates typically paid on liquid reserve assets.

It would appear that the social risks resulting from such borrowings are markedly greater than the private risks perceived and assumed by market participants. Whenever there are such large discrepancies between social and private costs—whenever, that is, private actions impose large externalities—there is a case for government action to realign incentives. This is as true for financial flows as it is for air or water pollution. Although there are real difficulties in restraining short-term foreign currency borrowing, given the ease with which regulations in this area can be evaded, with potentially harmful side effects, the search for a better policy mix must continue.

• • •

Economies with better financial institutions grow faster; those with weak ones are more vulnerable to financial crises and the slow growth that typically follows. How well countries address the information problems that they are supposed to address—screening and monitoring loans and enforcing repayment—has much to do with the overall performance of the economy. But how well they perform these functions depends on the incentives and new constraints they face, for financial markets both solve and create information problems.

If banks and security markets are monitors, who will monitor the monitors? Investors who entrust their funds to the financial market do some of the monitoring, but only imperfectly, partly because they have limited information. Governments have long sought to increase the information available to investors (through disclosure requirements). Governments have also gathered information themselves (through supervision) and acted on it. They also have created legal systems to discourage looting, fraud, pyramid schemes, the violation of minority shareholder rights, and the myriad other behaviors that undermine the efficiency and effectiveness of capital markets (where the private returns of some are at the expense of others).

Governments perform these roles through active support of the financial system and through the restraints they impose on the system. The exact policy and the best mix of policies depend on the capacities of the government and the circumstances of the country. As *World Development Report 1997* emphasized, one of the key tasks of governments is to strengthen its own capacities—and to better match its actions with those capacities and with circumstances.

The central role of finance in the economy has important implications for how countries respond to economic crises, particularly those associated with financial crises. Many of the lessons learned painfully from repeated financial crises around the globe have been reinforced by the recent experience in East Asia. It is important to preserve the informational and organizational capital of financial intermediaries, to the extent it has value. Because information is limited, suppliers of funds are not perfect substitutes, and it takes time to reestablish banking relationships. In the meantime the decline in finance can wreak havoc on the economy. So, without compromising the principle that shareholders and senior managers must lose when financial institutions fail, it is often prefer-

able to have failed banks taken over by (or merged into) stronger banks, or even recapitalized. It is because they recognize the importance of preserving the information held in banks that industrial countries experiencing bank crises have typically handled bank failure in other ways than by outright closure. As this chapter has suggested, it matters even more to developing countries to preserve and build upon the information that financial institutions contain.

Chapter 7

Increasing Our Knowledge of the Environment

BEHIND THE RISING PROSPERITY in the developing world lurks the shadow of lethal air pollution from motor vehicles, smokestacks, and hearths. All these sources and others emit tiny airborne particles that lodge deep in the lungs, causing severe and sometimes fatal respiratory problems. Every year in four Chinese cities alone—Chongqing, Beijing, Shanghai, and Shenyang—10,000 people die prematurely from exposure to these particles. And throughout the developing world such pollution kills hundreds of thousands of people and seriously damages the health of millions more. Workdays lost to respiratory illness run into the hundreds of millions and the corresponding economic costs into the billions of dollars.

These losses were once viewed as the price of economic development. Fortunately, the countries that have pioneered environmental protection in the developing world have shown this view to be gravely mistaken. Operating in very different political and institutional cultures, they have used pollution charges, grassroots community pressure, and command-and-control regulation to contain or even roll back air pollution at supportable cost. Across their diverse approaches lies an important unifying factor: the global community's accumulation and dissemination of knowledge—knowledge about measuring air quality, about evaluating health risks, about identifying pollution sources, about estimating abatement costs, about setting enforcement priorities, and about designing cost-effective regulatory instruments. As knowledge has accumulated and environmental policy strengthened, air quality has stabilized and even improved in many rapidly industrializing areas.

What is true for air pollution is true for many other types of environmental damage. Each year, diarrheal diseases from contaminated water kill about 2 million children and cause 900 million episodes of illness, most of which oral rehydration therapy and basic sanitation could have prevented. Annual losses from soil erosion range from 0.5 to 1.5 percent of GNP in many countries, but well-informed policies can trim these costs substantially. Greenhouse gas emissions will double within a generation at current growth rates, but effective policies and dissemination of information can greatly reduce them.

There is now general agreement about the importance of limiting environmental damage. We also have a good understanding of why government action is needed to preserve the environment. For example, pollution has adverse effects on others, but the polluter typically does not have to compensate them. When such spillover effects, or externalities, occur, the cost of pollution to society is greater than the cost to the polluter. There is then too much pollution because individuals and firms do not have the right incentives to reduce it. A factory that discharges pollutants into a river has no incentive to consider the damage inflicted on those downstream. A user of freon-based air conditioning has no incentive to take account of the damage freon causes to the atmosphere's ozone layer. Drivers have no incentive to reduce exhausts and improve air quality for their neighbors.

Effective public policies provide incentives to reduce pollution and natural resource degradation by aligning social and private costs. In some cases, legal systems can produce such alignment without direct government action. For instance, laws in some countries require polluters to compensate others for certain kinds of pollution damage. The assignment of property rights can also reduce the scope for environmental degradation; for example, a lake that has one owner is not likely to be overfished. But the holders of those rights may incur large transactions costs in enforcing them, and the assignment of property rights sometimes is simply not feasible—who, for example, should own the atmosphere?

Problems such as these have forced governments to do more to protect the environment. In some cases government regulators can give polluters the right incentive to clean up by charging them for the damage their activities cause. When information on discharges or the extent of their damage is not available, systems that monitor the more easily observable actions of polluters, such as the required installation of pollution control devices, may be desirable. With the right information, however, pollution charges are superior. Unlike technology standards, they put firms under continuous pressure to reduce pollution.

Information can also encourage pollution reduction. A government's regulations (including pollution charges) apply across its whole jurisdiction and may not be appropriate for all areas—environmental, social, and economic conditions may differ. In such cases, public disclosure of a polluter's emissions can complement formal regulation. Informed consumers may then buy fewer products from heavily polluting firms. Investors concerned about liability may become reluctant to finance them. And neighboring communities may insist that they improve their environmental performance.

Disseminating information on the implications of environmental degradation can also offer opportunities for improvement, but the impact of better information depends on people's ability and willingness to use it. That returns us to this Report's two main themes: narrowing knowledge gaps and addressing information problems.

This chapter discusses two main issues:

- *The importance of knowledge and information for environmental management.* Better environmental outcomes require more knowledge about environmental impacts and about technologies, as well as information about environmental performance such as the pollution generated by particular polluters.
- *The design of appropriate institutions for environmental management.* Effective management requires knowledge about the impact of alternative institutional arrangements, their information requirements, and the circumstances in which they will work well.

Knowledge for environmental management

The analysis of environmental degradation often centers on its relationship to economic development. Some argue that such degradation is the inevitable by-product of social and economic development, at least in its initial stages. Others argue that economic and social development will not suffer in the long run if natural resources are properly managed. Thus some see environmental management as a complement to development; others see the two as conflicting. But severe environmental degradation can occur even without development, simply from population pressure. This Report endorses a balanced view: good policies can support sustainable development strategies by protecting and even improving the environment while promoting economic growth. Such strategies call for good institutions, appropriate incentives, good information, and better knowledge of the environmental impacts of alternative policies.

The key aspects of the long, knowledge-intensive process of integrating environmental management with development are the following:

- *Understanding the environment and the processes that affect it* by identifying the sources of environmental degradation, its consequences, and the costs of reducing it, as the foundation for effective policy
- *Developing indicators of environmental performance* that policymakers at the local, regional, and national level can use
- *Using environmental information* to improve both public regulation and private decisionmaking, and
- *Managing environmental knowledge* by building the capacity to gather and disseminate knowledge, improving private sector environmental management, and broadening public policy models to include environmental variables.

Understanding the environment

We rely on markets to ensure the efficient supply of most goods and services. Prices determined by the intersection of demand and supply usually provide all the relevant information for efficient resource allocation, including the additional (marginal) benefit to consumers and to producers of an additional unit of output. The marvel of the price system is that no central planner has to know the details of consumers' preferences or firms' technological possibilities. But for the supply of clean air, clean water, and other environmental goods things are different. Such goods are not exchanged in markets. There are no prices to reflect consumers' marginal valuation of cleaner air or water or the cost to producers of providing them.

A collective decision must accordingly be made about how clean the environment should be. Different individuals may have different views, however, and these views have to be reconciled through the political process. To reach agreement, people have to know the consequences of different levels of pollution. Such knowledge is thus an essential part of decisions about environmental policy, but it can never be perfect. Consider, for example, the uncertainty about the impact of different levels of particulate air pollution on the health of different groups of people, including asthmatic children.

Under some conditions, society can use available knowledge to develop the system of environmental prices that the market has failed to create. Such prices, imposed on polluters in the form of pollution charges, are based on a collective decision about the marginal social cost of pollution. Appropriate pollution charges force polluters to pay that marginal social cost. This provides the correct incentive for producers to operate efficiently, by aligning the marginal social benefits with the marginal social costs. Once collective preferences are determined, such environmental prices work much as do prices for other goods.

But often the marginal social cost of pollution depends on the level of pollution. The appropriate charge cannot be determined until one knows what level of pollution will emerge, and that cannot be predicted without certain technical knowledge. Even then, there is likely to be considerable uncertainty, with adjustments having to be made over time. If pollution increases to a level higher than anticipated, the price charged for it may have to be increased. That is why monitoring levels of pollution is essential.

It might also prove impossible to levy charges on each firm or household that reflect its true contribution to pollution. That would require monitoring at the household or the firm level, which might be costly. Often, therefore, government action to protect the environment takes the form of regulation affecting pollution more directly. Cars may be limited to emissions below a certain level; coal-burning power plants may be required to install scrubbers that reduce sulfur dioxide emissions. For policies to be efficient, regulators must know the marginal costs associated with these tighter standards, to compare them with the marginal social benefits of pollution abatement. But such information can be difficult and expensive to acquire.

Incomplete information and knowledge also pose major problems for natural resource conservation. Data on environmental variables are often scarce and inadequate. And given the complexity of many ecological processes, translating environmental data into knowledge is difficult.

Some links between human activity and ecosystems are far from obvious. In Malaysia in the 1970s, supplies of the durian fruit began mysteriously to decline, threatening a $100-million-a-year industry. The durian trees were intact and apparently healthy, but were bearing less fruit. Then it was discovered that the flower of the durian tree was pollinated by a single species of bat, whose population was falling because of a decline in its primary source of food: flowering trees in mangrove swamps, which were being converted to shrimp farming.

In other instances, tackling the long-term effects of policies with environmental impacts requires sustained investment in monitoring and in updating knowledge. As discussed in the Overview, the green revolution has brought dramatic increases in agricultural yields, with beneficial effects on food security, farm income, and poverty alleviation. But concerns about the long-run environmental impact of the green revolution highlight the need for more knowledge.

Experience from Pakistan illustrates these concerns. In 1970 the success of the first generation of high-yielding varieties and the wider availability of irrigation led to predictions that Pakistan would soon become a net exporter of grain. For the next two decades, however, deficits in the domestic production of wheat—the major food staple—persisted, requiring imports of at least a million tons every other year. Consensus is still lacking on the causes of this disappointing performance, and it is certainly possible that they have nothing to do with natural resource degradation. Further observation and analysis will be needed to determine whether the benefits of high-yielding varieties were at least partly offset by accompanying nutrient depletion, soil compaction, declining soil organic matter, and widespread diffusion of specialized, potentially disease-prone cropping systems. But the findings of a recent study are at least cautionary: average production costs rose by 0.36 percent per year in one post–green revolution decade (1984–94), and degraded resources (especially soil) correlate with higher costs.

Knowledge takes time to evolve, be disseminated, and be accepted. Progress often occurs in bursts, first in the scientific community and eventually in society at large (Box 7.1). And political processes matter as much as scientific progress. The development community has been slow in fully accounting for the social and environmental consequences of large hydropower and forestry projects, for example. Increasingly, such accounting has been understood to be highly knowledge-intensive, requiring the participation of many stakeholders.

Knowledge can also be lost. For a long time indigenous knowledge was enough to guide environmental management. Traditional farming in Africa and Latin America, based on shifting agriculture, was efficient in managing nutrient cycles and regenerating soil fertility. But demographic pressure and commercial incentives favoring the mass planting of single crops displaced more diversified, subsistence-oriented systems, putting the survival of that knowledge—and the associated environmental control mechanisms—in jeopardy. Local and traditional knowledge is now used more extensively in the design of systems for the collection and analysis of information and in the promotion of sustainable farming practices.

Decisions on natural resource use, besides having spillover effects on current generations, may also affect future generations—a fact at the core of thinking about sustain-

Box 7.1

The slow evolution of knowledge about climate change

1824   Jean Baptiste Fourier first describes the natural greenhouse effect, comparing the action of the atmosphere to that of glass covering a container.

1850–70   The industrial revolution intensifies, starting a process of steadily growing greenhouse gas emissions.

1896, 1903, 1908   In three articles the Swedish scientist Svante Arrhenius hypothesizes that burning coal will increase the atmospheric concentration of carbon dioxide and warm the earth. He suggests that warming may be desirable.

1958   Continuous monitoring of carbon dioxide concentrations in the atmosphere begins at the Mauna Loa Observatory in Hawaii and at the South Pole.

1965   The U.S. President's Science Advisory Committee includes a chapter on atmospheric carbon dioxide in its report on environmental problems.

Early 1970s   Widespread concern develops over potential global climatic cooling induced by industrial and agricultural aerosols.

1979   The first World Climate Conference is held in Geneva. Concern about global warming is revived, but the conference statement is cautious about the issue.

1985–87   International meetings in Villach, Austria, and Bellagio, Italy, establish climate change as an international concern.

1988   An international group of scientific experts is organized as the Intergovernmental Panel on Climate Change (IPCC).

1990   The Second World Climate Conference in Geneva presents the results of the first IPCC assessment report. The IPCC estimates that a 60 percent cut in emissions would be needed to stabilize atmospheric carbon dioxide at the 1990 level, but no conclusive link between human activity and global warming is established.

1992   The United Nations Framework Convention on Climate Change is signed in Rio de Janeiro by more than 160 nations. The convention includes nominal objectives for some countries but no binding targets.

1995   The IPCC publishes its second assessment report, concluding that "the balance of evidence suggests that there is now a discernible human influence on the global climate."

1997   Agreement is reached on the Kyoto Protocol. Industrial countries and most of the economies in transition from central planning commit themselves to reducing greenhouse gas emissions by an average of 5.2 percent below 1990 levels in the period 2008–12.

able development. Thus sustainable development involves generating information about the spillover effects of current decisions across space and over time. It also means putting in place incentive systems that induce stakeholders to take that information into account.

According to a common interpretation of sustainable development, future generations will be no worse off than today's if they have at least an equivalent overall resource base consisting of a mix of natural, infrastructural, and knowledge capital. Some natural resources can be safely depleted, in this view, if the proceeds from their extraction are invested in the accumulation of other forms of productive capital. If human capital can substitute for natural resources, for example, a country may choose to reduce its stock of forested areas to invest the returns from logging in higher education.

But substitution is not always possible. To what extent can human-made capital (including knowledge) replace natural capital? Answering this question requires knowledge about some critical tradeoffs. Since such knowledge is still scarce, some strongly conflicting views are held. Some argue that opportunities for substitution are ample, others that substitution possibilities may be severely limited by poorly understood ecological thresholds. They caution

against policies with potentially irreversible effects, such as conversion of wetlands or forests and the loss of watershed protection and microclimate regulation. If the effects of a development decision are irreversible—or reversible only at very high social cost—a more cautious exploitation of natural resources may be called for than in conditions of full certainty or in the absence of irreversibility (Box 7.2).

Simply knowing the long-term effects of environmental problems—and the risks and limits of technological fixes—is not enough to ensure sustainability. Even with this knowledge, countries may lack the political incentives to implement market or institutional reforms. Political institutions are geared to the short term, and long-term programs are often difficult to implement, especially if they are costly or make powerful and vocal interest groups worse off. Overcoming this lack of institutional foresight is a key challenge for sustainable development.

Further problems can arise from environmental impacts that cross regional or national boundaries. Sulfur dioxide from power plants in the midwestern United States may bring acid rain to eastern states. Farmers in developing countries who clear forested land for subsistence agriculture have no incentive to take global impacts into account, whether or not they are aware of their contribution to global habitat loss and higher concentrations of atmospheric carbon dioxide. In these cases efficiency requires that environmental protection be undertaken within a broader political jurisdiction.

When the impacts are global, action has to be international. In recent years the international community has adopted a variety of conventions that seek to improve the global environment. At one extreme, the Montreal Protocol on ozone-depleting substances targets a specific problem and imposes a clearly defined schedule for action. It has been judged largely successful, possibly because of its specific focus and because of widespread agreement about the risks associated with ozone depletion. At the other extreme, Agenda 21, adopted by the 1992 Rio Earth Summit, includes an extremely broad set of environmental objectives but no common action plan. It is hard to identify particular successes for such a broad agenda, although it may well have contributed to international awareness of environmental problems.

Developing environmental performance indicators

Monitoring environmental quality is essential for environmental management. But our perception of environmental performance—and its effect on human welfare—depends on the framework in which this information is presented. The standard way of organizing country data on wealth and performance is the system of national accounts. But national accounts are geared toward macro-

economic management and are less suitable for assessing social welfare more broadly. Since they do not reflect depletion and degradation of the environment, they may give false policy signals to countries aiming for environmentally sustainable development. To monitor environmental quality, a different information framework with additional indicators is needed.

The most effective indicators are aggregates that summarize the underlying data to aid in diagnosing environmental problems. Equally important for policy are performance indicators: how have key aspects of environmental quality responded to the policy prescriptions applied? Some indicators measure environmental goods, such as the extent of protected lands or biodiversity. Others measure environmental bads, such as excess logging, soil loss, or air and water pollution. Still others monitor the effects of environmental degradation, such as the incidence of waterborne disease or species loss.

Environmental indicators need to present a coherent picture of the links between human activity and the environment. The OECD's pressure-state-response framework (Figure 7.1), the basis of almost all systems of environmental indicators, provides such coherence. The framework recognizes that indicators of both cause (pressure on the environment) and effect (the state of the environment) are needed to manage complex systems, as are response indicators to track policies and behavioral changes that mitigate environmental impacts. Within this framework,

Box 7.2

Uncertainty, irreversibility, and the value of information

The choice between conserving and developing natural resources is often rendered difficult by uneven information. Returns from development decisions (say, to convert a forest to industrial use) are known with a reasonable degree of confidence, whereas the benefits of conservation (say, the possibility of discovering valuable genetic resources or developing ecological tourism in a wilderness area) tend to be uncertain. But by forgoing immediate development, land managers leave open the option of acquiring better information on the comparative returns from alternative land uses.

Option value is defined as the expected value of future information from or about resources under conservation. Typically, option value is positive, which implies a gain from the decision to postpone development until more information is available on the benefits from conservation. Although its counterfactual nature makes the measurement of option value difficult, approximations have been attempted in a few cases.

In the late 1970s a previously unknown variety of teosinte, a wild relative of maize, was found in the remote Sierra de Manantlán region in Mexico. Besides being disease resistant, the newfound plant variety offers the potential for developing

a breed of perennial maize. If adopted on a large scale, perennial maize could significantly lower the labor and capital costs of production—and thus the price of maize.

This episode offers an interesting opportunity for applying the concept of option value with the benefit of hindsight. Had the wilderness area been converted to development, the new variety of teosinte might never have been found, and the possibility of developing a commercially viable variety of perennial maize would have been lost. But by preserving the wilderness, land managers decided to forgo possible development benefits—and serendipitously reaped conservation benefits instead.

Based on estimates of U.S. demand and supply for maize and on plausible assumptions about the returns from development of the wilderness area, the option value of conserving the wilderness area has been estimated at around $320 million. A short-sighted decisionmaker would have chosen to develop the area, whereas a more cautious land manager would have waited until more information was available on the benefits from conservation. The second choice would have been the right one, unless the immediate benefits from development exceeded $320 million.

Figure 7.1

The pressure-state-response framework

Monitoring environmental performance takes a sophisticated model of how society and nature interact.

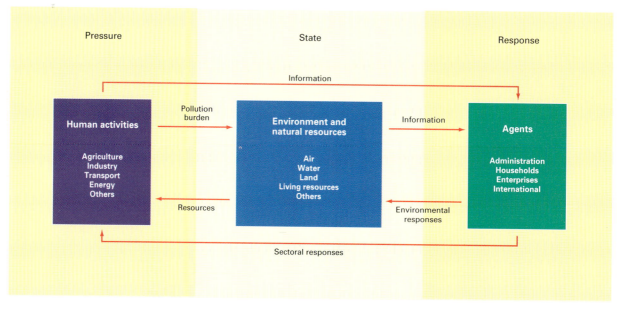

Source: OECD 1994.

well-structured sets of physical indicators can be constructed to inform both decisionmakers and the public about environmental change.

The need to better capture environmental degradation in national accounts has given rise to the concept of green national accounting, or "green GNP." Green accounting is intended to correct the national accounts by subtracting from GNP the costs associated with natural resource depletion and pollution damage. There is widespread agreement that such adjustments are conceptually appropriate. But the necessary supporting knowledge is often lacking. Estimation and valuation of environmental impacts remain more art than science in many cases; thus suggestions for adjustments to the national accounts have varied widely. Despite the many uncertainties, some countries have begun incorporating estimates of green GNP into policymaking. Among developing countries, the Philippines has one of the most advanced systems of green national accounts.

A sibling of green national accounting, genuine saving, has also been put forward as a direct indicator of whether a country is on a sustainable path. It measures the rate at which wealth is being created or destroyed—the true saving rate after accounting for investments in human

capital, depreciation of produced assets, and depletion and degradation of the environment. Negative genuine saving implies that total wealth is in decline. Policies leading to persistently negative genuine saving are policies for unsustainability.

Genuine saving departs from standard national accounting in several ways. It deducts from output values the value of the natural resources used up in producing that output. Deducting pollution damages—including lost welfare in human sickness and death—is also appropriate if society aims to maximize welfare, not just consumption of goods and services. And in recognition of the role of knowledge in accumulating wealth, estimates of genuine saving consider current education spending as an increase in saving, not in consumption as in traditional national accounts.

Genuine saving rates reveal whether countries are living off their capital stock, and many are: these rates have been negative in some countries for extended periods (Figure 7.2). In Ecuador genuine saving has been near zero or negative for much of the period the country has been exploiting its oil reserves. And the "lost decade" of the 1980s was characterized by negative genuine saving for many other countries in Latin America and the Caribbean. Genuine saving rates in Sub-Saharan Africa deteriorated sharply in the late 1970s and have been negative ever since, except in 1980 (Figure 7.3).

Genuine saving makes the growth-environment trade-off explicit, since countries planning to grow today and protect the environment tomorrow will exhibit depressed rates of genuine saving. Its role is to alert policymakers to unsustainable practices and trends. But responding to this signal requires more: it takes a broad understanding of environment-economy links at the macroeconomic, sectoral, and project levels; it also takes sound policy design and skillful environmental management. In Botswana, for example, natural resource accounts are a key instrument for developing public expenditure policy. The authorities recognize the value of resources and the importance of reinvesting resource rents. This understanding has led to better macroeconomic and environmental performance.

Figure 7.2

Genuine saving in Ecuador

Genuine saving—a measure that accounts for environmental losses—can fall well below conventional measures of saving.

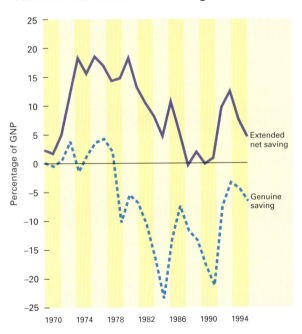

Note: Genuine saving is extended net saving adjusted for resource depletion and global environmental damage. Extended net saving is extended domestic investment (gross domestic investment plus expenditure on education) minus depreciation and foreign borrowing. Source: World Bank 1997c.

Figure 7.3

Genuine saving in selected world regions

Genuine saving has been low and sometimes negative in many developing countries.

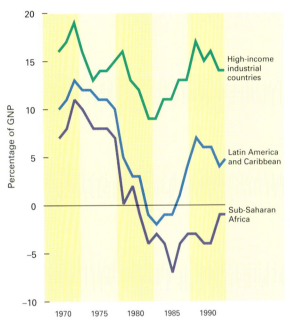

Note: Genuine saving is defined as in Figure 7.2. Source: World Bank 1997c.

Using environmental information

Recent evidence suggests a strong relationship between environmental regulation and economic development. *World Development Report 1992: Development and the Environment* argued that developing countries have plenty of opportunities to implement sustainable development policies. The efficient generation, dissemination, and use of knowledge—on the costs of inaction and on the benefits of environmental improvements—are keys to formulating and implementing these policies.

The information generated through monitoring the state of the environment can be used in several ways. First, it helps regulators determine whether to tighten or loosen environmental standards. For instance, some pollutants may have threshold concentrations, beyond which the risks of cancer or respiratory illness jump from negligible to significant. It is important to know whether the concentrations of such pollutants are nearing critical thresholds. Second, although pollution control is most effective when pollution from firms and households is directly monitored, a second-best approach is to monitor their pollution control activities. For example, pollution control devices on automobiles can be observed and tested, even if it is not practical to monitor emissions from each vehicle.

In some cases firms and households may respond directly to information about their polluting activities. Many do not want to contribute to environmental degradation, and they will respond as good citizens to information about the environmental consequences of their activities. Community groups, industry associations, and resource user associations can exert peer pressure on their members to act responsibly. But information alone does not provide a sufficient guide to action for individuals, firms, or their associations. Government regulation and penalties provide important incentives for adjusting pollution to socially sanctioned levels. Incentives may also be provided through pressure exerted by one interest group upon another: disseminating information about pollution by different firms can generate strong community pressure on them to reduce pollution, for example. In Indonesia, environmental regulators have significantly reduced water pollution by developing and publishing ratings of polluters' environmental performance (Box 7.3).

Care must be exercised, however, in using public disclosure as a tool for environmental regulation. The public may need help in interpreting the information, because the risks associated with different pollutants are not commonly known. Indonesia's ratings are developed from benchmark standards that reflect national pollution regulations; a poor rating informs the public that a firm is not in compliance with national environmental standards.

But in the United States and other OECD countries, such public disclosure programs as the Toxics Release Inventory have disseminated raw information on toxic emissions with no interpretation or risk assessment. Some chemicals labeled toxic in these programs are indeed quite dangerous, even in small doses. Others would be hazardous only after long exposure at very high levels. By treating all chemicals the same, such disclosure programs may alarm the public unnecessarily and pressure industry into adopting high-cost abatement programs that would yield few social benefits. In recent years, academic researchers and NGOs have enhanced the value of such disclosure programs by focusing public attention on the relative risks of different chemicals.

Sometimes firms themselves are in the best position to assess the environmental risks of their activities. In such cases it is reasonable to impose legal liability for pollution damage and for cleanup of toxic waste sites. But because many small firms do not have the capacity to judge the environmental impact of their emissions, legal liability cannot be imposed in all circumstances. Governments are often better positioned than firms to judge risk. Indeed, as governments have assumed more responsibility for environmental regulation, many firms have naturally come to assume that unregulated activities are not harmful.

Box 7.3

Public information for pollution control in Indonesia

The traditional approach to environmental regulation—through permits, monitoring, and enforcement—has often been slow, contentious, and costly, even in industrial countries. As a result, industrial and developing countries alike are trying new approaches to more effective pollution regulation. Indonesia's Program for Pollution Control, Evaluation, and Rating (PROPER), launched in 1995, is one such approach, which shows that local communities and market forces can be powerful allies in the struggle against industrial pollution.

PROPER was a response to a serious risk of water pollution damage due to weak formal regulatory enforcement accompanied by rapidly growing industry. Under the program a factory is assigned a color rating based on the government's evaluation of its environmental performance. A blue rating is given to factories in compliance with regulatory standards, and green to those whose emissions controls significantly exceed standards; the gold rating (yet to be awarded to any firm) is for world-class performers. Factories that fall somewhat short of compliance receive a red rating, and black is for those that have made no effort to control pollution and have caused serious environmental damage.

Armed with this information, local communities can negotiate emissions controls with neighboring factories, firms with good performance can earn goodwill in the market, investors can more accurately assess firms' environmental liabilities, and regulators can focus their limited resources on the worst offenders. During its first two years in operation, PROPER proved quite effective in moving poor performers toward compliance. More than 30 percent of the first 187 factories rated moved from red or black to blue status in 15 months. Some 400 factories are currently in the system, and Indonesia plans to extend coverage to 2,000 polluters by the year 2000. Inspired by these and other examples of public information in action, Colombia, Mexico, and the Philippines are starting their own public disclosure programs.

As relevant scientific data accumulate, knowledge about the environment and about complex economy-environment interactions is steadily improving. Better understanding of these interactions is essential for identifying environmental risk and efficiently managing natural resources. But nature is complex: some ecosystems may suffer irreversible damage after degradation has passed critical thresholds. Solid scientific results are still very scarce, and so any decisions about the environment are filled with uncertainty.

Better information can open new opportunities—and prevent costly mistakes—by allowing fine tuning of responses to environmental risk. The value of this information is then the net welfare gain from fine tuning. For climate change it has been estimated that resolving only some of the key uncertainties could be worth billions of dollars.

Better understanding of weather patterns also has value. Consider a farmer's decision about which crops to plant and when to plant them for next season's harvest. Among other factors, the choice depends on the weather pattern expected over the coming months. Therefore more reliable weather forecasts should provide significant benefits to farmers. Agricultural yields in parts of Latin America and Africa have been highly correlated with El Niño–Southern Oscillation (ENSO) events (Figure 7.4). Without reliable forecasts, farmers are forced to make planting decisions that are correct for an average season, and take the risk of serious damage from an unforeseen extreme weather event. With a better understanding of ENSO events and the ability to forecast them, farmers can receive long-term weather forecasts before they make their planting decisions. This should reduce the correlation between ENSO events and yields, and thus the incidence of ENSO-related famines.

The weather anomalies surrounding the 1997–98 El Niño also show the difficulty of understanding complex natural phenomena. Although scientists can now forecast weather patterns in an El Niño year with some confidence, they are often surprised by the magnitude of weather anomalies and their strong links with other phenomena. The intensity of recent forest fires in Southeast Asia—caused by human activity but aggravated by the dry conditions from El Niño—took many by surprise.

Another way of using environmental information is in the design of new technologies. Technological advance is often itself a major cause of environmental problems, but technological progress and innovation can also be part of the solution. Stimulated by environmental regulations that provide appropriate incentives, the supply of environmentally friendly technologies is expanding:

■ Modern computer mapping systems can monitor developments in the natural resource stock.
■ Pollution abatement technologies—such as electrostatic precipitators or flue gas desulfurization—reduce air emissions from power generation.
■ Equally important are substitution technologies, such as renewable energy sources or unleaded gasoline.

Even so, environmentally friendly technologies are undersupplied by the market, because (as discussed in Part One) the information they embody is a public good and because, as we have seen in this chapter, it is difficult to bring environmental benefits into the calculations of individual economic actors.

Moreover, reliance on technology to solve environmental problems is seldom enough. Ecological and chemical processes—and environment-economy links—are generally too complex to allow a simple technological fix. Often a solution to one environmental problem causes or aggravates another. Hydroelectric power, for example, is clean energy, causing no air pollution. But large dams and their reservoirs take up land, and if not carefully designed and sited can require the relocation of large numbers of people and damage ecosystems. Moreover, one technological alternative may not be a perfect substitute for the technique it seeks to replace. In the Republic of Yemen firewood is an important source of energy even in high-income urban households, because such alternatives as liquefied petroleum gas are considered inferior for the most important household use: baking bread.

Better knowledge about policy also makes an important contribution to environmental management. How do policies affect the environment? How can cost-effective policies be best designed? And how can tradeoffs between

Figure 7.4

Deviations from normal weather patterns and crop yields in Latin America

Better El Niño forecasts could be a boon to Latin America's farmers.

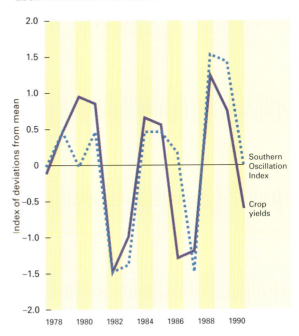

Note: The Southern Oscillation Index measures the direction and magnitude of the El Niño–Southern Oscillation; troughs mark El Niño events. Data are normalized deviations from annual averages. Underlying data for crop yields are from the Oaxaca Valles Centrales of Mexico. Source: Dilley 1997.

environmental and other objectives be assessed and responded to? For example, policymakers now realize that hidden subsidies in the sale of hydroelectric energy can lead to lower national income and diminished environmental quality.

With sophisticated knowledge management and decision support tools—and a better understanding of complex

social and natural systems—policymakers are now implementing broader, more integrated approaches to environmental management. Coastal zone management and pest control in agriculture are good examples (Box 7.4). Such integrated approaches are knowledge-intensive, but they can often achieve a given objective more cheaply. At China's Waigaoqiao thermal power plant, an integrated approach to sulfur emissions in the plant's urban airshed saved $100 million in flue gas desulfurization equipment. By installing such equipment in an older, more polluting plant closer to the urban center rather than in the new power station in the outskirts, the same air quality benefit was achieved more cheaply. Recognizing the cost-effectiveness of the proposal, the municipality agreed to an exception to the regulations and approved the arrangement.

Box 7.4

Integrated pest management in Indonesia

Farming systems that rely on the intensive use of chemical pesticides are frequently held responsible for several negative environmental effects: direct public health risks, pesticide resistance, and soil and water contamination. Integrated pest management (IPM) is an environmentally sound alternative to pesticide use. It encourages natural control of pests by using natural enemies, planting pest-resistant crop varieties, adopting cultural management, and, as a last resort, judiciously using pesticides.

In Indonesia until 1986, recurrent infestations of the brown plant hopper, induced by indiscriminate insecticide use, threatened rice production. Research had shown that the pest could be kept under good biological control by indigenous predators. A 1986 presidential decree banned 57 insecticides for use on rice and called for massive efforts to train government field staff and farmers in IPM. This validation of the approach allowed further important policy changes: complete removal of pesticide subsidies within two years (saving the government $120 million a year) and implementation of a national IPM program.

In 1989 the Indonesian government initiated one of the most aggressive IPM programs ever, with support from the U.S. Agency for International Development, the Food and Agriculture Organization, and later the World Bank. An IPM training project was added in 1993 to support the national program. Its objective is to train 800,000 farmers and trainers and provide policy support to strengthen the regulatory and environmental management of pesticides.

By 1997 the project had trained more than 600,000 farmers, including about 21,000 farmer trainers. Trained farmers carry out their own field investigations while relying on local and traditional knowledge to adapt broad concepts and practices of IPM to local conditions. They use community mechanisms to diffuse knowledge and support the adoption of IPM practices by other farmers.

IPM is an information-intensive technology that needs continuous inputs from research and other sources to maintain its dynamism at the farm level. And there are many more actors now: local governments, farmer groups, NGOs, and donors. The challenge is to ensure that farmers remain focused on the problem, through farmer-to-farmer extension, organizing farmer associations, developing informative media, and fostering participatory planning and implementation.

Managing environmental knowledge

Managing environmental knowledge, disseminating it, and building capacity for its efficient use are at least as important as creating such knowledge. That is why more environmental projects now include information systems and capacity building. The West African Newsmedia and Development Center, a regional NGO based in Benin, is targeting the media as a cost-effective means of disseminating environmental and development information. It has successfully built local capacity and integrated environmental issues into reporting by both print and broadcast media.

Better environmental management also requires creating appropriate incentives, for example by removing market distortions, resolving policy and information failures, and establishing compensation mechanisms where appropriate for those who lose from these changes. Given the right incentives and the ability to process relevant information, people will start exploiting opportunities that benefit both them and the environment. Ample evidence shows that this works for households, firms, and public entities. Mexico's Guadalajara Environmental Management Systems Pilot shows the power of managing environmental knowledge in the private sector (Box 7.5).

Data on the state and quality of the environment, even when incomplete, can be voluminous. Decisionmakers need tools and indicators that integrate and summarize data on environmental phenomena. Large, computer-based decision support tools can capture environment-economy links, to help decisionmakers set priorities and improve the design of response measures, for example by simulating the environmental consequences of different courses of action.

Consider such long-range pollutants as nitrogen oxides and sulfur dioxide. Their dispersion patterns are now reasonably well understood for many parts of the world, and information about the susceptibility of soils and species to acid deposits is gradually improving. This allows researchers to simulate the likely geographical distribution of environmental damage of emissions from different sources, and to compare deposits under different scenarios against critical loads—that is, the level of deposits beyond which ecosystems in an area would be seriously damaged (Figure 7.5).

Many environmental problems are caused by local market and policy imperfections but shared by countries worldwide, making the regional and global sharing of information important. For example, in Sub-Saharan Africa the Knowledge and Experience Resource Network supports local environmental planning and management in urban and rural communities. For preventing deforestation, networks of local centers collecting and analyzing information can be quite cost-effective (Box 7.6).

Building efficient environmental institutions

What is the best way to generate, transmit, and use environmental information—and to overcome the market imperfections that generally underlie environmental problems? Different institutional forms have different information requirements. For instance, market-based regulations that charge for emissions require monitoring of those emissions, which can be expensive and difficult. To set these charges appropriately, the government has to assess the marginal social cost of pollution—also difficult, even under the best conditions.

If the marginal social cost of pollution depends on the level of pollution, the information requirements are even greater. Either the government must have advance knowledge of the relationship between charges and resulting pollution levels before it sets the charge (which requires considerable information about technology), or it must be willing to adjust the charge if the resulting pollution varies from the desired level.

If the government issues tradable permits for pollution (Box 7.7), it must still monitor pollution levels. In addition, it must solve the difficult problem of distributing permits. This is an impediment to the use of tradable permits for pollution control.

Command-and-control regulation has a different set of information demands. Monitoring whether a particular technology is being used may be much easier than monitoring the level of pollution. But the choice of technology standards requires sophisticated knowledge of technologies—knowledge more likely to reside in regulated firms than in regulatory institutions. Different regulatory systems may also encounter different kinds of uncertainty. For instance, tradable permit systems may have little uncertainty about total emissions, but great uncertainty about the permit price that will be compatible with that level of emissions.

This section addresses the issue of informationally efficient mechanisms at four levels:

Box 7.5

Strengthening environmental management to boost performance

The Guadalajara Environmental Management Systems Pilot, begun in 1996, is helping 15 small and medium-size enterprises in that city implement an environmental management system based on an internationally known standard, ISO 14001. The standard does not set specific pollution control targets. Instead, it establishes the required elements of an effective environmental management system, including:

- An environmental policy, defined by top management and communicated throughout the organization
- Planning, including objectives and targets incorporated into a management program consistent with the environmental policy, defining responsibilities, resources, and a time frame
- Mechanisms for implementation of the environmental management program
- Procedures for monitoring and corrective action, and
- Periodic management review of the system, to ensure its continuing effectiveness.

Such systems do not just improve environmental management; they also appear to increase environmental performance. For many smaller firms the process has raised the environmental awareness and knowledge of all staff, from directors to production workers. In just a few months employees started to propose environmental improvements, and they were given the authority to implement them. Managers use the information thus generated as a marketing tool and to improve compliance with regulations. And setting measurable environmental goals and assigning responsibilities for meeting those goals have led to organizational changes that should sustain environmental improvement.

Keys to the success of the pilot have included:

- Getting nudges from large clients and suppliers
- Combing expert knowledge and local technical assistance, and
- Using simple analytical tools to process available information and achieve scheduled milestones.

- Using *markets* to reduce environmental damage when appropriate, through such market-based regulatory instruments as pollution charges and tradable emission permits
- Determining appropriate roles for *central and local governments*—for example, administering regulatory instruments, monitoring, enforcing, and ensuring that basic environmental performance standards are maintained

Figure 7.5

Acid deposits above critical loads in Asia: The RAINS model

Computer models can now simulate the likely distribution of environmental damage.

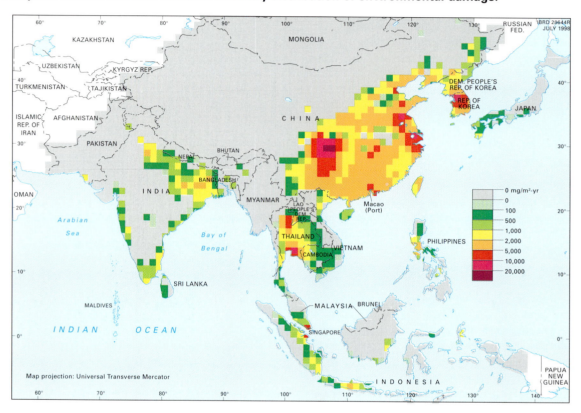

Note: The figure shows, for 2020, expected sulfur depositions in excess of what ecosystems can safely tolerate. Source: Amann and Cofala 1995.

Box 7.6

Building on local knowledge to monitor and understand deforestation

Deforestation is a widespread phenomenon but one that is often only partly understood. New approaches build on local sources to provide small-scale, locally verified information on forest conversion and its causes. As exemplified by the International Forestry Resources and Institutions (IFRI) Research Program at Indiana University in the United States, started in 1992, such information can be collected through a network of collaborating research centers throughout the world. The centers agree on a common research method to support the collection of primary data on forest conditions, management, and uses. They then interpret and analyze for policy purposes the information gathered in the field. And they promote the formation and strengthening of local capacity for assessment.

This approach differs from such conventional ways of understanding deforestation as global monitoring, primarily based on national inventories and satellite imagery, and the use of research stations, providing information on the effects of human activities on forest ecology. The new program complements these methods by narrowing knowledge gaps on the physical, ecological, socioeconomic, and institutional characteristics of deforestation—and on the interplay of demographic, political, policy, and socioeconomic forces that cause deforestation.

An important policy message that the new approach suggests is that the different forms of collective action need to be integrated. Addressing the information challenges of deforestation, which is local in its determinants but national and global in its effects, requires mobilizing many actors. The players include local communities and national researchers for the collection and interpretation of field data, the international academic community for the establishment of common methods, and the donor community for the provision of resources.

- Involving *communities and civil society* in environmental management, with particular attention to publication of environmental information, the role of traditional knowledge, and appropriate informal regulation by local organizations, and
- Expanding the scope for *international cooperation*, with appropriate arrangements for monitoring, disseminating information, and encouraging compliance by sovereign states.

Using markets to achieve environmental goals

Given the efficiency of markets in processing information and allocating goods and services, market-based approaches to environmental protection seem well worth exploring. Taxes and tradable permits can correct spillover problems in many cases. For example, the trading program for sulfur dioxide emissions rights in the United States cut those emissions by almost 50 percent, at a significantly lower cost than alternative instruments (Box 7.7).

One of the few large-scale applications of market-based instruments in developing countries is China's pollution levy. Under this scheme, which covers several thousand factories, firms are subject to a levy for discharging pollutants beyond a predetermined level. The scheme has provided an incentive for factories to cut their emissions while maintaining the flexibility to adjust rates to local circumstances: concentrations of important water pollutants in the provinces subject to the levy dropped by about 50 percent from 1987 to 1993.

An interesting form of market-based pollution control envisaged under the Kyoto Protocol to the Framework Convention on Climate Change is joint implementation, or greenhouse gas emission offsets that are international in scope. This system promotes cost-effective control of greenhouse gas emissions by giving abatement credits to countries that sponsor abatement activities in other countries. This allows industrial countries with high-cost abatement options to satisfy their abatement commitments by identifying and exploiting lower-cost options elsewhere. It has been estimated that seeking interregional efficiency through such measures could reduce the costs of compliance to about a third of those under a system of fixed targets for each country.

Creating markets for environmental goods sometimes runs into problems, however. If markets are to function well, schemes must account for information imperfections and uncertainties about compliance costs and environmental impacts. Where information is limited, monitoring and other transactions costs can be substantial. This can happen if there are many point sources, for example, or if emission cuts are measured against a counterfactual baseline, as is done under joint implementation and in many U.S. energy efficiency programs. Market-based in-

Box 7.7

Creating markets: The U.S. sulfur dioxide permit trading program

Trade in sulfur dioxide allowances was introduced in the United States in 1995 through an amendment to the 1990 Clean Air Act. The U.S. Acid Rain Program is the first long-term, large-scale pollution control program to rely on tradable emission permits. In its first phase it is limited to 260 of the country's most-polluting power generation units. After its full implementation in 2000, the program will cover practically all fossil fuel–based power plants on the mainland.

The potential gains have not yet been fully exploited, but the volume of emission trades is picking up, and the initially volatile market price has stabilized. Sulfur dioxide emissions have dropped sharply to a level well below the allowed cap. And the costs of compliance have been lower than expected, even though monitoring and transactions costs are relatively high, at about $120,000 per smokestack.

Emissions trading was not the only reason why compliance costs have remained low. Reduced transport costs made low-sulfur coal from the Midwest more widely and cheaply available. Combined with technical innovations facilitating the blending of high- and low-sulfur coal, this greatly increased the scope for fuel switching, an abatement option that tends to be cheaper than the principal technical solution, namely, flue gas desulfurization.

The Acid Rain Program has been crucial in allowing utilities to process new information more quickly and to react flexibly to new developments. For many power companies, permit prices provide useful information about sectorwide abatement costs, prompting them to revise their abatement strategy. Other utilities have been surprised by the new developments, finding that they had overinvested in sulfur dioxide abatement. The trading system, however, allowed them to "bank" their excessive emissions cuts against future caps. With modern allowance and emissions tracking systems, transactions costs have started to fall, the market is becoming more fluid, and efficiency gains are increasingly being realized.

Some tentative conclusions may be drawn from the experience thus far. Tradable permit systems work, but they have to be designed carefully, and they may not be the optimal solution under all circumstances. They do allow actors to react more efficiently to changes in market conditions, but they do not prevent them from making mistakes.

struments can also require a radical shift in thinking. Environmental goods have traditionally been free, and many cultures treat environmental goods (such as water in some Islamic countries) as special and beyond price. In the United States, where market-based pollution control is most advanced, it took years to create the necessary markets. Even so, market-based approaches can be a cost-effective solution for many environmental problems.

Sometimes markets more generally fail because information problems aggravate environmental difficulties or prevent their solution. Such problems can prevent the efficient monitoring of compliance with environmental standards and limit the access of poor households to capital and insurance markets—with repercussions for the environment. For example, lack of access to commercial insurance causes poor rural households to keep larger herds than would otherwise be necessary, as insurance against losses, and that in turn accelerates land degradation. Lack of access to credit may also prevent poor households from installing environmentally friendly technologies with high startup costs, such as solar home systems.

Innovative institutional structures, such as energy service companies and leasing and hire-purchase agreements, can mitigate such problems. Energy service companies, because they generally have a financial track record, have the access to credit that individual households may lack. This makes it possible for them to procure renewable energy technology in bulk, install it in client households, and operate it for a fee. Customers pay only for the energy services, not the equipment. By spreading the costs to consumers over the life of the system, energy service companies also allow for a more affordable payment scheme, and thus reach a larger customer base. Leasing and hire-purchase schemes work in a similar way, except that ownership of the equipment transfers to the customer once the loan is paid off. Such schemes could bring affordable electricity to an estimated additional 50 million poor households worldwide.

Sharing responsibility between central and local governments

When technological, social, and institutional conditions permit, establishing markets is a powerful way to bridge the information gap between providers and users of environmental goods and services. But governments have important complementary roles in providing and managing environmentally relevant information (such as environmental indicators) and in ensuring compliance.

In the traditional approach to pollution regulation, the government collects information on both the social damage from polluting activities and the private cost of abatement. It then identifies an optimal emissions level, to be enforced by regulation. This may be difficult in complex situations with many polluters, but it could be viable when there are a few major polluters, so that the government can gather the relevant information at reasonable cost.

The scale of a policy issue—local, national, or global—usually dictates the level of government best equipped to tackle it. For natural resources, decentralizing management to state and municipal governments is likely to be a cost-efficient way of addressing local spillovers. It can improve the exchange of environment-related information in several ways:

- Local governments, closer to the stakeholders in environmental problems, are likely to incur lower costs in gathering information about the private costs of (and the social benefits from) mitigating activities.
- State and municipal governments can take advantage of their knowledge of local conditions to apply centrally determined guidelines on emission standards or land zoning restrictions. They can also promote the adaptation of framework policies established by national ministries.
- Decentralization can shorten the feedback loop between making decisions, observing the effects, and adjusting the initial decisions.

Decentralizing environmental management has risks, however. It requires considerable human and institutional capital: doing it without adequately trained personnel, institutional backstopping, and recurrent funding may be counterproductive. Nor is it enough to promote stakeholder participation. Like those of central governments, the incentives of local governments are affected by the electoral cycle—which may be too short to properly address long-term concerns, or too long for issues that require frequent interaction with stakeholders. Local communities may thus have to be encouraged to voice their environmental concerns. And even where decentralization is the appropriate course, central governments need to retain some key roles in managing environmental information across jurisdictions.

Involving communities and civil society

Environmental issues span geographic boundaries. And even in open societies, formal regulation relies on fixed rules (concentration standards, charge rates) that reflect the preferences of well-organized interest groups. In regions with great social and environmental diversity, reliance on the two conventional systems of resource allocation—markets and government regulation—may not provide the best approach to environmental management. Other forms of social organization may also need to contribute.

Social norms and environmental performance. In recent development research, attention has shifted from transactional arrangements (markets, regulatory instruments, and the like) to the social and institutional foundations of efficient transactions. Students of economic development are paying closer attention to social capital—to the relationships and informal institutions that support successful developing communities. Legal scholars are giving more attention to the strong complementarity between informal behavioral norms and formal rules in successful governance. Environmental researchers are identifying similar patterns in local regulation of environmental damage. Formal and informal regulatory mechanisms almost always coexist, with the latter often dominating in developing countries where the former are weak.

The recent literature on pollution control contains many accounts of how industrial plants respond to community pressure. In some instances plants reduce their emissions by installing new treatment facilities. In others they compensate the community indirectly by providing drinking water or new facilities, such as temples and community halls. In still others they refuse to address pollution, especially when the source is not clearly identifiable. Polluters will be more responsive if their environmental reputation has market value, or if enhanced perception of risk causes their asset values or credit ratings to be downgraded in financial markets.

Innovative environmental policies now stress the complementary roles of communities, markets, and governments in disseminating information on pollution abatement and creating incentives for it. Policymakers are learning that pressure groups can complement regulation. The public may know that a given industry discharges pollutants into the environment, but it rarely knows how much each factory is discharging. It is the second piece of information that, when disclosed, puts pressure on the firm and gives it an incentive to comply with pollution standards. Box 7.3 showed how Indonesia has enhanced self-regulation through a program for rating and disclosing the environmental performance of large polluters. Recent research on Argentina, Chile, Mexico, and the Philippines has shown that their capital markets reward good environmental performance (Box 7.8).

Recent experience in Ciudad Juárez, Mexico, also shows that information and community pressure can reduce pollution even by small, informal enterprises (Box 7.9). The common failure to regulate such enterprises has been attributed to high marginal abatement costs, the inability of firms employing mostly low-skilled labor to adapt nimbly, and the need to sell homogeneous products in highly competitive markets. But Ciudad Juárez suggests that inappropriate institutional and informational arrangements deserve more of the blame.

In some cases the transition to sustainable environmental management may depend not so much on the availability of knowledge about appropriate technology, but on the right way of disseminating it. Community mechanisms, based on communication among different social strata and age groups, can provide innovative solutions (Box 7.10).

Local ecological information. In rural areas especially, local communities are both the source of key environmental information and the custodians of traditional environmental know-how. Local residents, the primary con-

Box 7.8

Information and pollution control incentives from capital markets

In the traditional regulatory model, profit-maximizing firms control pollution to the point where the rising marginal cost of abatement balances the expected incremental penalty for noncompliance. Yet polluters often control emissions even when expected regulatory penalties are very low. Regulation is clearly not the only incentive for pollution control, and recent research points to capital markets as having unrecognized potential here. They create incentives for pollution control when they revise their judgments about firms' value in response to favorable or unfavorable information about their environmental performance.

The impact of firm-specific environmental news on market value works through various channels. Reports of high levels of emissions by a firm can signal to investors the inefficiency of its production processes. They can also invite stricter scrutiny by regulators, environmental groups, and the polluter's neighbors. And they can result in a loss of reputation among environmentally conscious consumers. All these changes may impose costs on the firm and lower its expected stream of profits and thus its share price. In the same way, announcing good environmental performance or investments in cleaner technologies can enhance expected profits.

Recently a World Bank team studied the reaction of stock markets in Argentina, Chile, Mexico, and the Philippines to news about environmental performance. None of the four countries has a strong record of enforcing environmental regulations. Yet a firm's share price was found to rise by an average of 20 percent when its good environmental performance was publicly recognized by the authorities, and to fall from 4 to 15 percent in response to publicized citizens' complaints about pollution.

These results suggest that global capital markets are using information about environmental performance, and that financial decisions are an important missing link in explaining polluters' behavior. Public provision of reliable information about environmental performance can thus influence polluters indirectly, through financial markets, even when it is difficult to confront them directly, through formal regulation.

duit for fundamental data on forest ecology and use, are thus a basic link in network-based approaches to the study and analysis of deforestation (see Box 7.6). In the effort to protect biodiversity, taxonomic information is important for establishing priorities, determining baselines against which to measure the effectiveness of conservation efforts, and guiding screening and other activities to identify genetic traits of indigenous species that may be of use in developing new drugs or improved plant varieties.

Box 7.9

Information, community pressure, and adoption of clean technology in Ciudad Juárez, Mexico

From an environmental perspective, there are good reasons to assume the worst about small plants in pollution-intensive industries. Many unlicensed microenterprises operate with unskilled labor in highly competitive markets, so it seems likely that they would be either unwilling or unable to control pollution effectively. Take Mexico's 20,000 small, traditional brick kilns. Fired with highly polluting cheap fuels, such as used tires, garbage, used motor oil, and wood scrap, these kilns are a leading source of air pollution in many cities, and an especially serious health hazard to those who happen to live near brickmaking *colonias*. But regulating them by conventional means would appear impossible.

Traditional brickmaking typifies labor-intensive, low-technology production in the urban informal sector. The four main tasks—mixing earth and clay, molding the mixture into bricks, drying the bricks in the sun, and firing them in a primitive adobe kiln—are all performed by hand. The average kiln employs six workers and generates about $100 a month in profits. Most brickmakers live next to their kilns in rudimentary houses with no sewers or running water. The average kiln owner has three years of schooling, and about a quarter are illiterate.

In the early 1990s a coalition led by a private association, Federación Mexicana de Asociaciones Privadas (FEMAP), began introducing clean-burning propane into the brickmaking *colonias* of Ciudad Juárez. This amounted to significant technological change, not just simple fuel switching, because it involved substantial fixed costs: transactions costs, learning costs, costs of procuring propane burners, and costs to mod-

ify the kilns to withstand higher temperatures. Other obstacles included the brickmakers' financing constraints, their lack of appreciation of the health damage caused by burning debris, the economic attraction of cheap but dirty fuels, and a virtual absence of formal regulatory pressure. Nevertheless, by late 1993 between 40 and 70 percent of the 300 or so brickmakers in Ciudad Juárez had adopted propane as their primary fuel.

How did FEMAP defy the conventional wisdom? A research team at Resources for the Future, a U.S.-based, nonprofit environmental organization, identified three keys to its success. First, it provided appropriate information: local universities set up training programs for kiln operators and educated them and the surrounding communities about the health threat. Second, the propane company encouraged kiln operators to switch by providing free access to all the needed combustion equipment except the burner itself. Third, project organizers worked with leaders of local trade and community organizations to pressure brickmakers to adopt propane.

Ciudad Juárez's experience shows both the promise and the limits of informal regulation. In the early 1990s, with propane only about half again as costly as debris, the FEMAP initiative induced widespread adoption of a cleaner technology by informal sector polluters. But the recent elimination of fuel subsidies by the Mexican government has dramatically increased the price of propane relative to debris. Faced with this additional change in incentives, most of the kiln operators reverted to traditional fuels. Powerful though it may be, informal regulation has not repealed the laws of economics.

Costa Rica is experimenting with the direct involvement of local people in developing its biodiversity inventory of the country's wild lands. By combining local traditional knowledge with basic formal training in taxonomy, Costa Rica's INBio (Instituto Nacional de Biodiversidad) is developing a new profession, that of the parataxonomist, responsible for the basic field work for the inventory. Not merely a collector, the parataxonomist is also the initial cataloguer of specimens and a more immediate link to the communities in and around Costa Rica's wild lands.

Sustainable agriculture. In many parts of the developing world, new market opportunities offered by global economic integration, often coupled with subsidization of inputs, give incentives to commercial farmers to pursue short-term increases in yields through the use of agrochemicals or wasteful use of water. Meanwhile, credit-constrained subsistence farmers, often displaced from more fertile areas toward the agricultural frontier, are forced to convert wilderness areas to cultivation and cannot invest in soil-conserving techniques. In both cases the appropriate generation, dissemination, and use of knowledge on sustainable farming practices are essential. Knowledge-

intensive agriculture has important direct and indirect roles in conserving natural resources. Sustainable intensification of agriculture through biotechnology and integrated pest and nutrient management contributes to the conservation of resources in existing cultivated areas. It also helps reduce pressure to convert forests and other wild habitats to new production.

Governments in many developing countries are considering complementary approaches to traditional public extension schemes, to encourage technological progress in rural areas. Communities may have important skills for adapting general principles of agricultural sustainability to local conditions, and they are often effective transmitters of knowledge. A small group of trained farmers may inspire more trust than outside extension officials and thus have a better chance to promote innovations. They also provide efficient feedback to professional extensionists on the successes and failures of new technologies (see Box 7.4).

Ecolabeling. Consumers in high-income economies tend to be relatively sensitive to the environmental pedigree of the goods and services they buy, whether produced domestically or imported. If consumers can be provided with credible information on the "greenness" of their purchases, the powerful market incentives that result can induce producers to switch to environmentally friendly products and processes. For this to work, however, it is not enough for a given market to be environment-friendly. Mechanisms are needed to convey information about the actual practices that producers are following.

Consumers may be less interested in the certification of products with environmental impacts far back in the production chain. But for products with more discernible health benefits, such as organically farmed vegetables, new, ecolabeling-based markets seem more promising. In Canada food retailers and organic producers alike believe that a solid niche market of 10 to 15 percent could exist for organic products by 2000.

Developing countries seeking to tap new markets created by ecolabeling must meet three main requirements. First, internationally recognized standards of certification have to be established and promoted. For this international NGOs have to help in mobilizing the needed technical, financial, and consensus-oriented political resources. Second, a network of private independent certifiers needs to be encouraged at the country level, and the potential for governments to monitor compliance with internationally recognized standards needs to be explored. Third, national and local NGOs—in partnership with the private sector, and supported as necessary by funding from foundations or development agencies—have to disseminate information about "green" market opportunities and knowledge of sustainable production technologies to developing-country producers.

International cooperation

Solving environmental problems that reach across national boundaries requires international cooperation. The most successful approach thus far to limiting acid deposition in Europe has been through a European Acid Rain agreement. Similarly, the Vienna Convention and its associated protocols have been essential in protecting the ozone layer.

Collaboration on transboundary problems (discussed more fully in Chapter 9) is in many respects more difficult than dealing with local ones. Objective information about compliance with international agreements can be hard to come by, as the costs of global monitoring are often high, and many international treaties rely on a system of self-monitoring whereby each signatory reports on compliance in its own territory. More important, institutional mechanisms to compel sovereign states to comply with environmental regulation generally do not exist internationally. Although in some instances countries agree to act for the common good, successful international environmental agreements generally have to be in the self-interest of all participating parties.

Economic theory casts some doubt on the feasibility of such arrangements. Even when collaboration is beneficial

Box 7.10

Disseminating knowledge on sustainable irrigation in Brazil

In many countries the irrigation sector is the largest water user, accounting for up to 80 percent of consumption. It is also a wasteful user, because of poorly maintained infrastructure, inefficient technology, and negligent management. Low-value crops are often grown with expensive irrigation water that could be put to better use on higher-value crops or outside agriculture altogether. In addition to the high cost to governments of subsidizing irrigation systems, widespread irrigation contributes to drainage and salinization problems and groundwater pollution, and thus to the abandonment of formerly fertile land.

Often the problem is that knowledge about appropriate technology is likewise inefficiently distributed. A counter-example comes from a World Bank project in the Formosa irrigation district in Brazil's northeastern state of Bahia. When the project started, farmers in the local water user association were reluctant to adopt efficient water management options, such as water-saving sprinkler systems and higher-value crops. Water charges did not cover operation and maintenance costs, and the system was unsustainable.

In 1995 an analysis of the reasons for the limited interest in change led to an emphasis on involving the farmers' children, and thus to Projeto Amanhã (Project Tomorrow). A vocational school was founded to teach the younger generation about better irrigation, new agricultural techniques, and plant nursery management. With 120 students per class, the school has expanded to offer classes on sewing, furniture building, and beef and poultry production. Students also learn how to run sawmills and repair tractors. The school has 100 hectares of land planted with high-value crops for educational purposes. With the revenues from all these activities, it is self-sufficient.

The school has turned the project around. The water user association, which administers Projeto Amanhã, now has both older and younger members and is recovering between 80 and 100 percent of the irrigation district's operation and maintenance costs. The young people have convinced their parents to try new technologies and to plant high-value crops. One 1996 graduate reported that, before the project, his mother and eight siblings had barely survived by planting beans on their 15-hectare plot. Now he has started to grow high-value mangoes, bananas, and passionfruit, in the process increasing his family's net annual income 30-fold, from about $400 to $12,000.

to all countries, it is usually even more attractive for countries to free-ride on agreements undertaken by others. Moreover, there is some evidence that international cooperation may be most likely where it is least needed—where unilateral action by countries would have gone a long way toward solving the problem anyway. The high transactions costs of multiparty negotiations are another impediment.

With modern monitoring and communications tools reducing transactions costs, and with international trade strengthening the economic links between countries, the number of regional and international environmental agreements has been growing in recent years. Cooperative efforts are under way to protect the Red Sea, the Aral Sea, and Lake Victoria. True, not all international environmental agreements have been successful. But several examples—such as the Vienna Convention—suggest it is not impossible to overcome the incentives for countries to free-ride. The challenge is to design—through side payments, fostering of global markets, or other incentives—agreements in which participation and continuing compliance are in the interest of all parties.

• • •

This chapter has identified two main issues in the relationships linking knowledge, information, and environmental management. The first concerns the role of knowledge and information in identifying environmental problems and solutions. Environmental degradation is the result of a complex pattern of market, policy, and information failures. And although policymakers, industries, and the public are growing more aware of the seriousness of environmental problems, better understanding their causes, and identifying solutions, important knowledge gaps and information barriers remain.

To get environmental concerns into the mainstream of development efforts, the coherent and systematic measurement of environmental quality and its integration with indicators of social welfare are essential. Good progress has been made in the construction and use of environmental indicators and in devising greener national accounting aggregates. But attempts to measure sustainable development—with indicators that tightly link economic and environmental phenomena—are still in their infancy. And more work is needed to show how (and how much) a better quantitative understanding of sustainable development can affect economic policy.

Use of these environmental indicators must proceed down from the macro level to sectors and projects. At the sectoral level this means more strategic environmental assessments: comprehensive analyses of the environmental implications of policies, strategies, and programs for a given sector or geographic area (such as an urban area, coastal zone, or watershed). At the project level a broad toolkit of instruments is needed to ensure that investment projects are environmentally sound.

The second issue concerns institutions: what forms of social organization are best suited to deal with different environmental problems? Promising new approaches to informationally efficient environmental management are starting to emerge, supported by the information revolution, which increases transparency, allows the involvement of broader groups of better-informed stakeholders, and generally reduces the transactions costs of monitoring and trading environmental commodities. At the core of today's environmental agenda is identifying creative ways of combining markets, governments, and civil societies to promote efficient mechanisms for the generation, diffusion, and use of sound environmental knowledge.

Chapter 8

Addressing Information Problems That Hurt the Poor

THE SEARCH FOR BETTER WAYS to enable the poor to improve their lives is at the heart of every chapter of this Report. Part One investigated how poor countries could narrow the knowledge gap separating them from more technologically advanced countries by improving the ways they acquire, absorb, and communicate knowledge. Part Two has so far examined how to address information problems in finance and the environment, both of which profoundly affect the well-being of poor people. This chapter focuses on specific information problems that affect the poor and describes how governments and international development institutions can work with poor people to address these problems. These efforts will make it easier for people to lift themselves out of poverty.

Nearly 1.3 billion people, about one-quarter of the world's population, live on the equivalent of about $1 a day or less at 1985 international prices, or roughly the equivalent of $1.50 a day at 1997 prices in the United States. Most of the world's poor live in East and South Asia (Figure 8.1). Nearly 3 billion people, roughly half of world population, subsist on the scarcely more generous figure of $3 a day at 1997 U.S. prices.

Can working with the poor to address information failures really make a dent in a global poverty problem of such overwhelming proportions? No one knows for sure. Even so, many countries have promising initiatives under way to address the information problems that most hurt the poor. This chapter describes a few of these initiatives and the problems they address, in the hope of inspiring others to find new ways of helping the poor.

The chapter begins by recalling that listening to the poor is fundamental to all efforts to reduce poverty, and es-

pecially important in addressing information problems. Next, the chapter considers how mechanisms for aggregating and disseminating information are inadequate for giving poor people access to credit and insurance, why this lack of access is damaging to the poor, and what can be done to address such problems. Recognizing that the information problems that hinder credit and insurance will persist no matter what is done to address them, the chapter also considers other measures that can help, such as savings programs for the poor and self-selecting safety nets. And because poverty is multifaceted, the chapter concludes by highlighting the benefits from coordinating the efforts of all agencies and NGOs addressing those many facets.

Listening to the poor

Effective communication involves listening as well as talking—a simple truth too often overlooked in development work. People who work for donor governments, multilateral institutions, and developing-country governments recognize that there is much knowledge that the poor do not possess. But in their eagerness to give them this knowledge, they forget that the poor know a great deal that they do not. Like all people, the poor know their own circumstances, their own needs, and their own worries and aspirations better than anybody. They often have information about where they live—whether savanna or slum—that is not readily apparent to outsiders.

Listening to the poor means more than simply showing up and asking what is on their minds—although this, too, can be worthwhile. It means giving the poor the means to speak, through schooling and communications. It means learning systematically from household surveys and other

Figure 8.1

Poverty by developing region

The world's poor are concentrated in East and South Asia.

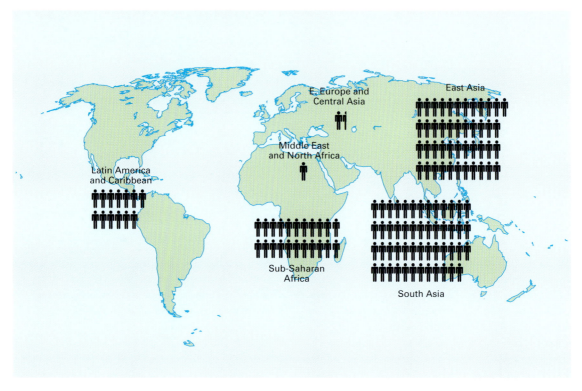

Note: Each figure represents 10 million persons living on $1 a day or less at 1985 international prices. Source: World Bank 1998d.

instruments and incorporating what is learned in the design of policy. It also means involving beneficiaries in project design and implementation. By listening, and by responding in ways that show that they have heard, donors and governments alike increase the odds that they will earn the trust of those they are trying to help. Trust is important to the poor as they select, apply, and adapt the knowledge most appropriate to their circumstances. Here we consider four aspects of listening to the poor: giving the poor voice, learning about the poor from the poor, communicating through local channels, and providing the information the poor need.

Giving the poor voice

Part One showed in detail the importance of education and telecommunications in closing the knowledge gap between and within countries, focusing on how poor countries and poor people obtain the knowledge they lack. Here we merely spotlight that the benefits of education and telecommunications are not limited to the knowledge

received. A girl who learns to read also learns to write—even if only to fill out a job application form—and that increases her ability to speak on her own behalf. Similarly, a poor person with access to a telephone can get advice from a doctor or a veterinarian—or complain to authorities about the poor quality of health services or the venality of the local irrigation officials. An important part of listening to the poor, then, is ensuring that the poor have the means to speak for themselves.

As Chapter 3 emphasized, education is critical in helping the poor absorb knowledge. One important reason why children from poor households are much less likely to enroll in school and stay there is that many poor parents are illiterate. Lacking education, they are ill equipped to understand its value and therefore less likely than other parents to sacrifice for their children's education. Here government support for education can be especially important.

But education is also important for giving voice to the poor. As people learn, they become more aware of their own circumstances and compare them against possible alternatives. They also discover ways to overcome the obstacles they face. With this awareness comes the ability to articulate concerns and desires, to make suggestions, to voice complaints. For example, in China, where concern is mounting over deteriorating environmental conditions, complaints about air pollution are much more frequent in provinces with higher literacy rates, even after income and air quality are held constant. Researchers estimate that an increase in a province's literacy rate from 60 percent to 84 percent would almost double the number of complaints, from 7.5 to 13.9 per 100,000 people.

This finding strengthens the rationale for public action to ensure that the poor have access to education. The policies for improving enrollments and educational quality discussed in Chapter 3 have enormous implications for the poor. They include targeting education subsidies and programs to those with few or illiquid resources; to mothers, who are the parent more likely to influence a child's education; and to basic education. They also include innovative management, such as stimulating community and parental oversight of schools even in poor areas and fostering lifelong education.

Access to telecommunications—especially telephones, e-mail, and the Internet—can also strengthen the voice of the poor, whether in marketing village handicrafts or in advocating policies that address their needs. Chapter 4 offered some striking examples: the use of e-mail by a small business loan program in Vietnam, the Panamanian women who posted pictures of their handicrafts on the Web, the subsistence farmers in the Philippines who became pineapple specialists thanks to telex and fax machines, the farmer's associations in Mexico that used computers to monitor their rural credit program, the small farmers in Sri Lanka who used the new telephone service to get current information on fruit prices.

New technology has made possible the rapid expansion of telecommunications networks. And private competition, with appropriate government regulation and incentives, provides a means of rapidly extending cheaper telecommunications to isolated communities. Chapter 4 showed how such competition is lowering costs and increasing the availability of telecommunications in Ghana, and how auctions of subsidies are making it attractive to provide pay phones in poor, remote regions in Chile.

Not surprisingly, poor people spend less on acquiring knowledge than other people do. What is perhaps surprising is that they spend even less on some knowledge goods, such as radios, telephones, newspapers, and books, than their lower incomes would suggest. The reason is that the poor must devote a much larger share of their more limited income on food, shelter, and other survival essentials. In Bulgaria and South Africa, household surveys show that the poor spend a smaller share of their income on

newspapers and (in Bulgaria) books than do the nonpoor (Figure 8.2). Illiteracy is part of the reason, of course. This is unfortunate, because basic education and access to media can have powerful effects (Box 8.1). But even for means of communication that do not require literacy, such as telephones and radios, the poor are at a disadvantage: ownership per capita of radios is much lower among the poor (Figure 8.2). Policies to improve literacy (Chapter 3) and increase poor people's access to media and telecommunications (Chapter 4) will help redress this imbalance.

Learning about poor people—from poor people
Learning about the poor often involves systematic learning through household surveys and other instruments. At other times it involves being available and quiet, so that the poor, not used to being heard from, recognize that rare opportunity to make their views known.

A 1988 living standards survey of households in Jamaica revealed some surprising information about two programs designed to help the poor: subsidies for basic foodstuffs, and food stamps for low-income households. Health clinics were the primary channel for identifying food stamp beneficiaries. Although policymakers were worried at first that malnourished children were not being brought to the clinics, the survey found that food stamps targeted to low-income households were much more effective than general subsidies for basic foodstuffs in reaching the poor (Figure 8.3). Ninety-four percent of malnourished children were visiting clinics, validating the design of the program.

Quantitative techniques are enriched when complemented by qualitative methods of listening to the poor. For example, one promising approach to learning from the poor is the beneficiary assessments that the World Bank uses in its social fund projects, in which communities receive funding for projects they themselves have selected. Initially applied early in the project cycle to identify the priorities of the poor, the assessments are now also a feature of project monitoring and evaluation.

In Zambia the first such assessments from project beneficiaries came from village officials, who gave high ratings to some parts of projects for addressing their priorities. Other beneficiaries, however, knew little about what was being proposed and gave them low ratings. This disparity led the project teams to look more into the politics and power structures of the communities involved. To incorporate the views of the poor, the teams established open consultations in public village meetings. All those taking part signed the minutes, which were posted in community centers. Over time, detailed field manuals were developed and community project committees strengthened. In a recent assessment, the beneficiaries gave 9 of 10 projects high ratings for responding to their needs.

Figure 8.2

Share of the poor in consumption of knowledge goods in Bulgaria and South Africa

The poor consume less than their share of knowledge goods.

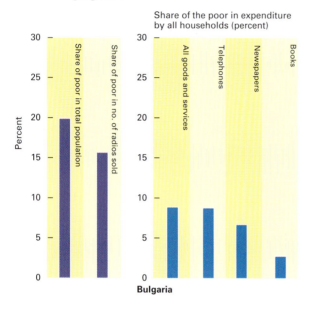

Bulgaria

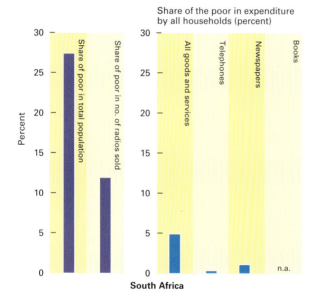

South Africa

n.a. Not available

Note: Data for Bulgaria are from a 1995 survey of 2,500 households; data for South Africa are from a 1993 survey of 9,000 households. Data in the two righthand charts are shares of monthly expenditure on the indicated good. Source: World Bank, various years.

Box 8.1

Education and the mass media: A powerful combination

Recent evidence points to the power of the joint impact of education and the media. Many studies have shown that mothers' education has a strong, positive effect on child health, but very little is known about how this effect is achieved. Recent work indicates that a mother's education improves child health by increasing the mother's ability to obtain and process information.

Using 1986 data from northeastern Brazil, one study found that parents who regularly made use of mass media, for example who read a newspaper, had healthier children (as measured by height for age). In fact, when these variables are added to the analysis, a mother's years of schooling no longer have a significant independent effect on child height. One interpretation of this finding is that both maternal education and information are essential for improved child health: education is necessary for mothers to process information, but access to relevant information through the mass media is necessary for education to have an effect.

Another study on education and child health, this one for Morocco using survey data from 1990–91, reveals more about the nature of the information that mothers obtain. Mothers' basic health knowledge was found to have a direct effect on child health, and education and access to the media together were shown to be the vehicles for acquiring that knowledge.

Beneficiary participation in the design and implementation of projects is an important way to learn what the poor need. A study published in 1995 of 121 rural water supply projects in 49 countries found that 7 of every 10 projects succeeded when the intended beneficiaries took an active part in project design, but that only 1 in 10 succeeded when they did not. Government support for a participatory approach greatly enhanced the likelihood of participation—and of success. People were willing to offer their views and contribute their efforts when they believed that others would do the same. Whether they were afraid that others would get their say and that they themselves would not, or whether they were willing to make an effort only if everyone was going to do their share, makes little difference. Either way, the government nudged communities to a high degree of information sharing, participation, and community ownership, all of which contributed to project success.

Such local knowledge aside, the poor also sometimes have knowledge valuable to the rest of society. Recall from Chapter 2 how agricultural researchers in Colombia and Rwanda invited local women to choose which of several new bean varieties to plant in their fields, and how the yields from their selections outperformed those of the scientists by 60 to 90 percent.

The danger of failing to ask the right questions—and of not creating a venue for the poor to speak out—was brought home forcefully to the designers of a donor-funded irrigation program in Nepal. They had assumed that irrigation was entirely lacking, but a project delay luckily allowed the donor to discover that the farmers had already installed 85 fully functioning irrigation systems. It pays to listen.

Working through local channels and earning people's trust
Studies show repeatedly that people are strongly influenced by their peers, especially when it comes to adopting new ideas. This is likely to be especially true for the poor, given high illiteracy rates in many societies and a lack of resources to acquire knowledge through other means. People's tendency to learn from their peers makes it important, when working with the poor, to use traditional knowledge channels and to foster new ones.

Working through local groups has been effective in Kenya, where farmers have organized themselves into cooperatives to market their crops, obtain credit, and improve their farming techniques. The national extension program works through these cooperatives and sometimes directly with individual farmers. In a recent survey in seven Kenyan districts, 4 of every 10 farmers attributed their awareness of better practices to other farmers—but fewer than 3 in 10 to extension workers. Farmer-to-farmer communication was most important in the diffusion of simple practices, such as plant spacing, which most farmers adopted. Extension workers contributed more in the diffusion of more complex practices, such as pesticide use, adopted by only a small proportion of the farmers.

Group-centered extension seems particularly effective in diffusing information among female farmers: in the same Kenyan survey, 65 percent of female-headed households that had received extension advice, but only 55 percent of male-headed households, reported that the advice was highly applicable to their work. Group-centered extension programs thus need to be adapted in ways that are sensitive to the characteristics and knowledge of local farmer groups.

Peer influence was also strongly evident in an 11-year study of a family planning program in 70 Bangladeshi villages. Households in villages where contraception was already prevalent were significantly more likely to adopt contraception. Moreover, Hindus tended to be influenced only by fellow Hindus, and Muslims only by Muslims.

Simply involving local groups and individuals is not enough for effective dissemination, however. It takes winning the trust of the community—and that takes time (Box 8.2). Given the importance of trust, it is not surpris-

Figure 8.3

Distribution of welfare benefits by household income in Jamaica

Food stamps found their way to Jamaica's poor better than did subsidies.

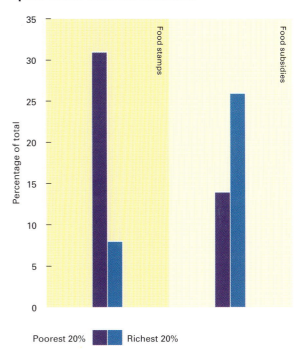

Note: Data are for 1989. Source: Grosh 1992.

ing that the diffusion of knowledge appears to be faster in villages where the social network is more densely knit.

To measure the density and importance of social connections in rural Tanzania in 1995, researchers asked households to list the groups they belonged to: churches, mosques, burial societies, credit associations, political organizations. They then constructed an index of social capital incorporating various aspects of membership: whether it was voluntary or restricted, the transparency of decisionmaking, and the effectiveness of the group. Villages rich in social capital had higher incomes than those with little. They were also much more likely to use fertilizer, agrochemical inputs, and improved seeds.

These examples confirm that learning about the poor and earning their trust require listening. Precisely because the poor have fewer opportunities to voice their concerns than others, and because information failures hurt them more than others, governments and other organizations that seek to assist the poor have a special obligation to listen well. The power to do good—or to do inadvertent harm—is immense.

Box 8.2

Trust and health services in Brazil's Ceará State

Ceará is one of Brazil's poorest states, with a third of its people in extreme poverty. To serve them, a preventive health program begun in the late 1980s hired 7,300 workers (mostly women) as community health agents at the minimum wage, and 235 nurses to supervise them. The government recruited people already concerned about community health and reinforced their dedication by giving them varied tasks as well as responsibility for results. This engendered a more client-centered and problem-solving approach to service delivery. The agents also made building trust part of their job. Their efforts were supported by a sustained media campaign to promote the program in newspapers, radio, and television. The government also awarded prizes for outstanding performance and invited dignitaries to visit communities producing results.

Gradually people came to trust the health workers. Mothers who formerly hid their children began to see the health agents as friends of the community. Within a few years, vaccination coverage for measles and polio in Ceará increased from 25 percent of children to 90 percent, and infant mortality rates declined from 102 per 1,000 live births to 65 per 1,000.

Providing knowledge the poor can use—in a manner they can use

The Overview began by noting that although knowledge has the potential to easily travel the world, it is not always used effectively. For example, millions of children the world around continue to die from diarrheal disease. Because diarrhea kills chiefly through dehydration, oral rehydration therapy can save millions of lives. The therapy involves having the child drink a simple solution that can be made at home from salt, sugar, and water, or by adding water to a commercially manufactured packet containing these ingredients. With government subsidies, the packets typically cost a few cents a dose. Yet even this rather simple technology has not always been delivered in a form the poor can use. Listening to the poor and considering what would work best for them from the outset could save many more lives.

An international campaign to reduce infant and child mortality by promoting oral rehydration therapy has indeed saved the lives of millions of children. But the remedy, despite its promise, is not consistently accessible to all. For very poor households the cumulative cost of oral rehydration packets becomes prohibitive if many bouts of illness must be treated. Similarly, many families do not have firewood to boil water, as previously required by some commercial solutions. Government subsidies to make the packets affordable have also proved a problem. When the

Arab Republic of Egypt's successful dissemination initiative discontinued subsidies in 1991, the rate of adoption plummeted. Households that could have used home remedies did not because commercial solutions had undermined confidence in them. Sadly, infant mortality saw a resurgence. Renewed efforts and support have since reversed some of the setbacks.

The approach taken by the United Nations Children's Fund (UNICEF) in Nepal shows the advantages of listening to the poor and providing knowledge the poor can use. In the early 1980s, deaths from diarrhea-induced dehydration were rising steadily among Nepalese children. Many of the more than 45,000 children who died each year could have been saved through oral rehydration therapy, but only 2 percent of Nepalese households were familiar with it. Because ready-made packets were scarce, the UNICEF program, initiated in the mid-1980s, promoted homemade solutions rather than the commercial alternative. But the promotional material described the treatment in words that applied to both. Rather than depress sales of ready-made packets, the program added to their credibility and increased local demand for them. And with more knowledge of what is involved in the cure, local communities are better able to sustain their use of some form of oral rehydration. The outreach program, having reached 96 percent of the population, helped more than halve the incidence of diarrhea-related child mortality.

The importance of providing knowledge that the poor can use, in a manner in which they can use it, can also be seen in AIDS prevention. Scientists know how the disease is spread and the precautions to be taken. But this information becomes useful to the poor only if those who would share it take time to listen to them, to understand local conditions, and to work with local leaders to develop prevention programs suited to those conditions. The same is true of agricultural extension programs and of fresh approaches to resolving poor people's lack of access to credit and insurance.

Improving access to credit and insurance

The Overview described how farmers with smaller plots, and those who leased the land they worked, were among the last to adopt the new seeds and techniques of the green revolution. With access to neither credit nor insurance, and with few resources of their own to fall back on, poor farmers could ill afford to chance the new technology. They had little choice but to wait until others had shown the value of the advances.

This lack of access to credit and insurance, at the heart of many of the disadvantages the poor face, is the direct outgrowth of an information failure, as discussed in Chapter 5. Wealthy savers lack information about the poor, and so cannot lend to them with confidence. That means the poor can seldom borrow, or can borrow only at high interest rates. Similarly, insurers lack a reliable means of assessing the effort that a farmer puts into cultivating a crop. Pests and storms may be easily observed and documented, but a farmer's effort cannot. That makes it difficult for an insurance agent or court to discern what really led to the failure of an insured crop—and therefore difficult for farmers to obtain insurance.

The insufficiency of coping mechanisms

Inability to borrow or to obtain insurance limits poor people's ability to smooth consumption over time. To have a buffer against disaster, they must save either cash or grain that can be readily tapped in an emergency. Their lack of access to credit and insurance also means that the poor bear much more risk than others do. A study in rural southwestern China covering the period 1985–90 found that, for the poorest tenth of households, the loss of one year's income due to crop failure led on average to a 40 percent decline in consumption the following year—a devastating outcome. In contrast, for the richest third of households the average consumption decline following a crop failure was only 10 percent of their income—far more tolerable.

Given the risks that the poor must endure, they naturally seek to reduce their exposure. Often this means forgoing productive investments in a child's education, in a new piece of farm machinery, or in new seeds or fertilizer. A study from central India found that the choices that poorer households made to minimize risk—such as planting less of their land with new seed varieties—significantly reduced their income (Box 8.3). Lacking credit and insurance, the poor thus face a bitter tradeoff: accept risk that could lead to disastrous fluctuations in income, or minimize risk in ways that perpetuate poverty.

When hit by a drop in income, poor households often must pull their children out of school to work at home. A study of six villages in India showed that a 10 percent decline in income across agricultural seasons leads to a decline in school attendance of about five days. Because erratic school attendance means in the end less schooling, and thus lower productivity and income for these children when they grow up, this form of self-insurance perpetuates poverty. Efforts to expand educational opportunities for the poor may thus meet with limited success without better understanding of the risks and constraints the poor face. On the plus side, the development of rural financial markets—and of financial markets more generally—may prove an unexpected boon for the schooling of poor children.

To ensure their economic security, many poor people maintain a close relationship with some individual or network with reasons to trust them. They may join village groups, where they can obtain both credit and mutual insurance (Box 8.4). Share tenancy, credit contracts with

contingent repayment provisions, and long-term labor contracts can also provide some insurance. Yet another response is interlinked transactions, in which workers borrow from employers, or borrowers go to work for the local moneylender. In such systems, good knowledge of the attributes of friends, relatives, and neighbors verifies quality, and social sanctions rather than formal legal systems enforce repayment.

Although useful and at times ingenious, these coping mechanisms are typically less effective than more formal

Box 8.3

Why are poor farmers slow to adopt new technologies?

New agricultural technologies are continually being developed and promoted. Recent innovations include improved, high-yielding varieties of staple grains such as sorghum and rice. The new technologies offer farmers greater expected yields and profits than traditional practices, but the innovations have often been adopted slowly, especially by the poor, because poor farmers cannot insure against risk.

Households can offset fluctuations in income through such coping mechanisms as loans, asset sales, grain storage, and transfers from family and neighbors. This enables them to maintain a more stable level of consumption despite fluctuating income. When households cannot smooth their consumption through these mechanisms, as often the poor cannot, they smooth their income instead by avoiding risky, but on average more profitable, opportunities.

How does income smoothing affect farming decisions? Using data collected by the International Crops Research Institute for the Semi-Arid Tropics (ICRISAT), in central India, one study found a positive correlation between consumption smoothing and risk taking. For instance, small farmers—a group with limited capacity to smooth consumption—planted only about 9 percent of their land with relatively risky, high-yielding varieties, whereas large farmers with better access to coping mechanisms planted about 36 percent with high-yielding seeds.

Another study based on the ICRISAT data shows that farmers who are poor and living in riskier environments choose a safer but less profitable portfolio of assets. In particular, for farmers in the poorest quartile of the wealth distribution, a reduction in a key source of risk (variation in the timing of the monsoon) by one standard deviation would lead to changes in investment behavior that would raise profits by up to 35 percent. But the same reduction in risk would have virtually no effect on the investment behavior of the wealthiest households: thanks to their ability to smooth consumption, risk was less of a problem for them. Since the poorest households are least able to smooth consumption, they are the ones that rely most on income smoothing in the face of risk, even if the cost is sharply reduced farm profits and having to forgo improved technologies.

Box 8.4

Mutual insurance

Islamic law prohibits charging interest on loans and even the setting of fixed repayment periods. In the words of the Koran, if a debtor is in trouble, there should be postponement to the time of ease. Clearly this dampens the incentive to lend, so how do Muslim households cope?

Data from four Muslim villages near Zaria, in northern Nigeria, from 1988–89, show the importance of interhousehold insurance against income shortfalls. Of 400 households, only a tenth reported not having engaged in any borrowing or lending over the survey period, whereas more than half had both borrowed and lent. Loans were made within tightly knit groups whose members had almost perfect information about each other's needs, activities, and circumstances. Almost all lending was between inhabitants of the same village or between relatives. The loans were very informal, based purely on trust, with no written contract. Repayment was enforced by the threat of exclusion from future borrowing. Indeed, lenders regarded only 1 loan in 20 to be in default.

But what happens when drought afflicts an entire village? When everyone is in trouble, who can afford to forbear? More than half the variation (58 percent) in agricultural output in the region was caused by such aggregate shocks. Although there appeared to be no direct outside lending in the northern Nigeria study, funds did flow between villages through networks and connections with outsiders—here the established Hausa tradition of long-distance trading plays a key role. Such loans between villages are nevertheless far less prevalent than loans within them.

credit and insurance arrangements. Evidence suggests that mutual insurance and kinship networks, because they are restricted to small communities and groups, do not fully insure the poor against an economic shock, especially when that shock affects a whole village or community. So unless credit and insurance choices for the poor can be improved, income inequality and inequitable growth will persist.

Government responses to imperfect credit and insurance markets

Information failures prevent the poor from enjoying full access to credit and insurance, and the adjustments they make to compensate can be costly. Government policies can respond to these problems in three main ways:

- By dealing with underlying asset problems of the poor, for example by improving the distribution of land and strengthening the legal institutions needed for collateral, thus bypassing the need for information

- By establishing institutions that directly address information problems, for example through peer monitoring in microcredit, and
- By recognizing that credit and insurance markets will always be imperfect, and developing complementary programs in other areas to help the poor finance themselves, for example through well-targeted savings programs, safety nets, and education subsidies.

Dealing with fundamental problems that reduce the need for information. Land titling and registration programs increase the value of land as collateral, thus reducing lenders' enforcement costs. And by providing security of tenure, they create incentives to invest in land to increase its productivity. In Thailand one study found that farmers with title to their land who offer land as collateral could borrow more from financial institutions than farmers who lacked title—in the Lop Buri region 52 percent more. Economic outcomes were also far better among titled farmers. They invested more in their land, used more inputs such as irrigation and fertilizer, and obtained higher yields than untitled farmers. Similar evidence has been documented for other countries in Asia, Latin America, and the Caribbean.

But land titling does not always improve access to credit, especially for the poor. Two surveys of 250 farm households in rural Paraguay in the early 1990s concluded that titling provided better access to formal credit for farmers with 15 to 50 hectares of land, but had almost no impact for farmers with smaller parcels. Small farmers were squeezed out of formal credit markets even after receiving title to their land, perhaps because of the high transactions costs of small loans. So, if titling is to alleviate poverty, rural financial reform may be needed as well.

Land titling efforts have been even more disappointing in Africa. A 1993 study of 10 regions in Ghana, Kenya, and Rwanda found that land registration had no effect on access to credit. There land could not serve as collateral because there is no active market in land. Land titling in any case seldom supplants traditional land use rights based on custom, and conflicts between the two systems are frequent. And titling land to facilitate access to credit presumes that sources of institutional credit exist, but in the Africa study there were none.

Hence land reform and land titling, although effective in some instances, are no panacea. Other measures to improve the ability of the poor to pledge collateral—such as more transparent property laws, fewer restrictions on property transfers, and better court systems—can all make the few assets the poor have more usable as collateral. Even where such programs are effective, scope remains for innovative measures to directly address the information problems that limit poor people's access to credit.

Improving information flows among the poor. The best-known mechanisms for improving the flow of information among the poor, and their access to credit, are the group lending schemes for microcredit. These enable an outside lender to tap a source of information that poor people have in abundance: information about each other. Bangladesh's Grameen Bank, Bolivia's BancoSolidario (BancoSol), and similar microfinance programs have quieted skeptics with repayment rates well above 90 percent. Techniques include progressive lending, which start borrowers with very small pilot loans on which repayment installments begin immediately, and training for borrowers in the business of lending.

In Grameen Bank's group lending model, would-be borrowers first form groups of five. Although the loans go to individuals, all group members understand that if any member defaults, none will receive subsequent loans. This gives them an incentive to monitor each other's performance, increasing the probability of repayment. Since the groups form voluntarily, borrowers can use their knowledge of their neighbors to exclude the riskiest, thus mitigating another common problem for lenders.

Group lending also provides opportunities to learn how to gain access to credit markets. This is helpful because many Grameen clients have never borrowed from formal institutions. The group structure compensates for this by providing a way for members to enter credit relationships in the company of neighbors and to keep abreast of each other's ideas and progress. Weekly group meetings facilitate such learning. Myrada, a rural Indian NGO, employs a similar strategy but goes a step further in seeking to establish self-sustaining links between banks and the rural poor (Box 8.5).

In progressive lending, the small initial loans ($50 or less) build up to larger amounts over time. The first loans, although too small to be profitable to lenders, help them determine the creditworthiness of borrowers. They also give borrowers a low-risk opportunity to learn about lending arrangements and to develop strategies for larger loans. Estimates for BancoSol suggest that 10 to 15 percent of its small borrowers will default. Progressive lending allows bank staff to address credit problems while the amounts are small.

Most microfinance contracts, unlike conventional loans, require borrowers to start repaying soon after disbursement, usually well before investments bear fruit. Borrowers make payments in small, regular (typically weekly) installments until the principal and interest are fully paid. The arrangement alerts lenders to possible repayment problems early on. It also reduces risk for the lender in another way. Since borrowers must have other household income to begin repayment so soon after disbursement, meeting the repayment schedule signals to the lender that borrowers

Box 8.5

Addressing information problems to provide credit to the poor in southern India

In rural southern India an NGO called Myrada wants to put itself out of business in five years by forging links between bankers and the poor. To integrate its credit management groups (*sanghas*) into the commercial banking system, it requires sangha members to assume responsibility for maintaining their own financial records, for forming and enforcing their own lending rules, and for participating in regional organizations (called apex bodies) run by elected sanghas representatives.

The apex bodies teach members how to resolve disputes, select and train new members, and negotiate with commercial bankers for progressively larger loans. Most important, the apex bodies take on long-term management of the sanghas when Myrada staff leave. Myrada is thus a temporary broker for bankers and the poor. Its objective is to help the poor become "bank-friendly," and the banks more "poor-friendly."

Myrada's most mature project, in Holalkere, involves 214 sanghas and about 4,400 people. By mid-1996, three years after the apex bodies were granted full managerial oversight of the sanghas, 81 sanghas were meeting without Myrada's supervision and were receiving loans directly from commercial banks. Perhaps more important, the sanghas are now role models for neighboring villages, with at least three new ones having formed without any assistance from Myrada.

have an independent means to repay if projects do not fare as well as hoped. But early repayment also excludes the poorest households or increases their chance of default.

Externalities are associated with group lending schemes: those who bear the startup costs provide a social facility that benefits all who join. Since startup costs cannot easily be recouped, such schemes may be undersupplied. Thus there is a role for government to encourage the formation of such institutions. It should enable farmers to form groups by themselves, making use of existing self-help groups and grassroots organizations. Beyond providing the impetus for group formation, government may also provide management training, educate members about joint liability and loan recovery practices, provide extension services, and introduce accounting systems and loan evaluation procedures to ensure the success of group lending programs. Government can also play a role in disseminating information about successful group lending schemes.

Innovative measures to help the poor weather shortfalls

No matter how effective the efforts just described, information problems will persist, and the poor will continue to have a tough time getting credit and insurance. Governments can ease these problems through a variety of programs that help the poor weather unforeseen shortfalls in their income.

Savings schemes

One promising approach is in savings. Many observers have assumed that poor households cannot save, but mounting evidence suggests this is not true. The poor do save, but they often lack a secure and liquid vehicle for the small sums they can put aside. The benefits to poor households from improving savings mechanisms may turn out to be larger than those from trying to fix dysfunctional credit markets. One important advantage of these microsavings services is that they are not hampered by information problems.

Bank Rakyat Indonesia (BRI), which operates in rural villages through its Unit Desa program, shows the value of safe, convenient savings. The program started in the early 1980s with a focus on credit, but bank managers quickly realized that attracting deposits could reduce their capital costs while providing households a much-wanted means to build assets. Now the bank finds that many more households are interested in saving than in borrowing. By 1996 the program had attracted deposits from 16.1 million low-income households and lent to 2.5 million—a decade before, it had had no deposits. Many of the savings accounts are small, averaging less than $190, and the average depositor is much poorer than the average borrower.

Convenience, liquidity, and safety—the latter strengthened by BRI's being state-owned—tend to be more important for small savers than the going interest rate on deposits. BRI has also adopted novel ways of encouraging saving. For example, it holds a lottery with small monthly prizes as well as annual prizes such as motorcycles, cars, even houses. Depositors receive a free allotment of lottery numbers in proportion to their average balance over the month. The idea has been very popular, and Bolivia's BancoSol adopted it in 1993.

Targeted transfers

Because information problems in credit and insurance markets deprive the poor of opportunities to diffuse risk, basic social services should be publicly provided, at least to the very poor, who are least likely to be able to purchase credit and insurance. Well-targeted safety nets can also reduce the costly adjustments that the poor would otherwise have to make.

Short-term relief programs can expand income-generating opportunities for the poor, reduce inequality in asset-holdings over the long run, and reduce the need for later public action to alleviate poverty. After natural disaster struck a number of villages in India, public employment programs cushioned the effects on the poor. These programs, together with institutional credit, reduced distress sales of land by poor farmers whose crops had been devastated. In a village in Bangladesh, by contrast, there were no comparable measures to help the poor, and many distress sales occurred. That further polarized land ownership, aggravating inequalities in income and access to credit.

Targeting safety net programs, and government services more generally, is a serious challenge—and a classic information problem. How does the government find and identify the poor? After all, many of them live their lives far removed from the formal economy. And because they harbor a lifelong distrust of authority, many will not present themselves on the mere promise of public benefits. So they remain invisible. Meanwhile, the lure of government largesse attracts many who are not poor.

Means-testing, or restricting eligibility for relief to those meeting certain economic criteria, is a standard approach used in industrial countries to target the needy. But means-testing requires the government to evaluate applicants' claims about their incomes, and often about their assets and earning capacities. And to guard against fraud, information from the applicants must be cross-checked against information from other sources—lenders, other public agencies, potential employers. This can be a major administrative burden for a developing country—on top of the cost of the assistance itself.

One solution is to distribute assistance according to criteria that correlate with need but are easier to observe: for instance, to large families or the elderly (Box 8.6). Governments may also pool information from reputable nongovernmental sources, such as local charitable organizations or microfinance institutions. Giving people an incentive to report abuses is yet another way of working against willful exploitation of the system.

A second solution is self-selection: designing programs so that only the truly needy seek them out. Rather than rely on administrative discretion in selecting beneficiaries, many antipoverty programs can encourage self-selection by the poor. For example, if the wage rate is low enough in a workfare program, only poor jobseekers will participate, and they will move on to other jobs when they become available. A low wage rate can also allow benefits to be spread among more of the poor. A 1997 World Bank project in Argentina offered low-wage work on community projects in poor areas during a period of unusually high unemployment. More than half the participants were from the poorest 10 percent of the population.

Another means of encouraging self-selection improved the effectiveness of a food price subsidy program in Tunisia initiated in the early 1990s. Using information from

Box 8.6

Delivering pensions to the poor in South Africa

Direct cash transfers, in theory an efficient way of redistributing income and reducing poverty, are rarely used in developing countries, for two main reasons. First, determining who is most needy is often difficult, because much economic activity takes place in the informal sector, through exchanges in kind and through "off-the-books" cash transactions. Second, verifying the identity of those who collect payments is often difficult. South Africa has gotten around this problem by combining means-testing with an age threshold—age being a characteristic that is relatively easy to verify and, in rural South Africa, closely correlated with poverty.

The social pension system pays a fixed sum to women over 60 and men over 65 whose means (defined as the sum of their income and a value assigned to their assets) fall below a specified floor. The benefit is reduced for those whose means exceed the floor on a rand-for-rand basis; pensions are not paid to those whose income exceeds a specified ceiling.

To ensure that the payments are disbursed only to those who have qualified, program staff travel in vans equipped with automated teller machines that use fingerprint reading technology. They visit villages once a month, disbursing cash directly to qualified individuals and recording the transactions. The program, begun in 1993, reaches about 80 percent of elderly rural South Africans of African descent, and smaller proportions of elderly people in other racial groups. The program also reaches poor children: among families of African descent, one in three children lives in a household where an elderly person receives a means-tested pension.

household surveys that identified differences in consumption patterns of the poor and the nonpoor, the government designed and marketed, and then subsidized, certain foodstuffs that had the same nutritional value as nonsubsidized foods but were perceived as less desirable. For example, milk subsidies were shifted to reconstituted milk packaged in less convenient half-liter cartons; this discouraged consumption by the rich, who preferred local fresh milk in bottles. Cooking oil subsidies were shifted to a generic mixed oil product purchased from bulk oil drums, and away from varieties of pure olive and vegetable oil marketed to the rich and the middle class in brand-name bottles.

Self-targeting cannot be the only targeting mechanism for some kinds of programs, however. Cash transfers and highly subsidized student loans, for example, will appeal to many people, including the nonpoor. Such situations may require means-testing that includes some easily observable characteristic, as has been done with pensions in South Africa.

Coordinating efforts at poverty reduction

Because the poor face so many interrelated problems, a program that provides credit for income generation, but that does not help the poor evaluate investment opportunities and does not answer the need for training, will be less than fully effective. Similarly, an agency promoting such credit might be working at cross-purposes with an NGO trying to do the same. Hence the need not just to expand the scope of programs, but also to coordinate the efforts of the many organizations working to reduce poverty.

Indonesia's P4K program (whose name is the Indonesian abbreviation for a phrase meaning "guidance in increasing incomes for small farmers") builds on a partnership among the Ministry of Agriculture, Bank Rakyat Indonesia, and local governments to reduce poverty among more than 350,000 families. P4K is administered in 10 provinces by the Ministry of Agriculture's Agency for Agricultural Education and Training, with provincial managers and staff located in agricultural information centers. The key to the program's success lies in coordinating the different institutions so that each complements the others. The agency's field workers serve as contacts with the clients. Local governments help conduct socioeconomic surveys to identify poor villages. They then direct benefits to those with average annual incomes equivalent to less than 320 kilograms of rice per capita (about $80). BRI provides credit for income-generating activities through 40,000 self-help groups, which harness resources and facilities provided by the government and the private sector. The results: household incomes are up between 41 and 54 percent, and arrears on credit extended are as little as 2 percent of the total.

Microfinance institutions are beginning to tackle the interrelated problems of the poor. Some institutions lend only if borrowers agree to enter educational programs. Some use group meetings not just to collect payments and disburse loans but also to discuss legal rights and other business issues. And some, like the Grameen Bank, promote social development by fostering the opening of schools. Grameen's expansion has fueled rapid growth in the number of schools supported by groups of borrowers and in the number of children attending these schools (Figure 8.4).

Grameen's cellular phone enterprise typifies the expansion of its income-generating activities. Grameen Phone, a nationwide mobile telephone company, enables poor women in villages to purchase mobile telephones as economic investments. They then sell telephone services to whole villages or individual clients. The program offers a

Figure 8.4

Grameen Bank lending and schools run by Grameen Bank groups

As the Grameen Bank has expanded, so has its impact on education.

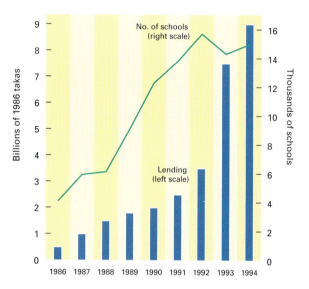

Note: Lending data are annual disbursements. Source: Khandker, Khalily, and Khan 1998.

credit, BRAC finds that its clients can build quickly on their new knowledge, making both the credit and the training component much more effective than either would be separately.

Today more than 10 million people borrow from microfinance programs worldwide, but the movement remains young. To push it along, several consortia link microfinance institutions, many of them small and dispersed, into a global network. In three of these consortia—Women's World Banking, the Microfinance Network, and the Consultative Group to Assist the Poorest—participants share experiences and technical assistance. Learning from success and from failure is being facilitated by access to the Internet, which is promoting the rapid and open exchange of news, opinions, and ideas among practitioners, academics, and development organizations around the world.

•   •   •

Poverty is multifaceted and often self-perpetuating. The poor lack education, adequate health care, access to credit, and such basic assets as land. Many of these problems are linked to each other and to both gaps in knowledge and imperfections in information, which force the poor into economic relationships that limit their productivity. Given the dire consequences of sudden income shocks, the poor naturally avoid risk where they can. But this locks them into a vicious cycle of low-risk, low-return activities that keeps them in poverty.

This vicious cycle can be broken: innovations have come from listening to the poor and adapting institutions to their needs. Land titling, microcredit, microsavings, and better safety nets make it possible, by addressing information problems, to assist the needy while minimizing fiscally burdensome benefits for those less deserving. These innovations will not end poverty overnight, nor are they a substitute for other policies to ensure sustainable, pro-poor growth. But they are crucial elements in a successful antipoverty strategy. And recognizing how information problems lead to market imperfections is a key step in designing realistic policies that will make it possible for the poor to improve their lives.

double benefit: the women gain an instrument of power, and the villages a connection to the marketplaces and business centers of the world.

Another multifaceted effort is the human rights and legal education program of the Bangladesh Rural Advancement Committee (BRAC). More than 250,000 clients, most of them women, have learned about their legal rights in business and family relationships, and many have taken steps to protest illegal divorces or to pursue their rightful claims to inheritances. BRAC also provides clients with training in growing vegetables, raising livestock, operating fisheries, producing silk, and engaging in environmentally sensitive forestry. By combining training with

Chapter 9

What Can International Institutions Do?

INTERNATIONAL INSTITUTIONS, COUNTRY DONORS, and the broader development community are rapidly coming to understand that knowledge is central to development—that knowledge *is* development. This entire Report implies roles for the World Bank and other international institutions in helping countries to close knowledge gaps and overcome information problems. These ideas should inform the lending and aid programs of these institutions, helping guide their project selection and design as well as their policy support activities. The development community can help countries develop the infrastructure and institutions they need to acquire and absorb knowledge, for example through supporting telecommunications projects and education reform (as discussed in Part One). It can also help them develop the institutional frameworks to minimize information problems, for example by improving laws against fraud, piloting community-monitored environmental projects, or working to improve access to credit for the poor (as considered in Part Two).

This chapter focuses on another set of roles that development institutions are taking on. With the recognition that knowledge is development, they are realigning their way of doing business and placing the creation, transfer, and management of knowledge at the center of their activities. Consider first the *creation* of knowledge. Chapter 1 introduced the idea of knowledge as a public good. Once placed in the public domain, it is free for others to use, and it can be disseminated widely at virtually no cost. This implies that people can often benefit from knowledge without paying the costs of creating it. Because the creators of knowledge cannot recoup their costs, the market will not supply enough knowledge, and gov-

ernments must decide whether to step in to finance its creation. In some instances, the spillover benefits of knowledge extend beyond national boundaries, so that no single government is willing to spend the resources to create it; even if it does make an effort, it will supply too little. International institutions can thus solve what might otherwise be a difficult problem of coordinating the actions of many countries to create knowledge that the world needs.

The green revolution is a case in point. Without an international effort, its breakthroughs in agriculture would not have occurred, or would have occurred only much later, leaving countless small-scale farmers and landless laborers destitute. Provision of such international public goods is a responsibility of international institutions and is the first topic addressed in this chapter.

Although knowledge created as an international public good can contribute to development, it is knowledge created in developing countries themselves that usually is most important. Every policy reform, every new program, every additional project creates new knowledge about what works and what doesn't work in development. But codifying this huge reservoir of knowledge and making it accessible is far from costless, and probably too enormous a labor for any one country to undertake. Another role for international institutions and other providers, then, is to help countries with the daunting task of sifting through international experience, extracting relevant knowledge, experimenting with it, and adapting it to local conditions. This two-way *exchange* of knowledge—from developing countries to development institutions and back again—is the topic of the chapter's second section.

That raises the question of how to manage knowledge, for knowledge created or adapted is only as good as the system that keeps it organized, accessible, and dynamic. Organizations have always managed knowledge, formally or informally, but new technologies offer formerly unimagined possibilities that require a rethinking of traditional systems. The third section of this chapter explores these possibilities for knowledge *management,* highlighting the choices that organizations must make and identifying some special challenges for development institutions. We also describe knowledge management efforts currently under way at the World Bank and plans to make relevant materials about development more widely available.

Knowledge creation: An international public good

Many types of knowledge are international public goods. No one country or private organization has the incentive to do the necessary research to create this knowledge, and international institutions can help fill this gap. Indeed, as already noted, most knowledge has the properties of a public good: there is no marginal cost to an additional person using the knowledge, and it is often difficult to exclude nonpaying users, which means that the private returns to knowledge creation may be low. Governments can and do act to protect some types of knowledge from uncompensated use by establishing intellectual property rights, which increase the returns to knowledge creation by making exclusion possible. But for some types of knowledge, such as basic research, exclusion is either impossible or has been deemed undesirable because the cost—the resulting underutilization of knowledge—would outweigh the benefit. These types of knowledge are an international public good, and their efficient supply requires international collective action. The need is even more acute when the knowledge is itself about the production of an international public good, such as how to protect the ozone layer or stem global warming.

International support for basic research

Agricultural knowledge is generally an international public good, and the Consultative Group for International Agricultural Research (CGIAR) is an outstanding example of how international institutions can act to provide such goods where other institutions, public or private, cannot. By researching higher-yielding varieties of staple crops for developing countries, the CGIAR was instrumental in sowing the seeds of the green revolution (see the Overview).

Formed in 1971, the CGIAR is an international research organization whose members include both industrial and developing countries as well as private foundations and international organizations. Its impact far exceeds its resources, especially in the development of new agricultural technologies that have raised crop yields and helped food production more than keep pace with global demand. Through its sponsorship of 16 international agricultural research centers, it has developed new, yield-enhancing crop varieties, helped alleviate the scourge of agricultural pests and disease, and trained thousands of plant scientists and research technicians. The benefit-cost ratios of the CGIAR's undertakings demonstrate its high returns: for example, those for its rice programs are 17 to 1, and those for its wheat programs an astounding 190 to 1.

Today, however, the CGIAR is having to redefine its role (Box 9.1). Stronger IPRs and new biotechnological methods broaden the scope for private research efforts. The risk is that the poor will not have access to these innovations.

Box 9.1

Plow ahead or prune back? The challenges facing the CGIAR

In the past decade or so, the CGIAR has expanded its research horizons to include environmental issues, forestry, and aquatic resources, because of the complexity of today's world and the intertwined relationship between agricultural and environmental concerns. The CGIAR seeks to improve the yield of complex farming systems in an environmentally positive manner. Yet with declining overseas development aid, the CGIAR, like many other development organizations, has had to reexamine its research priorities, retaining only those where it has clear comparative advantage. Despite these funding constraints, the CGIAR continues to work toward strengthening global food security and helping farmers meet the day-to-day challenges of keeping their environment healthy and their farming sustainable. In a world where 90 million new mouths must be fed every year and where national research systems in developing countries are still weak, the nature of agricultural research remains such that continuing, if not strengthened, international sponsorship and participation by the CGIAR and groups like it seems essential.

The CGIAR has to respond to new developments in the institutional environment for agricultural research. Changes in national agricultural and science policies, in the international trading system, and, most important, in the incentives for private research all point to a need for the CGIAR to continually reexamine its activities and strategy. Whether within countries or globally, the reinforcement of IPRs, both in genetic resources and in biotechnological methods, has whetted the appetite of private firms to undertake plant research, which could result in the poor losing access to innovations in these areas. Moreover, if private researchers discover and patent promising new biotechnological tools, the need for public research may diminish. The CGIAR is meeting these challenges by becoming more constructively engaged with private research, while maintaining its relationships with national agricultural research systems and advanced research institutes.

Engaging the private sector through market incentives

On many knowledge frontiers, the skewed distribution of global wealth implies that the strongest incentives for private research are for innovations that interest primarily the richer countries. These innovations may or may not be high priorities for poorer countries, particularly in the area of health research. Some major diseases—malaria and tuberculosis, for example—afflict poorer countries far more than they do richer ones. Research and development will not be adequately targeted to these diseases without international support. The treatments for some other diseases, such as AIDS, are beyond the means of the poor. For such diseases a special effort must be made to develop affordable remedies. Yet the World Health Organization has estimated that, in the early 1990s, 95 percent of health-related R&D was devoted to issues of concern primarily to the industrial countries, and only 5 percent to the health concerns of the far more populous developing world.

One international effort launched recently seeks to develop a vaccine for AIDS. Many believe that technical advances in creating a vaccine hold the world's best hope of checking the spread of this disease. A low-cost, effective AIDS vaccine would solve technical, political, and economic problems. And the mere possibility that interventions in favor of vaccine development could eventually result in the eradication of AIDS is enough to command consideration of such interventions by the global community.

If technical changes to combat AIDS were already moving rapidly in the right direction, there would be little justification for public action. But the evidence suggests that existing, market-based incentives are biased in favor of developing a profitable treatment for AIDS, and against developing an inexpensive vaccine to prevent it. The reason is that effective demand for new treatments is strong, coming from AIDS patients in high-income economies, whereas demand for a vaccine from those at high risk in developing countries is weak. The tragedy is that a vaccine promises far greater spillover benefits: by limiting the spread of AIDS, it protects even those who never purchase or use the vaccine. An ounce of prevention is thus still worth a pound of cure, but in this case the unequal distribution of global income distorts the terms of that trade.

The question of how to create the knowledge to produce an AIDS vaccine is thus an important one. One possibility is for a new international organization to try to acquire the requisite skills and do the necessary clinical trials. But these require huge investments, which the major pharmaceutical companies are the obvious candidates to make. So development institutions are looking into a new approach to encourage private pharmaceutical companies to undertake research relevant to developing countries (Box 9.2).

Fostering collective action

Another area of research with strong international public good dimensions is the environment. Here cross-border externalities are legion: political and administrative boundaries, both within and among nations, mean nothing to the forces of the biosphere. Such problems as climate change, loss of biodiversity, ozone depletion, and the pollution of international waters are local in origin but global in effect. Because the costs of poor environmental policies accrue to the world, no one country has the incentive to research effective strategies for protecting environmental health. Problems of coordination also arise: how to foster collective action by dozens of nations to solve major problems that affect them all, at times unequally.

Environmental problems are thus largely knowledge problems. And to solve them, the international community has taken action through such mechanisms as the Global Environment Facility (GEF), a unique example of global collective action (Box 9.3). The GEF tackles three major challenges. First, any meaningful assessment of the

Box 9.2

Can contingent lending spur efforts toward an AIDS vaccine?

The World Bank and other development institutions are investigating a new financing mechanism for AIDS research: a contingent loan. Such a mechanism might reduce the uncertainty about projections of the price and quantity of future vaccine sales in developing countries, while leaving key product R&D in the hands of the private pharmaceutical firms. Under a contingent loan scheme, the international community would make binding commitments to lend to developing countries sufficient funds to buy large amounts of an AIDS vaccine, once such a vaccine has been invented and demonstrated safe and effective. By assuring the pharmaceutical firms of a future market, the scheme would reduce the risks to which those firms are exposed, giving them a stronger incentive to conduct the necessary research.

The contingent loan approach is not without its problems. Even with adequate investment in basic research, the financial incentive provided may prove insufficient, in the eyes of the private decisionmakers, to outweigh all the risks in bringing an AIDS vaccine to market—especially when many other potentially lucrative avenues remain open for investment. And on the supply side, no amount of funds committed or research undertaken can guarantee that an AIDS vaccine can actually be produced. As in any technical endeavor, no one can know if something will succeed before it has been tried. But a virtue of the contingent loan approach is that the costs are limited: if no vaccine emerges, nothing will have to be paid out.

threats to the global environment, and of how to mitigate those threats, requires collecting, interpreting, and analyzing information from as many countries as possible. To this end, the GEF promotes international efforts—such as the Global Biodiversity Assessment and the Global International Waters Assessment—to collect and disseminate scientific and technical knowledge on planetary environmental issues. It also assists developing countries through a special program to enable them to take stock of strategic knowledge related to biological resources and climate change. This includes, for example, taking inventories of sinks and sources of greenhouse gases.

Second, once generated, this global environmental knowledge—standing alone or embedded in technologies—needs to be disseminated across countries. Within the GEF, information gathered at the national level is shared internationally through reports to the global conventions. The GEF also fosters market-based approaches to the diffusion of environment-friendly technologies. In the area of climate change, the GEF has mobilized $4.5 billion to be used in transferring to developing countries the knowledge and technologies required to promote energy efficiency, the use of renewable energy, and the reduction of greenhouse gas emissions.

Third, incentives are needed to mobilize human and financial resources around the globe, to translate knowledge about the global environment into policy action. One key to the GEF's achievements is the incentive for cooperation that its way of operating inspires. Science-based technical and operational criteria for determining the eligibility of funding proposals are established in the GEF's operational strategy. These ensure transparency in funding decisions. And because they are designed to maximize global environmental benefits, they encourage broad support from the donor community. The GEF operational strategy also explicitly recognizes that promoting a healthy global environment must go hand in hand with supporting national efforts for sustainable development.

Exchanging and adapting knowledge

Most knowledge that is beneficial for developing countries is not the product of internationally sponsored research, vital though such research can be. It is rather the consequence of actions taken in developing countries themselves. Local knowledge creation—and its transfer from one country to another—thus has the potential to unleash powerful development forces. Learning from others, assimilating that knowledge, and adapting it to local circumstances offer the opportunity to make rapid advances without repeating others' mistakes.

If sharing knowledge about development successes and setbacks is so important, why don't countries do more of it? Part of the answer lies in the sheer difficulty of the task.

Assessing the merits of alternative project interventions, or carrying out rigorous analyses of the policy experiments of dozens of other countries, is beyond the capacity of most developing economies. But partly it is a matter of incentives: the global benefits of a systematic analysis of policy experiments exceed those that accrue to any single country. Here we examine how international development agencies can support these efforts in three dimensions: innovating, adapting, and evaluating projects; assessing policy changes and outcomes; and building local capacity for policy analysis and evaluation.

Innovating and adapting at the project level

Development assistance can help create the local knowledge necessary for local public institutions to succeed. Properly managed, foreign aid can encourage better delivery of public services: primary schools in El Salvador, water supply in Guinea, road maintenance in Tanzania, telecommunications regulation in Argentina. It can do this both by helping with particular development projects and through providing advice and analysis, and often through a combination of the two.

By supporting efforts initiated domestically, donors can help countries at every stage of a development project: from designing the first pilots to bringing those pilots to scale to evaluating the outcomes. Adaptation is crucial in all this, because one size often does not fit all. In many cases, if knowledge is to be effective, it must be locally created or re-created, domestically owned, and internalized. Good principles must always be adapted to new circumstances, and here domestic stakeholders—governments, businesses, and citizens—must take the lead. Effective adaptation also requires that governments and donors elicit and really listen to feedback from those whom the project is supposed to benefit.

Donors are also becoming more flexible about allowing adjustments to projects in midstream, and they are encouraging "structured learning." Under this approach, information gathered in the course of a project's implementation is fed back into its design, allowing continual improvements in service delivery. An example is the World Bank's support of Brazil's PROSANEAR sanitation project. Sponsored in part by the Caixa Econômica Federal (a state-owned bank specializing in lending for housing and sanitation projects), PROSANEAR uses an inexpensive but effective strategy for sewage collection that relies on a high degree of community participation and shared responsibility. Communities monitor household use and system performance, and they manage their own repairs. The project's most striking feature is the Caixa's commitment to adjust the project's design in light of experience.

Development agencies and NGOs can also assist countries by supporting the diffusion of information about service provision drawn from their experience in implementing many projects in different countries with different institutional structures. West Africa's AGETIPs (*agences d'exécution des travaux d'intérêt public*) are one example of an innovative mode of public contracting that has spread well beyond its country of origin. Started in Senegal, AGETIPs are based on the idea that public services of superior quality need not rely on direct public provision by government agencies. These not-for-profit associations instead enter into contractual arrangements with governments to carry out infrastructure projects. After Senegal's successful experience—in which AGETIPs, through soliciting bids from and contracting with private suppliers, reduced construction costs and delays—other African countries adopted this model with help from the World Bank.

Development institutions can encourage the diffusion of such reforms by bearing some of the startup costs. In Guinea a World Bank loan facilitated a contractual ar-

rangement in which a private management agency took over the operation of a publicly subsidized water system. The loan paid the difference between the system's costs and the revenues that could be recovered from users. Thanks to this financing, the subsidy, rather than being eliminated suddenly, could be reduced gradually as the operation moved to a commercial basis.

In numerous cases of public sector innovation—from parental involvement in school management to concessions for water supply—development assistance has contributed to better public services by supporting innovation and evaluation and by promoting the replication in other countries of a pioneer country's success. Development agencies, especially when intimately involved in reforms, can thus provide a means of disseminating lessons from the innovators to the followers. That is precisely what happened with the Road Maintenance Initiative in Africa (Box 9.4).

Many donors also have an established capacity to evaluate projects by drawing on cross-country evidence and experience in ways that no single country could. Project evaluation benefits the country in which the project is located, particularly if the feedback results in continuous improvement. But when properly disseminated, the results of careful evaluation can benefit other countries as well. In this sense project evaluation is yet another international public good: one country bears the additional costs of learning, but many other countries ultimately benefit.

Donors can help secure these benefits by financing rigorous independent evaluations. In fact, much of the value of development projects comes through the ex post evaluation of innovative activities, whether successful or unsuccessful. Thorough evaluation includes listening to project beneficiaries and taking into account their measures of a project's success or failure. It also requires analysis, which means not only recording perceptions of what constitutes best practice, but also digging into what really works, why it works, and what the most important contributing factors are. Analysis is needed not only to ensure continual improvement, but also because all too often what is "best practice" depends on both the details of a program and the context in which it is applied. Only careful analysis can determine which practices suit which contexts.

Modern scientific method shows us how best to conduct such analyses. Where possible, project evaluators engage in controlled experiments, in which similar groups receive different "treatments" and the outcomes are analyzed using statistical techniques. For instance, the close monitoring of family planning services in "treatment" and "control" areas in rural Bangladesh has provided far and away the most powerful evidence on the impact of family planning programs. Such knowledge will prove useful around the globe. And in Kenya a well-designed experiment has

Box 9.4

Maintaining roads by building institutions in Africa

In Africa nearly a third of the road network as measured by value has become unpassable because of poor maintenance. To address this problem, a group of donor agencies including the United Nations Commission for Africa and the World Bank launched the Road Maintenance Initiative in 1987. The undertaking began with workshops with domestic stakeholders, to build a consensus on the need for institutional change and its direction. These workshops revealed that it was pointless to focus on road maintenance as an isolated problem. Instead, poor maintenance was recognized as merely a symptom—weak and unsuitable institutional arrangements for managing and financing roads were the real culprit. The next stage was to devise a process that would build effective institutions, bringing in the main users of roads—farmers, businessmen, transport operators—as full partners, since it is they who bear the costs of poor roads.

This type of institution building cannot, of course, solve all the problems related to road maintenance. Part of the difficulty stems from poor original construction, which in turn may have resulted from poor governance and corrupt inspectors. Further problems arise from failure to set and enforce weight limits on roads—a serious shortcoming given that heavy trucks do the most damage to roads. Nevertheless, the Road Maintenance Initiative has had considerable success, and its experience confirms some of the basic features of successful institution building:

- First, establishing a consensus on problems and solutions requires patience, because it takes time to analyze and think through solutions and to implement them in a self-sustaining fashion—it took five years for the Road Maintenance Initiative to show results.
- Second, lasting reform requires domestic interest and commitment. Only after the private sector became convinced that there was hope for improved roads, and the public agencies became convinced that gains were possible, did the process take on a life of its own.
- Third, ideas do spread from country to country. With each round of implementation, other African countries have learned both the pros and the cons of alternative approaches.

examined the impact of textbooks on learning by teaming independently financed researchers with small NGOs.

Disseminating and adapting the results of policy research
Any one country can accumulate only so much experience of its own with policy problems. To gather enough knowledge about how to deal with hyperinflation, for example, or regulation of the telecommunications industry, countries have to look abroad, drawing on the experiences of other countries that have faced similar challenges. But carrying out careful analyses of policy experiments in many other nations is beyond the capacity of most developing countries. Even if their capacity were greater, they would carry out too little research of this type. Once created, the knowledge would spill across borders—whether through published reports or through informal observation leading to demonstration effects—and would benefit other countries. But the country doing the research will not take these benefits fully into account in deciding how much research to do.

The policy research of development institutions aims to fill this gap, by analyzing and codifying policy reforms around the world so that this information can be used worldwide. For example, it was only in the late 1970s that development agencies began to fully appreciate the value of openness to international markets as a spur to economic growth. In the two decades since, development agencies have worked to disseminate research showing the benefits of a reasonable degree of openness, encouraging insular economies to learn from the success of the more open ones.

It is hard to assess the impact of this dissemination, but clearly the past decade has seen a worldwide trend toward economic liberalization and greater openness. Of 35 countries that undertook major trade liberalizations over this period, almost all were influenced by the successful cases that had gone before. This influence would have been much less potent without systematic efforts to demonstrate and disseminate the lessons of success and failure.

Other examples suggest that much good can come from knowledge dissemination sponsored by development agencies, even when unaccompanied by substantial financial transfers. Vietnam, for example, was plagued in the mid-1980s by hyperinflation, a huge fiscal deficit, poor incentives for production, and stagnant income per capita. The country began to reform in 1986, but because of its political estrangement from the West, it received no large-scale financial assistance. Vietnam did, however, receive a significant amount of technical assistance and policy advice, financed by the Nordic countries and the United Nations Development Programme (UNDP). Both the World Bank and the International Monetary Fund were active in delivering this assistance and advice. Only after a marked policy improvement between 1988 and 1992 did significant amounts of financial assistance begin to flow into the country in a sustained way (Figure 9.1). But by then a sharp improvement in economic performance had already taken place: income per capita was growing strongly, and inflation had fallen off dramatically, from over 400 percent in 1988 to 32 percent in 1992.

The important lesson from Vietnam's turnabout is that donor agencies can help with policy reform and institutional development before providing large amounts of money. Studies of Vietnam's reform point to the useful-

Figure 9.1

Aid flows and GDP per capita in Vietnam

Vietnam's policy reforms boosted growth even before aid flows increased.

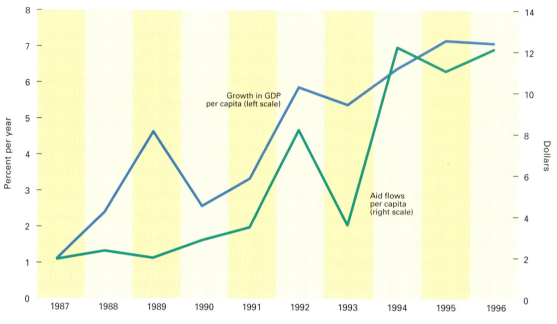

Source: World Bank data.

ness of international agencies during this period and to some of the innovative approaches adopted. To take just one example, the Asia Foundation and the World Bank organized a series of workshops in which domestic private firms and government policymakers publicly debated economic reform priorities for the first time. Stimulating policy debate and the interaction of civil society and government is one of the most useful roles that development agencies can play. It seldom costs a lot of money, but it can have a very large payoff.

Another example comes from recent research on pension reform. Many developing economies have public pension schemes that operate on a pay-as-you-go basis, with current contributions paid out mostly to current recipients. The benefit-tax ratios of these schemes remain viable as long as there are many workers and few retirees, but will become unworkable as the ratio of retirees to workers climbs. A 1994 World Bank report, *Averting the Old Age Crisis,* showed how a low-cost form of international assistance can stimulate reform of pension policy. In the wake of that Report, donors have helped a wide range of countries—among them Argentina, China, Hungary, Mexico, Poland, and Uruguay—study the long-term fiscal and dis-

tributional consequences of their old-age security systems. These countries were able to draw on the lessons of, for example, the successful Chilean pension reform. Once the public understood that current benefit-tax ratios were not sustainable, political support for reform increased.

Although it cannot be proved (or disproved), it seems likely that development agencies have an important role in creating and disseminating knowledge about successful policies. Increasingly, donors are shifting their focus from finance to ideas. An example is the United Kingdom, whose recent white paper on international development states:

Research is an important weapon in the fight against poverty. Without research, many development interventions would fail or be much less successful; and research has significant multiplier effects—solutions to the causes of poverty in one part of the developing world may well be replicable in another. The principle of shared knowledge is an important component of the partnerships which are essential to development. The government sees the continued investment in knowledge generation as a key element in achieving its aims and objectives for international development.

The impact of the adaptation and dissemination of ideas is obviously difficult to measure, but recent research has quantified one measure of the importance of analytical work, namely, the increased returns it generates on development projects. Empirical analysis of the performance of World Bank projects shows the value of the effort that goes into producing the economic memoranda, public expenditure reviews, poverty assessments, and other reports that underpin the policy dialogue with government, and of the wide range of sectoral reports that provide the foundation for specific lending operations. Even after statistically controlling for differences among countries, sectors, economic conditions, and amounts of staff input for project preparation and supervision, this research finds that analytical work—both macroeconomic and sectoral—improves project performance. Indeed, one additional week of analytical work by World Bank staff increases the benefits of an average-size Bank-financed project by four to eight times the cost of that week of staff time. And because analytical work typically relates to more than one project, the overall benefit is even larger: up to 12 to 15 times the cost. Moreover, these are just the benefits to projects financed by the Bank. If the changes inspired by the Bank's analysis affect other donor-financed projects, or even perhaps all government projects as well as policies, the returns to analytical work could be truly astronomical.

Building local capacity for policy analysis

Policymakers and communities in developing countries often have information, or local knowledge, that is not readily transferable to international institutions. It is often most efficient for development institutions to transfer internationally available knowledge to well-trained government officials or other local residents, who can then merge that knowledge with local knowledge to devise locally appropriate policies or projects. For this reason, donors often help create domestic capacity for policy analysis and devise mechanisms that allow a strong civil society to engage government in a dialogue on policy.

The African Economic Research Consortium, which supports research by Africans on African economic policies, is one such innovative effort to create and sustain policy analysis capabilities outside governments (Box 9.5). Another is an effort funded by the U.S. Agency for International Development to raise the quality of education by creating the capacity, outside ministries of education, to do serious analysis of educational reforms. This effort, initiated in several countries in Africa, looks to create a competitive element in policy analysis so that the government does not retain a monopoly on information and technical

Box 9.5

The African Economic Research Consortium: A successful experiment in capacity building

The African Economic Research Consortium, which started from a small effort in 1984 by Canada's International Development Research Center, has grown into a continent-wide organization supported by 16 donor agencies and NGOs. The consortium works to raise the quality of economic analysis through three mechanisms. It provides small grants to support the research endeavors of individual researchers, allowing them to supplement their (generally low) salaries while still maintaining time for study. It also provides a mechanism for review, discussion, and exchange among African researchers, to raise the quality of analysis through seminars and peer review as well as by linking African and non-African scholars working on similar issues. And it oversees a master's program in economics to train future analysts. The World Bank has for quite some time been involved in all three aspects of the consortium's work, providing financing, making staff specialists available for research seminars, and assisting in developing and delivering training courses.

There are clear signs that the consortium has fostered progress. Independent evaluations find that it has raised the esprit de corps of African economists and enhanced the amount and the quality of African research. Many early participants in the consortium are moving into positions as policymakers, where they can draw on their expertise and that of the network of researchers throughout Africa. Perhaps the best sign of the capacity of consortium members for policy analysis comes from an independent reviewer, who commented on their "excellent critiques of the analytical work of the [World] Bank and other international institutions."

capacity. Greater competition and enhanced analytical skills should accelerate the rate at which good policies are learned from international experience, adapted to local conditions, and adopted.

One of the main traditional solutions when a country lacks certain needed skills has been to provide technical assistance. This has often entailed spending considerable sums financing foreign experts, in the hope of alleviating critical short-term constraints and improving long-term human and institutional development. Technical assistance has had some important successes but overall has been disappointing, especially with regard to the long-term benefits. A UNDP evaluation in 1993 concluded with a fourfold censure: "There is a growing sense that technical cooperation does not work well, that as presently practiced it is ineffective, that such benefits as it brings are extremely costly, and that, in any case, it has little lasting impact."

Of course, the more a country or public agency is driving its own reform program, the more receptive it may be to technical assistance and institution building. Freestanding technical assistance provided by international consultants and the insertion of individual technical experts into government agencies have served some purposes. But when such assistance is not driven by domestic demand for expertise, foreign experts too often fail to be integrated into agencies in ways that allow the transfer of capacity. That is why technical assistance as a mechanism to promote effective public sector institutions has had only limited success. In many environments there is no way around a slow process to create the capacity for policy analysis and dialogue, both in the government and in civil society.

Some countries have used donor-financed short-term training opportunities to upgrade the technical skills of their staff and have achieved significant performance improvements. But many others have been unsuccessful. The reason is probably that lack of technical skills is not the key constraint. If public sector officials do not have the incentive to perform, if they are politically blocked from performing, or if they lack the materials or the resources to perform, additional training in what to do if they had the incentive, power, and resources is irrelevant.

Managing knowledge for economic development

The management of knowledge through systematic sharing is becoming more explicit in organizations around the world, including those involved in development assistance. The idea that knowledge for development should be shared is obviously not new. But the transfer of knowledge is inherently difficult, since even those who have knowledge may not be conscious of what they know or how significant it is. Knowledge is thus "sticky" and tends to stay in people's heads. In response to this stickiness, communities have always used interactive knowledge-sharing mechanisms—from palavers under the baobab, village square debates, and town meetings to conclaves, professional consultations, workshops, and conferences.

Many factors have transformed the way organizations view knowledge and knowledge sharing, but perhaps most pivotal is the dramatically extended reach of knowledge through new information technology (Chapter 4). Thanks to the plummeting costs of communications and computing and the extraordinary growth and accessibility of the World Wide Web, organizations with operations and employees around the world can now mobilize expertise from any source and rapidly apply it to new situations. And their clients are coming to expect to benefit not merely from the know-how of the particular team assigned to the particular task, but from the very best that the organization as a whole has to offer. Knowledge sharing is thus enabling—and forcing—institutions that are already international in scope to become truly global in character.

Which organizations are most actively taking up the challenge of formal knowledge management? The major international consulting firms were among the early adopters, but its popularity is spreading rapidly across all sectors of business in the United States and Europe. In the field of economic development, the recent Global Knowledge 97 conference, convened jointly by the Government of Canada and the World Bank, brought together participants from scores of development organizations—multilateral, bilateral, NGO, and private sector—to discuss issues of knowledge sharing, access, participation, and the new information technologies (Box 9.6). At the level of the individual organization, comprehensive programs for sharing knowledge typically emerge when the organization's know-how is perceived as critical to its mission, when the value of that know-how is high, and when the enterprise is geographically dispersed.

To take just one example, Skandia AFS, a Stockholm-based provider of financial services, began consciously to manage its stock of knowledge in 1991 to support a global expansion. As it founded each new startup, the firm initially used the administrative resources of an established business unit in the host country. This reuse of existing knowledge helped reduce lead times and startup costs, increasing productivity and quality. The company was soon completing two startups a year, not just one, having shrunk the lead time to seven months (the industry average was seven years at the time).

The diverse efforts of organizations around the world to share knowledge are being pursued under various labels: knowledge management, knowledge sharing, intellectual capital management, intellectual asset management. Whatever the label, an organization embarking on this course must confront some key choices about the dimensions of its knowledge management system. This section describes some of those choices and the tensions that underlie them—and some additional challenges that apply primarily to development institutions.

Key dimensions of knowledge management programs

The most important decisions that an organization must make in establishing its knowledge management system are the following: deciding with whom to share, deciding what to share, deciding how to share, and deciding *to* share. Knowledge sharing is a social process, which tends to occur in a community where there is trust and openness among members. In undertaking knowledge-sharing programs, many organizations, including the World Bank, have found that the nurturing of knowledge-based communities, or communities of practice (economists, educators, environmental scientists, and the like), is a sine qua non.

Box 9.6

Bilateral-multilateral cooperation to promote global knowledge sharing

In June 1997 the Government of Canada and the World Bank co-hosted Global Knowledge 97, a conference that brought together in Toronto more than 1,700 participants from scores of countries. The organizers worked together with a large number of public and private organizations to explore the vital role of knowledge in sustainable development, and the ways in which the information revolution transforms the development process. The conference examined the new opportunities for partnership and dialogue created by the information revolution; the challenges for equity and access posed by new technologies; the ways in which information and knowledge can serve economic and social empowerment; and the ways in which the international development community must adapt to address these new opportunities and challenges. The conference also featured cybercafes, videoconference links with sites around the globe, and a Knowledge and Technology Forum highlighting innovative uses of technology to address development challenges.

As a follow-up, the organizers established an evolving Global Knowledge Partnership. The partnership includes public, private commercial, and not-for-profit organizations committed to sharing information and resources to promote broad access to, and effective use of, knowledge that can promote sustainable, equitable development. Members cooperate through a variety of initiatives, including pilot projects, conferences and workshops, capacity-building initiatives, information sharing, and project coordination.

The conference also led to the creation of a Global Knowledge Partnership site on the World Wide Web, with information in English, French, and Spanish. The website is the center for a growing dialogue; an information resource on tools, partnerships, and best practices; and the forum for a continuing Global Knowledge Virtual Conference. This on-line conference brings together individuals committed to ensuring that the world's poor are full partners both in the benefits of the information age and in building and sharing knowledge for sustainable and equitable development.

Such communities are typically based on the affinity created by common education, work practices, interests, or experience, where practitioners face a common set of problems in a particular knowledge area and share an interest in finding new solutions, or more effective solutions, to those problems. Some asymmetry of knowledge is essential for these communities to become dynamic, living entities: some members of the community must have knowledge that others in the community want and need. Various mechanisms are available to strengthen such communities, including specific work objectives, the provision of ade-

quate resources and management support, and the recognition, both formal and informal, of individual contributions.

Deciding with whom to share. The first major decision concerns the intended beneficiaries. Knowledge-sharing programs may aim at sharing with either an internal or an external audience. Internal knowledge-sharing programs typically aim at making the existing business work better, faster, or cheaper, by arming front-line staff with higher-quality, more up-to-date, and more easily accessible tools and inputs. This improved access allows them to add value for clients or reduce costs. Internal knowledge sharing was the thrust of the initial knowledge-sharing initiatives in the major international consulting firms in the early 1990s.

More recently, some of these firms—such as Arthur Andersen and Ernst & Young—have started offering external knowledge-sharing services so that clients can have direct on-line access to the firm's know-how. Arthur Andersen makes some of its knowledge resources available on-line through its KnowledgeSpace™ service, and Ernst & Young provides answers to clients through its on-line consulting service Ernie™. The World Bank's strategy for sharing knowledge has been explicitly external from the outset. Its objective is to make know-how and experience accessible not only internally, to World Bank staff, but externally to clients, partners, and stakeholders around the world—and in the process to reach many who now have little or no access to its expertise.

External knowledge sharing poses greater risks than do internal programs. It raises complex issues of confidentiality, copyright, and, in the private sector, the protection of proprietary assets. But it may also offer greater benefits. Some analysts believe that, in the next five years, knowledge-sharing programs will broaden from their current employee focus to encompass suppliers, business partners, and customers.

Deciding what to share. The knowledge that knowledge-sharing programs seek to make available comes in various types. Some programs, such as that of Manpower, Inc., provide customers with content that enables them to better use the firm's services. Others, such as those of Broderbund Software Inc. and Symantec Corporation, provide on-line service and support aimed at helping customers make better use of the software they have purchased. Still others, such as those of the international consulting firms and the World Bank, aim at sharing the know-how and best practices that make up the core expertise of the organization (Box 9.7).

The question of what to share encompasses both the type of knowledge and its quality. In organizing knowledge-sharing programs, it is common to put processes in place to ensure that the content shared reaches a minimum threshold of value and reliability. Some programs—for

Box 9.7

Knowledge management at the World Bank

Recently a World Bank task team leader in the Republic of Yemen urgently needed to respond to a client about setting up management information systems in an education ministry. Not so long ago, such a request would have had to wait until the team leader returned to headquarters, where he could consult with colleagues and perhaps search libraries and databases for the answer. Using the Bank's knowledge management system, however, the team leader simply contacted the education advisory service in the Bank's Human Development Network, which, in collaboration with the relevant community of practice, ascertained that there was similar and relevant experience in Kenya. The information was dispatched to Yemen, enabling the team leader to respond to the client within 48 hours, rather than weeks later.

An Indonesian official needed to know the international experience on private sector involvement in vocational training. Again through the help of the Human Development Network, the relevant Bank task team leader was quickly able to provide the official a comprehensive analysis, performed jointly with the United Nations Industrial Development Organization. He was even able to suggest some potential partners, identified through the International Finance Corporation, a Bank affiliate.

Launched in October 1996, the World Bank's knowledge management system seeks to make the Bank a clearinghouse for knowledge about development—not just a corporate memory bank of best practices, but also a collector and disseminator of the best development knowledge from outside organizations. By 2000, according to plan, relevant parts of the system will be made externally accessible, so that clients, partners, and stakeholders around the world can have access to the Bank's know-how. Now moving ahead rapidly on a broad front, the Bank's sectoral networks are leading the effort through the following activities:

- Building communities of practice
- Developing an on-line knowledge base
- Establishing help desks and advisory services
- Building a directory of expertise
- Making key statistics available
- Providing access to transaction information
- Providing a space for professional conversation, and
- Establishing external access and outreach to clients, partners, and stakeholders.

Knowledge management is expected to change the way the World Bank operates internally and to transform its relationships with all those it deals with on the outside.

---

example, that of OneWorld Online (Box 9.8)—make no explicit distinction between levels of reliability once an initial threshold has been met. This allows users to draw their own conclusions about its value. Other programs, particularly those that offer external knowledge sharing, provide explicit guidance on whether the material has been authenticated. Most knowledge-sharing systems also allow, to varying degrees, the inclusion of new and promising ideas that have not yet been authenticated and in this sense are not yet knowledge.

Knowledge-sharing programs have to cope with adapting know-how to the local context in which it is to be applied. Where this know-how is extremely robust and the local context largely predictable, adaptation may not pose much of a problem. But in most areas of development assistance, know-how is typically less than fully robust, and the local context almost always unpredictable. Knowledge of the local context and of local know-how thus becomes very important. This realization has spurred the effort to incorporate local knowledge into development-oriented knowledge management systems.

A recently launched initiative will expand the World Bank's knowledge management system to incorporate local knowledge from countries and sectors in which the Bank is active. Gathered through field interviews, participatory community assessments, and focus-group meetings with NGOs, this knowledge is being catalogued by country, region, sector, and theme, to be made widely available to practitioners everywhere. By taking into account and complementing traditional practices in the least-developed countries, this approach should make knowledge available to far greater numbers of the poor. It may also ensure greater acceptance of development solutions.

Deciding how to share. Knowledge management programs can be seen as having both a collecting and a connecting dimension. The first "how" question is how to balance the two. The connecting dimension involves linking people who need to know with those who do know, thus developing new capabilities for nurturing knowledge and acting knowledgeably. Connecting is necessary because knowledge is embodied in people and in the relationships within and between organizations. Information becomes knowledge as it is interpreted and made concrete in light of the individual's understanding of the context.

For example, help desks and advisory services (small teams of experts whom one can call to obtain specific know-how or help in solving a problem) can be very effective in the short term to connect people and get quick answers to questions, thus accelerating turnaround time and adding value for clients. At the World Bank such services have tended to prove more immediately productive than has the building of knowledge bases, which takes longer. Organizational "yellow pages" (lists of people indicating which of them knows what) can enable staff to connect to the right people and know-how more efficiently. But an organization that focuses entirely on connecting, with little or no attempt at collecting, can be very inefficient. Such organizations will fail to get the leverage that true knowledge sharing offers—and may spend much time reinventing wheels.

The collecting dimension relates to the capture and dissemination of know-how through information and communications technologies aimed at codifying, storing, and retrieving content, which in principle is continuously updated through computer networks. Through such collections of content, what is learned is made readily accessible. Even where comprehensive collections exist, their effective use may still require knowledgeable and skilled interpretation and alignment with the local context. Reading a newspaper article on brain surgery, after all, does not qualify one to conduct the operation. Thus it is that an organization focused completely on collecting, and making little or no effort to connect people, tends to end up with a repository of static, little-used documents.

Most knowledge management programs—particularly organization-wide programs such as those at Ernst & Young, Arthur Andersen, and the World Bank—aim at an integrated approach to managing knowledge, combining the benefits of both the connecting and the collecting dimension. They achieve a balance between connecting individuals who need to know with those who do know, and collecting what is learned as a result of these connections, filtering it, and making it easily accessible. When collected documents are linked to their authors' websites or e-mail addresses or offer other interactive possibilities, allowing for more accurate interpretation and more in-depth learning, they can become dynamic—and thus much more useful.

A second "how" question concerns the choice of appropriate technology for knowledge sharing. There are many examples of systems that are not quick, not easy to use, and not easy to maintain. It is no trivial task to develop tools that reliably support knowledge sharing in an appropriate and user-friendly way, particularly when the scope of sharing is organization-wide. Most of the technological tools now available tend to help disseminate know-how, but offer less assistance in using it. Tools that assist in knowledge creation are even less well developed. Some of the more user-friendly technologies are the traditional ones: face-to-face discussions, the telephone, and flip charts.

In choosing information technology for knowledge-sharing programs, an organization must keep several im-

Box 9.8

Sharing knowledge at OneWorld Online

OneWorld Online (www.oneworld.org) is an electronic gateway for the public to the issues of sustainable development. It draws on the websites of over 250 partner organizations spanning government departments, research institutes, NGOs, news services, and international agencies. Among them are the European Centre for Development Policy Management (the Netherlands), the Institute of Development Studies (United Kingdom), the International Institute for Sustainable Development (Canada), the Centre for Science and Environment (India), and the Inter Press Service (Italy). These resources sum to a virtual library on development and global justice issues, encompassing more than 70,000 articles in six languages. Unlike in a bibliographic database, however, the documents are available in full text form and are free for anyone to read.

The partners of OneWorld Online came together because Internet users are generally looking for knowledge about a development theme, not about this or that organization. Thus, packaging the materials of these various organizations under topic headings makes them much more readily available. The headings include guides to key development themes, think tanks for professionals, news from a global perspective, educational resources, radio programming, and training opportunities. The service is proving very popular: the website receives more than 4 million hits a month from more than 120 countries on average, 60 of them in the developing world.

Owned by a charity and run by a team of 15 people based near Oxford, in the United Kingdom, OneWorld Online is establishing additional editorial centers in the Netherlands, India, Africa, and Central America. These are intended to provide a genuinely "one world" perspective, especially through the use of languages other than English. They also work to support local NGOs in maximizing the Internet's potential as a tool for development.

A central feature of OneWorld Online's website is a specialized search engine dedicated solely to sustainable development. This offers the user a way to avoid the needle-in-a-haystack approach of all-purpose search engines. Users of the OneWorld search engine know that the domain searched contains only relevant material of known date and provenance.

portant questions in mind. Is the technology responsive to users' needs, pitched to users' abilities, and well integrated with other technologies used by the organization? Can items be easily found and retrieved? Is new material entered in a way that preserves the quality of the system, and is obsolete material removed promptly?

Deciding to *share.* Even if the organization has a clear vision and answers to these questions—what, how, and with whom to share—its knowledge management efforts will founder if they are not backed by senior managers. A real commitment to sharing requires substantial changes in resource allocation and organizational procedures.

First, formal knowledge programs can require a sizable commitment of financial resources. The typical organization-wide knowledge management program may consume as much as 5 percent of the total enterprise budget. The large international consulting companies are believed to spend on average between 6 and 12 percent of their revenues on knowledge-sharing activities and infrastructure.

Second, the organization's incentive structure must be altered to reinforce its knowledge-sharing system. An open, sharing culture will promote the success of knowledge management programs, and incentives can help in turn to make such a culture a reality. Some organizations such as Price Waterhouse and Ernst & Young have made knowledge sharing an integral part of their formal personnel evaluation systems, apparently to good effect. Knowledge fairs (company-wide events at which knowledge professionals present their services to communities of practice) and knowledge-sharing awards have also been used. A recent study of successful knowledge management projects has identified a knowledge-friendly culture and supporting incentives as two of the factors critical for success in almost all of them—but emphasizes that other factors, such as the appropriate technical and organizational infrastructure, may be even more important.

Third, the organization must be prepared to accept some ambiguity, or at least to rely on nontraditional measures, when evaluating the impact of knowledge sharing. Measuring that impact, whether in terms of return on investment (for private companies) or in terms of development success (for international development institutions), remains problematic. In principle, inputs lead to activities, which generate outputs, which in turn produce outcomes, which in turn result in an overall impact. But measurement problems arise at each link of this chain.

It is difficult to disentangle knowledge-sharing inputs and outputs from other operational activities, although the formal definition of specific knowledge management activities has proved helpful. Outcomes can be illuminated by the use of surveys, focus groups, and groupware sessions, but often it is not easy to interpret what the results mean for the system as a whole. Impact can be assessed through correlations with other measures, but causal connections are difficult to trace and often speculative at best. The study just cited shows just how difficult and speculative: in deciding which knowledge management projects were "successful," the authors had to rely on input, usage, and qualitative measures to supplement limited information about financial returns.

The bottom line is that few organizations, if any, have devised credible measures to establish a causal relationship between spending on organization-wide knowledge sharing and specific improvements in key performance measures. The assessment usually comes down to a qualitative judgment: is it working?

Knowledge management for development assistance: Special challenges

Like other organizations, international institutions and the development community today enjoy an unprecedented opportunity to use new technologies for knowledge management to get better and faster results on the ground. But their choices have broader ramifications, requiring decisions not only on the technical issues but also on the larger principles at the heart of the development process. Now that new technology makes sharing much easier and cheaper than ever before, it is vital that these tools be used for the public good. To achieve this, collaboration and openness become the dominant principles of operation, particularly in international assistance (Box 9.9).

International institutions should take care to orient knowledge-sharing programs to the needs and technological capabilities of users in developing countries. Part of this challenge is one of technical design. Systems must be geared to users who have limited technical means, such as low-speed modems and little computing capacity, so that their low-end technology is not a barrier to access. Systems should use public rather than proprietary software where possible and provide alternative means of access for those without computers. User fees for access to knowledge bases should be avoided, if they risk limiting access for low-income users.

Also part of the challenge is the authentication of content. Since human beings often fully trust only the knowledge they themselves have helped create, development knowledge bases will reach their full potential only if practitioners in developing countries take part in building them. For explicit know-how, participation can be facilitated by opening knowledge bases for comment and review and by providing the means to register alternative views. For know-how that remains tacit, active participation by developing countries is needed in all phases of knowledge creation—for example, in project design and in building new knowledge bases.

A prerequisite for knowledge sharing is free information flows. So far, the Internet has been open and inclusive in spirit, although there have been efforts to encroach on that freedom. Some countries have banned access to the Internet entirely; others use prohibitive pricing to preclude access for much of their population. Continued vigilance is thus needed to ensure that the Internet remains a

Box 9.9

Knowledge partnerships for the environment

Sustainable development requires a wide range of stake-holders working together toward common goals. The World Bank is therefore trying to serve as a knowledge hub, facilitating the interchange of knowledge among stakeholders and, especially, between the institutions of the industrial and the developing world.

Much of the knowledge shared will be knowledge about the environment. In sustainable forestry, the Bank has set ambitious targets to protect large areas of the world's remaining tropical forests. Achieving these targets will require the commitment of and support from a wide range of stakeholders. To this end, a range of partnerships and on-line discussions have been established, involving among others the Bank, the World Wildlife Fund Alliance, and the CEO Forum, a group that represents the world's top private forestry companies.

A second example is the Bank's partnership with the Biodiversity Conservation Information System (BCIS), a consortium of 12 of the world's leading conservation NGOs. The consortium's members are working to improve access to their large databases on protected areas, threatened ecosystems and species, and environmental law. Through partnership with the BCIS, the World Bank can add its knowledge resources and make a wealth of information available to its operational staff and clients. Just as important, it can help increase the flow of data and knowledge from its country operations back to the international system, while ensuring that those engaged in project-based activities have access to the best available environmental data and practices.

truly international and freely accessible public good. Any approach to limit access under whatever guise—commercial priorities, moral values, national pride, linguistic predilection—must be weighed against the enormous opportunity costs of interfering with free information flows.

The same logic that drives the international community to manage its knowledge applies with equal force to developing countries. They must establish their own knowledge bases, authenticate them from their own experience, interpret what is meaningful from their own perspectives, and create a future that meets their needs. As international institutions learn how to share knowledge more effectively, they can and should help developing countries to understand what is at stake in managing knowledge and

to nurture similar capacities. This will be a large-scale and long-term undertaking.

• • •

Now that knowledge is recognized as central to development, the development community is taking on a new set of tasks related to the creation, transfer, and management of knowledge. Because no one country or organization will create all the international public goods that are needed, it is up to the entire development community to pitch in to do so. But the agenda is daunting: a cure for malaria, a vaccine for AIDS, restoration of the ozone layer—to name only a few of the challenges. The Consultative Group for International Agricultural Research has shown what is possible, but also what is no longer possible in today's world. Whichever of these public goods the development community addresses, the roster of players will have to extend beyond governments, the major philanthropies, and international organizations to enlist businesses and NGOs. This should ease the burden but will complicate the process of public good creation in this new age of partnership.

Because knowledge of successful development practices is too often locked in a few people's heads, another major task for the development community—another global public good—is to assess the merits of alternative policy actions and to conduct rigorous policy experiments in a wide variety of settings. Transferring the knowledge produced by project evaluation and policy research, and adapting it to local circumstances, can avoid mistakes and propel the development process forward. But the adaptation is the trickiest part and will require adequate local capacity.

A vital element in building this capacity is developing systems for managing and sharing knowledge. Global corporations and international institutions have recently begun to do this for their own operations, greatly abetted by advances in computing and communications. As they refine these systems, they are opening them to their clients, so that the institutions can respond faster to client needs and deliver products and services of the highest possible quality. For the World Bank and the rest of the development community, the advent of knowledge management is beginning to stimulate true exchanges of knowledge, not just one-way transfers. And as developing countries begin to put their own knowledge management systems in place, the opportunities for creating and exchanging knowledge about all aspects of development will soar.

Chapter 10

What Should Governments Do?

THE OVERVIEW PROPOSED THAT WE LOOK at development in a new way: that we look at the knowledge gaps between and within countries and at the information problems that undermine markets and hinder government action. These gaps and these failures are especially severe in poorer countries and work especially to the detriment of the poor. Subsequent chapters examined these problems in detail and considered some of the many ways in which countries around the world are addressing them. The knowledge perspective has reinforced some well-known lessons, such as the crucial importance of universal education, and focused fresh attention on other needs, such as tertiary education. It has also cast into sharp relief the need to recognize and compensate for information problems and the resulting market failures.

The general principle that institutions should act on their comparative strengths suggests that governments should focus on those responsibilities that the private sector is unlikely to shoulder, or to shoulder well. That is, governments should concentrate on activities whose spillover effects (externalities) are especially important, that have clear public good characteristics, or that address distributional concerns. As we have seen throughout the Report, public action is important in narrowing knowledge gaps and addressing information problems. This final chapter sketches a strategy for public action based on the Report's three main conclusions.

First, narrowing the gaps in know-how that separate poor countries from rich—and poor people from non-poor—can increase economic growth in developing countries, raise incomes, reduce environmental degradation, and generally improve the quality of life, especially for the poor. The first section of this chapter suggests how governments can address these issues.

Second, even if we could magically close all knowledge gaps, developing countries would still be disadvantaged by information failures. Therefore, addressing information problems—such as a banker's lack of knowledge about a poor borrower's creditworthiness, or a consumer's lack of knowledge about the quality of goods in the marketplace—can improve the functioning of market and nonmarket institutions, making it easier for people to partake in the economy and improve their lives. The second section of this chapter summarizes how governments can address these information problems.

Third, no matter what governments do to narrow knowledge gaps and improve information flows, these problems can never be eliminated. Policies work best when they are based on the recognition that knowledge is not freely available to all, and that many markets for the things that matter most to our well-being are far from perfect. The Report therefore concludes with a discussion of policymaking amid persistent knowledge gaps and information failures.

Formulate a national strategy to narrow knowledge gaps

The opportunities for countries and companies to move to better practice—for narrowing the knowledge gaps within and between countries—are nothing short of stupendous, and they apply not just to industry but across the entire economy. Grasping those opportunities requires openness to outside ideas. It also requires the right incentives and institutions. And it requires strong local efforts to acquire, adapt, and use knowledge effectively. Strategies to close knowledge gaps should focus on three issues:

- What policies foster the acquisition of knowledge?
- What policies enhance a country's learning capacities?
- What policies improve the effectiveness of communications and reduce the costs?

As countries search for the answers, competing priorities will vie for attention and resources, often posing explicit dilemmas and tradeoffs: Should countries acquire knowledge abroad or create it at home? Should education systems extend basic literacy at the expense of investment in tertiary education? Often the issue is balance, and the balance shifts with a country's stage of development and its circumstances.

Tap global knowledge and create local knowledge

Acquiring knowledge involves a combination of tapping knowledge from abroad and creating knowledge at home. Because no country can create all the knowledge it needs, learning from others is a critical component of a successful strategy for all countries, even the more technologically advanced. Even low-income economies must build the capacity to adapt imported knowledge and to create knowledge that cannot be obtained internationally. The precise approach will vary according to a country's situation. Some newly industrializing economies in Asia have stepped up their investment in original research and development, even as they continue to learn from abroad. Some low-income economies find that they learn most effectively from the middle-income economies. And some economies in transition from central planning, given their already high educational attainment, continue to pursue advanced basic research, even as they catch up on manufacturing techniques.

To build their knowledge base, developing countries should explore all the means available of acquiring knowledge from abroad and creating it locally. They should:

- Find new and better ways of producing goods and services through trade—ever more important as the structure of trade shifts from commodities and simple manufactured goods to increasingly knowledge-intensive products
- Work with foreign direct investors that are leaders in innovation, spurring domestic producers to try to match best practice and to tap potential knowledge spillovers
- Get access to new proprietary technical knowledge through technology licensing
- Stimulate domestic innovation and get access to global knowledge through establishing laws and institutions for the protection of intellectual property rights

- Attract back home talented people who have studied or worked abroad, and
- Promote domestic R&D to make it more responsive to the market.

Trade. Openness to trade is essential. One of the main reasons the East Asian economies were able to grow so fast for so long was their ability to build strong links with world markets and to draw upon the technology flowing through those markets. They did this with policies ranging from trade liberalization to export promotion, some of which offset protectionist biases favoring domestic industries. Export promotion and diversification are also valuable, since domestic producers, to be competitive internationally, must meet international standards and adopt up-to-date technology. Exporters also receive much technical information from buyers and suppliers, and importers get access to knowledge embodied in new goods and services. But for trade to expand, countries also need good standards, measurement, testing, and quality control systems, so that domestic products and services can compete in the global market. These standards need not be set by government, as we saw with the ISO 9000 certification standards described in Chapter 2.

Foreign direct investment. Countries with more open trade regimes are likely to attract competitive, outward-oriented foreign investment, which brings efficient technology and management into the economy. Hong Kong (China), Indonesia, Malaysia, Singapore, Taiwan (China), and Thailand have been particularly welcoming, and their growth spurts were closely linked to surges in foreign direct investment. In contrast, Sub-Saharan Africa has been less open to foreign trade and investment. Partly as a result, the region has attracted only about 1 percent of worldwide foreign direct investment to developing countries, and it has lagged behind other regions in acquiring knowledge and in economic growth. To attract foreign investment, developing countries also need appropriate infrastructure—both "hard" infrastructure, such as transport and communications, and "soft," institutional infrastructure, such as effective legal, financial, and educational systems.

Technology licensing. Technology licensing has become increasingly important, since new knowledge is expanding rapidly. Governments can facilitate the inflow of such knowledge by not restricting access to technology licensing or restricting the terms of such contracts. Instead, by encouraging the creation of domestic information centers, where local firms can obtain information on foreign technology, countries can reduce their firms' disadvantages in licensing negotiations.

Intellectual property rights. As the world moves toward a knowledge-based economy, producers of knowledge are seeking stronger enforcement of intellectual property rights—and that has mixed effects on the production of new knowledge and the closing of knowledge gaps. Well-designed intellectual property rights regimes try to balance the private incentives for the creation of knowledge against the social benefits from its dissemination. This balance is difficult to achieve because most of the producers of knowledge reside in industrial countries. But as Chapter 2 showed, adequate intellectual property rights are necessary if countries are to get access to foreign technology through foreign direct investment and technology transfers. They are also important in stimulating the domestic creation of knowledge, which in many developing countries will grow as they strengthen their human and technological capabilities.

How should developing countries respond to the trend toward strengthened intellectual property rights? The answer is twofold. First, they should negotiate internationally for intellectual property rights regimes that give adequate consideration to their urgent need to narrow the knowledge gap—while maintaining incentives for knowledge producers everywhere to continue their creative activity. Furthermore, as new technological developments bring in new issues for negotiation—biotechnology and information technologies, for example—developing countries will need to keep up with these trends and represent their own interests. Second, developing countries should establish and enforce intellectual property rights standards that comply with international practice, because adhering to those standards is necessary to get access to foreign technology through foreign direct investment and technology transfer—and to get access to foreign markets through trade.

Developing-country governments can also continue efforts to negotiate for definitions of intellectual property rights that recognize the value of indigenous knowledge and reward those who create and preserve it. For example, in 1990 world sales of modern medicines derived from plants discovered by indigenous peoples were estimated at $43 billion. Yet only a tiny fraction of this went to the people and groups who had preserved the traditional knowledge of these medicinal plants or to the countries where the plants were found. Developing countries thus need to increase their capability to negotiate better terms with foreign firms who would profit from this knowledge. To do so, they must participate actively in evolving international agreements on intellectual property rights and biodiversity.

People. A final important channel for the acquisition of knowledge from abroad is expatriate nationals. Today more than a million students from developing countries are enrolled in higher education programs abroad, and many will stay where they have studied. Many of the best-trained at home, finding few opportunities to use their new knowledge in their own countries, will also end up emigrating.

This continuing brain drain has led some developing economies to establish programs to encourage expatriates to return. Korea and Taiwan, China, offered well-trained expatriates good job opportunities and strong financial and tax incentives to return home to teach or work. China, India, and Taiwan, China, have tapped the expertise of their overseas nationals without bringing them back, by offering special opportunities for trade and investment.

Are all modes of knowledge transfer equally conducive to domestic learning? Probably not. The most appropriate form of know-how is that which matches the sophistication of the technology with domestic capabilities. Licensing coupled with a strong domestic technological effort may be appropriate for firms in a newly industrializing economy, whereas foreign direct investment may be a more suitable approach for a lower-income economy. The East Asian economies drew on the full range of possibilities, the precise mix differing with the base of capabilities and the technological vision of government. Their experience shows that there is more than one solution, and that the most effective strategies make the most of all available channels for tapping global knowledge as well as creating it locally.

Creating knowledge at home. Developing countries, in addition to taking advantage of the large global stock of knowledge, should develop the capability to create knowledge at home. We saw in the Overview how agricultural knowledge had to be adapted to local conditions for the green revolution to take hold. Even in manufacturing, knowledge from other countries must often be adapted to differences in climate, consumer tastes, and availability of complementary inputs. And some types of knowledge must be built from the ground up. Examples include knowledge of the local environment and social customs, often vital for effective policy. For these and other reasons, a balanced strategy for narrowing knowledge gaps must include the capacity to create locally the knowledge that cannot be obtained from abroad.

Governments can encourage research either directly through public R&D or indirectly through incentives for private R&D. Direct government R&D includes that financed at universities, government research institutes, science parks, and research-oriented graduate schools. Indirect support for R&D includes preferential finance, tax concessions, matching grants, and the promotion of national R&D projects. For most developing countries, however, local research should focus on essential needs. And maintaining core strengths in basic science and technology may be necessary not only to maintain access to the global pool of knowledge but also to adapt that knowledge to local uses.

Many public research institutions lack either information on the needs of the productive sector or incentives to respond to those needs. That is why Brazil, China, India, Korea, and Mexico have launched vast programs to reform their public R&D laboratories and focus them on the needs of the productive sector, as Chapter 2 discussed. The measures include restructuring the labs so they behave like corporations, capping the government contribution to their budgets to provide incentives for researchers to seek corporate sponsorship, improving the pay and recognition of researchers, and giving firms direct incentives to place research contracts with them.

Only a few developing economies—Korea, Singapore, and Taiwan, China, among them—have provided the right incentives for significant private R&D, and allowed their publicly funded R&D institutes to focus on more basic precommercial research. But continuing strong government support is essential in some other crucial areas, such as research to adapt international advances in agriculture and health to a country's circumstances.

Increase people's capabilities to absorb knowledge

An effective strategy to narrow knowledge gaps must include measures to increase people's capacity to use knowledge. Ensuring universal access to basic education is the crucial first step, but it is not enough. Countries must also ensure that they have enough highly trained personnel, including engineers and scientists. This requires strong secondary schools and universities, especially for engineering and science. And it means providing opportunities for lifelong learning after students complete their formal education. To meet these needs with a limited budget, all countries, especially the poorest, must obtain the best possible return for their educational dollar.

To address these problems, governments should consider the following possibilities:

- Decentralize education to give more power to those with the most information about educational needs and how to meet them: students, parents, teachers, and local school administrators
- Focus public resources on those who need them most, for example by targeting subsidies to the poor and to girls
- Provide support for higher education, especially in the sciences and engineering, while ensuring access for the poor, and
- Use new learning technologies to improve the quality of education and to broaden access.

Decentralize to give power to those with the most information. Achieving educational goals often does not mean spending more, but rather improving the quality and delivery of education. Although increasing spending to reduce class size, for example, would almost surely improve educational quality, equivalent improvements are often possible even within existing budgets, by increasing efficiency and reforming the way education is provided.

Education systems confront complex information problems, and addressing these problems can help improve educational quality. One way to do this is to move from a top-down to a more client-driven approach, placing power in the hands of those closest to the education process and thus with the most information. As Chapter 3 showed, the many experiments under way throughout the developing world offer a great opportunity to learn what works and what does not. For example, in El Salvador, teacher absenteeism has declined in community-managed schools, even in the poorest communities, because parents closely monitor teacher performance.

Focus public resources on those who need them most. Despite the high private returns to education, many people cannot take advantage of educational opportunities because they cannot pay the cost. Education requires considerable private resources, even for education that is "free" in the sense that no fees are charged. Time spent in school is time not spent on other tasks: working for a wage or in a family enterprise, or caring for younger siblings, a task that often falls to girls. For the poor, these opportunity costs may make education unaffordable, especially when access to credit is lacking. Governments can alleviate these problems through a variety of mechanisms: higher subsidies to schools in poorer areas, direct stipends for disadvantaged students (like those recently provided to girls in Bangladesh), and student loans for higher education.

Support tertiary education, especially in engineering and the sciences. Many low-income economies have programs of tertiary education that prepare workers for scarce civil service positions but do not improve technical skills. Often it is more effective to focus public resources on the preparation of engineers and scientists capable of absorbing and adapting advanced technology. Korea achieved universal primary enrollment before its economic takeoff, and it moved quickly to expand tertiary education and train its own scientists and engineers. Today its enrollment shares in mathematics, computer science, and engineering are similar to those in many OECD countries. Strengthening tertiary education need not require more government spending, especially in the long run. Because advanced training confers significant benefits on those who receive it, governments can often increase tuition charges while still ensuring access for low-income students, for example through expanded student loan programs.

The transition economies face special problems. They need to improve the content, delivery, and funding of education to respond to market demands and tight budgets, especially in science and engineering. Some of the transition economies had first-rate scientific and engineering establishments, now threatened by underfunding and a brain drain. Maintaining quality and redirecting research and teaching to reflect the new reality will prove a challenge.

Use new learning technologies to improve quality and broaden access. New technology for teacher training and distance education has greatly increased the opportunities and reduced the cost of adult learning outside traditional campus settings. In China half the 92,000 students who graduate with degrees in engineering and technology each year are taught through distance learning provided by traditional universities. The African Virtual University is trying to increase university enrollments and improve the quality and relevance of instruction in business, science, and engineering throughout the Sub-Saharan region. So far it has installed 27 satellite receiver terminals, and to compensate for the dearth of scientific journals in African universities it has developed a digital library.

In sum, an effective education system is crucial to increasing people's capacity to absorb knowledge. Reforming education systems to achieve this goal involves more than simply spending more from the public purse. Governments must apply their resources to the array of institutions and activities associated with lifelong learning: preschool programs, basic formal schooling, higher formal schooling, formal training programs, on-the-job learning, information dissemination programs, and informal education. The most effective public actions will be those that focus directly on the information problems that underlie market failures—or that address distributional concerns.

Build the capacity for people to communicate

The new information and communications technologies let people share knowledge today at an ever more affordable cost. The potential is thus great for developing countries to take advantage of the new technologies to upgrade education systems, improve policy formation and execution, and widen the range of new opportunities for businesses. To realize this potential, countries need to make the effective use of information technologies a key thrust of their national development strategies, as Malaysia has done. Countries should:

- Ensure competition and appropriate regulation, to unleash private initiative to provide communications infrastructure and services and expand the use of new technologies, and
- Ensure that services are extended to remote areas and the poor, by moving away from traditional cross-subsidy schemes, and working instead in partnership with the private sector or end-users to determine the required government support.

Ensure competition, private provision, and regulation. Chile, Ghana, the Philippines, and dozens of other developing countries are privatizing their telecommunications industries. Their experience shows that access to services expands much faster in privatized markets where competition prevails. Governments should speed their efforts to privatize and, more important, to introduce competition along with privatization to avoid private monopolies replacing public ones. For example, competition among international suppliers of telecommunications services can ensure that a large part of the gains from technological progress in the communications industry accrues to the countries hosting those international suppliers. But all too often, developing countries rely on one international supplier.

Access also expands rapidly when government encourages the emergence of new private providers, particularly in value-added services and cellular phones. Sri Lanka licensed four private cellular companies and has seen access explode. Malaysia and the Philippines have about one cellular phone for every two traditional wire-based lines, which is five times the ratio for France or Belgium. Cellular phones are proliferating in many other developing countries as consumers see them as a good substitute for hard-to-get or poorly working traditional telephone service.

Although competition is increasing in telecommunications, it is still far from perfect. Even the United States, with one of the most competitive telecommunications industries in the world, does not yet have enough competition to put regulation aside. Developing countries need strong regulatory authorities, not to choke competition but to enhance it. In Poland, poor regulation so thwarted the benefits of liberalization that of the 200 or so new telecommunications licenses awarded since 1990, only 12 were in use in 1996. The reasons included unfavorable terms for revenue sharing between new licensees and the dominant state operator, limited access to the state operator's network, slow negotiation of agreements for interconnection with that network, and prohibitions against new licensees setting up their own transmission facilities. An important new role for regulation is to ensure that a dominant operator—be it public or private—does not engage in anticompetitive practices, for example by withholding essential technical and commercial information needed to price interconnections.

Regulation will take different forms in countries at different stages of development and with different needs, but there is much to learn from Chile, Ghana, Poland, and the United States. One task of the regulatory authority is to help competing operators reach a reasonable agreement when they cannot do so themselves. For instance, Guatemala requires the regulator to choose among the parties' final offers for connectivity charges. If one party stubbornly maintains an unreasonable position, the regulator is likely to choose the other's price. (If a country's regulatory skills are scarce, this task can be outsourced.) State-owned operators must also be deprived of the sovereign immunity that protects them from legal action.

Monopoly power is a concern not only in telephone service but in the mass media as well. Some countries are troubled about concentration of ownership of television stations, or of print and broadcast media more broadly. Another worry is that privatizing state-controlled media may curtail cultural diversity. Providers who compete for a mass market tend to offer similar products, leaving those with more specialized interests lacking adequate service. (This is one of the reasons behind public radio and television.) Fortunately the new information and communications technologies can enhance diversity: cable and satellite television can deliver far more stations at low cost than conventional broadcasting ever could. One private company, for example, is about to launch three satellites, one each to cover Africa, Latin America, and Asia, to beam a variety of world-class programs to low-income consumers.

Provide access to rural areas and the poor. In many developing countries entrepreneurs have brought telephone access even to the poorest. Senegal in 1995 had more than 2,000 privately owned "telecenters," each with a pay phone and a fax machine; this was four times the number just two years before. In many instances, however, providing access to the rural poor requires government support. South Africa's multipurpose community information centers suggest a model. Its Universal Service Agency, established in 1996, provides each center with two years' worth of startup costs, plus field workers to offer technical support. A 1997 survey of these centers found that 67 percent had a telephone, 31 percent a computer, and 8 percent Internet access.

As Chile's auctions of telephone subsidies show, market-like mechanisms can determine the extent of required government support and help allocate public funding. In 1994 the government established a special fund to award subsidies competitively to projects providing telephone service to small towns and remote areas. The fund is achieving its objectives in a cost-effective way because many private providers have requested less subsidy than assumed—and in many cases no subsidy at all. If the fund's performance is maintained, 97 percent of Chileans will have access to basic telecommunications services by the end of 1998.

Address information problems to foster markets

A sound national knowledge strategy requires that governments seek ways to improve information flows that make a market economy function better. But governments, like every actor in every economy, are themselves subject to information failure. So policymakers must consider the strengths and limits of government capabilities relative to those of the market. This echoes one of the key findings of *World Development Report 1997: The State in a Changing World,* namely, that when deciding the scope and nature of public action, policymakers must balance the market failure they seek to address against the government's capacity to address it.

Part Two of this Report spelled out the need to address information problems in finance, the environment, and assistance to the poor—three areas of special relevance to developing countries. Here we consider three types of action that cut across these and all other parts of the economy, and the role of government in each:

- Provide and elicit information to verify quality
- Monitor and enforce performance to support market transactions, and
- Ensure two-way information flows between citizens (especially the poor) and government.

Advanced economies tend to have much better developed mechanisms for each of these actions than do developing ones. As economies grow more complex, requiring sophisticated transactions over long distances, traditional information mechanisms such as local reputation to establish quality or reliability become inadequate. The lack of alternative institutions can lead to serious inefficiencies and even to the breakdown of markets. Governments thus have to ensure that information crucial to markets but otherwise unavailable is collected and shared. They must decide case by case whether to address these problems directly—for example, by inspecting products and certifying quality—or to create mechanisms for other players, such as firms, voluntary associations, and citizen groups, to address them.

Provide and elicit information

For some products and services, markets alone are sufficient. A person can easily decide whether a haircut is worth the price, and the economic loss from a bad haircut is small, temporary, and mostly confined to the customer. Sometimes, however, buyers cannot readily determine quality, and the damage from a wrong purchase may be lasting or widespread. That is true, for example, when buyers cannot determine the wholesomeness of food, the soundness of banks, or the profitability of a company offering shares on the stock market. In such cases governments can greatly improve market outcomes by providing and eliciting information that would not otherwise be available. They can:

- Establish product standards to ensure, for example, the quality of food and promote exports
- Make information available and set standards for services such as education
- Set standards for accounting

- Establish disclosure requirements for banks and firms
- Create self-revelation mechanisms—systems of incentives that lead firms and individuals to reveal information they would otherwise keep hidden, and
- Ensure the transparency of public institutions.

There are compelling reasons for governments to be active in these areas. Often the information in question is a public good or has important spillover effects, so that the private sector by itself will not invest enough in collecting and disseminating the information. As in other situations, governments should focus their limited resources in areas where the market is least likely to provide adequate solutions, and where government action has the greatest potential to improve outcomes.

Establish standards for product quality. In most countries with weak institutions and poorly developed markets, only the government has the authority and the credibility to define and enforce standards, so that quality can be recognized and rewarded in the market. This Report has presented many examples of such direct government action. In India the National Dairy Development Board defined and monitored standards in the milk market, to the benefit of both consumers and producers (Chapter 5). Government action can also ensure the quality of a wide range of exports, enhancing the ability of firms to compete in the global marketplace, as Malaysia has done with its promotion of international quality standards.

In other cases government can encourage private quality standards instead of trying to develop and impose its own. An example is the ISO 9000 standards of product quality, developed and publicized by the private sector. These standards provide buyers with important information about the quality controls in place during production. Adherence to such standards is particularly important for developing-country exporters seeking to establish a reputation for quality in competitive import markets. Because the private sector has already developed the standards, governments need only publicize them and encourage exporters to use them. Similarly, private credit rating agencies can complement government supervision. Drawing on publicly provided information, they perform an important service by processing it and disseminating their findings.

Make information about educational options more accessible. How do parents know the quality of instruction being offered by schools? Governments can help by requiring schools and training programs to disclose overall test scores and summaries of placement records of their students. They can also accredit schools directly, after inspecting and evaluating them, and they can release information about school performance. Sometimes governments can encourage private voluntary accreditation agencies to provide the information instead, as in the Philippines. Many countries rely on a combination, using mandatory government ac-

creditation for basic education and voluntary private accreditation for higher levels. In the United States, for example, university accreditation is handled almost entirely by private agencies.

Set standards for accounting. Accounting standards are crucial for investors to assess a firm's financial history and the breakdown of its financial assets and liabilities (the balance sheet), revenues and expenses (the income statement), and liquidity (the cash flow statement). If governments fail to establish standards or require disclosure of this information by listed firms, equity markets will remain weak, and firms must rely more heavily on loans and direct financing. This impedes the efficient allocation of capital and limits the possibilities for distributing risk. The result will be higher debt-equity ratios, making firms and countries highly vulnerable to external shocks.

Many low-income economies have weak accounting systems, often with few trained accountants and in some cases no uniform system of accounts. In such settings equity markets are apt to be nonexistent or very small, dominated by foreign players who have better access to information. As a result, and despite rapid growth in equity markets over the past decade, banks still account for the lion's share of the financial sector in most developing countries. Improvements in accounting standards are important for the efficiency of the financial system—and for growth. Studies show that countries with sound accounting systems—for example, with standards that produce comprehensive and comparable corporate financial statements—have more-developed financial intermediaries and faster growth. One study estimated that raising accounting standards in Argentina in the early 1990s to the average then prevailing in the OECD countries would have boosted the country's GDP growth rate by 0.6 percentage point a year.

Establish standards and disclosure requirements for banks and firms. Setting standards and disclosure requirements for banks and other financial institutions is especially important—and difficult. Because a bank's assets consist mainly of the promises of borrowers to repay loans, accurate and consistent information on the status of those loans is critical to assessing a bank's viability. Without this information, it can be difficult to gauge the health of the entire economy. For example, in Mexico before the 1994 crisis, banks reported overdue interest payments as nonperforming but continued to claim the loan itself as an asset, in contrast with the practice in the United States. When Mexican borrowers began to miss payments, the Mexican accounting system portrayed the situation as much better than U.S. rules would have revealed. The Mexican system, since reformed, is now more consistent with U.S. practice.

Banks play a key role in addressing the information problems involved in assessing the performance of firms, through monitoring their bank accounts and from past dealings. But who watches the watchdogs? It falls to the government to determine on behalf of the public the quality of the banks themselves. To do this, governments must establish consistent and rigorous accounting standards that require banks to reveal their assets, liabilities, and loan-loss provisions. But disclosure is not enough—bank regulators need to enforce standards as well.

Establishing standards and disclosure requirements for firms requires fewer government resources than does direct government action to obtain and disseminate the same information. Disclosure thus can be required even when governments face tight budgetary situations. But to be effective, disclosure requirements have to be backed by effective legal enforcement. And if markets are to rely on the information provided—whether voluntary or mandatory—they must have confidence in its accuracy. This requires effective enforcement of strong laws against fraud.

Create self-revelation mechanisms. In most of the approaches just described, information is ferreted out by an entity one step removed from the source. This entity may be the government or a third party, such as a private accreditation agency for schools or a credit rating agency for firms. In recent years some governments have discovered a promising alternative: sometimes, by creating the right mechanisms and incentives, they can encourage firms and individuals to reveal information that they would otherwise have kept hidden. These are called *self-revelation mechanisms.*

One such self-revelation approach uses auctions to induce producers with complex cost structures to reveal their true costs. Producers sometimes exaggerate the costs of providing a service, whether telecommunications or pollution abatement. Governments could counter this by launching extensive investigations into company finances or production processes. A less intrusive, less costly, and more effective approach uses market mechanisms to encourage producers to reveal this information themselves. Examples include the auction of telecommunications subsidies in Chile (Chapter 4) and the system of tradable pollution permits in the United States (Chapter 7).

Self-revelation has also been used to ensure that social benefits go to those who need them most. In many developing countries, food subsidies go to consumers at all income levels, draining scarce government funds. In Tunisia, household consumption surveys were used to design and market subsidized foodstuffs that appealed to the poor but that wealthier households snubbed. Public works programs have used similar self-selection mechanisms. A recent World Bank–supported project in Argentina offered jobs on community projects at a low wage, so that only the neediest were likely to apply (Chapter 8).

Ensure the transparency of public institutions. Public institutions, including governments and multilateral institutions, have a special obligation to disclose information about their operations—that is, to be transparent. Not only can a lack of transparency lead to corruption, weakening the state; it can also be used to hide mistakes and incompetence, limiting the ability of citizens to monitor the government and to choose effective leaders. Lack of transparency can generate uncertainty about future government policies, and this uncertainty can hurt the business environment, especially the environment for investing. And lack of transparency contributes to a lack of trust in government and to a lack of participation and ownership, all recognized as vital to the success of development.

A variety of concrete policies can help foster transparency. Involving local communities in monitoring public services improves their provision and checks abuses of local power. Removing barriers to competition reduces opportunities for corruption, such as those that arise with complex cross-subsidy schemes and special privileges associated with monopolies. Given the value of transparency, many governments have imposed disclosure requirements on themselves; an example is the Freedom of Information Act in the United States. Perhaps the most important safeguards of transparency are a literate citizenry and vigilant media. These not only strengthen public administration, for example by improving environmental monitoring, but also ensure that government acts in a timely manner to avert grave threats, such as famine.

Monitor and enforce performance

Ensuring that firms, banks, and individuals live up to their promises is a problem in all societies but tends to be especially severe in the weak institutional environments that characterize many developing countries. Three imperatives for policy are to:

- Develop a strong legal and judicial system, but
- Create incentives to minimize recourse to it, and
- Explore innovative alternative approaches to enforcement.

Develop a strong legal and judicial system. Typically the problem is not the absence of laws but the lack of credible enforcement. Fixing slow and corrupt courts is thus critical for successful economic reform. But even when the judicial system works well, litigation is costly. Thus the most effective arrangements create incentives for good behavior, so that recourse to the courts underpins the system but is regarded as a last resort. Areas in which a sound legal code supports monitoring and enforcement, and where information disclosure can minimize the need to rely on the courts, include bankruptcy, contract enforcement, bank regulation, and antifraud measures.

Because each party to a contract lacks full information about the other's intent and ability to comply, the legal framework must establish and enforce damages that may be collected for breach of contract. Here the balance is crucial. If damages are too difficult to collect, there will be too few incentives to fulfill contracts; if too easy, one party may falsely claim breach of contract in hopes of obtaining a windfall. The difference between the penalties under civil law and the harsher punishments of criminal law reflect this need for balance: persons proven guilty of deliberate fraud are punished more severely than those who proved unable to fulfill a contract despite a good-faith effort.

The interactions between sound laws, an effective judiciary, and self-enforcing arrangements are subtle and complex. For example, lack of information about a borrower's intention to repay can be overcome with collateral. But for collateral to be effective, property rights and land registration must be clearly established. Even where these exist, collateral will facilitate credit markets only if borrowers who default can be forced to relinquish collateral promptly. Similarly, firms are more likely to repay loans if a bankruptcy system gives creditors the means to seize the assets of a firm in default.

Create incentives to minimize recourse to the courts. As in quality verification, government and the private sector can act in complementary ways to improve monitoring and enforcement, if the government establishes the right incentives. For instance, insurance companies have a strong incentive to see that the firms they insure against fire do everything reasonably possible to prevent fires. So they typically enforce safety codes far more effectively than governments do. Governments can help by establishing liability laws so that real estate owners have incentives to acquire insurance in the first place. Governments must also take care that their actions do not undermine incentives for private sector enforcement. For instance, firms that provide earthquake insurance have an incentive to make sure that buildings they insure are built to specified standards. But if the government provides disaster-relief assistance to repair buildings every time an earthquake strikes, regardless of whether or not structures complied with the building code, that incentive will evaporate. In this case government has to keep from acting too much.

A similar relationship between government-set incentives and private action is apparent in bank regulation. The value of a bank as an ongoing concern (its franchise value) can prod bank owners to act prudently. At their best, these incentives do more to prevent overly risky lending than do capital adequacy standards. But sometimes, inadequate regulation combines with government policy in ways that erode franchise value unexpectedly. For example, in the United States in the 1970s and 1980s, savings and loan institutions recycled short-term deposits into large long-term loans. When interest rates rose in 1979, depositors took their money elsewhere, leaving the savings and loans insolvent. As their franchise values declined, these institutions, encouraged by deregulation, engaged in riskier lending, which culminated in their widespread failure later in the 1980s. That is why financial liberalization, which gives banks greater freedom to take on risk, coupled with low franchise values is such a dangerous cocktail.

Explore innovative alternatives. Innovative measures to address information problems and thereby improve monitoring and enforcement have recently emerged in markets ranging from finance to consumer goods. Underlying each of the examples discussed here is the idea that institutional arrangements—often but not always initiated by the government—can make it easier for private or community groups to monitor and enforce performance.

Requiring firms to disclose how much pollution they create often induces them to pollute less. The pressure works through a variety of channels, as it does in Indonesia's PROPER program, which discloses firms' compliance with water pollution regulations (Chapter 7). Armed with easy-to-understand compliance ratings of neighboring factories, local communities can pressure those factories to cut pollution. Moreover, because environmental reputation influences a firm's sales and share price, the disclosure of a company's environmental record creates incentives for that company to clean up beyond what regulation alone requires. Regulators, meanwhile, can focus their limited resources on the worst offenders, including those who refuse to disclose accurate pollution data.

Ecolabeling is another promising approach to giving private players the power to monitor and enforce environmental performance. Consumers often prefer goods produced in an environmentally sound manner—be it dolphin-safe tuna, recycled paper, or lumber harvested on a sustainable basis—and will sometimes pay a premium for them. Ecolabeling provides a mechanism for consumers to reward and encourage practices of which they approve. Governments could promote ecolabeling directly by establishing standards and inspecting producers to ensure compliance. Often, however, it is simpler and more effective to merely provide the legal framework and copyright protection that ensure accurate labeling and prevent the pirating of established labels.

Sometimes governments can actually create new interest groups to assist in monitoring and enforcement. One example is the requirement in some countries that banks issue long-term, uninsured, subordinated debt. Because the debt is uninsured, purchasers have a strong incentive to monitor the issuing banks. Even the price of the subordinated debt in secondary markets provides valuable information about the viability of banks. This "multiple eyes" approach also helps improve bank performance: because bank managers do not want the price of their subordinated debt to drop, they are inclined to manage the bank more prudently than otherwise.

Microfinance is another area in which creating new constituencies has improved monitoring and enforcement. To overcome a chronic lack of information about the ability of the poor to repay loans, microfinance programs lend through small groups of people who know each other well. Although the loans go to individuals, group members understand that if any member defaults, none will receive future loans. Borrowers thus have a strong incentive to monitor the use of funds by fellow group members and to use peer pressure to enforce repayment. By providing monitoring and enforcement where none existed before, these programs give participants access to credit at reasonable interest rates, often for the first time in their lives.

Ensure two-way information flows

The way governments convey information to citizens, especially the poor, is often critical. So are the ways they listen to citizens and what they learn from them. Examples throughout this Report show how governments can ensure a two-way exchange of information—from society to government and from government to society. The starting point in all this is listening to the poor. Countries should:

- Give the poor voice, especially through better educational opportunities and better access to telecommunications
- Learn about the poor from the poor
- Work through local channels and earn the trust of the poor, and
- Provide knowledge to the poor in a manner they can use.

Give the poor voice. With education comes a broader world view and the ability to articulate concerns and desires, to make suggestions, and to voice complaints. A girl who learns to read also learns to write—even if only to fill out a job application form—and that increases her ability to voice her own concerns. Access to telecommunications—especially telephones, e-mail, and the Internet—can also strengthen the voice of the poor, whether in marketing village handicrafts or in advocating policies that address their needs. A poor laborer with access to a telephone can interpret advice from a doctor or veterinarian—or complain to officials about the poor quality of public health services. Chapter 4 offered some striking examples: the use of e-mail by a small business loan program in Vietnam, the Panamanian women who posted pictures of their handicrafts on the World Wide Web, the subsistence farmers in the Philippines who became pineapple specialists thanks to telex and fax machines.

Giving the poor voice also means taking the time to listen and learn. Recall that the extension agents most effective at informing farmers about the green revolution's new techniques were those who listened and got a better understanding of farmers' needs and concerns. More recently, agricultural researchers in Colombia and Rwanda let women farmers select those bean varieties they felt would do best in their growing conditions. The women's selections outproduced the varieties selected by plant breeders at central research stations by 60 to 90 percent.

Results from efforts around the world suggest that giving voice to the public and listening to that voice can greatly improve government decisionmaking. A public budgeting initiative in Porto Alegre, Brazil, succeeded only because of the autonomy granted to the city and its urban planners, who enlisted the participation of beneficiaries in the design and implementation of projects. That enabled them to establish priorities and implement programs in accord with local needs. The initiative showed that sometimes the easiest way to learn what people want is simply to ask.

Enabling communities to monitor public actions and voice their preferences through a free and vigorous press can check the abuse of power and improve the quality of services. On behalf of the poor, India's vigorous media have provided early warnings of hunger and agitated for public action—action that is more likely to succeed in societies where information can flow freely and public desire for action can be expressed without fear of government retaliation.

Learn about the poor. Learning about the poor often involves systematic learning through household surveys and other instruments. A living standards survey of households in Jamaica revealed some surprising information about two programs designed to help the poor: subsidies for basic foodstuffs and food stamps for low-income households. Policymakers were especially worried that malnourished children were not being brought to the clinics that are the primary channel for identifying food stamp beneficiaries. But the survey found that food stamps targeted to low-income households were much more effective than general subsidies for basic foodstuffs in reaching the poor.

Many ways of listening to and learning from the poor are now taking hold. Perhaps the most important is involving poor people in the design and implementation of projects intended to benefit them. One set of numbers reveals the power of beneficiary participation, which at last the development community is recognizing as fundamental. Of 121 rural water supply projects in 49 countries, those that involved beneficiaries in project design achieved a success rate of 7 in 10, compared with only 1 in 10 for projects that did not involve them. The study also found that governments have a key role in fostering beneficiary participation.

Work through local channels—and earn trust. Studies show repeatedly that people are strongly influenced by their peers, and that working through traditional channels of communication is especially important for transmitting new ideas. This is likely to be particularly true for the poor, given their high illiteracy rates and lack of resources to acquire knowledge through other means. Recent studies of the success of the new preventive health program in Ceará State, Brazil, show that people learn best from their peers. And a study covering 70 villages in the Matlab district of Bangladesh found that peer influence was the key determinant of whether people adopted new family planning techniques. In each instance, working closely with local communities made it possible to communicate valuable information to people who would otherwise have rejected or even feared it. Working through local groups has also been effective in Kenya, where farmers have organized themselves into cooperatives to market their crops, obtain credit, and improve their farming techniques. The national extension program works through these cooperatives and sometimes directly with individual farmers.

Earning the trust of the poor is thus the key to effective exchanges of knowledge, and involving local people is a powerful means of disseminating new knowledge, whether about new seeds, new contraceptive methods, or new curricula. Given the importance of trust, it is not surprising that the diffusion of knowledge appears to be faster in villages where the social network is more densely knit. To measure the density and importance of social connections in rural Tanzania, researchers asked households to list the groups they belonged to: churches, mosques, burial societies, credit associations, political organizations. Villages rich in social capital had higher incomes than those with little. They were also much more likely to use fertilizer, agrochemical inputs, and improved seeds.

Provide knowledge to the poor. The approach taken by the United Nations Children's Fund (UNICEF) in Nepal shows the advantage of providing knowledge the poor can use. The program there promoted homemade solutions rather than the commercial alternative, but the promotional material described the treatment in words that applied to both. Rather than depress sales of ready-made packets, the program added to their credibility and increased local demand for them. And with more knowledge of what is involved in the cure, local communities are better able to sustain their use of some form of oral rehydration. Having reached 96 percent of the population, the program helped more than halve the incidence of diarrhea-related child mortality.

The importance of providing knowledge that the poor can use, in a manner in which they can use it, can also be seen in AIDS prevention. Scientists know how the disease is spread and the precautions to be taken. But this information becomes useful to the poor only if those providing it understand local conditions and work with local leaders to develop prevention programs suited to those conditions. This was done in Ethiopia and Namibia, where community street theaters have been more effective in preventing AIDS than have radio, television, or print materials.

Recognize the persistence of knowledge gaps and information problems

No matter what governments do, knowledge gaps and information failures will persist. Even countries that pursue an aggressive, knowledge-based development strategy will not be free of these problems. Policymakers have to live with imperfection:

■ In many instances, policymakers have to make key decisions in the absence of full knowledge.
■ In all instances, they must keep in mind that even policies unrelated to knowledge and information will play out in an economy subject to information failures—and thus to market failures.

Policymaking amid persistent knowledge gaps
Chapter 3 pointed to some of the positive spillovers from education: educated farmers show the way for uneducated ones, educated mothers have healthier children, and so on. In other instances, actions that benefit a firm or an individual have negative spillovers: water pollution from firms and air pollution from automobiles are prime examples. An important role of government is to maximize well-being by altering incentives to take these spillovers into account, for example by providing education stipends and taxing water pollution and gasoline consumption. But because spill-overs are difficult to measure, policymakers can seldom know their precise magnitude. This is not to say that governments should ignore them. The appropriate course is trial and error, using the tools at government's disposal to readjust incentives to achieve socially desirable outcomes.

The need for an effective policy response is greatest when action—or inaction—risks irreversible damage to human well-being. We do not know precisely the future impact of today's carbon emissions on global warming. But given the risks, it is prudent to err on the side of caution and to restrict emissions in the most cost-effective way possible. Similarly, we cannot know in advance which salamander or orchid contains a cure for cancer, or how diverse species support one another and maintain the entire web of life. So the prudent course is to preserve fragile and unique ecosystems, even when this means forgoing short-term economic gains from converting forests into pasture, or wetlands into ports. In other areas, such as health care, failure to act may have irreversible consequences. Although measures of the long-term effects of childhood malnutrition are less then perfect, we know these effects are likely to be permanent, and that prudent governments should ensure that every child has enough to eat.

In these and other cases, policymakers are also hampered by lack of knowledge about the impact of specific policies. Indeed, most policies, even those that do not involve spillovers or irreversible consequences, must be decided in the midst of persistent knowledge gaps. In part, this dilemma stems from imperfect knowledge of human nature: people respond to policies in unpredictable ways. The problem is worse in developing countries, where the capacity to design and implement policies is less fully developed, and where the technology for recording and analyzing information about people's responses is often lacking.

There are many examples where the availability of information to the government is critical to the implementation of government programs. For example, unless government can effectively monitor sales, it cannot impose a sales tax. Traditionally, many developing countries have relied heavily on trade taxes as a source of revenue, not so much because they wanted to restrict trade, but because traded goods must pass through a few easily identifiable checkpoints, and can thus be monitored and taxed. Fortunately, more developing countries are taking advantage of the plummeting costs and increased ease of use of new technologies to expand the scope of taxes that can be effectively administered. In Central and South America, several countries have increased the quality and the quantity of information they gather about individual taxpayers. Nationwide taxpayer identification numbers and computerized files are used to monitor taxpayer characteristics, transactions reported by third parties, and collection and delinquency records.

Policymaking amid persistent information failures
Possibly the most difficult challenge in policy design is recognizing information failures and modifying policy accordingly. The difficulties that arise from failing to take persistent information failures into account can be seen in two very different regions: the transition economies of Central and Eastern Europe and the financially troubled economies of East Asia.

The transition economies show all too painfully the cost of not having institutions to address information problems. Once the inefficiencies of central planning were replaced with a market system of prices, profits, and private property, one might have expected output to soar. Instead, it plummeted—and has yet to recover nearly a decade after the transition began. Part of the explanation is that the pace, sequencing, and manner of the transition destroyed institutions for mediating information faster than new institutions for a market economy could be created.

After the Soviet Union broke up in 1991, Soviet productive capacity remained in place, and many of the myriad price and trade distortions under the old system were re-

moved. Yet in 10 of the 15 countries of the former Soviet Union, GDP has shrunk by around half (Figure 10.1). What accounts for this collapse? Under central planning many firms relied on a single supplier for inputs. When markets were freed, new opportunities appeared for producers all along the chain of production. Bargaining relationships were altered, and often the outcome was a failure to reach a resolution. Yet information—and markets—were insufficient for firms to identify an alternative source of supply. Often bargaining broke down because of information problems, especially along production chains that linked many specialized producers. Not surprisingly, output fell most for goods with the most complex production processes.

In East Asia the problems have been very different. The economies there have been very successful in closing knowledge gaps: in acquiring, absorbing, and communicating knowledge. They have dealt less well with the information problems in their economies, and these explain in part their current difficulties. In the 1990s, several of the East Asian economies liberalized short-term capital flows before they had ensured that their financial institutions were on a sound footing. As a result, when capital flows reversed sharply in 1997, banks were too weak to withstand the strain. The liberalization of financial mar-

Figure 10.1

Trends in GDP in six former Soviet republics

Output has halved in parts of the former Soviet Union.

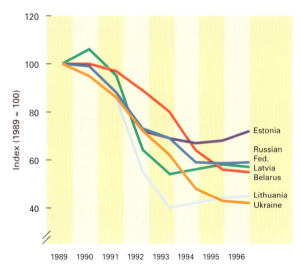

Source: Reprinted with permission from Blanchard and Kremer 1997. Copyright © by the President and Fellows of Harvard College and the Massachusetts Institute of Technology.

kets preceded the establishment of adequate supervisory and regulatory capacity, so regulators either did not know how vulnerable the banks were or lacked the enforcement power to shore up the system. That shows that however desirable financial reforms may be, they need to take account of the consequences of information problems for the financial system and for the entire economy.

As East Asia's experience also shows, governments have an especially important role in regulating formal financial markets, because of their profound effect on the entire economy—and this regulation must take into account that information in the financial sector will always be imperfect. Appropriate regulation includes monitoring banks' risk management systems, their capital reserves, and their individual transactions. Standards for the adequacy of capital are important, because banks with enough capital have incentives to make only good loans. Banks whose capital has fallen to zero or worse have a tendency to gamble—they have nothing to lose, and a high payoff from the gamble may give them new life. Such gambling has contributed greatly to financial crises throughout the world. And because regulation and enforcement are sometimes inadequate, governments must provide backup systems, including deposit insurance (to discourage bank runs) and a central bank (to act as lender of last resort).

In the new global economy, monitoring and enforcement in the financial sector have become more important than ever. With money moving rapidly across borders, a financial crisis in one country can quickly spread to others. Volatile capital flows have deepened, and may have caused, financial crises and economic recessions in several countries. These outcomes mean that the risk borne by investors differs from the risk borne by society. And this provides the reason for government action—to find policies that discourage volatile short-term capital flows while maintaining the flows needed for trade and long-term investment, especially foreign direct investment. Countries have tried a variety of mechanisms to do this. Brazil has a tax on capital

inflows. Chile has a mandatory deposit scheme. Colombia has restrictions on bank exposure. And other mechanisms are under consideration, including proposals to restrict or eliminate corporate income tax deductions for interest payments on foreign-denominated, short-term debt. Will they work? Only time and nimble refinements will tell. The sole certainty in all this is the uncertainty.

Enlightening the way forward

Recent development thinking has been based on the assumption that markets work well enough to ensure development and alleviate poverty. Our growing understanding of information constraints suggests that markets alone are often inadequate; societies also require policies and institutions to facilitate the acquisition, adaptation, and dissemination of knowledge, and to mitigate information failures, especially as they affect the poor. This view implies an expanded mandate for public action. Yet governments, like markets, are hampered by information failures. In deciding which problems to address, policymakers balance the size of the information problem and the resulting market failure against the capacity of the government to improve the situation. The appropriate course of action will vary depending on the circumstances. In all countries, however, openness to learning, recognition that there is much we do not know, and a willingness to make midcourse adjustments will enhance the prospects of success.

We began by comparing knowledge to light. When we look back in 25 years on development's progress in the first quarter of the 21st century, which countries will stand out? It will surely be those that have mastered the acquisition of knowledge, increased the capacity to absorb it, and improved the means of communication for all their citizens. It will be those that have also found ways around information failures and improved the effectiveness of markets. It will thus be those that have extended the power and reach of knowledge to enlighten the lives of people everywhere.

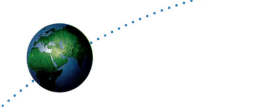

Technical Note

TABLE 1.2 WAS CONSTRUCTED by Easterly, Levine, and Pritchett by performing a variance decomposition of the three studies listed in the table. They started with the following equation:

Growth of GDP per capita =

TFP growth + 0.4 × Growth of capital per capita,

where the coefficient 0.4 is taken as the share of capital in GDP. They then decomposed the variance of growth of GDP per capita as follows:

Variance (growth of GDP per capita) =

Variance (TFP growth)

+ $(0.4)^2$ Variance (growth of capital per capita)

+ 2 × 0.4 × Covariance (TFP growth, growth of capital per capita).

The first line of the table then reports the value obtained for the second term of the right-hand side of the equation, expressed as a percentage of total variance in growth of GDP per capita; the third and fourth lines of the table do the same for the first and third terms, respectively. The second line of the table is the sum of the third and fourth lines.

The figure in *Box 1.3* was constructed by first estimating an equation in which countries' growth rates of GDP

per capita were regressed against several independent variables, including some considered to contribute to countries' access to knowledge and capability to use knowledge. Data for 74 countries and averages for three decades (1965–75, 1975–85, and 1985–95) were pooled, so as to exploit information across those decades. To avoid reverse causation affecting the results, values for the independent variables were taken at the beginning of each decade over which the dependent variable was averaged.

The dependent variable in the equation (GROWTH) is growth of real GDP per capita in 1985 international dollars. Data from the *Penn World Tables 5.6* (NBER 1998) were used for 1965 to 1992, and from World Bank 1998d for 1980 to 1995. For the overlapping years the observations from the two sources were averaged.

Independent variables consisted of three control variables (OPENNESS, TELEF100, and SCHOOL) and three state variables (GOVERNMENT, INCOME, and INVESTMENT). OPENNESS is a country's openness to trade as measured by the sum of imports and exports as a percentage of nominal GDP; data are from NBER 1998. TELEF100 is the number of telephone main lines per 100 inhabitants; data are from the International Telecommunication Union database. SCHOOL is average years of schooling in the population; data come from the TFP Project of the World Bank's Development Data Group.

GOVERNMENT is the share of general-government spending in real GDP in 1985 international dollars; data are from NBER 1998. INCOME is real GDP per capita;

Table TN1

Results of the regression of GDP growth on access to and capability to use knowledge

Independent variable	Regression coefficient	t statistic
Constant	−0.27	−1.80
OPENNESS	1.03×10^{-4} *	2.20
TELEF100	6.66×10^{-4} *	2.08
Log of (1 + SCHOOL)	0.012 *	2.29
GOVERNMENT	−0.001 **	−3.95
Log of INCOME	0.086 *	2.07
Square of log of INCOME	−0.006 *	−2.36
INVESTMENT	9.08×10^{-4} **	3.28
Adjusted R^2	0.24	
No. of observations	197	

** Significant at the 1 percent level.
 * Significant at the 5 percent level.

Source: World Bank staff calculations.

data are from NBER 1998 for 1975 to 1992, and from World Bank 1998d for the remaining years. INVESTMENT is the share of investment in real GDP; data are from NBER 1998.

Table TN1 presents the results. The point estimates for the log of INCOME and its square were close to those in Easterly and Levine 1996. This result supports the idea that there is convergence, but that countries that are very far behind converge very slowly if at all. Values for the other coefficients were close to those found in other research.

Next, on the basis of the estimated equation, average growth rates for the sample were calculated by fixing the state variables at their average levels and varying the control variables to take "low" and "high" values. "Low" values are those 1 standard deviation or more below the average, and "high" values those 1 standard deviation or more above the average.

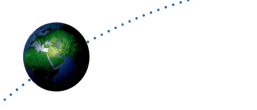

Bibliographical Note

THIS REPORT HAS DRAWN on a wide range of World Bank documents and on numerous outside sources. World Bank sources include ongoing research as well as country economic, sector, and project work. These and other sources are listed alphabetically by author or organization in two groups: background papers commissioned for this Report and a selected bibliography. The background papers, some of which will be made available through the Policy Research Working Paper series, and the rest through the *World Development Report* office, synthesize relevant literature and Bank work. The views they express are not necessarily those of the World Bank or of this Report.

In addition to the principal sources listed, many persons, both inside and outside the Bank, provided valuable advice and guidance. Special thanks are owed to the following: Pranab Bardhan, Gregory Ingram, Jean-Jacques Laffont, Dilip Mookherjee, Jonathan Morduch, Christopher Udry, and John Williamson. Special thanks are also owed to the executive directors of the Bank for their invaluable comments.

Additional comments and suggestions were provided by James Adams, Kulsum Ahmed, Mir A. Altaf, Katherine Bain, Rema Balasundram, Michael Baxter, Tamara Belt, Paul Bermingham, Natasha Beschomer, Deepak Bhattasali, Tyler Biggs, James Bond, François Bourguignon, Derek Byerlee, William Byrd, Ajay Chhibber, John Daly, Paul David, Asli Demirgüç-Kunt, Shantayanan Devarajan, Donna Dowsett-Coirolo, Jacquelin Dubow, Gunnar Eskeland, Gershon Feder, Osvaldo Feinstein, Habib Fetini, Carsten Fink, Kenneth Flamm, Emmanuel Forestier, Jason Furman, Alan Gelb, Christiaan Grootaert, Sanjeev Gupta, Jeffrey Hammer, Ian G. Heggie, John Heilbrunn, Peter Heller, Lauritz Holm-Nielsen, Zahid Hussain, Carollyne Hutter, Jonathan Isham, Hannan Jacoby, Ian Johnson, Christine Jones, Daoud L. Khairallah, Nalin Kishore, Mathieu Credo Koumoin, Michael Kremmer, Kathie Krumm, Pierre Landell-Mills, Carol Lee, Fred Levy, Katherine Marshall, Jean Roger Mercier, Pradeep Mitra, Raja Mitra, Joel Mokyr, Dilip Mookherjee, Mohamed Muhsin, Mustapha Kamel Nabli, Vikram Nehru, Richard Nelson, Richard Newfarmer, Maris O'Rourke, Mead Over, Howard Pack, John Page, Phil Pardy, Guillermo Perry, Guy Pfeffermann, Boris Pleskovic, Carl Pray, Danny Quah, Vijaya Ramachandaram, Dani Rodrik, Alexander Rondos, Mark Rosenzweig, Alan Ruby, Kamal Saggi, Joanne Salop, Marcelo Selowsky, Ismail Serageldin, Paul Siegelbaum, Peter Smith, Anil Srivastava, Anna Stahmer, Inder Sud, Hong Tan, Vinod Thomas, Brigida Tuason, Dina Umali-Deininger, Rudolf V. Van Puymbroeck, Keshav Varma, Walter Vergara, Robert Watson, Björn Wellenius, George West, Stuart Whitehead, John Williamson, L. Colin Xu, and Willem Zijp. Adrienne Brusselars, Meta de Coquereaumont, Wendy Guyette, Glen Guymon, Paul Holtz, Daphne Levitas, Terra Lynch, Heidi Manley, Laurel Morais, and Alison Smith, all with Communications Development of Washington, D.C., provided valuable editorial advice. Other valuable assistance was also provided by Carol Best, Emily Khine, Elizabete de Lima, Michelle Mason, and George Moore.

A wide range of consultations was undertaken for the Report. We particularly wish to thank the following organizations and individuals for arranging consultation meetings: the Canadian Government and the Economic Development Institute of the World Bank for consultation during the Global Knowledge 97 conference in Toronto; the Danish Ministry of Foreign Affairs; the Finnish Ministry of Foreign Affairs; the German Ministry of Cooperation; the National Council for Economic Research, New Delhi; Vivek Bharati in the World Bank Resident Mission, New Delhi; the Organisation for Economic Cooperation and Development, Paris; Austin Hu in the Resident Mission, Beijing; Andrew Rogerson; Keiko Itoh in the Resident Mission, London; the Overseas Development Institute; the Institute of Innovation Research; Mika Iwasaki in the Resident Mission, Tokyo. We would also like to acknowledge generous support from the trust funds of Denmark, Norway, and Switzerland to finance background studies for the report.

We wish to thank the numerous participants in the consultations—*in Beijing:* Jing Chen, Xiaozhu Chen, Xianhong Deng, Zhenglai Deng, Xuan Feng, Austin Hu, Kathie Krumm, Xiaomin Lai, Zhang Lansong, Hanlin Li, Jingwen Li, Shantong Li, Wangrong Li, Xiaofu Li, Dexiu Ma, Yang Ma, Weifang Min, Xiaoguang Ouyang, Hong Sheng, Jikang Wang, Jinkang Wu, Haungzhong Xie, Huixing Xu, Peizeng Xuan, Xiaozhun Yi, Yongding Yu, Weiying Zhang, Xiangchen Zhang, Dihua Zhao; *in Berlin:* K. Y. Amoako, Ela Bhatt, Lajos Bokros, H. E. Carlos Bresser-Pereira, Heinz Buhler, Harald Fuhr, Cecilia Gallardo de Cano, Tasso Gereissati, Heba Handoussa, Nguyen Thi Hang, Ingomar Hauchler, Jerzy Hausner, Alan Hirsch, Gudrun Kochendörfer-Lucius, Klaus König, Armin Laschet, Henrietta Mensa-Bonsu, Joerg Meyer-Stamer, Solita Monsod, Wolf Preuss, Oleg D. Protsenco, Wolfgang Schmitt, Carl-Dieter Spranger, Claudia M. Von Monbart; *in Copenhagen:* Poul Engberg-Pedersen, Jens Krummholt, Frode Neergaard, Klaus Winkel; *in Helsinki:* Marja Erola, Kaarina Rautal; *in London:* Geoff Barnard, Heather Budge-Reid, Charles Clift, Ben Fine, Caroline Harper, Robert Lamb, Rosemary McGee, Andy Norton, Andrew Scott, Paul Spray, Koy Thompson, Patrick Watt, Alex Wilks; *in New Delhi:* Andre Beteille, Vivek Bharati, Vinayak Chatterji, Mrinal Datta Chowhary, Bibek Debroy, Ashok Desai, Ashok Ganguly, James Hanson, P. V. Indiresan, L. C. Jain, Edwin Lim, Rakesh Mohan, Deepak Nayyar, R. S. Paroda, R. K. Pachauri, V. S. Raju, S. Ramchandran, Jairam Ramesh, C. N. R. Rao, N. C. Saxena, Pronab Sen, N. Seshagiri, Harshavardhan Singh, Parvinder Singh, S. Sundareshan, Suresh Tendulkar, Mark Tully; *in New York:* Nancy Barry, Joseph Foumbi, Morten Giersing, Marjorie Newman-Williams, Kenneth Prewitt; *in Ottawa:* Brent Herbert-Copley, Caroline Pestieau; *in Paris:* Graham Vickery, Wing-Yin Yu; *in Toronto:* the 70 NGO and government participants in the special breakout session on the Report; *in Tokyo:* Dong-Se Cha, Hong-Tack Chun, Akira Goto,

Tomoko Hirai, Farrukh Iqbal, Mika Iwasaki, Rumiko Kakishima, Young-Ki Lee, Hiroyuki Maeda, Masaki Omura, Sadao Nagaoka, Ikujiro Nonaka, Naoki Suzjuki, Kazuo Takahashi, Hirotaka Takeuchi, Shujiro Urata; *in Washington, at a meeting with the Academic Advisory Group to the Report:* Paul David, Robert Evenson, Joseph Greenwald, Richard Nelson, Howard Pack, Vernon Ruttan, Luc Soete; *at a meeting with the Knowledge Management Board of the World Bank:* Roberto Chavez, Boris Cournede, Stephen Denning, Osvaldo Feinstein, Patrick Grasso, David Gray, Patty Hamsher, Nagy Hanna, Adnan Hassan, Patrice Mallet, Klaus Tilmes; *at a meeting with the Private Sector Advisory Group to the Report:* Debra Amidon, Robert Buckman, Marc Demarest, Neil Duffy, Leif Edvinsson, Peter Ewell, Peter Henschel, Robert Hiebeler, Dan Holtshouse, Cynthia Johnson, Bipin Junnarkar, Steven Kerr, Esko Kilpi, James Mingle, Carla O'Dell, Howard Pack, Edna Pasher, Paul Pederson, Alan Powell, Hubert St. Onge, Tom Stewart, Susan Stucky, Karl Erik Sveiby, Mike Thalacker, Rob Vander Spek, Vivienne Wee, Anders Wijkman, and Karl Wiig.

Overview

The comparison of Korea and Ghana is based on data from Summers and Heston 1994 and World Bank 1993b. Data on the number of new varieties of rice and maize released by national research organizations are from Byerlee and Moya 1993 and López-Pereira and Morris 1994. Foster and Rosenzweig 1996 is the source of the finding that more-educated farmers adopted green revolution techniques more rapidly and that returns to education among farmers rose in those areas with the greatest potential gains from adoption of new varieties. The estimate of income loss to farmers due to slow adoption and inefficient use of high-yielding varieties is from Foster and Rosenzweig 1995. The southern Indian survey of the boost in the real incomes of small farmers when they did adopt new seeds is from the Rosenzweig background paper. The survey of incomes and nutrient intakes among farmers in southern India is reported in Hazell and others 1991. The Mookherjee background paper discusses Porto Alegre's public budgeting initiative. Other material in the Overview is documented in the bibliographical notes for other chapters.

Chapter 1

The quotation from Thomas Jefferson is from David 1993. Reasons for the shifting relationship between income and infant mortality are based on the discussion of improving health standards in World Bank 1993c. The study of the effect of maternal education on infant mortality is Filmer and Pritchett 1997, which also shows mortality rates in 45 developing countries. Box 1.1 draws on information provided by Luis Saenz. Reference to the effect of smoke on children and women can be found in World Bank 1996. Figures on the effect of the level of education of the household head on household incomes and poverty rates in Vietnam come from World Bank 1995b.

The total factor productivity approach is described in Solow 1956. Box 1.2 is based on Young 1995, Kim and Lau 1992, Krugman 1994, Klenow and Rodriguez-Clare 1997b, and Stiglitz 1996. Studies of the contribution of education to growth in U.S. GDP per capita are from Denison 1985. The study of total factor productivity in 98 countries is Klenow and Rodriguez-Clare 1997b. The quotation from Alfred Marshall is from Marshall 1890. The two authors who pioneered the incorporation of purposeful investment in education, innovation, and adaptation of knowledge in growth models are Romer 1990 and Lucas 1988. Box 1.3 is based on World Bank staff calculations (see the Technical Note). One study of the effect of institutional quality and sound policy on economic growth is Olson, Sarna, and Swamy 1997. Figures on the growth of international trade between 1960 and 1995 are based on World Bank 1998d; figures on the proportion of that trade that is between multinationals and their affiliates are from World Bank 1997d.

Estimates of the proportion of GDP in major OECD countries that is based on the production and distribution of knowledge are made by OECD 1996b. Statistics on the number of patents issued worldwide are from the Braga, Fink, and Sepulveda background paper. Projections of average product cycles for the U.S. and Japanese automobile industries are from Wester 1993. The hypothetical example of the $500 Boeing 767, illustrating the dramatic fall in costs and gains in performance of information technology, is from WHO 1988. The statistic on the growth in telephone traffic from 1975 to 1995 is from World Bank 1997d.

Chapter 2

This chapter draws on Evenson and Westphal 1995. The study of productivity in 200 firms in Kenya is RPED 1998, which also contains the surveys in Ghana and Zimbabwe showing similar results. The section on acquiring global technical knowledge draws on Lall's background paper (b) and Dahlman 1994. The figure on average productivity in Kenya's spinning is from Pack 1987. The percentages of the world's R&D and of its scientific publications produced by the more industrialized nations are from UNESCO 1996 and European Commission 1994, respectively. The lesson from Japan on the value of importing is discussed in Nagaoka 1989. The change in the structure of international trade since the 1970s is discussed in the Lall background paper (b). Box 2.1 is based on Plaza and Sananikone 1997. The survey cited in that box is UNIDO 1995. The improvements made by Sudarshan Chemical Industries are discussed in Chemical Week 1994.

The statistic on multinationals' share of U.S. patents is from the Kumar background paper. On subcontracting by Intel's Malaysian plant see World Bank 1993b. The studies cited in Box 2.2 are Levine and Renelt 1992, Malhotra 1995, and World Bank 1993b. Notes on *maquiladoras* and their relative isolation from the rest of the Mexican economy were provided by Alpha Southwest Corporation.

The statistic on the growth of technology transfer payments is from IMF, various years. An account of the Korean firms' licensing negotiations is in Enos 1991. The effort by Japan's Ministry of International Trade and Industry to weaken the bargaining power of foreign licensers in the 1950s and 1960s is described in Nagaoka 1989. The story of U.S. knowledge sharing with Europeans under the Marshall Plan is told in Silberman and Weiss 1992. UNESCO 1997 provides data on numbers of students from developing countries who get their tertiary education abroad. Success stories among developing economies that have instituted programs to counter brain drain are presented in Dahlman and Sananikone 1990 and in Kim 1997. How Côte d'Ivoire diminished the incentive of its textile producers to move toward efficient production is described in Mytelka 1985. The account of Brazil's attempt to develop a national computer industry is in Dahlman 1993. Evidence that making subsidies contingent on export performance ensured the use of technology sophisticated enough for East Asian economies to compete in world markets is from Westphal 1990. Box 2.3 draws on Ray 1998. The different ways in which Japan, Korea, and Taiwan, China, emphasized a government role in promoting industry are discussed in World Bank 1993b. How Hong Kong (China) and Singapore followed more conventional outward policies with much less state intervention is discussed in World Bank 1993b and Dahlman 1994. For an early study of technology exports from developing countries see Dahlman and Sercovich 1984. Box 2.4 draws on the Braga, Fink, and Sepulveda background paper. Box 2.5 is based on Mansfield 1994 and 1995. The background paper by Braga, Fink, and Sepulveda discusses the cost of developing, testing, and marketing a new drug in the United States. Analysts who have found that IPR protection has a small positive impact on economic growth across countries are Mazzoleni and Nelson forthcoming and Mansfield 1994 and 1995. The figures on the increase in the number of developing countries to sign the Paris or Berne conventions on IPRs are from the World Intellectual Property Organization (WIPO) and are given in the Braga, Fink, and Sepulveda background paper. Box 2.6 is taken from the Braga, Fink, and Sepulveda background paper. The same paper explores new IPR challenges for developing countries in biotechnology and information technology and discusses the WIPO Copyright Treaty and the WIPO Performance and Phonograms Treaty.

The study of technology institutions and policies in China, Japan, Korea, Mexico, and Taiwan, China, is Ergas and others 1997. The figures for the proportion of GDP spent on R&D in developing countries compared with industrial countries is from the Lall background paper (b), which also describes the expansion of private firms into R&D in developing countries in the past 15 years and Korea's strategy to promote domestic R&D. Box 2.7 is based on World Bank 1997f. The estimate of the return on agricultural research is from Alston and others 1998. Lack of IPR protection for critical agricultural technologies is discussed in the Pray background paper. Programs to reform public R&D laboratories in Brazil, China, India, Korea, and Mexico and focus them on the needs of the productive sector are described in the Lall background paper (b). Figures on Korea's ascendancy in private R&D and the reasons for it are given in Kim 1997. The statistics on sales of medicines derived from plants discovered by indigenous peoples and the statistic on natural pharmaceuticals in the United States are from Brush and Sabinsky 1995 and UNICEF 1995. Oral rehydration as a contrary example of where local knowledge was ignored is discussed in UNICEF 1995 and Werner and Sanders 1997. Box 2.8 is based on Quisumbing and others 1995. Box 2.9 draws on ESMAP 1991b.

Chapter 3
The studies of labor markets that find an association between wages and basic schooling are Glewwe 1998 (for Ghana), Knight and Sabot 1990 (for Kenya and Tanzania), Alderman and others 1996 (for Pakistan), and Moll 1998 (for South Africa). Studies from Côte d'Ivoire, Pakistan, and Peru on "sheepskin" or credentialing effects of education are van der Gaag and Vijverberg 1989, Tayyeb 1991, and King 1990.

See the bibliographical note to the Overview for references to studies that find greater productivity and a greater likelihood of profiting from technological improvements among more-educated farmers. Orazem and Vodopivec 1995 find that more-educated Slovenian workers experienced smaller declines in employment and real wages. Jejeebhoy 1995 is the source of evidence that persons with more schooling are more likely to adopt new contraceptive technology. Beneficial effects on IQ, innate ability, and cognitive development are discussed in Sternberg and Grigorenko 1997. Box 3.1 is based on Young 1997. On the four ways in which schooling enables mothers to raise healthier children see Glewwe 1997, Thomas and Strauss 1992, Barrera 1990, Frankenberg 1995, Rosenzweig and Schultz 1982, and Thomas, Lavy, and Strauss 1996. Examples of how schooling complements health services and reduces mortality rates among children can be found in Alderman and Lavy 1996. On the rela-

tionship between educational attainment and condom use see Filmer 1997.

The study of educational attainment among inventors in India is from Deolalikar and Evenson 1990. Evidence for the association between mathematics and science test performance and subsequent growth is in Hanushek 1995.

Box 3.2 is based on Murphy, Shleifer, and Vishny 1992. Box 3.3 draws on OECD 1996a and Amsden 1989. The trend toward including linkages between universities and the private sector is discussed in Lee 1996.

See the bibliographical note to the Overview for documentation of the fact that farmers with basic schooling gained a substantial advantage over farmers with no schooling as they acquired experience. Westphal, Rhee, and Pursell 1981 argue that Korea's rapid rate of technological learning was due to the short intervals between construction of successive industrial plants. Tan and Batra 1995 discuss the fact that larger firms are more likely to train their workers formally.

The fact that children of more-educated parents, particularly mothers, obtain more education is discussed in Alderman, Orazem, and Paterno 1996. The study that estimated the proportion of educated people in an Indian village that was optimal for learning about new farm technologies is Yamauchi 1997. The source of the ratio of males with and without high school diplomas within the ambit of the U.S. criminal justice system is Council of Economic Advisers 1995. A recent study showing a lack of correlation between public spending on education and economic growth is Devarajan, Swaroop, and Zou 1996, and a study finding a lack of correlation between such spending and educational outcomes is Hanushek and Kim 1996. Editions of *World Development Report* for 1988, 1990, 1991, and 1997 discuss the efficiency and equity issues bedeviling education, as do several World Bank strategy papers on education: see, for example, World Bank 1995a. Assessments showing that students have not mastered skills that the curriculum was intended to teach are from Glewwe 1998 and Glewwe, Kremer, and Moulin 1997. Box 3.4 draws on Knowles and others 1998.

For a discussion of the role of decentralization see Lauglo and McLean 1985. A discussion of decentralization of education as a means of overcoming information problems with monitoring and incentives is in Pritchett and Filmer forthcoming. King and Ozler 1998 examine Nicaragua's experience with school reform and its effect on test scores. On the post–civil war improvement and expansion of El Salvador's community-managed schools see Jimenez and Sawada 1998. Evidence of how information affected behavior during the AIDS epidemic in Thailand is from World Bank 1997b. Box 3.5 is based on Middleton, Ziderman, and Van Adams 1993.

Accreditation is discussed in Cooney and Paqueo-Arrezo 1993. Estimates of private rates of return to education are from Psacharopoulos 1994. Surveys from 21 countries showing income to be a major constraint are described in Behrman and Knowles 1997. Results for Peru are from Jacoby 1994, and those for Vietnam are from Glewwe and Jacoby 1995. The study of student selection for higher education in Colombia is Jimenez and Tan 1987. The statistics provided on higher education in the Philippines are from James 1991. The cross-country review of government-financed student loan programs is that by Albrecht and Ziderman 1991. Box 3.6 draws on Harding 1995 and Harrison 1997. The figure for the share of noneducational expenses in tertiary education budgets in francophone Africa is from World Bank 1995a.

The source for the information on curriculum development in Europe and Central Asia is Heyneman 1998. Documentation on distance education in Latin America is from World Bank 1998a. Background on interactive radio instruction can be found in Bosch 1997. A recent assessment of computer-aided instruction is in Osin 1998. The gains from computer-assisted instruction are documented in Kulik, Kulik, and Baangert-Drowns 1985. A review of distance education and virtual universities is in Perraton and Potashnik 1997. Box 3.7 is based on World Bank forthcoming (b).

Chapter 4

The discussion of the information revolution and the forces driving it draws on Bond 1997a. The story of how community street theaters have communicated information on AIDS prevention is from McIntyre 1998. The statistics on the rise of computing power per dollar invested and on the falling cost of voice transmission circuits are from Bond 1997a. Box 4.1 is based on the Flamm background paper (a) and information provided by the Energy, Mining, and Telecommunications Department of the World Bank. Figures on the rate of growth in the world supply of information technology and on the industrial countries' share in its production are from Mansell and Wehn 1998.

Examples of the uses of technology by individual investors in China are taken from Smith 1997. The example of the use of information technology to improve opportunities for generating income in Vietnam is from 24 Hours in Cyberspace 1996; the example from Panama was provided by Daniel Salcedo. Box 4.2 is from Clottes 1997, with additional material provided by Rema Balasundram.

Examples of the use of telecommunications and computer links to provide marketing information to farmers in Costa Rica, and of cellular phones to inform Ivorian farmers of current international cocoa prices, are taken, respectively, from Zijp 1994 (quoting Annis 1992) and Rischard

1996. The use by Filipino farmers of telex and fax machines for research and marketing, and the description of how Mexican farmer associations used computers to monitor the government's rural credit program, are described in Zijp 1994. Saunders, Warford, and Wellenius 1993 report on the impact of telephone service on fruit farmers in Sri Lanka, on the small grocer in Uruguay, and on the spare parts distributor in Kenya. The examples from Kenya and Morocco of how governments can use technology to improve governance by sharing knowledge among policymaking institutions and think tanks are from Schware and Kimberley 1995 and Hanna 1991, respectively. Box 4.3 draws on Schware and Kimberley 1995. The information technology objectives in Malaysia's national development strategy were provided by the Malaysia Country Management Unit of the World Bank and presented in Multimedia Development Corporation 1998. The discussion of the Y2K problem and Box 4.4 are based on material provided by the Information Support Group and the Information for Development program at the World Bank.

The survey of Internet users in Africa is discussed in Menou 1998. Figures on telephone density in South Asia, Sub-Saharan Africa, and the United States are from the International Telecommunication Union database, as are figures showing that the majority of people on waiting lists for telephones are in developing countries. The figure on annual telecommunications investment in developing countries is from Clottes 1997.

General references for the section on competition and the role of public policy are drawn from Stiglitz 1998, which also documents the high capital cost of telephone installation in many developing countries. The share of private telephones in Sub-Saharan Africa is from the International Telecommunication Union database. Box 4.5 is based on Braga 1997. Figures on price competition for cellular phones in Sri Lanka are from World Bank data. Changes since the 1980s in the way information infrastructure is supplied, priced, financed, used, and regulated are discussed in Smith 1995.

Box 4.6 draws on Braga and others 1998. Statistics on the availability of pay phones in Africa and Singapore are from the International Telecommunication Union database. Stories on obstacles to telephone communication in poor countries are from Hope 1997 and Wade-Barrett 1997. Wellenius 1997b describes and gives figures for what happened in Chile and the Philippines when they adopted competitive telecommunications systems. The IENTI Telecommunications Reform database documents Uganda's initiative in bringing about competition in telephone services. Wellenius 1997b discusses the benefits to consumers of competition in cellular service in Ghana. Box 4.7 is based on information received from Paul Bermingham.

The principles for privatization in the telecommunications sector are discussed in Stiglitz 1998. How poor regulation thwarted the benefits of liberalization in Poland is described in Wellenius 1997b. Regulatory measures in Guatemala to open up competitive pricing of connectivity charges are described in Spiller and Cardilli 1997. Measures for bringing telephone access to the poor are described in Zongo 1997 for Senegal; information on such measures for South Africa was provided by staff in the Energy Management and Communications department of the World Bank. Spiller and Cardilli 1997 describe how Chile and New Zealand have successfully privatized. The Chilean model of competitive bidding for subsidies is discussed in Wellenius 1997a. The private company that will bring world-class programs to low-income consumers in Africa, Latin America, and Asia through low-orbit satellites is WorldSpace (see WorldSpace 1998).

Chapter 5

The role of guilds as providers of quality control in medieval Europe and in the Arab world in the 19th century is discussed in Kuran 1989. Box 5.1 is based on Klitgaard 1991. Dimitri 1997 is the source of the discussion of quality problems in the fresh fruit market in the United States. For a discussion of quality problems in the labor market, and of the 1986 survey in West Bengal, India, documenting territorial segmentation of the labor market, see Bardhan and Rudra 1986. Box 5.2 is from Aleem 1993.

The discussion of sharecropping is based on Stiglitz 1974. Statistics on the proportion of land under share tenancy in different countries are drawn from Otsuka, Chuma, and Hayami 1992. Box 5.3 is based on Shaban 1987. For a discussion of tenancy arrangements in rural Tunisia see Laffont and Matoussi 1995. Land reforms in Brazil to address the productivity problems of poor farmers are discussed in World Bank 1997e. The discussion of permanent labor contracts and the figures on their decline in two Indian villages are drawn from Ray 1998.

Chapter 6

For a general review of the role of finance in development see Levine 1997. Some basic references for information-related market failures in finance are Stiglitz 1993 and Stiglitz and Weiss 1981. The informational foundations of banking are treated at a detailed theoretical level in Freixas and Rochet 1997. Box 6.1 is based on Kane 1994. Evidence from Ecuador and India on the relationship of productivity to access to credit is from Caprio and Demirgüç-Kunt 1997. Box 6.2 draws on Jorion 1997. The dynamic feedback of weakening collateral values is developed in a systematic way by Kiyotaki and Moore 1997. The point that financial markets do not provide full incentives for information gathering derives from Gross-

man and Stiglitz 1980. Details of the modifications to Botswana's system of land ownership, which strengthened collateral, were provided by Quill Hermans. Box 6.3 was written by Randi Ryterman. James 1987 provides evidence that announcement of a bank loan agreement boosts the stock price of the borrowing firm. The quotation from Walter Bagehot is from Bagehot 1873. The discussion of international differences in accounting standards and legal systems, including differential protection of managers, creditors, and shareholders, is based on the work of La Porta and others 1998. The related analysis of quantitative links between these accounting and legal differences and growth is based on Levine, Loayza, and Beck 1998. An analytical discussion of the "looting" problem is in Akerlof and Romer 1993. The discussion of the relationship between liquid stock exchanges and economic growth draws on Levine and Zervos 1998. The point about the need for a different approach to legal system design in transition economies is from Black, Kraakman, and Hay 1998. Box 6.4 is based in part on Weiss and Nikitin 1998. Box 6.5 draws on Garcia 1996 and White 1997. The contribution of complex derivatives in the Mexican exchange rate crisis is described by Garber 1998. Box 6.6 was written by Gerard Caprio. The Suffolk Bank system of private regulation is described by Calomiris and Kahn 1996. For discussion of evidence that mild restraints on deposit interest rates may have contributed to growth in some East Asian economies see World Bank 1993b. For economic evidence linking capital account with financial market vulnerability see Demirgüç-Kunt and Detragiache 1997. On the theory of financial restraint see Hellman, Murdock, and Stiglitz 1997.

Additional material and suggestions were provided by Cheryl Gray, Quill Hermans, Karla Hoff, Chad Leechor, Ross Levine, Don McIsaac, and Barbara Opper.

Chapter 7

The chapter draws on a wide range of sources, including Dasgupta and Mäler 1994, Tietenberg 1997, Thomas, Kishor, and Belt 1997, and World Bank 1998b. Figures on pollution in four Chinese cities are from World Bank 1997a. Figures and other evidence on disease and damage from environmental degradation come from Crosson and Anderson 1991, Esrey 1990, and Nelson 1990. The anecdote on the durian tree in Malaysia is based on Lewin 1987 and World Bank 1992. Data on wheat production and resource degradation in Pakistan are from Byerlee 1992, Byerlee and Siddiq 1994, and Ali 1998.

The chronology in Box 7.1 was taken from Handel and Risbey 1992 and Jäger 1992, with updates. The notion of sustainable development based on the substitution of human-made for natural capital is discussed by many authors; see, for example, Pezzey 1989.

In Box 7.2 the notion of option value is from Arrow and Fisher 1974; the estimate of the option value of conserving the wilderness area of Sierra de Manantlán is from Fisher and Hanemann 1990. Suggestions for effective indicators of environmental quality are drawn from World Bank 1997c. The notion of genuine saving and the figures for Latin America and the Caribbean and for Sub-Saharan Africa are from World Bank 1997c. Box 7.3 is based on World Bank 1998b. The example of Botswana's natural resource accounts was provided by Kirk Hamilton. Nordhaus and Popp 1997 estimate the value of information about climate change. The discussion of El Niño forecasting is based on information provided by Maxx Dilley and Robert Watson. The anecdote about firewood use in the Republic of Yemen comes from ESMAP 1991a. World Bank 1997a reports on the Waigaoqiao thermal power plant in China. Box 7.4 is based on a summary of the project provided by Dely Gapasin.

The example of the West African Newsmedia and Development Center is taken from Ariasingam, Abedin, and Chee 1997. Box 7.5 is based on information supplied by Kulsum Ahmed and Paul Martin. On the Sub-Saharan African Knowledge and Experience Resource Network see MELISSA 1998. Box 7.6 is based on Ostrom and Wertime 1995. Box 7.7 is based on information from Maureen Cropper and Donald Larson and on the analysis by Schmalensee and others 1997. On China's scheme for reducing water pollution see Wang and Wheeler 1996. The estimate of the benefits of market-based greenhouse gas abatement is based on Richels and others 1996. On joint implementation and related mechanisms see UNFCCC 1998. The link between lack of insurance and land degradation is described by Dasgupta and Mäler 1994. The discussion of energy service companies is based on Cabraal, Cosgrove-Davies, and Schaeffer 1996. The estimate of increased affordability of energy comes from the Solar Electric Light Company, Chevy Chase, Md. Some issues related to the decentralization of environmental management functions are discussed in Lutz and Caldecott 1996. For recent literature on how industry responds to community environmental pressure see World Bank 1998b. Box 7.8 is from World Bank 1998b. Box 7.9 is based on Blackman and Bannister 1998. Box 7.10 is based on a summary of the project provided by Karin Kemper and Donald Larson.

Information on the work of parataxonomists in Costa Rica can be found in Reid 1993. The projection of demand for organic products in Canada is from Weymes 1990. The discussion of free riding in international agreements is based on Barrett 1992.

Contributions, comments, and suggestions received from Kulsum Ahmed, Tamara Belt, Anil Cabraal, Ken Chomitz, Luis Constantino, Maureen Cropper, Chona Cruz, John Dixon, Francisco Ferreira, Dely Gapasin, Kirk Hamilton, Ian Johnson, Karin Kemper, Nalin Kishor, Kanta Kumari, Donald Larson, Vladimir Litvak, Paul Martin, Douglas Olson, Ramesh Ramankutty, Richard Reidinger, Frank Rittner, Larry Simpson, and Vinod Thomas are gratefully acknowledged.

Chapter 8

Statistics on poverty in the introductory section are from World Bank data. Researchers' estimates of the impact of an increase in literacy on environmental awareness are from Dasgupta and Wheeler 1997. Box 8.1 draws on Thomas, Strauss, and Henriques 1991. The Jamaican living standards survey providing information about food supplementation in poor households is discussed in Grosh 1992. The study of 121 rural water supply projects in 49 countries is Narayan and Pritchett 1995. On the donor-funded irrigation program in Nepal that nearly missed the fact that farmers had already installed their own systems see Ostrom 1995. Cooperative groups in Kenya and the effectiveness of group-centered extension among female farmers are described in Bindlish and Evenson 1993 and Purcell and Anderson 1997. The study showing evidence of peer influence in a family planning program in Bangladesh is Munshi and Mayaux 1998. Box 8.2 draws on Tendler 1994 and Tendler and Freedheim 1994. The survey in rural Tanzania to measure the density and importance of social capital is Narayan and Pritchett 1997. Issues in promoting oral rehydration therapy are described in UNICEF 1997 and Werner and Sanders 1997.

Jalan and Ravallion 1998 study the effects of individual and covariate shocks to income on rural southern Chinese households of varying wealth. The study of ICRISAT data on farmers' choices of traditional versus high-yielding rice varieties, reported in Box 8.3, is Morduch 1995; Binswanger and Rosenzweig 1993 relate farm profits to the predictability of the monsoon. Jacoby and Skoufias 1997 examine the response of school attendance to seasonal income fluctuations in India. Box 8.4 is based on Udry 1994.

The findings in Thailand that farmers with land title, who could offer collateral, could borrow significantly more than those without are from Feder, Onchan, and Raparla 1986, as is evidence that farmers with title in Thailand and other countries invested more in their land and obtained better access to credit. Feder 1991 gathers evidence for other countries. Qualifying evidence from Paraguay on the value of land titling in providing access to credit is from Olinto 1997. The study of land titling in Ghana, Kenya, and Rwanda is Bruce and Migot-Adholla 1994. The discussion of the Grameen Bank and other microfinance institutions draws on Morduch 1998. Box 8.5 draws on Woolcock 1998.

Information on the Unit Desa program in Indonesia is from Jonathan Morduch. How short-term relief programs combined with institutional credit reduced distress sales of land in India after a natural disaster is described in Cain 1983. Self-selection programs of assistance are discussed in Subbarao and others 1997; the 1997 World Bank project in Argentina is described in an internal World Bank report. Tuck and Lindert 1996 describe the food price subsidy program in Tunisia. Box 8.6 is based on Case and Deaton 1996.

The discussion of P4K in Indonesia is drawn from International Fund for Agricultural Development 1994. For a discussion of the Grameen Bank's programs to promote social development see Khandker, Khalily, and Khan 1998. Grameen's cellular phone enterprise is discussed by Yunus 1996. Details of the human rights and legal education of the Bangladesh Rural Advancement Committee were provided by Jonathan Morduch. Morduch 1998 describes the formation of consortia to link microfinance programs globally.

Chapter 9

Information for the section on knowledge creation and for Boxes 9.1, 9.2, and 9.3 was provided by the Consultative Group on International Agricultural Research, Mead Over, and the Global Environment Facility.

The section on transferring and adapting knowledge draws heavily on World Bank forthcoming (a). The account of the workings of PROSANEAR comes from World Bank 1994b and other World Bank documents. The description of AGETIPs is taken from Dia 1995. The story of Guinea's water sector is from a 1996 edition of *Viewpoint,* a World Bank internal newsletter published by the Industry and Energy Department. Box 9.4 draws from Heggie 1995. Family planning services in rural Bangladesh are described in World Bank forthcoming (a). The allusion to the Kenya textbook experiment draws on Glewwe, Kremer, and Moulin 1997. The reference for the Vietnam story is World Bank forthcoming (a). World Bank 1994a discusses international assistance and pension reform. The recent U.K. white paper on international development is United Kingdom Secretary of State for International Development 1997. The discussion of the return to analytical work is drawn from Deininger, Squire, and Basu forthcoming. Information for Box 9.5 came from an internal Bank document. The quotation from the United Nations Development Programme evaluation is from Berg 1993.

Descriptions of the spread of formal knowledge management programs in Europe and the United States appear in American Productivity and Quality Center 1996, 1997, and 1998. Desisto and Harris 1998 predict that during the next five years knowledge sharing programs will shift from an internal to an external focus. Box 9.6 draws on material supplied by Bruce Ross-Larson. Box 9.7 draws on material supplied by Roberto Chavez. On the question of the choice of appropriate technology for knowledge sharing, a general discussion is in Davenport and Prusak 1998. Box 9.8 was written by Peter Armstrong. Willmott 1998 discusses the fact that many systems are still not quick, easy to use, or easy to maintain. Davenport and Prusak 1998 further note that we do not yet have useful technology to assist with knowledge creation and discuss more traditional modes of communication as tools for knowledge sharing.

Studies of the costs of knowledge management programs have been produced by the Gartner Group (Bair and Hunter 1998), including estimates of knowledge management expenditure in budgets for enterprises or, in the case of consulting companies, in revenue (Hunter 1998). American Productivity and Quality Center 1996 documents how organizations like Price Waterhouse and Ernst & Young have made knowledge sharing an integral part of their formal personnel evaluation systems. On the use of knowledge-sharing awards, see a general discussion in Davenport and Prusak 1998, and the description of the Texas Instruments "Not Invented Here But I Used It Anyway" award in American Productivity and Quality Center 1997. The use of incentives is identified as a critical success factor in Davenport, De Long, and Beers 1998; the study of whether knowledge management programs actually succeed appears in the same source. Box 9.9 was written by David Gray.

Chapter 10

Much of the material in this chapter summarizes discussions in other chapters. Documentation is provided in the bibliographical note for the chapter where the original discussion appears.

King and Anne 1993 reports on the provision of educational stipends to girls in Bangladesh. Aiyer 1996 describes how Mexican accounting methods failed to show the true status of bank loans. On the role of India's media in warning of famine and agitating for public action see Drèze and Sen 1989 and Ram 1990. The source for the statement that several South and Central American countries have increased the quality and quantity of information about individual taxpayers is the Mookherjee background paper.

Background papers

Barton, John. "Biotechnology Patenting."
Behrman, Jere. "Empirical Evidence on Asymmetric Information, Markets and Policies in Developing Economies."
Belussi, Fiorenza. "Policies for the Development of Knowledge-Intensive Local Production Systems."

Braga, Carlos, Carsten Fink, and Claudia Paz Sepulveda. "Intellectual Property Rights and Economic Development."

Centre for Information Society Development in Africa, CSIR South Africa, and the Centre for Tele-Information, Technical University of Denmark. "Knowledge in Development: Multi-Media, Multi-Purpose Community Information Centres as Catalysts for Building Innovative Knowledge-Based Societies."

Flamm, Kenneth. "Assessing the Rate of Technological Advance in Information Technology: Quantitative Measurements and Methodological Issues." (a)

———. "Semiconductor Trade Disputes: Defining the World Trading System in High Technology Products." (b)

Johnson, Daniel, and Robert Evenson. "Invention in Less-Developed Countries."

Kumar, Nagesh. "Multinational Enterprises and Technology Generation: Locational Patterns, Their Determinants and Implications."

Kuznetsov, Yevgeny. "Public Policy in the World of Uncertainty and Change: Facilitating Social Learning."

Lall, Sanjaya. "Exports of Manufactures by Developing Countries: Emerging Patterns of Trade and Location." (a)

———. "Putting Knowledge to Work for Development." (b)

Maskus, Keith. "Price Effects and Competition Aspects of Intellectual Property Rights in Developing Countries."

Mitra, Raja. "Harnessing Information and Knowledge for Economic Development." (a)

———. "Knowledge Clusters and Regional Inequalities." (b)

Mookherjee, Dilip. "Information Systems and Public Policy in LDCs."

Pray, Carl. Untitled.

Radosevic, Slavo. "Post-Socialist Transformation of Countries of the Central and Eastern Europe and Knowledge-Based Economy: The Evidence and Main Analytical Issues." (a)

———. "Building Knowledge-Based Economy in Countries of Central and Eastern Europe: Policy Implications." (b)

Rosenzweig, Mark. "Social Learning and Economic Growth. Empirical Evidence."

Sternberg, Robert, Elena Grigorenko, and Donald Bundy. "Measuring Human Development: The Role of General Indices of Cognitive Ability in Assessing the Impact of Education and Targeted Interventions on Child Development."

Thomas, Vinod, Nalin Kishor, and Tamara Belt. "Embracing the Power of Knowledge for a Sustainable Environment."

Selected bibliography

Acemoglu, Daron. 1997. "Training and Innovation in an Imperfect Labor Market." *Review of Economic Studies* 64(2): 445–64.

Aghion, Philippe, and Patrick Bolton. 1997. "A Theory of Trickle-Down Growth and Development." *Review of Economic Studies* 64(2): 151–72.

Aiyer, Sri-Ram. 1996. "Anatomy of Mexico's Banking System following the Peso Crisis." Report No. 45 (revised). Regional Studies Program, Latin America and the Caribbean Technical Department, World Bank, Washington, D.C.

Akerlof, George A. 1976. "The Economics of Caste and of the Rat Race and Other Woeful Tales." *Quarterly Journal of Economics* 90(4): 599–617.

Akerlof, George A., and Paul M. Romer. 1993. "Looting: The Economic Underworld of Bankruptcy for Profit." *Brookings Papers on Economic Activity* 2(1): 2–60.

Albrecht, Douglas, and Adrian Ziderman. 1991. *Deferred Cost Recovery for Higher Education: Student Loan Programs in Developing Countries.* World Bank Discussion Paper No. 137. Washington, D.C.: World Bank.

Alderman, Harold, J. Behrman, D. Ross, and R. Sabot. 1996. "The Returns to Endogenous Human Capital in Pakistan's Rural Wage Labor Market." *Oxford Bulletin of Economics and Statistics* 58(1): 29–55.

Alderman, Harold, and Victor Lavy. 1996. "Household Responses to Public Health Services: Cost and Quality Trade-offs." *World Bank Research Observer* 11(1): 3–22.

Alderman, Harold, Peter F. Orazem, and Elizabeth M. Paterno. 1996. "School Quality, School Cost, and the Public/Private School Choices of Low-Income Households in Pakistan." Working Paper Series on Impact Evaluation of Education Reforms, Paper No. 2. Development Research Group, World Bank, Washington, D.C.

Alderman, Harold, and G. Shively. 1996. "Price Movements and Economic Reform in Ghana: Implications for Food Security." In David Sahn, ed., *Economic Reform and the Poor in Africa.* Oxford, U.K.: Clarendon Press.

Aleem, Irfan. 1993. "Imperfect Information, Screening and Cost of Informal Lending: A Study of a Rural Credit Market in Pakistan." In Karla Hoff, Avishay Braverman, and Joseph E. Stiglitz, eds., *The Economics of Rural Organization: Theory, Practice, and Policy.* London, U.K.: Oxford University Press.

Ali, Mubarak. 1998. "Technical Change and Resource Productivity in Pakistan's Agriculture: An Analysis by Cropping System." Asian Vegetable Research and Development Center, Tainan, Taiwan, China.

Alston, J. M., C. C. Marra, P. G. Pardey, and T. J. Wyatt. 1998. "Research Returns Redux: A Meta-Analysis of Agricultural R&D Evaluations." IFPRI Research Report (draft). International Food Policy Research Institute, Washington, D.C.

Amann, Markus, and Janusz Cofala. 1995. "Scenarios of Future Acidification in Asia: Exploratory Calculations." In *RAINS-ASIA Technical Report: The Development of an Integrated Model for Sulfur Deposition.* Washington, D.C.: World Bank.

American Productivity and Quality Center. 1996. *Knowledge Management Consortium Benchmarking Study: Best-Practice Report.* Houston, Tex.

———. 1997. *Using Information Technology to Support Knowledge Management, Consortium Benchmarking Study: Best-Practice Report.* Houston, Tex.

———. 1998. *Knowledge Management and the Learning Organization: A European Perspective.* Houston, Tex.

Amsden, Alice. 1989. *Asia's Next Giant: South Korea and Late Industrialization.* New York, N.Y.: Oxford University Press.

Annis, Sheldon. 1992. "Evolving Connectedness Among Environmental Groups and Grassroots Organizations in Protected Areas of Central America." *World Development* 20: 587–95.

Aoki, Masahiko, Kevin Murdock, and Masahiro Okuno-Fujiwara. 1997. "Beyond the East Asian Miracle: Introducing the Market-Enhancing View." In Masahiko Aoki, Kyung-Ki

Kim, and Masahiro Okuno-Fujiwara, eds., *The Role of Government in East Asian Economic Development: Comparative Institutional Analysis.* New York, N.Y.: Oxford University Press.

Aoki, R., and T. J. Prusa. 1993. "International Standards for Intellectual Property Protection and R&D Incentives." *Journal of International Economics* 35(2): 251–73.

Ariasingam, David L., Esme Abedin, and Nina Chee. 1997. "Environmental Education. Building Constituencies." Report No. 17319. Environmental Education Program, World Bank, Washington, D.C.

Arnott, Richard, and Joseph E. Stiglitz. 1994. "Moral Hazard and Nonmarket Institutions: Dysfunctional Crowding Out or Peer Monitoring?" *American Economic Review* 81(1): 179–90.

Arrow, Kenneth, and Anthony C. Fisher. 1974. "Environmental Preservation, Uncertainty, and Irreversibility." *Quarterly Journal of Economics* 88(2): 312–19.

Bagehot, Walter. 1873. *Lombard Street: A Description of the Money Market.* London, U.K.: H. S. King. Reprinted, Homewood, Ill.: Richard D. Irwin, 1962.

Bair, J., and R. Hunter. 1998. "Introducing the KM Project Viability Assessment." Research Note KM: SPA-03-5005. Gartner Group, Stamford, Conn.

Banerjee, A. 1992. "Simple Model of Herd Behavior." *Quarterly Journal of Economics* 107(3): 797–817.

Banerjee, Abhijit, and Andrew Newman. 1993. "Occupational Choice and the Process of Development." *Journal of Political Economy* 101(2): 274–98.

Bardhan, Pranab. 1997. "The Nature of Institutional Impediments to Economic Development." Working Paper No. 96066. Center for International and Development Economic Research, University of California, Berkeley.

Bardhan, Pranab, and A. Rudra. 1986. "Labor Mobility and the Boundaries of the Village Moral Economy." *Journal of Peasant Studies* 13(3): 90–99.

Barr, Nicholas, ed. 1994. *Labor Markets and Social Policy in Central and Eastern Europe: The Transition and Beyond.* New York, N.Y.: Oxford University Press.

Barrera, Albino. 1990. "The Role of Maternal Schooling and Its Interactions with Public Health Programs in Child Health Production." *Journal of Development Economics* 32(1): 69–91.

Barrett, Scott. 1992. "The Problem of Global Environmental Protection." In Dieter Helm, ed., *Economic Policy toward the Environment.* Oxford, U.K.: Blackwell.

Bartel, Ann P., and Frank R. Lichtenberg. 1987. "The Comparative Advantage of Educated Workers in Implementing New Technology." *Review of Economics and Statistics* 69(1): 1–11.

Bartholomew, Philip, and Benton Gup. 1998. "A Survey of Bank Failures in the Non-U.S. G-10 Countries since 1980." Paper presented at the Western Economics Association meetings, Lake Tahoe, Nev., June.

Baskin, Jonathan Barron. 1988. "The Development of Corporate Financial Markets in Britain and the United States, 1600–1914: Overcoming Asymmetric Information." *Business History Review* 62(1): 199–237.

Beanton, Albert E., Ina V. S. Mullis, Michael O. Martin, Eugenio J. Gonzalez, Dana L. Kelly, and Teresa A. Smith. 1996. *Mathematics Achievement in the Middle School Years: IEA's Third International Mathematics and Science Study.* Boston, Mass.: Center for the Study of Testing, Evaluation, and Educational Policy, and Boston College.

Behrman, Jere R., and James C. Knowles. 1997. "How Strongly is Child Schooling Associated with Household Income?" University of Pennsylvania, Philadelphia, Penn., and Abt Associates, Bethesda, Md.

Berg, Elliott. 1993. *Rethinking Technical Cooperation: Reforms for Capacity Building in Africa.* New York, N.Y.: United Nations Development Programme.

Biggs, T., M. Shah, and P. Srivastava. 1995. *Technological Capabilities and Learning in African Enterprises.* World Bank Technical Paper No. 286. Washington, D.C.: World Bank

Bindlish, Vishva, and Robert Evenson. 1993. *Evaluation of the Performance of T&V Extension in Kenya.* World Bank Technical Paper No. 208. Africa Technical Department, World Bank, Washington, D.C.

Binswanger, Hans P., Klaus Deininger, and Gershon Feder. 1988. "Power, Distortions, Revolt and Reform in Agricultural Land Relations." In Jere R. Behrman and T. N. Srinivasan, eds., *Handbook of Development Economics,* vol. IIIB. Amsterdam: North-Holland.

Binswanger, Hans, and Mark Rosenzweig. 1993. "Wealth, Weather, Risk, and the Composition and Profitability of Agricultural Investments." *Economic Journal* 103(4): 56–78.

Black, Bernard, Reiner Kraakman, and Jonathan Hay. 1998. "Corporate Law From Scratch." In Roman Frydman, Cheryl Gray, and Andrzej Rapaczynski, eds., *Corporate Governance in Central Europe and Russia: Insiders and the State.* Budapest: Central European University Press.

Blackman, Allen, and Geoffrey Bannister. 1998. "Community Pressure and Clean Technologies in the Informal Sector: An Econometric Analysis of the Adoption of Propane by Traditional Brickmakers in Ciudad Juárez, Mexico." *Journal of Environmental Economics and Management* 35(1): 1–21.

Blanchard, Olivier, and Michael Kremer. 1997. "Disorganization." *Quarterly Journal of Economics* 112: 1091–1126.

Bond, James. 1997a. "The Drivers of the Information Revolution—Cost, Computing Power and Convergence." In *The Information Revolution and the Future of Telecommunications.* Washington, D.C: World Bank.

———. 1997b. "How Information Infrastructure is Changing the World." In *The Information Revolution and the Future of Telecommunications.* Washington, D.C.: World Bank.

———. 1997c. "Telecommunications is Dead, Long Live Networking—The Effect of the Information Revolution on the Telecom Industry." In *The Information Revolution and the Future of Telecommunications.* Washington, D.C: World Bank.

Bosch, Andrea. 1997. "Interactive Radio Instruction: Twenty-Three Years of Improving Educational Quality." Education and Technology Series No. 1(1). Human Development Department Education Group—Education and Technology Team, World Bank, Washington, D.C.

Bowles, Samuel, and Herbert Gintis. 1996. "Efficient Redistribution: New Rules for Markets, States, and Communities." *Politics and Society* 24: 307–42.

Braga, Carlos A. Primo. 1997. "Liberalizing Telecommunications and the Role of the World Trade Organization." In *The Information Revolution and the Future of Telecommunications.* Washington, D.C.: World Bank.

Braga, Carlos A. Primo, and Carsten Fink. 1997. "The Private Sector and the Internet." In *The Information Revolution and the Future of Telecommunications.* Washington, D.C.: World Bank.

Braga, Carlos A. Primo, Emmanuel Forestier, Charles Kenny, and Peter Smith. 1998. "Developing Countries and the Telecommunications Accounting Rate Regime: A Role for the World Bank." Energy Mining and Telecommunications Department (IENTI), Telecommunication and Informatics Division, World Bank, Washington, D.C.

Braverman, Avishay, and Joseph E. Stiglitz. 1982. "Sharecropping and the Interlinking of Agrarian Markets." *American Economic Review* 72(4): 695–715.

Bruce, John W., and S. E. Migot-Adholla. 1994. *Searching for Land Tenure Security in Africa.* Dubuque, Ia.: Kendall/Hunt.

Brush, S. B., and D. Sabinsky. 1995. *Valuing Local Knowledge: Indigenous People and Intellectual Property Rights.* Washington, D.C.: Island Press.

Buckley, Stephen. 1997. "The Lives and Deaths of an Ethiopian Midwife." *Washington Post,* October 7, 1997.

Burnside, Craig, and David Dollar. 1997. "Aid Policies and Growth." Policy Research Working Paper No. 1777. World Bank, Washington, D.C.

Byerlee, Derek. 1992. "Technical Change, Productivity, and Sustainability in Irrigated Cropping System of South Asia: Emerging Issues in the Post-Green Revolution Era." *Journal of International Development* 4(5): 477–96.

Byerlee, Derek, and Piedad Moya. 1993. "Impacts of International Wheat Breeding Research in the Developing World, 1966–1990." Centro Internacional de Mejoramiento de Maiz y Trigo (CIMMYT with CGIAR), Mexico City.

Byerlee, Derek, and A. Siddiq. 1994. "Has the Green Revolution Been Sustained? The Quantitative Impact of the Seed-Fertilizer Revolution in Pakistan Revisited." *World Development* 22(9): 1345–61.

Cabraal, Anil, Mac Cosgrove-Davies, and Loretta Schaeffer. 1996. *Best Practices for Photovoltaic Household Electrification Programs. Lessons from Experiences in Selected Countries.* World Bank Technical Paper No. 324. Asia Technical Department, World Bank, Washington, D.C.

Cain, Mead. 1983. "Fertility as an Adjustment to Risk." Working Paper No. 100. Population Council, Center for Policy Studies, New York, N.Y.

Calomiris, C. W., and C. M. Kahn. 1996. "The Efficiency of Self-Regulated Payments Systems: Learning from the Suffolk System." *Journal of Money, Credit, and Banking* 28(4): 766–97.

Caprio, J. G., Jr., and A. Demirgüç-Kunt. 1997. "The Role of Long-Term Finance." Policy Research Working Paper No. 1746. Policy Research Department, Finance and Private Sector Development Division, World Bank, Washington, D.C.

Case, Anne, and Angus Deaton. 1996. "Large Cash Transfers to the Elderly in South Africa." NBER Working Paper No. 55721. National Bureau of Economic Research, Cambridge, Mass.

Castro-Leal, Florencio, Julia Dayton, Lionel Demery, and Kalpana Mehra. 1997. "Public Social Spending in Africa: Do the Poor Benefit?" Working Paper. Poverty Reduction and Economic Management Network, Poverty Division, World Bank, Washington, D.C.

CGIAR (Consultative Group on International Agricultural Research). 1994–95. *Annual Report.* Washington, D.C.: CGIAR Secretariat.

Chemical Week. 1994. "Indian Industry Flocks to ISO 9000 to Boost Already Booming Exports." November 4.

Clottes, Francoise. 1997. "The Information Revolution and the Role of Government." In *The Information Revolution and the Future of Telecommunications.* Washington, D.C.: World Bank.

Cooney, Robert P., and Eliza Paqueo-Arrezo. 1993. "Higher Education Regulation in the Philippines: Issues of Control, Quality Assurance, and Accreditation." *Higher Education Policy* 25(6): 25–28.

Council of Economic Advisers. 1995. *Economic Report of the President 1995.* Washington, D.C.: Government Printing Office.

Crosson, Pierre R., and Jock R. Anderson. 1991. *Global Food: Resources and Prospects.* Washington, D.C.: World Bank.

Dahlman, Carl J. 1993. "Electronics Development Strategy: The Robot Government." In Björn Wellenius, Arnold Miller, and Carl J. Dahlman, eds., *Developing the Electronics Industry.* Washington, D.C.: World Bank.

———. 1994. "Technology Strategy in East Asian Developing Economies." *Journal of Asian Economics* 5(Winter): 541–72.

Dahlman, Carl J., and Ousa Sananikone. 1990. "Technology Strategy in the Economy of Taiwan: Exploiting Foreign Linkages and Investing in Local Capability." Industry and Energy Department, Policy Planning and Research, World Bank, Washington, D.C.

Dahlman, Carl J., and Francisco C. Sercovich. 1984. "Local Development and Exports of Technology: The Comparative Advantages of Argentina, Brazil, India, the Republic of Korea, and Mexico." World Bank Staff Working Paper No. 667. World Bank, Washington, D.C.

Dasgupta, Monica. 1994. "What Motivates Fertility Decline? A Case Study from Punjab, India." In B. Egero and M. Hammerskjold, eds., *Understanding Reproductive Change.* Lund, Sweden: Lund University Press.

Dasgupta, Partha, and Karl-Göran Mäler. 1994. "Poverty, Institutions, and the Environmental-Resource Base." Environment Paper No. 9. World Bank, Washington, D.C.

Dasgupta, Susmita, Hua Wang, and David Wheeler. 1997. "Surviving Success: Policy Reform and the Future of Industrial Pollution in China." Working Paper No. 1856. Development Research Group, World Bank, Washington, D.C.

Dasgupta, Susmita, and David R. Wheeler. 1997. "Citizen Complaints as Environmental Indicators: Evidence from China." Policy Research Working Paper No. WPS1704. Environment Department, Pollution Control and Waste Management, World Bank, Washington, D.C.

Datt, Gaurav, and Martin Ravallion. 1998. "Farm Productivity and Rural Poverty in India." *Journal of Development Studies* 34(3): 62–85.

Davenport, Thomas K., D. W. De Long, and Michael C. Beers. 1998. "Successful Knowledge Management Projects." *Sloan Management Review* 39(1): 43–57.

Davenport, Thomas K., and Laurence Prusak. 1998. *Working Knowledge: How Organizations Manage What They Know.* Boston, Mass.: Harvard Business School Press.

David, Paul A. 1993. "Knowledge, Property, and the System Dynamics of Technological Change." In Lawrence M. Summers and Shekhar Shah, eds., *Proceedings of the World Bank Annual Conference on Development Economics.* Washington, D.C.: World Bank.

Davis, Lance E., and Robert J. Cull. 1994. *International Capital Markets and American Economic Growth: 1820–1914.* Cambridge, U.K.: Cambridge University Press.

Deininger, Klaus, Lyn Squire, and Swati Basu. Forthcoming. "Does Economic Analysis Improve the Quality of Foreign Assistance?" *World Bank Economic Review*.

Demirgüç-Kunt, A., and E. Detragiache. 1998. "Financial Liberalization and Financial Fragility." In *Annual World Bank Conference on Development Economics*. Washington, D.C.: World Bank.

Denison, Edward F. 1962. *The Sources of Economic Growth in the United States and the Alternatives before Us*. New York, N.Y.: Committee for Economic Development.

———. 1985. *Trends in American Economic Growth, 1929–1982*. Brookings Institution: Washington, D.C.

Deolalikar, Anil, and Robert Evenson. 1990. "Private Inventive Activity in Indian Manufacturing: Its Extent and Determinants." In R. E. Evenson and G. Ranis, eds., *Science and Technology: Lessons for Development Policy*. Boulder, Colo.: Westview Press.

Desisto, R., and K. Harris. 1998. "Powerful Marketing and Sales Solutions with KM." Research Note KM: SPA-04-1863. Gartner Group, Stamford, Conn.

Devarajan, Shantayanan, Vinaya Swaroop, and Heng-fu Zou. 1996. "The Composition of Public Expenditure and Economic Growth." *Journal of Monetary Economics* 37(2): 313–44.

Dia, Mamadou. 1995. *Africa's Management and Beyond: Reconciling Indigenous and Transplanted Institutions*. Washington, D.C.: World Bank.

Dilley, Maxx. 1997. "Climatic Factors Affecting Annual Maize Yields in the Valley of Oaxaca, Mexico." *International Journal of Climatology* 17(3): 1549–57.

Dimitri, Carolyn. 1997. "Grower-Wholesaler Fruit Marketing Contracts in the Early 1900s: A Rationale for Institutional Innovation." Agriculture and Resource Economics Department, University of Maryland, College Park, Md.

Downing, Robert J., Ramesh Ramankutty, and Jitendra J. Shah. 1997. *RAINS-ASIA. An Assessment Model for Acid Deposition in Asia*. Directions for Development Series. Washington, D.C.: World Bank.

Drèze, Jean, Peter Lanjouw, and Naresh Sharma. 1997. "Credit in Rural India: A Case Study." DERP Working Paper No. 6. Suntory and Toyota International Centres for Economics and Related Disciplines, London School of Economics, London.

Drèze, Jean, and Amartya Sen, eds. 1989. *Hunger and Public Action*. Oxford, U.K.: Oxford University Press.

Easterly, William. 1997. "The Ghosts of Financing Gap: How the Harrod-Domar Growth Model Still Haunts Development Economics." Policy Research Working Paper No. 1807. World Bank, Washington, D.C.

Easterly, William, and Ross Levine. 1996. "Africa's Growth Tragedy: Policies and Ethnic Division." Discussion Paper No. 536. Harvard Institute for International Development, Cambridge, Mass.

Easterly, William, Ross Levine, and Lant Pritchett. Forthcoming. "Stylized Facts and the Growth Models Who Love Them." Development Research Group, World Bank, Washington, D.C.

Enos, John. 1991. *The Creation of Technological Capability in Developing Countries*. London, U.K.: Pinter.

Ergas, H., M. Goldman, E. Ralph, and G. Felker. 1997. *Technology Institutions and Policies: Their Role in Developing Technological Capability in Industry*. World Bank Technical Paper No. 383. World Bank, Washington, D.C.

ESMAP (Energy Sector Management Assistance Programme). 1991a. "Republic of Yemen. Household Energy Strategy Study, Phase I. A Preliminary Study of Northern Governorates." Report No. 126/91. World Bank, Washington, D.C.

———. 1991b. "Rwanda: Commercialization of Improved Charcoal Stoves and Carbonization Techniques." Mid-Term Progress Report No. 141/91. World Bank, Washington, D.C.

Esrey, Steven A. 1990. *Health Benefits from Improvements in Water Supply and Sanitation: Survey and Analysis of the Literature of Selected Diseases*. Technical Report No. 66. Arlington, Va.: Water and Sanitation for Health Project.

Ethier, W. J., and J. R. Markusen. 1996. "Multinational Firms, Technology Diffusion, and Trade." *Journal of International Economics* 41(1): 1–28.

European Commission. 1994. *The European Report on Science and Technology Indicators*. Brussels.

Evans, Philip B., and Thomas S. Wurster. 1997. "Strategy and the New Economics of Information: Competing in the Information Economy." *Harvard Business Review* 75(9): 71–82.

Evenson, Robert L., and Larry Westphal. 1995. "Technological Change and Technology Strategy." In Jere Behrman and T. N. Srinavasan, eds., *Handbook of Development Economics*, vol. 3A. Amsterdam: Elsevier.

FAO (Food and Agriculture Organization). Various years. *FAO Production Yearbook*. Rome.

Feder, Gershon. 1991. "Land Tenure and Property Rights: Theory and Implications for Development Policy." *World Bank Economic Review* 5(1): 135–53.

Feder, Gershon, Tongroj Onchan, and Tejaswi Raparla. 1986. *Land Ownership, Security, and Access to Credit in Rural Thailand*. Discussion Paper No. ARU 53. Washington, D.C.: World Bank.

Filmer, Deon. 1997. "The Socioeconomic Correlates of Sexual Behavior: Results from an Analysis of DHS Data." Development Research Group, World Bank, Washington, D.C.

Filmer, Deon, and Lant Pritchett. 1997. *Child Mortality and Public Spending on Health: How Much Does Money Matter?* Policy Research Working Paper No. 1864. Washington, D.C.: World Bank.

Fisher, Anthony C., and W. Michael Hanemann. 1986. "Option Value and the Extinction of Species." *Advances in Applied Micro-Economics* 4: 169–90.

———. 1990. "Option Value: Theory and Measurement." *European Review of Agricultural Economics* 17(2): 167–80.

Foster, Andrew, and Mark Rosenzweig. 1993. "Information Flows and Discrimination in Labor Markets in Rural Areas in Developing Countries." In Lawrence H. Summers and Shekhar Shah, eds., *Proceedings of the World Bank Annual Conference on Development Economics 1992*. Washington, D.C.: World Bank.

———. 1995. "Learning by Doing and Learning from Others: Human Capital and Technical Change in Agriculture." *Journal of Political Economy* 103(6): 1176–1209.

———. 1996. "Technical Change and Human Capital Returns and Investments: Evidence from the Green Revolution." *American Economic Review* 86(4): 931–53.

Frankenberg, Elizabeth. 1995. "The Effects of Access to Health Care on Infant Mortality in Indonesia." *Health Transition Review* 5(1): 143–63.

Freixas, X., and J.-C. Rochet. 1997. *Microeconomics of Banking.* Cambridge, Mass.: MIT Press.

Froot, Kenneth, Paul O'Connell, and Mark Seasholes. 1998. "The Portfolio Flows of International Investors." Paper presented at the CEPR/World Bank Conference, London, May 8–9.

Garber, P. 1998. "Derivative Products in Exchange Rate Crises." In Reuven Glick, ed., *Managing Capital Flows and Exchange Rates: Lessons from the Pacific Basin.* New York, N.Y.: Cambridge University Press.

Garcia, Gillian. 1996. "Deposit Insurance: Obtaining the Benefits and Avoiding the Pitfalls." Working Paper No. 96/83. International Monetary Fund, Washington, D.C.

Ghatak, Maitreesh. 1996. "Strategic Complementarities in Discriminatory Behavior." Department of Economics, University of Chicago.

Glewwe, Paul. 1997. "How Does Schooling of Mothers Improve Child Health? Evidence from Morocco." LSMS Working Paper No. 128. World Bank, Washington, D.C.

———. 1998. *The Economics of School Quality Investments in Developing Countries: An Empirical Study of Ghana.* London, U.K.: Macmillan Press.

Glewwe, Paul, and Hanan Jacoby. 1995. "Economic Analysis of Delayed Primary School Enrollment in a Low-Income Country: The Role of Early Childhood Nutrition." *Review of Economics and Statistics* 77(2): 156–69.

Glewwe, Paul, Michael Kremer, and Sylvie Moulin. 1997. "Textbooks and Test Scores: Evidence from a Prospective Evaluation in Kenya." Development Research Group, World Bank, Washington, D.C.

Gould, David M., and William C. Gruben. 1996. "The Role of Intellectual Property Rights in Economic Growth." *Journal of Development Economics* 48(3): 328–50.

Grabowski, Richard. 1994. "The Successful Developmental State: Where Does It Come From?" *World Development* 22(3): 413–22.

Greif, Avner. 1994. "Cultural Beliefs and the Organization of Society: A Historical and Theoretical Reflection on Collectivist and Individualist Societies." *Journal of Political Economy* 102(5): 912–50.

———. 1996. "Contracting, Enforcement, and Efficiency: Economics Beyond the Law." In Michael Bruno and Boris Pleskovic, eds., *Annual World Bank Conference on Development Economics.* Washington, D.C.: World Bank.

Grosh, Margaret E. 1992. "Jamaican Food Stamps Programme: A Case Study in Targeting." *Food Policy* 17 (February): 23–40.

Grossman, S. J., and J. Stiglitz. 1980. "On the Impossibility of Informationally Efficient Markets." *American Economic Review* 70(3): 393–408.

Haggard, Stephan, J. McMillan, and C. Woodruff. 1996. "Trust and Search in Vietnam's Emerging Private Sector." Discussion Paper Series No. 1506. Center for Economic Policy Research, University of California at San Diego, San Diego, Calif.

Handel, M. D., and J. S. Risbey. 1992. *An Annotated Bibliography on Greenhouse Effect Change.* Report No. 1. Center for Global Change Science. Cambridge, Mass.: Massachusetts Institute of Technology.

Hanna, Nagy K. 1991. *The Information Technology Revolution and Economic Development.* World Bank Discussion Paper No. 120. Washington, D.C.: World Bank.

Hanushek, Eric A. 1995. "Schooling, Labor Force Quality, and Economic Growth." NBER Working Paper No. 5399. National Bureau of Economic Research, Cambridge, Mass.

Hanushek, Eric A., and Dongwook Kim. 1996. "Schooling, Labor Force Quality, and the Growth of Nations." University of Rochester and Korea Development Institute.

Harding, Ann. 1995. "Financing Higher Education: An Assessment of Income-Contingent Loan Options and Repayment Patterns over the Life-Cycle." *Education Economics* 3(2): 173–231.

Harris, Robert G., and C. Jeffrey Kraft. 1997. "Meddling Through: Regulated Local Telephone Competition in the United States." *Journal of Economic Perspectives* 11(4): 93–112.

Harrison, Mark. 1997. "Government Financing of Higher Education in Australia: Rationale and Performance." *Australian Economic Review* 30(2): 225–39.

Hazell, Peter B. R., and C. Ramasamy, with contributions by P. K. Aiyasamy and others. 1991. *The Green Revolution Reconsidered: The Impact of High-Yielding Rice Varieties in South India.* Baltimore, Md.: Johns Hopkins University Press.

Heggie, Ian Graeme. 1995. *Managing and Financing Roads: An Agenda for Reform.* World Bank Technical Paper No. 275. Washington, D.C.: World Bank.

Hellman, T., K. Murdock, and J. Stiglitz. 1997. "Financial Restraint: Towards a New Paradigm." In M. Aoki, M. Okuno-Fujiwara, and H. Kim, eds., *The Role of Government in East Asian Economic Development: Comparative Institutional Analysis.* New York, N.Y.: Oxford University Press.

Heyneman, Stephen J. 1998. "From the Party/State to Multi-Ethnic Democracy: Education and Its Influence on Social Cohesion in the Europe and Central Asia Region." Europe and Central Asia Regional Office, Human Development Sector Unit, World Bank, Washington, D.C.

Hoff, Karla. 1994. Book review of Anne Krueger's *Political Economy of Policy Reform in Developing Countries* (MIT Press). *Journal of Economic Literature* 32(3): 1933–34.

———. 1996. "Market Failures and the Distribution of Wealth: A Perspective from the Economics of Information." *Politics and Society* 24: 411–32.

———. 1998. "Adverse Selection and Institutional Adaptation." Department of Economics Working Paper 98-2. Department of Economics, University of Maryland, College Park, Md.

Hoff, Karla, Avishay Braverman, and Joseph E. Stiglitz, eds. 1993. *The Economics of Rural Organization: Theory, Practice, and Policy.* London, U.K.: Oxford University Press.

Hoff, Karla, and Andrew Lyon. 1995. "Non-Leaky Buckets: Optimal Redistributive Taxation and Agency Costs." *Journal of Public Economics* 58(3): 365–90.

Hoff, Karla, and Joseph E. Stiglitz. 1990. "Imperfect Information and Rural Credit Markets—Puzzles and Policy Perspectives." *World Bank Economic Review* 4(3): 235–50.

Hope, Kerin. 1997. "Albania Has Only 1.4 Fixed-Wire Telephones for Every 100 Inhabitants." *Financial Times*, February 19.

Hunter, R. 1998. "KM in Government: This is Not the Consulting Industry." Research Note KM: KA-03-6492. Gartner Group, Stamford, Conn.

IENTI Telecommunication Reform Database. www.worldbank. org.html/fpd/ienti/ienti/html.

IMF (International Monetary Fund). Various years. *International Financial Statistics.* Washington, D.C.

International Fund for Agricultural Development. 1994. "Interim Evaluation Report." Rome.

Isham, Jon, Deepa Narayan, and Lant Pritchett. 1995. "Establishing Causality with Subjective Data." *World Bank Economic Review* 9(2): 175–200.

Jacoby, Hanan. 1994. "Borrowing Constraints and Progress through School: Evidence from Peru." *Review of Economics and Statistics* 76(2): 151–60.

Jäger, Jill. 1992. "From Conference to Conference." *Climatic Change* 20: iii–vii.

Jakoby, Hannan, and Emmanuel Skoufias. 1997. "Risk, Financial Markets, and Human Capital in a Developing Country." *Review of Economic Studies* 64(3): 311–35.

Jalan, Jvotsna, and Martin Ravallion. 1998. "Are the Poor Less Well Insured? Evidence on Vulnerability to Income Risk in Rural China." Policy Research Working Paper No. 1863. Development Research Group, World Bank, Washington, D.C.

James, Christopher. 1987. "Some Evidence on the Uniqueness of Bank Loans." *Journal of Financial Economics* 19(2): 217–36.

James, Estelle. 1991. "Private Higher Education: The Philippines as a Prototype." *Higher Education* 21(2): 189–206.

Jejeebhoy, Shireen. 1995. *Women's Education, Autonomy, and Reproductive Behaviour.* Oxford, U.K.: Clarendon Press.

Jimenez, Emmanuel, and Marlaine E. Lockheed, eds. 1991. "Private versus Public Education: An International Perspective." *International Journal of Educational Research* 15(5): 353–498.

Jimenez, Emmanuel, Marlaine E. Lockheed, and Vicente Paqueo. 1991. "Relative Efficiency of Private and Public Schools in Developing Countries." *World Bank Research Observer* 6(7): 205–18.

Jimenez, Emmanuel, and Yasuyuki Sawada. 1998. "Do Community-Managed Schools Work? An Evaluation of El Salvador's EDUCO Program." Working Paper Series on Impact Evaluation of Education Reforms, Paper No. 8. Development Research Group, World Bank, Washington, D.C.

Jimenez, Emmanuel, and Jee-Peng Tan. 1987. *Selecting the Brightest for Post-Secondary Education in Colombia: The Impact on Equity.* Discussion Paper No. EDT 61. Washington, D.C: World Bank.

Jorgenson, Dale, and Zvi Griliches. 1966. "Sources of Measured Productivity Change." *Review of Economic Studies* 34(99): 249–82.

Jorion, P. 1997. *Value at Risk: The New Benchmark for Controlling Market Risk.* Chicago: Irwin Professional Publishers.

Kane, E. J. 1994. "Difficulties of Transferring Risk-Based Capital Requirements to Developing Countries." Policy Research Working Paper No. 1244. Policy Research Department, Finance and Private Sector Development Division, World Bank, Washington, D.C.

Khandker, Shahidur K. R., Baqui Khalily, and Zahed Khan. 1998. *Grameen Bank: Performance and Sustainability.* World Bank Discussion Paper No. 306. Washington, D.C.: World Bank.

Kim, Hyung-ki, and Jun Ma. 1997. "The Role of Government in Acquiring Technological Capability: The Case of the Petrochemical Industry in East Asia." In Masahiko Aoki, Kyung-Ki Kim, and Masahiro Okuno-Fujiwara, eds., *The Role of Government in East Asian Economic Development: Comparative Institutional Analysis.* New York, N.Y.: Oxford University Press.

Kim, Jong-Il, and Lawrence J. Lau. 1992. "Sources of Economic Growth of the Newly Industrialized Countries on the Pacific Rim." CEPR Publication No. 295. Center for Economic Policy and Research, Stanford University, Stanford, Calif.

Kim, K., and D. Leipziger. 1993. "Korea: The Lessons of East Asia—A Case of Government Led Development." Report No. 12481. World Bank, Washington, D.C.

Kim, K., and J. K. Park. 1985. *Sources of Economic Growth in Korea.* Seoul: Korea Development Institute.

Kim, Linsa. 1997. *Imitation to Innovation: The Dynamics of Korean Technological Learning.* Boston, Mass.: Harvard Business Review Press.

King, Elizabeth M. 1990. "Does Education Pay in the Labor Market? Women's Labor Force Participation, Occupation, and Earnings in Peru." LSMS Working Paper No. 67. World Bank, Washington, D.C.

King, Elizabeth M., and M. Anne, eds. 1993. *Women's Education in Developing Countries: Barriers, Benefits, and Policies.* Baltimore, Md.: Johns Hopkins University Press.

King, Elizabeth M., and Berk Ozler. 1998. "What's Decentralization Got to Do with Learning? The Case of Nicaragua's School Autonomy Reform." Working Paper Series on Impact Evaluation of Education Reforms Paper No. 9. Development Research Group, World Bank, Washington, D.C.

Kiyotaki, Nobuhiro, and John Moore. 1997. "Credit Cycles." *Journal of Political Economy* 105(2): 211–48.

Klenow, Peter J., and Andrés Rodriguez-Clare. 1997a. "Economic Growth: A Review Essay." *Journal of Monetary Economics* 40(December): 597–617.

———. 1997b. "The Neoclassical Revival in Growth Economics: Has It Gone Too Far?" In *NBER Macroeconomics Annual for 1997.* Cambridge, Mass.: MIT Press.

Klitgaard, Robert. 1991. *Adjusting to Reality: Beyond "State versus Market" in Economic Development.* San Francisco, Calif.: Institute for Contemporary Studies Press.

Knack, Stephen, and Philip Keefer. 1997. "Does Social Capital Have an Economic Payoff? A Cross-Country Investigation." *Quarterly Journal of Economics* 112(4): 1251–88.

Knight, John B., and Richard H. Sabot. 1990. *Education, Productivity, and Inequality: The East African Natural Experiment.* New York, N.Y.: Oxford University Press.

Knowles, James, Jere R. Behrman, Benjamin E. Dikono, and Keith McInnes. 1998. "Key Issues in the Financing of Viet Nam's Social Services." In *Financing of Social Services Project: Report to the Government of Viet Nam and the Asian Development Bank.* Bethesda, Md.: Abt Associates.

Kranton, Rachel. 1996. "Reciprocal Exchange: A Self-Sustaining System." *American Economic Review* 86(4): 830–51.

Krueger, Anne O. 1993. *Political Economy of Policy Reform in Developing Countries.* Cambridge, Mass.: MIT Press.

Krugman, Paul. 1994. "Myth of Asia's Miracle." *Foreign Affairs* 73(November–December):62–78.

Kulik, James A., Chen-Lin C. Kulik, and Robert L. Baangert-Drowns. 1985. "Effectiveness of Computer-Based Education in Elementary Schools." *Computers in Human Behavior* 1(1): 59–74.

Kuran, T. 1989. "The Craft Guilds of Tunis and Their Amins: A Study in Institutional Atrophy." In M. K. Nabli and J. B. Nugent, eds., *The New Institutional Economics and Development: Theory and Applications to Tunisia.* Amsterdam: North Holland.

Laffont, Jean-Jacques, and Mohamed Salah Matoussi. 1995. "Moral Hazard, Financial Constraints, and Sharecropping in El Oulja." *Review of Economic Studies* 62(3): 381–99.

La Porta, Rafael, Florencia Lopez de Silanes, Andrei Shleifer, and Robert W. Vishny. 1996. "Law and Finance." Research Working Paper No. 5661. National Bureau of Economic Research, Cambridge, Mass.

———. 1997a. "Trust in Large Organizations." *American Economic Review* 87(3): 333–38.

———. 1997b. "Legal Determinants of External Finance." *Journal of Finance* 52(4): 1131–50.

———. 1998. "Agency Problems and Divided Policies Around the World." NBER Working Paper No. 6594. National Bureau of Economic Research, Cambridge, Mass.

Laporte, Bruno, and Dena Ringold. 1997. *Trends in Education Access and Financing during the Transition in Central and Eastern Europe.* Washington, D.C : World Bank.

Lauglo, Jon, and Martin McLean, eds. 1985. *The Control of Education: International Perspectives on the Centralization-Decentralization Debate.* London, U.K.: Heinemann Educational Books.

Lee, Y. S. 1996. "Technology Transfer and the Research University: A Search for the Boundaries of University-Industry Collaboration." *Research Policy* 25(6): 843–63.

Levine, Ross. 1997. "Financial Development and Economic Growth: View and Agenda." *Journal of Economic Literature* 35(2): 688–727.

———. Forthcoming. "Law, Finance, and Economic Growth." *Journal of Financial Intermediation.*

Levine, Ross, Norman Loayza, and Thorsten Beck. 1998. "Financial Intermediation and Growth: Causality and Causes." Development Research Group, World Bank, Washington, D.C.

Levine, R., and D. Renelt. 1992. "A Sensitivity Analysis of Cross-Country Growth Regression." *American Economic Review* 82(4): 942–63.

Levine, Ross, and Sara Zervos. 1998. "Stock Markets, Banks, and Economic Growth." *American Economic Review* 99(3): 537–58.

Lewin, R. 1987. "Domino Effect Involved in Ice Age Extinctions." *Science* 238(4): 1509–10.

Lin, Justin Yifu, and Jeffrey B. Nugent. 1995. "Institutions and Economic Development." In Jere R. Behrman and T. N. Srinivasan, *Handbook of Development Economics,* vol. 3A, pp. 2303–70. Amsterdam: North-Holland.

López-Pereira, Miguel A., and Michael L. Morris. 1994. "Impacts of International Maize Breeding Research in the Developing World, 1966–9." Centro Internacional de Mejoramiento de Maiz y Trigo (CIMMYT with CGIAR), Mexico City.

Lucas, Robert. 1988. "On the Mechanics of Economic Development." *Journal of Monetary Economics* 22(1): 3–42.

Lutz, Ernst, and Julian Caldecott, eds. 1996. *Decentralization and Biodiversity Conservation.* Washington, D.C.: World Bank.

Macro International. Various years. *Demographic Health Surveys.* (Final reports, by country). Calverton, Md.

McIntyre, Peter. 1998. *Puppeteers with a Purpose.* New York, N.Y.: UNICEF.

Maddison, Angus. 1995. *Monitoring the World Economy, 1820–1992.* Paris: Development Centre of the OECD.

Malhotra, R. 1995. "The Road Less Traveled: The Role of the Private Sector in MENA Development." Research paper for the Europe and Central Asia/Middle East and North Africa Technical, Private Sector, and Finance Division, World Bank, Washington, D.C.

Mansell, Robin, and Uta Wehn. 1998. *Knowledge Societies: Information Technology for Sustainable Development.* New York, N.Y.: Oxford University Press.

Mansfield, Edwin. 1994. *Intellectual Property Protection, Foreign Direct Investment and Technology Transfer.* Discussion Paper No. 19. Washington, D.C.: International Finance Corporation.

———. 1995. *Intellectual Property Protection, Direct Investment, and Technology Transfer: Germany, Japan, and the United States.* Discussion Paper No. 27. International Finance Corporation, Washington, D.C.

Marshall, Alfred. 1890. *Principles of Economics.* Cambridge, U.K.: Cambridge University Press. Reprinted London, U.K.: Macmillan, 1961.

Maskus, K. E., and M. Penubarti. 1995. "How Trade Related are Intellectual Property Rights?" *Journal of International Economics* 39(1): 227–48.

Matsuyama, Kiminori. 1997. "Economic Development as Coordination Problems." In Masahiko Aoki, Kyung-Ki Kim, and Masahiro Okuno-Fujiwara, eds., *The Role of Government in East Asian Economic Development: Comparative Institutional Analysis,* pp. 134–60. New York, N.Y.: Oxford University Press.

Mazzoleni, Roberto, and Richard Nelson. Forthcoming. "The Benefits and Costs of Stronger Patent Protection: A Contribution to Debate." World Bank, Washington, D.C.

Meinzen-Dick, Ruth, Richard B. Reidinger, and Andrew Manzardo. 1995. "Participation in Irrigation." Participation Paper No. 003. Environment Department, World Bank, Washington, D.C.

MELISSA (Managing the Environment Locally in Sub-Saharan Africa). 1998. www.melissa.org.

Menou, Michel J. 1998. "Studies of the Impact of Electronic Networking on Development: Report of the Mid-Project Meeting of the CABECA Survey of African Internet Use." Pan African Development Information System, Addis Ababa.

Michie, R. C. 1977. *The London and New York Stock Exchanges 1850–1914.* London, U.K.: Allen & Unwin.

Middleton, John, Adrian Ziderman, and Arvil Van Adams. 1993. *Skills for Productivity: Vocational Education and Training in Developing Countries.* New York, N.Y.: Oxford University Press.

Mitchell, B. R. 1992. *International Historical Statistics: Europe, 1750–1970.* New York, N.Y.: Stockton Press.

Moll, Peter. 1998. "Primary Schooling, Cognitive Skills, and Wages in South Africa." *Economica* 65: 263–84.

Mookherjee, Dilip. 1996. "Informational Rents and Property Rights in Land." In John Roemer, ed., *Property Rights, Incentives, and Welfare.* London: Macmillan Press.

Morduch, Jonathan. 1995. "Income Smoothing and Consumption Smoothing." *Journal of Economic Perspectives* 9(3): 103–14.

———. 1998. "The Microfinance Innovation." Department of Economics, Harvard University, Cambridge, Mass.

Multimedia Development Corporation. 1998. *Unlocking the Full Potential of the Information Age.* Kuala Lumpur, Malaysia.

Munshi, Kaivan, and Jacques Mayaux. 1998. "Social Effects in the Demographic Transition: Evidence from Matlab, Bangladesh." Boston University.

Munshi, Kaivan D., and Kirit S. Parikh. 1994. "Milk Supply Behavior in India: Data Integration, Estimation, and Implications for Dairy Development." *Journal of Development Economics* 45(2): 201–23.

Murphy, Kevin M., Andrei Shleifer, and Robert W. Vishny. 1992. "Transition to a Market Economy: Pitfalls of Partial Reform." *Quarterly Journal of Economics* 107(I): 889–906.

Mytelka, Lynn K. 1985. "Stimulating Effective Technology Transfer: The Case of Textiles in Africa." In Nathan Rosenberg and Claudio Frischtak, eds., *International Technology Transfer.* New York, N.Y.: Praeger.

Nagaoka, Sadeo. 1989. "Overview of Japanese Industrial Technology Development." Departmental Working Paper No. 10583. Industry Development Division, Industry and Energy Department, Policy Planning and Research, World Bank, Washington, D.C.

Nalebuff, Barry, and Joseph E. Stiglitz. 1983. "Prizes and Incentives: Towards a General Theory of Compensation and Competition." *Bell Journal of Economics* 14(1): 21–43.

Narayan, Deepa, and Lant H. Pritchett. 1995. "The Contribution of People's Participation: Evidence from 121 Rural Water Supply Projects." Report No. 14904. Environmentally and Socially Sustainable Development Work in Progress. World Bank, Washington, D.C.

———. 1997. "Cents and Sociability: Household Income and Social Capital in Rural Tanzania." Policy Research Working Paper No. 1796. World Bank, Washington, D.C.

Nelson, Ridley. 1990. *Dryland Management: The "Desertification" Problem.* World Bank Technical Paper No. 116. Washington, D.C.: World Bank.

Nordhaus, William D., and David Popp. 1997. "What is the Value of Scientific Knowledge? An Application to Global Warming Using the PRICE Model." *Energy Journal* 18(1): 1–45.

North, Douglass. 1990. *Institutions, Institutional Change, and Economic Performance.* Cambridge, U.K.: Cambridge University Press.

OECD (Organisation for Economic Co-operation and Development). 1994. *Environmental Indicators—OECD Core Set.* Paris.

———. 1996a. "Educational Policy Review: Korea." Directorate for Education, Employment, Labour, and Social Affairs, DEELSA/ED(96)9, Paris.

———. 1996b. "The Knowledge Based Economy." In *Science, Technology, and Industry Outlook.* Paris.

———. 1997a. *Eco-Labelling: Actual Effects of Selected Programmes.* Paris.

———. 1997b. *Processes and Production Methods (PPMs): Conceptual Framework and Considerations on Use of PPM-Based Trade Measures.* Paris.

Olinto, Pedro. 1997. "Land Tenure Insecurity, Credit Rationing, and Household Asset Accumulation: Panel Data Evidence from Rural Paraguay." Ph.D. diss. University of Wisconsin-Madison.

Olson, Mancur, Naveen Sarna, and Anand V. Swamy. 1997. "Governance and Growth: A Simple Hypothesis Explaining Cross-Country Differences in Productivity Growth." IRIS Working Paper. Center for Institutional Reform and the Informal Sector, University of Maryland, College Park, Md.

Orazem, Peter, and Milan Vodopivec. 1995. "Winners and Losers in Transition: Returns to Education, Experience, and Gender in Slovenia." *World Bank Economic Review* 9(2): 201–30.

Osin, Luis. 1998. "Computers in Education in Developing Countries: Why and How." Education and Technology Series, Paper No. 3(1). Human Development Department Education Group—Education and Technology Team, World Bank, Washington, D.C.

Ostrom, Elinor. 1995. "Incentives, Rule of the Game, and Development." In Michael Bruno and Boris Pleskovic, eds., *Annual Bank Conference on Development Economics 1995.* Washington, D.C.: World Bank.

Ostrom, Elinor, and Mary Beth Wertime. 1995. *IFRI Research Strategy.* International Forestry Resources and Institutions, Indiana University. http://www.indiana.edu/~ifri/research/ifrirestrat.htm.

Otsuka, K., H. Chuma, and Y. Hayami. 1992. "Land and Labor Contracts in Agrarian Economies." *Journal of Economic Literature* 30(4): 1965–2018.

Pack, Howard. 1987. *Productivity, Technology, and Industrial Development: A Case Study in Textiles.* New York, N.Y.: Oxford University Press.

Pack, Howard, and Larry Westphal. 1986. "Industrial Strategy and Technology Change: Theory versus Reality." *Journal of Development Economics* 22(1): 87–128

Parente, S. L., and E. C. Prescott. 1994. "Barriers to Technology Adoption and Development." *Journal of Political Economy* 102(2): 298–321.

Perraton, Hilary, and Michael Potashnik. 1997. "Teacher Education at a Distance." Education and Technology Series 2(2). Human Development Department Education Group—Education and Technology Team, World Bank, Washington, D.C.

Pezzey, John. 1989. "Economic Analysis of Sustainable Growth and Sustainable Development." Working Paper No. 15. Environment Department, World Bank, Washington, D.C.

Plaza, S., and O. Sananikone. 1997. "Standardization and Competitiveness: Issues and Implications for Developing Countries." Private Sector Development Department, World Bank. Washington, D.C.

Pritchett, Lant, and Deon P. Filmer. Forthcoming. "What Education Production Functions Really Show: A Positive Theory of Education Expenditures." *Economics of Education Review.*

Psacharopoulos, George. 1994. "Returns to Investment in Education: A Global Update." *World Development* 22(9): 1325–43.

Purcell, Dennis L., and Jock R. Anderson. 1997. "Agricultural Extension and Research: Achievements and Problems in National Systems." Operations Evaluation Study, World Bank, Washington, D.C.

Quisumbing, Agnes R., Lynn R. Brown, Hillary S. Feldstein, L. Haddad, and Christine Pena. 1995. *Women: The Key to Food Security.* Washington, D.C.: International Food Policy Research Institute.

Ram, M. 1990. "An Independent Press and Anti-Hunger Strategies." In Jean Drèze and Amartya Sen, eds., *The Political Economy of Hunger,* vols. 1, 2, and 3. Oxford, U.K.: Oxford University Press.

Rapaczynski, Andrzej. 1996. "The Roles of the State and the Market in Establishing Property Rights." *Journal of Economic Perspectives* 10(2): 87–103.

Rapp, Robert. 1975. "The Unmaking of the Mediterranean Trade Hegemony: International Trade Rivalry and the Commercial Revolution." *Journal of Economic History* 35(2): 499–525.

Ray, Debraj. 1998. *Development Economics.* Princeton, N.J.: Princeton University Press.

Reid, Walter V., ed. 1993. *Biodiversity Prospecting: Using Genetic Resources for Sustainable Development.* Washington, D.C.: World Resources Institute.

Richels, R., J. Edmonds, H. Gruenspecht, and T. Wigley, with contributions from Henry Jacoby, A. Manne, S. Peck, T. Teisberg, M. Wise, and Z. Yang. 1996. "The Berlin Mandate: The Design of Cost-Effective Mitigation Strategies." Report of the Subgroup on the Regional Distribution of the Costs and Benefits of Climate Change Policy Proposals. Energy Modeling Forum No. 14. Stanford University, Stanford, Calif.

Rischard, Jean-François. 1996. "Connecting Developing Countries to the Information Technology Revolution." *SAIS Review* 16(Winter/Spring): 93–107.

Rodrik, Dani. 1998. "Who Needs Capital Account Convertibility?" John F. Kennedy School of Government, Harvard University, Cambridge, Mass.

Romer, David. 1985. "Financial Intermediation, Reserve Requirements, and Inside Money: A General Equilibrium Analysis." *Journal of Monetary Economics* 16(9): 175–94.

Romer, Paul M. 1990. "Endogenous Technological Change." *Journal of Political Economy* 98(October): S71–S102.

———. 1993. "Two Strategies for Economic Development: Using Ideas and Producing Ideas." In Lawrence M. Summers and Shekhar Shah, eds., *Proceedings of the World Bank Annual Conference on Development Economics.* Washington, D.C.: World Bank.

Rosenberg, Nathan. 1982. *Inside the Black Box: Technology and Economics.* Cambridge, U.K.: Cambridge University Press.

Rosenzweig, M., and T. P. Schultz. 1982. "Child Mortality and Fertility in Colombia: Individual and Community Effects." *Health Policy and Education* 2: 305–48.

RPED (Regional Program on Enterprise Development). 1998. "Productivity Growth and Learning Mechanisms in Sub-Saharan Africa: Findings from the Regional Program on Enterprise Development." World Bank, Washington, D.C.

Sadoulet, Elisabeth, Seiichi Fukui, and Alain de Janvry. 1994. "Efficient Share Tenancy Contracts under Risk: The Case of Two Rice-Growing Villages in Thailand." *Journal of Development Economics* 45(2): 225–43.

Sah, Raaj K., and Joseph E. Stiglitz. 1989. "Sources of Technological Divergence between Developed and Less Developed Economies." In G. Calvo, R. Findlay, P. Kouri, and J. Braga de Macedo, eds., *Debt, Stabilization, and Development.* London, U.K.: Blackwell.

Sarel, Michael. 1997. "Growth in East Asia: What We Can and What We Cannot Infer." *Economic Issues No. 1.* International Monetary Fund, Washington, D.C.

Saunders, Robert, Jeremy Warford, and Björn Wellenius. 1993. *Telecommunications and Economic Development.* Baltimore, Md.: Johns Hopkins University Press.

Schmalensee, Richard, Paul L. Joskow, A. Denny Ellerman, Juan Pablo Montero, and Elizabeth M. Bailey. 1997. "An Interim Evaluation of Sulfur Dioxide Emission Trading." Massachussetts Institute of Technology, Cambridge, Mass.

Schneider, Robert R. 1995. "Government and the Economy on the Amazon Frontier." Environment Paper No. 11. World Bank, Washington, D.C.

Schware, Robert, and Paul Kimberley. 1995. *Information Technology and National Trade Facilitation: Making the Most of Global Trade.* World Bank Technical Paper Nos. 316 and 317. World Bank, Washington, D.C.

Serageldin, Ismail, and David Steeds, eds. 1996. *Rural Well-Being: From Vision to Action.* Washington, D.C.: World Bank.

Shaban, Radwan Ali. 1987. "Testing between Competing Models of Sharecropping." *Journal of Political Economy* 95(5): 893–920.

Shabbir, Tayyeb. 1991. "Sheepskin Effects in the Returns to Education in a Developing Country." *Pakistan Development Review* 30(1): 1–19.

Siamwalla, A., C. Pinthong, N. Poapongsakorn, P. Satsanguan, P. Nettarayak, W. Mingmaneenakin, and Y. Tubpun. 1990. "The Thai Rural Credit System: Public Subsidies, Private Information, and Segmented Markets." *World Bank Economic Review* 4(2): 271–96.

Silberman, James M., and Charles Weiss, Jr. 1992. "Restructuring for Productivity: The Technical Assistance Program of the Marshall Plan as a Precedent for the Former Soviet Union." Industry and Services Paper No. 64. Industry and Energy Department, World Bank, Washington, D.C.

Smith, Craig S. 1997. "Stock Market Mania is Sweeping China; Speculators Abound." *Wall Street Journal,* August 27.

Smith, Peter. 1995. "Subscribing to Monopoly. The Telecom Monopolist's Lexicon—Revisited." *Viewpoint* Note No. 53. Internal newsletter, Industry and Energy Department, World Bank, Washington, D.C.

Solow, Robert. 1956. "A Contribution to the Theory of Economic Growth." *Quarterly Journal of Economics* 70(1): 65–94.

Spiller, Pablo T., and Carlo G. Cardilli. 1997. "The Frontier of Telecommunications Deregulation: Small Countries Leading the Pack." *Journal of Economic Perspectives* 11(4): 127–38.

Sternberg, Robert, and Elena Grigorenko. 1997. "Interventions for Cognitive Development in Children 0–3 Years Old." In Mary Emming Young, ed., *Early Child Development. Investing in the Future.* Amsterdam: Elsevier.

Stiglitz, Joseph E. 1974. "Incentives and Risk Sharing in Sharecropping." *Review of Economic Studies* 41(1): 219–55.

———. 1989a. "Markets, Market Failures, and Development." *American Economic Review* 79(2): 197–203.

———. 1989b. "Rational Peasants, Efficient Institutions, and a Theory of Rural Organization: Methodological Remarks for Development Economics." In Pranab Bardhan, ed., *The Eco-*

nomic Theory of Agrarian Institutions. Oxford, U.K.: Clarendon Press.

——. 1993. "The Role of the State in Financial Markets." In *Proceedings of the Annual World Bank Conference on Development Economics.* Washington, D.C.: World Bank.

——. 1994. *Whither Socialism?* Cambridge, Mass.: MIT Press.

——. 1996. "Economic Growth Revisited." *Industrial and Corporate Change* 3(1): 65–110.

——. 1998. "Creating Competition in Telecommunications." Address to a Conference on Managing the Telecommunications Sector Post-Privatization, George Washington University, Washington, D.C., April 27.

Stiglitz, Joseph E., and Andrew Weiss. 1981. "Credit Rationing in Markets with Imperfect Information." *American Economic Review* 71(3): 393–410.

Subbarao, K., Aniruddha Bonnerjee, Jeanine Braithwaite, Soniya Carvalho, Kene Ezemenari, Carol Graham, and Alan Thompson. 1997. *Safety Net Programs and Poverty Reduction: Lessons from Cross-Country Experience.* Directions in Development Series. Washington, D.C.: World Bank.

Summers, Robert, and Alan Heston. 1994. "Differential-Productivity Hypothesis and Purchasing-Power Parities: Some New Evidence." *Review of International Economics* 2(October): 227–43.

Tan, Hong W., and Geeta Batra. 1995. "Enterprise Training in Developing Countries: Incidence, Productivity Effects, and Policy Implications." Working Paper No. 15373. World Bank, Washington, D.C.

Tendler, Judith. 1994. "New Lessons from Old Projects : The Workings of Rural Development in Northeast Brazil." Operations Evaluation Study. World Bank, Washington, D.C.

Tendler, Judith, and Sara Freedheim. 1994. "Trust in a Rent-Seeking World: Health and Government Transformed in Northeast Brazil." *World Development* 22(12): 1771–91.

Thomas, Duncan, Victor Lavy, and John Strauss. 1996. "Public Policy and Anthropometric Outcomes in Côte d'Ivoire." *Journal of Public Economics* 61: 155–92.

Thomas, Duncan, and John Strauss. 1992. "Prices, Infrastructure, Household Characteristics, and Child Height." *Journal of Development Economics* 39(10): 301–33.

Thomas, Duncan, John Strauss, and Maria-Helena Henriques. 1991. "How Does Mother's Education Affect Child Height?" *Journal of Human Resources* 26(2): 183–211.

Thomas, Vinod, Nalin M. Kishor, and Tamara C. Belt. 1997. *Embracing the Power of Knowledge for a Sustainable Environment.* Washington, D.C.: World Bank.

Tietenberg, Tom. 1997. "Information Strategies for Pollution Control." Paper presented at the Eighth Annual Meetings of the European Association of Environmental and Resource Economists, Tilburg, The Netherlands. http://www.colby.edu/personal/thtieten.

Tuck, Laura, and Kathy Lindert. 1996. *From Universal Food Subsidies to a Self-Targeted Program: A Case Study in Tunisian Reform.* World Bank Discussion Paper No. 351. Washington, D.C.: World Bank.

24 Hours in Cyberspace. 1996. "Emailing a Future: Loan Program Sows Hope in Vietnam and Cambodia." www.cyber24.com/htm1/2_229.htm.

Tzannatos, Zafiris, and Geraint Johnes. 1996 *Training and Skills Development in the East Asian NIC's: A Comparison and*

Lessons for Developing Countries. PSP Discussion Paper Series. Washington, D.C.: World Bank.

Udry, Christopher. 1994. "Risk, Insurance, and Default in a Rural Credit Market: An Empirical Investigation in Northern Nigeria." *Review of Economic Studies* 61(3): 495–526.

UNCSTD (United Nations Commission on Science and Technology for Development). 1997. "Building Innovative Knowledge Societies for Sustainable Development." New York, N.Y.

UNESCO (United Nations Education, Scientific, and Cultural Organization). 1996. *The World Science Report.* Paris.

——. 1997. *Statistical Yearbook.* Paris.

——. 1998. *World Education Report.* Paris: UNESCO Publishing.

UNFCCC (United Nations Framework Convention on Climate Change). 1998. www.unfccc.org.

UNICEF (United Nations Children's Fund). 1995. *The State of the World's Children: 1995.* New York, N.Y.: Oxford University Press.

——. 1997. *The State of the World's Children: 1997.* New York, N.Y.: Oxford University Press.

UNIDO (United Nations Industrial Development Organization). 1995. *Trade Implications of International Standards for Quality and Environmental Management Systems ISO 9000/ISO 14000: Survey Results.* Vienna.

United Kingdom Secretary of State for International Development. 1997. *Eliminating World Poverty: A Challenge for the 21st Century."* White Paper on International Development. London.

USAID (U.S. Agency for International Development). 1993. "Policy Dialogue and Reform in the Education Sector." Advocacy Series, Education and Development. Washington, D.C.

van der Gaag, Jacques, and Wim Vijverberg. 1989. "Wage Determinants in Côte d'Ivoire: Experience, Credentials, and Human Capital." *Economic Developments and Cultural Change* 27(2): 371–81.

Vergara, W., and D. Babelon. 1990. *The Petrochemical Industry in Developing Asia.* World Bank Technical Paper No. 113. Industry and Energy Series. Washington, D.C.: World Bank.

Wade-Barrett, Carmen. 1997. "Telecommunications of Jamaica Has Installed Some 160,000 Lines over the Last Three Years." Inter Press Service, June 30.

Wang, Hua, and David Wheeler. 1996. "Pricing Industrial Pollution in China: An Econometric Analysis of the Levy System." Working Paper No. 1644. Policy Research Department, World Bank, Washington, D.C.

Weiss, Andrew, and Georgiy Nikitin. 1998. "Performance of Czech Companies by Ownership Structure." Paper presented at the William Davidson Institute (University of Michigan) conference on Finance in Transition Economies. Boston University, May.

Wellenius, Björn. 1997a. "Extending Telecommunications Service to Rural Areas—The Chilean Experience." *Viewpoint* (February) Note No. 105. Internal newsletter, Industry and Energy Department, World Bank, Washington, D.C.

——. 1997b. "Telecommunications Reform—How to Succeed: Public Policy for the Private Sector." *Viewpoint* (October) Note No. 130. Internal newsletter, Industry and Energy Department, World Bank, Washington, D.C.

Werner, David, and David Sanders. 1997. *Questioning the Solution: The Politics of Primary Health Care and Child Survival.* Atlantic Highlands, N.J.: Zed Books.

Wester, Gregory. 1993. "Vehicle Product Cycles and Their Market Effects." *Review of the U.S. Economy* (November): 47–51.

Westphal, Larry E. 1990. "Industrial Policy in an Export-Propelled Economy: Lessons from South Korea's Experience." *Journal of Economic Perspectives* 4(4): 41–59.

Westphal, Larry E., Yung W. Rhee, and Gary Pursell. 1981. "Korean Industrial Competence: Where It Came From." Staff Working Paper No. 469. World Bank, Washington, D.C.

Weymes, R., ed. 1990. *Organic Farming—Is There a Future? Initial Results of a 1990 Canada-Wide Survey.* Proceedings of a conference on Transition to Organic Agriculture, University of Saskatchewan, Saskatoon, Saskatchewan.

White, Eugene. 1997. "Deposit Insurance." In Gerard Caprio, Jr., and Dimitri Vittas, eds., *Reforming Financial Systems: Historical Implications for Policy.* New York, N.Y.: Cambridge University Press.

WHO (World Health Organization). 1988. *Informatics and Telematics in Health: Present and Potential Uses.* Geneva.

Willmott, Hugh. 1998. *Knowledge Management: A Real Business Guide.* London, U.K.: Caspian Publishing, Ltd.

Woolcock, Michael. 1998. "Social Theory, Development Policy, and Poverty Alleviation: A Comparative-Historical Analysis of Group-Based Banking in Developing Economies." Ph.D. diss. Brown University, Department of Sociology.

World Bank. 1991. "Peru: Poverty Assessment and Social Policies and Programs for the Poor." Report No. 11191-PE. Latin America and the Caribbean Region, Country Department 1, World Bank, Washington, D.C. http://www.worldbank.org/lsms.

———. 1992. *World Development Report 1992: Development and the Environment.* New York, N.Y.: Oxford University Press.

———. 1993a. "Peru Poverty Assessment and Social Policies and Programs for the Poor." Macroeconomic Analysis Sector Report No. 11191. World Bank, Washington, D.C.

———. 1993b. *The East Asian Miracle: Economic Growth and Public Policy.* World Bank Policy Research Report. New York, N.Y.: Oxford University Press.

———. 1993c. *World Development Report 1993: Investing in Health.* New York, N.Y.: Oxford University Press.

———. 1994a. *Averting the Old Age Crisis.* World Bank Policy Research Report. New York, N.Y.: Oxford University Press.

———. 1994b. *World Development Report 1994: Infrastructure for Development.* New York, N.Y.: Oxford University Press.

———. 1995a. *Priorities and Strategies for Education: A World Bank Review.* Washington, D.C.: World Bank.

———. 1995b. *Vietnam Poverty Assessment and Strategy.* Washington, D.C.: World Bank.

———. 1996. *Rural Energy and Development: Improving Energy Supply for Two Billion People.* Washington, D.C.: World Bank.

———. 1997a. *Clean Water, Blue Skies: China's Environment in the Next Century.* Washington, D.C.: World Bank.

———. 1997b. *Confronting AIDS: Public Priorities in a Global Epidemic.* New York, N.Y.: Oxford University Press.

———. 1997c. *Expanding the Measure of Wealth: Indicators of Environmentally Sustainable Development.* Environmentally Sustainable Development Studies and Monographs Series No. 17. Washington, D.C.: World Bank.

———. 1997d. *Global Economic Prospects and the Developing Countries.* Washington, D.C.: World Bank.

———. 1997e. "Land Reform and Poverty Alleviation Pilot." Public Information Center (PIC) No. 4974. World Bank, Washington, D.C.

———. 1997f. "Science and Technology Reform Support: Project for Brazil." Project Appraisal Document No. 17178. World Bank, Washington, D.C.

———. 1997g. *World Development Indicators.* Washington, D.C.: World Bank.

———. 1997h. *World Development Report 1997: The State in a Changing World.* New York, N.Y.: Oxford University Press.

———. 1998a. *Latin America and the Caribbean: Education and Technology at the Crossroads.* Washington, D.C.: World Bank.

———. 1998b. NIPR (New Ideas in Pollution Regulation). http://www.worldbank.org/nipr.

———. 1998c. *Rethinking Aid: What Works, What Doesn't, and Why?* New York, N.Y.: Oxford University Press.

———. 1998d. *World Development Indicators.* Washington, D.C.: World Bank.

———. Forthcoming-(a). *Dividends and Disappointments: Learning from the Successes and Failures of Aid.* A World Bank Policy Research Report. Washington, D.C.: World Bank.

———. Forthcoming-(b). "The Expansion of Learning." World Bank, Washington, D.C.

———. Various years. *Living Standards Measurement Surveys.* Washington, D.C. World Bank.

WorldSpace. 1998. "WorldSpace: The Technology." www.worldspace.com/text/technology.html.

Yamauchi, Futoshi. 1997. "Information, Neighborhood Effects, and the Investment in Human Capital: Learning School Returns in a Dynamic Context." Department of Economics, University of Pennsylvania, Philadelphia, Penn.

Young, Alwyn. 1995. "The Tyranny of Numbers: Confronting the Statistical Realities of the East Asian Growth Experience." *Quarterly Journal of Economics* 110 (August): 643–80.

Young, Mary Eming, ed. 1997. *Early Child Development. Investing in the Future.* Amsterdam: Elsevier.

Yunus, Muhammad. 1996. "Socially Responsible Actions to Promote Rural Well-Being." In Ismail Serageldin and David Steeds, eds., *Rural Well-Being: From Vision to Action.* Washington, D.C.: World Bank.

Zijp, Willem. 1994. *Improving the Transfer and Use of Agricultural Information. A Guide to Information Technology.* World Bank Discussion Paper No. 247. World Bank, Washington, D.C.

Zongo, Gaston. 1997. "Impact Socioeconomique et Financier des Télécentres Privés." Paper presented to the ICTP/ITU Workshop on the Economic Quantification of the Impact of Telecommunications in Development, Trieste, Italy, February 26 and March 1.

Appendix

International Statistics on Knowledge

Table A.1. Tertiary enrollments by field of study

Data on education are compiled by the United Nations Educational, Scientific, and Cultural Organization (UNESCO) from official responses to surveys and from reports provided by education authorities in each country. The data in the table are based on both the International Standard Classification of Education (ISCED) level categories and field of study. Students enrolled in ISCED levels 5 through 7 programs are included in the table. Level 5 students are in programs leading to an award not equivalent to a first university degree, designed to prepare them for particular vocational fields in which they can qualify. Level 6 students are enrolled in programs leading to a first university degree or equivalent qualification, such as a Bachelor's degree. Level 7 students are enrolled in programs leading to a post-graduate degree or equivalent qualification.

ISECD *field of study* refers to the student's main area of specialization. *Natural science* includes biology, chemistry, geology, physics, astronomy, meteorology, and oceanography. *Mathematics and computer science* include general programs in mathematics, statistics, actuarial science, and computer science. *Engineering* includes chemical engineering and materials techniques, electrical, electronic, industrial, metallurgical, mining, and mechanical engineering, surveying, and agricultural, forestry and fishery engineering techniques. *Transport and communications* includes air crew and ships' officers programs, railway operating trades, road motor vehicle operation programs, and postal service programs.

Enrollment ratios are compiled by World Bank staff using UNESCO's electronic database corresponding to its *Statistical Yearbook, 1997*. Because classifications by field of study and data collection practices sometimes differ across countries and over time within countries, readers are encouraged to consult country-specific notes in UNESCO's *Statistical Yearbook, 1997* (Table 3.11).

Table A.2. Assessment of legal infrastructure

Values of the indexes in the table are from Levine forthcoming; the indexes are composites of indicators taken from La Porta and others 1998, who compiled their data from national sources and the *International Country Risk Guide*. The data thus reflect conditions prevailing at the time of their survey (1995–96). The index of creditors' rights is a combination of three indicators. The first, AUTOSTAY, equals one if a country's laws impose an automatic stay on the assets of a firm upon its filing a reorganization petition, and equals zero if no such restriction appears in the legal code. This restriction prevents bankers from gaining possession of collateral. MANAGES, the second indicator, equals one (and zero otherwise) if a firm continues to manage its property pending resolution of a reorganization, rather than being replaced by a team selected by the courts or the creditors. SECURED equals one (and zero otherwise) if secured creditors receive first priority in the distribution of proceeds from the disposition of a bankrupt firm's assets. MANAGES should thus be negatively correlated, and SECURED positively associated, with the activities of banks. The creditors' rights index is defined as SECURED minus AUTOSTAY minus MANAGES and ranges therefore from 1 (best) to –2 (worst).

Shareholders' rights is a similar amalgamation of five indicators whose values can equal zero or one. The indicator PROXY takes on a value of one if shareholders may vote in person or by mail. CUMULATIVE equals one if the law or code allows shareholders to cast all of their votes for one candidate. BLOCKED equals one if the law or code does not allow firms to require that shareholders deposit shares prior to a general shareholders' meeting (thus preventing them from selling those shares for a number of days). MINOR equals one if minority shareholders may challenge management decisions or the right to step out of the company by requiring it to purchase shares when they object to certain fundamental changes. MEETING equals one if the minimum percentage of share capital that a shareholder must own in order to call for an extraordinary shareholders' meeting is less than or equal to 10 percent.

Finally, enforcement is a combination of two variables whose values can range from 1 to 10. RULELAW is an assessment of the law and order tradition in the country over the period 1982–95. CONRISK is an assessment for the same period of the government's ability to modify a contract unilaterally after it has been signed. Data for both variables are from the *International Country Risk Guide*.

Table A.1. Tertiary enrollments by field of study

Economy	Natural science % of 20–24 age group 1990–95[a]	Natural science % female 1990–95[a]	Mathematics and computer science % of 20–24 age group 1990–95[a]	Mathematics and computer science % female 1990–95[a]	Engineering % of 20–24 age group 1990–95[a]	Engineering % female 1990–95[a]	Transport and communications % of 20–24 age group 1990–95[a]	Transport and communications % female 1990–95[a]
Albania	0.3	55.8	0.0	45.5	0.9	26.2	. .	. .
Algeria	1.4	52.7	0.8	36.0	2.5	26.6	0.0	13.9
Angola	0.1	40.1	. .	. .	0.1	21.1	. .	. .
Argentina	2.8	. .	. .	. .	3.9	. .	. .	. .
Australia	5.2	45.4	1.8	25.6	7.5	10.0	. .	. .
Austria	2.5	39.5	2.8	21.5	4.5	10.4	. .	. .
Belarus	0.1	. .	. .	. .	9.1	30.6	. .	. .
Belgium	1.2	39.1	1.4	22.9	3.4	14.6	0.0	18.7
Benin	0.4	9.9	0.0	. .	. .	. .	. .	. .
Bolivia	0.5	. .	0.9	. .	2.9	. .	. .	. .
Brazil	0.3	52.0	0.7	40.4	1.1	19.2	0.0	21.0
Bulgaria	0.9	61.3	0.6	55.3	8.4	42.6	0.4	42.0
Burkina Faso	0.2	7.3	0.0	5.4	. .	. .	. .	. .
Burundi	0.1	24.0	0.0	17.6	0.0	3.6	. .	. .
Cameroon	0.8	16.8	. .	. .	0.1	0.8	. .	. .
Canada	2.2	46.4	2.5	30.0	4.9	14.3	0.2	6.7
Central African Republic	0.1	7.3	0.0	. .	0.1	3.4	. .	. .
Chad	0.0	3.5	0.0	3.3	0.0	. .	. .	. .
Chile	0.7	46.7	0.3	. .	6.9	19.1	. .	. .
China	0.1	. .	0.1	. .	0.8	. .	0.1	. .
Hong Kong, China	3.0	28.9	1.5	25.1	3.7	6.2	0.0	32.3
Colombia	0.3	46.4	0.3	43.9	4.9	30.7	. .	. .
Congo, Rep.	0.4	9.4	0.0	25.0	. .	. .	. .	. .
Costa Rica	0.4	. .	1.2	. .	2.5	. .	0.0	. .
Côte d'Ivoire	0.8	8.0	0.3	18.7	0.2	8.7	0.0	18.9
Croatia	0.3	58.9	0.2	29.6	6.6	19.3	0.9	13.8
Czech Republic	0.7	38.1	0.4	13.8	5.9	19.8	0.2	20.6
Denmark	1.6	40.3	1.7	26.1	4.6	20.2	0.1	7.5
Ecuador	0.7	. .	0.0	. .	2.6	. .	. .	. .
Egypt, Arab Rep.	0.5	37.1	0.1	23.8	1.0	19.8	. .	. .
El Salvador	0.0	57.6	0.4	50.0	2.6	24.0	. .	. .
Estonia	0.9	40.8	0.6	44.4	6.6	14.8	0.4	14.1
Ethiopia	0.0	16.0	0.0	19.1	0.1	8.1	. .	. .
Finland	2.9	50.9	3.5	18.4	12.7	14.1	. .	. .
France	7.1	36.4	. .	. .	1.2	21.2	. .	. .
Georgia	2.7	65.0	0.4	52.2	8.9	31.8	0.9	48.3
Germany	2.2	33.3	1.8	24.1	5.8	9.7	0.0	2.9
Ghana	0.1	17.3	0.0	11.5	0.1	2.8	. .	. .
Greece	2.0	37.4	1.8	32.5	6.1	19.6	0.3	9.0
Guinea	0.3	5.8	. .	. .	0.2	3.8	. .	. .
Honduras	0.0	48.7	0.6	6.6	1.8	31.3	. .	. .
Hungary	0.3	36.7	0.2	20.1	1.9	20.2	0.9	23.5
India	1.1	33.3	. .	. .	0.3	7.9	. .	. .
Indonesia	0.2	34.0	0.8	34.3	1.8	14.2	0.1	20.5
Ireland	5.4	51.1	1.2	32.3	3.9	11.6	. .	. .
Israel	2.1	52.4	1.6	34.7	6.2	23.9	. .	. .
Italy	2.2	51.9	1.0	43.1	4.2	13.1	0.1	43.1
Jamaica	0.5	. .	0.2	. .	0.4	. .	. .	. .
Japan	0.7	17.6	0.2	20.2	9.0	10.8	0.0	6.2
Jordan	1.4	57.1	2.5	41.3	3.1	17.7	0.0	. .
Kazakhstan	1.9	70.7	1.1	25.9	2.3	28.7	0.5	48.3
Kenya	0.2	12.6	. .	. .	. .	. .	. .	. .
Korea, Rep.	3.8	33.7	2.8	25.9	13.5	9.9	0.0	35.0
Kyrgyz Republic	1.1	65.3	0.5	72.4	0.4	38.0	0.3	3.9
Lao PDR	0.0	40.7	0.1	22.9	0.2	11.2	0.1	5.3
Latvia	0.6	49.5	1.2	31.2	2.8	19.6	0.5	9.0
Lebanon	1.3	52.0	0.6	37.6	1.1	20.0	. .	. .
Lesotho	0.2	33.0	0.0	28.3	0.1	13.7	. .	. .
Macedonia, FYR	0.8	70.7	0.5	65.8	4.2	26.4	0.1	21.8
Madagascar	0.7	36.0	0.1	20.9	0.1	12.4	. .	. .
Malawi	0.0	20.9	. .	. .	0.1	5.3	. .	. .
Malaysia	0.5	46.1	0.3	51.0	0.8	14.4	. .	. .
Mali	0.0	2.8	0.0	4.9	0.1	1.9	0.0	20.3
Mauritania	0.3	16.4	0.0	13.2	0.1	6.6	. .	. .
Mauritius	0.1	44.2	0.1	30.8	0.3	4.1	. .	. .
Mexico	0.5	54.6	1.2	41.2	2.7	14.0	0.0	9.9
Moldova	0.1	. .	0.0	. .	9.6	42.2	0.8	21.6
Mongolia	0.7	62.4	0.3	51.2	2.5	45.7	0.1	50.3
Morocco	2.8	29.0	. .	. .	0.1	13.7	0.0	1.7
Mozambique	0.1	28.8	0.0	25.5	0.1	6.8	. .	. .

Table A.1. *(continued)*

Economy	Natural science		Mathematics and computer science		Engineering		Transport and communications	
	% of 20–24 age group 1990–95[a]	% female 1990–95[a]	% of 20–24 age group 1990–95[a]	% female 1990–95[a]	% of 20–24 age group 1990–95[a]	% female 1990–95[a]	% of 20–24 age group 1990–95[a]	% female 1990–95[a]
Namibia	0.4	35.2	..	..	..	..	..	..
Nepal	0.8	12.9	..	..	0.1	8.6	..	..
Netherlands	1.4	32.4	0.7	10.2	4.8	12.8	0.1	5.7
New Zealand	4.8	42.3	0.4	30.3	3.0	13.3	0.2	11.6
Nicaragua	0.3	76.0	0.8	53.5	1.9	26.5	..	..
Nigeria	0.5	..	..	..	0.3	..	..	..
Norway	3.0	40.0	0.4	27.6	5.2	18.6	0.3	8.1
Oman	0.3	62.8	0.1	59.0	0.4	8.9	..	..
Pakistan	0.3	15.8	..	..	0.4	2.0	..	..
Panama	0.8	48.9	0.6	53.1	5.0	31.8	..	..
Papua New Guinea	0.1	20.6	0.0	32.5	0.2	6.3	..	..
Paraguay	0.3	80.2	0.7	46.0	0.5	17.2	..	..
Peru	0.7	..	..	..	4.0	..	..	..
Philippines	0.5	67.9	2.1	54.4	3.9	18.3	0.9	0.8
Poland	0.8	62.8	0.5	56.3	4.9	18.1	0.2	10.0
Portugal	1.0	59.8	1.7	46.2	6.0	28.3	0.0	..
Romania	0.6	72.1	0.5	57.8	4.5	28.1	0.1	11.6
Russian Federation	1.6	51.8	1.6	55.0	14.8	24.2	0.5	36.0
Saudi Arabia	1.0	51.2	0.3	32.4	0.5	4.6	0.1	..
Senegal	0.6	9.3	0.0	12.4	0.1	30.2	..	..
Slovak Republic	0.9	48.0	0.1	22.5	8.7	28.5	..	..
Slovenia	0.7	54.0	0.1	38.1	5.6	21.4	0.9	29.3
South Africa	0.7	45.9	0.9	34.9	0.6	5.8	..	..
Spain	2.9	50.4	2.5	31.8	6.2	22.3	..	..
Sri Lanka	0.5	44.0	0.0	33.4	0.4	12.4	..	..
Sweden	1.8	47.0	2.3	27.3	6.2	19.4	0.1	13.9
Switzerland	2.3	29.8	0.6	14.4	4.4	4.7	0.0	3.5
Syrian Arab Republic	1.4	41.9	0.1	30.7	1.0	32.5	..	..
Tajikistan	..	..	..	..	3.2	17.2	..	..
Tanzania	0.0	11.9	0.0	2.7	0.1	4.0	0.0	19.1
Thailand	1.3	41.7	0.0	50.5	1.7	5.9	0.0	..
Togo	0.3	7.4	..	..	0.1	2.3	..	..
Trinidad and Tobago	0.7	51.3	..	..	0.9	20.9	0.0	..
Tunisia	1.5	37.2	0.3	22.1	0.8	16.8	0.1	24.2
Turkey	0.7	45.2	0.5	33.0	2.5	16.8	0.0	14.2
Uganda	0.1	26.8	0.0	17.9	0.1	9.1	..	..
Ukraine	..	..	..	..	10.6	..	..	..
United Arab Emirates	0.5	76.5	0.3	66.5	0.4	22.4	..	..
United Kingdom	2.6	44.4	2.2	25.2	4.7	12.3	..	..
United States	2.6	..	2.7	..	4.2	..	0.6	..
Uruguay	0.4	..	..	..	3.6	..	..	..
Yemen, Rep.	0.1	23.9	0.0	26.4	0.2	10.5	..	..
Zimbabwe	0.2	24.1	0.1	36.5	0.7	6.4	..	..

a. Data are for the most recent year available.

Table A.2.   Assessment of legal infrastructure

Economy	Creditors' rights	Shareholders' rights	Enforcement	Economy	Creditors' rights	Shareholders' rights	Enforcement
Systems of English origin				*Systems of French origin*			
Australia	−1	4	9.36	Argentina	−1	4	5.13
Canada	−1	4	9.48	Belgium	0	0	9.74
Hong Kong, China	1	4	8.52	Brazil	−2	3	6.31
India	1	2	5.14	Chile	−1	3	6.91
Ireland	−1	3	8.38	Colombia	−2	1	4.55
Israel	1	3	6.18	Ecuador	1	2	5.93
Kenya	1	3	5.54	Egypt	1	2	5.11
Malaysia	1	3	7.11	France	−2	2	9.09
New Zealand	0	4	9.65	Greece	−1	1	6.40
Nigeria	1	3	3.55	Indonesia	1	2	5.04
Pakistan	1	4	3.95	Italy	−1	0	8.75
Singapore	1	3	8.72	Jordan	—	1	4.61
South Africa	0	4	5.85	Mexico	−2	0	5.95
Sri Lanka	—	2	3.58	Netherlands	−1	2	9.68
Thailand	1	3	6.91	Peru	−2	2	3.59
United Kingdom	1	4	9.10	Philippines	−2	4	3.77
United States	−1	5	9.50	Portugal	−1	2	8.63
Zimbabwe	1	3	4.36	Spain	0	2	8.10
Average	0.41	3.39	6.94	Turkey	−1	2	5.57
				Uruguay	0	1	6.15
Systems of German origin				Venezuela	—	1	6.34
Austria	0	2	9.80	Average	−0.84	1.76	6.44
Germany	0	1	9.50				
Japan	0	3	9.34	*Systems of Scandinavian origin*			
Korea	1	2	6.97	Denmark	0	3	9.66
Switzerland	−1	1	9.99	Finland	−1	2	9.58
Taiwan, China	0	3	8.84	Norway	−1	3	9.86
Average	0	2	9.07	Sweden	−1	2	9.79
					Average	−0.75	2.50	9.72

— Not available.

Note: Scores for creditors' rights range from −2 to 1; scores for shareholders' rights range from 1 to 5; values for enforcement range from 1 to 10.
Source: La Porta and others 1998; Levine, Loayza, and Beck 1998.

Selected

World Development Indicators

Contents

Introduction to Selected World Development Indicators

SELECTED WORLD DEVELOPMENT INDICATORS provides a core set of standard indicators drawn from the World Bank's development databases. The layout of the 21 tables retains the tradition of presenting comparative socioeconomic data for more than 130 economies for the most recent year for which data are available and for an earlier year. An additional table presents basic indicators for 77 economies with sparse data or with populations of less than 1 million.

The indicators presented here are a selection from more than 500 included in the 1998 *World Development Indicators*. Published annually, *World Development Indicators* adopts an integrated approach to the measurement of development progress. Its opening chapter reports on the prospects for and record of social and economic progress in developing countries, measured against six international goals. Its five main sections recognize the contribution of a wide range of factors: human capital development, environmental sustainability, macroeconomic performance, private sector development, and the global links that influence the external environment for development. *World Development Indicators* is complemented by a separately published CD-ROM database that gives access to over 1,000 data tables and 500 time-series indicators for 223 countries and regions.

Organization of Selected World Development Indicators

Tables 1 and 2, *World view,* offer an overview of key development issues: How rich or poor are the people in each economy? What is their real level of welfare as reflected in child malnutrition and mortality rates? What is the life expectancy of newborns? What percentage of adults are illiterate?

Tables 3 to 7, *People,* show the rate of progress in social development during the past decade. Data on population growth, labor force participation, and income distribution are included. New this year is a table on the prevalence and depth of poverty. Measures of well-being such as malnutrition and access to health care, school enrollment ratios, and gender differences in access to educational attainment are also provided.

Tables 8 to 10, *Environment,* bring together key indicators on land use and agricultural output, water resources, energy consumption, and carbon dioxide emissions.

Tables 11 to 15, *Economy,* present information on the structure and growth of the world's economies, including government finance statistics and a summary of the balance of payments.

Tables 16 to 19, *States and markets,* look at the roles of the public and the private sector in creating the necessary infrastructure for economic growth. These tables present information on private investment, stock markets, and the economic activities of the state (including military expenditure), as well as a full table of indicators on information technology and research and development.

Tables 20 and 21, *Global links,* contain information on trade and financial flows, including aid and lending to developing countries.

Because the World Bank's primary business is providing lending and policy advice to its low- and middle-income members, the issues covered in these tables focus mainly on these economies. Where available, information on the high-income economies is also provided for comparison. Readers may wish to refer to national statistical publications and publications of the Organisation for Economic Co-operation and Development and the European Community for more information on the high-income economies.

Classification of economies

As in the rest of the Report, the main criterion used in the Selected World Development Indicators to classify economies and broadly distinguish stages of economic development is gross national product (GNP) per capita. Countries are classified into three categories according to income. The classification used in this edition has been updated to reflect the World Bank's current operational guidelines. The GNP per capita cutoff levels are as follows: low-income, $785 or less in 1997; middle-income, $786 to $9,655; and high-income, $9,656. A further division at GNP per capita $3,125 is made between lower-middle-income and upper-middle-income economies. Economies are further classified by region. See the table on Classification of economies at the end of the Report for a list of economies in each group (including those with populations of less than 1 million).

Data sources and methodology

Socioeconomic data presented here are drawn from several sources: primary data collection by the World Bank, member-country statistical publications, research institutes such as the World Resources Institute, and international organizations such as the United Nations and its specialized agencies, the International Monetary Fund, and the Organisation for Economic Co-operation and Development (see the list of Data Sources following the Technical Notes for a complete listing). Although international standards of coverage, definition, and classification apply to most statistics reported by countries and international agencies, there are inevitably differences in coverage, currentness, and the capabilities and resources devoted to basic data collection and compilation. For some topics, competing sources of data require review by World Bank staff to ensure that the most reliable data available are presented. In some instances, where available data are deemed too weak to provide reliable measures of levels and trends or do not adequately adhere to international standards, the data are not shown.

The data presented are generally consistent with those in the 1998 *World Development Indicators*. However, data have been revised and updated wherever new information has become available. Differences may also reflect revisions to historical series and changes in methodology. Thus data of different vintages may be published in different editions of Bank publications. Readers are advised not to compile data series across publications. Consistent time-series data are available in the 1998 *World Development Indicators CD-ROM*.

All dollar figures are in current U.S. dollars unless otherwise stated. The various methods used to convert from national currency figures are described in the Technical Notes.

Summary measures

The summary measures at the bottom of each table are totals (indicated by *t* if the aggregates include estimates for missing data and nonreporting economies, or by an *s* for simple sums), weighted averages (*w*), or median values (*m*) calculated for groups of economies. The countries excluded from the main tables (those presented in Table 1a) have been included in the summary measures where data are available or, if no data are available, by assuming that they follow the trend of reporting countries. This gives a more consistent aggregated measure by standardizing country coverage for each period shown. Where missing information accounts for a third or more of the overall estimate, however, the group measure is reported as not available.

Terminology and country coverage

The term "country" does not imply political independence but may refer to any territory for which authorities report separate social or economic statistics. Data are shown for economies as they were constituted in 1997, and historical data are revised to reflect current political arrangements. Throughout the tables, exceptions are noted.

As of July 1, 1997, China resumed its exercise of sovereignty over the Special Administrative Region of Hong Kong. Data for China do not include data for Taiwan, China, unless otherwise noted.

Data are shown separately whenever possible for the countries formed from the former Czechoslovakia: the Czech Republic and the Slovak Republic.

Data are shown separately for Eritrea whenever possible; in most cases prior to 1992, however, they are included in the data for Ethiopia.

Data for Germany refer to the unified Germany, unless otherwise noted.

Data for Jordan refer to the East Bank only, unless otherwise noted.

In 1991 the Union of Soviet Socialist Republics was formally dissolved into 15 countries: Armenia, Azerbaijan, Belarus, Estonia, Georgia, Kazakhstan, the Kyrgyz Republic, Latvia, Lithuania, Moldova, the Russian Federation, Tajikistan, Turkmenistan, Ukraine, and Uzbekistan. Whenever possible, data are shown for the individual countries.

Data for the Republic of Yemen refer to that country as it is constituted from 1990 onward; data for previous years refer to the former People's Democratic Republic of Yemen and the former Yemen Arab Republic, unless otherwise noted.

Whenever possible, data are shown for the individual countries formed from the former Yugoslavia: Bosnia and Herzegovina, Croatia, the former Yugoslav Republic of

Macedonia, Slovenia, and the Federal Republic of Yugoslavia (Serbia and Montenegro).

Table layout

The table format of this edition conforms to that of the *World Development Indicators*: economies are listed in alphabetical order, and summary measures are placed at the bottom of the table. Economies with populations of fewer than 1 million and those with sparse data are not shown in the main tables but are included, where possible, in the aggregates. Basic indicators for these economies may be found in Table 1a. A ranking of economies by GNP per capita, a traditional feature of the Selected World Development Indicators layout, is now included as an indicator in Table 1.

Technical notes

Because data quality and intercountry comparisons are often problematic, readers are encouraged to consult the Technical Notes, the Classification of Economies table, and the footnotes to the tables. For more extensive docu-

mentation see the 1998 *World Development Indicators.* The Data Sources section following the Technical Notes lists sources that contain more comprehensive definitions and descriptions of the concepts used.

For more information about the Selected World Development Indicators and the World Bank's other statistical publications, please contact:

Information Center, Development Data Group
The World Bank
1818 H Street, N.W.
Washington, D.C. 20433
Hotline: (800) 590-1906 or (202) 473-7824
Fax: (202) 522-1498
E-mail: info@worldbank.org
World Wide Web: http://www.worldbank.org/wdi

To order World Bank publications, e-mail your request to books@worldbank.org, or write to World Bank Publications at the address above, or call (202) 473-1155.

The World by Income

This map presents economies classified according to World Bank estimates of 1997 GNP per capita. Not shown on the map due to space constraints are: American Samoa (upper middle income); Fiji, Kiribati, Samoa, Tonga (lower middle income); French Polynesia (high income); Tuvalu (no data).

Low $785 or less
Lower middle $786 to $3,125
Upper middle $3,126 to $9,655
High $9,656 or more

No data

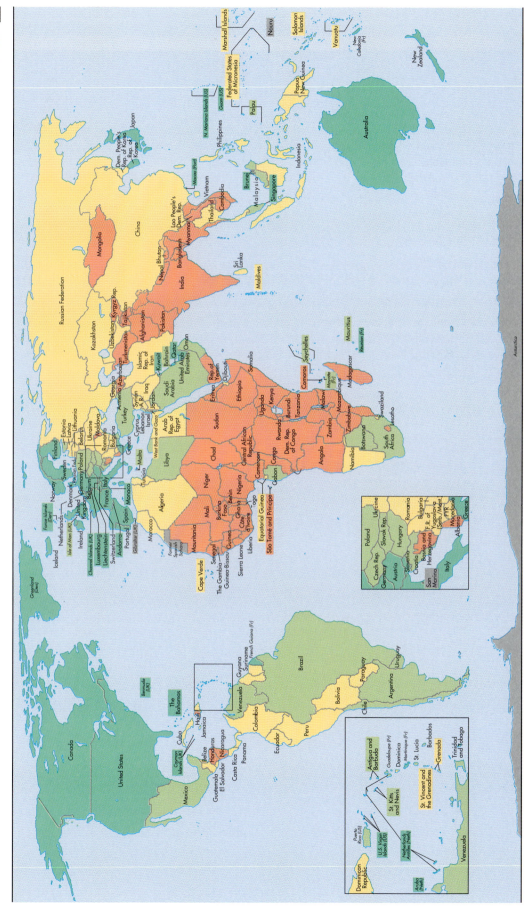

Table 1. Size of the economy

Economy	Population Millions 1997	Land area Thousands of sq. km 1995	Population density People per sq. km 1997	Gross national product (GNP) Billions of dollars 1997[a]	Rank 1997	Avg. annual growth rate (%) 1996–97	GNP per capita Dollars 1997[a]	Rank 1997	Avg. annual growth rate (%) 1996–97	GNP measured at PPP[b] Billions of dollars 1997	Per capita Dollars 1997	Rank 1997
Albania	3	27	119	2.5	111	..	750	84	..	..	..	..
Algeria	29	2,382	12	43.8	49	2.0	1,490	67	–0.1	134.5[c]	4,580[c]	54
Angola	11	1,247	9	3.8	102	15.4	340	107	12.1	10.8	940	109
Argentina	36	2,737	13	305.7	18	6.1	8,570	28	4.7	355.0	9,950	30
Armenia	4	28	133	2.0	118	5.6	530	95	5.4	8.6	2,280	79
Australia	19	7,682	2	380.0	14	2.9	20,540	16	1.8	373.2	20,170	15
Austria	8	83	97	225.9	21	2.1	27,980	8	1.9	177.5	21,980	9
Azerbaijan	8	87	87	3.9	101	3.1	510	96	2.6	11.6	1,520	96
Bangladesh	124	130	920	33.2	52	5.4	270	116	3.7	129.6	1,050	106
Belarus	10	207	50	22.1	57	11.1	2,150	58	11.5	49.7	4,840	52
Belgium	10	33	310	268.4	19	..	26,420	9	..	227.3	22,370	8
Benin	6	111	49	2.2	114	5.3	380	104	2.3	7.3	1,260	100
Bolivia	8	1,084	7	7.4	81	..	950	79	..	..	..	..
Brazil	164	8,457	19	773.4	8	2.4	4,720	34	1.1	1,019.9	6,240	47
Bulgaria	8	111	76	9.4	74	–6.8	1,140	74	–6.1	32.0	3,860	61
Burkina Faso	11	274	38	2.6	109	6.8	240	121	4.0	10.8[c]	990[c]	108
Burundi	7	26	244	1.2	128	3.7	180	130	1.1	3.9	590	120
Cambodia	11	177	57	3.2	106	..	300	115	..	..	..	..
Cameroon	14	465	29	9.1	77	8.4	650	90	5.3	27.9	1,980	84
Canada	30	9,221	3	583.9	9	3.6	19,290	18	2.6	661.6	21,860	10
Central African Republic	3	623	5	1.1	129	5.6	320	112	3.4	5.2[c]	1,530[c]	95
Chad	7	1,259	5	1.6	125	6.8	240	122	4.2	7.2	1,070	104
Chile	15	749	19	73.3	40	7.6	5,020	32	6.1	176.6	12,080	27
China	1,227	9,326	129	1,055.4	7	8.9	860	81	7.8	4,382.5	3,570	65
Hong Kong, China	7	1	6,218	164.4	26	5.2	25,280	13	2.1	159.6	24,540	4
Colombia	38	1,039	35	86.8	38	..	2,280	55	..	251.7	6,720	40
Congo, Dem. Rep.	47	2,267	19	5.1	89	..	110	131	..	35.8[c]	790[c]	115
Congo, Rep.	3	342	8	1.8	122	0.5	660	89	–2.2	3.8	1,380	98
Costa Rica	4	51	66	9.3	76	2.6	2,640	52	0.7	22.5	6,410	44
Côte d'Ivoire	15	318	44	10.2	73	6.9	690	87	4.2	24.2	1,640	93
Croatia	4	56	85	20.7	59	..	4,610	36	..	..	..	..
Czech Republic	10	77	134	53.5	46	0.7	5,200	31	0.8	117.3	11,380	28
Denmark	5	42	123	171.4	24	3.4	32,500	5	3.1	120.0	22,740	7
Dominican Republic	8	48	162	13.5	69	11.7	1,670	62	9.8	36.8	4,540	55
Ecuador	12	277	41	19.0	64	4.4	1,590	63	2.3	57.5	4,820	53
Egypt, Arab Rep.	60	995	58	71.2	41	4.9	1,180	72	3.0	177.3	2,940	72
El Salvador	6	21	273	10.7	70	3.5	1,810	61	0.9	16.7	2,810	73
Estonia	1	42	35	4.8	93	6.4	3,330	47	7.7	7.3	5,010	50
Ethiopia	60	1,000	56	6.5	86	5.3	110	132	2.0	30.7	510	122
Finland	5	305	17	123.8	32	4.6	24,080	14	4.3	97.6	18,980	18
France	59	550	106	1,526.0	4	2.3	26,050	11	1.9	1,280.3	21,860	11
Gabon	1	258	4	4.9	90	6.4	4,230	38	3.8	7.5	6,540	42
Georgia	5	70	78	4.6	94	..	840	82	..	10.7	1,980	85
Germany	82	349	234	2,319.5	3	..	28,260	7	..	1,748.3	21,300	13
Ghana	18	228	75	6.6	85	3.1	370	106	0.5	32.3[c]	1,790[c]	88
Greece	11	129	81	126.2	31	3.4	12,010	24	3.1	137.5	13,080	25
Guatemala	11	108	98	16.8	66	3.6	1,500	66	0.9	43.1	3,840	62
Guinea	7	246	27	3.9	100	7.2	570	92	4.6	12.8	1,850	87
Guinea-Bissau	1	28	38	0.3	133	7.4	240	123	5.0	1.2	1,070	105
Haiti	7	28	260	2.5	110	1.1	330	108	–0.8	8.6[c]	1,150[c]	101
Honduras	6	112	53	4.4	95	7.6	700	86	4.5	13.8	2,200	81
Hungary	10	92	111	45.0	48	3.9	4,430	37	4.3	71.1	7,000	39
India	961	2,973	313	373.9	15	5.0	390	102	3.2	1,587.0	1,650	92
Indonesia	200	1,812	107	221.9	22	4.4	1,110	75	2.8	690.7	3,450	67
Ireland	4	69	52	66.4	43	7.5	18,280	19	7.3	60.7	16,740	20
Israel	6	21	269	87.6	37	..	15,810	22	..	99.0	16,960	19
Italy	57	294	195	1,155.4	6	1.3	20,120	17	1.2	1,152.1	20,060	16
Jamaica	3	11	233	4.0	99	1.9	1,560	65	1.0	8.9	3,470	66
Japan	126	377	333	4,772.3	2	0.5	37,850	2	0.2	2,950.7	23,400	6
Jordan	4	89	47	7.0	82	4.4	1,570	64	1.5	15.2	3,430	68
Kazakhstan	16	2,671	6	21.8	58	1.3	1,340	69	2.2	53.7	3,290	69
Kenya	28	569	47	9.3	75	2.3	330	109	–0.1	31.2	1,110	102
Korea, Rep.	46	99	456	485.2	11	4.8	10,550	25	3.8	621.1	13,500	24
Kyrgyz Republic	5	192	24	2.0	116	5.1	440	99	4.0	9.5	2,040	83
Lao PDR	5	231	20	1.9	120	6.5	400	101	3.8	6.3	1,290	99
Latvia	2	62	41	6.0	87	..	2,430	54	..	9.1	3,650	64
Lebanon	4	10	391	13.9	68	..	3,350	46	..	24.9	5,990	48
Lesotho	2	30	65	1.4	127	5.2	670	88	2.9	5.1[c]	2,480[c]	74
Lithuania	4	65	57	8.3	80	2.7	2,230	56	2.9	16.7	4,510	56
Macedonia, FYR	2	25	77	2.2	115	..	1,090	76	..	..	..	..
Madagascar	14	582	23	3.6	104	4.7	250	120	1.6	12.9	910	112
Malawi	10	94	104	2.3	113	3.1	220	124	0.5	7.2	700	118
Malaysia	21	329	61	98.2	35	7.5	4,680	35	5.2	229.3	10,920	29
Mali	10	1,220	8	2.7	108	6.6	260	118	3.5	7.6	740	116
Mauritania	2	1,025	2	1.1	130	5.9	450	98	3.2	4.5	1,870	86

Note: For data comparability and coverage, see the Technical Notes. Figures in italics are for years other than those specified.

Economy	Population Millions 1997	Land area Thousands of sq. km 1995	Population density People per sq. km 1997	Gross national product (GNP) Billions of dollars 1997[a]	Rank 1997	Avg. annual growth rate (%) 1996–97	GNP per capita Dollars 1997[a]	Rank 1997	Avg. annual growth rate (%) 1996–97	GNP measured at PPP[b] Billions of dollars 1997	Per capita Dollars 1997	Rank 1997
Mauritius	1	2	553	4.3	96	5.2	3,800	40	4.2	10.7	9,360	31
Mexico	95	1,909	48	348.6	16	8.0	3,680	42	6.2	770.3	8,120	35
Moldova	4	33	132	2.3	112	..	540	94	..	..	..	..
Mongolia	3	1,567	2	1.0	131	..	390	103	..	..	..	..
Morocco	28	446	59	34.4	51	−2.7	1,250	70	−4.4	86.1	3,130	70
Mozambique	19	784	22	1.7	124	8.6	90	133	5.7	9.7[c]	520[c]	121
Namibia	2	823	2	3.6	103	3.8	2,220	57	1.3	8.8[c]	5,440[c]	49
Nepal	23	143	150	4.8	92	2.7	210	125	0.0	24.7	1,090	103
Netherlands	16	34	456	402.7	13	3.2	25,820	12	2.7	332.8	21,340	12
New Zealand	4	268	13	60.5	45	1.9	16,480	21	1.0	60.9	16,600	21
Nicaragua	5	121	36	1.9	121	13.5	410	100	10.4	11.0[c]	2,370[c]	78
Niger	10	1,267	7	2.0	119	3.6	200	128	0.1	8.9[c]	920[c]	111
Nigeria	118	911	122	30.7	54	4.2	260	119	1.2	103.5	880	114
Norway	4	307	14	158.9	27	4.0	36,090	3	3.5	105.4	23,940	5
Oman	2	212	10	10.6	71	..	4,950	33	..	20.1	8,690	32
Pakistan	137	771	169	67.2	42	2.8	490	97	0.0	218.2	1,590	94
Panama	3	74	35	8.4	79	4.3	3,080	49	2.6	19.2	7,070	38
Papua New Guinea	5	453	9	4.2	98	−14.0	940	80	−15.9	10.8[c]	2,390[c]	77
Paraguay	5	397	12	10.2	72	14.5	2,010	60	11.6	19.7	3,870	60
Peru	25	1,280	19	60.8	44	1.7	2,460	53	−0.1	108.7	4,390	57
Philippines	73	298	236	89.3	36	5.8	1,220	71	3.6	269.2	3,670	63
Poland	39	304	127	138.9	28	6.8	3,590	43	6.7	246.6	6,380	46
Portugal	10	92	108	103.9	33	3.4	10,450	26	3.3	137.6	13,840	23
Romania	23	230	98	32.1	53	−6.6	1,420	68	−6.3	96.8	4,290	58
Russian Federation	147	16,889	9	403.5	12	..	2,740	51	..	618.4	4,190	59
Rwanda	8	25	259	1.7	123	15.1	210	126	−2.0	4.9	630	119
Saudi Arabia	20	2,150	9	128.9	30	..	6,790	29	..	..	..	..
Senegal	9	193	43	4.9	91	4.4	550	93	1.6	14.6	1,670	90
Sierra Leone	5	72	63	0.9	132	..	200	129	..	2.4	510	123
Singapore	3	1	4,896	101.8	34	8.8	32,940	4	7.2	89.6	29,000	1
Slovak Republic	5	48	111	19.8	60	6.1	3,700	41	5.9	42.0	7,850	36
Slovenia	2	20	99	19.3	63	..	9,680	27	..	24.9	12,520	26
South Africa	38	1,221	30	130.2	29	1.3	3,400	45	−0.5	286.9[c]	7,490[c]	37
Spain	39	499	79	570.1	10	3.2	14,510	23	3.1	617.6	15,720	22
Sri Lanka	18	65	280	14.8	67	6.9	800	83	5.8	45.5	2,460	75
Sweden	9	412	21	232.0	20	1.8	26,220	10	1.7	168.4	19,030	17
Switzerland	7	40	178	313.5	17	..	44,320	1	..	186.2	26,320	3
Syrian Arab Republic	15	184	77	17.1	65	2.0	1,150	73	−0.6	44.5	2,990	71
Tajikistan	6	141	42	2.0	117	2.2	330	110	0.7	5.6	930	110
Tanzania	31	884	34	6.6	83	..	210	127	..	..	..	..
Thailand	61	511	116	169.6	25	−0.4	2,800	50	−1.3	399.3	6,590	41
Togo	4	54	76	1.4	126	5.0	330	111	2.1	7.8	1,790	89
Trinidad and Tobago	1	5	251	5.5	88	6.4	4,230	39	5.5	8.4	6,410	45
Tunisia	9	155	58	19.4	61	11.5	2,090	59	9.7	46.2	4,980	51
Turkey	64	770	80	199.5	23	8.1	3,130	48	6.4	409.7	6,430	43
Turkmenistan	5	470	10	2.9	107	..	630	91	..	6.6	1,410	97
Uganda	20	200	96	6.6	84	5.3	320	113	2.3	21.3[c]	1,050[c]	107
Ukraine	50	579	89	52.4	47	−3.0	1,040	77	−2.3	109.3	2,170	82
United Arab Emirates	3	84	29	42.7	50	..	17,360	20	..	..	..	..
United Kingdom	59	242	243	1,220.2	5	3.4	20,710	15	3.2	1,208.9	20,520	14
United States	268	9,159	29	7,690.1	1	3.8	28,740	6	2.9	7,690.1	28,740	2
Uruguay	3	175	18	19.4	62	3.4	6,020	30	2.8	27.3	8,460	34
Uzbekistan	24	414	55	23.9	56	2.2	1,010	78	0.3	58.0	2,450	76
Venezuela	23	882	25	78.7	39	7.4	3,450	44	5.3	194.3	8,530	33
Vietnam	77	325	227	24.5	55	..	320	114	..	128.3	1,670	91
Yemen, Rep.	16	528	29	4.3	97	..	270	117	..	11.8	720	117
Zambia	9	743	12	3.6	105	7.9	380	105	5.3	8.4	890	113
Zimbabwe	11	387	28	8.6	78	2.1	750	85	0.0	26.2	2,280	80
World	5,829 t	130,129 t	44 w	29,925.7 t		3.2 w	5,130 w		1.8 w	36,950.6 t	6,330 w	
Low income	2,048	30,175	65	721.7		5.0	350		2.8	2,869.9	1,400	
Middle income	2,855	68,983	40	5,401.9		4.9	1,890		3.8	12,989.8	4,550	
Lower middle income	2,285	46,158	48	2,817.9		..	1,230		..	8,594.9	3,760	
Upper middle income	571	22,825	24	2,584.0		4.7	4,520		3.2	4,394.9	7,700.0	
Low & middle income	4,903	99,158	48	6,123.6		4.9	1,250		3.3	15,859.7	3,230.0	
East Asia & Pacific	1,753	15,869	108	1,707.3		6.8	970		5.6	6,247.3	3,560	
Europe & Central Asia	471	23,844	20	1,105.8		..	2,320		..	2,089.1	4,390	
Latin America & Carib.	494	20,064	24	1,916.8		4.4	3,880		2.7	3,288.7	6,660	
Middle East & N. Africa	283	10,972	25	582.7		..	2,060		..	1,297.3	4,580	
South Asia	1,289	4,781	260	501.9		4.8	390		2.9	2,032.0	1,580	
Sub-Saharan Africa	614	23,628	25	309.1		4.2	500		1.2	905.3	1,470	
High income	926	30,971	30	23,802.1		2.8	25,700		2.2	21,090.9	22,770	

a. Preliminary World Bank estimates calculated using the World Bank *Atlas* method; figures in italics refer to 1996. b. Purchasing power parity; see the Technical Notes.
c. The estimate is based on regression; others are extrapolated from the latest International Comparison Programme benchmark estimates.

Table 2.   Quality of life

Economy	Growth of private consumption per capita Avg. annual growth rate (%) 1980–96 Uncorrected	Distribution-corrected	Prevalence of child malnutrition % of children under age 5 1990–96	Under-5 mortality rate Per 1,000 1980	1996	Life expectancy at birth Years 1996 Males	Females	Adult illiteracy rate % of people 15 and above 1995 Males	Females	Urban population % of total 1980	1997	Access to sanitation in urban areas % of urban pop. with access 1995
Albania	..	..	..	..	40	69	75	..	..	34	38	..
Algeria	−1.9	−1.2	10	139	39	68	72	26	51	43	57	..
Angola	−7.4	..	35	..	209	45	48	..	..	21	32	34
Argentina	..	..	2	38	25	69	77	4	4	83	89	100
Armenia	−5.4	..	..	..	20	69	76	..	..	66	69	..
Australia	1.6	1.1	..	..	7	75	81	..	..	86	85	..
Austria	2.0	1.5	..	..	6	74	80	..	..	65	64	100
Azerbaijan	..	..	10	..	23	65	74	..	..	53	56	..
Bangladesh	0.0	0.0	68	207	112	57	59	51	74	11	19	77
Belarus	−4.5	−3.5	..	..	17	63	74	..	..	57	72	..
Belgium	1.7	1.3	..	..	7	73	80	..	..	95	97	100
Benin	−0.8	..	24	205	140	52	57	51	74	27	40	54
Bolivia	−0.7	−0.4	16	171	102	59	63	10	24	46	62	64
Brazil	0.0	0.0	7	86	42	63	71	17	17	66	80	55
Bulgaria	−0.7	−0.5	..	..	20	67	75	..	..	61	69	100
Burkina Faso	0.0	..	33	241	158	45	47	71	91	9	17	42
Burundi	−0.8	..	38	195	176	45	48	51	78	4	8	..
Cambodia	..	..	38	..	170	52	55	20	47	12	22	..
Cameroon	−2.5	..	15	172	102	55	58	25	48	31	46	73
Canada	1.3	0.9	..	..	7	76	82	..	..	76	77	..
Central African Republic	−2.4	..	23	193	164	46	51	32	48	35	40	..
Chad	−0.4	..	..	206	189	47	50	38	65	19	23	73
Chile	3.2	1.4	1	37	13	72	78	5	5	81	84	100
China	7.7	4.5	16	60	39	68	71	10	27	20	32	58
Hong Kong, China	5.3	..	..	12	6	76	81	4	12	92	95	..
Colombia	1.3	0.6	8	58	31	67	73	9	9	64	74	76
Congo, Dem. Rep.	−4.2	..	34	..	..	51	54	13	32	29	29	..
Congo, Rep.	−0.4	..	24	..	145	49	54	17	33	41	60	11
Costa Rica	0.7	0.4	2	29	15	75	79	5	5	43	50	..
Côte d'Ivoire	−2.6	−1.6	24	157	150	53	55	50	70	35	45	59
Croatia	..	..	..	..	10	68	77	..	..	50	57	72
Czech Republic	..	..	1	..	10	70	77	..	..	64	66	..
Denmark	1.6	1.2	..	..	6	73	78	..	..	84	85	100
Dominican Republic	0.6	0.3	6	92	47	69	73	18	18	51	63	76
Ecuador	−0.2	−0.1	17	98	40	67	73	8	12	47	60	87
Egypt, Arab Rep.	2.0	1.3	9	175	66	64	67	36	61	44	45	20
El Salvador	2.8	1.4	11	125	40	66	72	27	30	42	46	78
Estonia	7.8	4.7	..	..	16	63	76	..	..	70	74	..
Ethiopia	−1.7	..	48	213	177	48	51	55	75	11	16	..
Finland	1.4	1.1	..	..	5	73	81	..	..	60	64	100
France	1.7	1.1	..	..	6	74	82	..	..	73	75	100
Gabon	−4.9	..	15	..	145	53	57	26	47	34	52	79
Georgia	..	..	..	..	19	69	77	..	..	52	59	..
Germany	..	..	..	..	6	73	80	..	..	83	87	100
Ghana	0.1	0.1	27	157	110	57	61	24	47	31	37	50
Greece	1.9	..	..	..	9	75	81	..	..	58	60	100
Guatemala	−0.4	−0.1	33	140	56	64	69	38	51	37	40	78
Guinea	0.9	0.5	24	..	210	46	47	50	78	19	31	..
Guinea-Bissau	−1.0	−0.4	23	..	223	42	45	32	58	17	23	32
Haiti	−0.8	..	28	200	130	54	57	52	58	24	33	42
Honduras	−0.3	−0.1	18	101	50	65	69	27	27	35	45	89
Hungary	1.4	1.0	..	..	13	65	75	..	..	57	66	100
India	2.3	1.6	66	173	85	62	63	35	62	23	27	70
Indonesia	4.3	2.8	40	124	60	63	67	10	22	22	37	73
Ireland	2.8	1.8	..	..	7	74	79	..	..	55	58	100
Israel	3.3	2.1	..	19	9	75	79	..	..	89	91	..
Italy	2.2	1.5	..	..	7	75	81	..	..	67	67	100
Jamaica	3.8	2.2	10	34	14	72	77	19	11	47	55	89
Japan	2.9	..	3	..	6	77	83	..	..	76	78	..
Jordan	−1.2	−0.7	10	64	35	69	72	7	21	60	73	..
Kazakhstan	..	..	1	..	30	60	70	..	..	54	60	..
Kenya	0.9	0.4	23	115	90	57	60	14	30	16	30	69
Korea, Rep.	7.1	..	..	18	11	69	76	1	3	57	83	..
Kyrgyz Republic	..	..	..	..	36	62	71	..	..	38	39	87
Lao PDR	..	..	40	..	140	52	54	31	56	13	22	30
Latvia	..	..	..	..	18	63	76	..	..	68	73	..
Lebanon	..	..	9	..	36	68	71	10	20	74	88	..
Lesotho	−2.8	−1.2	21	..	113	57	60	19	38	13	26	1
Lithuania	..	..	..	..	13	65	76	..	..	61	73	..
Macedonia, FYR	..	..	..	..	18	70	74	..	..	54	61	..
Madagascar	−2.7	−0.2	32	175	135	57	60	..	..	18	28	12
Malawi	−0.6	..	28	271	217	43	43	28	58	9	14	70
Malaysia	3.3	1.7	23	..	14	70	74	11	22	42	55	100
Mali	−1.1	..	31	291	220	48	52	61	77	19	28	58
Mauritania	−0.4	−0.2	48	..	155	52	55	50	74	27	54	..

Note: For data comparability and coverage, see the Technical Notes. Figures in italics are for years other than those specified.

Economy	Growth of private consumption per capita Avg. annual growth rate (%) 1980–96		Prevalence of child malnutrition % of children under age 5 1990–96	Under-5 mortality rate Per 1,000		Life expectancy at birth Years 1996		Adult illiteracy rate % of people 15 and above 1995		Urban population % of total		Access to sanitation in urban areas % of urban pop. with access 1995
	Uncorrected	Distribution-corrected		1980	1996	Males	Females	Males	Females	1980	1997	
Mauritius	5.4	..	15	38	20	68	75	13	21	42	41	..
Mexico	−0.3	−0.1	14	76	36	69	75	8	13	66	74	81
Moldova	..	..	..	..	24	64	71	..	..	40	53	96
Mongolia	..	..	12	..	71	64	67	..	..	52	62	..
Morocco	1.7	1.0	10	147	67	64	68	43	69	41	53	69
Mozambique	−1.7	..	47	285	214	44	46	42	77	13	36	53
Namibia	−0.6	..	26	108	92	55	57	..	..	23	38	77
Nepal	5.2	3.3	49	179	116	57	57	59	86	7	11	51
Netherlands	1.5	1.1	..	..	6	75	80	..	..	88	89	100
New Zealand	0.9	..	..	..	7	73	79	..	..	83	86	..
Nicaragua	−2.7	−1.3	24	120	57	65	70	35	33	53	63	34
Niger	−6.3	−4.0	43	300	..	44	49	79	93	13	19	71
Nigeria	−3.0	−1.7	35	196	130	51	55	33	53	27	41	61
Norway	1.5	1.1	..	..	6	75	81	..	..	71	74	100
Oman	..	..	14	..	20	69	73	..	..	32	79	98
Pakistan	1.5	1.1	40	161	123	62	65	50	76	28	35	53
Panama	1.9	0.8	7	47	25	72	76	9	10	50	56	..
Papua New Guinea	−0.4	−0.2	30	..	85	57	58	19	37	13	17	82
Paraguay	2.0	0.8	4	59	45	68	74	7	9	42	54	..
Peru	−0.9	−0.5	11	126	58	66	71	6	17	65	72	62
Philippines	0.8	0.4	30	69	44	64	68	5	6	38	56	..
Poland	0.6	0.4	..	..	15	68	77	..	..	58	64	100
Portugal	2.9	..	..	..	8	72	79	..	..	29	37	100
Romania	0.0	0.0	6	..	28	65	73	..	..	49	57	85
Russian Federation	..	..	3	..	25	60	73	..	..	70	77	..
Rwanda	−1.8	−1.3	29	218	205	39	42	30	48	5	6	..
Saudi Arabia	..	..	..	..	28	69	71	29	50	66	84	..
Senegal	−1.0	−0.5	22	218	88	49	52	57	77	36	45	83
Sierra Leone	−2.4	−0.9	29	335	284	35	38	55	82	24	35	17
Singapore	4.9	..	14	13	5	74	79	4	14	100	100	97
Slovak Republic	−3.2	−2.5	..	..	13	69	77	..	..	52	60	..
Slovenia	..	..	..	..	6	71	78	..	..	48	52	95
South Africa	−0.1	0.0	9	..	66	62	68	18	18	48	50	79
Spain	2.3	1.6	..	..	6	73	81	..	..	73	77	100
Sri Lanka	2.6	1.8	38	48	19	71	75	7	13	22	23	..
Sweden	0.7	0.5	..	..	5	76	82	..	..	83	83	100
Switzerland	0.6	0.4	..	..	6	75	82	..	..	57	62	100
Syrian Arab Republic	0.4	..	..	74	36	66	71	14	44	47	53	100
Tajikistan	..	..	..	..	38	66	72	..	..	34	32	83
Tanzania	..	..	29	176	144	49	52	21	43	15	26	97
Thailand	5.6	3.0	13	58	38	67	72	4	8	17	21	..
Togo	−0.9	..	25	175	138	49	52	33	63	23	32	56
Trinidad and Tobago	−1.2	..	7	39	15	70	75	1	3	63	73	60
Tunisia	0.8	0.5	9	100	35	69	71	21	45	52	63	..
Turkey	−1.3	..	10	133	47	66	71	8	28	44	72	99
Turkmenistan	..	..	..	..	50	62	69	..	..	47	45	70
Uganda	1.7	1.0	26	180	141	43	43	26	50	9	13	75
Ukraine	..	..	..	..	17	62	73	..	..	62	71	70
United Arab Emirates	−0.5	..	7	..	17	74	76	21	20	72	85	..
United Kingdom	2.6	1.7	..	..	7	74	80	..	..	89	89	..
United States	1.8	1.1	..	..	8	74	80	..	..	74	77	..
Uruguay	3.1	..	4	43	22	70	77	3	2	85	91	..
Uzbekistan	..	..	4	..	35	66	72	..	..	41	42	46
Venezuela	−0.7	−0.4	5	42	28	70	76	8	10	79	86	64
Vietnam	..	..	45	60	48	66	70	4	9	19	20	43
Yemen, Rep.	..	..	30	198	130	54	54	..	..	20	35	70
Zambia	−4.0	−2.1	29	149	202	44	45	14	29	40	44	40
Zimbabwe	0.6	..	16	107	86	55	57	10	20	22	33	98
World	2.9 w	2.0 w		132 w	73 w	65 w	69 w	21 w	38 w	40 w	46 w	.. w
Low income	0.9	1.0		175	113	58	60	35	59	22	28	65
Middle income	4.6	2.8		85	43	66	71	12	25	38	49	67
Lower middle income	5.8	3.4		85	44	66	71	12	27	32	42	62
Upper middle income	0.1	0.1		82	37	66	73	12	17	62	74	..
Low & middle income	3.0	2.1		133	80	63	67	21	39	32	40	..
East Asia & Pacific	6.8	4.0		75	47	67	70	9	24	21	33	62
Europe & Central Asia	..	..		..	30	64	73	..	..	58	68	..
Latin America & Carib.	0.1	0.0		82	41	66	73	12	15	65	74	..
Middle East & N. Africa	0.6	..		141	63	66	68	28	50	48	58	..
South Asia	2.1	1.5		174	93	61	63	38	64	22	27	68
Sub-Saharan Africa	−1.8	..		193	147	51	54	34	53	23	32	..
High income	2.4	..		..	7	74	81	a	a	75	78	..

a. UNESCO estimates illiteracy to be less than 5 percent.

Table 3.   Population and labor force

	Population						Labor force							
	Total Millions		Avg. annual growth rate (%)		Aged 15–64 Millions		Total Millions		Avg. annual growth rate (%)		Female % of labor force		Children aged 10–14 % of age group	
Economy	1980	1997	1980–90	1990–97	1980	1997	1980	1997	1980–90	1990–97	1980	1997	1980	1997
Albania	3	3	2.1	0.2	2	2	1	2	2.6	0.8	39	41	4	1
Algeria	19	29	2.9	2.3	9	17	5	9	3.7	4.1	21	26	7	1
Angola	7	11	2.7	3.1	4	6	3	5	2.2	2.8	47	46	30	27
Argentina	28	36	1.5	1.3	17	22	11	14	1.3	2.1	28	32	8	4
Armenia	3	4	1.4	0.9	2	2	1	2	1.6	0.8	48	48	0	0
Australia	15	19	1.5	1.2	10	12	7	9	2.3	1.3	37	43	0	0
Austria	8	8	0.2	0.6	5	5	3	4	0.5	0.5	40	41	0	0
Azerbaijan	6	8	1.5	0.9	4	5	3	3	1.0	1.4	47	44	0	0
Bangladesh	87	124	2.4	1.6	44	69	41	63	2.8	2.1	42	42	35	29
Belarus	10	10	0.6	0.0	6	7	5	5	0.5	–0.1	50	49	0	0
Belgium	10	10	0.1	0.3	6	7	4	4	0.2	0.5	34	40	0	0
Benin	3	6	3.1	2.9	2	3	2	3	2.7	2.6	47	48	30	27
Bolivia	5	8	2.0	2.4	3	4	2	3	2.6	2.6	33	38	19	13
Brazil	121	164	2.0	1.4	70	106	48	74	3.2	1.7	28	35	19	15
Bulgaria	9	8	–0.2	–0.7	6	6	5	4	–0.4	–0.9	45	48	0	0
Burkina Faso	7	11	2.6	2.8	3	5	4	6	2.0	2.1	48	47	71	48
Burundi	4	7	2.8	2.6	2	3	2	4	2.6	2.6	50	49	50	49
Cambodia	6	11	2.9	2.7	4	6	3	5	2.8	2.4	56	53	27	24
Cameroon	9	14	2.8	2.9	5	7	4	6	2.4	3.0	37	38	34	24
Canada	25	30	1.2	1.2	17	20	12	16	1.9	1.1	40	45	0	0
Central African Republic	2	3	2.4	2.2	1	2	1	2	1.7	1.8	48	47	39	30
Chad	4	7	2.4	2.5	2	4	2	3	2.1	2.5	43	44	42	38
Chile	11	15	1.6	1.6	7	9	4	6	2.7	2.1	26	33	0	0
China	981	1,227	1.5	1.1	586	829	539	726	2.2	1.1	43	45	30	10
Hong Kong, China	5	7	1.2	1.9	3	5	2	3	1.6	1.9	34	38	6	0
Colombia	28	38	1.9	1.8	16	23	9	16	3.9	2.7	26	38	12	6
Congo, Dem. Rep.	27	47	3.3	3.2	14	23	12	19	2.8	2.9	45	44	33	29
Congo, Rep.	2	3	3.1	2.9	1	1	1	1	3.1	2.6	43	43	27	26
Costa Rica	2	4	2.8	2.1	1	2	1	1	3.8	2.5	21	30	10	5
Côte d'Ivoire	8	15	3.8	2.9	4	8	3	5	3.1	2.3	32	33	28	20
Croatia	5	..	0.4	..	3	3	2	2	0.3	0.0	40	44	0	0
Czech Republic	10	10	0.1	–0.1	6	7	5	6	0.2	0.4	47	47	0	0
Denmark	5	5	0.0	0.4	3	4	3	3	0.7	0.0	44	46	0	0
Dominican Republic	6	8	2.2	1.9	3	5	2	3	3.1	2.7	25	30	25	15
Ecuador	8	12	2.5	2.2	4	7	3	4	3.5	3.1	20	27	9	5
Egypt, Arab Rep.	41	60	2.5	2.0	23	36	14	22	2.5	2.8	26	29	18	10
El Salvador	5	6	1.0	2.4	2	3	2	2	1.7	3.6	27	35	17	15
Estonia	1	1	0.6	–1.2	1	1	1	1	0.4	–1.1	51	49	0	0
Ethiopia	38	60	3.1	2.3	19	30	17	27	2.9	2.4	42	41	46	42
Finland	5	5	0.4	0.4	3	3	2	3	0.6	0.1	46	48	0	0
France	54	59	0.5	0.5	34	38	24	26	0.4	0.8	40	45	0	0
Gabon	1	1	3.3	2.6	0	1	0	1	2.4	1.7	45	44	29	17
Georgia	5	5	0.7	–0.1	3	4	3	3	0.4	–0.1	49	47	0	0
Germany	78	82	0.1	0.5	52	56	37	41	0.6	0.3	40	42	0	0
Ghana	11	18	3.3	2.7	6	10	5	8	3.1	2.7	51	51	16	13
Greece	10	11	0.5	0.5	6	7	4	4	1.2	0.9	28	37	5	0
Guatemala	7	11	2.8	2.8	4	6	2	4	2.9	3.4	22	27	19	15
Guinea	4	7	2.5	2.6	2	4	2	3	2.1	2.3	47	47	41	33
Guinea-Bissau	1	1	1.8	2.1	0	1	0	1	1.3	1.9	40	40	43	38
Haiti	5	7	1.9	2.1	3	4	3	3	1.3	1.8	45	43	33	24
Honduras	4	6	3.3	3.0	2	3	1	2	3.6	3.8	25	31	14	8
Hungary	11	10	–0.3	–0.3	7	7	5	5	–0.8	0.0	43	44	0	0
India	687	961	2.1	1.8	395	587	300	416	1.9	2.0	34	32	21	13
Indonesia	148	200	1.8	1.7	83	127	59	94	2.9	2.5	35	40	13	9
Ireland	3	4	0.3	0.5	2	2	1	1	0.4	1.6	28	34	1	0
Israel	4	6	1.8	3.2	2	4	1	2	2.3	3.9	34	40	0	0
Italy	56	57	0.1	0.2	36	39	23	25	0.8	0.4	33	38	2	0
Jamaica	2	3	1.2	1.0	1	2	1	1	2.1	1.8	46	46	0	0
Japan	117	126	0.6	0.3	79	87	57	67	1.1	0.6	38	41	0	0
Jordan	2	4	3.7	4.8	1	3	1	1	4.8	5.3	15	23	4	0
Kazakhstan	15	16	1.2	–0.4	9	11	7	8	1.1	–0.1	48	47	0	0
Kenya	17	28	3.4	2.6	8	15	8	13	3.6	2.7	46	46	45	40
Korea, Rep.	38	46	1.2	1.0	24	33	16	22	2.3	1.9	39	41	0	0
Kyrgyz Republic	4	5	1.9	0.7	2	3	2	2	1.6	1.3	48	47	0	0
Lao PDR	3	5	2.3	2.6	2	3	2	2	1.9	2.3	45	47	31	26
Latvia	3	2	0.5	–1.1	2	2	1	1	0.2	–1.1	51	50	0	0
Lebanon	3	4	1.9	1.9	2	3	1	1	2.9	2.9	23	29	5	0
Lesotho	1	2	2.7	2.1	1	1	1	1	2.3	2.4	38	37	28	22
Lithuania	3	4	0.9	–0.1	2	2	2	2	0.7	–0.2	50	48	0	0
Macedonia, FYR	2	2	0.1	0.7	1	1	1	1	0.6	1.2	36	41	1	0
Madagascar	9	14	2.9	2.7	4	7	4	7	2.5	2.8	45	45	40	35
Malawi	6	10	3.3	2.7	3	5	3	5	3.0	2.4	51	49	45	34
Malaysia	14	21	2.6	2.3	8	12	5	8	2.8	2.7	34	37	8	3
Mali	7	10	2.5	2.8	3	5	3	5	2.3	2.6	47	46	61	53
Mauritania	2	2	2.6	2.5	1	1	1	1	2.0	2.7	45	44	30	23

Note: For data comparability and coverage, see the Technical Notes. Figures in italics are for years other than those specified.

	Population						Labor force							
	Total Millions		Avg. annual growth rate (%)		Aged 15–64 Millions		Total Millions		Avg. annual growth rate (%)		Female % of labor force		Children aged 10–14 % of age group	
Economy	1980	1997	1980–90	1990–97	1980	1997	1980	1997	1980–90	1990–97	1980	1997	1980	1997
Mauritius	1	1	0.9	1.1	1	1	0	0	2.3	1.7	26	32	5	3
Mexico	67	95	2.3	1.8	34	58	22	38	3.5	2.8	27	32	9	6
Moldova	4	4	0.9	–0.1	3	3	2	2	0.2	0.1	50	49	3	0
Mongolia	2	3	2.9	2.1	1	1	1	1	3.1	2.9	46	46	4	2
Morocco	19	28	2.2	1.9	10	17	7	11	2.6	2.5	34	35	21	4
Mozambique	12	19	1.6	3.8	6	10	7	9	1.2	3.3	49	48	39	33
Namibia	1	2	2.7	2.6	1	1	0	1	2.4	2.5	40	41	34	20
Nepal	14	23	2.6	2.7	8	12	7	11	2.4	2.5	39	40	56	44
Netherlands	14	16	0.6	0.6	9	11	6	7	2.0	0.6	31	40	0	0
New Zealand	3	4	0.8	1.2	2	2	1	2	2.0	1.4	34	44	0	0
Nicaragua	3	5	2.9	3.0	1	3	1	2	2.9	4.0	28	37	19	13
Niger	6	10	3.3	3.3	3	5	3	5	3.0	2.9	45	44	48	45
Nigeria	71	118	3.0	2.9	38	62	30	47	2.6	2.8	36	36	29	25
Norway	4	4	0.4	0.5	3	3	2	2	0.9	0.8	40	46	0	0
Oman	1	2	3.9	5.0	1	1	0	1	3.4	4.7	7	16	6	0
Pakistan	83	137	3.1	2.9	44	74	29	49	2.9	3.3	23	27	23	17
Panama	2	3	2.0	1.8	1	2	1	1	3.0	2.5	30	34	6	3
Papua New Guinea	3	5	2.2	2.3	2	3	2	2	2.1	2.3	42	42	28	18
Paraguay	3	5	3.0	2.7	2	3	1	2	2.9	2.9	27	29	15	7
Peru	17	25	2.2	2.0	9	15	5	9	3.1	3.1	24	29	4	2
Philippines	48	73	2.6	2.3	27	43	19	30	2.9	2.7	35	37	14	7
Poland	36	39	0.7	0.2	23	26	19	19	0.1	0.5	45	46	0	0
Portugal	10	10	0.1	0.1	6	7	5	5	0.4	0.4	39	44	8	2
Romania	22	23	0.4	–0.4	14	15	11	11	–0.2	0.0	46	44	0	0
Russian Federation	139	147	0.6	–0.1	95	100	76	78	0.2	0.1	49	49	0	0
Rwanda	5	8	3.0	1.8	3	4	3	4	3.2	2.3	49	49	43	42
Saudi Arabia	9	20	5.2	3.4	5	11	3	7	6.5	3.2	8	14	5	0
Senegal	6	9	2.8	2.6	3	5	3	4	2.5	2.6	42	43	43	30
Sierra Leone	3	5	2.1	2.5	2	2	1	2	1.8	2.3	36	36	19	15
Singapore	2	3	1.7	1.9	2	2	1	2	2.3	1.7	35	38	2	0
Slovak Republic	5	5	0.6	0.2	3	4	2	3	0.9	0.7	45	48	0	0
Slovenia	2	2	0.5	–0.1	1	1	1	1	0.3	0.1	46	46	0	0
South Africa	27	38	2.2	1.7	15	24	10	15	2.5	2.0	35	38	1	0
Spain	37	39	0.4	0.2	23	27	14	17	1.3	1.0	28	36	0	0
Sri Lanka	15	18	1.4	1.2	9	12	5	8	2.3	1.8	27	36	4	2
Sweden	8	9	0.3	0.5	5	6	4	5	1.0	0.2	44	48	0	0
Switzerland	6	7	0.6	0.8	4	5	3	4	1.5	0.8	37	40	0	0
Syrian Arab Republic	9	15	3.3	2.9	4	8	2	4	3.0	3.3	23	26	14	4
Tajikistan	4	6	2.9	1.8	2	3	2	2	2.0	2.2	47	44	0	0
Tanzania	19	31	3.2	3.0	9	16	10	16	3.2	2.8	50	49	43	38
Thailand	47	61	1.7	1.2	26	41	24	35	2.6	1.5	47	46	25	15
Togo	3	4	3.0	3.0	1	2	1	2	2.6	2.7	39	40	36	28
Trinidad and Tobago	1	1	1.3	0.8	1	1	0	1	1.2	1.8	32	37	1	0
Tunisia	6	9	2.5	1.8	3	6	2	4	2.7	3.0	29	31	6	0
Turkey	44	64	2.3	1.8	25	41	19	29	2.9	2.2	35	36	21	22
Turkmenistan	3	5	2.5	3.4	2	3	1	2	2.3	3.5	47	46	0	0
Uganda	13	20	2.4	3.1	6	10	7	10	2.2	2.7	48	48	49	45
Ukraine	50	50	0.4	–0.4	33	34	26	25	–0.1	–0.4	50	49	0	0
United Arab Emirates	1	3	5.7	4.9	1	2	1	1	5.1	3.7	5	14	0	0
United Kingdom	56	59	0.2	0.3	36	38	27	29	0.6	0.3	39	44	0	0
United States	227	268	0.9	1.0	151	175	110	136	1.3	1.1	42	46	0	0
Uruguay	3	3	0.6	0.6	2	2	1	1	1.6	1.0	31	41	4	2
Uzbekistan	16	24	2.5	2.0	9	13	6	10	2.2	2.7	48	46	0	0
Venezuela	15	23	2.7	2.2	8	14	5	9	3.6	3.0	27	34	4	1
Vietnam	54	77	2.1	2.1	28	45	26	39	2.7	2.0	48	49	22	8
Yemen, Rep.	9	16	3.3	4.5	4	8	2	5	3.7	4.9	33	28	26	20
Zambia	6	9	3.0	2.8	3	5	2	4	3.1	2.8	45	45	19	16
Zimbabwe	7	11	3.3	2.3	3	6	3	5	3.6	2.3	44	44	37	28
World	4,427 t	5,829 t	1.7 w	1.5 w	2,595 t	3,644 t	2,034 t	2,784 t	2.0 w	1.6 w	39 w	40 w	20 w	13 w
Low income	1,384	2,048	2.4	2.1	759	1,171	611	902	2.3	2.3	37	36	27	21
Middle income	2,217	2,855	1.6	1.3	1,306	1,851	1,050	1,437	2.1	1.4	39	41	20	8
Lower middle income	1,794	2,285	1.6	1.2	1,063	1,491	883	1,193	2.1	1.3	41	43	22	8
Upper middle income	423	571	1.9	1.5	244	361	167	245	2.5	1.9	32	35	11	9
Low & middle income	3,600	4,903	2.0	1.6	2,066	3,023	1,662	2,339	2.2	1.8	38	39	23	14
East Asia & Pacific	1,359	1,753	1.6	1.3	796	1,155	704	979	2.3	1.4	42	44	27	10
Europe & Central Asia	428	471	0.9	0.1	276	311	215	234	0.6	0.5	47	46	3	4
Latin America & Carib.	358	494	2.0	1.7	200	306	130	206	3.0	2.3	28	34	13	9
Middle East & N. Africa	175	283	3.0	2.5	91	162	54	92	3.1	3.2	24	26	14	5
South Asia	902	1,289	2.2	1.9	508	767	389	558	2.1	2.2	34	33	23	16
Sub-Saharan Africa	379	614	2.9	2.7	196	322	171	269	2.7	2.6	42	42	35	30
High income	825	926	0.7	0.7	528	621	372	445	1.2	0.9	38	43	0	0

Table 4. Poverty

Economy	National poverty lines								International poverty lines				
		Population below the poverty line (%)				Population below the poverty line (%)				Population below $1 a day	Poverty gap at $1 a day	Population below $2 a day	Poverty gap at $2 a day
	Survey year	Rural	Urban	National	Survey year	Rural	Urban	National	Survey year	%	%	%	%
Albania	1996	..	..	19.6		..	..	..		..	..	..	..
Algeria	1988	16.6	7.3	12.2	1995	30.3	14.7	22.6	1995	<2	..	17.6	4.4
Angola		..	..			..	..	..		..	..	..	..
Argentina	1991	..	..	25.5		..	..	..		..	..	..	..
Armenia		..	..	..		..	..	..		..	..	..	..
Australia		..	..	..		..	..	..		..	..	..	..
Austria		..	..	..		..	..	..		..	..	..	..
Azerbaijan		..	..	..		..	..	..		..	..	..	..
Bangladesh	1991–92	46.0	23.3	42.7	1995–96	39.8	14.3	35.6		..	..	..	..
Belarus		..	..	..		..	..	..	1993	<2	..	6.4	0.8
Belgium		..	..			..	..	..		..	..	..	..
Benin	1995	..	..	33.0		..	..	..		..	..	..	..
Bolivia		..	..	..		..	..	..		..	..	..	..
Brazil	1990	32.6	13.1	17.4		..	..	..	1995	23.6	10.7	43.5	22.4
Bulgaria		..	..	..		..	..	..	1992	2.6	0.8	23.5	6.0
Burkina Faso		..	..	..		..	..	..		..	..	..	..
Burundi	1990	..	..	36.2		..	..	..		..	..	..	..
Cambodia		..	..	..		..	..	..		..	..	..	..
Cameroon	1984	32.4	44.4	40.0		..	..	..		..	..	..	..
Canada		..	..	..		..	..	..		..	..	..	..
Central African Republic		..	..	..		..	..	..		..	..	..	..
Chad		..	..	..		..	..	..		..	..	..	..
Chile	1992	..	..	21.6	1994	..	..	20.5	1992	15.0	4.9	38.5	16.0
China	1994	11.8	<2	8.4	1995	9.2	<2	6.5	1995	22.2	6.9	57.8	24.1
Hong Kong, China		..	..	..		..	..	..		..	..	..	..
Colombia	1991	29.0	7.8	16.9	1992	31.2	8.0	17.7	1991	7.4	2.3	21.7	8.4
Congo, Dem. Rep.		..	..	..		..	..	..		..	..	..	..
Congo, Rep.		..	..	..		..	..	..		..	..	..	..
Costa Rica		..	..	..		..	..	..	1989	18.9	7.2	43.8	19.4
Côte d'Ivoire		..	..	..		..	..	..	1988	17.7	4.3	54.8	20.4
Croatia		..	..	..		..	..	..		..	..	..	..
Czech Republic		..	..	..		..	..	..	1993	3.1	0.4	55.1	14.0
Denmark		..	..	..		..	..	..		..	..	..	..
Dominican Republic	1989	27.4	23.3	24.5	1992	29.8	10.9	20.6	1989	19.9	6.0	47.7	20.2
Ecuador	1994	47.0	25.0	35.0	1995	..	..	..	1994	30.4	9.1	65.8	29.6
Egypt, Arab Rep.		..	..	..		..	..	..	1990–91	7.6	1.1	51.9	15.3
El Salvador	1992	55.7	43.1	48.3		..	..	..		..	..	..	..
Estonia	1994	14.7	6.8	8.9		..	..	..	1993	6.0	1.6	32.5	10.0
Ethiopia		..	..	..		..	..	..	1981–82	46.0	12.4	89.0	42.7
Finland		..	..	..		..	..	..		..	..	..	..
France		..	..	..		..	..	..		..	..	..	..
Gabon		..	..	..		..	..	..		..	..	..	..
Georgia		..	..	..		..	..	..		..	..	..	..
Germany		..	..	..		..	..	..		..	..	..	..
Ghana	1992	34.3	26.7	31.4		..	..	..		..	..	..	..
Greece		..	..	..		..	..	..		..	..	..	..
Guatemala		..	..	..		..	..	..	1989	53.3	28.5	76.8	47.6
Guinea		..	..	..		..	..	..	1991	26.3	12.4	50.2	25.6
Guinea-Bissau	1991	60.9	24.1	48.8		..	..	..	1991	88.2	59.5	96.7	76.6
Haiti	1987	..	..	65.0		..	..	..		..	..	..	..
Honduras	1992	46.0	56.0	50.0		..	..	..	1992	46.9	20.4	75.7	41.9
Hungary	1993	..	..	25.3		..	..	..	1993	<2	..	10.7	2.1
India	1992	43.5	33.7	40.9	1994	36.7	30.5	35.0	1992	52.5	15.6	88.8	45.8
Indonesia	1987	16.4	20.1	17.4	1990	14.3	16.8	15.1	1995	11.8	1.8	58.7	19.3
Ireland		..	..	..		..	..	..		..	..	..	..
Israel		..	..	..		..	..	..		..	..	..	..
Italy		..	..	..		..	..	..		..	..	..	..
Jamaica	1992	..	..	34.2		..	..	..	1993	4.3	0.5	24.9	7.5
Japan		..	..	..		..	..	..		..	..	..	..
Jordan	1991	..	..	15.0		..	..	..	1992	2.5	0.5	23.5	6.3
Kazakhstan		..	..	..		..	..	..	1993	<2	..	12.1	2.5
Kenya	1992	46.4	29.3	42.0		..	..	..	1992	50.2	22.2	78.1	44.4
Korea, Rep.		..	..	..		..	..	..		..	..	..	..
Kyrgyz Republic	1993	48.1	28.7	40.0		..	..	..	1993	18.9	5.0	55.3	21.4
Lao PDR	1993	53.0	24.0	46.1		..	..	..		..	..	..	..
Latvia		..	..	..		..	..	..		..	..	..	..
Lebanon		..	..	..		..	..	..		..	..	..	..
Lesotho	1993	53.9	27.8	49.2		..	..	..	1986–87	48.8	23.8	74.1	43.5
Lithuania		..	..	..		..	..	..	1993	<2	..	18.9	4.1
Macedonia, FYR		..	..	..		..	..	..		..	..	..	..
Madagascar		..	..	..		..	..	..	1993	72.3	33.2	93.2	59.6
Malawi	1990–91	..	..	54.0		..	..	..		..	..	..	..
Malaysia	1989	..	..	15.5		..	..	..	1989	5.6	0.9	26.6	8.5
Mali		..	..	..		..	..	..		..	..	..	..
Mauritania	1990	..	..	57.0		..	..	..	1988	31.4	15.2	68.4	33.0

Note: For data comparability and coverage, see the Technical Notes. Figures in italics are for years other than those specified.

	National poverty lines								International poverty lines				
		Population below the poverty line (%)				Population below the poverty line (%)				Population below $1 a day	Poverty gap at $1 a day	Population below $2 a day	Poverty gap at $2 a day
Economy	Survey year	Rural	Urban	National	Survey year	Rural	Urban	National	Survey year	%	%	%	%
Mauritius	1992	..	..	10.6		..	..	..		..	..	..	..
Mexico	1988	..	..	10.1		..	..	..	1992	14.9	3.8	40.0	15.9
Moldova		..	..			..	..	..	1992	6.8	1.2	30.6	9.7
Mongolia	1995	33.1	38.5	36.3		..	..	..		..	..	..	..
Morocco	1984–85	32.6	17.3	26.0	1990–91	18.0	7.6	13.1	1990–91	<2	..	19.6	4.6
Mozambique		..	..	..		..	..	..		..	..	..	..
Namibia		..	..	..		..	..	..		..	..	..	..
Nepal	1995–96	44.0	23.0	42.0		..	..	..	1995	50.3	16.2	86.7	44.6
Netherlands		..	..	..		..	..	..		..	..	..	..
New Zealand		..	..	..		..	..	..		..	..	..	..
Nicaragua	1993	76.1	31.9	50.3		..	..	..	1993	43.8	18.0	74.5	39.7
Niger		..	..	..		..	..	..	1992	61.5	22.2	92.0	51.8
Nigeria	1985	49.5	31.7	43.0	1992–93	36.4	30.4	34.1	1992–93	31.1	12.9	59.9	29.8
Norway		..	..	..		..	..	..		..	..	..	..
Oman		..	..	..		..	..	..		..	..	..	..
Pakistan	1991	36.9	28.0	34.0		..	..	..	1991	11.6	2.6	57.0	18.6
Panama		..	..	..		..	..	..	1989	25.6	12.6	46.2	24.5
Papua New Guinea		..	..	..		..	..	..		..	..	..	..
Paraguay	1991	28.5	19.7	21.8		..	..	..		..	..	..	..
Peru	1986	64.0	45.0	52.0	1991	68.0	50.3	54.0		..	..	..	..
Philippines	1985	58.0	42.0	52.0	1991	71.0	39.0	54.0	1991	28.6	7.7	64.5	28.2
Poland	1993	..	..	23.8		..	..	..	1993	6.8	4.7	15.1	7.7
Portugal		..	..	..		..	..	..		..	..	..	..
Romania	1994	27.9	20.4	21.5		..	..	..	1992	17.7	4.2	70.9	24.7
Russian Federation	1994	..	..	30.9		..	..	..	1993	<2	..	10.9	2.3
Rwanda	1993	..	..	51.2		..	..	..	1983–85	45.7	11.3	88.7	42.3
Saudi Arabia		..	..	..		..	..	..		..	..	..	..
Senegal		..	..	..		..	..	..	1991–92	54.0	25.5	79.6	47.2
Sierra Leone	1989	76.0	53.0	68.0		..	..	..		..	..	..	..
Singapore		..	..	..		..	..	..		..	..	..	..
Slovak Republic		..	..	..		..	..	..	1992	12.8	2.2	85.1	27.5
Slovenia		..	..	..		..	..	..		..	..	..	..
South Africa		..	..	..		..	..	..	1993	23.7	6.6	50.2	22.5
Spain		..	..	..		..	..	..		..	..	..	..
Sri Lanka	1985–86	45.5	26.8	40.6	1990–91	38.1	28.4	35.3	1990	4.0	0.7	41.2	11.0
Sweden		..	..	..		..	..	..		..	..	..	..
Switzerland		..	..	..		..	..	..		..	..	..	..
Syrian Arab Republic		..	..	..		..	..	..		..	..	..	..
Tajikistan		..	..	..		..	..	..		..	..	..	..
Tanzania	1991	..	..	51.1		..	..	..	1993	10.5	2.1	45.5	15.3
Thailand	1990	..	..	18.0	1992	15.5	10.2	13.1	1992	<2	..	23.5	5.4
Togo	1987–89	..	..	32.3		..	..	..		..	..	..	..
Trinidad and Tobago	1992	..	..	21.0		..	..	..		..	..	..	..
Tunisia	1985	29.2	12.0	19.9	1990	21.6	8.9	14.1	1990	3.9	0.9	22.7	6.8
Turkey		..	..	..		..	..	..		..	..	..	..
Turkmenistan		..	..	..		..	..	..	1993	4.9	0.5	25.8	7.6
Uganda	1993	..	..	55.0		..	..	..	1989–90	69.3	29.1	92.2	56.6
Ukraine	1995	..	..	31.7		..	..	..		..	..	..	..
United Arab Emirates		..	..	..		..	..	..		..	..	..	..
United Kingdom		..	..	..		..	..	..		..	..	..	..
United States		..	..	..		..	..	..		..	..	..	..
Uruguay		..	..	..		..	..	..		..	..	..	..
Uzbekistan		..	..	..		..	..	..		..	..	..	..
Venezuela	1989	..	..	31.3		..	..	..	1991	11.8	3.1	32.2	12.2
Vietnam	1993	57.2	25.9	50.9		..	..	..		..	..	..	..
Yemen, Rep.	1992	19.2	18.6	19.1		..	..	..		..	..	..	..
Zambia	1991	88.0	46.0	68.0	1993	..	..	86.0	1993	84.6	53.8	98.1	73.4
Zimbabwe	1990–91	..	..	25.5		..	..	..	1990–91	41.0	14.3	68.2	35.5

Table 5. Distribution of income or consumption

Economy	Survey year	Gini index	Percentage share of income or consumption						
			Lowest 10%	Lowest 20%	Second 20%	Third 20%	Fourth 20%	Highest 20%	Highest 10%
Albania		..	..	..	..	..	..	..	..
Algeria	1995[a,b]	35.3	2.8	7.0	11.6	16.1	22.7	42.6	26.8
Angola		..	..	..	..	..	..	..	..
Argentina		..	..	..	..	..	..	..	..
Armenia		..	..	..	..	..	..	..	..
Australia	1989[c,d]	33.7	2.5	7.0	12.2	16.6	23.3	40.9	24.8
Austria	1987[c,d]	23.1	4.4	10.4	14.8	18.5	22.9	33.3	19.3
Azerbaijan		..	..	..	..	..	..	..	..
Bangladesh	1992[a,b]	28.3	4.1	9.4	13.5	17.2	22.0	37.9	23.7
Belarus	1993[c,d]	21.6	4.9	11.1	15.3	18.5	22.2	32.9	19.4
Belgium	1992[c,d]	25.0	3.7	9.5	14.6	18.4	23.0	34.5	20.2
Benin		..	..	..	..	..	..	..	..
Bolivia	1990[c,d]	42.0	2.3	5.6	9.7	14.5	22.0	48.2	31.7
Brazil	1995[c,d]	60.1	0.8	2.5	5.7	9.9	17.7	64.2	47.9
Bulgaria	1992[c,d]	30.8	3.3	8.3	13.0	17.0	22.3	39.3	24.7
Burkina Faso		..	..	..	..	..	..	..	..
Burundi		..	..	..	..	..	..	..	..
Cambodia		..	..	..	..	..	..	..	..
Cameroon		..	..	..	..	..	..	..	..
Canada	1994[c,d]	31.5	2.8	7.5	12.9	17.2	23.0	39.3	23.8
Central African Republic		..	..	..	..	..	..	..	..
Chad		..	..	..	..	..	..	..	..
Chile	1994[c,d]	56.5	1.4	3.5	6.6	10.9	18.1	61.0	46.1
China	1995[c,d]	41.5	2.2	5.5	9.8	14.9	22.3	47.5	30.9
Hong Kong, China		..	..	..	..	..	..	..	..
Colombia	1995[c,d]	57.2	1.0	3.1	6.8	10.9	17.6	61.5	46.9
Congo, Dem. Rep.		..	..	..	..	..	..	..	..
Congo, Rep.		..	..	..	..	..	..	..	..
Costa Rica	1996[c,d]	47.0	1.3	4.0	8.8	13.7	21.7	51.8	34.7
Côte d'Ivoire	1988[a,b]	36.9	2.8	6.8	11.2	15.8	22.2	44.1	28.5
Croatia		..	..	..	..	..	..	..	..
Czech Republic	1993[c,d]	26.6	4.6	10.5	13.9	16.9	21.3	37.4	23.5
Denmark	1992[c,d]	24.7	3.6	9.6	14.9	18.3	22.7	34.5	20.5
Dominican Republic	1989[c,d]	50.5	1.6	4.2	7.9	12.5	19.7	55.7	39.6
Ecuador	1994[a,b]	46.6	2.3	5.4	8.9	13.2	19.9	52.6	37.6
Egypt, Arab Rep.	1991[a,b]	32.0	3.9	8.7	12.5	16.3	21.4	41.1	26.7
El Salvador	1995[c,d]	49.9	1.2	3.7	8.3	13.1	20.5	54.4	38.3
Estonia	1993[c,d]	39.5	2.4	6.6	10.7	15.1	21.4	46.3	31.3
Ethiopia		..	..	..	..	..	..	..	..
Finland	1991[c,d]	25.6	4.2	10.0	14.2	17.6	22.3	35.8	21.6
France	1989[c,d]	32.7	2.5	7.2	12.7	17.1	22.8	40.1	24.9
Gabon		..	..	..	..	..	..	..	..
Georgia		..	..	..	..	..	..	..	..
Germany	1989[c,d]	28.1	3.7	9.0	13.5	17.5	22.9	37.1	22.6
Ghana	1992[a,b]	33.9	3.4	7.9	12.0	16.1	21.8	42.2	27.3
Greece		..	..	..	..	..	..	..	..
Guatemala	1989[c,d]	59.6	0.6	2.1	5.8	10.5	18.6	63.0	46.6
Guinea	1991[a,b]	46.8	0.9	3.0	8.3	14.6	23.9	50.2	31.7
Guinea-Bissau	1991[a,b]	56.2	0.5	2.1	6.5	12.0	20.6	58.9	42.4
Haiti		..	..	..	..	..	..	..	..
Honduras	1996[c,d]	53.7	1.2	3.4	7.1	11.7	19.7	58.0	42.1
Hungary	1993[c,d]	27.9	4.1	9.7	13.9	16.9	21.4	38.1	24.0
India	1994[a,b]	29.7	4.1	9.2	13.0	16.8	21.7	39.3	25.0
Indonesia	1995[a,b]	34.2	3.6	8.4	12.0	15.5	21.0	43.1	28.3
Ireland	1987[c,d]	35.9	2.5	6.7	11.6	16.4	22.4	42.9	27.4
Israel	1992[c,d]	35.5	2.8	6.9	11.4	16.3	22.9	42.5	26.9
Italy	1991[c,d]	31.2	2.9	7.6	12.9	17.3	23.2	38.9	23.7
Jamaica	1991[a,b]	41.1	2.4	5.8	10.2	14.9	21.6	47.5	31.9
Japan		..	..	..	..	..	..	..	..
Jordan	1991[a,b]	43.4	2.4	5.9	9.8	13.9	20.3	50.1	34.7
Kazakhstan	1993[c,d]	32.7	3.1	7.5	12.3	16.9	22.9	40.4	24.9
Kenya	1992[a,b]	57.5	1.2	3.4	6.7	10.7	17.0	62.1	47.7
Korea, Rep.		..	..	..	..	..	..	..	..
Kyrgyz Republic	1993[c,d]	35.3	2.7	6.7	11.5	16.4	23.1	42.3	26.2
Lao PDR	1992[a,b]	30.4	4.2	9.6	12.9	16.3	21.0	40.2	26.4
Latvia	1993[c,d]	27.0	4.3	9.6	13.6	17.5	22.6	36.7	22.1
Lebanon		..	..	..	..	..	..	..	..
Lesotho	1986–87[a,b]	56.0	0.9	2.8	6.5	11.2	19.4	60.1	43.4
Lithuania	1993[c,d]	33.6	3.4	8.1	12.3	16.2	21.3	42.1	28.0
Macedonia, FYR		..	..	..	..	..	..	..	..
Madagascar	1993[a,b]	43.4	2.3	5.8	9.9	14.0	20.3	50.0	34.9
Malawi		..	..	..	..	..	..	..	..
Malaysia	1989[c,d]	48.4	1.9	4.6	8.3	13.0	20.4	53.7	37.9
Mali		..	..	..	..	..	..	..	..
Mauritania	1988[a,b]	42.4	0.7	3.6	10.3	16.2	23.0	46.5	30.4

Note: For data comparability and coverage, see the Technical Notes. Figures in italics are for years other than those specified.

Economy	Survey year	Gini index	Percentage share of income or consumption						
			Lowest 10%	Lowest 20%	Second 20%	Third 20%	Fourth 20%	Highest 20%	Highest 10%
Mauritius		..	..	..	..	..	..	..	..
Mexico	1992[a,b]	50.3	1.6	4.1	7.8	12.5	20.2	55.3	39.2
Moldova	1992[c,d]	34.4	2.7	6.9	11.9	16.7	23.1	41.5	25.8
Mongolia	1995[a,b]	33.2	2.9	7.3	12.2	16.6	23.0	40.9	24.5
Morocco	1990–91[a,b]	39.2	2.8	6.6	10.5	15.0	21.7	46.3	30.5
Mozambique		..	..	..	..	..	..	..	..
Namibia		..	..	..	..	..	..	..	..
Nepal	1995–96[a,b]	36.7	3.2	7.6	11.5	15.1	21.0	44.8	29.8
Netherlands	1991[c,d]	31.5	2.9	8.0	13.0	16.7	22.5	39.9	24.7
New Zealand		..	..	..	..	..	..	..	..
Nicaragua	1993[a,b]	50.3	1.6	4.2	7.9	12.6	20.0	55.2	39.8
Niger	1992[a,b]	36.1	3.0	7.5	11.8	15.5	21.1	44.1	29.3
Nigeria	1992–93[a,b]	45.0	1.3	4.0	8.9	14.4	23.4	49.4	31.4
Norway	1991[c,d]	25.2	4.1	10.0	14.3	17.9	22.4	35.3	21.2
Oman		..	..	..	..	..	..	..	..
Pakistan	1991[a,b]	31.2	3.4	8.4	12.9	16.9	22.2	39.7	25.2
Panama	1991[c,d]	56.8	0.5	2.0	6.3	11.3	20.3	60.1	42.5
Papua New Guinea	1996[a,b]	50.9	1.7	4.5	7.9	11.9	19.2	56.5	40.5
Paraguay	1995[c,d]	59.1	0.7	2.3	5.9	10.7	18.7	62.4	46.6
Peru	1994[a,b]	44.9	1.9	4.9	9.2	14.1	21.4	50.4	34.3
Philippines	1994[a,b]	42.9	2.4	5.9	9.6	13.9	21.1	49.6	33.5
Poland	1992[a,b]	27.2	4.0	9.3	13.8	17.7	22.6	36.6	22.1
Portugal		..	..	..	..	..	..	..	..
Romania	1992[c,d]	25.5	3.8	9.2	14.4	18.4	23.2	34.8	20.2
Russian Federation	1993[c,d]	31.0	3.0	7.4	12.6	17.7	24.2	38.2	22.2
Rwanda	1983–85[a,b]	28.9	4.2	9.7	13.2	16.5	21.6	39.1	24.2
Saudi Arabia		..	..	..	..	..	..	..	..
Senegal	1991[a,b]	54.1	1.4	3.5	7.0	11.6	19.3	58.6	42.8
Sierra Leone	1989[a,b]	62.9	0.5	1.1	2.0	9.8	23.7	63.4	43.6
Singapore		..	..	..	..	..	..	..	..
Slovak Republic	1992[c,d]	19.5	5.1	11.9	15.8	18.8	22.2	31.4	18.2
Slovenia	1993[c,d]	29.2	4.0	9.3	13.3	16.9	21.9	38.6	24.5
South Africa	1993[a,b]	58.4	1.4	3.3	5.8	9.8	17.7	63.3	47.3
Spain	1990[c,d]	32.5	2.8	7.5	12.6	17.0	22.6	40.3	25.2
Sri Lanka	1990[a,b]	30.1	3.8	8.9	13.1	16.9	21.7	39.3	25.2
Sweden	1992[c,d]	25.0	3.7	9.6	14.5	18.1	23.2	34.5	20.1
Switzerland	1982[c,d]	36.1	2.9	7.4	11.6	15.6	21.9	43.5	28.6
Syrian Arab Republic		..	..	..	..	..	..	..	..
Tajikistan		..	..	..	..	..	..	..	..
Tanzania	1993[a,b]	38.1	2.9	6.9	10.9	15.3	21.5	45.4	30.2
Thailand	1992[a,b]	46.2	2.5	5.6	8.7	13.0	20.0	52.7	37.1
Togo		..	..	..	..	..	..	..	..
Trinidad and Tobago		..	..	..	..	..	..	..	..
Tunisia	1990[a,b]	40.2	2.3	5.9	10.4	15.3	22.1	46.3	30.7
Turkey		..	..	..	..	..	..	..	..
Turkmenistan	1993[c,d]	35.8	2.7	6.7	11.4	16.3	22.8	42.8	26.9
Uganda	1992[a,b]	40.8	3.0	6.8	10.3	14.4	20.4	48.1	33.4
Ukraine	1992[c,d]	25.7	4.1	9.5	14.1	18.1	22.9	35.4	20.8
United Arab Emirates		..	..	..	..	..	..	..	..
United Kingdom	1986[c,d]	32.6	2.4	7.1	12.8	17.2	23.1	39.8	24.7
United States	1994[c,d]	40.1	1.5	4.8	10.5	16.0	23.5	45.2	28.5
Uruguay		..	..	..	..	..	..	..	..
Uzbekistan		..	..	..	..	..	..	..	..
Venezuela	1995[c,d]	46.8	1.5	4.3	8.8	13.8	21.3	51.8	35.6
Vietnam	1993[a,b]	35.7	3.5	7.8	11.4	15.4	21.4	44.0	29.0
Yemen, Rep.	1992[a,b]	39.5	2.3	6.1	10.9	15.3	21.6	46.1	30.8
Zambia	1993[a,b]	46.2	1.5	3.9	8.0	13.8	23.8	50.4	31.3
Zimbabwe	1990[a,b]	56.8	1.8	4.0	6.3	10.0	17.4	62.3	46.9

a. Refers to expenditure shares by percentiles of population. b. Ranked by per capita expenditure. c. Refers to income shares by percentiles of population. d. Ranked by income per capita.

Table 6.   Education

Economy	Public expenditure on education % of GNP		Net enrollment ratio % of relevant age group				Percentage of cohort reaching grade 4				Expected years of schooling			
			Primary		Secondary		Males		Females		Males		Females	
	1980	1995a	1980	1995	1980	1995	1980	1991	1980	1991	1980	1992	1980	1992
Albania	..	3.4	..	96	..	..	..	..	..	..	..	..	..	..
Algeria	7.8	..	81	95	31	56	92	97	91	96	9	11	6	9
Angola	..	..	70	..	..	..	..	..	..	..	8	..	7	..
Argentina	2.7	4.5	..	..	..	59	..	..	..	..	..	13	..	14
Armenia	..	..	..	..	..	..	..	..	..	..	..	..	..	..
Australia	5.5	5.6	100	98	70	89	..	..	..	..	12	13	12	14
Austria	5.6	5.5	99	100	..	90	..	..	..	..	11	15	11	14
Azerbaijan	..	3.0	..	..	..	..	..	..	..	..	..	..	..	..
Bangladesh	1.5	2.3	..	..	..	..	..	..	..	..	..	..	..	..
Belarus	5.2	5.6	..	95	..	..	..	..	..	..	..	..	..	..
Belgium	6.1	5.7	97	98	..	98	78	..	81	..	14	14	13	14
Benin	..	3.1	..	59	..	..	..	64	..	62	..	..	..	..
Bolivia	4.4	6.6	79	16	..	..	..	..	..	..	9	11	8	9
Brazil	3.6	..	80	90	14	19	..	..	..	..	9	..	9	..
Bulgaria	4.5	4.2	96	97	73	75	..	93	..	90	11	11	11	12
Burkina Faso	2.6	3.6	15	31	..	7	79	81	79	82	2	3	1	2
Burundi	..	2.8	20	52	..	5	83	78	83	76	3	5	2	4
Cambodia	..	..	..	..	..	..	..	..	..	..	..	..	..	..
Cameroon	3.2	..	..	..	15	..	81	..	81	..	8	..	6	..
Canada	6.9	7.3	..	95	..	92	..	..	..	..	15	17	15	18
Central African Republic	..	..	56	..	..	..	..	85	..	81	..	..	..	..
Chad	..	2.2	..	..	..	..	..	74	..	65	..	..	..	..
Chile	4.6	2.9	..	86	..	55	..	..	..	..	..	12	..	12
China	2.5	2.3	..	99	..	..	..	..	..	..	..	..	..	..
Hong Kong, China	..	2.8	95	91	61	71	100	..	100	..	12	..	12	..
Colombia	1.9	3.5	..	85	..	50	..	72	..	74	..	..	..	..
Congo, Dem. Rep.	2.6	..	..	61	..	23	77	..	70	..	..	7	..	4
Congo, Rep.	7.0	5.9	96	..	..	..	91	88	91	89	..	..	..	..
Costa Rica	7.8	4.5	89	92	39	43	80	90	84	91	10	10	10	9
Côte d'Ivoire	7.2	..	..	..	..	..	94	85	91	83	..	..	..	..
Croatia	..	5.3	..	82	..	66	..	..	..	..	..	11	..	11
Czech Republic	..	6.1	..	98	..	88	..	..	..	..	..	..	..	..
Denmark	6.9	8.3	96	99	88	86	..	98	..	98	14	15	14	15
Dominican Republic	2.2	1.9	..	81	..	22	..	..	..	..	..	10	..	10
Ecuador	5.6	3.4	..	92	..	..	..	..	..	..	..	..	..	..
Egypt, Arab Rep.	5.7	5.6	..	89	..	65	95	..	65	..	..	11	..	9
El Salvador	3.9	2.2	..	79	..	21	..	..	..	..	..	9	..	9
Estonia	..	6.6	..	94	..	77	..	..	..	..	..	12	..	13
Ethiopia	..	4.7	..	24	..	..	..	..	..	..	..	..	..	..
Finland	5.3	7.6	..	99	..	93	..	100	..	100	..	..	..	..
France	5.0	5.9	100	99	79	88	..	..	..	..	13	14	13	15
Gabon	2.7	..	..	..	..	..	82	..	79	..	..	..	..	..
Georgia	..	5.2	..	82	..	71	..	..	..	..	..	..	..	..
Germany	..	4.7	..	100	..	88	..	..	..	..	..	15	..	14
Ghana	3.1	..	..	..	..	..	87	..	82	..	..	..	..	..
Greece	..	3.7	103	..	..	85	98	..	98	..	12	13	12	13
Guatemala	..	1.7	58	..	13	..	..	..	..	..	..	..	..	..
Guinea	..	..	..	37	..	..	..	80	..	73	..	4	..	2
Guinea-Bissau	..	..	47	..	3	..	63	..	46	..	6	..	3	..
Haiti	1.5	..	38	..	..	..	..	60	..	60	..	..	..	..
Honduras	3.2	3.9	78	90	..	21	..	..	..	..	..	..	..	..
Hungary	4.7	6.0	95	93	..	73	96	97	96	97	9	12	10	12
India	2.8	3.5	..	..	..	..	..	..	..	..	..	..	..	..
Indonesia	1.7	..	88	97	..	42	..	..	..	..	..	10	..	9
Ireland	..	6.3	100	100	78	85	..	..	..	..	11	13	11	13
Israel	7.9	6.6	..	..	..	..	..	..	..	..	..	..	..	..
Italy	..	4.9	..	97	..	..	100	100	100	100	..	..	..	..
Jamaica	7.0	8.2	96	100	64	64	..	98	..	100	10	11	11	11
Japan	5.8	3.8	100	100	93	96	100	100	100	100	13	..	12	..
Jordan	..	6.3	93	..	68	..	95	100	95	97	12	11	12	12
Kazakhstan	..	4.5	..	..	..	..	..	..	..	..	..	..	..	..
Kenya	6.8	7.4	91	..	..	..	..	..	..	..	..	..	..	..
Korea, Rep.	3.7	3.7	100	99	70	96	96	100	96	100	12	14	11	13
Kyrgyz Republic	7.2	6.8	..	97	..	..	..	..	..	..	..	..	..	..
Lao PDR	..	2.4	..	68	..	18	..	..	..	..	..	8	..	6
Latvia	3.3	6.3	..	84	..	78	..	..	..	..	..	..	..	..
Lebanon	..	2.0	..	..	..	..	..	..	..	..	..	..	..	..
Lesotho	5.1	5.9	66	65	13	16	61	74	77	84	7	8	10	10
Lithuania	5.5	6.1	..	..	..	80	..	..	..	..	..	..	..	..
Macedonia, FYR	..	5.5	..	85	..	51	..	..	..	..	..	..	..	..
Madagascar	4.4	..	..	..	..	..	..	63	..	64	..	..	..	..
Malawi	3.4	5.7	43	100	..	66	62	73	55	68	..	6	..	5
Malaysia	6.0	5.3	..	91	..	..	..	98	..	99	..	..	..	..
Mali	3.8	2.2	20	25	..	..	..	..	..	..	..	2	..	1
Mauritania	..	5.0	..	60	..	..	..	82	..	83	..	..	..	..

Note: For data comparability and coverage, see the Technical Notes. Figures in italics are for years other than those specified.

PEOPLE

Economy	Public expenditure on education % of GNP		Net enrollment ratio % of relevant age group				Percentage of cohort reaching grade 4				Expected years of schooling			
			Primary		Secondary		Males		Females		Males		Females	
	1980	1995ª	1980	1995	1980	1995	1980	1991	1980	1991	1980	1992	1980	1992
Mauritius	5.3	4.3	79	96	..	..	..	99	..	99	..	..	..	..
Mexico	4.7	5.3	..	100	..	..	..	..	..	..	..	..	..	..
Moldova	..	6.1	..	..	..	..	..	..	..	..	..	..	..	..
Mongolia	..	5.6	..	80	..	57	..	..	..	..	..	..	..	..
Morocco	6.1	5.6	62	72	20	..	90	85	89	85	8	8	5	6
Mozambique	4.4	..	36	40	..	6	..	66	..	60	5	4	4	3
Namibia	1.5	9.4	..	92	..	36	..	..	..	..	..	12	..	13
Nepal	1.8	2.9	..	..	..	..	..	..	..	..	..	..	..	..
Netherlands	7.6	5.3	93	99	81	..	97	..	100	..	14	16	13	15
New Zealand	5.8	6.7	100	100	81	93	..	97	..	97	14	15	13	16
Nicaragua	3.4	..	98	83	23	27	51	..	55	..	8	8	9	9
Niger	3.1	..	21	..	4	..	82	..	79	..	..	3	..	1
Nigeria	6.4	..	..	..	..	..	..	..	..	..	..	..	..	..
Norway	7.2	8.3	98	99	84	94	99	..	100	..	13	15	13	16
Oman	2.1	4.6	43	71	10	56	..	..	..	..	5	8	2	7
Pakistan	2.0	..	..	..	..	..	..	..	..	..	..	..	..	..
Panama	4.8	5.2	89	..	46	..	87	85	88	88	11	11	11	11
Papua New Guinea	..	..	..	..	..	..	..	68	..	67	..	..	..	..
Paraguay	1.5	2.9	89	89	..	33	..	79	..	81	..	9	..	8
Peru	3.1	..	86	91	..	53	85	..	83	..	11	..	10	..
Philippines	1.7	2.2	94	100	45	60	..	..	..	..	10	11	11	11
Poland	..	4.6	98	97	70	83	..	..	..	..	12	12	12	12
Portugal	3.8	5.4	98	100	..	78	..	..	..	..	..	..	..	..
Romania	3.3	3.2	..	92	..	73	..	..	..	..	..	11	..	11
Russian Federation	3.5	4.1	..	100	..	..	..	..	..	..	..	..	..	..
Rwanda	2.7	..	59	76	..	8	83	72	84	75	..	6	..	6
Saudi Arabia	4.1	5.5	49	62	21	48	91	..	90	..	7	9	5	8
Senegal	..	3.6	37	54	..	..	93	94	90	90	..	6	..	4
Sierra Leone	3.8	..	..	..	..	..	..	..	..	..	11	..	11	..
Singapore	2.8	3.0	99	..	..	..	..	..	..	..	..	..	..	..
Slovak Republic	..	4.4	..	..	..	..	..	..	..	..	..	..	..	..
Slovenia	..	5.8	..	100	..	..	..	..	..	..	..	..	..	..
South Africa	..	6.8	..	96	..	52	..	..	..	..	..	12	..	12
Spain	..	5.0	100	100	74	94	95	97	95	98	13	14	12	15
Sri Lanka	2.7	3.1	..	..	..	..	..	97	..	98	..	..	..	..
Sweden	9.0	8.0	..	100	..	96	99	..	100	..	12	14	13	14
Switzerland	5.0	5.5	..	100	..	..	92	..	94	..	14	15	13	14
Syrian Arab Republic	4.6	..	89	91	39	39	94	95	91	95	11	10	8	9
Tajikistan	8.2	8.6	..	..	..	..	..	..	..	..	..	..	..	..
Tanzania	4.4	..	68	48	..	..	..	89	..	90	..	..	..	..
Thailand	3.4	4.2	..	..	..	..	..	..	..	..	..	..	..	..
Togo	5.6	5.6	..	85	..	..	90	84	84	79	..	11	..	6
Trinidad and Tobago	4.0	4.5	90	88	..	64	..	..	..	..	11	11	11	11
Tunisia	5.4	6.8	82	97	23	..	94	93	90	93	10	11	7	10
Turkey	2.8	3.4	..	96	..	50	..	99	..	98	..	..	..	..
Turkmenistan	..	..	..	..	..	..	..	..	..	..	..	..	..	..
Uganda	1.2	..	39	..	..	..	..	..	..	..	..	..	..	..
Ukraine	5.6	7.7	..	..	..	..	..	..	..	..	..	..	..	..
United Arab Emirates	1.3	1.8	74	83	..	71	..	94	..	93	8	11	7	12
United Kingdom	5.6	5.5	100	100	79	92	..	..	..	..	13	15	13	15
United States	6.7	5.3	95	96	..	89	..	..	..	..	14	16	15	16
Uruguay	2.3	2.8	..	95	..	..	93	99	99	99	..	..	..	..
Uzbekistan	6.4	9.5	..	..	..	..	..	..	..	..	..	..	..	..
Venezuela	4.4	5.2	82	88	14	20	..	..	..	..	..	10	..	11
Vietnam	..	2.7	95	..	..	..	..	..	..	..	..	..	..	..
Yemen, Rep.	..	7.5	..	..	..	..	..	..	..	..	..	..	..	..
Zambia	4.5	1.8	77	77	..	16	..	..	..	..	..	..	..	..
Zimbabwe	6.6	8.5	..	..	..	..	..	81	..	80	..	..	..	..
World	4.4 m	5.2 m	..	.. w	..	..	..	..	..	..	..	..	..	..
Low income	3.4	5.5	..	95	..	..	..	..	..	..	..	..	..	..
Middle income	4.1	4.5	..	95	..	..	..	..	..	..	..	..	..	..
Lower middle income	4.5	4.4	..	92	..	..	..	..	..	..	..	..	..	..
Upper middle income	4.0	4.6	..	..	..	..	..	..	..	..	..	..	..	..
Low & middle income	3.9	4.5	..	99	..	..	..	..	..	..	..	..	..	..
East Asia & Pacific	2.1	2.6	..	99	..	..	..	..	..	..	..	..	..	..
Europe & Central Asia	5.0	5.6	..	96	..	..	..	..	..	..	..	..	..	..
Latin America & Carib.	3.9	3.9	..	91	..	..	..	..	..	..	..	..	..	..
Middle East & N. Africa	5.0	5.6	..	..	..	..	..	..	..	..	..	..	..	..
South Asia	2.0	3.0	..	..	..	..	..	..	..	..	..	..	..	..
Sub-Saharan Africa	4.1	5.3	..	..	..	..	..	..	..	..	..	..	..	..
High income	5.6	5.5	..	98	..	..	..	..	..	..	..	..	..	..

a. Data are from UNESCO's publication, *World Education Report, 1998*. They are not yet available in time series.

Table 7.   Health

Economy	Public expenditure on health % of GDP 1990–95[a]	Access to safe water % of population with access 1980	1995	Access to sanitation % of population with access 1980	1995	Infant mortality rate Per 1,000 live births 1980	1996	Contraceptive prevalence rate % of women aged 15–49 1990–96	Total fertility rate Births per woman 1980	1996	Maternal mortality ratio Per 100,000 live births 1990–96
Albania	2.7	*92*	..	..	..	47	37	..	3.6	2.6	28[b]
Algeria	3.3	*77*	..	..	..	98	32	51	6.7	3.4	140[b]
Angola	4.0	..	*32*	..	*16*	153	124	..	6.9	6.8	1,500[c]
Argentina	4.3	..	*64*	..	*89*	35	22	..	3.3	2.7	100[c]
Armenia	3.1	..	..	..	..	26	16	..	2.3	1.6	21[b]
Australia	6.0	*99*	95	*99*	*90*	11	6	..	1.9	1.8	9[c]
Austria	5.9	*100*	..	*85*	100	14	5	..	1.6	1.4	10[c]
Azerbaijan	1.4	..	..	..	..	30	20	..	3.2	2.1	44[b]
Bangladesh	1.2	..	79	..	*35*	132	77	45	6.1	3.4	850[c]
Belarus	5.3	..	..	*50*	100	16	13	..	2.0	1.3	22[b]
Belgium	7.0	..	..	*99*	100	12	7	..	1.7	1.5	10[c]
Benin	1.7	..	*50*	..	*20*	120	87	17	7.0	5.9	500[d]
Bolivia	2.7	..	60	..	*44*	118	67	45	5.5	4.4	370[d]
Brazil	2.7	..	*72*	..	*41*	67	36	77	3.9	2.4	160[d]
Bulgaria	4.0	*96*	..	..	*99*	20	16	..	2.0	1.2	20[b]
Burkina Faso	2.3	*35*	78	*5*	*18*	121	98	8	7.5	6.7	930[c]
Burundi	0.9	..	..	..	..	121	97	..	6.8	6.4	1,300[c]
Cambodia	0.7	..	*13*	..	..	201	105	..	4.7	4.6	900[c]
Cameroon	1.0	..	*41*	..	*40*	94	54	16	6.5	5.5	550[c]
Canada	6.8	*97*	100	*60*	*85*	10	6	..	1.7	1.7	6[c]
Central African Republic	1.9	*16*	18	..	..	117	96	14	5.8	5.0	700[d]
Chad	3.4	..	*24*	..	*21*	147	115	..	5.9	5.6	900[d]
Chile	2.5	..	..	..	*83*	32	12	..	2.8	2.3	180[b]
China	2.1	..	*90*	..	*21*	42	33	85	2.5	1.9	115[e]
Hong Kong, China	1.9	..	..	..	..	11	4	..	2.0	1.2	7[c]
Colombia	3.0	..	*76*	..	*63*	45	25	72	3.8	2.7	100[c]
Congo, Dem. Rep.	0.2	..	..	..	..	111	90	..	6.6	6.3	..
Congo, Rep.	1.8	..	*47*	..	*9*	89	90	..	6.2	6.0	890[c]
Costa Rica	6.3	..	..	..	..	20	12	..	3.7	2.7	55[c]
Côte d'Ivoire	1.4	*20*	*72*	*17*	*54*	108	84	11	7.4	5.1	600[d]
Croatia	8.5	..	*96*	..	*68*	21	9	..	..	1.6	12[b]
Czech Republic	7.7	..	..	..	..	16	6	69	2.1	1.2	7[b]
Denmark	5.3	*100*	100	*100*	100	8	6	..	1.5	1.8	9[c]
Dominican Republic	2.0	..	*71*	..	*78*	74	40	64	4.2	3.1	110[c]
Ecuador	2.0	..	*70*	..	*64*	67	34	57	5.0	3.1	150[c]
Egypt, Arab Rep.	1.6[f]	*90*	64	*70*	*11*	120	53	48	5.1	3.3	170[c]
El Salvador	1.2	..	*55*	..	*68*	81	34	53	5.3	3.5	300[c]
Estonia	6.3	..	..	..	..	17	10	..	2.0	1.3	52[b]
Ethiopia	1.7	*4*	*27*	..	*10*	155	109	4	6.6	7.0	1,400[c]
Finland	5.7	..	100	*100*	100	8	4	..	1.6	1.8	11[c]
France	8.0	..	100	*85*	*96*	10	5	..	1.9	1.7	15[c]
Gabon	0.6	..	*67*	..	*76*	116	87	..	4.5	5.0	500[c]
Georgia	0.8	..	..	..	..	25	17	..	2.3	1.5	19[b]
Germany	8.2	..	..	..	100	12	5	..	1.4	1.3	22[c]
Ghana	1.3	..	56	..	*27*	100	71	20	6.5	5.0	740[c]
Greece	5.5	..	..	..	96	18	8	..	2.2	1.4	10[c]
Guatemala	0.9	..	60	..	*66*	81	41	32	6.2	4.6	190[d]
Guinea	1.2	..	*62*	*12*	*70*	185	122	2	6.1	5.7	880[d]
Guinea-Bissau	1.1	*24*	23	..	*20*	168	134	..	6.0	6.0	910[c]
Haiti	1.3	..	*28*	..	24	123	72	18	5.9	4.3	600[d]
Honduras	2.8	..	65	..	62	70	44	47	6.5	4.5	220[c]
Hungary	6.8	..	..	..	94	23	11	..	1.9	1.5	14[b]
India	0.7	..	*81*	..	*29*	116	65	43	5.0	3.1	437[d]
Indonesia	0.7	..	*62*	..	*51*	90	49	55	4.3	2.6	390[d]
Ireland	5.4	..	..	..	100	11	5	60	3.2	1.9	10[c]
Israel	2.1	..	99	..	70	15	6	..	3.2	2.6	7[c]
Italy	5.4	*99*	..	*99*	100	15	6	..	1.6	1.2	12[c]
Jamaica	3.0	..	70	..	74	21	12	..	3.7	2.3	120[c]
Japan	5.7	..	..	..	85	8	4	..	1.8	1.4	8[b]
Jordan	3.7	*89*	89	*76*	100	41	30	..	6.8	4.4	150[c]
Kazakhstan	2.2	..	..	..	..	33	25	..	2.9	2.1	53[b]
Kenya	1.9	..	53	..	77	72	57	..	7.8	4.6	650[c]
Korea, Rep.	1.8	..	89	..	100	26	9	..	2.6	1.7	30[b]
Kyrgyz Republic	3.7	..	75	..	53	43	26	..	4.1	3.0	32[b]
Lao PDR	1.3	..	39	..	19	127	101	..	6.7	5.7	650[c]
Latvia	4.4	..	..	..	..	20	16	..	2.0	1.2	15[b]
Lebanon	2.1	*92*	..	*59*	..	48	31	..	4.0	2.7	300[c]
Lesotho	3.5	*18*	*52*	*12*	*6*	108	74	23	5.6	4.6	610[c]
Lithuania	5.1	..	..	..	..	20	10	..	2.0	1.4	13[b]
Macedonia, FYR	7.3	..	..	..	..	54	16	..	2.5	2.1	22[b]
Madagascar	1.1	..	*29*	..	3	138	88	17	6.5	5.7	660[d]
Malawi	2.3	..	45	..	53	169	133	22	7.6	6.5	620[d]
Malaysia	1.4	..	88	*75*	91	30	11	..	4.2	3.4	43[b]
Mali	2.0	..	37	..	31	184	120	7	7.1	6.7	580[d]
Mauritania	1.8	..	..	..	..	120	94	..	6.3	5.1	800[c]

Note: For data comparability and coverage, see the Technical Notes. Figures in italics are for years other than those specified.

PEOPLE

Economy	Public expenditure on health % of GDP 1990–95[a]	Access to safe water % of population with access 1980	1995	Access to sanitation % of population with access 1980	1995	Infant mortality rate Per 1,000 live births 1980	1996	Contraceptive prevalence rate % of women aged 15–49 1990–96	Total fertility rate Births per woman 1980	1996	Maternal mortality ratio Per 100,000 live births 1990–96
Mauritius	2.2	..	98	..	100	32	17	75	2.7	2.1	112[b]
Mexico	2.8	..	83	..	66	51	32	..	4.5	2.9	110[c]
Moldova	4.9	..	..	..	50	35	20	..	2.4	1.9	33[b]
Mongolia	4.8	..	..	50	40	82	53	..	5.3	3.3	65[g]
Morocco	1.6	32	52	50	40	99	53	50	5.4	3.3	372[g]
Mozambique	4.6	9	32	10	21	155	123	..	6.5	6.1	1,500[c]
Namibia	3.7	..	..	..	34	90	61	29	5.9	4.9	220[d]
Nepal	1.2	11	48	0	20	132	85	..	6.1	5.0	1,500[c]
Netherlands	6.7	100	100	100	100	9	5	..	1.6	1.5	12[c]
New Zealand	5.7	87	..	..	..	13	6	..	2.0	2.0	25[c]
Nicaragua	4.3	..	61	..	31	90	44	44	6.2	4.0	160[c]
Niger	1.6	..	53	..	15	150	118	4	7.4	7.4	593[d]
Nigeria	0.3	..	39	..	36	99	78	6	6.9	5.4	1,000[c]
Norway	6.6	..	..	100	100	8	4	..	1.7	1.9	6[c]
Oman	2.5	15	..	..	79	41	18	..	9.9	7.0	..
Pakistan	0.8	38	60	16	30	124	88	14	7.0	5.1	340[c]
Panama	5.4	..	83	..	87	32	22	..	3.7	2.6	55[c]
Papua New Guinea	2.8	..	28	..	22	67	62	..	5.7	4.7	370[d]
Paraguay	1.0	..	..	..	30	50	24	51	4.8	3.9	190[d]
Peru	2.6	..	60	..	44	81	42	55	4.5	3.1	280[c]
Philippines	1.3	..	..	..	..	52	37	48	4.8	3.6	208[d]
Poland	4.8	67	..	50	100	21	12	..	2.3	1.6	10[b]
Portugal	4.5	57	..	..	100	24	7	..	2.2	1.4	15[c]
Romania	3.6	77	..	50	49	29	22	57	2.4	1.3	41[b]
Russian Federation	4.1	..	..	..	..	22	17	34	1.9	1.3	53[b]
Rwanda	1.9	..	..	..	..	128	129	21	8.3	6.1	1,300[c]
Saudi Arabia	3.1	91	93	76	86	65	22	..	7.3	6.2	18[b]
Senegal	2.5	..	50	..	58	91	60	7	6.7	5.7	510[d]
Sierra Leone	1.6	..	34	13	11	190	174	..	6.5	6.5	1,800[c]
Singapore	1.3	100	100	..	97	12	4	..	1.7	1.7	10[c]
Slovak Republic	6.0	..	..	43	51	21	11	..	2.3	1.5	8[b]
Slovenia	7.4	..	..	..	90	15	5	..	2.1	1.3	5[b]
South Africa	3.6	..	70	..	46	67	49	69	4.6	2.9	230[c]
Spain	6.0	98	99	95	100	12	5	..	2.2	1.2	7[c]
Sri Lanka	1.4	..	..	..	..	34	15	..	3.5	2.3	30[b]
Sweden	6.0	..	..	85	100	7	4	..	1.7	1.7	7[c]
Switzerland	7.2	..	100	85	100	9	5	..	1.6	1.5	6[c]
Syrian Arab Republic	..	71	85	45	78	56	31	40	7.4	4.0	179[b]
Tajikistan	6.4	..	..	..	62	58	32	..	5.6	3.7	74[b]
Tanzania	3.0	..	49	..	86	108	86	18	6.7	5.6	530[d]
Thailand	1.4	..	81	..	70	49	34	..	3.5	1.8	200[c]
Togo	1.7	..	..	..	..	110	87	..	6.6	6.2	640[c]
Trinidad and Tobago	2.6	..	82	..	56	35	13	..	3.3	2.1	90[c]
Tunisia	3.0	72	..	46	..	69	30	60	5.2	2.8	..
Turkey	2.7	67	92	..	94	109	42	..	4.3	2.6	180[c]
Turkmenistan	2.8	..	85	..	60	54	41	..	4.9	3.3	44[b]
Uganda	1.6	..	34	..	57	116	99	15	7.2	6.7	550[g]
Ukraine	5.0	..	97	50	49	17	14	..	2.0	1.3	30[b]
United Arab Emirates	2.0	100	98	75	95	55	15	..	5.4	3.5	..
United Kingdom	5.8	..	100	..	96	12	6	..	1.9	1.7	9[b]
United States	6.6	..	90	98	85	13	7	..	1.8	2.1	12[c]
Uruguay	2.0	..	83	..	82	37	18	..	2.7	2.2	85[c]
Uzbekistan	3.5	..	..	..	18	47	24	..	4.8	3.4	24[b]
Venezuela	2.3	..	79	..	58	36	22	..	4.1	3.0	200[b]
Vietnam	1.1	..	36	..	21	57	40	..	5.0	3.0	105[b]
Yemen, Rep.	1.2	..	52	..	51	141	98	..	7.9	7.2	1,400[c]
Zambia	2.4	..	43	..	23	90	112	26	7.0	5.8	230[d]
Zimbabwe	2.0	..	74	5	58	82	56	58	6.8	3.9	280[d]
World	3.2 w	..	78 w	..	47 w	80 w	54 w		3.7 w	2.8 w	
Low income	0.9	..	71	..	30	117	80		5.6	4.1	
Middle income	3.0	..	84	..	36	57	35		3.2	2.3	
Lower middle income	2.5	..	84	..	31	56	37		3.1	2.2	
Upper middle income	3.3	..	..	..	..	59	31		3.8	2.6	
Low & middle income	2.7	..	..	..	..	87	59		4.1	3.0	
East Asia & Pacific	1.7	..	84	..	29	56	39		3.1	2.2	
Europe & Central Asia	4.4	..	..	..	..	41	24		2.5	1.8	
Latin America & Carib.	2.9	..	73	..	57	59	33		4.1	2.8	
Middle East & N. Africa	2.4	..	..	..	..	96	50		6.1	4.0	
South Asia	1.2	..	78	..	30	120	73		5.3	3.4	
Sub-Saharan Africa	1.6	..	45	..	37	115	91		6.6	5.6	
High income	6.9	..	..	..	92	13	6		1.9	1.7	

a. Data are for the most recent year available. b. Official estimate. c. UNICEF-WHO estimate based on statistical modeling. d. Indirect estimate based on a sample survey. e. Based on a survey covering 30 provinces. f. Data are for 1997. g. Based on a sample survey.

Table 8. Land use and agricultural productivity

	Cropland % of land area		Irrigated land % of cropland		Arable land Hectares per capita		Agricultural productivity 1987 dollars				Food production index 1989–91 = 100	
							Agr. value added per agricultural worker		Agr. value added per hectare of agr. land			
Economy	1980	1995	1979–81	1994–96	1979–81	1994–96	1979–81	1994–96	1979–81	1992–94	1979–81	1994–96
Albania	26	26	53.0	48.4	0.22	0.18	908	1,161	565	752	..	..
Algeria	3	3	3.4	6.9	0.37	0.27	2,713	3,612	109	180	71	115
Angola	3	3	2.2	2.1	0.41	0.28	..	149	..	9	92	126
Argentina	10	10	5.8	6.3	0.89	0.72	6,248	7,028	51	62	95	116
Armenia	..	25	..	44.7	..	0.15	..	1,275	..	261	..	78
Australia	6	6	3.5	4.9	2.97	2.65	17,222	22,256	16	21	92	118
Austria	20	18	0.2	0.3	0.20	0.18	10,695	15,659	956	1,088	92	101
Azerbaijan	..	23	..	50.0	..	0.21	..	..	..	..	..	55
Bangladesh	70	67	17.1	37.3	0.10	0.07	187	226	587	863	79	103
Belarus	..	30	..	1.9	..	0.59	..	3,023	..	380	..	68
Belgium	..	..	..	..	..	..	..	..	..	..	..	..
Benin	16	17	0.3	0.5	0.39	0.26	374	563	188	321	63	126
Bolivia	2	2	6.6	3.7	0.35	0.29	1,135	..	42	42	71	120
Brazil	6	8	3.3	4.9	0.32	0.32	1,217	2,384	93	119	70	117
Bulgaria	38	38	28.3	19.0	0.43	0.48	4,446	6,240	650	513	105	68
Burkina Faso	10	13	0.4	0.7	0.40	0.33	155	182	64	93	63	121
Burundi	46	43	0.7	1.3	0.24	0.15	218	177	212	270	80	94
Cambodia	12	22	4.9	4.5	0.30	0.39	..	131	..	86	51	116
Cameroon	15	15	0.2	0.3	0.68	0.46	861	827	252	313	83	114
Canada	5	5	1.3	1.6	1.86	1.54	12,317	30,202	131	154	80	111
Central African Republic	3	3	..	..	0.81	0.60	456	516	96	119	80	111
Chad	3	3	0.2	0.4	0.70	0.51	148	198	6	10	91	117
Chile	6	6	29.6	29.9	0.36	0.28	1,729	3,042	79	150	72	125
China	11	10	45.1	51.8	0.10	0.08	113	193	106	184	61	144
Hong Kong, China	7	7	43.5	28.6	0.00	0.00	..	..	..	..	97	52
Colombia	5	6	7.7	16.6	0.13	0.07	1,579	2,172	123	165	76	109
Congo, Dem. Rep.	3	3	0.1	0.1	0.26	0.17	218	219	83	113	72	106
Congo, Rep.	0	0	0.7	0.6	0.08	0.06	544	629	21	28	80	112
Costa Rica	10	10	12.1	23.8	0.12	0.09	2,544	3,790	280	373	73	123
Côte d'Ivoire	10	13	1.4	1.7	0.24	0.21	1,527	1,354	195	212	71	118
Croatia	..	22	..	0.2	..	0.23	..	..	..	..	..	57
Czech Republic	..	44	..	0.7	..	0.30	..	..	..	..	..	82
Denmark	63	55	14.5	20.1	0.52	0.45	18,790	38,131	1,166	1,684	83	102
Dominican Republic	29	39	11.7	13.7	0.19	0.17	1,325	1,587	251	262	85	104
Ecuador	9	11	19.4	8.1	0.20	0.14	1,267	1,790	194	259	77	131
Egypt, Arab Rep.	2	3	100.0	100.0	0.06	0.05	757	1,331	2,691	2,990	68	118
El Salvador	35	37	14.8	15.8	0.12	0.10	1,417	1,300	733	674	91	107
Estonia	..	27	..	..	..	0.76	..	6,266	..	526	..	56
Ethiopia	..	12	..	1.7	..	0.20	..	181	..	116	90	..
Finland	..	..	..	..	0.54	0.50	20,171	31,457	2,100	2,072	93	92
France	34	35	4.6	8.0	0.32	0.32	13,699	30,035	838	1,113	94	101
Gabon	2	2	0.9	0.8	0.42	0.29	1,412	1,516	67	74	80	107
Georgia	..	16	..	42.0	..	0.15	..	..	..	..	..	71
Germany	36	35	3.7	3.9	0.15	0.14	..	..	..	..	91	89
Ghana	16	20	0.2	0.1	0.18	0.17	813	684	215	227	73	143
Greece	30	27	24.2	38.0	0.30	0.23	5,595	7,726	685	766	91	102
Guatemala	16	18	5.0	6.5	0.18	0.13	..	1,240	..	503	70	111
Guinea	3	4	12.8	10.9	0.13	0.10	..	225	..	54	97	126
Guinea-Bissau	10	12	6.0	5.0	0.32	0.28	186	292	54	78	69	111
Haiti	32	33	7.9	9.6	0.10	0.08	..	..	..	..	106	91
Honduras	16	18	4.1	3.6	0.43	0.29	959	1,490	200	268	88	104
Hungary	58	54	3.6	4.2	0.47	0.47	..	4,679	..	485	91	73
India	57	57	22.8	29.5	0.24	0.18	304	404	338	520	68	115
Indonesia	14	17	16.2	15.2	0.12	0.09	422	481	376	519	64	119
Ireland	16	19	..	..	0.33	0.37	..	..	..	..	83	105
Israel	20	21	49.3	44.6	0.08	0.06	..	..	..	..	86	108
Italy	42	37	19.3	24.7	0.17	0.14	10,516	17,876	1,650	1,964	101	102
Jamaica	22	22	13.6	14.3	0.08	0.07	711	1,045	433	591	86	116
Japan	13	12	62.6	61.8	0.04	0.03	9,832	16,712	11,279	12,445	94	98
Jordan	4	5	11.0	18.2	0.14	0.08	3,129	2,769	224	461	61	148
Kazakhstan	..	12	..	7.0	..	2.00	..	..	..	..	..	70
Kenya	8	8	0.9	1.5	0.23	0.15	268	240	68	90	68	101
Korea, Rep.	22	20	59.6	66.5	0.05	0.04	1,950	5,302	5,229	6,961	78	115
Kyrgyz Republic	..	7	..	77.6	..	0.25	..	69	..	4	..	81
Lao PDR	3	4	15.4	18.4	0.21	0.19	..	..	..	..	71	115
Latvia	..	28	..	..	..	0.68	..	3,870	..	349	..	57
Lebanon	30	30	28.1	28.7	0.07	0.05	..	..	..	..	58	117
Lesotho	..	..	..	..	0.22	0.16	291	194	35	24	89	109
Lithuania	..	46	..	..	..	0.79	..	..	..	..	..	65
Macedonia, FYR	..	26	..	9.9	..	0.31	..	..	..	..	..	96
Madagascar	5	5	21.5	35.0	0.29	0.20	190	178	26	34	82	104
Malawi	14	18	1.3	1.6	0.21	0.17	162	156	145	153	91	102
Malaysia	15	23	6.7	4.5	0.07	0.09	2,235	4,052	941	942	55	122
Mali	2	3	2.9	2.6	0.31	0.33	251	259	24	33	80	114
Mauritania	0	0	25.1	23.6	0.12	0.09	..	..	5	7	86	100

Note: For data comparability and coverage, see the Technical Notes. Figures in italics are for years other than those specified.

Economy	Cropland % of land area		Irrigated land % of cropland		Arable land Hectares per capita		Agricultural productivity 1987 dollars Agr. value added per agricultural worker		Agr. value added per hectare of agr. land		Food production index 1989–91 = 100	
	1980	1995	1979–81	1994–96	1979–81	1994–96	1979–81	1994–96	1979–81	1992–94	1979–81	1994–96
Mauritius	53	52	15.0	17.0	0.10	0.09	1,764	3,762	1,607	1,902	89	104
Mexico	13	14	20.3	23.5	0.35	0.27	1,372	1,518	109	123	85	117
Moldova	..	66	..	14.1	..	0.41	..	..	..	..	..	63
Mongolia	1	1	3.0	6.1	0.71	0.54	..	..	..	..	88	80
Morocco	18	21	15.0	13.5	0.39	0.33	565	919	78	111	56	101
Mozambique	4	4	2.1	3.4	0.24	0.17	..	92	..	12	99	106
Namibia	1	1	0.6	0.8	0.64	0.51	1,295	1,458	8	9	108	107
Nepal	16	21	22.5	31.0	0.16	0.13	173	198	271	406	65	109
Netherlands	24	27	58.5	61.5	0.06	0.06	23,131	41,245	3,489	5,932	87	104
New Zealand	13	12	5.2	9.1	0.80	0.44	10,693	13,373	86	132	91	117
Nicaragua	11	23	6.0	3.3	0.41	0.55	3,268	3,697	212	155	118	120
Niger	..	..	..	..	0.63	0.53	292	256	57	63	101	120
Nigeria	33	36	0.7	0.7	0.39	0.28	479	684	111	150	58	132
Norway	..	..	..	..	0.20	0.22	19,593	34,809	3,172	3,403	92	99
Oman	0	0	92.7	98.4	0.01	0.01	1,041	..	155	*328*	63	88
Pakistan	26	28	72.7	79.8	0.24	0.16	323	466	227	382	66	125
Panama	7	9	5.0	4.8	0.22	0.19	1,954	2,320	208	246	86	102
Papua New Guinea	1	1	..	..	0.01	0.01	671	752	1,756	2,186	86	106
Paraguay	4	6	3.4	3.0	0.52	0.46	1,698	2,204	49	54	61	113
Peru	3	3	33.0	41.2	0.19	0.16	..	..	..	..	78	123
Philippines	29	32	14.0	16.7	0.11	0.08	777	780	782	835	86	116
Poland	49	48	0.7	0.7	0.41	0.37	..	1,359	..	366	88	83
Portugal	34	33	20.1	20.9	0.25	0.23	..	..	..	715	72	97
Romania	46	43	21.9	31.3	0.44	0.41	..	3,007	..	393	111	97
Russian Federation	..	8	..	4.0	..	0.88	..	..	..	..	..	71
Rwanda	41	47	0.4	0.3	0.15	0.13	306	206	445	378	90	72
Saudi Arabia	1	2	28.9	38.7	0.20	0.20	1,641	..	23	..	31	95
Senegal	12	12	2.6	3.1	0.42	0.28	328	375	92	118	75	106
Sierra Leone	7	8	4.1	5.4	0.14	0.11	365	344	117	123	85	95
Singapore	13	2	..	..	0.00	0.00	8,791	20,215	18,956	72,942	154	42
Slovak Republic	..	33	..	18.6	..	0.28	..	..	..	497	..	76
Slovenia	..	14	..	0.7	..	0.12	..	..	..	..	..	96
South Africa	11	13	8.4	8.1	0.46	0.40	2,361	2,870	45	49	93	98
Spain	41	40	14.8	17.8	0.42	0.39	..	8,699	..	496	82	95
Sri Lanka	29	29	28.4	29.2	0.06	0.05	489	561	592	801	98	108
Sweden	..	..	..	..	0.36	0.31	18,485	28,590	1,263	1,577	100	96
Switzerland	10	11	6.2	5.8	0.06	0.06	..	..	..	..	96	97
Syrian Arab Republic	31	32	9.6	18.1	0.60	0.37	3,426	..	212	..	94	134
Tajikistan	..	6	..	83.5	..	0.14	..	..	..	..	..	70
Tanzania	3	4	4.1	4.9	0.12	0.11	..	..	..	..	77	98
Thailand	36	40	16.4	23.5	0.35	0.29	375	554	338	488	80	108
Togo	43	45	0.3	0.3	0.76	0.51	404	461	119	189	77	117
Trinidad and Tobago	23	24	17.8	18.0	0.06	0.06	4,822	3,586	1,801	1,245	102	105
Tunisia	30	31	4.9	7.4	0.51	0.32	1,384	2,286	142	232	68	99
Turkey	37	35	9.6	15.3	0.57	0.40	1,208	1,168	354	404	76	105
Turkmenistan	..	3	..	87.8	..	0.31	..	..	..	..	..	121
Uganda	28	34	0.1	0.1	0.32	0.27	..	592	..	515	71	107
Ukraine	..	59	..	7.5	..	0.64	..	..	..	..	..	70
United Arab Emirates	0	1	237.7	86.8	0.01	0.02	8,928	..	970	2,076	47	169
United Kingdom	29	25	2.0	1.8	0.12	0.10	..	..	..	..	92	101
United States	21	21	10.8	11.4	0.83	0.71	17,719	..	156	261	95	113
Uruguay	8	7	5.4	10.7	0.48	0.40	5,379	6,535	65	80	87	123
Uzbekistan	..	11	..	88.9	..	0.18	..	1,228	..	150	..	108
Venezuela	4	4	3.6	5.2	0.19	0.13	3,103	3,270	110	139	78	120
Vietnam	20	21	24.1	29.6	0.11	0.08	..	801	..	2,640	64	127
Yemen, Rep.	3	3	19.9	31.3	0.16	0.10	..	..	..	..	75	113
Zambia	7	7	0.4	0.9	0.89	0.59	116	100	6	7	74	97
Zimbabwe	7	8	3.1	4.5	0.36	0.27	294	266	34	41	82	92
World	11 w	11 w	16.6 w	17.6 w	0.27 w	0.24 w	.. w	.. w	.. w	.. w	80 w	116 w
Low income	13	14	18.6	22.8	0.26	0.19	..	397	142	183	73	116
Middle income	9	10	20.9	18.2	0.19	0.22	..	..	..	197	72	124
Lower middle income	10	10	30.2	21.8	0.14	0.20	..	..	..	256	68	133
Upper middle income	8	9	8.3	10.1	0.39	0.33		..	..	*126*	81	109
Low & middle income	10	11	19.8	19.9	0.22	0.21	..	459	..	206	72	122
East Asia & Pacific	11	12	..	..	0.12	0.09	..	..	..	..	65	139
Europe & Central Asia	..	13	..	9.8	..	0.61	..	..	..	..	..	..
Latin America & Carib.	7	8	9.8	11.1	0.33	0.28	1,586	2,292	90	116	80	115
Middle East & N. Africa	5	6	23.5	31.2	0.29	0.21	1,918	..	185	..	67	118
South Asia	44	45	27.8	35.1	0.23	0.17	290	383	337	519	70	115
Sub-Saharan Africa	6	7	3.7	4.0	0.36	0.26	458	392	53	68	79	113
High income	..	..	..	..	0.46	0.41	..	..	..	..	92	106

Table 9.   Water use, deforestation, and protected areas

Economy	Freshwater resources Cu. meters per capita 1996	Annual freshwater withdrawals					Access to safe water % of population with access 1995		Annual deforestation 1990–95		Nationally protected areas 1994[e]	
		Billion cu. m[a]	% of total resources[a]	% for agriculture[b]	% for industry[b]	% for domestic use[b]	Urban	Rural	Square kilometers	Avg. annual % change	Thousand square km	% of total land area
Albania	13,542	0.2[c]	0.4	76	18	6	..	..	0	0.0	0.3	1.2
Algeria	483	4.5	32.4	60[d]	15[d]	25[d]	..	..	234	1.2	119.2	5.0
Angola	16,577	0.5	0.3	76[d]	10[d]	14[d]	69	15	2,370	1.0	26.4	2.1
Argentina	19,705	27.6[c]	4.0	73	18	9	73	17	894	0.3	43.7	1.6
Armenia	2,411	3.8	41.8	72[d]	15[d]	13[d]	..	..	–84	–2.7	2.1	7.6
Australia	18,731	14.6[c]	4.3	33	2	65	..	..	–170	0.0	940.8	12.2
Austria	6,986	2.4	4.2	9[d]	58[d]	33[d]	..	..	0	0.0	20.8	24.2
Azerbaijan	1,068	15.8	195.1	74[d]	22[d]	4[d]	..	..	0	0.0	1.9	2.2
Bangladesh	11,153	22.5	1.7	96	1	3	42	80	88	0.8	1.0	0.7
Belarus	3,612	3.0	8.1	19	49	32	..	..	–688	–1.0	2.7	1.2
Belgium	827	9.0	107.5	4	85	11	..	..	0	0.0	0.8	..
Benin	1,829	0.2	1.5	67[d]	10[d]	23[d]	41	53	596	1.2	7.8	7.0
Bolivia	39,536	1.2	0.4	85	5	10	75	27	5,814	1.2	92.3	8.5
Brazil	32,163	36.5	0.7	59	19	22	85	31	25,544	0.5	321.9	3.8
Bulgaria	2,154	13.9	77.2	22	76	3	..	..	–6	0.0	3.7	3.3
Burkina Faso	1,640	0.4	2.2	81[d]	0[d]	19[d]	..	..	320	0.7	26.6	9.7
Burundi	561	0.1	2.8	64[d]	0[d]	36[d]	..	..	14	0.4	0.9	3.5
Cambodia	8,574	0.5	0.6	94	1	5	20	12	1,638	1.6	30.0	17.0
Cameroon	19,596	0.4	0.1	35[d]	19[d]	46[d]	71	24	1,292	0.6	20.5	4.4
Canada	95,097	45.1	1.6	12	70	18	..	..	–1,764	–0.1	823.6	9.0
Central African Republic	42,166	0.1	0.0	74[d]	5[d]	21[d]	18	18	1,282	0.4	61.1	9.8
Chad	2,269	0.2	1.2	82[d]	2[d]	16[d]	48	17	942	0.8	114.9	9.1
Chile	32,458	16.8[c]	3.6	89	5	6	..	..	292	0.4	137.3	18.3
China	2,304	460.0	16.4	87	7	6	93	89	866	0.1	580.8	6.2
Hong Kong, China	..	..	..	..	..	..	..	..	..	..	..	..
Colombia	28,571	5.3	0.5	43	16	41	88	48	2,622	0.5	93.8	9.0
Congo, Dem. Rep.	20,670	0.4	0.0	23[d]	16[d]	61[d]	..	..	..	..	99.2	4.4
Congo, Rep.	345,619	0.0	0.0	11[d]	27[d]	62[d]	..	..	416	0.2	11.8	3.4
Costa Rica	27,600	1.4[c]	1.4	89	7	4	..	..	414	3.0	6.5	12.5
Côte d'Ivoire	5,346	0.7	0.9	67[d]	11[d]	22[d]	59	81	308	0.6	19.9	6.3
Croatia	12,870	..	..	..	..	..	98	80	0	0.0	3.9	6.9
Czech Republic	5,642	2.7	4.7	2[d]	57[d]	41[d]	..	..	–2	0.0	10.7	13.8
Denmark	2,090	1.2	10.9	43	27	30	100	100	0	0.0	13.9	32.7
Dominican Republic	2,511	3.0	14.9	89	6	5	74	67	264	1.6	10.5	21.7
Ecuador	26,842	5.6	1.8	90	3	7	82	55	1,890	1.6	111.1	40.1
Egypt, Arab Rep.	47	55.1	1,967.9	85[d]	9[d]	6[d]	82	50	0	0.0	7.9	0.8
El Salvador	3,270	1.0[c]	5.3	89	4	7	78	37	38	3.3	0.1	0.2
Estonia	8,663	3.3	26.0	3[d]	92[d]	5[d]	..	..	–196	–1.0	4.1	10.4
Ethiopia	1,889	2.2	2.0	86[d]	3[d]	11[d]	90	20	624	0.5	60.2	6.0
Finland	21,463	2.2	2.0	3	85	12	100	100	166	0.1	27.4	9.0
France	3,084	37.7	21.0	15	69	16	100	100	–1,608	–1.1	56.0	10.2
Gabon	145,778	0.1	0.0	6[d]	22[d]	72[d]	80	30	910	0.5	10.5	4.1
Georgia	10,737	4.0	6.9	42[d]	37[d]	21[d]	..	..	0	0.0	1.9	2.7
Germany	1,172	46.3	48.2	20[d]	70[d]	11[d]	..	..	0	0.0	91.9	26.3
Ghana	1,729	0.3[c]	1.0	52[d]	13[d]	35[d]	70	49	1,172	1.3	11.0	4.9
Greece	4,310	5.0	11.2	63	29	8	..	..	–1,408	–2.3	2.2	1.7
Guatemala	10,615	0.7[c]	0.6	74	17	9	91	43	824	2.1	13.3	7.7
Guinea	33,436	0.7	0.3	87[d]	3[d]	10[d]	61	62	748	1.1	1.6	0.7
Guinea-Bissau	14,628	0.0	0.1	36[d]	4[d]	60[d]	18	27	104	0.4	..	..
Haiti	1,499	0.0	0.4	68	8	24	37	23	8	3.4	0.1	0.4
Honduras	9,084	1.5	2.7	91	5	4	81	53	1,022	2.3	8.6	7.7
Hungary	589	6.8	113.5	36	55	9	..	..	–88	–0.5	5.7	6.2
India	1,957	380.0[c]	20.5	93	4	3	85	79	–72	0.0	143.4	4.8
Indonesia	12,839	16.6	0.7	76	11	13	78	54	10,844	1.0	185.6	10.2
Ireland	12,962	0.8[c]	1.7	10	74	16	..	..	–140	–2.7	0.5	0.7
Israel	299	1.9	108.8	79[d]	5[d]	16[d]	..	..	0	0.0	3.1	14.9
Italy	2,778	56.2	35.3	59	27	14	..	..	–58	–0.1	22.8	7.7
Jamaica	3,259	0.3[c]	3.9	86	7	7	92	48	158	7.2	0.0	0.2
Japan	4,350	90.8	16.6	50	33	17	..	..	132	0.1	27.6	7.3
Jordan	158	0.5[c]	66.2	75[d]	3[d]	22[d]	..	..	12	2.5	2.9	3.3
Kazakhstan	4,579	37.9	50.3	79[d]	17[d]	4[d]	..	..	–1,928	–1.9	9.9	0.3
Kenya	738	2.1	10.1	76[d]	4[d]	20[d]	67	49	34	0.3	35.0	6.2
Korea, Rep.	1,451	27.6	41.8	46	35	19	..	..	130	0.2	6.9	7.0
Kyrgyz Republic	10,315	11.0	23.4	95[d]	3[d]	2[d]	..	..	0	0.0	2.8	1.5
Lao PDR	9,840	1.0	2.1	82	10	8	40	39	..	..	24.4	10.6
Latvia	6,707	0.7	4.2	14[d]	44[d]	42[d]	..	..	–250	–0.9	7.8	12.5
Lebanon	1,030	1.3[c,e]	30.7	68[d]	4[d]	28[d]	..	..	52	7.8	0.0	0.4
Lesotho	2,571	0.1	1.0	56[d]	22[d]	22[d]	14	64	0	0.0	0.1	0.2
Lithuania	4,206	4.4	28.2	3	90	7	..	..	–112	–0.6	6.3	9.8
Macedonia, FYR	..	..	..	..	..	..	..	..	2	0.0	2.2	8.5
Madagascar	24,590	16.3	4.8	99[d]	0[d]	1[d]	83	10	1,300	0.8	11.2	1.9
Malawi	1,747	0.9	5.1	86[d]	3[d]	10[d]	52	44	546	1.6	10.6	11.3
Malaysia	22,174	9.4[c]	2.1	47	30	23	100	74	4,002	2.4	14.8	4.5
Mali	6,001	1.4	2.3	97[d]	1[d]	2[d]	36	38	1,138	1.0	40.1	3.3
Mauritania	171	1.6[c]	407.5	92[d]	2[d]	6[d]	..	..	0	0.0	17.5	1.7

Note: For data comparability and coverage, see the Technical Notes. Figures in italics are for years other than those specified.

ENVIRONMENT

Economy	Freshwater resources Cu. meters per capita 1996	Annual freshwater withdrawals Billion cu. m[a]	% of total resources[a]	% for agriculture[b]	% for industry[b]	% for domestic use[b]	Access to safe water % of population with access 1995 Urban	Rural	Annual deforestation 1990–95 Square kilometers	Avg. annual % change	Nationally protected areas 1994[e] Thousand square km	% of total land area
Mauritius	1,940	0.4[c]	16.4	77[d]	7[d]	16[d]	95	100	0	0.0	0.0	2.0
Mexico	3,836	77.6[c]	21.7	86	8	6	91	62	5,080	0.9	98.5	5.1
Moldova	231	3.7	370.0	23	70	7	..	..	0	0.0	0.1	0.2
Mongolia	9,776	0.6	2.2	62	27	11	..	..	0	0.0	61.7	3.9
Morocco	1,110	10.9	36.2	92[d]	3[d]	5[d]	98	14	118	0.3	3.7	0.8
Mozambique	5,547	0.6	0.6	89	2[d]	9[d]	17	40	1,162	0.7	0.0	0.0
Namibia	3,913	0.3	4.0	68[d]	3[d]	29[d]	..	..	420	0.3	102.2	12.4
Nepal	7,714	2.7	1.6	95	1	4	64	49	548	1.1	11.1	8.1
Netherlands	644	7.8	78.1	34	61	5	100	100	0	0.0	4.3	11.5
New Zealand	89,959	2.0	0.6	44	10	46	..	..	−434	−0.6	60.7	22.9
Nicaragua	38,862	0.9[c]	0.5	54	21	25	81	27	1,508	2.5	9.0	7.4
Niger	375	0.5	14.3	82[d]	2[d]	16[d]	46	55	0	0.0	84.2	6.6
Nigeria	1,929	3.6	1.6	54[d]	15[d]	31[d]	63	26	1,214	0.9	29.7	3.3
Norway	87,651	2.0	0.5	8	72	20	..	..	−180	−0.2	55.4	18.0
Oman	456	1.2	123.2	93[d]	2[d]	5[d]	..	..	0	0.0	9.9	17.6
Pakistan	1,858	155.6[c]	62.7	96[d]	2[d]	2[d]	77	52	550	2.9	37.2	4.8
Panama	53,852	1.3	0.9	77	11	12	84	..	636	2.1	13.3	17.8
Papua New Guinea	181,993	0.1	0.0	49	22	29	84	17	1,332	0.4	0.8	0.2
Paraguay	18,971	0.4	0.5	78	7	15	..	17	3,266	2.6	15.0	3.7
Peru	1,647	6.1	15.3	72	9	19	74	24	2,168	0.3	41.8	3.3
Philippines	4,492	29.5[c]	9.1	61	21	18	..	..	2,624	3.5	6.1	2.0
Poland	1,279	12.3	24.9	11	76	13	..	..	−120	−0.1	30.7	10.1
Portugal	3,827	7.3	19.2	48	37	15	..	..	−240	−0.9	5.8	6.3
Romania	1,637	26.0	70.3	59	33	8	..	..	12	0.0	10.7	4.7
Russian Federation	29,191	117.0	2.7	23[d]	60[d]	17[d]	..	..	0	0.0	705.4	3.9
Rwanda	937	0.8	12.2	94[d]	2[d]	5[d]	..	..	4	0.2	3.3	13.3
Saudi Arabia	124	17.0[c]	709.2	90[d]	1[d]	9[d]	..	..	18	0.8	62.0	2.9
Senegal	3,093	1.4	5.2	92[d]	3[d]	5[d]	82	28	496	0.7	21.8	11.3
Sierra Leone	34,557	0.4	0.2	89[d]	4[d]	7[d]	58	21	426	3.0	0.8	1.1
Singapore	197	0.2[c]	31.7	4	51	45	100	..	0	0.0	0.0	4.9
Slovak Republic	5,765	1.8	5.8	..	..	..	..	..	−24	−0.1	10.2	21.1
Slovenia	..	..	..	..	..	..	..	..	0	0.0	1.1	5.4
South Africa	1,190	13.3	29.7	72[d]	11[d]	17[d]	..	..	150	0.2	69.7	5.7
Spain	2,809	30.8	27.9	62	26	12	..	..	0	0.0	42.5	8.5
Sri Lanka	2,361	6.3[c]	14.6	96	2	2	..	..	202	1.1	8.0	12.3
Sweden	19,903	2.9	1.7	9	55	36	..	..	24	0.0	29.8	7.3
Switzerland	6,008	1.2	2.8	4	73	23	100	100	0	0.0	7.3	18.5
Syrian Arab Republic	483	14.4	205.9	94[d]	2[d]	4[d]	92	78	52	2.2	..	..
Tajikistan	11,186	12.6	19.0	88[d]	7[d]	5[d]	..	..	0	0.0	0.9	0.6
Tanzania	2,623	1.2	1.5	89[d]	2[d]	9[d]	65	45	3,226	1.0	139.4	15.7
Thailand	1,833	31.9	29.0	90	6	4	89	72	3,294	2.6	70.2	13.7
Togo	2,719	0.1	0.8	25[d]	13[d]	62[d]	..	..	186	1.4	6.5	11.9
Trinidad and Tobago	3,932	0.2[c]	2.9	35	38	27	83	80	26	1.5	0.2	3.1
Tunisia	385	3.1	87.2	89[d]	3[d]	9[d]	..	..	30	0.5	0.4	0.3
Turkey	3,126	31.6	16.1	72[d]	11[d]	16[d]	98	85	0	0.0	10.7	1.1
Turkmenistan	217	22.8	2,280.0	91	8	1	..	..	0	0.0	11.1	2.4
Uganda	1,976	0.2	0.5	60	8	32	47	32	592	0.9	19.1	9.6
Ukraine	1,047	34.7	65.3	30	54	16	..	..	−54	−0.1	4.9	0.9
United Arab Emirates	59	2.1	1,406.7	92[d]	1[d]	7[d]	98	98	0	0.0	..	..
United Kingdom	1,208	11.8	16.6	3	77	20	100	100	−128	−0.5	51.1	21.2
United States	9,270	467.3	19.0	42[d]	45[d]	13[d]	..	..	−5,886	−0.3	1,302.1	11.4
Uruguay	18,420	0.7[c]	1.1	91	3	6	..	..	4	0.0	0.3	0.2
Uzbekistan	702	82.2	504.3	84[d]	12[d]	4[d]	..	..	−2,260	−2.7	2.4	0.6
Venezuela	38,367	4.1[c]	0.5	46	11	43	80	75	5,034	1.1	263.2	29.8
Vietnam	4,990	28.9	7.7	78	9	13	53	32	1,352	1.4	13.3	4.1
Yemen, Rep.	260	2.9	71.5	92[d]	1[d]	7[d]	88	17	0	0.0	..	..
Zambia	8,703	1.7	2.1	77[d]	7[d]	16[d]	64	27	2,644	0.8	63.6	8.6
Zimbabwe	1,254	1.2	8.7	79[d]	7[d]	14[d]	99	65	500	0.6	30.7	7.9
World	7,342 w	..	..	68 w	22 w	10 w	.. w	.. w	101,724 s	0.3 w	8,603.2 s	6.7 w
Low income	5,096	..	..	92	4	3	79	67	37,622	0.7	1,421.1	4.9
Middle income	8,241	..	..	73	18	9	..	80	75,666	0.4	3,571.0	5.2
Lower middle income	6,401	..	..	75	17	8	..	81	33,358	0.2	2,354.1	5.2
Upper middle income	15,656	..	..	66	18	16	..	..	42,308	0.5	1,216.9	5.3
Low & middle income	6,961	..	..	80	13	7	..	..	113,288	0.4	4,992.1	5.1
East Asia & Pacific	5,072	..	..	84	8	7	89	82	29,826	0.8	966.3	6.2
Europe & Central Asia	11,410	..	..	52	37	11	..	..	−5,798	−0.1	856.7	3.6
Latin America & Carib.	22,011	..	..	77	11	12	..	..	57,766	0.6	1,303.4	6.5
Middle East & N. Africa	854	..	..	84	8	8	..	..	800	0.9	290.8	3.0
South Asia	3,017	..	..	95	3	2	83	74	1,316	0.2	212.4	4.4
Sub-Saharan Africa	7,821	..	..	85	4	10	..	..	29,378	0.7	1,362.5	5.8
High income	9,378	..	..	40	45	15	..	..	−11,564	−0.2	3,611.2	11.9

a. Data refer to any year from 1980 to 1996, unless otherwise noted. b. Unless otherwise noted, sectoral withdrawal percentages are estimated for 1987. c. Data refer to estimates for years before 1980 (see World Bank 1998b). d. Data refer to years other than 1987 (see World Bank 1998b). e. Data may refer to earlier years. They are the most recent reported by the World Conservation Monitoring Center in 1994.

Table 10. Energy use and emissions

Economy	Commercial energy use					GDP per unit of energy use 1987 $ per kg		Net energy imports % of commercial energy use		Carbon dioxide emissions			
	Thousand metric tons of oil equivalent		Kg of oil equivalent per capita		Avg. annual % growth					Total Million metric tons		Per capita Metric tons	
	1980	1995	1980	1995	1980–95	1980	1995	1980	1995	1980	1995	1980	1995
Albania	2,674	1,020	1,001	314	−6.4	0.7	1.8	−14	8	4.8	1.8	1.8	0.6
Algeria	12,078	24,346	647	866	4.2	4.1	2.7	−452	−349	66.2	91.3	3.5	3.2
Angola	937	959	133	89	0.5	..	7.7	−722	−2,631	5.3	4.6	0.8	0.4
Argentina	39,716	53,016	1,413	1,525	1.9	2.8	2.5	8	−25	107.5	129.5	3.8	3.7
Armenia	1,070	1,671	346	444	−1.8	2.1	0.6	−18	85	..	3.6	..	1.0
Australia	70,372	94,200	4,790	5,215	2.2	2.4	2.8	−22	−98	202.8	289.8	13.8	16.0
Austria	23,449	26,383	3,105	3,279	1.3	4.5	5.5	67	68	52.2	59.3	6.9	7.4
Azerbaijan	15,001	13,033	2,433	1,735	−3.9	..	0.2	1	−13	..	42.6	..	5.7
Bangladesh	2,809	8,061	32	67	7.4	4.5	3.0	60	26	7.6	20.9	0.1	0.2
Belarus	2,385	23,808	247	2,305	10.3	..	0.7	−8	88	..	59.3	..	5.7
Belgium	46,100	52,378	4,682	5,167	1.6	2.9	3.2	83	78	127.2	103.8	12.9	10.2
Benin	149	107	43	20	−3.3	7.9	18.4	100	−117	0.5	0.6	0.1	0.1
Bolivia	1,599	2,939	299	396	3.2	2.9	2.0	−122	−52	4.5	10.5	0.8	1.4
Brazil	73,041	122,928	602	772	4.2	3.4	2.7	65	40	183.4	249.2	1.5	1.6
Bulgaria	28,476	22,878	3,213	2,724	−2.5	0.7	1.0	74	57	75.3	56.7	8.5	6.7
Burkina Faso	144	162	21	16	1.1	11.2	16.4	100	100	0.4	1.0	0.1	0.1
Burundi	58	144	14	23	6.4	13.9	7.7	98	97	0.1	0.2	0.0	0.0
Cambodia	393	517	60	52	2.1	..	2.6	97	96	0.3	0.5	0.0	0.0
Cameroon	774	1,556	89	117	3.3	9.7	6.1	−269	−246	3.9	4.1	0.4	0.3
Canada	192,942	233,328	7,845	7,879	1.6	1.7	2.0	−7	−50	420.9	435.7	17.1	14.7
Central African Republic	59	94	26	29	2.6	18.2	13.6	71	74	0.1	0.2	0.0	0.1
Chad	93	101	21	16	0.6	6.2	10.7	100	100	0.2	0.1	0.0	0.0
Chile	7,732	15,131	694	1,065	5.4	2.3	2.4	50	71	27.9	44.1	2.5	3.1
China	413,176	850,521	421	707	5.1	0.3	0.7	−4	−2	1,476.8	3,192.5	1.5	2.7
Hong Kong, China	5,628	13,615	1,117	2,212	6.2	5.3	5.4	100	100	16.4	31.0	3.3	5.0
Colombia	13,962	24,120	501	655	3.5	2.1	2.1	7	−125	39.8	67.5	1.4	1.8
Congo, Dem. Rep.	1,487	2,058	55	47	2.2	4.4	2.3	1	5	3.5	2.1	0.1	0.0
Congo, Rep.	262	367	157	139	2.6	5.7	6.6	−1,193	−2,361	0.4	1.3	0.2	0.5
Costa Rica	949	1,971	415	584	6.0	4.2	3.3	81	81	2.5	5.2	1.1	1.6
Côte d'Ivoire	1,435	1,362	175	97	1.2	6.7	8.4	87	68	4.7	10.4	0.6	0.7
Croatia	..	6,852	..	1,435	..	..	..	..	43	..	17.0	..	3.6
Czech Republic	45,766	39,013	4,473	3,776	−1.2	..	0.8	13	22	..	112.0	..	10.8
Denmark	19,734	20,481	3,852	3,918	0.7	4.4	5.7	95	24	62.9	54.9	12.3	10.5
Dominican Republic	2,211	3,801	388	486	4.3	2.1	1.9	98	96	6.4	11.8	1.1	1.5
Ecuador	4,209	6,343	529	553	2.6	2.3	2.2	−156	−231	13.4	22.6	1.7	2.0
Egypt, Arab Rep.	15,176	34,678	371	596	5.4	1.8	1.6	−120	−71	45.2	91.7	1.1	1.6
El Salvador	1,004	2,322	221	410	5.7	4.4	2.5	59	70	2.1	5.2	0.5	0.9
Estonia	..	5,126	..	3,454	..	..	0.8	..	39	..	16.4	..	11.1
Ethiopia	624	1,178	17	21	4.9	..	7.4	91	87	1.8	3.5	0.0	0.1
Finland	25,022	28,670	5,235	5,613	1.5	2.9	3.3	72	55	54.9	51.0	11.5	10.0
France	190,109	241,322	3,528	4,150	2.1	4.1	4.3	75	47	482.7	340.1	9.0	5.8
Gabon	831	644	1,203	587	−4.3	5.1	7.9	−994	−2,804	4.8	3.5	6.9	3.2
Georgia	4,474	1,850	882	342	−3.3	..	..	−5	74	..	7.7	..	1.4
Germany	358,995	339,287	4,585	4,156	−0.2	..	..	49	58	..	835.1	..	10.2
Ghana	1,303	1,564	121	92	2.7	3.6	4.6	57	66	2.4	4.0	0.2	0.2
Greece	15,960	23,698	1,655	2,266	3.2	3.3	2.8	77	62	51.7	76.3	5.4	7.3
Guatemala	1,443	2,191	209	206	3.6	5.0	4.4	84	73	4.5	7.2	0.6	0.7
Guinea	356	422	80	64	1.3	..	6.7	89	86	0.9	1.1	0.2	0.2
Guinea-Bissau	31	40	38	37	2.1	3.9	5.8	100	100	0.1	0.2	0.2	0.2
Haiti	241	357	45	50	0.1	6.8	3.3	92	91	0.8	0.6	0.1	0.1
Honduras	636	1,401	174	236	5.1	5.6	3.8	89	83	2.1	3.9	0.6	0.7
Hungary	28,556	25,103	2,667	2,454	−1.0	0.8	1.0	49	47	82.5	55.9	7.7	5.5
India	93,897	241,291	137	260	6.5	1.9	1.7	21	18	347.3	908.7	0.5	1.0
Indonesia	25,904	85,785	175	442	8.9	2.0	1.6	−266	−97	94.6	296.1	0.6	1.5
Ireland	8,484	11,461	2,495	3,196	2.2	3.1	4.4	78	69	25.2	32.2	7.4	9.0
Israel	8,607	16,650	2,219	3,003	5.0	3.4	3.5	98	97	21.1	46.3	5.4	8.4
Italy	138,629	161,360	2,456	2,821	1.4	4.8	5.4	86	82	371.9	410.0	6.6	7.2
Jamaica	2,164	3,003	1,015	1,191	2.7	1.3	1.2	100	100	8.4	9.1	4.0	3.6
Japan	346,567	497,231	2,968	3,964	2.8	5.5	6.1	88	80	907.4	1,126.8	7.8	9.0
Jordan	1,713	4,323	785	1,031	5.2	2.7	1.9	100	96	4.7	13.3	2.2	3.2
Kazakhstan	76,799	55,432	5,153	3,337	−3.1	..	0.3	0	−16	..	221.5	..	13.3
Kenya	1,991	2,907	120	109	3.5	3.1	3.4	95	82	6.2	6.7	0.4	0.3
Korea, Rep.	41,426	145,099	1,087	3,225	9.6	1.8	1.8	77	86	125.2	373.6	3.3	8.3
Kyrgyz Republic	1,938	2,315	534	513	5.0	..	0.5	−13	41	..	5.5	..	1.2
Lao PDR	107	184	33	40	2.6	..	9.6	−121	−20	0.2	0.3	0.1	0.1
Latvia	566	3,702	222	1,471	22.9	12.1	1.3	54	91	..	9.3	..	3.7
Lebanon	2,376	4,486	791	1,120	3.2	0.0	1.3	97	98	6.2	13.3	2.1	3.3
Lesotho	..	..	..	..	..	..	..	..	..	..	..	..	..
Lithuania	11,353	8,510	3,326	2,291	−3.2	..	0.8	98	61	..	14.8	..	4.0
Macedonia, FYR	..	2,572	..	1,308	..	..	..	..	37	..	..	..	..
Madagascar	391	484	45	36	1.6	6.9	5.8	90	83	1.6	1.1	0.2	0.1
Malawi	334	374	54	38	1.6	3.1	3.8	70	59	0.7	0.7	0.1	0.1
Malaysia	9,522	33,252	692	1,655	9.8	2.4	1.9	−58	−88	28.0	106.6	2.0	5.3
Mali	164	207	25	21	1.7	10.8	12.1	87	80	0.4	0.5	0.1	0.0
Mauritania	214	231	138	102	0.5	3.8	5.0	100	100	0.6	3.1	0.4	1.3

Note: For data comparability and coverage, see the Technical Notes. Figures in italics are for years other than those specified.

ENVIRONMENT

Economy	Commercial energy use					GDP per unit of energy use 1987 $ per kg		Net energy imports % of commercial energy use		Carbon dioxide emissions			
	Thousand metric tons of oil equivalent		Kg of oil equivalent per capita		Avg. annual % growth					Total Million metric tons		Per capita Metric tons	
	1980	1995	1980	1995	1980–95	1980	1995	1980	1995	1980	1995	1980	1995
Mauritius	339	435	351	388	2.6	3.7	6.6	94	92	0.6	1.5	0.6	1.3
Mexico	98,904	133,371	1,486	1,456	2.2	1.3	1.3	–51	–51	255.0	357.8	3.8	3.9
Moldova	..	4,177	..	963	..	..	..	..	99	..	10.8	..	2.5
Mongolia	1,943	2,576	1,168	1,045	1.8	..	..	38	15	6.8	8.5	4.1	3.4
Morocco	4,518	8,253	233	311	4.4	3.4	2.8	86	95	15.9	29.3	0.8	1.1
Mozambique	1,123	662	93	38	–1.6	1.2	3.4	–15	76	3.2	1.0	0.3	0.1
Namibia	..	..	..	..	..	..	..	..	..	..	..	..	..
Nepal	174	700	12	33	9.3	12.6	6.4	91	86	0.5	1.5	0.0	0.1
Netherlands	65,000	73,292	4,594	4,741	1.4	3.0	3.7	–11	10	152.6	135.9	10.8	8.8
New Zealand	9,190	15,409	2,952	4,290	3.9	3.3	2.7	39	19	17.6	27.4	5.6	7.6
Nicaragua	696	1,159	248	265	3.4	5.5	3.1	94	74	2.0	2.7	0.7	0.6
Niger	210	330	38	37	2.0	12.1	7.5	93	83	0.6	1.1	0.1	0.1
Nigeria	9,879	18,393	139	165	3.4	2.6	1.9	–968	–468	68.1	90.7	1.0	0.8
Norway	18,819	23,715	4,600	5,439	1.8	3.9	4.7	–196	–669	90.4	72.5	22.1	16.6
Oman	1,010	4,013	917	1,880	9.2	3.9	3.1	–1,361	–1,031	5.9	11.4	5.3	5.3
Pakistan	11,451	31,536	139	243	7.0	1.9	1.6	39	41	31.6	85.4	0.4	0.7
Panama	1,419	1,783	725	678	1.6	3.3	3.9	94	89	3.5	6.9	1.8	2.6
Papua New Guinea	705	1,000	228	232	2.4	3.9	4.6	89	–150	1.8	2.5	0.6	0.6
Paraguay	544	1,487	173	308	7.1	6.0	3.4	89	–141	1.5	3.8	0.5	0.8
Peru	8,233	10,035	476	421	0.6	0.7	0.7	–36	16	23.5	30.6	1.4	1.3
Philippines	13,357	21,542	276	307	3.6	2.5	2.0	79	72	36.5	61.2	0.8	0.9
Poland	124,557	94,472	3,501	2,448	–2.0	0.5	0.7	3	0	456.2	338.0	12.8	8.8
Portugal	10,291	19,245	1,054	1,939	4.6	3.5	2.7	86	90	27.1	51.9	2.8	5.2
Romania	63,751	44,026	2,872	1,941	–2.9	0.5	0.7	19	32	191.8	121.1	8.6	5.3
Russian Federation	764,349	604,461	5,499	4,079	–3.0	0.5	0.5	2	–54	..	1,818.0	..	12.3
Rwanda	190	211	37	33	–0.7	9.2	6.3	85	78	0.3	0.5	0.1	0.1
Saudi Arabia	35,355	82,742	3,772	4,360	5.2	2.7	1.2	–1,408	–468	130.7	254.3	14.0	13.4
Senegal	875	866	158	104	–0.3	4.2	6.1	100	95	2.8	3.1	0.5	0.4
Sierra Leone	310	326	96	72	0.5	2.7	2.2	100	100	0.6	0.4	0.2	0.1
Singapore	6,049	21,389	2,651	7,162	10.0	2.3	2.0	100	100	30.1	63.7	13.2	21.3
Slovak Republic	20,646	17,447	4,142	3,272	–1.3	..	0.9	84	72	..	38.0	..	7.1
Slovenia	4,269	5,583	2,245	2,806	0.7	..	..	62	54	..	11.7	..	5.9
South Africa	59,051	88,882	2,175	2,405	1.8	1.3	1.0	–13	–31	211.3	305.8	7.8	8.3
Spain	68,583	103,491	1,834	2,639	3.2	3.6	3.5	77	70	200.0	231.6	5.3	5.9
Sri Lanka	1,411	2,469	96	136	2.7	3.4	3.8	91	84	3.4	5.9	0.2	0.3
Sweden	40,984	50,658	4,932	5,736	1.3	3.4	3.4	61	38	71.4	44.6	8.6	5.0
Switzerland	20,814	25,142	3,294	3,571	1.7	7.4	7.5	66	56	40.9	38.9	6.5	5.5
Syrian Arab Republic	5,343	14,121	614	1,001	5.9	1.9	1.3	–78	–143	19.3	46.0	2.2	3.3
Tajikistan	1,650	3,283	416	563	8.9	..	0.5	–20	60	..	3.7	..	0.6
Tanzania	1,023	947	55	32	0.8	..	..	92	86	1.9	2.4	0.1	0.1
Thailand	12,093	52,125	259	878	11.1	2.8	2.1	96	63	40.1	175.0	0.9	2.9
Togo	195	185	75	45	0.9	6.4	7.1	99	100	0.6	0.7	0.2	0.2
Trinidad and Tobago	3,860	6,925	3,567	5,381	4.0	1.5	0.7	–240	–88	16.7	17.1	15.4	13.3
Tunisia	3,083	5,314	483	591	4.0	2.4	2.4	–99	14	9.4	15.3	1.5	1.7
Turkey	31,314	62,187	704	1,009	4.9	1.9	1.8	45	58	76.3	165.9	1.7	2.7
Turkmenistan	7,948	13,737	2,778	3,047	–6.9	..	..	–1	–137	..	28.3	..	6.3
Uganda	320	430	25	22	2.8	..	24.8	52	57	0.6	1.0	0.1	0.1
Ukraine	97,893	161,586	1,956	3,136	2.1	..	0.2	–12	50	..	438.2	..	8.5
United Arab Emirates	8,576	28,454	8,222	11,567	7.5	3.6	..	–995	–388	36.3	68.3	34.8	27.8
United Kingdom	201,168	221,911	3,571	3,786	1.0	2.8	3.5	2	–15	585.1	542.1	10.4	9.3
United States	1,801,406	2,078,265	7,928	7,905	1.3	2.1	2.6	14	20	4,515.3	5,468.6	19.9	20.8
Uruguay	2,206	2,035	757	639	0.7	3.4	4.4	89	77	5.8	5.4	2.0	1.7
Uzbekistan	4,821	46,543	302	2,043	11.6	..	0.3	4	–6	..	98.9	..	4.3
Venezuela	35,011	47,140	2,354	2,158	1.7	1.3	1.2	–280	–298	89.6	180.2	6.0	8.3
Vietnam	4,024	7,694	75	104	4.1	..	7.8	32	–79	16.8	31.7	0.3	0.4
Yemen, Rep.	1,364	2,933	160	192	5.3	..	..	100	–493	1.2	..	0.1	..
Zambia	1,685	1,302	294	145	–2.1	1.3	1.7	32	31	3.5	2.4	0.6	0.3
Zimbabwe	2,797	4,673	399	424	4.4	1.6	1.4	28	24	9.6	9.7	1.4	0.9
World	6,325,980 t	8,244,516 t	1,456 w	1,474 w	3.2 w	2.2 w	2.4 w	0 w	0 w	13,585.7	22,700.2 t	3.4 w	4.0 w
Low income	182,583	388,774	133	198	6.2	2.4	1.9	–36	–20	560.6	1,334.4	0.4	0.7
Middle income	2,335,343	3,175,039	1,064	1,139	5.5	1.0	1.0	–39	–37	4,252.9	10,231.4	2.2	3.7
Lower middle income	1,695,439	2,296,701	953	1,030	7.5	0.8	0.8	–14	–23	2,513.1	7,733.7	1.6	3.5
Upper middle income	639,904	876,338	1,536	1,579	2.1	1.7	1.5	–103	–74	1,739.8	2,497.7	4.3	4.5
Low & middle income	2,517,926	3,563,813	705	751	5.6	1.1	1.1	–38	–35	4,813.5	11,565.9	1.5	2.5
East Asia & Pacific	514,939	1,082,697	391	657	5.3	..	0.9	–12	–8	1,832.7	4,140.0	1.4	2.5
Europe & Central Asia	1,336,389	1,279,103	3,340	2,712	8.8	..	0.6	8	–10	886.9	3,722.0	..	7.9
Latin America & Carib.	319,888	463,321	893	969	2.7	2.2	2.0	–26	–39	850.5	1,219.8	2.4	2.6
Middle East & N. Africa	142,738	315,726	822	1,178	5.2	3.3	1.8	–591	–240	500.5	982.9	2.9	3.9
South Asia	110,649	286,730	123	231	6.6	2.0	1.7	23	21	392.4	1,024.1	0.4	0.8
Sub-Saharan Africa	93,323	136,236	248	238	2.0	2.1	1.9	–118	–113	350.5	477.1	0.9	0.8
High income	3,808,064	4,680,703	4,808	5,118	1.7	2.9	3.3	27	24	8,772.1	11,134.4	12.0	12.5

Table 11. Growth of the economy

	Gross domestic product		GDP implicit deflator		Agriculture value added		Industry value added		Services value added		Exports of goods and services		Gross domestic investment
Economy	1980–90	1990–97	1980–90	1990–97	1980–90	1990–97	1980–90	1990–97	1980–90	1990–97	1980–90	1990–97	1990–97
Albania	1.5	1.8	–0.4	58.1	1.9	*8.2*	2.1	*–11.0*	–0.4	7.2	..	..	*41.8*
Algeria	2.8	0.8	8.1	23.6	4.6	2.3	2.3	0.2	3.8	0.3	4.1	2.7	–4.4
Angola	*3.7*	0.7	*5.9*	1,058.9	*0.5*	*–5.7*	*6.4*	5.1	*2.2*	*–3.0*	*13.3*	5.6	8.4
Argentina	–0.3	4.5	389.0	13.0	0.9	1.0	–0.9	4.6	0.0	5.0	3.7	9.1	10.9
Armenia	3.3	*–21.2*	1.4	*860.5*	–3.9	*–0.6*	5.1	*–28.7*	4.6	*–19.7*	..	..	*–17.7*
Australia	3.4	3.7	7.2	1.2	3.3	*–1.2*	2.9	*2.2*	3.7	*4.6*	6.9	*7.6*	*5.2*
Austria	2.2	1.6	3.3	2.9	1.1	*–1.1*	1.9	*1.3*	2.4	*2.0*	4.9	*3.7*	*2.3*
Azerbaijan	..	–15.1	..	447.8	..	..	..	..	..	..	..	..	..
Bangladesh	4.3	4.5	9.5	4.7	2.7	1.7	4.9	6.8	5.7	5.8	7.7	15.7	13.4
Belarus	..	–6.5	..	564.8	..	*–9.8*	..	*–10.0*	..	*–5.6*	..	..	*–17.1*
Belgium	1.9	*1.2*	4.4	*2.8*	2.0	*3.3*	..	..	..	..	4.6	*4.5*	*–0.7*
Benin	3.2	4.5	1.1	10.6	5.1	5.1	1.3	4.1	2.4	4.1	–3.1	3.3	2.3
Bolivia	–0.2	3.8	333.1	10.9	..	..	..	..	..	..	5.2	6.1	5.8
Brazil	2.8	3.1	284.5	475.2	2.8	3.9	2.0	2.5	3.6	3.7	7.5	6.0	4.0
Bulgaria	4.0	*–3.5*	1.8	79.8	–2.1	*–3.3*	5.2	*–4.9*	4.8	*–0.6*	–3.5	0.6	*–15.4*
Burkina Faso	3.7	3.3	3.3	7.0	3.1	4.1	3.7	1.9	4.7	2.7	–0.4	*–2.4*	3.2
Burundi	4.4	–3.7	4.4	15.4	3.1	–2.8	4.5	–8.0	5.4	–3.0	3.4	–3.2	–10.4
Cambodia	..	6.2	..	37.9	..	*2.1*	..	*11.3*	..	*8.4*	..	..	..
Cameroon	3.3	0.1	5.6	6.2	2.1	3.2	5.9	–3.8	2.6	0.5	5.9	4.7	–1.7
Canada	3.4	2.1	4.4	1.4	1.5	*0.7*	2.9	1.8	..	..	6.0	9.4	1.8
Central African Republic	1.4	1.2	7.9	5.9	1.6	1.5	1.4	0.1	1.1	0.7	–1.2	0.6	–0.9
Chad	3.8	1.8	2.9	7.3	2.3	5.4	8.1	0.0	7.6	–0.5	6.5	3.7	..
Chile	4.1	*7.2*	20.9	*13.6*	5.6	*5.5*	3.7	*6.2*	4.2	*8.2*	7.0	*8.6*	*11.5*
China	10.2	11.9	5.9	11.6	5.9	4.4	11.1	16.3	13.6	9.5	11.5	15.8	14.1
Hong Kong, China	6.9	5.3	7.7	6.7	..	..	..	..	..	..	14.4	11.1	11.1
Colombia	3.7	*4.5*	..	..	2.9	*1.2*	5.0	*2.9*	3.1	*6.8*	7.5	*5.5*	*20.8*
Congo, Dem. Rep.	1.6	*–6.6*	62.9	2,746.5	2.5	*3.0*	0.9	*–15.9*	1.2	*–17.4*	9.6	*–8.8*	*–5.0*
Congo, Rep.	3.6	0.7	0.5	8.9	3.4	0.9	5.2	0.6	2.5	0.5	4.8	6.3	–0.6
Costa Rica	3.0	3.7	23.6	18.0	3.1	2.9	2.8	3.5	3.1	4.0	6.1	8.7	0.9
Côte d'Ivoire	0.9	3.0	2.7	9.3	0.3	2.6	4.4	4.2	0.0	2.8	1.9	5.0	14.4
Croatia	..	..	..	218.1	..	..	..	..	..	..	..	..	..
Czech Republic	*1.7*	*–1.0*	*1.5*	17.7	..	..	..	..	..	..	..	..	*0.9*
Denmark	2.4	2.3	5.5	1.8	3.1	*1.7*	2.9	*1.9*	..	..	4.4	*3.4*	*2.4*
Dominican Republic	3.0	5.0	21.6	11.4	0.4	3.9	3.6	5.6	3.5	5.0	1.5	9.1	8.6
Ecuador	2.0	3.1	..	..	4.4	2.7	1.2	4.1	1.8	2.6	5.4	6.6	3.0
Egypt, Arab Rep.	5.3	3.9	13.7	10.5	2.7	2.9	5.2	4.2	6.6	3.8	5.2	3.8	2.7
El Salvador	0.2	*5.8*	16.3	*10.6*	–1.1	*1.2*	0.1	*5.3*	0.7	*7.5*	–3.4	*11.6*	*11.8*
Estonia	2.1	–4.3	2.3	92.1	..	–6.5	..	–11.6	..	–1.7	..	..	–10.1
Ethiopia[a]	*2.3*	4.5	*3.6*	8.9	*1.4*	3.0	*1.8*	4.1	*3.1*	6.9	*2.0*	8.6	21.4
Finland	3.3	1.1	6.8	1.7	–0.2	*0.9*	3.3	*1.0*	..	..	2.2	*9.3*	*–5.4*
France	2.4	1.3	6.0	1.9	2.0	*0.1*	1.1	*–0.3*	3.0	*1.6*	3.7	3.5	*–2.1*
Gabon	0.6	2.6	1.9	9.8	1.2	*–2.3*	1.5	2.7	–0.3	3.3	3.0	4.7	1.2
Georgia	0.4	*–26.2*	1.9	2,279.5	..	..	..	..	..	..	..	..	..
Germany[b]	2.2	..	..	2.5	1.7	..	1.2	..	2.9	..	..	..	..
Ghana	3.0	4.3	42.1	28.0	1.0	2.7	3.3	4.3	6.4	6.1	2.5	7.1	4.7
Greece	1.8	1.8	18.0	11.3	–0.1	*3.1*	1.3	*–0.8*	..	..	7.2	*4.6*	*1.0*
Guatemala	0.8	4.1	14.6	12.3	*2.3*	2.9	*2.1*	3.9	*2.1*	4.7	–2.1	7.3	3.9
Guinea	..	4.1	..	7.9	..	4.4	..	3.0	..	4.4	..	2.4	0.3
Guinea-Bissau	4.0	3.8	56.6	45.7	4.7	5.5	2.2	2.7	3.7	1.4	–1.7	14.9	–6.5
Haiti	–0.2	–3.8	7.5	23.9	..	..	..	..	..	..	1.2	2.1	–2.9
Honduras	2.7	3.4	5.7	20.4	2.7	3.1	3.3	3.8	2.5	3.8	1.1	2.9	7.9
Hungary	1.6	–0.4	8.6	22.5	0.6	–5.0	–2.6	1.1	3.6	–3.2	4.0	*1.0*	*8.1*
India	5.8	*5.9*	8.0	*9.4*	3.1	*3.0*	7.1	*7.1*	6.7	*7.5*	5.9	*13.7*	*8.9*
Indonesia	6.1	7.5	8.5	8.5	3.4	*2.8*	6.9	*10.2*	7.0	*7.5*	2.9	9.2	10.0
Ireland	3.2	6.5	6.6	1.8	..	..	..	..	..	..	9.0	11.8	*–2.4*
Israel	3.5	*6.4*	101.5	*12.2*	..	..	..	..	..	..	5.5	9.5	*11.5*
Italy	2.4	1.1	10.0	4.5	0.1	*1.4*	..	..	..	..	4.1	*8.1*	*–2.2*
Jamaica	2.0	*0.8*	18.6	*36.1*	0.6	*6.7*	2.4	*–0.2*	1.9	*0.8*	5.4	*0.4*	*4.9*
Japan	4.0	1.4	1.7	0.6	1.3	*–2.0*	4.2	*0.2*	3.9	*2.0*	4.5	*3.9*	*0.2*
Jordan	2.6	7.2	4.3	3.9	6.8	–2.8	1.7	10.0	2.1	6.4	5.9	9.3	10.3
Kazakhstan	..	–10.5	..	604.9	..	..	..	..	..	..	..	..	..
Kenya	4.2	2.0	9.1	15.4	3.3	0.8	3.9	2.0	4.9	3.6	4.3	2.3	3.5
Korea, Rep.	9.5	7.2	6.1	5.3	2.8	2.1	12.1	7.5	9.0	7.8	12.0	15.7	6.3
Kyrgyz Republic	..	*–12.3*	..	256.2	..	..	..	..	..	..	..	..	..
Lao PDR	*3.7*	6.7	*37.5*	12.2	..	..	..	..	..	..	..	..	..
Latvia	3.4	*–10.7*	0.0	*112.0*	2.3	*–13.0*	4.3	*–20.2*	3.0	*–2.0*	..	..	*–32.0*
Lebanon	78.2	8.3	1.6	27.7	..	..	..	..	..	..	..	..	..
Lesotho	4.3	7.6	13.8	8.0	2.2	4.0	7.1	*11.8*	5.2	*6.0*	4.1	9.9	12.7
Lithuania	..	–4.5	..	139.9	..	..	..	..	..	..	..	..	..
Macedonia, FYR	..	..	..	149.4	..	..	..	..	..	..	..	..	..
Madagascar	1.1	0.8	17.1	23.6	2.5	1.7	0.9	1.1	0.3	1.0	–1.7	4.0	–0.9
Malawi	2.3	3.6	14.4	33.3	2.0	4.7	2.9	1.9	3.5	2.7	2.5	3.3	–7.9
Malaysia	5.2	8.7	1.7	4.4	3.8	*1.9*	7.2	*11.2*	4.2	*8.6*	10.9	14.0	15.1
Mali	2.9	3.3	3.6	10.0	3.3	3.4	4.3	7.0	2.1	1.8	5.2	6.4	6.3
Mauritania	1.7	4.3	8.4	5.7	1.7	5.0	4.9	3.7	0.4	4.0	3.6	0.1	*4.0*

Note: For data comparability and coverage, see the Technical Notes. Figures in italics are for years other than those specified.

	Average annual % growth												
	Gross domestic product		GDP implicit deflator		Agriculture value added		Industry value added		Services value added		Exports of goods and services		Gross domestic investment
Economy	1980–90	1990–97	1980–90	1990–97	1980–90	1990–97	1980–90	1990–97	1980–90	1990–97	1980–90	1990–97	1990–97
Mauritius	6.2	5.1	9.5	6.2	2.9	0.3	10.3	5.5	5.4	6.3	10.4	5.5	0.4
Mexico	1.1	1.8	71.5	18.5	0.8	1.2	1.1	1.8	1.2	1.9	7.0	9.8	0.1
Moldova	..	..	..	307.7	..	..	..	..	..	..	..	..	..
Mongolia	4.9	-0.6	-1.6	89.3	0.6	7.6	6.0	-5.1	5.5	-2.1	..	..	..
Morocco	4.2	2.0	7.1	3.7	6.7	-0.7	3.0	2.1	4.2	2.9	6.8	6.4	-0.1
Mozambique	1.7	6.9	38.3	44.2	5.5	4.6	-5.2	2.3	13.6	10.4	0.7	9.3	3.6
Namibia	1.3	4.1	13.2	9.7	0.0	4.3	1.1	2.9	-0.2	4.2	1.2	4.4	4.1
Nepal	4.6	5.0	11.1	9.6	4.0	2.2	6.0	7.7	4.8	6.6	5.6	24.1	5.2
Netherlands	2.3	2.3	1.6	2.0	3.4	3.7	1.6	1.2	2.6	2.3	4.5	4.2	-0.5
New Zealand	1.7	3.2	10.8	1.8	3.9	0.9	1.1	3.8	1.8	3.4	4.0	6.2	8.1
Nicaragua	-2.6	5.7	..	..	-5.8	8.7	2.1	-4.8	-1.6	2.0	-7.8	10.6	9.8
Niger	0.1	1.5	1.9	7.2	1.7	2.3	-1.7	1.3	-0.3	0.9	-2.9	-0.8	3.0
Nigeria	1.6	2.7	16.7	35.1	3.3	2.6	-1.1	0.5	3.8	4.8	-0.3	3.6	0.7
Norway	2.8	3.9	5.6	1.9	-0.2	4.4	3.3	5.2	2.7	2.8	5.2	5.4	..
Oman	8.3	6.0	-3.6	-2.9	7.9	..	10.3	..	6.0	..	..	..	..
Pakistan	6.3	4.4	6.7	11.4	4.3	3.8	7.3	5.5	6.8	5.0	8.1	4.4	3.8
Panama	0.5	4.8	1.9	2.8	2.5	2.2	-1.3	7.9	0.6	4.5	0.4	0.1	15.0
Papua New Guinea	1.9	7.6	5.3	6.9	1.8	4.8	1.9	13.6	2.0	4.0	3.3	9.8	3.7
Paraguay	2.5	3.1	24.4	16.1	3.6	2.9	-0.3	2.4	3.4	3.5	11.5	7.8	3.8
Peru	-0.3	6.0	..	..	..	5.6	..	6.5	..	5.8	-1.7	9.1	12.9
Philippines	1.0	3.3	14.9	8.7	1.0	1.9	-0.9	3.7	2.8	3.7	3.5	11.5	5.8
Poland	1.8	3.9	53.8	29.5	-0.7	-1.6	-1.3	4.7	2.8	3.0	4.5	11.5	8.7
Portugal	2.9	1.7	18.1	6.3	..	..	..	..	..	..	8.6	6.0	..
Romania	0.5	0.0	2.5	124.5	..	-0.4	..	-2.1	..	-2.8	..	..	-7.5
Russian Federation	2.8	-9.0	2.4	394.0	..	-8.2	..	-11.0	..	-8.4	..	-13.2	..
Rwanda	2.5	-6.3	4.0	20.4	0.5	-5.8	2.5	-11.2	5.5	-6.9	3.4	-15.3	10.6
Saudi Arabia	-1.2	1.7	-4.9	0.8	13.4	..	-2.3	..	-1.2	..	..	..	..
Senegal	3.1	2.4	6.5	6.9	3.3	2.2	4.1	3.7	2.8	2.1	3.8	1.0	6.9
Sierra Leone	0.6	-3.3	64.0	37.7	3.1	-1.5	1.7	-6.4	-2.7	-3.9	0.2	-18.4	-12.8
Singapore	6.6	8.5	2.2	2.9	-6.2	1.8	5.4	9.1	7.5	8.4	10.8	13.3	9.8
Slovak Republic	2.0	0.4	1.8	12.7	1.6	1.9	2.0	-7.2	0.8	6.4	..	14.1	-1.0
Slovenia	..	..	..	32.1	..	..	..	..	..	..	..	..	..
South Africa	1.2	1.5	14.9	10.1	2.9	2.5	0.0	0.8	2.3	1.8	1.9	5.2	13.0
Spain	3.2	1.6	9.3	4.6	..	-4.8	..	..	..	..	5.7	10.1	-1.5
Sri Lanka	4.2	4.9	11.0	9.9	2.2	1.5	4.6	6.5	4.7	6.1	6.8	8.4	6.4
Sweden	2.3	0.9	7.4	2.6	1.5	-1.9	2.8	-0.7	..	..	4.3	7.8	..
Switzerland	2.2	-0.1	3.7	2.3	..	..	..	..	..	..	3.4	1.8	..
Syrian Arab Republic	1.5	6.9	15.3	8.7	-0.6	..	6.6	..	0.4	..	3.6	..	..
Tajikistan	..	-16.4	..	394.3	..	..	..	..	..	..	..	..	..
Tanzania[c]	..	..	..	24.9	..	..	..	..	..	..	..	..	..
Thailand	7.6	7.5	3.9	5.0	4.0	3.6	9.9	10.3	7.3	7.9	14.0	12.8	10.3
Togo	1.6	2.2	4.9	8.6	5.2	14.7	1.1	2.0	-0.3	-20.6	0.1	1.3	-4.4
Trinidad and Tobago	-2.5	1.5	2.4	6.3	-5.8	1.7	-5.5	1.3	-3.3	1.1	8.9	-4.9	9.0
Tunisia	3.3	4.8	7.4	4.6	2.8	-0.1	3.1	4.3	3.6	5.2	5.6	5.0	1.7
Turkey	5.3	3.6	45.2	78.2	1.3	1.2	7.8	4.6	4.4	3.7	16.9	10.9	4.0
Turkmenistan	..	-9.6	..	1,074.2	..	..	..	..	..	..	..	..	..
Uganda	3.1	7.2	113.8	17.5	2.3	3.8	6.0	13.0	3.0	8.5	2.3	16.7	9.9
Ukraine	..	-13.6	..	800.5	..	..	..	..	..	..	..	..	..
United Arab Emirates	-2.0	3.4	0.7	1.8	9.6	..	-4.2	..	3.4	..	0.0	..	..
United Kingdom	3.2	1.9	5.7	3.1	..	..	..	..	..	..	3.9	5.3	..
United States	2.9	2.5	4.2	2.4	4.0	..	2.8	..	2.9	..	4.7	7.0	..
Uruguay	0.4	3.7	..	..	0.1	4.4	-0.2	0.4	0.9	5.6	4.3	5.9	6.0
Uzbekistan	..	-3.5	..	546.5	..	-1.8	..	-6.0	..	-2.3	..	..	-7.6
Venezuela	1.1	1.9	19.3	46.7	3.0	1.1	1.6	3.1	0.5	1.0	2.8	5.3	2.8
Vietnam	4.6	8.6	210.8	19.9	4.3	5.2	..	..	..	..	..	..	..
Yemen, Rep.	..	..	..	26.3	..	..	..	..	..	..	..	..	..
Zambia	0.8	-0.5	42.2	75.2	3.6	0.8	1.0	-2.6	0.1	1.1	-3.4	-1.9	2.6
Zimbabwe	3.4	2.0	11.6	22.6	3.1	3.8	3.2	-0.8	3.0	2.7	4.3	10.5	5.8
World	3.1 w	2.3 w			2.8 w	1.8 w	3.3 w	1.6 w	3.3 w	2.3 w	5.2 w	7.0 w	.. w
Low income	4.3	4.2			2.6	3.5	5.3	5.1	5.0	5.6	3.3	7.8	7.8
Middle income	2.8	2.5			3.5	2.3	..	..	3.2	4.8	..	..	7.2
Lower middle income	3.7	2.2			..	2.8	..	..	..	..	..	..	..
Upper middle income	1.7	2.9			2.4	1.6	1.2	3.0	2.0	3.5	6.0	8.9	5.9
Low & middle income	3.0	2.8			3.2	2.9	4.3	..	3.5	4.9	..	..	7.2
East Asia & Pacific	7.8	9.9			4.7	3.8	8.9	14.5	8.9	8.4	8.8	13.5	12.7
Europe & Central Asia	2.9	-5.4			..	..	..	..	..	..	..	..	..
Latin America & Carib.	1.8	3.3			1.9	2.6	1.5	2.8	2.0	3.8	5.3	7.3	5.9
Middle East & N. Africa	0.4	2.6			4.6	3.2	1.3	..	1.1	..	..	..	..
South Asia	5.7	5.7			3.2	2.9	6.9	6.9	6.6	7.1	6.4	12.4	8.6
Sub-Saharan Africa	1.7	2.1			1.7	4.6	1.1	1.4	2.4	2.4	2.2	4.7	7.2
High income	3.2	2.1			2.2	0.8	3.2	0.7	3.3	1.9	5.1	6.7	..

a. Data prior to 1992 include Eritrea. b. Data prior to 1990 refer to the Federal Republic of Germany before unification. c. Data cover mainland Tanzania only.

Table 12. Structure of output

Economy	Gross domestic product Millions of dollars		Value added as a % of GDP							
			Agriculture		Industry		Manufacturing		Services	
	1980	1997	1980	1997	1980	1997	1980	1997	1980	1997
Albania	..	2,276	34	55	45	21	..	..	21	23
Algeria	42,345	45,997	10	12	54	51	9	9	36	37
Angola	..	7,396	..	7	..	68	..	6	..	25
Argentina	76,962	322,730	6	6	41	31	29	..	52	63
Armenia	..	1,401	18	44	58	35	..	25	25	20
Australia	160,109	391,045	5	4	36	28	19	15	58	68
Austria	78,539	206,239	4	2	36	31	25	20	60	68
Azerbaijan	..	4,399	..	22	..	18	..	18	..	60
Bangladesh	12,950	32,838	50	30	16	17	11	9	34	53
Belarus	..	22,462	..	16	..	41	..	35	..	43
Belgium	118,915	264,400	2	1	..	..	22	19	..	..
Benin	1,405	2,137	35	38	12	14	8	8	52	48
Bolivia	2,500	8,108	..	13	..	27	..	3	..	60
Brazil	234,526	786,466	11	14	44	36	33	23	45	50
Bulgaria	20,040	9,484	14	10	54	33	..	..	32	57
Burkina Faso	1,709	2,441	33	35	22	25	16	19	45	40
Burundi	920	1,137	62	58	13	18	7	18	25	24
Cambodia	..	3,095	..	50	..	15	..	5	..	35
Cameroon	6,741	9,115	29	41	23	20	9	10	48	39
Canada	263,193	603,085	..	..	..	..	..	..	..	..
Central African Republic	797	954	40	54	20	18	7	9	40	28
Chad	1,033	1,603	45	39	9	15	..	12	46	46
Chile	27,572	74,292	7	..	37	..	21	..	55	..
China	201,688	825,020	30	20	49	51	41	40	21	29
Hong Kong, China	28,495	171,401	1	0	32	15	24	7	67	84
Colombia	33,397	85,202	19	16	32	20	23	16	49	64
Congo, Dem. Rep.	14,922	6,904	25	64	33	13	14	5	42	23
Congo, Rep.	1,706	2,298	12	10	47	57	7	6	42	33
Costa Rica	4,815	9,350	18	15	27	24	19	17	55	61
Côte d'Ivoire	10,175	10,251	26	27	20	21	13	18	54	51
Croatia	..	19,081	..	12	..	25	..	20	..	62
Czech Republic	29,123	54,890	7	..	63	..	..	..	30	..
Denmark	66,322	161,107	..	..	..	..	..	..	..	..
Dominican Republic	6,631	14,936	20	13	28	32	15	17	52	55
Ecuador	11,733	18,887	12	12	38	37	18	22	50	51
Egypt, Arab Rep.	22,913	75,482	18	16	37	32	12	25	45	53
El Salvador	3,574	10,416	38	13	22	27	16	21	40	60
Estonia	..	4,617	..	7	..	28	..	16	..	65
Ethiopia[a]	5,179	6,330	56	56	12	7	8	..	32	37
Finland	51,306	116,170	..	..	..	..	..	..	..	..
France	664,595	1,396,540	4	2	34	26	24	19	62	71
Gabon	4,279	5,435	7	7	60	52	5	5	33	42
Georgia	..	3,028	24	35	36	35	28	20	40	29
Germany	..	2,100,110	..	1	..	..	..	24	..	..
Ghana	4,445	6,762	58	47	12	17	8	9	30	36
Greece	48,613	119,111	..	..	..	..	..	..	..	..
Guatemala	7,879	17,784	..	24	..	19	..	14	..	57
Guinea	..	3,998	..	26	..	36	..	5	..	38
Guinea-Bissau	111	265	42	54	19	11	..	7	39	35
Haiti	1,462	2,360	..	42	..	14	..	..	..	44
Honduras	2,566	4,490	24	20	24	28	15	16	52	52
Hungary	22,163	44,845	..	7	..	32	..	24	..	61
India	172,321	359,812	38	27	26	30	18	19	36	43
Indonesia	78,013	214,593	24	16	42	42	13	25	34	41
Ireland	20,080	72,037	..	..	..	..	..	..	..	..
Israel	22,598	91,965	..	..	..	..	..	..	..	..
Italy	449,913	1,145,370	6	3	..	..	28	21	..	..
Jamaica	2,652	4,051	8	8	38	36	17	17	54	55
Japan	1,059,254	4,201,636	4	2	42	38	29	25	54	60
Jordan	3,962	7,927	8	5	28	30	13	16	64	65
Kazakhstan	..	21,039	..	13	..	30	..	6	..	57
Kenya	7,265	9,899	33	29	21	17	13	11	47	54
Korea, Rep.	62,803	442,543	15	6	40	43	28	26	45	51
Kyrgyz Republic	..	1,754	..	52	..	19	..	8	..	29
Lao PDR	..	1,753	..	52	..	21	..	15	..	28
Latvia	..	5,024	12	9	51	33	46	22	37	58
Lebanon	..	14,962	..	12	..	27	..	17	..	61
Lesotho	369	950	24	14	29	41	7	16	47	45
Lithuania	..	9,265	..	13	..	32	..	20	..	55
Macedonia, FYR	..	2,061	..	11	..	25	..	..	..	64
Madagascar	4,042	3,552	30	32	16	13	..	12	54	55
Malawi	1,238	2,424	44	36	23	18	14	14	34	46
Malaysia	24,488	97,523	22	13	38	46	21	34	40	41
Mali	1,686	2,532	48	49	13	17	7	7	38	34
Mauritania	709	1,068	30	25	26	29	..	10	44	46

Note: For data comparability and coverage, see the Technical Notes. Figures in italics are for years other than those specified.

| Economy | Gross domestic product Millions of dollars | | Value added as a % of GDP | | | | | | | |
| | | | Agriculture | | Industry | | Manufacturing | | Services | |
	1980	1997	1980	1997	1980	1997	1980	1997	1980	1997
Mauritius	1,132	4,151	12	10	26	32	15	23	62	58
Mexico	223,505	334,766	8	5	33	26	22	20	59	68
Moldova	..	1,803	..	50	..	23	..	8	..	27
Mongolia	..	862	15	31	33	35	..	..	52	34
Morocco	18,821	33,258	18	20	31	31	17	17	51	49
Mozambique	2,028	1,944	37	39	35	23	..	..	27	38
Namibia	2,172	3,453	24	14	39	34	9	12	37	52
Nepal	1,946	4,899	62	43	12	22	4	10	26	35
Netherlands	171,861	360,472	3	3	32	27	18	18	64	70
New Zealand	22,395	64,999	11	..	31	..	22	..	58	..
Nicaragua	2,144	1,971	23	34	31	22	26	16	45	44
Niger	2,508	1,858	43	38	23	18	4	7	34	44
Nigeria	64,202	36,540	21	45	46	24	8	8	34	32
Norway	63,419	153,403	4	2	35	30	15	12	61	68
Oman	5,989	13,438	3	..	69	..	1	..	28	..
Pakistan	23,690	64,360	30	26	25	25	16	17	46	50
Panama	3,810	8,244	10	8	21	18	12	9	69	73
Papua New Guinea	2,548	5,165	33	26	27	40	10	8	40	33
Paraguay	4,579	10,180	29	23	27	22	16	14	44	55
Peru	20,661	62,431	10	7	42	37	20	23	48	56
Philippines	32,500	83,125	25	20	39	32	26	22	36	48
Poland	57,068	135,659	..	6	..	39	..	..	..	55
Portugal	28,729	97,357	..	..	..	..	..	..	..	..
Romania	..	35,204	..	21	..	40	..	..	..	39
Russian Federation	..	440,562	9	7	54	39	..	..	37	54
Rwanda	1,163	1,771	50	39	23	24	17	18	27	37
Saudi Arabia	156,487	125,266	1	..	81	..	5	..	18	..
Senegal	3,016	4,542	16	18	21	18	13	12	63	63
Sierra Leone	1,199	940	33	44	21	24	5	6	47	32
Singapore	11,718	96,319	1	0	38	36	29	26	61	64
Slovak Republic	..	19,565	..	5	..	31	..	..	..	64
Slovenia	..	17,905	..	5	..	38	..	28	..	57
South Africa	78,744	129,094	7	5	50	39	23	24	43	57
Spain	211,542	531,419	..	3	..	..	..	..	..	..
Sri Lanka	4,024	15,128	28	22	30	26	18	17	43	52
Sweden	125,557	227,751	..	..	..	..	..	..	..	..
Switzerland	102,719	293,400	..	..	..	..	..	..	..	..
Syrian Arab Republic	13,062	17,115	20	..	23	..	..	..	56	..
Tajikistan	..	1,990	..	..	..	..	..	..	..	..
Tanzania[b]	..	6,707	..	48	..	21	..	7	..	31
Thailand	32,354	157,263	23	11	29	40	22	29	48	50
Togo	1,136	1,279	27	40	25	22	8	9	48	38
Trinidad and Tobago	6,236	5,894	2	2	60	43	9	8	38	55
Tunisia	8,742	19,069	14	14	31	28	12	18	55	58
Turkey	68,790	181,464	26	17	22	28	14	18	51	55
Turkmenistan	..	4,399	..	..	..	..	..	..	..	..
Uganda	1,245	6,555	72	44	4	17	4	8	23	39
Ukraine	..	44,007	..	13	..	39	..	..	..	48
United Arab Emirates	29,629	45,147	1	..	77	..	4	..	22	..
United Kingdom	537,383	1,271,710	..	..	..	..	..	..	..	..
United States	2,709,000	7,745,705	3	..	33	..	22	..	64	..
Uruguay	10,132	18,180	14	9	34	26	26	18	53	65
Uzbekistan	..	23,857	..	26	..	27	..	8	..	47
Venezuela	69,256	67,316	5	4	46	47	16	18	49	49
Vietnam	..	24,893	..	27	..	31	..	..	..	42
Yemen, Rep.	..	5,442	..	18	..	49	..	11	..	34
Zambia	3,884	4,051	14	16	41	41	18	30	44	43
Zimbabwe	6,679	8,512	16	28	29	32	22	19	55	41
World	10,674,160 t	28,157,012 t	7 w	.. w	38 w	.. w	24 w	.. w	55 w	.. w
Low income	448,604	717,238	35	31	26	27	15	16	38	42
Middle income	2,579,064	5,186,786	15	12	45	38	..	..	40	50
Lower middle income	..	2,658,209	18	14	45	40	..	..	37	46
Upper middle income	1,188,996	2,503,695	9	10	46	34	23	..	45	56
Low & middle income	3,017,430	5,909,683	18	16	42	36	22	..	40	48
East Asia & Pacific	410,579	1,572,402	28	19	44	45	32	33	28	36
Europe & Central Asia	..	1,091,827	..	11	..	36	..	..	..	53
Latin America & Carib.	786,542	1,875,869	10	10	40	33	27	21	50	57
Middle East & N. Africa	460,257	..	12	..	48	..	9	..	40	..
South Asia	219,283	483,896	38	27	25	28	17	18	37	44
Sub-Saharan Africa	267,180	320,252	22	25	36	30	14	16	42	45
High income	7,816,706	22,321,973	3	..	36	..	24	..	61	..

a. Data prior to 1992 include Eritrea. b. Data cover mainland Tanzania only.

Table 13. Structure of demand

	% of GDP											
	Private consumption		General government consumption		Gross domestic investment		Gross domestic saving		Exports of goods and services		Resource balance	
Economy	1980	1997	1980	1997	1980	1997	1980	1997	1980	1997	1980	1997
Albania	56	94	9	13	35	21	35	–7	23	13	0	–27
Algeria	43	54	14	10	39	27	43	36	34	33	4	9
Angola	. .	5	. .	43	. .	24	. .	53	. .	74	. .	29
Argentina	76	82	a	a	25	19	24	18	5	9	–1	–1
Armenia	47	115	16	13	29	10	37	–28	. .	24	9	–38
Australia	59	61	18	18	25	21	24	21	16	21	–2	0
Austria	55	56	18	20	29	25	27	24	36	39	–2	–1
Azerbaijan	. .	83	. .	8	. .	28	. .	10	. .	19	. .	–19
Bangladesh	92	77	6	14	15	17	2	10	6	16	–13	–8
Belarus	. .	59	. .	23	. .	25	. .	17	. .	44	. .	–7
Belgium	63	62	18	15	22	18	19	23	62	73	–3	5
Benin	96	80	9	10	15	18	–5	10	23	25	–20	–8
Bolivia	100	75	0	14	0	18	0	11	0	19	0	–7
Brazil	70	66	9	16	23	20	21	18	9	6	–2	–2
Bulgaria	55	71	6	12	34	14	39	17	36	65	5	3
Burkina Faso	95	78	10	12	17	25	–6	9	10	13	–23	–16
Burundi	91	91	9	10	14	5	–1	0	9	8	–14	–5
Cambodia	. .	87	. .	8	. .	21	. .	5	. .	26	. .	–16
Cameroon	70	77	10	8	21	10	20	14	27	27	–1	4
Canada	55	60	19	20	24	18	25	21	28	38	2	2
Central African Republic	94	84	15	9	7	9	–9	7	25	21	–16	–2
Chad	100	92	4	7	3	19	–9	1	17	17	–12	–18
Chile	71	65	12	9	21	28	17	26	23	27	–4	–2
China	51	49	15	11	35	35	35	40	6	20	0	5
Hong Kong, China	60	61	6	9	35	34	34	31	90	132	–1	–4
Colombia	70	72	10	10	19	21	20	17	16	17	1	–3
Congo, Dem. Rep.	82	88	8	4	10	6	10	8	16	35	0	2
Congo, Rep.	47	46	18	19	36	26	36	35	60	77	0	9
Costa Rica	66	64	18	13	27	24	16	23	26	46	–10	–1
Côte d'Ivoire	63	66	17	12	27	16	20	23	35	47	–6	7
Croatia	. .	66	. .	30	. .	15	. .	3	. .	42	. .	–11
Czech Republic	. .	51	. .	22	31	35	. .	27	. .	55	. .	–8
Denmark	56	54	27	25	19	17	17	21	33	34	–1	4
Dominican Republic	77	70	8	12	25	23	15	18	19	27	–10	–5
Ecuador	60	64	15	14	26	18	26	22	25	32	0	4
Egypt, Arab Rep.	69	78	16	10	28	18	15	12	31	21	–12	–6
El Salvador	72	87	14	9	13	16	14	3	34	21	1	–12
Estonia	. .	61	. .	25	. .	27	. .	14	. .	73	. .	–13
Ethiopiab	83	79	14	12	9	20	3	10	11	16	–6	–11
Finland	54	53	18	22	29	16	28	25	33	38	–1	8
France	59	60	18	19	24	18	23	21	22	23	–1	2
Gabon	26	48	13	11	28	21	61	42	65	59	33	21
Georgia	56	100	13	7	29	4	31	–7	. .	17	2	–11
Germany	. .	57	. .	20	. .	23	. .	23	. .	24	. .	1
Ghana	84	82	11	10	6	16	5	7	8	25	–1	–9
Greece	71	. .	12	14	24	. .	18	. .	16	16	–6	–10
Guatemala	79	84	8	5	16	14	13	11	22	18	–3	–4
Guinea	. .	80	. .	8	. .	14	. .	12	. .	21	. .	–2
Guinea-Bissau	73	89	28	7	28	19	–1	4	13	23	–29	–15
Haiti	82	. .	10	9	17	. .	8	. .	22	8	–9	–20
Honduras	70	63	13	15	25	32	17	22	36	37	–8	–10
Hungary	61	64	10	10	31	27	29	26	39	39	–2	–1
India	73	68	10	10	21	25	17	22	7	12	–4	–3
Indonesia	51	63	11	7	24	31	38	31	34	28	14	–1
Ireland	. .	55	19	15	. .	15	. .	30	48	75	–13	15
Israel	50	58	39	29	22	24	11	13	40	29	–11	–10
Italy	61	61	15	16	27	18	24	22	22	28	–3	4
Jamaica	64	71	20	16	16	27	16	14	51	55	0	–13
Japan	59	60	10	10	32	29	31	30	14	9	–1	1
Jordan	79	67	29	22	37	33	–8	11	40	49	–44	–22
Kazakhstan	. .	68	. .	12	. .	23	. .	20	. .	31	. .	–3
Kenya	62	70	20	17	29	19	18	13	28	32	–11	–6
Korea, Rep.	64	55	12	11	32	35	24	34	34	38	–7	–1
Kyrgyz Republic	. .	87	. .	17	. .	19	. .	–4	. .	31	. .	–23
Lao PDR	. .	. .	. .	. .	. .	31	. .	12	. .	23	. .	–19
Latvia	59	70	8	20	26	19	33	10	. .	46	7	–9
Lebanon	. .	101	. .	16	. .	27	. .	–17	. .	10	. .	–43
Lesotho	133	85	26	17	43	86	–59	–2	20	25	–102	–91
Lithuania	. .	70	. .	18	. .	21	. .	11	. .	52	. .	–10
Macedonia, FYR	. .	72	. .	18	. .	17	. .	10	. .	41	. .	–7
Madagascar	89	88	12	7	15	12	–1	5	13	22	–16	–8
Malawi	70	79	19	16	25	13	11	5	25	25	–14	–7
Malaysia	51	45	17	11	30	43	33	44	58	90	3	1
Mali	92	74	10	12	16	26	–2	14	16	24	–18	–11
Mauritania	68	74	25	13	36	19	7	13	37	47	–29	–6

Note: For data comparability and coverage, see the Technical Notes. Figures in italics are for years other than those specified.

	% of GDP											
	Private consumption		General government consumption		Gross domestic investment		Gross domestic saving		Exports of goods and services		Resource balance	
Economy	1980	1997	1980	1997	1980	1997	1980	1997	1980	1997	1980	1997
Mauritius	75	68	14	9	21	26	10	22	51	61	−10	−4
Mexico	65	66	10	10	27	21	25	23	11	22	−2	2
Moldova	..	66	..	20	..	28	..	14	..	52	..	−14
Mongolia	44	64	29	16	63	22	27	20	21	44	−36	−2
Morocco	68	68	18	16	24	21	14	16	17	25	−10	−5
Mozambique	103	63	21	15	0	45	−24	23	21	26	−24	−23
Namibia	44	59	17	31	29	20	39	9	76	49	10	−11
Nepal	82	83	7	9	18	22	11	8	12	24	−7	−14
Netherlands	61	60	17	14	22	19	22	26	51	53	0	6
New Zealand	62	63	18	14	21	22	20	23	30	30	−1	1
Nicaragua	82	84	20	13	17	28	−2	3	24	41	−19	−25
Niger	75	85	10	13	28	10	15	2	25	16	−14	−8
Nigeria	56	65	12	11	21	18	31	24	29	15	10	5
Norway	50	..	19	21	25	..	31	..	43	41	6	9
Oman	28	..	25	..	22	..	47	..	63	..	25	..
Pakistan	83	73	10	12	18	19	7	14	12	17	−12	−4
Panama	45	53	18	15	28	29	38	32	98	94	9	3
Papua New Guinea	61	36	24	24	25	27	15	40	43	57	−10	13
Paraguay	76	67	6	13	32	23	18	20	15	22	−13	−2
Peru	57	68	11	11	29	25	32	21	22	13	3	−4
Philippines	67	72	9	13	29	25	24	16	24	46	−5	−9
Poland	67	64	9	18	26	22	23	18	28	26	−3	−4
Portugal	..	..	13	18	33c	25c	..	..	25	33	−13	−7
Romania	60	70	5	11	40	25	35	19	35	27	−5	−7
Russian Federation	62	63	15	11	22	22	22	25	..	23	0	3
Rwanda	83	90	12	9	16	19	4	0	14	6	−12	−19
Saudi Arabia	22	42	16	26	22	20	62	32	71	42	41	12
Senegal	78	77	22	10	15	19	0	13	28	33	−16	−5
Sierra Leone	79	99	21	11	17	9	0	−10	28	12	−17	−19
Singapore	53	39	10	9	46	37	38	51	215	187	−9	14
Slovak Republic	..	49	..	24	..	38	..	27	..	57	..	−11
Slovenia	..	57	..	20	..	23	..	22	..	55	..	−1
South Africa	50	62	13	21	28	16	36	17	36	28	8	1
Spain	66	62	13	17	23	21	21	21	16	24	−2	0
Sri Lanka	80	72	9	11	34	27	11	18	32	33	−23	−9
Sweden	51	52	29	26	21	15	19	22	29	40	−2	7
Switzerland	..	..	14	15	27c	..	..	..	36	36	−3	4
Syrian Arab Republic	67	..	23	..	28	..	10	..	18	..	−17	..
Tajikistan	..	71	..	11	..	17	..	18	..	114	..	1
Tanzania[d]	..	83	..	13	..	21	..	3	..	22	..	−15
Thailand	65	55	12	10	29	41	23	35	24	39	−6	−6
Togo	54	78	22	11	28	15	23	11	51	34	−5	−4
Trinidad and Tobago	46	59	12	12	31	16	42	29	50	53	11	14
Tunisia	62	61	14	16	29	24	24	23	40	42	−5	−1
Turkey	77	71	12	12	18	24	11	18	5	22	−7	−6
Turkmenistan	..	..	..	..	..	..	..	..	..	..	..	..
Uganda	..	82	11	10	..	15	..	8	19	11	−7	−7
Ukraine	..	58	..	22	..	23	..	20	..	46	..	−2
United Arab Emirates	17	..	11	..	28	..	72	..	78	..	43	..
United Kingdom	59	..	22	21	17	..	19	..	27	28	2	−1
United States	64	68	17	16	20	18	19	16	10	11	−1	−2
Uruguay	76	76	12	13	17	12	12	11	15	18	−6	−2
Uzbekistan	..	66	..	25	..	16	..	9	..	31	..	−7
Venezuela	55	66	12	5	26	17	33	30	29	37	7	13
Vietnam	..	77	..	7	..	27	..	14	..	46	..	−13
Yemen, Rep.	..	73	..	18	..	22	..	9	..	46	..	−13
Zambia	55	81	26	10	23	15	19	9	41	30	−4	−6
Zimbabwe	68	60	19	21	17	25	14	19	23	37	−3	−6
World	61 w	63 w	15 w	15 w	24 w	22 w	24 w	22 w	19 w	21 w	1 w	1 w
Low income	73	71	11	11	20	22	16	18	13	19	−5	−4
Middle income	58	62	13	13	27	25	28	25	22	26	1	0
Lower middle income	58	60	15	13	29	27	28	27	..	27	..	..
Upper middle income	59	64	12	14	25	22	29	21	25	23	5	−1
Low & middle income	61	63	13	13	26	25	26	24	20	25	0	−1
East Asia & Pacific	53	53	14	10	32	34	33	36	16	28	1	3
Europe & Central Asia	64	64	13	15	25	23	23	21	..	31	..	..
Latin America & Carib.	67	67	10	12	24	20	23	20	15	17	−2	1
Middle East & N. Africa	46	55	18	17	29	26	36	28	35	28	7	2
South Asia	75	69	9	11	21	24	15	20	8	13	−6	−4
Sub-Saharan Africa	63	65	14	17	23	18	23	18	30	28	2	0
High income	61	63	16	16	24	21	23	21	19	20	0	0

a. General government consumption figures are not available separately; they are included in private consumption. b. Data prior to 1992 include Eritrea. c. Includes statistical discrepancy. d. Data cover mainland Tanzania only.

Table 14.   Central government finances

| | % of GDP | | | | | | | | | | % of total expenditure[b] | | | |
| | Current tax revenue | | Current nontax revenue | | Current expenditure | | Capital expenditure | | Overall deficit/surplus[a] | | Goods and services | | Social services[c] | |
Economy	1980	1996	1980	1996	1980	1996	1980	1996	1980	1996	1980	1996	1980	1996
Albania	..	16.6	..	4.5	..	25.5	..	5.5	..	−9.0	..	26.3	..	33.0
Algeria	..	..	..	..	..	..	..	..	..	..	..	..	..	..
Angola	..	..	..	..	..	..	..	..	..	..	..	..	..	..
Argentina	10.4	11.9	5.2	1.0	18.2	13.4	0.0	1.1	−2.6	−1.1	57.1	22.4	28.6	65.1
Armenia	..	..	..	..	..	..	..	..	..	..	..	..	..	..
Australia	19.6	23.1	2.2	2.4	21.2	26.6	1.5	0.9	−1.5	−1.0	21.7	22.4	46.7	55.9
Austria	31.3	33.1	2.6	3.1	33.3	39.1	3.3	3.1	−3.3	−5.2	26.2	24.7	71.6	70.0
Azerbaijan	..	..	..	..	..	..	..	..	..	..	..	..	..	..
Bangladesh	7.7	..	3.6	..	..	..	..	..	2.5	..	..	..	17.3	..
Belarus	..	..	..	..	..	..	..	..	..	..	..	..	..	..
Belgium	41.4	43.2	1.9	1.4	46.3	46.8	4.3	2.5	−8.1	−3.9	22.6	18.6	61.3	..
Benin	..	..	..	..	..	..	..	..	..	..	..	..	..	..
Bolivia	..	14.4	..	2.5	..	17.9	..	4.9	..	−2.3	..	35.8	..	40.8
Brazil	17.8	19.7	4.8	6.1	18.6	32.3	1.6	0.8	−2.4	−6.7	20.0	13.3	40.0	40.5
Bulgaria	..	25.1	..	8.5	..	48.5	..	1.3	..	−16.0	..	19.3	..	25.3
Burkina Faso	10.4	..	1.2	..	9.9	..	2.3	..	0.2	..	66.6	..	28.9	..
Burundi	13.2	11.2	0.8	2.2	13.1	15.8	10.9	6.1	−3.9	−6.5	39.3	46.7	..	25.3
Cambodia	..	..	..	..	..	..	..	..	..	..	..	..	..	..
Cameroon	15.0	9.4	1.3	3.6	10.6	11.6	5.2	1.1	0.5	0.2	55.0	53.0	25.6	21.2
Canada	16.2	18.5	2.5	2.4	21.0	..	0.3	..	−3.5	−3.7	21.8	..	45.6	48.6
Central African Republic	15.0	..	1.5	..	20.7	..	1.3	..	−3.5	..	67.0	..	29.1	..
Chad	..	..	..	..	..	..	..	..	..	..	..	..	..	..
Chile	25.6	18.3	6.4	3.3	25.3	16.2	2.7	3.3	5.4	2.1	41.2	28.8	59.1	66.7
China	..	5.2	..	0.4	..	..	..	..	..	−1.7	..	..	..	1.9
Hong Kong, China	..	..	..	..	..	..	..	..	..	..	..	..	..	..
Colombia	10.3	13.6	1.7	2.7	9.2	..	4.1	..	−1.8	..	36.2	..	44.3	..
Congo, Dem. Rep.	8.3	4.5	1.1	0.4	9.9	7.4	2.4	0.2	−0.8	0.0	65.1	94.5	22.1	1.6
Congo, Rep.	27.0	..	8.3	..	21.8	..	17.7	..	−5.2	..	..	..	..	..
Costa Rica	16.8	23.5	1.0	3.2	19.9	27.7	5.2	2.9	−7.4	−3.9	52.4	47.1	62.6	59.7
Côte d'Ivoire	21.1	..	1.7	..	22.7	..	9.0	..	−10.8	..	..	..	..	..
Croatia	..	42.9	..	2.6	..	41.2	..	5.5	..	−0.5	..	51.9	..	61.4
Czech Republic	..	34.1	..	1.8	..	33.3	..	4.1	..	0.0	..	15.4	..	54.4
Denmark	31.3	35.3	4.1	5.3	36.6	41.9	2.8	1.5	−2.7	−2.0	21.6	19.0	57.1	54.9
Dominican Republic	11.1	14.7	3.2	1.5	11.7	9.0	5.2	6.5	−2.6	0.8	49.9	38.2	35.7	41.6
Ecuador	12.2	13.9	0.5	1.8	11.9	12.4	2.3	3.3	−1.4	0.0	28.3	46.9	43.9	..
Egypt, Arab Rep.	28.9	22.6	16.6	14.3	36.5	30.2	9.0	7.1	−6.4	0.3	38.4	31.5	25.8	32.2
El Salvador	11.1	11.6	0.5	0.4	14.3	11.2	2.8	2.2	−5.7	−0.5	49.7	50.8	34.2	36.6
Estonia	..	30.9	..	2.3	..	30.7	..	2.7	..	−0.2	..	44.7	..	56.0
Ethiopia	12.8[d]	..	3.5[d]	..	16.3[d]	..	3.3[d]	..	−3.1[d]	..	85.2[d]	..	19.5[d]	..
Finland	25.1	27.9	2.1	4.9	25.2	40.6	3.0	2.1	−2.2	−9.8	21.5	17.0	53.4	56.6
France	36.7	38.8	2.9	2.6	37.4	44.7	2.1	2.0	−0.1	−5.4	30.5	24.0	70.2	..
Gabon	23.6	..	11.9	..	..	..	..	..	6.1	..	..	..	..	..
Georgia	..	..	..	..	..	..	..	..	..	..	..	..	..	..
Germany	..	29.4	..	2.0	..	32.1	..	1.5	..	−2.1	34.4	31.7	69.4	..
Ghana	6.4	..	0.5	..	9.8	..	1.1	..	−4.2	..	48.2	..	35.8	..
Greece	22.6	19.7	2.7	2.3	24.7	29.1	4.6	4.5	−4.1	−13.8	44.6	28.8	51.5	35.4
Guatemala	8.7	7.7	0.7	0.7	7.0	6.6	5.1	2.3	−3.4	−0.7	49.7	51.8	31.6	39.3
Guinea	..	..	..	..	..	..	..	..	..	..	..	..	..	..
Guinea-Bissau	..	..	..	..	..	..	..	..	..	..	..	..	..	..
Haiti	9.3	..	1.3	..	13.9	..	3.5	..	−4.7	..	81.5	..	..	..
Honduras	13.6	..	0.9	..	..	..	..	..	..	..	..	..	..	..
Hungary	44.9	..	8.6	..	48.7	..	7.5	..	−2.8	..	19.5	..	26.9	..
India	9.8	10.3	1.9	3.4	11.7	14.5	1.6	1.7	−6.5	−5.1	28.7	23.2	..	..
Indonesia	20.2	14.7	1.0	2.3	11.7	8.7	10.4	6.0	−2.2	1.2	25.2	30.0	12.6	39.0
Ireland	30.9	34.7	3.9	1.9	40.4	36.8	4.6	3.5	−12.5	−2.0	18.8	18.0	52.8	58.0
Israel	43.3	33.4	7.1	5.1	67.4	40.9	2.8	3.9	−15.6	−4.7	50.0	33.0	27.8	54.5
Italy	29.3	40.7	2.5	3.0	39.1	47.9	2.2	2.7	−10.8	−7.2	17.7	17.4	50.7	..
Jamaica	27.9	..	1.2	..	..	..	..	..	−15.5	..	..	..	..	..
Japan	11.0	..	0.6	..	14.8	..	3.6	..	−7.0	..	12.9	..	..	..
Jordan	14.0	21.0	4.0	7.6	29.2	25.5	12.1	6.1	−9.3	1.1	42.6	61.6	25.9	41.1
Kazakhstan	..	..	..	..	..	..	..	..	..	..	..	..	..	..
Kenya	19.1	20.2	2.8	2.3	19.4	22.9	5.9	5.5	−4.5	−3.3	56.8	50.5	32.6	..
Korea, Rep.	15.5	18.6	2.2	2.7	14.8	14.4	2.4	4.2	−2.2	0.1	45.1	26.7	25.8	34.0
Kyrgyz Republic	..	..	..	..	..	..	..	..	..	..	..	..	..	..
Lao PDR	..	..	..	..	..	..	..	..	..	..	..	..	..	..
Latvia	..	25.5	..	4.9	..	30.2	..	1.4	..	−1.6	..	35.5	..	63.4
Lebanon	..	11.6	..	5.2	..	26.8	..	5.7	..	−15.6	..	29.2	..	19.4
Lesotho	29.5	..	4.8	..	..	..	..	..	..	..	..	..	..	..
Lithuania	..	22.0	..	0.8	..	23.4	..	2.0	..	−3.7	..	42.5	..	50.6
Macedonia, FYR	..	..	..	..	..	..	..	..	..	..	..	..	..	..
Madagascar	12.9	8.4	0.3	0.2	..	10.5	..	6.8	..	−1.3	..	25.3	..	22.7
Malawi	16.6	..	2.5	..	18.0	..	16.6	..	−15.9	..	37.1	..	16.1	..
Malaysia	23.4	20.1	2.8	4.9	18.6	17.8	9.9	4.2	−6.0	2.0	38.0	44.9	30.4	42.5
Mali	9.2	..	0.8	..	18.8	..	1.8	..	−4.5	..	46.2	..	21.8	..
Mauritania	..	..	..	..	..	..	..	..	..	..	..	..	..	..

Note: For data comparability and coverage, see the Technical Notes. Figures in italics are for years other than those specified.

	% of GDP										% of total expenditure[b]			
	Current tax revenue		Current nontax revenue		Current expenditure		Capital expenditure		Overall deficit/surplus[a]		Goods and services		Social services[c]	
Economy	1980	1996	1980	1996	1980	1996	1980	1996	1980	1996	1980	1996	1980	1996
Mauritius	18.4	16.2	2.4	2.4	22.7	18.7	4.6	3.6	−10.3	−4.0	41.7	47.0	46.5	48.3
Mexico	13.9	12.8	1.1	2.5	10.7	14.0	5.0	1.9	−3.0	−0.5	31.8	26.1	44.3	50.2
Moldova	..	..	..	..	..	..	..	..	..	..	..	..	..	..
Mongolia	..	18.7	..	5.3	..	17.5	..	4.0	..	−6.6	..	35.8	..	32.8
Morocco	20.4	23.9	2.9	4.7	22.8	26.2	10.3	7.2	−9.7	−4.4	46.9	48.7	27.2	26.9
Mozambique	..	..	..	..	..	..	..	..	..	..	..	..	..	..
Namibia	..	..	..	..	..	..	..	..	..	..	..	..	..	..
Nepal	6.6	8.8	1.3	2.0	..	..	..	..	−3.0	−4.5	..	..	15.5	..
Netherlands	44.2	42.6	5.3	2.9	48.3	46.6	4.6	1.9	−4.6	−2.3	15.6	15.5	64.2	63.9
New Zealand	30.7	32.8	3.5	2.9	35.9	31.5	2.4	0.8	−6.7	5.2	29.0	49.0	61.0	69.3
Nicaragua	20.3	23.9	2.4	1.5	24.9	22.3	5.7	10.9	−6.8	−0.6	60.0	30.0	33.5	46.8
Niger	12.3	..	2.2	..	9.5	..	9.1	..	−4.8	..	30.3	..	25.9	..
Nigeria	..	..	..	..	..	..	..	..	..	..	..	..	..	..
Norway	33.8	32.4	3.5	8.8	32.5	37.1	2.0	1.9	−1.7	1.6	20.4	19.9	41.9	49.8
Oman	10.7	8.6	27.5	22.3	30.3	32.0	8.2	4.4	0.4	−5.0	71.1	75.5	9.6	33.3
Pakistan	13.3	15.3	2.9	4.1	14.5	19.1	3.1	4.1	−5.7	−4.8	47.4	43.2	..	..
Panama	18.6	17.2	6.7	8.9	24.9	21.9	5.5	2.8	−5.2	2.9	49.8	54.4	39.8	69.0
Papua New Guinea	20.5	18.9	2.4	3.1	29.2	26.1	5.2	3.3	−1.9	−4.1	57.7	48.2	27.8	30.7
Paraguay	9.8	..	0.9	..	7.5	..	2.4	..	0.3	..	60.9	..	35.7	..
Peru	15.8	14.0	1.3	2.1	15.0	13.8	4.4	2.7	−2.4	2.4	44.7	37.5	..	..
Philippines	12.5	16.8	1.5	1.7	9.9	15.2	3.5	2.8	−1.4	0.3	60.4	45.6	24.1	26.0
Poland	..	36.1	..	3.6	..	40.4	..	1.8	..	−2.2	..	25.2	..	69.6
Portugal	24.1	32.1	1.9	3.4	28.7	38.8	4.4	5.3	−8.5	−5.5	33.8	39.3	48.4	..
Romania	10.1	24.1	35.2	3.3	29.7	27.6	15.0	3.4	0.5	−4.0	11.4	33.2	18.9	47.7
Russian Federation	..	17.4	..	1.1	..	26.5	..	1.3	..	−4.4	..	39.8	..	..
Rwanda	11.0	..	1.8	..	9.4	..	5.0	..	−1.7	..	57.5	..	..	..
Saudi Arabia	..	..	..	..	..	..	..	..	..	..	..	..	..	..
Senegal	20.7	..	1.5	..	21.2	..	1.9	..	0.9	..	72.1	..	37.3	..
Sierra Leone	13.6	7.7	1.5	0.4	19.7	11.1	5.0	3.7	−11.8	−5.8	..	35.1	..	..
Singapore	17.5	16.2	7.9	9.7	15.6	12.3	4.5	3.6	2.1	14.3	57.5	59.4	29.2	39.7
Slovak Republic	..	..	..	..	..	..	..	..	..	..	..	..	..	..
Slovenia	..	..	..	..	..	..	..	..	..	..	..	..	..	..
South Africa	20.5	26.0	3.0	1.7	19.2	30.9	3.0	3.0	−2.3	−5.9	46.6	26.9	..	..
Spain	22.2	28.9	1.9	2.3	23.7	36.2	3.0	2.0	−4.2	−7.2	40.0	16.4	69.1	49.5
Sri Lanka	19.1	16.9	1.1	2.1	24.7	22.2	16.7	5.2	−18.3	−7.8	31.2	36.9	24.3	33.4
Sweden	30.1	37.2	4.9	4.9	37.6	45.2	1.8	1.2	−8.1	−3.2	17.4	13.6	63.9	60.5
Switzerland	18.1	21.5	1.4	1.7	18.7	25.4	1.4	1.1	−0.2	−1.0	27.5	29.6	64.4	71.7
Syrian Arab Republic	10.5	19.2	16.3	4.5	30.3	15.9	17.9	9.8	−9.7	−1.8	..	..	17.6	17.4
Tajikistan	..	..	..	..	..	..	..	..	..	..	..	..	..	..
Tanzania	..	..	..	..	..	..	..	..	..	..	51.7	..	21.8	..
Thailand	13.2	16.9	1.2	1.6	14.5	10.3	4.4	5.8	−4.9	2.3	55.0	55.5	29.0	38.1
Togo	27.0	..	4.3	..	23.7	..	8.9	..	−2.0	..	52.3	..	40.0	..
Trinidad and Tobago	36.1	24.2	7.1	4.0	18.8	26.2	12.1	3.0	7.4	0.2	34.2	50.9	33.2	45.2
Tunisia	23.9	25.0	6.9	4.8	22.2	26.0	9.4	6.7	−2.8	−3.2	42.1	38.5	37.6	47.4
Turkey	14.3	15.2	3.7	3.1	15.5	24.6	5.9	2.2	−3.1	−8.3	46.5	32.6	23.8	19.0
Turkmenistan	..	..	..	..	..	..	..	..	..	..	..	..	..	..
Uganda	3.1	..	0.1	..	5.4	..	0.8	..	−3.1	..	..	..	24.2	..
Ukraine	..	..	..	..	..	..	..	..	..	..	..	..	..	..
United Arab Emirates	0.0	0.6	0.2	1.8	11.2	11.3	0.9	0.5	2.1	0.2	80.5	86.6	23.6	29.8
United Kingdom	30.6	33.7	4.6	2.8	36.4	39.9	1.8	2.1	−4.6	−5.3	31.6	29.6	45.8	51.7
United States	18.5	19.3	1.7	1.5	20.7	21.6	1.3	0.7	−2.8	−1.6	29.5	22.3	50.8	53.1
Uruguay	21.0	29.2	1.2	2.1	20.1	31.3	1.7	1.8	0.0	−1.6	47.6	29.4	62.3	76.1
Uzbekistan	..	..	..	..	..	..	..	..	..	..	..	..	..	..
Venezuela	18.9	14.5	3.4	6.1	14.7	15.7	4.0	2.4	0.0	1.0	50.2	20.0	..	..
Vietnam	..	..	..	..	..	..	..	..	..	..	..	..	..	..
Yemen, Rep.	..	9.9	..	10.0	..	21.9	..	2.8	..	−5.5	..	66.6	..	26.3
Zambia	23.1	16.7	1.8	1.4	33.2	13.9	4.0	6.9	−18.5	0.7	54.6	44.8	20.7	34.1
Zimbabwe	15.4	..	3.9	..	26.5	..	1.4	..	−8.8	..	55.5	..	28.6	..

a. Includes grants. b. Total expenditure includes lending minus repayments. c. Refers to education, health, social security, welfare, housing, and community amenities.
d. Includes Eritrea.

Table 15. Balance of payments current account and international reserves

	Goods and services				Net income		Net current transfers		Current account balance		Gross international reserves	
	Exports		Imports									
Economy	1980	1996	1980	1996	1980	1996	1980	1996	1980	1996	1980	1997
Albania	378	373	371	1,111	4	72	6	559	16	−107	..	342
Algeria	14,128	13,960	12,311	..	−1,869	..	301	..	249	..	7,062	9,668
Angola	..	3,167	..	3,017	..	−735	..	245	..	−340	..	..
Argentina	9,897	27,031	13,182	27,910	−1,512	−3,591	23	334	−4,774	−4,136	9,298	22,405
Armenia	..	368	..	888	..	44	..	185	..	−291	..	239
Australia	25,755	78,805	27,070	79,568	−2,695	−15,199	−425	105	−4,435	−15,857	6,369	17,542
Austria	26,650	91,614	29,921	94,418	−528	−202	−66	−984	−3,865	−3,990	17,729	21,982
Azerbaijan	..	757	..	1,443	..	−60	..	80	..	−666	..	466
Bangladesh	885	4,508	2,545	7,614	14	−6	..	..	−844	−1,637	332	1,609
Belarus	..	6,017	..	6,922	..	−65	..	62	..	−909	..	394
Belgium[a]	70,498	190,732	74,259	179,072	61	6,944	−1,231	−4,217	−4,931	14,387	27,998	20,637
Benin	226	405	421	477	8	−41	151	149	−36	36	15	256
Bolivia	1,030	1,380	136	1,752	−146	−188	13	287	−319	−272	554	1,362
Brazil	21,869	52,641	27,826	63,293	−7,018	−11,105	144	3,621	−12,831	−18,136	6,879	51,679
Bulgaria	9,302	6,824	7,995	6,540	−412	−472	..	..	953	−56	..	2,549
Burkina Faso	210	272	577	483	−3	−29	322	255	−49	15	75	348
Burundi	..	129	..	277	..	−9	..	151	..	−6	105	118
Cambodia	..	806	..	1,294	..	−45	..	235	..	−298	..	299
Cameroon	1,792	2,158	1,829	1,822	−628	−583	..	..	−564	−175	207	1
Canada	74,973	234,311	70,399	211,509	−10,764	−20,311	95	318	−6,095	2,808	15,480	18,696
Central African Republic	201	179	327	244	3	−23	81	63	−43	−25	62	179
Chad	71	190	79	411	−4	−7	24	191	12	−38	12	136
Chile	5,968	18,709	7,052	20,086	−1,000	−2,016	113	472	−1,971	−2,921	4,123	17,839
China*	23,637	171,678	18,900	154,127	451	−12,437	486	2,129	5,674	7,243	10,102	146,683
Hong Kong, China	..	..	..	..	..	..	..	..	..	..	..	92,919
Colombia	5,328	14,518	5,454	16,878	−245	−2,925	165	532	−206	−4,754	6,476	9,614
Congo, Dem. Rep.	1,658	2,001	1,905	..	−496	..	150	..	−593	..	380	83
Congo, Rep.	1,021	1,584	1,025	2,133	−162	−455	−1	−30	−167	−1,034	93	60
Costa Rica	1,195	3,790	1,661	3,901	−212	−186	15	154	−664	−143	197	1,261
Côte d'Ivoire	3,577	5,110	4,145	4,017	−553	−915	−706	−381	−1,826	−203	46	636
Croatia	..	8,008	..	10,194	..	−45	..	779	..	−1,452	..	2,690
Czech Republic	..	29,874	..	33,834	..	−722	..	384	..	−4,299	..	10,032
Denmark	21,989	67,237	21,727	58,198	−1,977	−4,609	−161	−1,565	−1,875	2,865	4,352	19,590
Dominican Republic	1,271	6,095	1,919	6,689	−277	−596	205	1,080	−720	−110	279	396
Ecuador	2,887	5,750	2,946	4,621	−613	−1,308	30	290	−642	111	1,254	2,210
Egypt, Arab Rep.	6,246	15,245	9,157	18,951	−318	539	..	..	−438	499	2,484	19,405
El Salvador	1,214	2,049	1,170	3,673	−62	−87	52	1,389	34	−322	382	1,446
Estonia	..	2,896	..	3,421	..	2	..	100	..	−423	..	760
Ethiopia[b]	569	783	782	1,647	7	−44	..	..	−126	−461	262	502
Finland	16,802	47,844	17,307	38,228	−783	−3,732	−114	−1,098	−1,403	4,787	2,452	8,884
France	153,197	365,375	155,915	334,186	2,680	−2,704	−4,170	−7,924	−4,208	20,561	75,621	54,651
Gabon	2,409	2,916	1,475	1,848	−426	−770	−124	−198	384	100	115	283
Georgia	..	479	..	798	..	87	..	190	..	−216	..	..
Germany[c]	224,224	604,077	225,599	576,283	914	−4,469	−12,858	−36,397	−13,319	−13,072	104,768	105,208
Ghana	1,210	1,728	1,178	2,393	−83	−140	81	482	30	−324	329	930
Greece	8,122	15,238	11,145	25,633	−273	−2,181	1,087	8,022	−2,209	−4,554	3,616	13,656
Guatemala	1,731	2,796	1,960	3,540	−44	−230	110	523	−163	−452	753	1,172
Guinea	..	761	..	948	..	−93	..	102	..	−177	..	122
Guinea-Bissau	17	24	75	80	−8	−15	−14	46	−80	−26	..	12
Haiti	306	192	481	782	−14	−10	89	463	−101	−138	27	83
Honduras	942	1,635	1,128	1,852	−152	−226	22	243	−317	−201	159	586
Hungary	10,302	16,933	10,944	18,099	−1,103	−1,434	..	..	−1,682	−1,678	..	8,509
India	11,265	42,690	17,378	54,505	356	−4,369	..	..	−2,897	−4,601	12,008	28,383
Indonesia	23,797	51,160	21,540	53,244	−3,073	−5,778	250	619	−566	−7,023	6,800	17,499
Ireland	9,610	54,066	12,044	46,566	−902	−8,279	1,204	2,184	−2,132	1,406	3,071	6,635
Israel	8,668	28,292	11,511	38,729	−757	−2,845	2,729	6,226	−871	−7,057	4,052	20,003
Italy	97,298	320,752	110,265	257,467	1,278	−14,967	1,101	−7,280	−10,587	41,040	62,453	75,043
Jamaica	1,363	3,180	1,408	3,640	−212	−320	121	535	−136	−245	105	683
Japan	146,980	468,002	156,970	446,679	770	53,553	−1,530	−8,993	−10,750	65,884	38,878	227,018
Jordan	1,181	3,663	2,417	5,420	36	−301	..	..	281	−226	1,742	2,365
Kazakhstan	..	6,966	..	7,546	..	−222	..	50	..	−752	..	2,225
Kenya	2,007	3,027	2,846	3,441	−194	−221	157	561	−876	−74	539	603
Korea, Rep.	21,924	155,109	25,687	175,763	−2,102	−2,526	592	119	−5,273	−23,061	3,096	20,497
Kyrgyz Republic	..	548	..	950	..	−80	..	78	..	−404	..	170
Lao PDR	..	427	..	787	..	−4	..	82	..	−283	..	148
Latvia	..	2,613	..	3,028	..	41	..	93	..	−280	..	776
Lebanon	..	1,413	..	7,596	..	290	..	2,550	..	−3,343	7,030	8,654
Lesotho	90	181	475	874	266	330	175	471	56	108	50	572
Lithuania	..	4,211	..	4,986	..	−91	..	144	..	−723	..	1,064
Macedonia, FYR	..	1,302	..	1,773	..	−30	..	..	..	−288	..	280
Madagascar	516	803	1,075	1,002	−44	−163	47	210	−556	−153	9	282
Malawi	313	385	487	873	−149	−86	63	124	−260	−450	76	166
Malaysia	14,098	83,322	13,526	86,595	−836	−4,236	−2	148	−266	−7,362	5,759	21,100
Mali	263	387	520	746	−17	−36	150	231	−124	−164	26	420
Mauritania	253	504	449	510	−27	−48	90	76	−133	22	147	204
* Data for Taiwan, China	21,495	131,722	22,361	122,275	48	3,240	−95	−1,660	−913	11,027	4,063	87,444

Note: For data comparability and coverage, see the Technical Notes. Figures in italics are for years other than those specified.

Millions of dollars

Economy	Goods and services				Net income		Net current transfers		Current account balance		Gross international reserves	
	Exports		Imports									
	1980	1996	1980	1996	1980	1996	1980	1996	1980	1996	1980	1997
Mauritius	574	2,701	690	2,767	−23	−40	22	123	−117	17	113	721
Mexico	22,622	106,900	27,601	100,288	−6,277	−13,067	834	4,531	−10,422	−1,923	4,175	28,855
Moldova	..	964	..	1,306	..	55	..	73	..	−214	..	366
Mongolia	475	508	1,272	521	−11	−25	0	..	−808	39	..	201
Morocco	3,233	9,246	5,207	10,980	−562	−1,309	1,130	2,416	−1,407	−627	814	4,194
Mozambique	399	411	844	1,055	22	−140	56	339	−367	−445	..	517
Namibia	..	1,591	..	1,868	..	97	..	263	..	84	..	251
Nepal	224	1,003	365	1,653	13	−3	..	..	−93	−569	272	627
Netherlands	90,380	225,473	91,622	199,932	1,535	6,376	−1,148	−6,658	−855	25,258	37,501	32,759
New Zealand	6,403	18,876	6,934	18,712	−538	−4,665	96	553	−973	−3,948	365	4,450
Nicaragua	495	807	907	1,299	−124	−300	124	275	−411	−435	75	382
Niger	617	321	956	457	−33	−47	97	31	−276	−152	133	57
Nigeria	27,071	14,743	20,014	9,836	−1,304	−2,639	−576	824	5,178	3,092	10,605	4,334
Norway	27,264	63,866	23,749	49,495	−1,922	−1,638	−515	−1,488	1,079	11,246	6,746	23,742
Oman	3,757	7,352	2,298	5,423	−257	−536	−260	−1,659	942	−265	704	1,634
Pakistan	2,958	10,317	5,709	15,174	−281	−1,956	..	..	−869	−4,208	1,570	1,790
Panama	3,422	7,426	3,394	7,530	−397	−108	40	152	−329	−60	117	1,150
Papua New Guinea	1,029	2,966	1,322	2,260	−179	−465	184	72	−289	313	457	381
Paraguay	701	3,936	1,314	4,951	−4	306	..	39	−618	−668	783	796
Peru	4,631	7,268	3,970	9,947	−909	−1,575	147	647	−101	−3,607	2,806	11,322
Philippines	7,235	26,795	9,166	33,317	−420	3,662	447	880	−1,904	−1,980	3,983	8,717
Poland	16,061	37,390	17,842	41,273	−2,357	−1,075	721	1,694	−3,417	−3,264	575	20,662
Portugal	6,674	33,764	10,136	41,729	−608	−352	3,006	6,826	−1,064	−1,491	13,893	20,369
Romania	12,087	9,648	13,730	12,503	−777	−309	0	593	−2,420	−2,571	2,512	4,676
Russian Federation	..	102,449	..	86,001	..	−5,213	..	164	..	11,399	..	17,727
Rwanda	165	86	319	363	2	−13	104	291	−48	1	187	153
Saudi Arabia	106,765	60,221	55,793	47,407	526	3,214	−9,995	−15,813	41,503	215	26,096	8,684
Senegal	807	1,550	1,215	1,821	−98	−168	120	382	−386	−58	25	394
Sierra Leone	275	128	471	206	−22	−21	53	26	−165	−73	31	50
Singapore	24,285	156,052	25,312	142,461	−429	1,702	−106	−1,010	−1,563	14,283	6,570	71,300
Slovak Republic	..	10,889	..	13,134	..	−47	..	201	..	−2,090	..	3,604
Slovenia	..	10,497	..	10,674	..	155	..	62	..	39	..	3,310
South Africa	28,627	33,309	22,073	32,716	−3,285	−2,552	239	−74	3,508	−2,033	7,924	5,957
Spain	32,140	146,404	38,004	141,304	−1,362	−5,928	1,646	2,584	−5,580	1,756	20,514	72,924
Sri Lanka	1,293	4,861	2,197	6,074	−26	−203	274	764	−655	−653	283	2,038
Sweden	38,151	101,620	39,878	84,809	−1,380	−8,303	−1,224	−2,616	−4,331	5,892	7,001	12,169
Switzerland	48,595	121,738	51,843	109,064	4,186	11,597	−1,140	−3,801	−201	20,470	64,847	63,157
Syrian Arab Republic	2,477	6,131	4,531	6,071	785	−399	1,520	624	251	285	828	..
Tajikistan	..	772	..	808	..	−68	..	20	..	−84	..	..
Tanzania	748	1,372	1,384	2,167	−14	−55	129	437	−521	−413	20	622
Thailand	7,939	71,416	9,996	83,482	−229	−3,385	210	760	−2,076	−14,692	3,029	26,916
Togo	550	402	691	444	−40	−45	86	30	−95	−57	85	123
Trinidad and Tobago	3,139	2,799	2,434	2,110	−306	−390	−42	−4	357	294	2,812	723
Tunisia	3,262	8,151	3,766	8,582	−259	−965	410	860	−353	−536	700	2,043
Turkey	3,621	45,354	8,082	48,331	−1,118	−2,920	2,171	4,447	−3,408	−1,450	3,304	19,788
Turkmenistan	..	1,691	..	1,532	..	..	..	4	..	43	..	..
Uganda	329	726	441	1,601	−7	−46	..	..	−121	−502	3	633
Ukraine	..	20,346	..	21,468	..	−573	..	509	..	−1,186	..	2,358
United Arab Emirates	..	..	..	..	..	..	..	..	..	..	2,350	8,354
United Kingdom	146,072	340,232	134,200	348,888	−418	13,163	−4,592	−7,396	6,862	−2,889	31,792	37,636
United States	271,800	848,646	290,730	956,004	29,580	−897	−8,500	−40,489	2,150	−148,726	171,360	134,880
Uruguay	1,526	3,799	2,144	3,962	−100	−206	9	74	−709	−296	2,402	2,070
Uzbekistan	..	4,161	..	5,175	..	−69	..	8	..	−1,075	..	..
Venezuela	19,968	25,258	15,130	14,837	329	−1,735	−439	138	4,728	8,824	13,385	17,735
Vietnam	..	9,695	..	12,870	..	−505	..	1,045	..	−2,636	..	1,990
Yemen, Rep.	..	2,409	..	3,044	..	−617	..	..	..	−70	..	1,038
Zambia	1,609	1,296	1,765	..	−205	..	−155	..	−516	..	206	239
Zimbabwe	1,610	2,344	1,730	2,515	−61	−294	31	40	−149	−425	420	383
World	2,400,597 t	6,689,040 t	2,405,428 t	6,522,540 t								
Low income	70,570	134,512	101,615	183,203								
Middle income	650,441	1,473,612	584,098	1,509,671								
Lower middle income	..	..	..	..								
Upper middle income	300,440	561,371	246,740	579,815								
Low & middle income	633,124	1,612,603	671,734	1,677,129								
East Asia & Pacific	77,284	447,383	85,244	422,216								
Europe & Central Asia	..	..	..	..								
Latin America & Carib.	121,191	320,894	142,086	318,469								
Middle East & N. Africa	205,272	169,488	148,981	160,504								
South Asia	17,450	65,583	29,271	85,500								
Sub-Saharan Africa	89,966	83,985	83,985	100,832								
High income	1,729,293	5,091,134	1,775,216	4,936,249								

a. Includes Luxembourg. b. Data prior to 1992 include Eritrea. c. Data prior to 1990 refer to the Federal Republic of Germany before unification.

Table 16.   Private sector finance

Economy	Private investment % of gross domestic fixed investment		Stock market capitalization Millions of dollars		No. of listed domestic companies		Interest rate spread (lending minus deposit rate) Percentage points		Domestic credit provided by the banking sector % of GDP	
	1980	1996	1990	1997	1990	1996	1990	1997	1990	1997
Albania	..	..	..	..	..	..	2.1	7.2	..	44.8
Algeria	67.4	74.8	..	..	..	..	..	..	74.7	42.4
Angola	..	68.9	..	..	..	..	..	..	..	..
Argentina	..	85.8	3,268	59,252	179	147	..	2.3	32.4	27.3
Armenia	..	33.6	..	7	..	10	..	28.0	62.2	9.1
Australia	..	..	107,611	311,988	1,089	1,135	6.8	..	104.0	87.9
Austria	..	..	11,476	33,953	97	106	..	..	123.0	130.8
Azerbaijan	..	..	..	..	..	..	..	..	57.2	11.1
Bangladesh	58.9	62.5	321	4,551	134	186	4.0	5.9	32.5	40.2
Belarus	..	..	..	..	..	..	..	32.0	..	17.7
Belgium	..	..	65,449	119,831	182	139	6.9	4.2	74.4	153.9
Benin	..	61.7	..	..	..	..	9.0	..	22.3	7.5
Bolivia	51.3	41.9	..	114	..	10	18.0	35.4	30.6	54.5
Brazil	89.7	86.2	16,354	255,478	581	551	..	..	87.4	43.8
Bulgaria	85.9	85.0	..	7	..	15	9.9	48.3	118.6	119.1
Burkina Faso	..	57.9	..	..	..	..	9.0	..	13.7	13.1
Burundi	8.1	15.7	..	..	..	..	..	..	24.4	20.5
Cambodia	..	68.6	..	..	..	..	..	10.4	..	7.5
Cameroon	77.8	95.5	..	..	..	..	11.0	10.5	31.0	16.3
Canada	..	..	241,920	486,268	1,144	1,265	1.3	1.4	86.6	101.9
Central African Republic	46.5	41.8	..	..	..	..	11.0	10.5	12.9	10.0
Chad	4.8	35.8	..	..	..	..	11.0	10.5	11.0	9.8
Chile	72.2	80.0	13,645	72,046	215	291	8.5	3.7	72.8	59.4
China	43.4	47.0	2,028	206,366	14	540	0.7	3.0	90.0	102.6
Hong Kong, China	85.1	86.8	83,397	449,381	284	561	3.3	3.5	132.1	168.0
Colombia	58.3	47.8	1,416	19,530	80	189	8.8	10.1	36.2	45.5
Congo, Dem. Rep.	42.4	..	..	..	..	..	..	..	25.3	1.6
Congo, Rep.	..	91.4	..	..	..	..	11.0	10.5	29.1	16.9
Costa Rica	61.3	75.1	311	782	82	114	11.4	9.5	29.8	38.1
Côte d'Ivoire	53.2	69.1	549	914	23	31	9.0	..	44.6	28.7
Croatia	..	59.6	..	581	..	61	501.0	11.2	..	46.4
Czech Republic	..	..	..	12,786	..	1,588	..	5.5	..	78.5
Denmark	..	..	39,063	71,688	258	237	6.2	5.1	65.1	58.7
Dominican Republic	68.4	66.5	..	..	..	..	15.3	7.6	31.3	31.2
Ecuador	59.7	78.3	69	1,946	65	42	–6.0	14.9	17.2	35.5
Egypt, Arab Rep.	30.1	59.1	1,765	20,830	573	646	7.0	4.0	107.1	86.8
El Salvador	44.8	78.0	..	450	..	49	3.2	4.2	32.1	41.5
Estonia	..	80.2	..	..	..	..	..	13.6	65.0	30.1
Ethiopia	..	63.9	..	..	..	..	3.6	4.5	67.3	45.1
Finland	..	..	22,721	63,078	73	71	4.1	3.3	84.4	63.7
France	..	..	314,384	591,123	578	686	6.0	2.8	106.3	102.1
Gabon	80.1	72.0	..	..	..	..	11.0	10.5	20.1	15.8
Georgia	..	73.7	..	..	..	..	..	..	..	..
Germany	..	..	355,073	670,997	413	681	4.5	6.4	110.0	136.7
Ghana	..	26.3	76	1,492	13	21	..	..	13.2	26.8
Greece	..	..	15,228	34,164	145	224	8.1	8.8	103.8	84.0
Guatemala	63.8	81.3	..	168	..	9	5.1	13.4	17.4	19.5
Guinea	..	57.7	..	..	..	..	0.2	4.0	5.5	6.7
Guinea-Bissau	..	32.5	..	..	..	..	13.1	4.5	43.5	7.4
Haiti	..	27.6	..	..	..	..	..	10.3	32.9	31.7
Honduras	62.1	62.7	40	338	26	111	8.3	10.8	40.9	29.3
Hungary	..	..	505	14,975	21	45	4.1	6.5	82.8	49.2
India	55.5	66.1	38,567	128,466	6,200	8,800	..	..	54.7	49.3
Indonesia	..	60.5	8,081	29,105	125	253	3.3	1.8	45.5	54.3
Ireland	..	..	..	12,243	..	76	5.0	6.1	58.0	84.4
Israel	..	..	3,324	45,268	216	655	12.0	5.6	100.9	79.4
Italy	..	..	148,766	258,160	220	244	7.3	4.9	90.8	95.0
Jamaica	..	..	911	1,887	44	46	6.6	22.4	34.7	33.5
Japan	..	..	2,917,679	3,088,850	..	53	3.4	2.1	267.4	295.8
Jordan	51.4	77.1	2,001	5,446	105	98	3.3	3.5	118.1	74.4
Kazakhstan	..	98.8	..	..	..	..	..	..	..	7.9
Kenya	54.7	44.5	453	1,846	54	56	5.1	13.5	52.7	55.2
Korea, Rep.	76.2	76.0	110,594	41,881	669	760	0.0	1.1	65.3	86.0
Kyrgyz Republic	..	87.5	..	5	..	27	..	9.8	..	26.2
Lao PDR	..	..	..	..	..	..	2.5	11.0	5.1	16.2
Latvia	..	89.3	..	148	..	34	..	9.3	..	13.0
Lebanon	..	71.8	..	..	..	..	23.0	6.9	132.8	122.4
Lesotho	..	36.8	..	..	..	..	7.4	6.2	30.1	–25.3
Lithuania	..	86.3	..	900	..	460	..	6.5	..	12.1
Macedonia, FYR	..	..	..	..	..	..	..	9.8	..	35.2
Madagascar	..	42.5	..	..	..	..	5.3	15.6	26.3	13.8
Malawi	21.4	84.3	..	..	..	..	8.9	19.0	20.6	10.7
Malaysia	62.6	69.8	48,611	93,608	282	621	1.3	1.8	77.9	166.6
Mali	..	54.4	..	..	..	..	9.0	..	13.4	12.0
Mauritania	..	68.3	..	..	..	..	5.0	..	54.8	8.0

Note: For data comparability and coverage, see the Technical Notes. Figures in italics are for years other than those specified.

Economy	Private investment % of gross domestic fixed investment		Stock market capitalization Millions of dollars		No. of listed domestic companies		Interest rate spread (lending minus deposit rate) Percentage points		Domestic credit provided by the banking sector % of GDP	
	1980	1996	1990	1997	1990	1996	1990	1997	1990	1997
Mauritius	64.0	64.8	268	1,676	13	40	5.4	9.8	45.1	72.5
Mexico	57.0	79.1	32,725	156,595	199	193	..	..	42.5	40.5
Moldova	..	78.5	..	..	..	..	..	9.8	62.9	21.9
Mongolia	..	..	..	..	..	..	..	36.9	68.7	10.2
Morocco	44.0	57.8	966	12,177	71	47	0.5	..	60.1	60.3
Mozambique	27.0	65.3	..	..	..	..	..	..	29.5	5.0
Namibia	42.0	62.2	21	473	3	12	10.6	7.5	19.2	52.7
Nepal	60.2	67.8	..	208	..	90	..	..	28.9	35.8
Netherlands	..	..	119,825	378,721	260	217	8.5	3.0	107.4	124.6
New Zealand	..	..	8,835	38,288	171	158	4.3	4.0	74.3	89.6
Nicaragua	..	38.6	..	..	..	..	12.5	8.6	206.5	148.6
Niger	..	50.6	..	..	..	..	9.0	..	16.1	10.1
Nigeria	..	62.5	1,372	3,646	131	183	5.5	6.7	23.7	15.8
Norway	..	..	26,130	57,423	112	158	4.6	2.3	89.5	74.7
Oman	34.1	..	945	2,673	55	143	1.4	2.4	16.6	29.2
Pakistan	36.1	52.5	2,850	10,966	487	782	..	..	50.8	49.9
Panama	..	83.8	226	831	13	16	3.6	3.6	52.7	74.5
Papua New Guinea	58.6	85.8	..	..	..	..	6.8	3.1	35.8	28.1
Paraguay	85.1	83.4	..	383	..	60	8.1	14.0	14.9	25.5
Peru	75.6	82.9	812	17,586	294	231	2,330.0	15.0	16.2	17.7
Philippines	69.0	81.1	5,927	31,361	153	216	4.6	6.1	26.8	83.4
Poland	..	81.9	144	12,135	9	83	462.3	6.1	19.5	35.3
Portugal	..	..	9,201	38,954	181	158	7.8	4.6	73.6	99.7
Romania	..	73.8	..	61	..	17	..	..	79.7	9.6
Russian Federation	..	91.1	244	128,207	13	73	..	29.8	..	0.0
Rwanda	..	70.0	..	..	..	..	6.3	..	17.0	13.1
Saudi Arabia	..	..	..	40,961	..	69	..	..	58.8	37.9
Senegal	62.1	70.3	..	..	..	..	9.0	..	33.7	22.0
Sierra Leone	..	64.4	..	..	..	..	12.0	18.1	26.3	52.3
Singapore	75.6	..	34,308	150,215	150	223	2.7	2.9	74.0	84.6
Slovak Republic	..	..	..	1,826	..	816	..	5.3	..	60.0
Slovenia	..	26.7	..	663	24	21	180.0	8.1	36.9	36.0
South Africa	50.8	..	137,540	232,069	732	626	2.1	4.6	102.5	77.0
Spain	..	..	111,404	242,779	427	357	5.3	2.1	108.9	105.9
Sri Lanka	77.4	..	917	2,096	175	235	−6.4	−2.2	43.2	32.2
Sweden	..	..	97,929	247,217	258	229	6.8	4.5	145.6	67.9
Switzerland	..	..	160,044	402,104	182	213	−0.9	3.5	179.0	183.4
Syrian Arab Republic	36.1	..	..	..	..	..	..	..	56.6	48.4
Tajikistan	..	..	..	..	..	..	..	..	..	..
Tanzania	..	..	..	..	..	..	..	21.4	39.2	14.2
Thailand	68.1	77.6	23,896	23,538	214	454	2.1	3.1	90.8	124.3
Togo	28.3	78.2	..	..	..	..	9.0	..	21.3	24.3
Trinidad and Tobago	..	88.0	696	1,405	30	23	6.9	8.4	58.5	59.2
Tunisia	46.9	51.0	533	4,263	13	30	..	..	62.5	67.2
Turkey	..	81.4	19,065	61,090	110	229	..	..	26.0	34.4
Turkmenistan	..	..	..	..	..	..	..	..	..	1.7
Uganda	..	63.9	..	..	..	..	7.4	9.6	17.7	6.1
Ukraine	..	..	..	..	..	..	..	30.9	83.3	14.9
United Arab Emirates	..	..	..	..	..	..	..	..	35.2	48.6
United Kingdom	..	..	848,866	1,740,246	1,701	2,433	2.3	3.0	122.9	131.0
United States	..	..	3,059,434	8,484,433	6,599	8,479	..	..	114.3	137.6
Uruguay	67.9	71.1	38	266	36	18	76.2	52.0	60.7	39.8
Uzbekistan	..	..	..	128	..	4	..	..	..	..
Venezuela	51.5	31.5	8,361	14,581	76	88	0.4	4.4	37.4	19.9
Vietnam	..	76.3	..	..	..	..	..	5.3	15.9	22.3
Yemen, Rep.	..	67.6	..	..	..	..	..	..	62.0	28.9
Zambia	..	48.7	..	229	..	5	9.4	12.2	64.5	42.6
Zimbabwe	77.1	90.4	2,395	1,969	57	64	2.9	12.6	41.7	61.3
World	.. w	68.1 w	9,399,355 s	20,177,662 s	29,189 s	42,404 s			125.7 w	139.1 w
Low income	53.9	65.0	46,507	56,860	7,086	10,375			47.0	42.1
Middle income	60.5	67.1	329,021	1,669,545	4,370	9,649			65.6	55.7
Lower middle income	55.5	62.4	47,225	569,132	1,848	4,110			69.9	65.6
Upper middle income	..	80.6	281,796	1,100,413	2,522	5,539			62.6	44.9
Low & middle income	59.5	66.8	375,528	1,725,742	11,456	20,024			62.6	54.0
East Asia & Pacific	50.5	56.9	86,515	692,427	774	2,084			76.5	88.3
Europe & Central Asia	..	84.5	19,065	103,563	110	3,428			..	31.9
Latin America & Carib.	70.6	80.2	78,506	481,799	1,748	2,191			62.3	35.7
Middle East & N. Africa	..	..	6,210	51,373	817	1,184			69.6	70.2
South Asia	54.4	64.4	42,655	139,879	6,996	10,102			52.4	48.3
Sub-Saharan Africa	..	64.8	142,577	257,364	1,011	1,056			58.6	82.5
High income	..	..	9,023,827	18,451,920	17,733	22,359			138.8	157.8

Table 17. Role of government in the economy

Economy	Subsidies and other current transfers % of total expenditure		Value added by state-owned enterprises % of GDP		Military expenditure % of GDP		Composite ICRG risk rating June 1998	Institutional Investor credit rating[a] March 1998	Highest marginal tax rate		
									Individual		Corporate % 1997
									% 1997	On income over (dollars) 1997	
	1985	1996	1985–90	1990–95	1985	1995	June 1998	March 1998	1997	1997	1997
Albania	..	48	..	..	5.3	1.1	53.3	11.1	..	..	..
Algeria	..	..	..	..	2.5	3.2	59.3	25.1	..	..	..
Angola	..	..	..	..	19.9	3.0	45.3	12.5	..	..	..
Argentina	59	60	2.7	1.3	3.8	1.7	74.3	41.6	33	120,000	33
Armenia	..	..	..	..	..	0.9	..	..	..	..	..
Australia	63	68	..	..	2.7	2.5	79.3	73.7	47	39,582	36
Austria	58	59	..	..	1.3	0.9	85.8	87.4	50	63,903	34
Azerbaijan	..	..	..	..	..	2.8	..	..	40	1,757	32
Bangladesh	..	..	3.1	3.4	1.7	1.7	66.5	27.2	..	..	..
Belarus	..	..	..	..	..	0.8	61.8	12.9	..	..	..
Belgium	56	59	2.8	..	3.1	1.7	81.8	82.0	55	75,507	39
Benin	..	..	..	..	2.2	1.2	..	17.3	..	..	..
Bolivia	27	34	13.9	13.8	3.3	2.3	70.0	26.5	13	..	25
Brazil	42	44	7.6	8.0	0.8	1.7	67.8	38.7	25	20,789	15
Bulgaria	..	36	..	..	14.1	2.8	65.3	22.9	40	2,630	36
Burkina Faso	9	..	..	..	1.9	2.9	60.5	20.1	..	..	..
Burundi	..	12	7.3	..	3.0	4.4	..	..	..	..	..
Cambodia	..	..	..	..	..	3.1	..	..	..	..	..
Cameroon	14	13	18.0	..	1.9	1.9	61.3	18.5	60	14,313	39
Canada	60	..	..	..	2.2	1.7	83.3	83.1	29	43,178	38
Central African Republic	..	..	4.1	..	1.8	..	..	..	..	..	..
Chad	2	..	..	..	2.0	3.1	..	..	..	..	..
Chile	51	52	14.4	8.1	4.0	3.8	79.5	63.2	45	6,588	15
China	..	..	..	..	4.9	2.3	74.0	57.6	45	12,051	30
Hong Kong, China	..	..	..	..	..	..	78.3	..	..	..	17
Colombia	48	..	7.0	..	1.6	2.6	55.3	46.9	35	49,934	35
Congo, Dem. Rep.	..	2	..	..	1.2	0.3	45.8	..	..	..	..
Congo, Rep.	..	..	15.1	..	4.0	2.9	45.8	..	..	..	45
Costa Rica	33	23	8.1	..	0.7	0.6	76.5	35.8	25	24,559	30
Côte d'Ivoire	..	..	..	..	..	..	..	..	10	4,489	35
Croatia	..	34	..	..	..	10.5	..	36.0	35	4,675	..
Czech Republic	..	71	..	..	..	2.3	78.0	..	40	27,660	39
Denmark	57	64	..	..	2.3	1.8	87.5	83.4	60	..	34
Dominican Republic	17	12	..	..	1.2	1.4	73.3	..	..	..	..
Ecuador	..	9	10.2	..	2.8	3.7	61.8	26.7	25	61,861	20
Egypt, Arab Rep.	31	24	..	..	12.8	5.7	70.8	..	32	14,749	40
El Salvador	11	22	1.8	..	5.7	1.1	76.3	29.0	30	22,857	25
Estonia	..	46	..	..	..	1.1	..	38.9	26	..	26
Ethiopia	7	..	..	..	6.7	2.2	64.5	17.5	..	..	..
Finland	67	67	..	..	1.7	2.0	88.0	77.9	38	65,352	28
France	63	64	11.2	..	4.0	3.1	80.5	89.3	..	..	33
Gabon	7	..	..	..	2.8	2.6	69.3	24.7	55	..	40
Georgia	..	..	..	..	..	2.4	..	10.6	..	..	..
Germany	55	57	..	..	..	..	83.8	92.3	53	77,406	30
Ghana	10	..	8.5	..	1.0	1.4	63.0	31.4	35	9,173	35
Greece	35	20	11.5	..	7.0	5.5	77.3	53.7	45	68,820	40
Guatemala	14	12	1.9	..	1.6	1.3	72.0	27.0	30	30,002	30
Guinea	..	..	..	..	..	1.5	61.5	16.4	..	..	..
Guinea-Bissau	5	..	..	..	2.9	2.8	44.0	..	..	..	..
Haiti	..	..	..	..	1.5	2.9	52.5	12.7	..	..	..
Honduras	..	..	5.5	..	3.5	1.4	65.8	19.8	40	196,382	15
Hungary	69	..	..	..	7.2	1.5	77.0	52.2	42	6,614	18
India	44	38	13.4	13.4	3.5	2.4	63.8	46.5	40	3,359	40
Indonesia	24	21	14.5	..	2.4	1.8	41.5	49.9	30	20,982	30
Ireland	57	60	..	..	1.7	1.3	86.8	78.0	48	15,732	36
Israel	33	45	..	..	20.3	9.6	69.5	52.5	50	57,730	36
Italy	57	56	..	..	2.2	1.8	83.3	76.6	51	196,005	37
Jamaica	1	..	..	..	0.9	0.8	74.8	30.1	25	1,449	33
Japan	52	..	..	..	1.0	1.0	79.5	90.8	50	258,398	38
Jordan	14	10	..	..	15.5	7.7	73.8	35.5	..	..	..
Kazakhstan	..	..	11.6	..	..	0.9	..	..	40	..	30
Kenya	18	5	11.6	..	2.3	2.3	60.5	26.7	35	374	35
Korea, Rep.	38	48	10.3	..	5.0	3.4	67.8	..	40	94,764	28
Kyrgyz Republic	..	..	..	..	..	0.7	..	..	..	..	..
Lao PDR	..	..	..	..	7.4	4.2	..	..	..	..	..
Latvia	..	55	..	..	..	0.9	..	34.0	25	..	25
Lebanon	..	21	..	..	..	3.7	55.8	32.5	..	..	..
Lesotho	5	..	..	..	5.3	1.9	..	..	..	..	..
Lithuania	..	46	..	..	..	0.5	..	..	33	..	29
Macedonia, FYR	..	..	..	..	..	3.3	..	..	..	..	..
Madagascar	..	8	..	..	1.9	0.9	64.5	..	..	..	..
Malawi	7	..	4.3	..	2.0	1.6	64.3	20.1	38	2,763	38
Malaysia	13	24	..	..	3.8	3.0	70.0	64.5	30	58,893	30
Mali	8	..	..	..	2.9	1.8	64.8	16.7	..	..	..
Mauritania	..	..	..	..	6.9	3.2	..	..	..	..	..

Note: For data comparability and coverage, see the Technical Notes. Figures in italics are for years other than those specified.

STATES AND MARKETS

Economy	Subsidies and other current transfers % of total expenditure		Value added by state-owned enterprises % of GDP		Military expenditure % of GDP		Composite ICRG risk rating	Institutional Investor credit rating[a]	Highest marginal tax rate Individual		Corporate %
									%	On income over (dollars)	
	1985	1996	1985–90	1990–95	1985	1995	June 1998	March 1998	1997	1997	1997
Mauritius	24	25	1.9	..	0.2	0.4	..	51.8	30	2,764	35
Mexico	21	43	6.7	4.9	0.7	1.0	68.5	45.2	35	21,173	34
Moldova	..	..	..	..	..	2.1	..	..	..	..	..
Mongolia	..	42	..	..	8.3	2.4	67.3	..	..	..	..
Morocco	15	12	16.8	..	6.0	4.3	71.5	41.5	44	6,814	35
Mozambique	..	..	..	..	9.9	5.4	57.5	16.1	..	..	..
Namibia	29	..	..	..	..	2.1	78.8	..	35	17,152	35
Nepal	..	..	..	..	1.1	0.9	..	25.5	..	..	..
Netherlands	69	71	..	..	3.0	2.1	87.0	90.5	60	55,730	36
New Zealand	51	37	..	..	2.0	1.3	79.3	73.4	33	21,848	33
Nicaragua	11	25	..	..	17.4	2.2	53.8	13.5	30	20,202	30
Niger	..	..	5.1	..	0.8	1.2	54.5	..	..	..	..
Nigeria	9	..	..	..	1.5	0.8	58.3	15.2	25	754	30
Norway	68	69	..	..	3.1	2.7	93.3	87.3	..	..	28
Oman	6	6	..	..	24.4	16.7	76.0	53.2	0	..	50
Pakistan	15	15	..	..	6.2	6.1	55.5	27.5	35	7,485	46
Panama	17	27	8.2	..	2.0	1.4	73.3	34.9	30	200,000	30
Papua New Guinea	16	32	..	..	1.5	1.4	68.5	33.2	35	14,900	25
Paraguay	23	..	4.8	4.5	1.1	1.4	68.5	32.8	0	..	30
Peru	11	33	6.4	5.7	6.7	1.7	65.8	33.5	30	49,923	30
Philippines	7	17	2.3	2.2	1.4	1.5	67.0	43.3	35	19,016	35
Poland	75	61	..	..	10.2	2.3	82.0	51.9	44	14,542	40
Portugal	45	37	15.1	..	2.9	2.6	84.5	72.7	40	39,247	40
Romania	27	51	..	..	6.9	2.5	62.0	34.5	60	3,600	38
Russian Federation	..	50	..	..	..	11.4	63.8	..	35	8,587	35
Rwanda	..	..	..	..	1.7	5.2	..	..	..	..	..
Saudi Arabia	..	..	..	..	22.7	13.5	73.5	55.4	0	..	45
Senegal	..	..	6.9	..	2.8	1.6	64.5	21.6	50	24,141	..
Sierra Leone	5	31	..	..	0.8	6.1	36.3	5.7	..	..	..
Singapore	10	12	..	..	5.9	4.7	90.0	82.9	28	285,836	26
Slovak Republic	..	..	..	..	..	3.0	76.8	..	42	33,861	..
Slovenia	..	..	..	..	..	1.5	..	55.5	..	..	..
South Africa	31	46	14.9	..	3.8	2.2	72.0	46.5	45	21,440	35
Spain	55	66	..	..	2.4	1.6	79.0	77.3	56	79,896	35
Sri Lanka	16	22	..	..	2.9	4.6	62.8	33.6	35	5,293	35
Sweden	64	71	..	..	3.0	2.8	83.8	77.1	30	30,326	28
Switzerland	..	63	..	..	2.4	1.6	88.3	92.6	13	460,382	46
Syrian Arab Republic	..	..	..	..	21.8	7.2	69.0	..	..	..	..
Tajikistan	..	..	..	..	..	3.7	..	..	..	..	..
Tanzania	22	..	12.9	..	3.8	1.8	60.3	19.3	35	14,075	35
Thailand	8	7	..	..	4.2	2.5	62.3	52.3	37	158,479	30
Togo	11	..	..	..	2.6	2.3	60.8	17.4	..	..	..
Trinidad and Tobago	..	21	9.1	..	..	1.7	78.3	..	35	8,103	35
Tunisia	29	29	..	..	3.6	2.0	73.5	48.0	..	..	..
Turkey	41	47	6.5	5.1	4.6	4.0	49.0	37.8	55	14,877	25
Turkmenistan	..	..	..	..	..	1.7	..	..	..	..	..
Uganda	..	..	..	..	2.0	2.3	63.8	21.2	30	4,800	30
Ukraine	..	..	..	..	..	2.9	67.0	20.5	..	..	..
United Arab Emirates	8	9	..	..	6.7	4.8	78.5	61.4	..	..	..
United Kingdom	55	56	3.4	..	5.1	3.0	83.0	..	40	44,692	33
United States	49	59	1.1	..	6.1	3.8	81.8	92.6	40	271,050	35
Uruguay	43	61	5.0	..	2.9	2.4	73.0	44.6	0	..	30
Uzbekistan	..	..	..	..	..	3.8	..	..	..	..	..
Venezuela	31	43	22.3	..	2.1	1.1	67.3	36.1	34	..	34
Vietnam	..	..	..	..	19.4	2.6	63.5	32.7	50	6,278	25
Yemen, Rep.	..	7	..	..	..	..	66.5	..	..	..	..
Zambia	..	15	32.2	..	..	2.8	61.8	17.5	30	1,376	35
Zimbabwe	37	..	10.8	11.3	5.7	4.0	57.0	33.6	40	5,597	38
World	28 m	.. m			5.2 w	2.8 w	68.5 m	35.8 m			
Low income	..						60.8	..			
Middle income	23	28					70.0	37.0			
Lower middle income	19	23					68.5	33.6			
Upper middle income	36	42					73.3	45.9			
Low & middle income	..	..					65.1	32.0			
East Asia & Pacific	..	18					67.2	49.9			
Europe & Central Asia	..	..					..	..			
Latin America & Carib.	..	26					70.0	33.5			
Middle East & N. Africa	..	13					71.2	41.5			
South Asia	..	26					63.3	27.5			
Sub-Saharan Africa	..	..					61.1	18.9			
High income	55	59					83.2	82.0			

a. This copyrighted material is reprinted with permission from Institutional Investor, Inc., 488 Madison Avenue, New York, N.Y. 10022.

Table 18. Power and transportation

| | Electric power | | | | Transportation | | | | | | |
| | Consumption per capita Kilowatt-hours | | Transmission and distribution losses % of output | | Paved roads % of total | | Goods transported by road Millions of ton-km | | Goods transported by rail Ton-km per $ million of GDP (PPP) | | Air passengers carried Thousands |
Economy	1980	1995	1980	1995	1990	1996	1990	1996	1990	1996	1996
Albania	1,083	623	4	51	..	30	..	*3*	..	..	29
Algeria	265	513	11	17	67	69	..	*20,000*	23,531	*17,681*	3,494
Angola	67	60	25	28	*25*	25	867	2,187	..	..	207
Argentina	1,170	1,519	13	18	29	29	..	..	35,012	..	7,779
Armenia	2,729	811	10	39	99	100	..	*18*	..	..	358
Australia	5,393	8,033	10	7	35	39	91,400	128,000	81,987	..	30,075
Austria	4,371	5,800	6	6	100	100	..	*64,400*	89,822	79,531	4,719
Azerbaijan	2,440	1,806	14	23	..	..	153,111	11,459	..	..	1,233
Bangladesh	16	57	35	32	*7*	7	..	..	7,927	..	1,252
Belarus	2,455	2,451	9	15	*66*	70	..	*350*	1,253,634	619,342	596
Belgium	4,402	6,752	5	5	..	..	..	*428*	46,734	32,214	5,174
Benin	36	43	20	50	20	20	..	..	..	..	75
Bolivia	226	356	10	12	4	6	..	..	35,721	..	1,783
Brazil	977	1,610	12	17	10	9	313,229	384,000	51,447	*50,730*	22,004
Bulgaria	3,349	3,415	10	13	92	92	806	39	333,884	202,772	718
Burkina Faso	..	..	..	..	17	16	..	..	..	..	138
Burundi	..	..	..	..	18	7	..	..	..	..	9
Cambodia	..	..	..	..	8	8	..	..	..	..	..
Cameroon	166	196	0	4	11	13	..	..	33,076	*33,723*	362
Canada	12,329	15,147	9	5	35	..	149,300	182,000	433,360	*266,190*	22,856
Central African Republic	..	..	..	..	..	..	..	..	..	..	75
Chad	..	..	..	..	1	1	..	..	..	..	93
Chile	877	1,698	12	10	14	14	..	..	15,418	*6,096*	3,622
China	253	637	8	7	..	..	335,810	463,000	600,269	360,383	51,770
Hong Kong, China	2,167	4,850	11	15	100	100	..	*14*	..	..	..
Colombia	572	948	16	21	12	12	..	..	2,376	..	8,342
Congo, Dem. Rep.	147	132	8	3	..	..	..	..	33,997	*4,387*	..
Congo, Rep.	94	207	1	0	10	10	..	..	*129,821*	*54,139*	253
Costa Rica	860	1,348	0	8	15	17	..	..	..	..	918
Côte d'Ivoire	192	159	7	4	9	10	..	..	15,597	*13,484*	179
Croatia	..	2,074	..	19	80	82	4	4	192,652	103,711	727
Czech Republic	3,595	4,654	7	8	100	100	..	686	..	196,511	1,394
Denmark	4,245	5,975	7	6	100	100	..	..	19,129	14,713	5,892
Dominican Republic	433	588	21	25	45	49	..	..	..	..	30
Ecuador	361	600	14	21	13	13	*44,978*	54,300	..	..	1,873
Egypt, Arab Rep.	380	896	13	..	72	78	..	..	24,060	*27,908*	4,282
El Salvador	295	507	13	13	14	20	5	4,273	..	..	1,800
Estonia	3,433	3,022	5	20	52	53	..	11	522,628	540,949	149
Ethiopia	16	22	8	3	15	15	..	..	2,466	..	743
Finland	7,779	12,785	6	2	61	64	..	374	100,727	70,489	5,597
France	3,881	5,892	7	6	..	100	..	*1,275*	50,320	39,290	40,300
Gabon	618	737	1	10	8	8	..	..	*42,898*	*61,672*	431
Georgia	1,910	1,057	16	25	94	94	460	*7*	..	..	205
Germany	5,005	5,527	4	5	99	99	288,200	294,160	..	39,068	40,118
Ghana	426	318	3	4	20	24	..	..	6,122	..	197
Greece	2,064	3,259	7	7	92	92	177	201	6,418	1,913	6,396
Guatemala	209	264	10	13	25	28	..	..	..	..	300
Guinea	..	..	..	..	15	17	..	..	..	..	36
Guinea-Bissau	..	..	..	..	8	10	..	..	..	..	21
Haiti	41	32	26	53	22	24	..	..	..	..	..
Honduras	219	333	14	28	21	20	..	..	..	..	498
Hungary	2,335	2,682	12	14	50	43	..	39	247,156	103,268	1,563
India	130	339	18	18	..	50	..	..	248,766	*177,267*	13,255
Indonesia	44	263	19	12	46	46	..	..	8,541	*6,843*	16,173
Ireland	2,528	4,139	10	9	94	94	..	..	14,213	9,314	7,677
Israel	2,826	4,836	5	4	100	100	..	..	16,539	*11,827*	3,695
Italy	2,831	4,163	9	7	100	100	..	..	20,922	18,432	25,838
Jamaica	482	2,049	17	11	64	71	..	..	..	..	1,388
Japan	4,395	6,937	4	4	69	74	..	..	11,937	*8,896*	95,914
Jordan	387	1,139	19	8	100	100	..	..	80,377	47,815	1,299
Kazakhstan	..	3,106	0	15	55	81	2,236	803	4,930,610	..	568
Kenya	93	123	16	16	13	14	..	..	79,482	*46,448*	779
Korea, Rep.	841	3,606	6	5	72	76	..	*410*	40,675	24,665	33,003
Kyrgyz Republic	1,556	1,666	6	28	90	91	330	110	..	..	488
Lao PDR	..	..	..	..	24	14	..	..	..	..	125
Latvia	2,664	1,789	26	32	13	38	..	*30*	1,214,852	*1,115,793*	407
Lebanon	789	1,224	10	13	95	95	..	..	..	..	775
Lesotho	..	..	..	..	18	18	..	..	..	..	17
Lithuania	2,715	1,711	12	15	82	88	*296*	89	991,207	491,829	214
Macedonia, FYR	..	2,443	..	12	59	64	6	3	..	..	287
Madagascar	..	..	..	..	15	12	..	..	..	..	542
Malawi	..	..	..	..	17	19	..	..	14,556	*10,172*	153
Malaysia	630	1,953	9	10	70	75	..	..	11,915	*6,867*	15,118
Mali	..	..	..	..	11	12	..	..	52,037	..	75
Mauritania	..	..	..	..	11	11	..	..	..	..	235

Note: For data comparability and coverage, see the Technical Notes. Figures in italics are for years other than those specified.

STATES AND MARKETS

| | Electric power | | | | Transportation | | | | | | |
| Economy | Consumption per capita Kilowatt-hours | | Transmission and distribution losses % of output | | Paved roads % of total | | Goods transported by road Millions of ton-km | | Goods transported by rail Ton-km per $ million of GDP (PPP) | | Air passengers carried Thousands |
	1980	1995	1980	1995	1990	1996	1990	1996	1990	1996	1996
Mauritius	..	..	..	..	93	93	..	..	..	..	718
Mexico	859	1,305	11	14	35	37	..	..	64,903	52,983	14,678
Moldova	1,495	1,517	8	18	87	87	..	41	..	..	190
Mongolia	..	..	..	..	10	8	39	2	1,132,960	..	662
Morocco	223	407	10	4	49	50	40,390	54,671	72,647	55,334	2,301
Mozambique	370	67	0	5	17	19	..	230	..	..	163
Namibia	..	..	..	..	11	12	..	..	294,413	131,387	237
Nepal	13	39	29	26	38	42	..	..	..	..	755
Netherlands	4,057	5,374	4	4	88	90	..	..	12,850	9,816	..
New Zealand	6,269	8,504	11	9	57	58	..	..	51,139	..	9,597
Nicaragua	315	272	14	28	11	10	..	..	..	..	51
Niger	..	..	..	..	29	8	..	..	..	..	75
Nigeria	68	85	36	32	30	19	597	..	3,231	1	221
Norway	18,289	23,892	9	7	69	72	..	244	..	..	12,727
Oman	663	2,891	4	..	21	30	..	..	..	..	1,620
Pakistan	125	304	29	23	54	57	..	..	41,402	25,084	5,375
Panama	826	1,089	13	19	32	34	..	..	..	..	689
Papua New Guinea	..	..	..	..	3	4	..	..	..	..	970
Paraguay	232	683	0	1	9	10	..	..	..	..	213
Peru	503	525	13	21	10	10	..	..	8,023	5,176	2,328
Philippines	353	337	2	16	..	..	..	..	..	..	7,263
Poland	2,470	2,324	10	13	62	65	..	1,640	464,040	290,148	1,806
Portugal	1,469	2,857	12	11	..	86	130	369	14,010	13,832	4,806
Romania	2,434	1,603	6	11	51	51	..	616,044	515,789	230,933	913
Russian Federation	4,706	4,172	8	10	74	79	68,000	18,000	2,760,928	1,790,023	22,117
Rwanda	..	..	..	..	9	9	..	..	..	..	..
Saudi Arabia	1,356	3,906	9	9	41	43	..	..	4,653	4,384	11,706
Senegal	97	91	10	13	27	29	..	..	51,761	30,617	155
Sierra Leone	..	..	..	..	11	11	..	..	..	..	15
Singapore	2,412	6,018	5	4	97	97	..	..	..	..	11,841
Slovak Republic	3,817	4,075	8	8	99	98	83,571	34,745	..	298,678	63
Slovenia	4,089	4,710	8	5	72	82	8	5	186,105	115,975	393
South Africa	3,263	3,874	8	6	30	42	..	..	443,958	336,265	7,183
Spain	2,401	3,594	9	10	74	99	..	589	22,505	15,998	27,759
Sri Lanka	96	208	15	18	32	40	2,990	3,020	5,834	4,027	1,171
Sweden	10,216	14,096	9	6	71	76	..	..	128,234	103,765	9,879
Switzerland	5,579	6,916	7	6	..	..	401,000	410,000	..	..	10,468
Syrian Arab Republic	354	698	18	..	72	23	..	..	49,114	29,013	599
Tajikistan	2,217	2,367	7	12	72	83	..	..	..	..	594
Tanzania	50	52	4	13	37	4	..	..	..	..	224
Thailand	279	1,199	10	8	55	98	..	..	14,804	..	14,078
Togo	..	..	..	..	21	32	..	..	..	..	75
Trinidad and Tobago	1,584	2,817	0	10	46	51	..	..	..	..	897
Tunisia	379	661	12	10	76	79	..	..	59,563	53,910	1,371
Turkey	439	1,057	12	16	..	25	65,800	135,781	30,633	17,619	8,464
Turkmenistan	1,720	1,109	12	10	74	81	..	..	..	..	523
Uganda	..	..	..	..	..	..	..	..	13,661	12,829	100
Ukraine	3,598	2,785	8	10	94	95	2,078,990	1,254,540	2,208,646	910,955	1,151
United Arab Emirates	5,623	7,752	7	..	94	100	..	..	..	..	4,063
United Kingdom	4,160	5,081	8	7	100	100	..	1,689	17,286	11,465	..
United States	8,914	11,571	9	7	58	61	..	..	360,925	365,655	571,072
Uruguay	977	1,574	15	19	74	90	..	..	12,076	18,789	504
Uzbekistan	2,085	1,731	9	10	79	87	..	..	..	..	1,566
Venezuela	2,067	2,518	12	21	36	39	..	..	..	..	4,487
Vietnam	50	146	18	22	24	25	..	..	16,279	20,223	2,505
Yemen, Rep.	59	99	0	26	9	8	..	..	..	..	..
Zambia	1,016	574	7	11	17	18	..	..	72,889	60,312	..
Zimbabwe	990	738	14	7	14	47	..	..	280,908	200,217	654
World	1,590 w	1,978 w	8 w	8 w	39 m	46 m					1,388,670 s
Low income	156	269	15	15	17	18					34,930
Middle income	919	1,183	10	14	51	51					274,253
Lower middle income	811	991	10	15	51	53					164,113
Upper middle income	1,376	1,962	10	13	51	51					110,140
Low & middle income	638	824	11	15	29	30					309,184
East Asia & Pacific	243	575	10	13	17	12					110,432
Europe & Central Asia	3,189	2,798	8	12	77	82					47,754
Latin America & Carib.	859	1,298	12	17	22	26					76,532
Middle East & N. Africa	485	1,122	10	15	67	54					36,896
South Asia	116	300	20	19	38	42					22,305
Sub-Saharan Africa	444	437	15	13	17	17					15,658
High income	5,557	7,748	7	6	85	92					1,079,486

Table 19.   Communications, information, and science and technology

Economy	Daily newspapers 1994	Radios 1996	Television sets 1996	Telephone main lines 1996	Mobile telephones 1996	Personal computers 1996	Internet hosts Per 10,000 people July 1997	Scientists and engineers in R&D Per million people 1981–95	High-technology exports % of mfg. exports 1996	No. of patent applications filed[a] 1995 Residents	No. of patent applications filed[a] 1995 Nonresidents
Albania	54	179	173	19	1	..	0.32	..	..	..	1,564
Algeria	46	..	68	44	0	3.4	0.01	..	15	28	114
Angola	11	58	51	5	0	..	0.02	..	..	..	..
Argentina	138	..	347	174	16	24.6	5.32	350	17	..	..
Armenia	23	..	216	154	0	..	0.88	..	..	..	15,570
Australia	258	..	666	519	208	311.3	382.44	2,477	39	9,325	28,156
Austria	472	345	493	466	74	148.0	108.25	1,604	24	2,419	63,707
Azerbaijan	28	..	212	85	2	..	0.11	..	..	221	31
Bangladesh	6	48	7	3	0	..	0.00	..	..	70	156
Belarus	187	322	292	208	1	..	0.44	3,300	..	626	16,625
Belgium	321	..	464	465	47	167.3	84.64	1,814	..	1,464	52,187
Benin	2	1,461	73	6	0	..	0.02	177	..	..	..
Bolivia	69	..	202	47	4	..	0.69	250	41	17	106
Brazil	45	222	289	96	16	18.4	4.20	165	18	2,757	23,040
Bulgaria	..	350	361	313	3	295.2	6.65	4,240	..	370	16,953
Burkina Faso	0	32	6	3	0	..	0.04	..	..	..	..
Burundi	3	82	2	2	0	..	0.01	32	..	..	1
Cambodia	..	121	9	1	2	..	0.01	..	..	..	..
Cameroon	4	326	75	5	0	..	0.05	..	3	..	..
Canada	189	..	709	602	114	192.5	228.05	2,322	24	3,039	40,565
Central African Republic	1	93	5	3	0	..	0.02	55	0	..	..
Chad	0	620	2	1	..	..	0.00	..	..	..	..
Chile	100	..	280	156	23	45.1	13.12	364	18	181	1,535
China	23	161	252	45	6	3.0	0.21	537	21	10,066	31,707
Hong Kong, China	719	..	388	547	216	150.5	74.84	..	27	23	1,938
Colombia	64	..	188	118	13	23.3	1.81	39	21	141	1,093
Congo, Dem. Rep.	3	102	41	1	0	..	0.00	..	..	3	15
Congo, Rep.	8	318	8	8	..	..	0.02	461	12	..	..
Costa Rica	99	..	220	155	14	..	12.14	539	14	..	..
Côte d'Ivoire	7	..	60	9	1	1.4	0.17	..	..	..	..
Croatia	575	..	251	309	14	20.9	14.08	1,977	17	265	335
Czech Republic	219	..	406	273	19	53.2	47.66	1,285	14	628	19,382
Denmark	365	..	533	618	250	304.1	259.73	2,647	25	2,257	59,810
Dominican Republic	34	..	84	83	8	..	0.03	..	19	..	..
Ecuador	72	..	148	73	5	3.9	0.90	169	11	8	270
Egypt, Arab Rep.	64	..	126	50	0	5.8	0.31	458	9	..	..
El Salvador	50	..	250	56	3	..	0.34	19	17	3	64
Estonia	242	..	449	299	47	6.7	45.35	3,296	19	16	14,751
Ethiopia	2	206	4	3	..	..	0.00	..	..	..	..
Finland	473	1,386	605	549	292	182.1	653.61	3,675	23	2,533	20,192
France	237	..	598	564	42	150.7	49.86	2,537	31	16,140	73,626
Gabon	16	..	76	32	6	6.3	0.00	189	32	..	..
Georgia	..	..	474	105	0	..	0.55	..	..	288	15,660
Germany	317	..	493	538	71	233.2	106.68	3,016	25	51,948	84,667
Ghana	18	..	41	4	1	1.2	0.15	..	..	..	42
Greece	156	..	442	509	53	33.4	18.76	774	13	452	44,697
Guatemala	23	..	122	31	4	2.8	0.79	99	15	5	57
Guinea	..	100	8	2	0	0.3	0.00	264	..	..	..
Guinea-Bissau	6	40	..	7	..	..	0.09	..	..	..	..
Haiti	6	60	5	8	..	..	0.00	..	..	..	..
Honduras	44	108	80	31	0	..	0.94	..	3	7	40
Hungary	228	..	444	261	46	44.1	33.29	1,157	19	1,117	19,770
India	..	105	64	15	0	1.5	0.05	151	10	1,545	5,021
Indonesia	20	..	232	21	3	4.8	0.54	181	18	..	..
Ireland	170	..	469	395	82	145.0	90.89	1,871	62	927	44,660
Israel	281	..	303	446	184	117.6	104.79	4,826	30	1,266	3,159
Italy	105	..	436	440	112	92.3	36.91	1,303	15	1,625	63,330
Jamaica	66	792	326	142	22	4.6	1.36	8	67	7	54
Japan	576	..	700	489	214	128.0	75.80	5,677	39	335,061	53,896
Jordan	48	325	175	60	3	7.2	0.38	106	26	..	..
Kazakhstan	..	..	275	118	0	..	0.70	..	..	1,031	16,368
Kenya	13	..	19	8	0	1.6	0.16	..	..	..	28,728
Korea, Rep.	404	1,208	326	430	70	131.7	28.77	2,636	39	59,249	37,308
Kyrgyz Republic	11	..	238	75	..	..	0.23	..	24	119	15,599
Lao PDR	3	134	10	6	1	1.1	0.00	..	..	..	..
Latvia	228	..	598	298	11	7.9	21.03	1,165	16	210	16,140
Lebanon	172	..	355	149	65	24.3	2.72	67	..	..	..
Lesotho	7	77	13	9	1	..	0.08	..	..	8	2,608
Lithuania	136	583	376	268	14	6.5	7.46	1,278	23	106	15,882
Macedonia, FYR	21	..	170	170	0	..	2.15	1,258	..	100	3,084
Madagascar	4	214	24	3	0	..	0.03	22	3	21	15,802
Malawi	2	902	..	4	0	..	0.00	..	3	5	28,868
Malaysia	124	..	228	183	74	42.8	19.30	87	67	141	3,911
Mali	4	168	11	2	0	..	0.03	..	..	..	..
Mauritania	0	188	82	4	..	5.3	0.00	..	..	..	..

Note: For data comparability and coverage, see the Technical Notes. Figures in italics are for years other than those specified.

STATES AND MARKETS

Economy	Daily newspapers 1994	Radios 1996	Television sets 1996	Telephone main lines 1996	Mobile telephones 1996	Personal computers 1996	Internet hosts Per 10,000 people July 1997	Scientists and engineers in R&D Per million people 1981–95	High-technology exports % of mfg. exports 1996	No. of patent applications filed[a] 1995 Residents	No. of patent applications filed[a] 1995 Nonresidents
Mauritius	68	..	219	162	18	31.9	1.84	361	1	3	4
Mexico	113	..	193	95	11	29.0	3.72	95	32	436	23,233
Moldova	24	216	307	140	0	2.6	0.39	..	9	271	15,606
Mongolia	88	78	63	39	0	..	0.07	..	2	130	15,847
Morocco	13	..	145	45	2	1.7	0.32	..	24	89	292
Mozambique	5	46	3	3	..	0.8	0.02	..	5	..	..
Namibia	102	..	29	54	4	12.7	2.16	..	..	..	..
Nepal	8	57	4	5	..	..	0.07	22	0	3	5
Netherlands	334	..	495	543	52	232.0	219.01	2,656	42	4,460	59,279
New Zealand	297	..	517	499	138	266.1	424.34	1,778	11	1,418	19,230
Nicaragua	30	..	170	26	1	..	1.60	214	40	..	35
Niger	1	61	23	2	..	..	0.04	..	..	..	..
Nigeria	18	..	55	4	0	4.1	0.00	15	..	..	..
Norway	607	..	569	555	287	273.0	474.63	3,434	24	1,278	20,398
Oman	30	394	591	86	6	10.9	0.00	..	8	..	..
Pakistan	21	..	24	18	0	1.2	0.07	54	3	21	678
Panama	62	..	229	122	..	..	1.44	..	..	16	62
Papua New Guinea	15	..	4	11	1	..	0.18	..	..	..	..
Paraguay	42	..	144	36	7	..	0.47	..	4	..	..
Peru	86	..	142	60	8	5.9	2.63	273	11	..	..
Philippines	65	168	125	25	13	9.3	0.59	90	62	..	..
Poland	141	533	418	169	6	36.2	11.22	1,083	11	2,598	19,491
Portugal	41	..	367	375	67	60.5	18.26	599	12	96	58,605
Romania	297	..	226	140	1	5.3	2.66	1,382	7	1,811	16,856
Russian Federation	267	341	386	175	2	23.7	5.51	4,358	..	17,611	23,746
Rwanda	0	76	..	3	..	..	0.01	12	..	..	..
Saudi Arabia	54	..	263	106	10	37.2	0.15	..	..	28	718
Senegal	6	..	38	11	0	7.2	0.31	342	55	..	..
Sierra Leone	2	..	17	4	..	..	0.00	..	..	..	5
Singapore	364	..	361	513	141	216.8	196.30	2,512	71	10	11,871
Slovak Republic	256	953	384	232	5	186.1	20.47	1,922	16	273	17,659
Slovenia	185	..	375	333	20	47.8	85.66	2,998	16	318	16,267
South Africa	33	179	123	100	22	37.7	30.67	..	..	5,549	5,501
Spain	104	1,273	509	392	33	94.2	31.00	1,098	17	2,329	68,922
Sri Lanka	25	195	82	14	4	3.3	0.33	173	3	76	15,944
Sweden	483	..	476	682	282	214.9	321.48	3,714	31	6,396	64,165
Switzerland	409	..	493	640	93	408.5	207.98	..	..	5,116	64,626
Syrian Arab Republic	18	..	91	82	..	1.4	0.00	..	..	43	12
Tajikistan	13	196	279	42	0	..	0.00	..	..	33	15,598
Tanzania	8	398	16	3	0	..	0.02	..	..	..	..
Thailand	48	204	167	70	28	16.7	2.11	173	36	..	..
Togo	2	381	14	6	..	..	0.01	..	..	..	..
Trinidad and Tobago	135	..	318	168	11	19.2	3.24	240	33	24	15,515
Tunisia	46	176	156	64	1	6.7	0.02	388	10	31	115
Turkey	44	..	309	224	13	13.8	3.60	209	8	206	1,506
Turkmenistan	..	..	163	74	..	..	0.00	..	..	..	8,420
Uganda	2	123	26	2	0	0.5	0.01	..	..	..	20,840
Ukraine	118	..	341	181	1	5.6	2.09	6,761	..	4,806	17,548
United Arab Emirates	161	..	276	302	79	65.5	7.66	..	..	..	..
United Kingdom	351	..	612	528	122	192.6	149.06	2,417	40	25,355	90,399
United States	228	..	806	640	165	362.4	442.11	3,732	44	127,476	107,964
Uruguay	237	..	305	209	25	22.0	3.18	..	10	..	..
Uzbekistan	7	..	190	76	0	..	0.06	1,760	..	1,039	15,873
Venezuela	215	..	180	117	35	21.1	2.06	208	14	..	..
Vietnam	8	..	180	16	1	3.3	0.00	334	..	23	16,959
Yemen, Rep.	17	45	278	13	1	..	0.00	..	0	..	..
Zambia	8	130	80	9	0	..	0.27	..	..	4	90
Zimbabwe	18	..	29	15	..	6.7	0.24	..	5	56	177
World	98 w	.. w	211 w	133 w	28 w	50.0 w	34.75 w				
Low income	12	..	47	11	0	..	0.06				
Middle income	62	..	252	78	8	12.1	2.38				
Lower middle income	54	186	246	62	5	8.2	0.87				
Upper middle income	96	..	255	140	19	27.7	8.44				
Low & middle income	49	163	177	52	5	8.7	1.53				
East Asia & Pacific	28	160	228	41	7	4.5	0.57				
Europe & Central Asia	171	..	353	185	5	17.1	6.53				
Latin America & Carib.	83	..	217	102	14	23.2	3.48				
Middle East & N. Africa	38	..	145	65	3	17.5	0.23				
South Asia	..	119	53	14	0	1.5	0.06				
Sub-Saharan Africa	11	..	43	14	..	..	2.03				
High income	303	..	611	540	131	224.0	203.46				

a. Other patent applications filed in 1995 include those with the African Intellectual Property Organization (27 by residents, 15,819 by nonresidents), the African Regional Industrial Property Organization (4 by residents, 15,032 by nonresidents), and the European Patent Office (35,390 by residents, 42,869 by nonresidents). Information provided by WIPO. The International Bureau of WIPO assumes no liability or responsibility with regard to the transformation of these data for this table.

Table 20. Global trade

Economy	Merchandise exports Millions of dollars 1980	1996	Mfg. % of total 1980	1996	Merchandise imports Millions of dollars 1980	1996	Mfg. % of total 1980	1996	Trade share of GDP (%) 1980	1996	Net barter terms of trade 1987 = 100 1980	1996
Albania	..	296[a]	..	..	..	1,283[a]	..	..	46	52	..	..
Algeria	15,624	12,609[a]	0	4	10,524	8,372[a]	72	65	65	56	..	..
Angola	1,902	4,472[a]	13	..	873	2,039[a]	73	..	..	118	..	..
Argentina	8,019	23,810	23	30	10,539	23,762	77	87	12	19	..	..
Armenia	..	290[a]	..	..	..	862[a]	..	..	..	86	..	..
Australia	21,279	53,252	22	30	19,870	60,897	75	86	34	42	122.6	102.5
Austria	17,478	57,822	83	88	24,415	67,142	69	82	74	78	..	..
Azerbaijan	..	618[a]	..	..	..	1,255[a]	..	..	..	62	..	..
Bangladesh	740	3,297[a]	68	..	1,980	6,898[a]	58	..	24	38	148.4	..
Belarus	..	5,122[a]	..	..	..	6,778[a]	..	..	..	96	..	..
Belgium[b]	63,967	168,010	69	77	71,192	157,860	58	73	127	140	..	..
Benin	49	255[a]	3	..	302	869[a]	62	..	66	57	..	..
Bolivia	1,036	1,087	3	16	655	1,601	78	83	38	47	..	..
Brazil	20,132	47,164	37	54	24,949	53,736	41	71	20	15	96.0	..
Bulgaria	10,372	4,543[a]	..	..	9,650	4,313[a]	..	..	66	127	..	..
Burkina Faso	90	216[a]	11	..	358	783[a]	64	..	43	41	119.9	..
Burundi	129	37[a]	4	..	106	125[a]	61	..	32	19	..	..
Cambodia	15	300[a]	64	..	108	1,647[a]	26	..	..	69	..	..
Cameroon	1,321	1,758	4	8	1,538	1,204	78	67	54	32	..	..
Canada	63,105	199,071	48	63	57,707	170,265	72	82	55	73	113.3	101.7
Central African Republic	111	115	26	43	80	180	75	61	66	41	..	..
Chad	72	125[a]	15	..	37	217[a]	72	56	65	72	..	..
Chile	4,584	14,979	9	15	5,123	16,810	60	78	50	55	595.3	..
China*	18,136	151,047	..	84	19,501	138,833	..	79	13	40	..	..
Hong Kong, China[c]	19,703	180,744	91	92	22,027	198,543	75	88	181	285	100.7	100.2
Colombia	3,945	10,976	20	34	4,663	13,863	69	78	32	37	123.8	89.7
Congo, Dem. Rep.	2,507	1,465[a]	6	..	1,117	1,331[a]	75	..	33	68	..	..
Congo, Rep.	955	1,833[a]	7	2	418	1,590[a]	65	71	120	164	..	..
Costa Rica	1,032	2,882	28	24	1,596	3,871	68	77	63	91	101.9	..
Côte d'Ivoire	2,979	4,996[a]	5	..	2,552	2,909[a]	68	..	76	83	133.2	..
Croatia	..	4,512	..	72	..	7,788	..	69	..	95	..	..
Czech Republic	..	21,882	..	84	..	27,709	..	79	..	117	..	..
Denmark	16,407	48,868	55	59	19,315	43,093	57	71	66	63	90.8	101.0
Dominican Republic	704	3,893[a]	24	77	1,426	6,300[a]	54	..	48	63	..	..
Ecuador	2,481	4,762	3	9	2,215	3,733	87	81	51	57	..	..
Egypt, Arab Rep.	3,046	3,534	11	32	4,860	13,020	59	60	73	46	..	..
El Salvador	720	1,023	35	41	976	2,670	61	66	67	54	..	..
Estonia	..	2,074	..	68	..	3,196	..	72	..	159	..	..
Ethiopia[d]	424	494[a]	0	..	721	1,492[a]	64	..	27	41	..	..
Finland	14,140	40,520	70	83	15,632	30,853	56	73	67	68	86.2	..
France	110,865	283,318	73	79	134,328	274,088	54	76	44	45	90.0	105.2
Gabon	2,189	3,146	5	2	674	898	78	75	96	96	..	..
Georgia	..	261[a]	..	..	..	884[a]	..	..	..	44	..	..
Germany[e]	191,647	511,728	85	87	185,922	443,043	52	71	..	46	85.9	..
Ghana	942	1,684[a]	1	..	1,129	3,219[a]	59	..	18	65	..	..
Greece	5,142	9,558[a]	47	50	10,531	26,881[a]	60	71	39	43	97.8	..
Guatemala	1,486	2,031	24	31	1,559	3,146	65	68	47	40	..	..
Guinea	374	774[a]	1	..	299	810[a]	62	..	..	41	..	..
Guinea-Bissau	11	56[a]	8	..	55	107[a]	69	..	52	42	..	..
Haiti	376	180[a]	63	..	536	865[a]	62	..	52	35	..	..
Honduras	813	845	12	31	1,009	1,922	72	69	80	100	..	..
Hungary	8,677	13,138	65	68	9,212	16,207	62	73	80	79	112.2	..
India	7,511	32,325[a]	59	74	13,819	36,055[a]	39	54	17	27	71.5	..
Indonesia	21,909	49,727	2	51	10,834	42,925	65	71	54	51	..	..
Ireland	8,473	45,565	54	82	11,133	35,750	66	77	108	134	93.0	90.6
Israel	5,540	20,504	82	91	8,023	29,796	57	82	91	69	95.0	109.3
Italy	77,640	250,718	84	89	98,119	202,908	45	68	47	51	85.1	108.7
Jamaica	942	1,347	63	69	1,178	2,916	39	65	102	123	..	..
Japan	129,542	410,481	95	95	139,892	347,496	19	55	28	17	65.5	..
Jordan	402	1,466[a]	34	49	2,394	4,293[a]	61	61	124	125	98.4	120.5
Kazakhstan	..	6,230[a]	..	..	..	4,261[a]	..	..	..	65	..	..
Kenya	1,313	2,203[a]	12	..	2,590	3,480[a]	56	..	67	70	144.3	109.6
Korea, Rep.	17,446	124,404	90	92	22,228	144,724	43	67	74	69	84.7	89.5
Kyrgyz Republic	..	507	..	38	..	838	..	48	..	86	..	..
Lao PDR	9	334[a]	34	..	85	642[a]	56	..	..	65	..	..
Latvia	..	1,443	..	61	..	2,319	..	62	..	102	..	..
Lebanon	930	1,153[a]	58	..	3,132	7,560[a]	63	..	..	69	..	..
Lesotho	..	..	..	..	..	..	..	..	142	136	..	..
Lithuania	..	3,356	..	60	..	4,559	..	61	..	115	..	..
Macedonia, FYR	..	1,119[a]	..	..	..	1,941[a]	..	..	..	86	..	..
Madagascar	387	616[a]	6	14	676	671[a]	73	65	43	42	..	..
Malawi	269	501[a]	6	7	440	687[a]	75	73	64	49	118.0	..
Malaysia	12,939	78,151	19	76	10,735	76,082	67	85	113	183	131.9	..
Mali	235	288[a]	1	..	491	1,159[a]	45	..	49	56	..	..
Mauritania	255	574[a]	0	..	287	616[a]	52	..	104	115	..	..
* Data for Taiwan, China	19,837	115,646	..	..	19,791	101,338	..	..	..	..	78.0	98.7

Note: For data comparability and coverage, see the Technical Notes. Figures in italics are for years other than those specified.

GLOBAL LINKS

Economy	Merchandise exports Millions of dollars 1980	1996	Mfg. % of total 1980	1996	Merchandise imports Millions of dollars 1980	1996	Mfg. % of total 1980	1996	Trade share of GDP (%) 1980	1996	Net barter terms of trade 1987 = 100 1980	1996
Mauritius	420	1,699	27	68	619	2,255	54	71	113	126	69.7	..
Mexico	15,442	95,199	12	78	19,591	97,630	75	80	24	42	..	..
Moldova	..	1,104a	..	23	..	1,522a	..	42	..	118	..	..
Mongolia	..	424	..	10	..	451	..	65	78	89	..	..
Morocco	2,403	4,742	24	50	4,182	8,254	47	57	45	55	103.4	77.2
Mozambique	511	226	18	17	550	783	70	62	66	84	..	..
Namibia	..	..	..	..	..	..	..	..	143	107	..	..
Nepal	94	358a	30	99	226	664a	73	47	30	60	..	..
Netherlands	73,871	177,228	50	63	76,889	160,700	53	72	103	100	96.9	102.3
New Zealand	5,262	13,789	20	29	5,515	14,716	65	83	62	59	95.9	105.6
Nicaragua	414	653	14	34	882	1,076	63	71	68	106	87.9	..
Niger	580	79a	2	..	608	567a	55	..	63	37	..	..
Nigeria	25,057	15,610a	0	..	13,408	6,433a	76	..	49	28	..	..
Norway	18,481	48,922	32	23	16,952	34,290	67	80	80	72	122.8	103.1
Oman	3,748	6,395a	3	14	1,732	4,610a	66	70	100	89	..	..
Pakistan	2,588	9,266	48	84	5,350	11,812	54	57	37	37	95.2	88.1
Panama	353	558	9	20	1,447	2,778	58	71	187	185	..	..
Papua New Guinea	1,133	2,554a	3	..	958	1,866a	61	..	97	101	..	..
Paraguay	310	1,043	12	17	615	3,107	60	67	44	46	..	..
Peru	3,266	5,226	17	16	2,573	7,947	73	71	42	29	..	..
Philippines	5,751	20,328	21	84	8,295	34,663	48	78	52	94	103.9	..
Poland	16,997	24,387	61	74	19,089	37,092	51	75	59	49	95.5	..
Portugal	4,629	23,184	70	86	9,293	33,979	52	74	63	74	..	..
Romania	12,230	8,084	..	77	13,201	11,435	..	65	75	60	..	..
Russian Federation	..	81,438a	..	..	..	43,318a	..	..	..	42	..	..
Rwanda	138	168a	0	..	155	385a	72	..	41	28	..	..
Saudi Arabia	109,113	58,177a	1	..	29,957	27,764a	82	79	101	72	..	..
Senegal	477	655a	15	50	1,038	1,672a	48	53	72	67	81.7	..
Sierra Leone	302	214a	40	..	268	334a	71	..	73	43	..	..
Singapore	19,375	124,794	47	84	24,003	131,083	54	83	440	356	109.0	89.4
Slovak Republic	..	8,824	..	68	..	10,924	..	61	..	126	..	..
Slovenia	..	8,309	..	90	..	9,412	..	77	..	111	..	..
South Africaf	25,539	18,132	18	49	18,551	26,861	62	72	64	52	108.8	117.0
Spain	20,827	101,417	72	78	33,901	122,842	38	72	34	47	92.2	114.7
Sri Lanka	1,043	4,097a	19	73	2,035	5,028a	52	75	87	79	93.8	109.4
Sweden	30,788	82,704	78	80	33,426	63,970	62	79	61	73	91.4	103.5
Switzerland	29,471	80,756	90	94	36,148	79,192	71	85	76	68	79.3	..
Syrian Arab Republic	2,108	3,980a	7	..	4,124	6,399a	55	..	54	..	214.9	97.0
Tajikistan	..	770a	..	..	..	668a	..	..	..	228	..	..
Tanzania	528	828a	14	..	1,211	1,642a	63	..	..	58	..	..
Thailand	6,369	55,789a	25	73	9,450	73,289a	51	81	54	83	116.5	..
Togo	335	363a	11	..	550	1,032a	59	..	107	69	..	..
Trinidad and Tobago	4,077	2,456	5	39	3,178	2,204	49	62	89	95	195.6	..
Tunisia	2,234	5,517	36	80	3,509	7,681	58	75	86	86	104.3	..
Turkey	2,910	23,045	27	74	7,573	42,733	43	69	17	49	..	..
Turkmenistan	..	1,693a	..	..	..	1,313a	..	..	..	..	..	..
Uganda	465	568a	1	..	417	725a	65	..	45	34	..	..
Ukraine	..	16,040a	..	..	..	24,042a	..	..	..	93	..	..
United Arab Emirates	21,618	28,096a	..	..	8,098	30,374a	74	..	112	139	..	..
United Kingdom	114,422	259,039	71	82	117,632	283,682	61	80	52	58	105.3	102.9
United States	212,887	575,477	66	78	250,280	814,888	50	78	21	24	88.8	101.2
Uruguay	1,059	2,391	38	36	1,652	3,322	56	74	36	38	..	..
Uzbekistan	..	2,671a	..	..	..	4,761a	..	..	..	69	..	..
Venezuela	19,293	22,633	2	12	10,669	8,902	79	77	51	61	215.2	148.9
Vietnam	123	7,016a	14	..	618	13,910a	55	..	..	97	..	..
Yemen, Rep.	23	4,538a	47	1	1,853	3,443a	63	59	..	91	..	..
Zambia	1,330	1,020a	16	..	1,100	1,106a	71	..	87	84	..	..
Zimbabwe	433	2,094	36	30	193	2,808	73	73	56	82	..	..
World	1,875,309 t	5,398,224 t	65 w	78 w	2,004,907 t	5,555,200 t	54 w	75 w	39 w	43 w		
Low income	..	..	27	..	..	..	57	..	30	42		
Middle income	..	..	..	..	..	..	..	..	43	52		
Lower middle income	..	..	..	..	..	..	..	..	..	55		
Upper middle income	219,035	494,404	23	57	194,621	517,056	63	76	46	47		
Low & middle income	..	..	..	..	..	..	..	..	40	52		
East Asia & Pacific	..	371,815	..	75	..	395,405	..	78	32	58		
Europe & Central Asia	..	..	..	..	..	..	..	..	..	64		
Latin America & Carib.	102,403	261,905	19	45	110,273	315,627	63	76	32	33		
Middle East & N. Africa	..	..	..	..	100,712	..	70	..	63	54		
South Asia	12,464	50,819	53	76	..	62,294	..	55	21	30		
Sub-Saharan Africa	..	..	..	..	..	..	..	..	59	56		
High income	1,333,696	4,048,665	73	81	1,488,876	4,145,913	52	75	38	40		

a. Data are from IMF, *Direction of Trade Statistics*. b. Includes Luxembourg. c. Includes reexports. d. Data prior to 1992 include Eritrea. e. Data prior to 1990 refer to the Federal Republic of Germany before unification. f. Data are for the South African Customs Union, which includes Botswana, Lesotho, Namibia, and South Africa.

Table 21.   Aid and financial flows

| | Millions of dollars | | | | External debt | | | Official development assistance | | | |
| | Net private capital flows | | Foreign direct investment | | Total Millions of dollars | | Present value % of GNP | Dollars per capita | | % of GNP | |
Economy	1980	1996	1980	1996	1980	1996	1996	1991	1996	1991	1996
Albania	31	92	0	90	..	781	32	99	68	29	8.1
Algeria	−442	−72	349	4	19,365	33,259	71	13	11	1	0.7
Angola	237	753	−335	300	..	10,612	310	29	49	10	15.8
Argentina	−203	14,417	1,836	4,285	27,157	93,841	31	9	8	0	0.1
Armenia	..	18	..	18	..	552	27	1	78	0	18.2
Australia	..	..	6,517	6,321	..	..	..	..	..	..	..
Austria	..	..	653	3,826	..	..	..	..	..	..	..
Azerbaijan	..	601	..	601	..	435	10	0	14	0	3.0
Bangladesh	70	92	3	15	4,230	16,083	30	17	10	8	3.9
Belarus	..	7	..	18	..	1,071	4	18	7	1	0.4
Belgium	..	..	..	..	..	..	..	..	..	..	..
Benin	1	2	1	2	424	1,594	57[a]	55	52	15	13.5
Bolivia	3	571	27	527	2,702	5,174	57[a]	76	112	10	13.3
Brazil	562	28,384	989	9,889	71,520	179,047	26	1	3	0	0.1
Bulgaria	−42	300	4	115	..	9,819	89	37	20	3	1.9
Burkina Faso	0	0	0	0	330	1,294	31[a]	46	39	15	16.5
Burundi	−5	0	1	1	166	1,127	47	46	32	22	18.1
Cambodia	0	290	0	294	..	2,111	54	10	44	6	14.5
Cameroon	−125	−28	−113	35	2,588	9,515	106	44	30	4	4.9
Canada	..	..	7,581	6,398	..	..	..	..	..	..	..
Central African Republic	0	5	1	5	195	928	51	58	50	13	16.1
Chad	−1	18	0	18	284	997	51	46	46	15	26.9
Chile	2,098	6,803	590	4,091	12,081	27,411	48	9	14	0	0.3
China	8,107	50,100	3,487	40,180	4,504	128,817	17	2	2	1	0.3
Hong Kong, China	..	..	..	..	..	..	..	6	2	0	0.0
Colombia	345	7,739	500	3,322	6,941	28,859	40	4	7	0	0.3
Congo, Dem. Rep.	−24	2	−12	2	4,770	12,826	127	12	4	6	2.8
Congo, Rep.	−100	−7	0	8	1,526	5,240	260	57	159	6	22.9
Costa Rica	23	387	163	410	2,744	3,454	37	56	−2	3	−0.1
Côte d'Ivoire	57	160	48	21	7,462	19,713	171[a]	51	67	7	9.9
Croatia	..	915	..	349	..	4,634	24	0	28	0	0.7
Czech Republic	876	4,894	207	1,435	..	20,094	42	22	12	1	0.2
Denmark	..	..	1,132	773	..	..	..	..	..	..	..
Dominican Republic	130	366	133	394	2,002	4,310	33	9	13	1	0.8
Ecuador	183	816	126	447	5,997	14,491	78	23	22	2	1.5
Egypt, Arab Rep.	698	1,434	734	636	19,131	31,407	35	94	37	14	3.3
El Salvador	8	48	2	25	911	2,894	26	57	55	6	3.1
Estonia	..	191	..	150	..	405	9	10	42	0	1.4
Ethiopia	−45	−205	12	5	824	10,077	149	21	15	21	14.3
Finland	..	..	812	1,118	..	..	..	..	..	..	..
France	..	..	13,813	21,972	..	..	..	..	..	..	..
Gabon	103	−114	74	−65	1,514	4,213	86	145	112	3	2.6
Georgia	..	40	..	40	..	1,356	26	0	59	0	7.1
Germany	..	..	2,532	−3,183	..	..	..	..	..	..	..
Ghana	−5	477	15	120	1,398	6,202	56[a]	58	37	14	10.5
Greece	..	..	..	..	..	..	..	..	..	..	..
Guatemala	44	5	48	77	1,166	3,785	23	21	20	2	1.4
Guinea	−1	41	18	24	1,133	3,240	61	64	44	14	7.8
Guinea-Bissau	2	1	2	1	140	937	248	118	164	48	67.5
Haiti	8	4	8	4	303	897	20	28	51	6	14.4
Honduras	77	65	44	75	1,472	4,453	92	58	60	11	9.2
Hungary	−308	1,618	0	1,982	9,764	26,958	62	61	18	2	0.4
India	1,873	6,404	162	2,587	20,581	89,827	22	3	2	1	0.6
Indonesia	3,219	18,030	1,093	7,960	20,938	129,033	64	10	6	2	0.5
Ireland	..	..	627	2,456	..	..	..	..	..	..	..
Israel	..	..	101	2,110	..	..	..	353	389	3	0.4
Italy	..	..	6,411	3,523	..	..	..	..	..	..	..
Jamaica	92	191	138	175	1,913	4,041	92	67	24	5	1.4
Japan	..	..	1,777	200	..	..	..	..	..	..	..
Jordan	254	−119	38	16	1,971	8,118	110	260	119	24	7.2
Kazakhstan	..	615	..	310	..	2,920	14	7	8	0	0.6
Kenya	124	−104	57	13	3,383	6,893	64	38	22	12	6.8
Korea, Rep.	..	..	788	2,325	..	..	..	1	−3	0	0.0
Kyrgyz Republic	..	46	..	46	..	789	37	0	51	0	13.9
Lao PDR	6	104	6	104	350	2,263	45	35	72	14	18.2
Latvia	..	331	..	328	..	472	9	1	32	0	1.6
Lebanon	12	740	6	80	510	3,996	33	36	57	3	1.8
Lesotho	17	38	17	28	72	654	33	69	53	13	8.7
Lithuania	..	469	..	152	..	1,286	16	1	24	0	1.2
Macedonia, FYR	..	8	..	8	..	1,659	74	0	53	0	5.3
Madagascar	7	5	22	10	1,249	4,175	97	38	27	18	9.1
Malawi	2	−3	0	1	831	2,312	76[a]	60	50	25	23.2
Malaysia	769	12,096	2,333	4,500	6,611	39,777	52	16	−22	1	−0.5
Mali	−8	23	−7	23	727	3,020	56[a]	53	51	19	19.4
Mauritania	6	25	7	5	843	2,363	157	107	117	21	26.4

Note: For data comparability and coverage, see the Technical Notes. Figures in italics are for years other than those specified.

GLOBAL LINKS

	Millions of dollars				External debt			Official development assistance			
	Net private capital flows		Foreign direct investment		Total Millions of dollars		Present value % of GNP	Dollars per capita		% of GNP	
Economy	1980	1996	1980	1996	1980	1996	1996	1991	1996	1991	1996
Mauritius	85	112	41	37	467	1,818	45	63	17	2	0.5
Mexico	8,240	23,647	2,634	7,619	57,378	157,125	44	3	3	0	0.1
Moldova	..	115	..	41	..	834	39	0	9	0	2.1
Mongolia	16	−15	0	5	0	524	36	31	81	24	21.3
Morocco	337	388	165	311	9,247	21,767	61	50	24	5	1.8
Mozambique	35	23	9	29	49	5,842	411[a]	74	51	84	59.8
Namibia	..	..	..	..	..	..	..	133	119	7	5.7
Nepal	−9	9	6	19	205	2,413	26	24	18	12	8.9
Netherlands	..	..	12,343	7,824	..	..	..	..	..	..	..
New Zealand	..	..	1,735	280	..	..	..	..	..	..	..
Nicaragua	21	41	0	45	2,189	5,929	322[a]	217	212	64	57.1
Niger	9	−24	−1	0	863	1,557	45[a]	48	28	16	13.2
Nigeria	467	706	588	1,391	8,921	31,407	114	3	2	1	0.6
Norway	..	..	1,003	3,960	..	..	..	..	..	..	..
Oman	−259	69	141	67	599	3,415	31	9	28	0	0.6
Pakistan	182	1,936	244	690	9,931	29,901	39	12	7	3	1.4
Panama	127	301	132	238	2,975	6,990	80	42	33	2	1.1
Papua New Guinea	204	414	155	225	719	2,359	37	101	87	11	8.0
Paraguay	67	202	76	220	954	2,141	22	34	20	2	1.0
Peru	59	5,854	41	3,581	9,386	29,176	43	28	17	2	0.7
Philippines	639	4,600	530	1,408	17,417	41,214	51	16	12	2	1.0
Poland	71	5,333	89	4,498	8,894	40,895	31	0	22	3	0.6
Portugal	..	..	2,610	618	..	..	..	..	..	..	..
Romania	4	1,814	0	263	9,762	8,291	23	14	10	1	0.6
Russian Federation	5,604	7,454	0	2,479	4,476	124,785	25	4	0	0	0.0
Rwanda	6	1	8	1	190	1,034	47	51	100	19	51.2
Saudi Arabia	..	..	..	..	..	..	..	3	1	0	0.0
Senegal	42	34	57	45	1,473	3,663	53	85	68	12	11.6
Sierra Leone	36	5	32	5	469	1,167	78	26	42	15	21.2
Singapore	..	..	5,575	9,440	..	..	..	3	4	0	0.0
Slovak Republic	278	1,265	0	281	670	7,704	41	22	26	1	0.7
Slovenia	..	1,219	..	186	..	4,031	21	0	41	0	0.4
South Africa	..	1,417	..	136	0	23,590	18	0	10	0	0.3
Spain	..	..	13,984	6,396	..	..	..	..	..	..	..
Sri Lanka	54	123	43	120	1,841	7,995	41	52	27	10	3.6
Sweden	..	..	1,982	5,492	..	..	..	..	..	..	..
Switzerland	..	..	4,961	3,512	..	..	..	..	..	..	..
Syrian Arab Republic	18	77	71	89	3,552	21,420	120	30	16	3	1.4
Tajikistan	..	16	..	16	..	707	24	0	19	0	5.6
Tanzania	5	143	0	150	2,452	7,412	114	41	29	25	15.6
Thailand	4,498	13,517	2,444	2,336	8,297	90,823	56	13	14	1	0.5
Togo	0	0	0	0	1,049	1,463	80	56	39	13	12.0
Trinidad and Tobago	−69	343	109	320	829	2,242	46	−1	13	0	0.3
Tunisia	−122	697	76	320	3,526	9,886	53	43	14	3	0.7
Turkey	1,782	5,635	684	722	19,131	79,789	47	28	4	1	0.1
Turkmenistan	..	355	..	108	..	825	18	0	5	0	0.5
Uganda	16	114	0	121	689	3,674	32[a]	39	35	20	11.3
Ukraine	..	395	..	350	..	9,335	18	7	7	0	0.9
United Arab Emirates	..	..	..	..	..	..	..	−3	3	0	0.0
United Kingdom	..	..	32,427	32,346	..	..	..	..	..	..	..
United States	..	..	47,918	76,955	..	..	..	..	..	..	..
Uruguay	−192	499	0	169	1,660	5,899	33	17	16	1	0.3
Uzbekistan	..	431	..	55	..	2,319	9	0	4	0	0.4
Venezuela	−126	4,244	451	1,833	29,344	35,344	51	2	2	0	0.1
Vietnam	16	2,061	16	1,500	6	26,764	123	4	12	2	4.0
Yemen, Rep.	30	100	−131	100	1,684	6,356	88	22	17	6	4.9
Zambia	194	33	203	58	3,261	7,113	161	110	67	30	18.6
Zimbabwe	85	42	−12	63	786	5,005	67	39	33	..	5.2
World[b]	.. s	.. s	191,595 s	314,696 s	.. s	.. s		15 w	13 w	1.4 w	1.0 w
Low income	3,053	15,328	1,502	9,433	119,328	435,070		14	12	4.7	3.5
Middle income	37,843	230,398	22,185	109,341	483,994	1,656,327		11	8	0.8	0.4
Lower middle income	..	..	..	..	189,872	863,959		10	8	1.2	0.7
Upper middle income	..	..	..	..	294,122	792,367		14	7	0.4	0.2
Low & middle income	41,881	245,725	23,687	118,774	603,321	2,091,397		14	11	1.5	0.9
East Asia & Pacific	18,443	101,272	10,347	58,681	64,600	477,219		5	5	1.0	0.6
Europe & Central Asia	7,787	33,786	1,097	14,755	75,503	366,141		19	17	0.8	0.6
Latin America & Carib.	12,601	95,569	8,188	38,015	257,263	656,388		13	17	0.5	0.5
Middle East & N. Africa	646	1,979	2,757	614	83,793	212,389		43	19	2.4	1.3
South Asia	2,173	8,743	464	3,439	38,015	152,098		7	4	2.3	1.1
Sub-Saharan Africa	195	4,376	834	3,271	84,148	227,163		33	26	6.3	5.3
High income	..	..	167,908	195,922	..	..		..	..	..	..

a. Data are from debt sustainability analysis undertaken as part of the Heavily Indebted Poor Countries Debt Initiative. Present value estimates for these countries are for public and publicly guaranteed debt only, and export figures exclude workers remittances.   b. Includes aid not allocated by country or region.

Note: Totals for low- and middle-income economies may not sum to regional totals because of unallocated amounts.

Table 1a. Key indicators for other economies

Economy	Population Thousands 1997	Land area Thousands of sq. km 1995	Population density People per sq. km 1997	Gross national product (GNP) Millions of dollars 1997[a]	GNP Avg. annual growth rate (%) 1996–97	GNP per capita Dollars 1997[a]	GNP per capita Avg. annual growth rate (%) 1996–97	GNP measured at PPP[b] Millions of dollars 1997	GNP measured at PPP[b] Per capita (dollars) 1997	Life expectancy at birth Years 1996	Adult illiteracy % of people 15 and above 1995	Carbon dioxide emissions Thousands of tons 1995
Afghanistan	24,844	652.1	38	..	..	..[c]	..	..	..	45	69	1,238
American Samoa	60	0.2	298	..	..	..[d]	..	..	..	..	..	..
Andorra	71	0.2	160	..	..	..[e]	..	..	..	..	..	..
Antigua and Barbuda	66	0.4	151	489	1.9	7,380	1.0	578	8,720	75	..	..
Aruba	80	0.2	421	1,181	..	16,640	..	..	..	..	..	..
Bahamas, The	289	10.0	29	3,288	..	11,830	..	..	..	73	2	1,707
Bahrain	619	0.7	897	4,514	..	7,820	..	..	..	73	15	14,832
Barbados	265	0.4	616	1,741	..	6,590	..	..	..	76	3	824
Belize	228	22.8	10	625	1.6	2,740	–1.0	939	4,110	75	..	414
Bermuda	62	0.1	1,242	2,128	..	34,950	..	..	..	75	..	..
Bhutan	736	47.0	16	296	5.7	400	2.8	..	..	53	58	238
Bosnia and Herzegovina	..	51.0	..	..	..	..[c]	..	..	..	..	..	1,843
Botswana	1,510	566.7	3	4,922	7.8	3,260	5.7	12,413	8,220	51	30	2,242
Brunei	295	5.3	56	7,151	..	25,090	..	..	..	75	12	8,233
Cape Verde	399	4.0	99	436	23.0	1,090	19.9	1,191[f]	2,980[f]	66	28	114
Cayman Islands	35	0.3	130	..	..	..[e]	..	..	..	..	..	..
Channel Islands	148	..	..	..	..	..[e]	..	..	..	78	..	..
Comoros	518	2.2	232	208	–0.4	400	–2.9	825[f]	1,590[f]	59	43	66
Cuba	11,091	109.8	101	..	..	..[g]	..	..	..	76	4	29,067
Cyprus	747	9.2	81	10,839	..	14,930	..	..	..	77	..	5,177
Djibouti	636	23.2	27	..	..	..[g]	..	..	..	50	54	370
Dominica	74	0.8	99	232	3.1	3,120	..	332	4,470	74	..	..
Equatorial Guinea	421	28.1	15	444	106.6	1,050	101.4	1,516	3,600	50	..	132
Eritrea	3,827	101.0	38	801	..	210	..	..	..	55	..	..
Faeroe Islands	47	1.4	30	..	..	..[e]	..	..	..	..	..	..
Fiji	815	18.3	45	2,009	1.0	2,470	–0.5	3,290	4,040	72	8	737
French Guiana	153	88.2	2	..	..	..[e]	..	..	..	..	..	872
French Polynesia	225	3.7	61	..	..	..[e]	..	..	..	72	..	..
Gambia, The	1,180	10.0	118	409	5.2	350	2.2	1,581	1,340	53	61	216
Greenland	58	341.7	0	..	..	..[e]	..	..	..	68	..	..
Grenada	99	0.3	290	296	2.7	3,000	2.9	440	4,450	..	..	..
Guadeloupe	426	1.7	252	..	..	..[d]	..	..	..	75	..	..
Guam	155	0.6	282	..	..	..[e]	..	..	..	74	..	..
Guyana	848	196.9	4	677	4.9	800	3.8	2,445	2,890	64	2	934
Iceland	272	100.3	3	7,513	4.9	27,580	..	6,127	22,500	79	..	1,803
Iran, Islamic Rep.	60,973	1,622.0	38	113,506	3.2	1,780	1.2	352,628	5,530	70	28	263,760
Iraq	21,970	437.4	50	..	..	..[g]	..	..	..	62	42	99,001
Isle of Man	72	0.6	120	..	..	..[d]	..	..	..	..	..	..
Kiribati	83	0.7	114	76	1.7	910	–0.5	..	..	60	..	..
Korea, Dem. Rep.	22,773	120.4	189	..	..	..[g]	..	..	..	63	..	256,986
Kuwait	1,637	17.8	92	35,152	..	22,110	..	38,577	24,270	77	21	48,720
Liberia	2,894	96.3	30	..	..	..[c]	..	..	..	49	62	319
Libya	5,292	1,759.5	3	..	..	..[d]	..	..	..	68	24	39,403
Liechtenstein	31	0.2	190	..	..	..[e]	..	..	..	..	..	..
Luxembourg	422	2.6	160	18,837	..	45,330	..	14,319	34,460	77	..	9,263
Macao	471	0.0	23,555	..	..	..[e]	..	..	..	77	..	1,231
Maldives	262	0.3	874	301	6.0	1,150	3.3	848	3,230	64	7	183
Malta	376	0.3	1,174	3,203	..	8,630	..	..	..	77	..	1,726
Marshall Islands	57	0.2	290	108	..	1,770	..	..	..	..	..	..
Martinique	388	1.1	366	..	..	..[e]	..	..	..	77	..	2,037
Mayotte	108	0.3	340	..	..	..[d]	..	..	..	..	..	..
Micronesia, Fed. Sts.	111	0.7	160	220	..	1,980	..	..	..	66	..	..
Monaco	32	0.0	16,840	..	..	..[e]	..	..	..	..	..	..
Myanmar	46,680	657.6	71	..	..	..[c]	..	..	..	60	17	7,031
Netherlands Antilles	204	0.8	250	..	..	..[c]	..	..	..	76	..	..
New Caledonia	202	18.6	10	..	..	..[e]	..	..	..	74	..	1,715
Northern Mariana Islands	63	0.5	110	..	..	..[e]	..	..	..	..	..	..
Palau	17	0.5	40	..	..	..[d]	..	..	..	..	..	..
Puerto Rico	3,792	8.9	428	25,380	..	7,010	..	..	..	75	..	15,535
Qatar	675	11.0	61	7,429	..	11,570	..	..	..	72	21	29,019
Reunion	673	2.5	269	..	..	..[e]	..	..	..	75	..	1,554
Samoa	173	2.8	61	199	4.0	1,150	3.1	..	..	69	..	132
São Tomé and Principe	138	1.0	144	38	–2.8	270	–5.1	..	..	64	25	77
Seychelles	78	0.5	173	537	2.4	6,880	0.6	..	..	71	21	..
Solomon Islands	401	28.0	14	362	1.5	900	–1.5	943[f]	2,350[f]	63	..	161
Somalia	10,130	627.3	16	..	..	..[c]	..	..	..	49	..	11
St. Kitts and Nevis	41	0.4	113	252	6.0	6,160	6.1	315	7,730	70	..	..
St. Lucia	159	0.6	261	576	3.5	3,620	2.7	801	5,030	70	..	..
St. Vincent and the Grenadines	112	0.4	288	281	5.0	2,500	4.3	486	4,320	73	..	..
Sudan	27,861	2,376.0	12	7,801	6.4	280	4.2	..	..	54	54	3,499
Suriname	437	156.0	3	544	5.6	1,240	4.3	1,197	2,740	71	7	2,151
Swaziland	952	17.2	55	1,369	2.6	1,440	–0.2	3,393	3,560	57	23	454
Tonga	98	0.7	136	179	0.0	1,830	–0.4	..	..	72	..	..
Vanuatu	177	12.2	15	233	3.0	1,310	0.4	536[f]	3,020[f]	64	..	62
Virgin Islands (U.S.)	97	0.3	286	..	..	..[e]	..	..	..	76	..	..
West Bank and Gaza	..	..	..	..	..	..[g]	..	..	..	68	..	..
Yugoslavia, FR (Serb./Mont.)	10,614	102.0	104	..	..	..[g]	..	..	..	72	..	33,035

a. Calculated using the World Bank *Atlas* method. b. Purchasing power parity; see the Technical Notes. c. Estimated to be low income ($785 or less). d. Estimated to be upper middle income ($3,126 to $9,655). e. Estimated to be high income ($9,656 or more). f. The estimate is based on regression; others are extrapolated from the latest International Comparison Programme benchmark estimates. g. Estimated to be lower middle income ($786 to $3,125).

Technical Notes

THESE TECHNICAL NOTES discuss the sources and methods used to compile the 148 indicators included in the 1998 Selected World Development Indicators. The notes follow the order in which the indicators appear in the tables.

Sources

The data published in the Selected World Development Indicators are taken from the 1998 *World Development Indicators.* Where possible, however, revisions reported since the closing date of that edition have been incorporated. In addition, newly released estimates of gross national product per capita for 1997 are included in Table 1.

The World Bank draws on a variety of sources for the statistics published in the *World Development Indicators*. Data on external debt are reported directly to the World Bank by developing member countries through the Debtor Reporting System. Other data are drawn mainly from the United Nations and its specialized agencies, the International Monetary Fund (IMF), and country reports to the World Bank. Bank staff estimates are also used to improve currentness or consistency. For most countries, national accounts estimates are obtained from member governments through World Bank economic missions. In some instances these are adjusted by staff to ensure conformity with international definitions and concepts. Most social data from national sources are drawn from regular administrative files, special surveys, or periodic census inquiries. The Data Sources section following the Technical notes lists the principal international sources used.

Data consistency and reliability

Considerable effort has been made to standardize the data, but full comparability cannot be assured, and care must be taken in interpreting the indicators. Many factors affect availability, comparability, and reliability: statistical systems in many developing economies are still weak; statistical methods, coverage, practices, and definitions differ widely; and cross-country and intertemporal comparisons involve complex technical and conceptual problems that cannot be unequivocally resolved. For

these reasons, although the data are drawn from the sources thought to be most authoritative, they should be construed only as indicating trends and characterizing major differences among economies rather than offering precise quantitative measures of those differences. Also, national statistical agencies tend to revise their historical data, particularly for recent years. Thus, data of different vintages may be published in different editions of World Bank publications. Readers are advised not to compile such data from different editions. Consistent time series are available on the *World Development Indicators 1998 CD-ROM*.

Ratios and growth rates

For ease of reference, ratios and rates of growth are usually shown in the *World Development Indicators* tables. Values in their original form are available on the *World Development Indicators 1998 CD-ROM*. Unless otherwise noted, growth rates are computed using the least-squares regression method (see "Statistical methods" below). Because this method takes into account all available observations during a period, the resulting growth rates reflect general trends that are not unduly influenced by exceptional values. To exclude the effects of inflation, constant-price economic indicators are used in calculating growth rates. Data in italics are for a year or period other than that specified in the column heading—up to two years before or after for economic indicators, and up to three years for social indicators, because the latter tend to be collected less regularly and change less dramatically over short periods.

Constant-price series

To facilitate international comparisons and incorporate the effects of changes in intersectoral relative prices on the national accounts aggregates, constant-price data for most economies are first partially rebased to three sequential base years and then "chain-linked" together and expressed in prices of a common base year, 1987. The base years are 1970 for the period from 1960 to 1975, 1980 for 1976 to 1982, and 1987 for 1983 and beyond.

During the chain-linking procedure, components of gross domestic product (GDP) by industrial origin are individually rescaled and summed to arrive at the rescaled GDP. In this process a rescaling deviation may occur between the constant-price GDP measured by industrial origin and the constant-price GDP measured by expenditure. Such rescaling deviations are absorbed under the heading **Private consumption, etc.** on the assumption that estimates of GDP by industrial origin are more reliable estimate than those by expenditure. Independent of the rescaling, data for value added in the services sector also include a statistical discrepancy as reported by the original source.

Summary measures

The summary measures for regions and income groups, presented at the end of most tables, are calculated by simple addition when they are expressed in levels. Aggregate growth rates and ratios are usually computed as weighted averages. The summary measures for social indicators are weighted by population or subgroups of population, except for infant mortality, which is weighted by the number of births. See the notes on specific indicators for more information.

For summary measures that cover many years, calculations are based on a uniform group of economies so that the composition of the aggregate does not change over time. Group measures are compiled only if the data available for a given year account for at least two-thirds of the full group, as defined for the 1987 benchmark year. As long as this criterion is met, economies for which data are missing are assumed to behave like those that provide estimates. Readers should keep in mind that the summary measures are estimates of representative aggregates for each topic, and that nothing meaningful can be deduced about behavior at the country level by working back from group indicators. In addition, the weighting process may result in discrepancies between subgroup and overall totals.

Table 1. Size of the economy

Population is based on the de facto definition, which counts all residents, regardless of legal status or citizenship, except for refugees not permanently settled in the country of asylum, who are generally considered part of the population of the country of origin. The indicators shown are midyear estimates (see the technical note for Table 3).

Land area is total area, excluding inland bodies of water, coastal waterways, and offshore territorial waters.

Population density is midyear population divided by land area. The indicator is calculated using the most recently available data.

Gross national product (GNP) is the sum of value added by all resident producers, plus any taxes (less subsidies) not included in the valuation of output, plus net receipts of primary income (employee compensation and property income) from nonresident sources. Data are converted from national currency to current U.S. dollars by the *World Bank Atlas* method (see "Statistical methods" below). **Average annual growth rate of GNP** is calculated from constant-price GNP in national currency units. **GNP per capita** is GNP divided by midyear population. It is converted into current U.S. dollars by the *Atlas* method. **Average annual growth rate of GNP per capita** is calculated from constant-price GNP per capita in national currency units. **GNP measured at PPP** is GNP converted to U.S. dollars by the pur-

chasing power parity (PPP) exchange rate. At the PPP rate, one dollar has the same purchasing power over domestic GNP that the U.S. dollar has over U.S. GDP; dollars converted by this method are sometimes called international dollars.

GNP, the broadest measure of national income, measures total value added from domestic and foreign sources claimed by residents. GNP comprises gross domestic product plus net receipts of primary income from nonresident sources. The World Bank uses GNP per capita in U.S. dollars to classify economies for analytical purposes and to determine borrowing eligibility. When calculating GNP in U.S. dollars from GNP reported in national currencies, the World Bank follows its *Atlas* conversion method. This involves using a three-year average of exchange rates to smooth the effects of transitory exchange rate fluctuations. (See "Statistical methods" below for further discussion of the *Atlas* method.) Note that growth rates are calculated from data in constant prices and national currency units, not from the *Atlas* estimates.

Because nominal exchange rates do not always reflect international differences in relative prices, Table 1 also shows GNP converted into international dollars using PPP exchange rates. PPP rates allow a standard comparison of real price levels between countries, just as conventional price indexes allow comparison of real values over time. The PPP conversion factors used here are derived from the most recent round of price surveys conducted by the International Comparison Programme, a joint project of the World Bank and the regional economic commissions of the United Nations. This round of surveys, completed in 1996 and covering 118 countries, is based on a 1993 reference year. Estimates for countries not included in the survey are derived from statistical models using available data.

Table 2. Quality of life

Growth of private consumption per capita is the average annual rate of change in private consumption divided by the midyear population. (See the definition of private consumption in the technical note to Table 12.) The distribution-corrected growth rate is 1 minus the Gini index (see the technical note to Table 5) multiplied by the annual rate of growth of private consumption. Improvements in private consumption per capita are generally associated with a reduction in poverty, but where the distribution of income or consumption is highly unequal, the poor may not share in the improvement. The relationship between the rate of poverty reduction and the distribution of income or consumption, as measured by an index such as the Gini index, is complicated. But Ravallion 1997 has found that the rate of poverty reduction is directly proportional to the distribution-corrected rate of growth of private consumption.

Prevalence of child malnutrition is the percentage of children under age 5 whose weight for age is less than -2 standard deviations from the median of the reference population, which is based on children from the United States, who are assumed to be well nourished. Weight for age is a composite indicator of both weight for height (wasting) and height for age (stunting). Estimates of child malnutrition are from national survey data on weight for age.

Under-5 mortality rate is the probability that a child born in the indicated year will die before reaching age 5, if the child is subject to current age-specific mortality rates. The probability is expressed as a rate per 1,000.

Life expectancy at birth is the number of years a newborn infant would live if patterns of mortality prevailing at the time of its birth were to stay the same throughout its life.

Age-specific mortality data such as infant and child mortality rates, along with life expectancy at birth, are probably the best general indicators of a community's current health status and are often cited as overall measures of a population's welfare or quality of life. The main sources of mortality data are vital registration systems and direct or indirect estimates based on sample surveys or censuses. Because civil registers with relatively complete vital registration systems are fairly uncommon, estimates must be obtained from sample surveys or derived by applying indirect estimation techniques to registration, census, or survey data. Indirect estimates rely on estimated actuarial ("life") tables, which may be inappropriate for the population concerned. Life expectancy at birth and age-specific mortality rates are generally estimates based on the most recently available census or survey; see the Primary data documentation table in the 1998 *World Development Indicators* (World Bank 1998b).

Adult illiteracy rate is the percentage of persons aged 15 and above who cannot, with understanding, read and write a short, simple statement about their everyday life. Literacy is difficult to define and to measure. The definition here is based on the concept of functional literacy: a person's ability to use reading and writing skills effectively in the context of his or her society. Measuring literacy using such a definition requires census or sample survey measurements under controlled conditions. In practice, many countries estimate the number of illiterate adults from self-reported data or from estimates of school completion. Because of these differences in method, comparisons across countries—and even over time within countries—should be made with caution.

Urban population is the share of the population living in areas defined as urban in each country.

Access to sanitation in urban areas is the percentage of the urban population served by connections to public sewers or household systems, such as pit privies, pour-flush latrines, septic tanks, or communal toilets, or other such facilities.

Table 3. Population and labor force

Total population includes all residents regardless of legal status or citizenship, except for refugees not permanently settled in the country of asylum, who are generally considered part of the population of their country of origin. The indicators shown are midyear estimates. Population estimates are usually based on national censuses, whereas intercensal estimates are interpolations or extrapolations based on demographic models. Errors and undercounting occur even in high-income countries; in developing countries such errors may be substantial because of limits on transportation, communication, and the resources required to conduct a full census. Moreover, the international comparability of population indicators is limited by differences in the concepts, definitions, data collection procedures, and estimation methods used by national statistical agencies and other organizations that collect population data. The data in Table 3 are provided by national statistical offices or by the United Nations Population Division.

Average annual population growth rate is the exponential rate of change for the period (see "Statistical methods").

Population aged 15–64 is the number of people in the age group that makes up the largest part of the economically active population, excluding children. In many developing countries, however, children under age 15 work full or part time, and in some high-income countries many workers postpone retirement past age 65.

Total labor force comprises people who meet the definition established by the International Labour Organisation (ILO) for the economically active population: all people who supply labor for the production of goods and services during a specified period. It includes both the employed and the unemployed. Although national practices vary, in general the labor force includes the armed forces and first-time jobseekers but excludes homemakers and other unpaid caregivers and workers in the informal sector. Data on the labor force are compiled by the ILO from census or labor force surveys. Despite the ILO's efforts to encourage the use of international standards, labor force data are not fully comparable because of differences among countries, and sometimes within countries, in definitions and methods of collection, classification, and tabulation. The labor force estimates reported in Table 3 were calculated by applying gender-specific activity rates from the ILO database to the World Bank's population estimates to create a labor force series consistent with those estimates. This procedure sometimes results in estimates that differ slightly from those published in the ILO's *Yearbook of Labour Statistics*.

Average annual labor force growth rate is calculated using the exponential end-point method (see "Statistical methods").

Females as a percentage of the labor force shows the extent to which women are active in the labor force. Estimates of females in the labor force are from the ILO database. These estimates are not comparable internationally, because in many countries large numbers of women assist on farms or in other family enterprises without pay, and countries differ in the criteria used to determine the extent to which such workers are to be counted in the labor force.

Children aged 10–14 in the labor force is the share of that age group that is active in the labor force. Reliable estimates of child labor are difficult to obtain. In many countries child labor is illegal or officially presumed not to exist, and therefore not reported or included in surveys or recorded in official data. Data are also subject to underreporting because they do not include children engaged in agricultural or household activities with their families.

Table 4. Poverty

Survey year is the year in which the underlying data were collected.

Rural population below the poverty line is the percentage of the rural population living below the rural poverty line. **Urban population below the poverty line** is the percentage of the urban population living below the urban poverty line. **Population below the national poverty line** is the percentage of the population living below the national poverty line. National estimates are based on population-weighted subgroup estimates from household surveys.

Population below $1 a day and **Population below $2 a day** are the percentages of the population living at those levels of consumption or income at 1985 prices, adjusted for purchasing power parity.

Poverty gap at $1 a day and **Poverty gap at $2 a day** are calculated as the average difference between the poverty line and actual income or consumption for all poor households, expressed as a percentage of the poverty line. This measure reflects the depth of poverty as well as its prevalence.

International comparisons of poverty data entail both conceptual and practical problems. Different countries have different definitions of poverty, and consistent comparisons between countries using the same definition can be difficult. National poverty lines tend to have greater purchasing power in rich countries, where more generous standards are used than in poor countries.

International poverty lines attempt to hold the real value of the poverty line constant between countries. The standard of $1 a day, measured in 1985 international prices and adjusted to local currency using PPP conversion factors, was chosen for *World Development Report 1990: Poverty* (World Bank 1990) because it is typical of the poverty lines in low-income economies. PPP conversion factors are used because they take into account the local prices of goods and services that are not traded internationally. However, these factors were designed not for making international poverty comparisons, but for comparing aggregates in the national accounts. As a result, there is no certainty that an international poverty line measures the same degree of need or deprivation across countries.

Problems can arise in comparing poverty measures within countries as well as between them. For example, the cost of food staples—and the cost of living generally—are typically higher in urban than in rural areas. So the nominal value of the urban poverty line should be higher than the rural poverty line. But it is not always clear that the difference between urban and rural poverty lines found in practice properly reflects the difference in the cost of living. For some countries the urban poverty line in common use has a higher real value—meaning that it allows poor people to buy more commodities for consumption—than does the rural poverty line. Sometimes the difference has been so large as to imply that the incidence of poverty is greater in urban than in rural areas, even though the reverse is found when adjustments are made only for differences in the cost of living.

Other issues arise in measuring household living standards. The choice between income and consumption as a welfare indicator is one. Incomes are generally more difficult to measure accurately, and consumption accords better with the idea of a standard of living than does income, which can vary over time even if the standard of living does not. But consumption data are not always available, and when they are not there is little choice but to use income. There are still other problems. Household survey questionnaires can differ widely, for example in the number of distinct categories of consumer goods they identify. Survey quality varies, and even similar surveys may not be strictly comparable.

Comparisons across countries at different levels of development also pose a potential problem, because of differences in the relative importance of consumption of nonmarket goods. The local market value of all consumption in kind (including consumption from a household's own production, particularly important in underdeveloped rural economies) should be included in the measure of total consumption expenditure. Similarly, the imputed profit from production of nonmarket goods should be included in income. This is not always done, although such omissions were a far bigger problem in surveys before the 1980s than today. Most survey data now include valuations for consumption or income from own production. Nonetheless, valuation methods vary: for example, some surveys use the price at the nearest market, whereas others use the average farmgate selling price.

The international poverty measures in Table 4 are based on the most recent PPP estimates from the latest version of the Penn World Tables (National Bureau of Economic Research 1997). It should be noted, however, that any revisions in the PPP conversion factor of a country to incorporate better price indexes can produce dramatically different poverty lines in local currency.

Whenever possible, consumption has been used as the welfare indicator for deciding who is poor. When only household income is available, average income has been adjusted to accord with either a survey-based estimate of mean consumption (when available) or an estimate based on consumption data from national accounts. This procedure adjusts only the mean, however; nothing can be done to correct for the difference in Lorenz (income distribution) curves between consumption and income.

Empirical Lorenz curves were weighted by household size, so they are based on percentiles of population, not of households. In all cases the measures of poverty have been calculated from primary data sources (tabulations or household data) rather than existing estimates. Estimates from tabulations require an interpolation method; the method chosen is Lorenz curves with flexible functional forms, which have proved reliable in past work.

Table 5. Distribution of income or consumption

Survey year is the year in which the underlying data were collected.

Gini index measures the extent to which the distribution of income (or, in some cases, consumption expenditure) among individuals or households within an economy deviates from a perfectly equal distribution. A Lorenz curve plots the cumulative percentages of total income received against the cumulative number of recipients, starting with the poorest. The Gini index measures the area between the Lorenz curve and a hypothetical line of absolute equality, expressed as a percentage of the maximum area under the line. As defined here a Gini index of zero would represent perfect equality, and an index of 100 would imply perfect inequality (one person or household accounting for all income or consumption).

Percentage share of income or consumption is the share that accrues to deciles or quintiles of the population ranked by income or consumption. Percentage shares by quintiles may not add up to 100 because of rounding.

Data on personal or household income or consumption come from nationally representative household surveys. The data in the table refer to different years between 1985 and 1996. Footnotes to the survey year indicate whether the rankings are based on income or consumption. Distributions are based on percentiles of population, not of households, with households ranked by income or expenditure per person. Where the original data from the household survey were available, they have been used to directly calculate the income or consumption shares by quintile. Otherwise, shares have been estimated from the best available grouped data.

The distribution indicators have been adjusted for household size, providing a more consistent measure of income or consumption per capita. No adjustment has been made for differences in the cost of living in different parts of the same country, because the necessary data are generally unavailable. For further details on the estimation method for low- and middle-income economies, see Ravallion and Chen 1996.

Because the underlying household surveys differ in method and in the type of data collected, the distribution indicators are not strictly comparable across countries. These problems are diminishing as survey methods improve and become more standardized, but strict comparability is still impossible. The income distribution and Gini indexes for the high-income economies are directly calculated from the Luxembourg Income Study database (Luxembourg Income Study 1997). The estimation method used here is consistent with that applied to developing countries.

The following sources of noncomparability should be noted. First, the surveys can differ in many respects, including whether they use income or consumption expenditure as the living standard indicator. Income is typically more unequally distributed than consumption. In addition, the definitions of income used in surveys are usually very different from the economic definition of income (the maximum level of consumption consistent with keeping productive capacity unchanged). Consumption is usually a much better welfare indicator, particularly in developing countries. Second, households differ in size (number of members) and in the extent of income sharing among members. Individuals differ in age and in consumption needs. Differences between countries in these respects may bias distribution comparisons.

Table 6. Education

Public expenditure on education is the percentage of GNP accounted for by public spending on public education plus subsidies to private education at the primary, secondary, and tertiary levels. It may exclude spending by religious schools, which play a significant role in many developing countries. Data for some countries and for some years refer to spending by the ministry of education of the central government only, and thus exclude education expenditures by other central government ministries and departments, local authorities, and others.

Net enrollment ratio is the number of children of official school age (as defined by the education system) enrolled in primary or secondary school, expressed as a percentage of the number of children of official school age for those levels in the population. Enrollment data are based on annual enrollment surveys, typically conducted at the beginning of the school year. They do not reflect actual attendance or dropout rates during the school year. Problems affecting cross-country comparisons of enrollment data stem from inadvertent or deliberate misreporting of age, and from errors in estimates of school-age popu-

lations. Age-sex structures from censuses or vital registration systems, the primary sources of data on school-age populations, are commonly subject to underenumeration (especially of young children).

Percentage of cohort reaching grade 4 is the share of children enrolled in primary school in 1980 and 1991 who reached the fourth grade in 1983 and 1994, respectively. Because tracking data for individual students are not available, aggregate student flows from one grade to the next are estimated using data on average promotion, repetition, and dropout rates. Other flows, caused by new entrants, reentrants, grade skipping, migration, or school transfers during the school year, are not considered. This procedure, called the reconstructed cohort method, makes three simplifying assumptions: that dropouts never return to school; that promotion, repetition, and dropout rates remain constant over the entire period in which the cohort is enrolled; and that the same rates apply to all pupils enrolled in a given grade, regardless of whether they previously repeated a grade.

Expected years of schooling is the average number of years of formal schooling that a child is expected to receive, including university education and years spent in repetition. It may also be interpreted as an indicator of the total educational resources, measured in school years, that a child will require over the course of his or her "lifetime" in school.

Data on education are compiled by the United Nations Educational, Scientific, and Cultural Organization (UNESCO) from official responses to surveys and from reports provided by education authorities in each country. Because coverage, definitions, and data collection methods vary across countries and over time within countries, data on education should be interpreted with caution.

Table 7. Health

Public expenditure on health consists of recurrent and capital spending from government (central and local) budgets, external borrowings and grants (including donations from international agencies and nongovernmental organizations), and social (or compulsory) health insurance funds. Because few developing countries have national health accounts, compiling estimates of public health expenditures is complicated in countries where state, provincial, and local governments are involved in health care financing. Such data are not regularly reported and, when reported, are often of poor quality. In some countries health services are considered social services, and so are excluded from health sector expenditures. The data on health expenditures in Table 7 were collected by the World Bank as part of its health, nutrition, and population strategy. No estimates were made for countries with incomplete data.

Access to safe water is the percentage of the population with reasonable access to an adequate amount of safe water (including treated surface water and untreated but uncontaminated water, such as from springs, sanitary wells, and protected boreholes). In urban areas the source may be a public fountain or standpipe located not more than 200 meters from the residence. In rural areas the definition implies that household members do not have to spend a disproportionate part of the day fetching water. An "adequate" amount of safe water is that needed to satisfy metabolic, hygienic, and domestic requirements: usually about 20 liters per person per day. The definition of safe water has changed over time.

Access to sanitation is the percentage of the population with at least adequate disposal facilities that can effectively prevent human, animal, and insect contact with excreta. Suitable facilities range from simple but protected pit latrines to flush toilets with sewerage. To be effective, all facilities must be correctly constructed and properly maintained.

Infant mortality rate is the number of infants who die before reaching one year of age, expressed per 1,000 live births in a given year (see the discussion of age-specific mortality rates in the technical note to Table 2).

Contraceptive prevalence rate is the percentage of women who are practicing, or whose sexual partners are practicing, any form of contraception. It is usually measured for married women aged 15–49 only. Contraceptive prevalence includes all methods: ineffective traditional methods as well as highly effective modern methods. Unmarried women are often excluded from the surveys, and this may bias the estimate. The rates are obtained mainly from demographic and health surveys and contraceptive prevalence surveys.

Total fertility rate is the number of children who would be born to a woman if she were to live to the end of her childbearing years and bear children in accordance with current age-specific fertility rates. Data are from vital registration systems or, in their absence, from censuses or sample surveys. Provided that the censuses or surveys are fairly recent, the estimated rates are considered reliable. As with other demographic data, international comparisons are limited by differences in data definition, collection, and estimation methods.

Maternal mortality ratio is the number of women who die during pregnancy or childbirth, per 100,000 live births. Maternal mortality ratios are difficult to measure because health information systems are often weak. Classifying a death as maternal requires a cause-of-death attribution by medically qualified staff, based on information available at the time of death. Even then, some doubt may remain about the diagnosis in the absence of an autopsy. In many developing countries, causes of death are assigned by nonphysicians and often attributed to "ill-defined causes." Maternal deaths in rural areas are often not reported. The data in Table 7 are official estimates from administrative records, survey-based indirect estimates, or estimates derived from a demographic model developed by the United Nations Children's Fund (UNICEF) and the World Health Organization (WHO). In all cases the standard errors of maternal mortality ratios are large, which makes this indicator particularly unsuitable for monitoring changes over a short period.

Table 8. Land use and agricultural productivity

Cropland includes land devoted to temporary and permanent crops, temporary meadows, market and kitchen gardens, and land temporarily fallow. Permanent crops are those that do not need to be replanted after each harvest, excluding trees grown for wood or timber. **Irrigated land** refers to areas purposely provided with water, including land irrigated by controlled flooding. **Arable land** includes land defined by the Food and Agricul-

ture Organization (FAO) as land devoted to temporary crops (double-cropped areas are counted once), temporary meadows for mowing or for pasture, land under market or kitchen gardens, and land temporarily fallow. Land abandoned as a result of shifting cultivation is not included.

The comparability of land use data from different countries is limited by variations in definitions, statistical methods, and the quality of data collection. For example, countries may define land use differently. The FAO, the primary compiler of these data, occasionally adjusts its definitions of land use categories and sometimes revises earlier data. Because the data reflect changes in data reporting procedures as well as actual changes in land use, apparent trends should be interpreted with caution.

Agricultural productivity refers to agricultural value added per agricultural worker and agricultural value added per hectare of agricultural land (the sum of arable land, permanent cropland, and permanent pasture) are measured in constant 1987 U.S. dollars. Agricultural value added includes that from forestry and fishing. Thus interpretations of land productivity should be made with caution. To smooth annual fluctuations in agricultural activity, the indicators have been averaged over three years.

Food production index covers food crops that are considered edible and that contain nutrients. Coffee and tea are excluded because, although edible, they have no nutritive value.

The food production index is prepared by the FAO, which obtains data from official and semiofficial reports of crop yields, area under production, and livestock numbers. Where data are not available, the FAO makes estimates. The index is calculated using the Laspeyres formula: production quantities of each commodity are weighted by average international commodity prices in the base period and summed for each year. The FAO's index may differ from those of other sources because of differences in coverage, weights, concepts, time periods, calculation methods, and use of international prices.

Table 9. Water use, deforestation, and protected areas

Freshwater resources consists of internal renewable resources, which include flows of rivers and groundwater from rainfall in the country but not river flows from other countries. Freshwater resources per capita are calculated using the World Bank's population estimates.

Data on freshwater resources are based on estimates of runoff into rivers and recharge of groundwater. These estimates are based on different sources and refer to different years, so cross-country comparisons should be made with caution. Because they are collected intermittently, the data may hide significant variations in total renewable water resources from one year to the next. These annual averages also disguise large seasonal and interannual variations in water availability within countries. Data for small countries and countries in arid and semiarid zones are less reliable than those for larger countries and countries with more rainfall.

Annual freshwater withdrawals refers to total water withdrawal, not counting evaporation losses from storage basins. Withdrawals also include water from desalination plants in countries where they are a significant source of water. Withdrawal data are for single years between 1980 and 1996 unless otherwise indicated. Caution is advised in comparing data on annual freshwater withdrawal, which are subject to variations in collection and estimation methods. Withdrawals can exceed 100 percent of renewable supplies when extraction from nonrenewable aquifers or desalination plants is considerable, when river flows from other countries are used substantially, or when there is significant reuse of water. Withdrawals for agriculture and industry are total withdrawals for irrigation and livestock production and for direct industrial use (including withdrawals for cooling thermoelectric plants), respectively. Withdrawals for domestic uses include drinking water, municipal use or supply, and use for public services, commercial establishments, and homes. For most countries sectoral withdrawal data are estimated for 1987–95.

Access to safe water refers to the percentage of people with reasonable access to an adequate amount of safe drinking water in their dwelling or within a convenient distance of their dwelling.

Information on access to safe water, although widely used, is extremely subjective, and such terms as "adequate" and "safe" may have very different meanings in different countries, despite official WHO definitions. Even in industrial countries, treated water may not always be safe to drink. Although access to safe water is equated with connection to a public supply system, this does not take account of variations in the quality and cost (broadly defined) of the service once connected. Thus crosscountry comparisons must be made cautiously. Changes over time within countries may result from changes in definitions or measurements.

Annual deforestation refers to the permanent conversion of forest area (land under natural or planted stands of trees) to other uses, including shifting cultivation, permanent agriculture, ranching, settlements, and infrastructure development. Deforested areas do not include areas logged but intended for regeneration or areas degraded by fuelwood gathering, acid precipitation, or forest fires. Negative numbers indicate an increase in forest area.

Estimates of forest area are from FAO 1997, which provides information on forest cover as of 1995 and a revised estimate of forest cover in 1990. Forest cover data for developing countries are based on country assessments that were prepared at different times and that, for reporting purposes, had to be adapted to the standard reference years of 1990 and 1995. This adjustment was made with a deforestation model designed to correlate forest cover change over time with certain ancillary variables, including population change and density, initial forest cover, and ecological zone of the forest area under consideration.

Nationally protected areas are totally or partially protected areas of at least 1,000 hectares that are designated as national parks, natural monuments, nature reserves, wildlife sanctuaries, protected landscapes and seascapes, or scientific reserves with limited public access. The data do not include sites protected under local or provincial law. Total land area is used to calculate the percentage of total area protected.

Data on protected areas are compiled from a variety of sources by the World Conservation Monitoring Centre, a joint venture of the United Nations Environment Programme, the World Wide Fund for Nature, and the World Conservation Union. Because of differences in definitions and reporting practices, cross-country comparability is limited. Compounding these problems, available data cover different periods. Designating land as a protected area does not necessarily mean, however, that protection is in force. For small countries whose protected areas may be smaller than 1,000 hectares, this limit will result in an underestimate of the extent and number of protected areas.

Table 10. Energy use and emissions

Commercial energy use refers to apparent consumption, which is equal to indigenous production plus imports and stock changes, minus exports and fuels supplied to ships and aircraft engaged in international transportation.

The International Energy Agency (IEA) and the United Nations Statistical Division (UNSD) compile energy data. IEA data for nonmembers of the Organisation for Economic Co-operation and Development (OECD) are based on national energy data that have been adjusted to conform with annual questionnaires completed by OECD member governments. UNSD data are compiled primarily from responses to questionnaires sent to national governments, supplemented by official national statistical publications and by data from intergovernmental organizations. When official data are not available, the UNSD prepares estimates based on the professional and commercial literature. The variety of sources affects the cross-country comparability of data.

Commercial energy use refers to domestic primary energy use before transformation to other end-use energy sources (such as electricity and refined petroleum products). The use of firewood, dried animal manure, and other traditional fuels is not included. All forms of commercial energy—primary energy and primary electricity—are converted into oil equivalents. To convert nuclear electricity into oil equivalents, a notional thermal efficiency of 33 percent is assumed; for hydroelectric power, 100 percent efficiency is assumed.

GDP per unit of energy use is the U.S. dollar estimate of real gross domestic product (at 1987 prices) per kilogram of oil equivalent of commercial energy use.

Net energy imports is calculated as energy use less production, both measured in oil equivalents. A minus sign indicates that the country is a net exporter.

Carbon dioxide emissions measures those emissions stemming from the burning of fossil fuels and the manufacture of cement. They include carbon dioxide produced during consumption of solid, liquid, and gas fuels and from gas flaring.

The Carbon Dioxide Information Analysis Center (CDIAC), sponsored by the U.S. Department of Energy, calculates annual anthropogenic emissions of carbon dioxide. These calculations are derived from data on fossil fuel consumption, based on the World Energy Data Set maintained by the UNSD, and from data on world cement manufacturing, based on the Cement Manufacturing Data Set maintained by the U.S. Bureau of Mines. Each year the CDIAC recalculates the entire time series from 1950 to the present, incorporating its most recent findings and the latest corrections to its database. Estimates exclude fuels supplied to ships and aircraft engaged in international transportation because of the difficulty of apportioning these fuels among the countries benefiting from that transport.

Table 11. Growth of the economy

Gross domestic product is gross value added, at purchasers' prices, by all resident and nonresident producers in the economy plus any taxes and minus any subsidies not included in the value of the products. It is calculated without deducting for depreciation of fabricated assets or for depletion and degradation of natural resources. Value added is the net output of a sector after adding up all outputs and subtracting intermediate inputs. The industrial origin of value added is determined by the International Standard Industrial Classification (ISIC), revision 2.

The **GDP implicit deflator** reflects changes in prices for all final demand categories, such as government consumption, capital formation, and international trade, as well as the main component, private final consumption. It is derived as the ratio of current to constant-price GDP. The GDP deflator may also be calculated explicitly as a Laspeyres price index in which the weights are base-period quantities of output.

Agriculture value added corresponds to ISIC divisions 11–13 and includes forestry and fishing. **Industry value added** comprises the following sectors: mining (ISIC divisions 10–14), manufacturing (ISIC divisions 15–37), construction (ISIC division 45), and electricity, gas, and water supply (ISIC divisions 40 and 41). **Services value added** corresponds to ISIC divisions 50–96.

Exports of goods and services represents the value of all goods and market services provided to the rest of the world. Included is the value of merchandise, freight, insurance, travel, and other nonfactor services. Factor and property income (formerly called factor services), such as investment income, interest, and labor income, is excluded, as are transfer payments.

Gross domestic investment consists of outlays on additions to the fixed assets of the economy plus net changes in the level of inventories. Additions to fixed assets include land improvements (fences, ditches, drains, and so on); plant, machinery, and equipment purchases; and the construction of buildings, roads, railways, and the like, including commercial and industrial buildings, offices, schools, hospitals, and private residential dwellings. Inventories are stocks of goods held by firms to meet temporary or unexpected fluctuations in production or sales.

Growth rates are annual averages calculated using constant-price data in local currency. Growth rates for regional and income groups are calculated after converting local currencies to U.S. dollars at the average official exchange rate reported by the IMF for the year shown or, occasionally, using an alternative conversion factor determined by the World Bank's Development Data Group. Methods of computing growth rates and the alternative conversion factors are described under "Statistical methods" below. For additional information on the calculation of GDP and its sectoral components, see the technical note to Table 12.

Table 12. Structure of output

For definitions of GDP and value added components (agriculture, industry, manufacturing, and services), see the technical note to Table 11.

Gross domestic product represents the sum of value added by all producers in economy. Since 1968 the United Nations' System of National Accounts (SNA) has called for estimates of GDP by industrial origin to be valued at either basic prices (excluding all indirect taxes on factors of production) or producer prices (including taxes on factors of production, but excluding indirect taxes on final output). Some countries, however, report such data at purchasers' prices—the prices at which final sales are made—and this may affect estimates of the distribution of output. Total GDP as shown in this table is measured at purchasers' prices. GDP components are measured at basic prices.

Among the difficulties faced by compilers of national accounts is the extent of unreported economic activity in the informal or secondary economy. In developing countries a large share of agricultural output is either not exchanged (because it is consumed within the household) or not exchanged for money. Financial transactions also may go unrecorded. Agricultural production often must be estimated indirectly, using a combination of methods involving estimates of inputs, yields, and area under cultivation.

The output of industry ideally should be measured through regular censuses and surveys of firms. But in most developing countries such surveys are infrequent and quickly go out of date, so many results must be extrapolated. The choice of sampling unit, which may be the enterprise (where responses may be based on financial records) or the establishment (where production units may be recorded separately), also affects the quality of the data. Moreover, much industrial production is organized not in firms but in unincorporated or owner-operated ventures not captured by surveys aimed at the formal sector. Even in large industries, where regular surveys are more likely, evasion of excise and other taxes lowers the estimates of value added. Such problems become more acute as countries move from state control of industry to private enterprise, because new firms go into business and growing numbers of established firms fail to report. In accordance with the SNA, output should include all such unreported activity as well as the value of illegal activities and other unrecorded, informal, or small-scale operations. Data on these activities need to be collected using techniques other than conventional surveys.

In sectors dominated by large organizations and enterprises, data on output, employment, and wages are usually readily available and reasonably reliable. But in the services sector the many self-employed workers and one-person businesses are sometimes difficult to locate, and their owners have little incentive to respond to surveys, let alone report their full earnings. Compounding these problems are the many forms of economic activity that go unrecorded, including the work that women and children do for little or no pay. For further discussion of the problems encountered in using national accounts data see Srinivasan 1994 and Heston 1994.

Table 13. Structure of demand

Private consumption is the market value of all goods and services, including durable products (such as cars, washing machines, and home computers), purchased or received as income in kind by households and nonprofit institutions. It excludes purchases of dwellings but includes imputed rent for owner-occupied dwellings. In practice, it may include any statistical discrepancy in the use of resources relative to the supply of resources.

Private consumption is often estimated as a residual, by subtracting from GDP all other known expenditures. The resulting aggregate may incorporate fairly large discrepancies. When private consumption is calculated separately, the household surveys on which a large component of the estimates are based tend to be one-year studies with limited coverage. Thus the estimates quickly become outdated and must be supplemented by price- and quantity-based statistical estimating procedures. Complicating the issue, in many developing countries the distinction between cash outlays for personal business and those for household use may be blurred.

General government consumption includes all current spending for purchases of goods and services (including wages and salaries) by all levels of government, excluding most government enterprises. It also includes most expenditure on national defense and security, some of which is now considered part of investment.

Gross domestic investment consists of outlays on additions to the fixed assets of the economy plus net changes in the level of inventories. For the definitions of fixed assets and inventories see the technical note to Table 11. Under the revised (1993) SNA guidelines, gross domestic investment also includes capital outlays on defense establishments that may be used by the general public, such as schools and hospitals, and on certain types of private housing for family use. All other defense expenditures are treated as current spending.

Investment data may be estimated from direct surveys of enterprises and administrative records or based on the commodity flow method, using data from trade and construction activities. The quality of public fixed investment data depends on the quality of government accounting systems, which tend to be weak in developing countries; measures of private fixed investment—particularly capital outlays by small, unincorporated enterprises—are usually very unreliable.

Estimates of changes in inventories are rarely complete but usually include the most important activities or commodities. In some countries these estimates are derived as a composite residual along with aggregate private consumption. According to national accounts conventions, adjustments should be made for appreciation of the value of inventories due to price changes, but this is not always done. In economies where inflation is high, this element can be substantial.

Gross domestic saving is the difference between GDP and total consumption.

Exports of goods and services represents the value of all goods and services (including transportation, travel, and other services such as communications, insurance, and financial services) provided to the rest of the world.

Exports and imports are compiled from customs returns and from balance of payments data obtained from central banks. Although data on exports and imports from the payments side provide reasonably reliable records of cross-border transactions, they may not adhere strictly to the appropriate valuation and timing definitions of balance of payments accounting or, more important, correspond with the change-of-ownership criterion. (In conventional balance of payments accounting, a transaction is recorded as occurring when ownership changes hands.) This issue has assumed greater significance with the increasing globalization of international business. Neither customs nor balance of payments data capture the illegal transactions that occur in many countries. Goods carried by travelers across borders in legal but unreported shuttle trade may further distort trade statistics.

Resource balance is the difference between exports of goods and services and imports of goods and services.

Table 14. Central government finances

Current tax revenue comprises compulsory, unrequited, nonrepayable receipts collected by central governments for public purposes. It includes interest collected on tax arrears and penalties collected on nonpayment or late payment of taxes and is shown net of refunds and other corrective transactions.

Current nontax revenue includes requited, nonrepayable receipts for public purposes, such as fines, administrative fees, or entrepreneurial income from government ownership of property, and voluntary, unrequited, nonrepayable current government receipts other than from governmental sources. This category does not include grants, borrowing, repayment of previous lending, sales of fixed capital assets or of stocks, land, or intangible assets, or gifts from nongovernmental sources for capital purposes. Together tax and nontax revenue make up the current revenue of the government.

Current expenditure includes requited payments other than for capital assets or for goods or services to be used in the production of capital assets, and unrequited payments for purposes other than permitting the recipients to acquire capital assets, compensating the recipients for damage or destruction of capital assets, or increasing the financial capital of the recipients. Current expenditure does not include government lending or repayments to the government, or government acquisition of equity for public policy purposes.

Capital expenditure is spending to acquire fixed capital assets, land, intangible assets, government stocks, and nonmilitary, nonfinancial assets. Also included are capital grants.

Overall deficit/surplus is current and capital revenue and official grants received, less total expenditure and lending minus repayment.

Goods and services expenditure comprises all government payments in exchange for goods and services, including wages and salaries.

Social services expenditure comprises expenditure on health, education, housing, welfare, social security, and community amenities. It also covers compensation for loss of income to the sick and temporarily disabled; payments to the elderly, the permanently disabled, and the unemployed; family, maternity, and child allowances; and the cost of welfare services such as care of the aged, the disabled, and children. Many expenditures relevant to environmental protection, such as pollution abatement, water supply, sanitation, and refuse collection are included indistinguishably in this category.

Data on government revenues and expenditures are collected by the IMF through questionnaires distributed to member governments, and by the OECD. In general, the definition of government excludes nonfinancial public enterprises and public financial institutions (such as the central bank). Despite the IMF's efforts to systematize and standardize the collection of public finance data, statistics on public finance are often incomplete, untimely, and noncomparable. Inadequate statistical coverage precludes the presentation of subnational data, making cross-country comparisons potentially misleading.

Total central government expenditure as presented in the IMF's *Government Finance Statistics Yearbook* (IMF, various years) is a more limited measure of general government consumption than that shown in the national accounts because it excludes consumption expenditures by state and local governments. At the same time, the IMF's concept of central government expenditure is broader than the national accounts definition because it includes government gross domestic investment and transfer payments.

Central government finances can refer to one of two accounting concepts: consolidated or budgetary. For most countries central government finance data have been consolidated into one account, but for others only budgetary central government accounts are available. Countries reporting budgetary data are noted in the Primary data documentation table in the 1998 *World Development Indicators* (World Bank 1998b). Because budgetary accounts do not necessarily include all central government units, the picture they provide of central government activities is usually incomplete. A key issue is the failure to include the quasi-fiscal operations of the central bank. Central bank losses arising from monetary operations and subsidized financing can result in sizable quasi-fiscal deficits. Such deficits may also result from the operations of other financial intermediaries, such as public development finance institutions. Also missing from the data are governments' contingent liabilities for unfunded pension and insurance plans.

Table 15. Balance of payments current account and international reserves

Exports of goods and services and **imports of goods and services** together comprise all transactions between residents of a country and the rest of the world involving a change in ownership of general merchandise, goods sent for processing and repairs, nonmonetary gold, and services.

Net income refers to compensation earned by workers in an economy other than the one in which they are resident, for work performed and paid for by a resident of that economy, and investment income (receipts and payments on direct investment, portfolio investment, other investment, and receipts on reserve assets). Income derived from the use of intangible assets is recorded under business services.

Net current transfers consists of transactions in which residents of an economy provide or receive goods, services, income, or financial items without a quid pro quo. All transfers not considered to be capital transfers are current transfers.

Current account balance is the sum of net exports of goods and services, income, and current transfers.

Gross international reserves comprises holdings of monetary gold, special drawing rights, reserves of IMF members held by the IMF, and holdings of foreign exchange under the control of monetary authorities. The gold component of these reserves

is valued at year-end London prices ($589.50 an ounce in 1980 and $290.20 an ounce in 1997).

The balance of payments is divided into two groups of accounts. The current account records transactions in goods and services, income, and current transfers. The capital and financial account records capital transfers; the acquisition or disposal of nonproduced, nonfinancial assets (such as patents); and transactions in financial assets and liabilities. Gross international reserves are recorded in a third set of accounts, the international investment position, which records the stock of assets and liabilities.

The balance of payments is a double-entry accounting system that shows all flows of goods and services into and out of an economy; all transfers that are the counterpart of real resources or financial claims provided to or by the rest of the world without a quid pro quo, such as donations and grants; and all changes in residents' claims on, and liabilities to, nonresidents that arise from economic transactions. All transactions are recorded twice: once as a credit and once as a debit. In principle, the net balance should be zero, but in practice the accounts often do not balance. In these cases a balancing item, net errors and omissions, is included in the capital and financial account.

Discrepancies may arise in the balance of payments because there is no single source for balance of payments data and no way to ensure that data from different sources are fully consistent. Sources include customs data, monetary accounts of the banking system, external debt records, information provided by enterprises, surveys to estimate service transactions, and foreign exchange records. Differences in recording methods—for example, in the timing of transactions, in definitions of residence and ownership, and in the exchange rate used to value transactions—contribute to net errors and omissions. In addition, smuggling and other illegal or quasi-legal transactions may be unrecorded or misrecorded.

The concepts and definitions underlying the data in Table 15 are based on the fifth edition of the IMF's *Balance of Payments Manual* (IMF 1993). That edition redefined as capital transfers some transactions previously included in the current account, such as debt forgiveness, migrants' capital transfers, and foreign aid to acquire capital goods. Thus the current account balance now more accurately reflects net current transfer receipts in addition to transactions in goods, services (previously nonfactor services), and income (previously factor income). Many countries still maintain their data collection systems according to the concepts and definitions in the fourth edition. Where necessary, the IMF converts data reported in earlier systems to conform with the fifth edition (see the Primary data documentation table in World Bank 1998b). Values are in U.S. dollars converted at market exchange rates.

Table 16. Private sector finance

Private investment covers gross outlays by the private sector (including private nonprofit agencies) on additions to its fixed domestic assets. When direct estimates of private gross domestic fixed investment are not available, such investment is estimated as the difference between total gross domestic investment and consolidated public investment. No allowance is made for the depreciation of assets. Because private investment is often estimated as the difference between two estimated quantities—domestic fixed investment and consolidated public investment—private investment may be undervalued or overvalued and subject to errors over time.

Market capitalization (also called market value) is the sum of the market capitalizations of all firms listed on domestic stock exchanges, where each firm's market capitalization is its share price at the end of the year times the number of shares outstanding. Market capitalization, presented as one measure used to gauge a country's level of stock market development, suffers from conceptual and statistical weaknesses such as inaccurate reporting and different accounting standards.

Listed domestic companies is the number of domestically incorporated companies listed on stock exchanges at the end of the year, excluding investment companies, mutual funds, and other collective investment vehicles.

Interest rate spread, also known as the intermediation margin, is the difference between the interest rate charged by banks on short- and medium-term loans to the private sector and the interest rate offered by banks to resident customers for demand, time, or savings deposits. Interest rates should reflect the responsiveness of financial institutions to competition and price incentives. However, the interest rate spread may not be a reliable measure of a banking system's efficiency to the extent that information about interest rates is inaccurate, banks do not monitor all bank managers, or the government sets deposit and lending rates.

Domestic credit provided by the banking sector includes all credit to various sectors on a gross basis, with the exception of credit to the central government, which is net. The banking sector includes monetary authorities, deposit money banks, and other banking institutions for which data are available (including institutions that do not accept transferable deposits but do incur such liabilities as time and savings deposits). Examples of other banking institutions include savings and mortgage loan institutions and building and loan associations.

In general, the indicators reported here do not capture the activities of the informal sector, which remains an important source of finance in developing economies.

Table 17. Role of government in the economy

Subsidies and other current transfers includes all unrequited, nonrepayable transfers on current account to private and public enterprises, and the cost to the public of covering the cash operating deficits on sales to the public by departmental enterprises.

Value added by state-owned enterprises is estimated as sales revenue minus the cost of intermediate inputs, or as the sum of their operating surplus (balance) and wage payments. State-owned enterprises are government-owned or -controlled economic entities that generate most of their revenue by selling goods and services. This definition encompasses commercial enterprises directly operated by a government department and those in which the government holds a majority of shares directly or indirectly through other state enterprises. It also includes enterprises in which the state holds a minority of shares, if the distribution of the remaining shares leaves the government with effective control. It excludes public sector activity—such as

education, health services, and road construction and maintenance—that is financed in other ways, usually from the government's general revenue. Because financial enterprises are of a different nature, they have generally been excluded from the data.

Military expenditure for members of the North Atlantic Treaty Organization (NATO) is based on the NATO definition, which covers military-related expenditures of the defense ministry (including recruiting, training, construction, and the purchase of military supplies and equipment) and other ministries. Civilian-type expenditures of the defense ministry are excluded. Military assistance is included in the expenditure of the donor country. Purchases of military equipment on credit are recorded at the time the debt is incurred, not at the time of payment. Data for other countries generally cover expenditures of the ministry of defense; excluded are expenditures on public order and safety, which are classified separately.

Definitions of military spending differ depending on whether they include civil defense, reserves and auxiliary forces, police and paramilitary forces, dual-purpose forces such as military and civilian police, military grants-in-kind, pensions for military personnel, and social security contributions paid by one part of government to another. Official government data may omit some military spending, disguise financing through extrabudgetary accounts or unrecorded use of foreign exchange receipts, or fail to include military assistance or secret imports of military equipment. Current spending is more likely to be reported than capital spending. In some cases a more accurate estimate of military spending can be obtained by adding the value of estimated arms imports and nominal military expenditures. This method may understate or overstate spending in a particular year, however, because payments for arms may not coincide with deliveries.

The data in Table 17 are from the U.S. Arms Control and Disarmament Agency (ACDA). The IMF's *Government Finance Statistics Yearbook* is a primary source for data on defense spending. It uses a consistent definition of defense spending based on the United Nations' classification of the functions of government and the NATO definition. The IMF checks data on defense spending for broad consistency with other macroeconomic data reported to it, but it is not always able to verify their accuracy and completeness. Moreover, country coverage is affected by delays or failure to report data. Thus most researchers supplement the IMF's data with independent assessments of military outlays by organizations such as ACDA, the Stockholm International Peace Research Institute, and the International Institute for Strategic Studies. However, these agencies rely heavily on reporting by governments, on confidential intelligence estimates of varying quality, on sources that they do not or cannot reveal, and on one another's publications.

Composite ICRG risk rating is an overall index taken from the *International Country Risk Guide* (ICRG). The ICRG (PRS Group 1998) collects information on 22 components of risk, groups these components into three major categories (political, financial, and economic), and calculates a single risk assessment index ranging from 0 to 100. Ratings below 50 indicate very high risk and those above 80 very low risk. Ratings are updated every month.

Institutional Investor **credit rating** ranks, from 0 to 100, the probability of a country's default. A high number indicates a low probability of default on external obligations. *Institutional Investor* country credit ratings are based on information provided by leading international banks. Responses are weighted using a formula that gives more importance to responses from banks with greater worldwide exposure and more sophisticated country analysis systems.

Risk ratings may be highly subjective, reflecting external perceptions that do not always capture a country's actual situation. But these subjective perceptions are the reality that policymakers face in the climate they create for foreign private inflows. Countries not rated favorably by credit risk rating agencies typically do not attract registered flows of private capital. The risk ratings presented here are not endorsed by the World Bank but are included for their analytical usefulness.

Highest marginal tax rate is the highest rate shown on the schedule of tax rates applied to the taxable income of individuals and corporations. The table also presents the income threshold above which the highest marginal tax rate applies for individuals.

Tax collection systems are often complex, containing many exceptions, exemptions, penalties, and other inducements that affect the incidence of taxation and thus influence the decisions of workers, managers, entrepreneurs, investors, and consumers. A potentially important influence on both domestic and international investors is the tax system's progressivity, as reflected in the highest marginal tax rate on individual and corporate income. Figures for individual marginal tax rates generally refer to employment income. For some countries the highest marginal tax rate is also the basic or flat rate, and other surtaxes, deductions, and the like may apply.

Table 18. Power and transportation

Electric power consumption per capita measures the production of power plants and combined heat and power plants less distribution losses and their own use. **Electric power transmission and distribution losses** measures losses occurring between sources of supply and points of distribution, and in distribution to consumers, including pilferage.

Data on electric power production and consumption are collected from national energy agencies by the International Energy Agency and adjusted by that agency to meet international definitions. Adjustments are made, for example, to account for establishments that, in addition to their main activities, generate electricity wholly or partly for their own use. In some countries self-production by households and small entrepreneurs is substantial because of their remoteness or because public power sources are unreliable, and these adjustments may not adequately reflect actual output.

Although own consumption and transmission losses are netted out, electric power consumption includes consumption by auxiliary stations, losses in transformers that are considered integral parts of those stations, and electricity produced by pumping installations. It covers electricity generated by all primary sources of energy—coal, oil, gas, nuclear, hydroelectric, geothermal, wind, tide and wave, and combustible renewables— where data are available. Neither production nor consumption

data capture the reliability of supplies, including frequency of outages, breakdowns, and load factors.

Paved roads is the percentage of roads that have been sealed with asphalt or similar road-building materials. **Goods transported by road** is the volume of goods transported by road vehicles, measured in millions of metric tons times kilometers traveled. **Goods transported by rail** measures the tonnage of goods transported times kilometers traveled per million dollars of GDP measured in PPP terms. **Air passengers carried** includes passengers on both domestic and international passenger routes.

Data for most transport industries are not internationally comparable, because unlike demographic statistics, national income accounts, and international trade data, the collection of infrastructure data has not been standardized internationally. Data on roads are collected by the International Road Federation (IRF), and data on air transport by the International Civil Aviation Organization. National road associations are the primary source of IRF data; in countries where such an association is absent or does not respond, other agencies are contacted, such as road directorates, ministries of transport or public works, or central statistical offices. As a result, the compiled data are of uneven quality.

Table 19. Communications, information, and science and technology

Daily newspapers is the number of copies distributed of newspapers published at least four times a week, per thousand people. **Radios** is the estimated number of radio receivers in use for broadcasts to the general public, per thousand people. Data on the number of daily newspapers in circulation and of radio receivers in use are obtained from statistical surveys by the United Nations Educational, Scientific, and Cultural Organization (UNESCO). In some countries definitions, classifications, and methods of enumeration do not entirely conform to UNESCO standards. For example, newspaper circulation data should refer to the number of copies distributed, but in some cases the figures reported are the number of copies printed. In addition, many countries impose radio license fees to help pay for public broadcasting, discouraging radio owners from declaring ownership. Because of these and other data collection problems, estimates of the number of newspapers and radios vary widely in reliability and should be interpreted with caution.

Television sets is the estimated number of sets in use, per thousand people. Data on television sets are supplied to the International Telecommunication Union (ITU) through annual questionnaires sent to national broadcasting authorities and industry associations. Some countries require that television sets be registered. To the extent that households do not register some or all of their sets, the number of registered sets may understate the true number.

Telephone main lines counts all telephone lines that connect a customer's equipment to the public switched telephone network. **Mobile phones** refers to users of portable telephones subscribing to an automatic public mobile telephone service using cellular technology that provides access to the public switched telephone network, per thousand people. Data on telephone main lines and mobile phones are compiled by the

ITU through annual questionnaires sent to telecommunications authorities and operating companies. The data are supplemented by annual reports and statistical yearbooks of telecommunications ministries, regulators, operators, and industry associations.

Personal computers is the estimated number of self-contained computers designed to be used by a single person, per thousand people. Estimates by the ITU of the number of personal computers are derived from an annual questionnaire, supplemented by other sources. In many countries mainframe computers are used extensively, and thousands of users can be connected to a single mainframe computer; in such cases the number of personal computers understates the total use of computers.

Internet hosts is the number of computers directly connected to the worldwide network of interconnected computer systems, per 10,000 people. Internet hosts are ascribed to countries based on the country code in the host's universal resource locator, even though this code does not necessarily indicate that the host is physically located in the country. All hosts lacking a country code identification are ascribed to the United States. Thus the data should be considered approximate. Estimates of the number of Internet hosts come from Network Wizards, Menlo Park, Calif.

Scientists and engineers in R&D is the number of people trained to work in any field of science who are engaged in professional research and development activity (including administrators), per million people. Most such jobs require completion of tertiary education.

UNESCO collects data on scientific and technical workers and R&D expenditure from its member states, mainly from official replies to UNESCO questionnaires and special surveys, as well as from official reports and publications, supplemented by information from other national and international sources. UNESCO reports either the stock of scientists and engineers or the number of economically active persons qualified to be scientists and engineers (people engaged in or actively seeking work in any branch of the economy on a given date). Stock data generally come from censuses and are less timely than measures of the economically active population. UNESCO supplements these data with estimates of the number of qualified scientists and engineers by counting the number of people who have completed education at ISCED (International Standard Classification of Education) levels 6 and 7. The data on scientists and engineers, normally calculated in terms of full-time equivalent staff, cannot take into account the considerable variations in quality of training and education.

High-technology exports consists of goods produced by industries (based on U.S. industry classifications) that rank among a country's top ten in terms of R&D expenditure. Manufactured exports are commodities in the Standard International Trade Classification (SITC), revision 1, sections 5–9 (chemicals and related products, basic manufactures, manufactured articles, machinery and transport equipment, and other manufactured articles and goods not elsewhere classified), excluding division 68 (nonferrous metals).

Industry rankings are based on a methodology developed by Davis 1982. Using input-output techniques, Davis estimated the technology intensity of U.S. industries in terms of the R&D expenditure required to produce a certain manufactured good. This methodology takes into account direct R&D expenditure by final producers as well as indirect R&D expenditure by suppliers of intermediate goods used in producing the final good. Industries, classified on the basis of the U.S. Standard Industrial Classification (SIC), were ranked according to their R&D intensity, and the top ten SIC groups (as classified at the three-digit level) were designated high-technology industries.

To translate Davis's industry classification into a definition of high-technology trade, Braga and Yeats 1992 used the concordance between the SIC grouping and the Standard International Trade Classification (SITC), revision 1, classification proposed by Hatter 1985. In preparing the data on high-technology trade, Braga and Yeats considered only SITC groups (classified at the four-digit level) that had a high-technology weight above 50 percent. Examples of high-technology exports include aircraft, office machinery, pharmaceuticals, and scientific instruments. This methodology rests on the somewhat unrealistic assumption that using U.S. input-output relations and trade patterns for high-technology production does not introduce a bias in the classification.

Patent applications filed is the number of documents, issued by a government office, that describe an invention and create a legal situation in which the patented invention can normally only be exploited (made, used, sold, imported) by, or with the authorization of, the patentee. The protection of inventions is limited in time (generally 20 years from the filing date of the application for the grant of a patent). Information on patent applications filed is shown separately for residents and nonresidents of the country. Data on patents are from the World Intellectual Property Organization, which estimates that at the end of 1995 about 3.7 million patents were in force in the world.

Table 20. Global trade

Merchandise exports shows the f.o.b. (free on board) value, in U.S. dollars, of goods provided to the rest of the world. **Merchandise imports** shows the c.i.f. (cost plus insurance and freight) value in U.S. dollars of goods purchased from the rest of the world. Data for manufacturing exports and imports refer to commodities in SITC sections 5 (chemicals), 6 (basic manufactures), 7 (machinery and transport equipment), and 8 (miscellaneous manufactured goods), excluding division 68.

Trade share of GDP is the sum of exports and imports of goods and services as recorded in the national accounts, divided by GDP at market prices.

Net barter terms of trade is the ratio of the export price index to the corresponding import price index, measured relative to the base year 1987.

The terms of trade, a measure of the relative prices of a country's exports and imports, can be calculated in a number of ways. The most common is the net barter, or commodity, terms of trade, constructed as the ratio of the export price index to the import price index. When the net barter terms of trade increase, a country's exports are becoming more valuable or its imports cheaper.

Data on merchandise trade come from customs reports of goods entering an economy or from reports of financial transactions related to merchandise trade recorded in the balance of payments. Because of differences in timing and definitions, estimates of trade flows from customs reports are likely to differ from those based on the balance of payments. Furthermore, several international agencies process trade data, each making estimates to correct for unreported or misreported data, and this leads to other differences in the available data.

The most detailed source of data on international trade in goods is the COMTRADE database maintained by the United Nations Statistical Division (UNSD). The IMF also collects customs-based data on exports and imports of goods.

The value of exports is recorded as the cost of the goods delivered to the frontier of the exporting country for shipment—the f.o.b. value. Many countries collect and report trade data in U.S. dollars. When countries report in local currency, the UNSD applies the average official exchange rate for the period shown.

The value of imports is generally recorded as the cost of the goods when purchased by the importer plus the cost of transport and insurance to the frontier of the importing country—the c.i.f. value. Goods transported through a country en route to another country are excluded.

Total exports and shares of exports in manufacturing were estimated by World Bank staff from the COMTRADE database. Where necessary, data on total exports were supplemented from the IMF's *Direction of Trade Statistics* (IMF, various years). The classification of commodity groups is based on the SITC, revision 1. Shares may not sum to 100 percent because of unclassified trade.

Data on imports of goods are derived from the same sources as data on exports. In principle, world exports and imports should be identical. Similarly, exports from an economy should equal the sum of imports by the rest of the world from that economy. But differences in timing and definition result in discrepancies in reported values at all levels.

Table 21. Aid and financial flows

Net private capital flows consists of private debt and nondebt flows. Private debt flows include commercial bank lending, bonds, and other private credits; nondebt private flows are foreign direct investment and portfolio equity investment. **Foreign direct investment** is net inflows of investment to acquire a lasting management interest (10 percent or more of voting stock) in an enterprise operating in an economy other than that of the investor. It is the sum of equity capital flows, reinvestment of earnings, other long-term capital flows, and short-term capital flows as shown in the balance of payments.

The data on foreign direct investment are based on balance of payments data reported by the IMF, supplemented by data on net foreign direct investment reported by the OECD and official national sources. The internationally accepted definition of foreign direct investment is that provided in the fifth edition of the IMF's *Balance of Payments Manual* (IMF 1993). The OECD has also published a definition, in consultation with the IMF, Eurostat, and the United Nations. Because of the multiplicity of

sources and differences in definitions and reporting methods, more than one estimate of foreign direct investment may exist for a country, and data may not be comparable across countries.

Foreign direct investment data do not give a complete picture of international investment in an economy. Balance of payments data on foreign direct investment do not include capital raised in the host economies, which has become an important source of financing for investment projects in some developing countries. There is also increasing awareness that foreign direct investment data are limited because they capture only cross-border investment flows involving equity participation and omit nonequity cross-border transactions such as intrafirm flows of goods and services. For a detailed discussion of the data issues see Volume 1, Chapter 3, of the World Bank's *World Debt Tables 1993–94* (World Bank 1993b).

Total external debt is debt owed to nonresidents repayable in foreign currency, goods, or services. It is the sum of public, publicly guaranteed, and private nonguaranteed long-term debt, use of IMF credit, and short-term debt. Short-term debt includes all debt having an original maturity of one year or less and interest in arrears on long-term debt. **Present value of external debt** is the sum of short-term external debt plus the discounted sum of total debt service payments due on public, publicly guaranteed, and private nonguaranteed long-term external debt over the life of existing loans.

Data on the external debt of low- and middle-income economies are gathered by the World Bank through its Debtor Reporting System. World Bank staff calculate the indebtedness of developing countries using loan-by-loan reports submitted by these countries on long-term public and publicly guaranteed borrowing, along with information on short-term debt collected by the countries or from creditors through the reporting systems of the Bank for International Settlements and the OECD. These data are supplemented by information on loans and credits from major multilateral banks and loan statements from official lending agencies in major creditor countries, and by estimates from World Bank country economists and IMF desk officers. In addition, some countries provide data on private nonguaranteed debt. In 1996, 34 countries reported their private nonguaranteed debt to the World Bank; estimates were made for 28 additional countries known to have significant private debt.

The present value of external debt provides a measure of future debt service obligations that can be compared with such indicators as GNP. It is calculated by discounting debt service (interest plus amortization) due on long-term external debt over the life of existing loans. Short-term debt is included at its face value. Data on debt are in U.S. dollars converted at official exchange rates. The discount rate applied to long-term debt is determined by the currency of repayment of the loan and is based on the OECD's commercial interest reference rates. Loans from the International Bank for Reconstruction and Development and credits from the International Development Association are discounted using a reference rate for special drawing rights, as are obligations to the IMF. When the discount rate is greater than the interest rate of the loan, the present value is less than the nominal sum of future debt service obligations.

Official development assistance (ODA) consists of disbursements of loans (net of repayments of principal) and grants made on concessional terms by official agencies of the members of the Development Assistance Committee (DAC) and certain Arab countries to promote economic development and welfare in recipient economies listed by DAC as developing. Loans with a grant element of more than 25 percent are included in ODA, as are technical cooperation and assistance. Also included are aid flows (net of repayments) from official donors to the transition economies of Eastern Europe and the former Soviet Union and to certain higher-income developing countries and territories as determined by DAC. These are sometimes referred to as "official aid" and are provided under terms and conditions similar to those for ODA. Data for aid as a share of GNP are calculated using values in U.S dollars converted at official exchange rates.

The data cover bilateral loans and grants from DAC countries, multilateral organizations, and certain Arab countries. They do not reflect aid given by recipient countries to other developing countries. As a result, some countries that are net donors (such as Saudi Arabia) are shown in the table as aid recipients.

The data do not distinguish among different types of aid (program, project, or food aid; emergency assistance; peacekeeping assistance; or technical cooperation), each of which may have a very different effect on the economy. Technical cooperation expenditures do not always directly benefit the recipient economy to the extent that they defray costs incurred outside the country, for salaries and benefits of technical experts and for overhead of firms supplying technical services.

Because the aid data in Table 21 are based on information from donors, they are not consistent with information recorded by recipients in the balance of payments, which often excludes all or some technical assistance—particularly payments to expatriates made directly by the donor. Similarly, grant commodity aid may not always be recorded in trade data or in the balance of payments. Although estimates of ODA in balance of payments statistics are meant to exclude purely military aid, the distinction is sometimes blurred. The definition used by the country of origin usually prevails.

Statistical methods

This section describes the calculation of the least-squares growth rate, the exponential (end-point) growth rate, the Gini index, and the World Bank's *Atlas* methodology for calculating the conversion factor used to estimate GNP and GNP per capita in U.S. dollars.

Least-squares growth rate

The least-squares growth rate, r, is estimated by fitting a least-squares linear regression trend line to the logarithmic annual values of the variable in the relevant period. More specifically, the regression equation takes the form

$$\log X_t = a + bt,$$

which is equivalent to the logarithmic transformation of the geometric growth rate equation,

$$X_t = X_o (1 + r)^t.$$

In these equations, X is the variable, t is time, and $a = \log X_o$ and $b = log (1 + r)$ are the parameters to be estimated. If b^* is the least-squares estimate of b, then the average annual growth rate, r, is obtained as [antilog $(b^*)-1$] and is multiplied by 100 to express it as a percentage.

The calculated growth rate is an average rate that is representative of the available observations over the period. It does not necessarily match the actual growth rate between any two periods. Assuming that geometric growth is the appropriate "model" for the data, the least-squares estimate of the growth rate is consistent and efficient.

Exponential growth rate

The growth rate between two points in time for certain demographic data, notably labor force and population, is calculated from the equation:

$$r = \ln(p_n/p_1)/n,$$

where p_n and p_1 are the last and first observations in the period, n is the number of years in the period, and ln is the natural logarithm operator.

This growth rate is based on a model of continuous, exponential growth. To obtain a growth rate for discrete periods comparable to the least-squares growth rate, take the antilog of the calculated growth rate and subtract 1.

The Gini index

The Gini index measures the extent to which the distribution of income (or, in some cases, consumption expenditures) among individuals or households within an economy deviates from a perfectly equal distribution. A Lorenz curve plots the cumulative percentages of total income received against the cumulative percentage of recipients, starting with the poorest individual or household. The Gini index measures the area between the Lorenz curve and a hypothetical line of absolute equality, expressed as a percentage of the maximum area under the line. Thus a Gini index of zero presents perfect equality, whereas an index of 100 percent implies maximum inequality.

The World Bank employs a numerical analysis program, POVCAL, to estimate values of the Gini index; see Chen, Datt, and Ravallion 1992.

World Bank Atlas method

The *Atlas* conversion factor for any year is the average of a country's exchange rate (or alternative conversion factor) for that year and its exchange rates for the two preceding years, after adjusting them for differences in rates of inflation between the country and the Group of Five (G-5) countries (France, Germany, Japan, the United Kingdom, and the United States.) The inflation rate for the G-5 countries is represented by changes in the SDR deflators. This three-year averaging smooths annual fluctuations in prices and exchange rates for each country. The *Atlas* conversion factor is applied to the country's GNP. The resulting GNP in U.S. dollars is divided by the midyear population for the latest of the three years to derive GNP per capita.

The following formulas describe the procedures for computing the conversion factor for year t:

$$e_t^* = \frac{1}{3}\left[e_{t-2}\left(\frac{p_t}{p_{t-2}} \Big/ \frac{p_t^{S\$}}{p_{t-2}^{S\$}} \right) + e_{t-1}\left(\frac{p_t}{p_{t-1}} \Big/ \frac{p_t^{S\$}}{p_{t-1}^{S\$}} \right) + e_t \right]$$

and for calculating GNP per capita in U.S. dollars for year t:

$$Y_t^{\$} = (Y_t / N_t)/e_t^*$$

where

Y_t = current GNP (local currency) for year t
p_t = GNP deflator for year t

e_t = average annual exchange rate (national currency to the U.S. dollar) for year t
N_t = midyear population for year t, and
$P_t^{S\$}$ = SDR deflator in U.S. dollar terms for year t.

Alternative conversion factors
The World Bank systematically assesses the appropriateness of official exchange rates as conversion factors. An alternative conversion factor is used when the official exchange rate is judged to diverge by an exceptionally large margin from the rate effectively applied to domestic transactions of foreign currencies and traded products, the case for only a small number of countries (see the Primary data documentation table in World Bank 1998b). Alternative conversion factors are used in the *Atlas* method and elsewhere in the Selected World Development Indicators as single-year conversion factors.

Data Sources

ACDA (Arms Control and Disarmament Agency). 1997. *World Military Expenditures and Arms Transfers 1996.* Washington, D.C.

Ahmad, Sultan. 1992. "Regression Estimates of Per Capita GDP Based on Purchasing Power Parities." Policy Research Working Paper 956. World Bank, International Economics Department, Washington, D.C.

Ball, Nicole. 1984. "Measuring Third World Security Expenditure: A Research Note." *World Development* 12(2):157–64.

Bos, Eduard, My T. Vu, Ernest Massiah, and Rodolfo A. Bulatao. 1994. *World Population Projections, 1994–95 Edition.* Baltimore, Md.: Johns Hopkins University Press.

Braga, C. A. Primo, and Alexander Yeats. 1992. "How Minilateral Trading Arrangements May Affect the Post-Uruguay Round World." World Bank, International Economics Department, Washington, D.C.

Council of Europe. 1995. *Recent Demographic Developments in Europe and North America.* Strasbourg, France: Council of Europe Press.

Davis, Lester. 1982. *Technology Intensity of U.S. Output and Trade.* Washington, D.C.: U.S. Department of Commerce.

Eurostat (Statistical Office of the European Communities). Various years. *Demographic Statistics.* Luxembourg: Statistical Office of the European Communities.

FAO (Food and Agriculture Organization). Various years. *Production Yearbook.* FAO Statistics Series. Rome.

———. 1997. *State of the World's Forests 1997.* Rome.

Happe, Nancy, and John Wakeman-Linn. 1994. "Military Expenditures and Arms Trade: Alternative Data Sources." IMF Working Paper 94/69. International Monetary Fund, Policy Development and Review Department, Washington, D.C.

Heston, Alan. 1994. "A Brief Review of Some Problems in Using National Accounts Data in Level of Output Comparison and Growth Studies," *Journal of Development Economics* 44: 29–52.

ICAO (International Civil Aviation Organization). 1997. *Civil Aviation Statistics of the World: 1996. ICAO Statistics Yearbook,* 22nd ed. Montreal.

IEA (International Energy Agency). 1997a. *Energy Statistics and Balances of Non-OECD Countries 1994–95.* Paris.

———. 1997b. *Energy Statistics of OECD Countries 1994–95.* Paris.

IFC (International Finance Corporation). 1997a. *Emerging Stock Markets Factbook 1997.* Washington, D.C.

———. 1997b. *Trends in Private Investment in Developing Countries 1997.* Washington, D.C.

ILO (International Labour Organisation). Various years. *Yearbook of Labour Statistics.* Geneva.

———. 1995a. *Labour Force Estimates and Projections, 1950–2010.* Geneva.

———. 1995b. *Estimates of the Economically Active Population by Sex and Age Group and by Main Sectors of Economic Activity.* Geneva.

———. 1996. *Year Book of Labour Statistics.* Geneva.

IMF (International Monetary Fund). Various years. *Director of Trade Statistics Yearbook.* Washington, D.C.

———. Various years. *Government Finance Statistics Yearbook.* Washington, D.C.

———. Various years. *International Financial Statistics.* Washington, D.C.

———. 1986. *A Manual on Government Finance Statistics.* Washington, D.C.

———. 1993. *Balance of Payments Manual.* 5th ed. Washington, D.C.

Institutional Investor. 1998. New York. (March).

IRF (International Road Federation). 1995. *World Road Statistics 1990–94.* Geneva.

Luxembourg Income Study. 1997. *LIS Database.* http://lissy.ceps.lu/index.htm.

National Bureau of Economic Research. 1997. *Penn World Tables Mark 5.6.* http://nber.harvard.edu/pwt56.html.

OECD (Organisation for Economic Co-operation and Development). Various years. *Development Co-operation.* Paris.

———. 1988. *Geographical Distribution of Financial Flows to Developing Countries.* Paris.

———. 1996a. *National Accounts 1960–1994.* Vol. 1, *Main Aggregates.* Paris.

———. 1996b. *National Accounts 1960–1994.* Vol. 2, *Detailed Tables.* Paris.

———. 1997. *Development Co-operation: 1996 Report.* Paris.

PRS Group. 1998. *International Country Risk Guide.* June. East Syracuse, N.Y.

Price Waterhouse. 1997a. *Corporate Taxes: A Worldwide Summary.* New York.

———. 1997b. *Individual Taxes: A Worldwide Summary.* New York.

Ravallion, Martin, and Shaohua Chen. 1996. "What Can New Survey Data Tell Us about Recent Changes in Living Standards in Developing and Transitional Economies?" World Bank, Policy Research Department, Washington, D.C.

Srinivasan, T. N. 1994. "Database for Development Analysis: An Overview." *Journal of Development Economics* 44(1): 3–28.

UNCTAD (United Nations Conference on Trade and Development). Various years. *Handbook of International Trade and Development Statistics.* Geneva.

UNESCO (United Nations Educational, Scientific, and Cultural Organization). Various years. *Statistical Yearbook.* Paris.

UNICEF (United Nations Children's Fund). 1997. *The State of the World's Children 1997.* Oxford, U.K.: Oxford University Press.

UNIDO (United Nations Industrial Development Organization). 1996. *International Yearbook of Industrial Statistics 1996.* Vienna.

United Nations. Various years. *Energy Statistics Yearbook.* New York.

———. Various years. *Levels and Trends of Contraceptive Use.* New York.

———. Various issues. *Monthly Bulletin of Statistics.* New York.

———. Various years. *Population and Vital Statistics Report.* New York.

———. Various years. *Statistical Yearbook.* New York.

———. Various years. *Update on the Nutrition Situation.* Administrative Committee on Co-ordination, Subcommittee on Nutrition. Geneva.

———. Various years. *Yearbook of International Trade Statistics.* New York.

———. 1968. *A System of National Accounts: Studies and Methods.* Series F, No. 2, Rev. 3. New York.

———. 1985. *National Accounts Statistics: Compendium of Income Distribution Statistics.* New York.

———. 1996a. *World Urbanization Prospects, 1996 Revision.* New York.

———. 1996b. *World Population Prospects: The 1996 Edition.* New York.

U.S. Bureau of the Census. 1996. *World Population Profile.* Washington, D.C.: U.S. Government Printing Office.

WHO (World Health Organization). Various years. *World Health Statistics.* Geneva.

———. Various years. *World Health Statistics Report.* Geneva.

———. 1991. *Maternal Mortality: A Global Factbook.* Geneva.

WHO and UNICEF. 1996. *Revised 1990 Estimates on Maternal Mortality: A New Approach.* Geneva.

World Bank. 1993a. *Purchasing Power of Currencies: Comparing National Incomes Using ICP Data.* Washington, D.C.

———. 1993b. *World Debt Tables 1993–94.* Washington, D.C.

———. 1998a. *Global Development Finance 1998.* Washington, D.C.

———. 1998b. *World Development Indicators.* Washington, D.C.

World Resources Institute, UNEP (United Nations Environment Programme), UNDP (United Nations Development Programme), and World Bank. 1996. *World Resources 1996–97: A Guide to the Global Environment.* New York: Oxford University Press.

World Resources Institute in collaboration with UNEP (United Nations Environment Programme) and UNDP (United Nations Development Programme). 1998. *World Resources 1998–99: A Guide to the Global Environment.* New York, N.Y.: Oxford University Press.

Table 1. Classification of economies by income and region, 1998

Income group	Subgroup	Sub-Saharan Africa		Asia		Europe and Central Asia		Middle East and North Africa		Americas
		East and Southern Africa	West Africa	East Asia and Pacific	South Asia	Eastern Europe and Central Asia	Rest of Europe	Middle East	North Africa	
Low-income		Angola Burundi Comoros Congo, Dem. Rep.[a] Eritrea Ethiopia Kenya Lesotho Madagascar Malawi Mozambique Rwanda Somalia Sudan Tanzania Uganda Zambia Zimbabwe	Benin Burkina Faso Cameroon Central African Republic Chad Congo, Rep. Côte d'Ivoire Gambia, The Ghana Guinea Guinea-Bissau Liberia Mali Mauritania Niger Nigeria São Tomé and Principe Senegal Sierra Leone Togo	Cambodia Lao PDR Mongolia Myanmar Vietnam	Afghanistan Bangladesh Bhutan India Nepal Pakistan	Albania Armenia Azerbaijan Bosnia and Herzegovina Kyrgyz Republic Moldova Tajikistan Turkmenistan		Yemen, Rep.		Haiti Honduras Nicaragua
Middle-income	Lower	Djibouti Namibia Swaziland	Cape Verde Equatorial Guinea	China Fiji Indonesia Kiribati Korea, Dem. Rep. Marshall Islands Micronesia, Fed. Sts. Papua New Guinea Philippines Samoa Solomon Islands Thailand Tonga Vanuatu	Maldives Sri Lanka	Belarus Bulgaria Georgia Kazakhstan Latvia Lithuania Macedonia, FYR[b] Romania Russian Federation Ukraine Uzbekistan Yugoslavia, Fed. Rep.[c]		Iran, Islamic Rep. Iraq Jordan Syrian Arab Republic West Bank and Gaza	Algeria Egypt, Arab Rep. Morocco Tunisia	Belize Bolivia Colombia Costa Rica Cuba Dominica Dominican Republic Ecuador El Salvador Grenada Guatemala Guyana Jamaica Panama Paraguay Peru St. Vincent and the Grenadines Suriname
	Upper	Botswana Mauritius Mayotte Seychelles South Africa	Gabon	American Samoa Malaysia Palau		Croatia Czech Republic Estonia Hungary Poland Slovak Republic	Isle of Man Turkey	Bahrain Lebanon Oman Saudi Arabia	Libya Malta	Antigua and Barbuda Argentina Barbados Brazil Chile Guadeloupe Mexico Puerto Rico St. Kitts and Nevis St. Lucia Trinidad and Tobago Uruguay Venezuela
Subtotal:	157	26	23	22	8	26	3	10	5	34

Table 1. *(continued)*

| Income group | Subgroup | Sub-Saharan Africa | | Asia | | Europe and Central Asia | | Middle East and North Africa | | Americas |
		East and Southern Africa	West Africa	East Asia and Pacific	South Asia	Eastern Europe and Central Asia	Rest of Europe	Middle East	North Africa	
High-income	OECD countries			Australia Japan Korea, Rep. New Zealand			Austria Belgium Denmark Finland France Germany Greece Iceland Ireland Italy Luxembourg Netherlands Norway Portugal Spain Sweden Switzerland United Kingdom			Canada United States
	Non-OECD countries	Reunion		Brunei French Polynesia Guam Hong Kong, China^d Macao New Caledonia N. Mariana Islands Singapore Taiwan, China		Slovenia	Andorra Channel Islands Cyprus Faeroe Islands Greenland Liechtenstein Monaco	Israel Kuwait Qatar United Arab Emirates		Aruba Bahamas, The Bermuda Cayman Islands French Guiana Martinique Netherlands Antilles Virgin Islands (U.S.)
Total:	211	27	23	35	8	27	28	14	5	44

a. Formerly Zaire.
b. Former Yugoslav Republic of Macedonia.
c. Federal Republic of Yugoslavia (Serbia/Montenegro).
d. On July 1, 1997, China resumed its sovereignty over Hong Kong.

For operational and analytical purposes, the World Bank's main criterion for classifying economies is gross national product (GNP) per capita. Every economy is classified as low-income, middle-income (subdivided into lower-middle and upper-middle), or high-income. Other analytical groups, based on geographic regions, exports, and levels of external debt, are also used.

Low-income and middle-income economies are sometimes referred to as developing economies. The use of the term is convenient; it is not intended to imply that all economies in the group are experiencing similar development or that other economies have reached a preferred or final stage of development. Classification by income does not necessarily reflect development status.

This table classifies all World Bank member economies and all other economies with populations of more than 30,000. *Income group:* Economies are divided among income groups according to 1997 GNP per capita, calculated using the World Bank *Atlas* method. The groups are: low-income, $785 or less; lower-middle-income, $785–$3,125; upper-middle-income, $3,126–$9,655; and high-income, $9,655 or more.

World Development Indicators 1998

The second annual edition of the World Bank's flagship statistical reference—*World Development Indicators 1998*. This award-winning publication provides an expanded view of the world economy for 148 countries—with chapters focusing on people, economy, environment, states and markets, world view, and global links as well as introductions highlighting recent research on major development issues. The 1998 edition includes some key indicators for 1997.

416 pages Stock no. 14124 (ISBN 0-8213-4124-3) $60.00

Also Available on CD-ROM

This comprehensive database contains underlying time-series data for the *World Development Indicators* and *World Bank Atlas,* **now covering 1965-1996 for most indicators with some extending to 1997**. Powerful features allow you to generate maps and charts and download your results to other software programs. Requires Windows 3.1.™

Individual Version: Stock no. 14125 (ISBN 0-8213-4125-1) $275.00

Network Version: Stock no. 14126 (ISBN 0-8213-4126-X) $550.00

World Bank Atlas 1998

One of the Bank's most popular offerings, the *Atlas* is designed as a companion to the *World Development Indicators*. Tables, charts, and colorful maps address the development themes of people, economy, environment, states and markets, world view, and global links. This easy-to-use book is an international standard in statistical compilations and an ideal reference for office or classroom. Text, maps, and references appear in English, French, and Spanish.

64 pages Stock no. 14127 (ISBN 0-8213-4127-8) $20.00

World Bank Publications

For US customers, contact The World Bank, P.O. Box 960, Herdon, VA 20172-0960. Phone: (703) 661-1580, Fax: (703) 661-1501. Shipping and handling: US$5.00. For airmail delivery outside the US, charges are US$13.00 for one item plus US$6.00 for each additional item. Payment by US$ check drawn on a US bank payable to the World Bank or by VISA, MasterCard, or American Express. Customers outside the US may also contact their local World Bank distributor.

Quantity	Title	Stock #	Price	Total Price
_____	_____	_____	_____	_____
_____	_____	_____	_____	_____
_____	_____	_____	_____	_____

❏ Bank check ❏ VISA ❏ MasterCard ❏ American Express

Subtotal cost US$ _____

Shipping and handling US$ _____

Total US$ _____

_____
credit card account number

_____
Expiration Date   Signature (required to validate all orders)

PLEASE PRINT CLEARLY

Name _____

Address _____

City _____   State _____   Postal Code _____

Country _____   Telephone _____

DISTRIBUTORS OF WORLD BANK PUBLICATIONS

Prices and credit terms vary from country to country. Consult your local distributor before placing an order.

ARGENTINA
Oficina del Libro Internacional
Av. Cordoba 1877
1120 Buenos Aires
Tel: (54 1) 815-8354
Fax: (54 1) 815-8156
E-mail: olilibro@satlink.com

AUSTRALIA, FIJI, PAPUA NEW GUINEA, SOLOMON ISLANDS, VANUATU, AND SAMOA
D.A. Information Services
648 Whitehorse Road
Mitcham 3132
Victoria
Tel: (61) 3 9210 7777
Fax: (61) 3 9210 7788
E-mail: service@dadirect.com.au
URL: http://www.dadirect.com.au

AUSTRIA
Gerold and Co.
Weihburggasse 26
A-1011 Wien
Tel: (43 1) 512-47-31-0
Fax: (43 1) 512-47-31-29
URL: http://www.gerold.co/at.online

BANGLADESH
Micro Industries Development
  Assistance Society (MIDAS)
House 5, Road 16
Dhanmondi R/Area
Dhaka 1209
Tel: (880 2) 326427
Fax: (880 2) 811188

BELGIUM
Jean De Lannoy
Av. du Roi 202
1060 Brussels
Tel: (32 2) 538-5169
Fax: (32 2) 538-0841

BRAZIL
Publicacões Tecnicas Internacionais Ltda.
Rua Peixoto Gomide, 209
01409 Sao Paulo, SP.
Tel: (55 11) 259-6644
Fax: (55 11) 258-6990
E-mail: postmaster@pti.uol.br
URL: http://www.uol.br

CANADA
Renouf Publishing Co. Ltd.
5369 Canotek Road
Ottawa, Ontario K1J 9J3
Tel: (613) 745-2665
Fax: (613) 745-7660
E-mail: order.dept@renoufbooks.com
URL: http://www.renoufbooks.com

CHINA
China Financial & Economic Publishing House
8, Da Fo Si Dong Jie
Beijing
Tel: (86 10) 6333-8257
Fax: (86 10) 6401-7365

China Book Import Centre
P.O. Box 2825
Beijing

Chinese Corporation for Promotion of Humanities
No. 18, Xi Si Bei San Tial
Xi Cheng District
Beijing 100034
Fax: (86 10) 6615-5168

COLOMBIA
Infoenlace Ltda.
Carrera 6 No. 51-21
Apartado Aereo 34270
Santafé de Bogotá, D.C.
Tel: (57 1) 285-2798
Fax: (57 1) 285-2798

COTE D'IVOIRE
Center d'Edition et de Diffusion Africaines (CEDA)
04 B.P. 541
Abidjan 04
Tel: (225) 24 6510;24 6511
Fax: (225) 25 0567

CYPRUS
Center for Applied Research
Cyprus College
6, Diogenes Street, Engomi
P.O. Box 2006
Nicosia
TTel: (357 2) 59-0730
Fax: (357 2) 66-2051

CZECH REPUBLIC
USIS, NIS Prodejna
Havelkova 22
130 00 Prague 3
Tel: (420 2) 2423 1486
Fax: (420 2) 2423 1114
URL: http://www.nis.cz/

DENMARK
SamfundsLitteratur
Rosenoerns Allé 11
DK-1970 Frederiksberg C
Tel: (45 35) 351942
Fax: (45 35) 357822
URL: http://www.sl.cbs.dk

ECUADOR
Libri Mundi
Libreria Internacional
P.O. Box 17-01-3029
Juan Leon Mera 851
Quito
Tel: (593 2) 521-606; (593 2) 544-185
Fax: (593 2) 504-209
E-mail: librimu1@librimundi.com.ec
E-mail: librimu2@librimundi.com.ec

CODEU
Ruiz de Castilla 763, Edif. Expocolor
Primer piso, Of. #2
Quito
Tel/Fax: (593 2) 507-383; 253-091
E-mail: codeu@impsat.net.ec

EGYPT, ARAB REPUBLIC OF
Al Ahram Distribution Agency
Al Galaa Street
Cairo
Tel: (20 2) 578-6083
Fax: (20 2) 578-6833

The Middle East Observer
41, Sherif Street
Cairo
Tel: (20 2) 393-9732
Fax: (20 2) 393-9732

FINLAND
Akateeminen Kirjakauppa
P.O. Box 128
FIN-00101 Helsinki
Tel: (358 0) 121 4418
Fax: (358 0) 121-4435
E-mail: akatilaus@stockmann.fi
URL: http://www.akateeminen.com/

FRANCE
Editions Eska
5, avenue de l'Opéra
75001 Paris
Tel: (33 1) 42-86-56-00
Fax: (33 1) 42-60-45-35

GERMANY
UNO-Verlag
Poppelsdorfer Allee 55
53115 Bonn
Tel: (49 228) 949020
Fax: (49 228) 217492
URL: http://www.uno-verlag.de
E-mail: unoverlag@aol.com

GHANA
Epp Books Services
P.O. Box 44
TUC
Accra

GREECE
Papasotiriou S.A.
35, Stournara Str.
106 82 Athens
Tel: (30 1) 364-1826
Fax: (30 1) 364-8254

HAITI
Culture Diffusion
5, Rue Capois
C.P. 257
Port-au-Prince
Tel: (509) 23 9260
Fax: (509) 23 4858

HONG KONG, CHINA; MACAO
Asia 2000 Ltd.
Sales & Circulation Department
302 Seabird House
22-28 Wyndham Street, Central
Hong Kong, China
Tel: (852) 2530-1409
Fax: (852) 2526-1107
E-mail: sales@asia2000.com.hk
URL: http://www.asia2000.com.hk

HUNGARY
Euro Info Service
Margitszgeti Europa Haz
H-1138 Budapest
Tel: (36 1) 350 80 24, 350 80 25
Fax: (36 1) 350 90 32
E-mail: euroinfo@mail.matav.hu

INDIA
Allied Publishers Ltd.
751 Mount Road
Madras - 600 002
Tel: (91 44) 852-3938
Fax: (91 44) 852-0649

INDONESIA
Pt. Indira Limited
Jalan Borobudur 20
P.O. Box 181
Jakarta 10320
Tel: (62 21) 390-4290
Fax: (62 21) 390-4289

IRAN
Ketab Sara Co. Publishers
Khaled Eslamboli Ave., 6th Street
Delafrooz Alley No. 8
P.O. Box 15745-733
Tehran 15117
Tel: (98 21) 8717819; 8716104
Fax: (98 21) 8712479
E-mail: ketab-sara@neda.net.ir

Kowkab Publishers
P.O. Box 19575-511
Tehran
Tel: (98 21) 258-3723
Fax: (98 21) 258-3723

IRELAND
Government Supplies Agency
Oifig an tSoláthair
4-5 Harcourt Road
Dublin 2
Tel: (353 1) 661-3111
Fax: (353 1) 475-2670

ISRAEL
Yozmot Literature Ltd.
P.O. Box 56055
3 Yohanan Hasandlar Street
Tel Aviv 61560
Tel: (972 3) 5285-397
Fax: (972 3) 5285-397

R.O.Y. International
PO Box 13056
Tel Aviv 61130
Tel: (972 3) 649 9469
Fax: (972 3) 648 6039
E-mail: royil@netvision.net.il

Palestinian Authority/Middle East
Index Information Services
P.O.B. 19502 Jerusalem
Tel: (972 2) 6271219
Fax: (972 2) 6271634

ITALY
Licosa Commissionaria Sansoni SPA
Via Duca Di Calabria, 1/1
Casella Postale 552
50125 Firenze
Tel: (55) 645-415
Fax: (55) 641-257
E-mail: licosa@ftbcc.it
URL: http://www.ftbcc.it/licosa

JAMAICA
Ian Randle Publishers Ltd.
206 Old Hope Road, Kingston 6
Tel: 876-927-2085
Fax: 876-977-0243
E-mail: irpl@colis.com

JAPAN
Eastern Book Service
3-13 Hongo 3-chome, Bunkyo-ku
Tokyo 113
Tel: (81 3) 3818-0861
Fax: (81 3) 3818-0864
E-mail: orders@svt-ebs.co.jp
URL: http://www.bekkoame.or.jp/~svt-ebs

KENYA
Africa Book Service (E.A.) Ltd.
Quaran House, Mfangano Street
P.O. Box 45245
Nairobi
Tel: (254 2) 223 641
Fax: (254 2) 330 272

KOREA, REPUBLIC OF
Dayang Books Trading Co.
International Division
783-20, Pangba Bon-Dong, Socho-ku
Seoul
Tel: (82 2) 536-9555
Fax: (82 2) 536-0025
E-mail: seamap@chollian.net

Eulyoo Publishing Co., Ltd.
46-1, Susong-Dong
Jongro-Gu
Seoul
Tel: (82 2) 734-3515
Fax: (82 2) 732-9154

LEBANON
Librairie du Liban
P.O. Box 11-9232
Beirut
Tel: (961 9) 217 944
Fax: (961 9) 217 434

MALAYSIA
University of Malaya Cooperative
  Bookshop, Limited
P.O. Box 1127
Jalan Pantai Baru
59700 Kuala Lumpur
Tel: (60 3) 756-5000
Fax: (60 3) 755-4424
E-mail: umkoop@tm.net.my

MEXICO
INFOTEC
Av. San Fernando No. 37
Col. Toriello Guerra
14050 Mexico, D.F.
Tel: (52 5) 624-2800
Fax: (52 5) 624-2822
E-mail: infotec@rtn.net.mx
URL: http://rtn.net.mx

Mundi-Prensa Mexico S.A. de C.V.
c/Rio Panuco, 141-Colonia Cuauhtemoc
06500 Mexico, D.F.
Tel: (52 5) 533-5658
Fax: (52 5) 514-6799

NEPAL
Everest Media International Services (P.) Ltd.
GPO Box 5443
Kathmandu
Tel: (977 1) 472 152
Fax: (977 1) 224 431

NETHERLANDS
De Lindeboom/Internationale Publicaties b.v.–
P.O. Box 202, 7480 AE Haaksbergen
Tel: (31 53) 574-0004
Fax: (31 53) 572-9296
E-mail: lindeboo@worldonline.nl
URL: http://www .worldonline.nl/~lindeboo

NEW ZEALAND
EBSCO NZ Ltd.
Private Mail Bag 99914
New Market
Auckland
Tel: (64 9) 524-8119
Fax: (64 9) 524-8067

Oasis Official
P.O. Box 3627
Wellington
Tel: (64 4) 499 1551
Fax: (64 4) 499 1972
E-mail: oasis@actrix.gen.nz
URL: http://www.oasisbooks.co.nz/

NIGERIA
University Press Limited
Three Crowns Building Jericho
Private Mail Bag 5095
Ibadan
Tel: (234 22) 41-1356
Fax: (234 22) 41-2056

NORWAY
SWETS Norge AS
Book Department, Postboks 6512 Etterstad
N-0606 Oslo
Tel: (47 22) 97-4500
Fax: (47 22) 97-4545

PAKISTAN
Mirza Book Agency
65, Shahrah-e-Quaid-e-Azam
Lahore 54000
Tel: (92 42) 735 3601
Fax: (92 42) 576 3714

Oxford University Press
5 Bangalore Town
Sharae Faisal
PO Box 13033
Karachi-75350
Tel: (92 21) 446307
Fax: (92 21) 4547640
E-mail: ouppak@TheOffice.net

Pak Book Corporation
Aziz Chambers 21, Queen's Road
Lahore
Tel: (92 42) 636 3222; 636 0885
Fax: (92 42) 636 2328
E-mail: pbc@brain.net.pk

PERU
Editorial Desarrollo SA
Apartado 3824, Lima 1
Tel: (51 14) 285380
Fax: (51 14) 286628

PHILIPPINES
International Booksource Center Inc.
1127-A Antipolo St, Barangay, Venezuela
Makati City
Tel: (63 2) 896 6501; 6505; 6507
Fax: (63 2) 896 1741

POLAND
International Publishing Service
Ul. Piekna 31/37
00-677 Warzawa
Tel: (48 2) 628-6089
Fax: (48 2) 621-7255
E-mail: books%ips@ikp.atm.com.pl
URL: http://www .ipscg.waw.pl/ips/export/

PORTUGAL
Livraria Portugal
Apartado 2681, Rua Do Carmo 70-74
1200 Lisbon
Tel: (1) 347-4982
Fax: (1) 347-0264

ROMANIA
Compani De Librarii Bucuresti S.A.
Str. Lipscani no. 26, sector 3
Bucharest
Tel: (40 1) 613 9645
Fax: (40 1) 312 4000

RUSSIAN FEDERATION
Isdatelstvo <Ves Mir>
9a, Kolpachniy Pereulok
Moscow 101831
Tel: (7 095) 917 87 49
Fax: (7 095) 917 92 59

**SINGAPORE; TAIWAN, CHINA
MYANMAR; BRUNEI**
Hemisphere Publication Services
41 Kallang Pudding Road #04-03
Golden Wheel Building
Singapore 349316
Tel: (65) 741-5166
Fax: (65) 742-9356
E-mail: ashgate@asianconnect.com

SLOVENIA
Gospodarski Vestnik Publishing Group
Dunajska cesta 5
1000 Ljubljana
Tel: (386 61) 133 83 47; 132 12 30
Fax: (386 61) 133 80 30
E-mail: repansekj@gvestnik.si

SOUTH AFRICA, BOTSWANA
For single titles:
Oxford University Press Southern Africa
Vasco Boulevard, Goodwood
P.O. Box 12119, N1 City 7463
Cape Town
Tel: (27 21) 595 4400
Fax: (27 21) 595 4430
E-mail: oxford@oup.co.za

For subscription orders:
International Subscription Service
P.O. Box 41095
Craighall
Johannesburg 2024
Tel: (27 11) 880-1448
Fax: (27 11) 880-6248
E-mail: iss@is.co.za

SPAIN
Mundi-Prensa Libros, S.A.
Castello 37
28001 Madrid
Tel: (34) 914 363700
Fax: (34) 915 753998
E-mail: libreria@mundiprensa.es
URL: http://www .mundiprensa.com/

Mundi-Prensa Barcelona
Consell de Cent, 391
08009 Barcelona
Tel: (34 3) 488-3492
Fax: (34 3) 487-7659
E-mail: barcelona@mundiprensa.es

SRI LANKA, THE MALDIVES
Lake House Bookshop
100, Sir Chittampalam Gardiner Mawatha
Colombo 2
Tel: (94 1) 32105
Fax: (94 1) 432104
E-mail: LHL@sri.lanka.net

SWEDEN
Wennergren-Williams AB
P. O. Box 1305
S-171 25 Solna
Tel: (46 8) 705-97-50
Fax: (46 8) 27-00-71
E-mail: mail@wwi.se

SWITZERLAND
Librairie Payot Service Institutionnel
Côtes-de-Montbenon 30
1002 Lausanne
Tel: (41 21) 341-3229
Fax: (41 21) 341-3235

ADECO Van Diermen EditionsTechniques
Ch. de Lacuez 41
CH1807 Blonay
Tel: (41 21) 943 2673
Fax: (41 21) 943 3605

THAILAND
Central Books Distribution
306 Silom Road
Bangkok 10500
Tel: (66 2) 235-5400
Fax: (66 2) 237-8321

**TRINIDAD & TOBAGO
AND THE CARRIBBEAN**
Systematics Studies Ltd.
St. Augustine Shopping Center
Eastern Main Road, St. Augustine
Trinidad & Tobago, West Indies
Tel: (868) 645-8466
Fax: (868) 645-8467
E-mail: tobe@trinidad.net

UGANDA
Gustro Ltd.
PO Box 9997, Madhvani Building
Plot 16/4 Jinja Rd.
Kampala
Tel: (256 41) 251 467
Fax: (256 41) 251 468
E-mail: gus@swiftuganda.com

UNITED KINGDOM
Microinfo Ltd.
P.O. Box 3, Omega Park, Alton,
Hampshire GU34 2PG
England
Tel: (44 1420) 86848
Fax: (44 1420) 89889
E-mail: wbank@microinfo.co.uk
URL: http://www .microinfo.co.uk

The Stationery Office
51 Nine Elms Lane
London SW8 5DR
Tel: (44 171) 873-8400
Fax: (44 171) 873-8242
URL: http://www.theso.co.uk/

VENEZUELA
Tecni-Ciencia Libros, S.A.
Centro Cuidad Comercial Tamanco
Nivel C2, Caracas
Tel: (58 2) 959 5547; 5035; 0016
Fax: (58 2) 959 5636

ZAMBIA
University Bookshop, University of Zambia
Great East Road Campus
P.O. Box 32379
Lusaka
Tel: (260 1) 252 576
Fax: (260 1) 253 952

ZIMBABWE
Academic and Baobab Books (Pvt.) Ltd.
4 Conald Road, Graniteside
P.O. Box 567
Harare
Tel: 263 4 755035
Fax: 263 4 781913

BOOKSELLERS OF WORLD BANK PUBLICATIONS

Prices vary from country to country. Consult your local bookseller for prices and availability.

BULGARIA
Humanities Research Center
P.O. Box 1784
1784 Sofia
Tel: (359 2) 76 81 57
Fax: (359 2) 76 35 34; 76 27 84
E-mail: chr@mgu.bg

HUNGARY
Foundation for Market Economy
112 Pf 249
1519 Budapest
Tel: (36 1) 204 2951; 204 2948
Fax: (36 1) 204 2953
E-mail: ipargazd@hungary.net

JORDAN
Global Development Forum
P.O. Box 941488
Amman 11194
Tel: (962 6) 5537701
Fax: (962 6) 5537702
E-mail: gdf@index.com.jo

KENYA
Legacy Books
Loita House, Loita Street, Mezz. 1
P.O. Box 68077
Nairobi
Tel: (254 2) 330853/221426
Fax: (254 2) 330854/561654
E-mail: Legacy@form-net.com

KOREA, Republic of
Sejong Books, Inc.
81-4 Neung-dong
Kwangjin-ku
Seoul 143-180
Tel: (82 2) 498-0300
Fax: (82 2) 3409-0321
E-mail: sjbk@mail.nuri.net
URL: http://203.248.78.1/sejong/

NEPAL
Bazaar International
GPO Box 2480
Kathmandu
Tel: (977 1) 22-29-83
Fax: (977 1) 22-94-37

SLOVAK REPUBLIC
Slovart G.T.G. Ltd.
Krupinská 4
P.O. Box 152
852 99 Bratislava 5
Tel: (42 7) 839471; 839472; 839473
Fax: (42 7) 839485
E-mail: gtg@internet.sk

THAILAND
Chulalongkorn University Book Center
Phyathai Road
Bangkok 10330
Tel: (66 2) 218 7292
Fax: (66 2) 255 4441

TURKEY
Dünya Infotel, A.S.
100 Yil Mahallesi
34440 Bagcilar-Istanbul
Tel: (90 212) 629 0808
Fax: (90 212) 629 4689; 629 4627
E-mail: dunya@dunya-gazete.com.tr
URL: http://www.dunya.com/

UNITED ARAB EMIRATES
Al Hamim Stationary & Bookshop
P.O. Box 5027
Sharjah
Tel: (971 6) 734687
Fax: (971 6) 384473
Pager: (971 6) 9760976

URUGUAY
Librería Técnica Uruguaya
Colonia 1543, Piso 7, Of. 702
Casilla de Correo 1518
Montevideo 11000
Tel: (598 2) 490072
Fax: (598 2) 41 34 48